SQL Cookbook™

Other resources from O'Reilly

Related titles

SQL Tuning

Mastering Oracle SQL

SQL Pocket Reference

SQL in a Nutshell

MySQL Cookbook™

Learning SQL

Database in Depth

Transact-SQL Cookbook™

oreilly.com

oreilly.com is more than a complete catalog of O'Reilly books. You'll also find links to news, events, articles, weblogs, sample chapters, and code examples.

oreillynet.com is the essential portal for developers interested in open and emerging technologies, including new platforms, programming languages, and operating systems.

Conferences

O'Reilly brings diverse innovators together to nurture the ideas that spark revolutionary industries. We specialize in documenting the latest tools and systems, translating the innovator's knowledge into useful skills for those in the trenches. Visit *conferences.oreilly.com* for our upcoming events.

Safari Bookshelf (*safari.oreilly.com*) is the premier online reference library for programmers and IT professionals. Conduct searches across more than 1,000 books. Subscribers can zero in on answers to time-critical questions in a matter of seconds. Read the books on your Bookshelf from cover to cover or simply flip to the page you need. Try it today for free.

SQL Cookbook™

Anthony Molinaro

O'REILLY®

Beijing · Cambridge · Farnham · Köln · Sebastopol · Tokyo

SQL Cookbook™
by Anthony Molinaro

Copyright © 2006 O'Reilly Media, Inc. All rights reserved.
Printed in the United States of America.

Published by O'Reilly Media, Inc., 1005 Gravenstein Highway North, Sebastopol, CA 95472.

O'Reilly books may be purchased for educational, business, or sales promotional use. Online editions are also available for most titles (*safari.oreilly.com*). For more information, contact our corporate/institutional sales department: (800) 998-9938 or *corporate@oreilly.com*.

Editor:	Jonathan Gennick
Production Editor:	Darren Kelly
Production Services:	nSight, Inc.
Cover Designer:	Karen Montgomery
Interior Designer:	David Futato

Printing History:

December 2005:	First Edition.

ISBN: 978-0-596-00976-2
[LSI]

To my mom:
You're the best! Thank you for everything.

Table of Contents

Preface

SQL is *the* language in the database world. If you're developing for or reporting from relational databases, your ability to put data into a database and then get it back out again ultimately comes down to your knowledge of SQL. Yet many practitioners use SQL in a perfunctory manner, and are unaware of the power at their disposal. This book aims to change all that, by opening your eyes to what SQL can really do for you.

The book you're holding in your hands is a cookbook. It's a collection of common SQL problems and their solutions that I hope you'll find helpful in your day-to-day work. Recipes are categorized into chapters of related topics. When faced with a new SQL problem that you haven't solved before, find the chapter that best seems to apply, skim through the recipe titles, and hopefully you will find a solution, or at least inspiration for a solution.

More than 150 recipes are available in this 600-plus page book, and I've only scratched the surface of what can be done using SQL. The number of different SQL solutions available for solving our daily programming problems is eclipsed only by the number of problems we need to solve. You won't find all possible problems covered in this book. Indeed, such coverage would be impossible. You will, however, find many common problems and their solutions. And in those solutions lie techniques that you'll learn how to expand upon and apply to other, new problems that I never thought to cover.

 My publisher and I are constantly on the lookout for new, cookbook-worthy SQL recipes. If you come across a good or clever SQL solution to a problem, consider sharing it; consider sending it in for inclusion in the next edition of this book. See "Comments and Questions" for our contact information.

Why I Wrote This Book

Queries, queries, queries. My goal from the beginning of this project has not been so much to write a "SQL Cookbook" as to write a "Query Cookbook." I've aimed to create a book comprised of queries ranging from the relatively easy to the relatively difficult in hopes the reader will grasp the techniques behind those queries and use them to solve his own particular business problems. I hope to pass on many of the SQL programming techniques I've used in my career so that you, the reader, will take them, learn from them, and eventually improve upon them; through this cycle we all benefit. Being able to retrieve data from a database seems so simple, yet in the world of Information Technology (IT) it's crucial that the operation of data retrieval be done as efficiently as possible. Techniques for efficient data retrieval should be shared so that we can all be efficient and help each other improve.

Consider for a moment the outstanding contribution to mathematics by Georg Cantor, who was the first to realize the vast benefit of studying sets of elements (studying the set itself rather than its constituents). At first, Cantor's work wasn't accepted by many of his peers. In time, though, it was not only accepted, but set theory is now considered the foundation of mathematics! More importantly, however, it was not through Cantor's work alone that set theory became what it is today; rather, by sharing his ideas, others such as Ernst Zermelo, Gottlob Frege, Abraham Fraenkel, Thoralf Skolem, Kurt Gödel, and John von Neumann developed and improved the theory. Such sharing not only provided everyone with a better understanding of the theory, it made for a better set theory than was first conceived.

Objectives of This Book

Ultimately, the goal of this book is to give you, the reader, a glimpse of what can be done using SQL outside of what is considered the typical SQL problem domain. SQL has come a very long way in the last ten years. Problems typically solved using a procedural language such as C or JAVA can now be solved directly in SQL, but many developers are simply unaware of this fact. This book is to help make you aware.

Now, before you take what I just said the wrong way, let me state that I am a firm believer in, "If it ain't broke, don't fix it." For example, let's say you have a particular business problem to solve, and you currently use SQL to simply retrieve your data while applying your complex business logic using a language other than SQL. If your code works and performance is acceptable, then great. I am in no way suggesting that you scrap your code for a SQL-only solution; I only ask that you open your mind and realize that the SQL you programmed with in 1995 is not the same SQL being used in 2005. Today's SQL can do so much more.

Audience for This Book

This text is unique in that the target audience is wide, but the quality of the material presented is not compromised. Consider that both complex and simple solutions are provided, and that solutions for five different vendors are available when a common solution does not exist. The target audience is indeed wide:

The SQL novice

> Perhaps you have just purchased a text on learning SQL, or you are fresh into your first semester of a required database course and you want to supplement your new knowledge with some challenging real world examples. Maybe you've seen a query that magically transforms rows to columns, or that parses a serialized string into a result set. The recipes in this book explain techniques for performing these seemingly impossible queries.

The non-SQL programmer

> Perhaps your background is in another language and you've been thrown into the fire at your current job and are expected to support complex SQL written by someone else. The recipes shown in this book, particularly in the later chapters, break down complex queries and provide a gentle walk-through to help you understand complex code that you may have inherited.

The SQL journeyman

> For the intermediate SQL developer, this book is the gold at the end of the rainbow (OK, maybe that's too strong; please forgive an author's enthusiasm for his topic). In particular, if you've been coding SQL for quite some time and have not found your way onto window functions, you're in for a treat. For example, the days of needing temporary tables to store intermediate results are over; window functions can get you to an answer in a single query! Allow me to again state that I have no intention of trying to force-feed my ideas to an already experienced practitioner. Instead, consider this book as a way to update your skill set if you haven't caught on to some of the newer additions to the SQL language.

The SQL expert

> Undoubtedly you've seen these recipes before, and you probably have your own variations. Why, then, is this book useful to you? Perhaps you've been a SQL expert on one platform your whole career, say, SQL Server, and now wish to learn Oracle. Perhaps you've only ever used MySQL, and you wonder what the same solutions in PostgreSQL would look like. This text covers different relational database management systems (RDBMSs) and displays their solutions side by side. Here's your chance to expand your knowledge base.

How to Use This Book

Be sure to read this preface thoroughly. It contains necessary background and other information that you might otherwise miss if you dive into individual recipes. The section on "Platform and Version" tells you what RDBMSs this book covers. Pay special attention to "Tables Used in This Book," so that you become familiar with the example tables used in most of the recipes. You'll also find important coding and font conventions in "Conventions Used in This Book." All these sections come later in this preface.

Remember that this is a cookbook, a collection of code examples to use as guidelines for solving similar (or identical) problems that you may have. Do not try to *learn* SQL from this book, at least not from scratch. This book should act as a supplement to, not a replacement for, a complete text on learning SQL. Additionally, following the tips below will help you use this book more productively:

- This book takes advantage of vendor-specific functions. *SQL Pocket Guide* by Jonathan Gennick has all of them and is convenient to have close to you in case you don't know what some of the functions in my recipes do.

- If you've never used window functions, or have had problems with queries using GROUP BY, read Appendix A first. It will define and prove what a group is in SQL. More importantly, it gives a basic idea of how window functions work. Window functions are one of the most important SQL developments of the past decade.

- Use common sense! Realize that it is impossible to write a book that provides a solution to every possible business problem in existence. Instead, use the recipes from this book as templates or guidelines to teach yourself the techniques required to solve your own specific problems. If you find yourself saying, "Great, this recipe works for this particular data set, but mine is different and thus the recipe doesn't work quite correctly," that's expected. In that case, try to find commonality between the data in the book and your data. Break down the book's query to its simplest form and add complexity as you go. All queries start with SELECT ...FROM..., so in their simplest form, all queries are the same. If you add complexity as you go, "building" a query one step, one function, one join at a time, you will not only understand how those constructs change the result set, but you will see how the recipe is different from what you actually need. And from there you can modify the recipe to work for your particular data set.

- Test, test, and test. Undoubtedly any table of yours is bigger than the 14 row EMP table used in this book, so please test the solutions against your data, at the very least to ensure that they perform well. I can't possibly know what your tables look like, what columns are indexed, and what relationships are present in your schema. So please, do not blindly implement these techniques in your production code until you fully understand them and how they will perform against your particular data.

- Don't be afraid to experiment. Be creative! Feel free to use techniques different from what I've used. I make it a point to use many of the functions supplied by the different vendors in this book, and often there are several other functions that may work as well as the one I've chosen to use in a particular recipe. Feel free to plug your own variations into the recipes of this book.

- Newer does not always mean better. If you're not using some of the more recent features of the SQL language (for example, window functions), that does not necessarily mean your code is not as efficient as it can be. There are many cases in which traditional SQL solutions are as good or better than any new solution. Please keep this in mind, particularly in the Appendix B, *Rozenshtein Revisited*. After reading this book, you should not come away with the idea that you need to update or change all your existing code. Instead, only realize there are many new and extremely efficient features of SQL available now that were not available 10 years ago, and they are worth the time taken to learn them.

- Don't be intimidated. When you get to the solution section of a recipe and a query looks impossible to understand, don't fear. I've gone to great lengths to not only break down each query starting from its simplest form, but to show the intermediate results of each portion of a query as we work our way to the complete solution. You may not be able to see the big picture immediately, but once you follow the discussion and see not only how a query is built, but the results of each step, you'll find that even convoluted-looking queries are not hard to grasp.

- Program defensively when necessary. In an effort to make the queries in this book as terse as humanly possible without obscuring their meaning, I've removed many "defensive measures" from the recipes. For example, consider a query computing a running total for a number of employee salaries. It could be the case that you have declared the column of type VARCHAR and are (sadly) storing a mix of numeric and string data in one field. You'll find the running total recipe in this book does not check for such a case (and it will fail as the function SUM doesn't know what to do with character data), so if you have this type of "data" ("problem" is a more accurate description), you will need to code around it or (hopefully) fix your data, because the recipes provided do not account for such design practices as the mixing of character and numeric data in the same column. The idea is to focus on the technique; once you understand the technique, sidestepping such problems is trivial.

- Repetition is the key. The best way to master the recipes in this book is to sit down and code them. When it comes to code, reading is fine, but actually coding is even better. You must read to understand why things are done a certain way, but only by coding will you be able to create these queries yourself.

Be advised that many of the examples in this book are contrived. The problems are not contrived. They are real. However, I've built all examples around a small set of tables containing employee data. I've done that to help you get familiar with the example data, so that, having become familiar with the data, you can focus on the technique that each recipe illustrates. You might look at a specific problem and think: "I would never need to do that with employee data." But try to look past the example data in those cases and focus on the technique that I'm illustrating. The techniques are useful. My colleagues and I use them daily. We think you will too.

What's Missing from This Book

Due to constraints on time and book size, it isn't possible for a single book to provide solutions for all the possible SQL problems you may encounter. That said, here are some additional items that did not make the list:

Data Definition
Aspects of SQL such as creating indexes, adding constraints, and loading data are not covered in this book. Such tasks typically involve syntax that is highly vendor-specific, so you're best off referring to vendor manuals. In addition, such tasks do not represent the type of "hard" problem for which one would purchase a book to solve. Chapter 4, however, does provide recipes for common problems involving the insertion, updating, and deleting of data.

XML
It is my strong opinion that XML recipes do not belong in a book on SQL. Storing XML documents in relational databases is becoming increasingly popular, and each RDBMS has their own extensions and tools for retrieving and manipulating such data. XML manipulation often involves code that is procedural and thus outside the scope of this book. Recent developments such as XQUERY represent completely separate topics from SQL and belong in their own book (or books).

Object-Oriented Extensions to SQL
Until a language more suitable for dealing with objects comes along, I am strongly against using object-oriented features and designs in relational databases. At the present time, the object-oriented features available from some vendors are more suitable for use in procedural programming than in the sort of set-oriented problem-solving for which SQL is designed.

Debates on Points of Theory
You won't find arguments in this book about whether SQL is relational, or about whether NULL values should exist. These sort of theoretical discussions have their place, but not in a book centered on delivering SQL solutions to real-life problems. To solve real-life problems, you simply have to work with the tools available to you at the time. You have to deal with what you have, not what you wish you had.

If you wish to learn more about theory, any of Chris Date's "Relational Database Writings" books would be a good start. You might also pick up a copy of his most recent book, *Database in Depth* (O'Reilly).

Vendor Politics

This text provides solutions for five different RDBMSs. It is only natural to want to know which vendor's solution is "best" or "fastest." There is plenty of information that each vendor would gladly provide to show that their product is "best"; I have no intention of doing so here.

ANSI Politics

Many texts shy away from the proprietary functions supplied by different vendors. This text embraces proprietary functions. I have no intention of writing convoluted, poorly performing SQL code simply for the sake of portability. I have never worked in an environment where the use of vendor-specific extensions was prohibited. You are paying for these features; why not use them?

Vendor extensions exist for a reason, and many times offer better performance and readability than you could otherwise achieve using standard SQL. If you prefer ANSI-only solutions, fine. As I mentioned before, I am not here to tell you to turn all your code upside down. If what you have is strictly ANSI and it works for you, great. When it comes down to it, we all go to work, we all have bills to pay, and we all want to go home at a reasonable time and enjoy what's still left of our days. So, I'm not suggesting that ANSI-only is wrong. Do what works and is best for you. But, I want to make clear that if you're looking for ANSI-only solutions, you should look elsewhere.

Legacy Politics

The recipes in this text make use of the newest features available at the time of writing. If you are using old versions of the RDBMSs that I cover, many of my solutions will simply not work for you. Technology does not stand still, and neither should you. If you need older solutions, you'll find that many of the SQL texts available from years past have plenty of examples using older versions of the RDBMSs covered in this book.

Structure of This Book

This book is divided into 14 chapters and 2 appendices:

Chapter 1, *Retrieving Records*

Introduces very simple queries. Examples include how to use a WHERE clause to restrict rows from your result set, providing aliases for columns in your result set, using an inline view to reference aliased columns, using simple conditional logic, limiting the number of rows returned by a query, returning random records, and finding NULL values. Most of the examples are very simple, but some of them appear in more complex recipes, so it's a good idea to read this chapter if you're relatively new to SQL or aren't familiar with any of the examples listed for this chapter.

Chapter 2, *Sorting Query Results*

Introduces recipes for sorting query results. The ORDER BY clause is introduced and is used to sort query results. Examples increase in complexity ranging from simple, single-column ordering, to ordering by substrings, to ordering based on conditional expressions.

Chapter 3, *Working with Multiple Tables*

Introduces recipes for combining data from multiple tables. If you are new to SQL or are a bit rusty on joins, I strongly recommend you read this chapter before reading Chapter 5 and later. Joining tables is what SQL is all about; you must understand joins to be successful. Examples in this chapter include performing both inner and outer joins, identifying Cartesian productions, basic set operations (set difference, union, intersection), and the effects of joins on aggregate functions.

Chapter 4, *Inserting, Updating, Deleting*

Introduces recipes for inserting, updating, and deleting data, respectively. Most of the examples are very straightforward (perhaps even pedestrian). Nevertheless, operations such as inserting rows into one table from another table, the use of correlated subqueries in updates, an understanding of the effects of NULLs, and knowledge of new features such as multi-table inserts and the MERGE command are extremely useful for your toolbox.

Chapter 5, *Metadata Queries*

Introduces recipes for getting at your database metadata. It's often very useful to find the indexes, constraints, and tables in your schema. The simple recipes here allow you to gain information about your schema. Additionally, "dynamic" SQL examples are shown here as well, i.e., SQL generated by SQL.

Chapter 6, *Working with Strings*

Introduces recipes for manipulating strings. SQL is not known for its string parsing capabilities, but with a little creativity (usually involving Cartesian products) along with the vast array of vendor-specific functions, you can accomplish quite a bit. This chapter is where the book begins to get interesting. Some of the more interesting examples include counting the occurrences of a character in a string, creating delimited lists from table rows, converting delimited lists and strings into rows, and separating numeric and character data from a string of alphanumeric characters.

Chapter 7, *Working with Numbers*

Introduces recipes for common number crunching. The recipes found here are extremely common and you'll learn how easily window functions solve problems involving moving calculations and aggregations. Examples include creating running totals; finding mean, median, and mode; calculating percentiles; and accounting for NULL while performing aggregations.

Chapter 8, *Date Arithmetic*

Is the first of two chapters dealing with dates. Being able to perform simple date arithmetic is crucial to everyday tasks. Examples include determining the number of business days between two dates, calculating the difference between two dates in different units of time (day, month, year, etc.), and counting occurrences of days in a month.

Chapter 9, *Date Manipulation*

Is the second of the two chapters dealing with dates. In this chapter you will find recipes for some of the most common date operations you will encounter in a typical work day. Examples include returning all days in a year, finding leap years, finding first and last days of a month, creating a calendar, and filling in missing dates for a range of dates.

Chapter 10, *Working with Ranges*

Introduces recipes for identifying values in ranges, and for creating ranges of values. Examples include automatically generating a sequence of rows, filling in missing numeric values for a range of values, locating the beginning and end of a range of values, and locating consecutive values.

Chapter 11, *Advanced Searching*

Introduces recipes that are crucial for everyday development and yet sometimes slip through the cracks. These recipes are not any more difficult than others, yet I see many developers making very inefficient attempts at solving the problems these recipes solve. Examples from this chapter include finding knight values, paginating through a result set, skipping rows from a table, finding reciprocals, selecting the top *n* records, and ranking results.

Chapter 12, *Reporting and Warehousing*

Introduces queries typically used in warehousing or generating complex reports. This chapter was meant to be the majority of the book as it existed in my original vision. Examples include converting rows into columns and vice versa (cross-tab reports), creating buckets or groups of data, creating histograms, calculating simple and complete subtotals, performing aggregations over a moving window of rows, and grouping rows based on given units of time.

Chapter 13, *Hierarchical Queries*

Introduces hierarchical recipes. Regardless of how your data is modeled, at some point you will be asked to format data such that it represents a tree or parent-child relationship. This chapter provides recipes accomplishing these tasks. Creating tree-structured result sets can be cumbersome with traditional SQL, so vendor-supplied functions are particularly useful in this chapter. Examples include expressing a parent-child relationship, traversing a hierarchy from root to leaf, and rolling up a hierarchy.

Chapter 14, *Odds 'n' Ends*

Is a collection of miscellaneous recipes that didn't seem to fit into any other problem domain, but that nevertheless are interesting and useful. This chapter is different from the rest in that it focuses on vendor-specific solutions only. This is the only chapter of the book where each recipe highlights only one vendor. The reasons are twofold: first, this chapter was meant to serve as more of a fun, geeky chapter. Second, some recipes exist only to highlight a vendor-specific function that has no equivalent in the other RDBMSs (examples include SQL Server's PIVOT/UNPIVOT operators and Oracle's MODEL clause). In some cases, though, you'll be able to easily tweak a solution provided in this chapter to work for a platform not covered in the recipe.

Appendix A, *Window Function Refresher*

Is a window function refresher along with a solid discussion of groups in SQL. Window functions are new to most, so it is appropriate that this appendix serves as a brief tutorial. Additionally, in my experience I have noticed that the use of GROUP BY in queries is a source of confusion for many developers. This chapter defines exactly what a SQL group is, and then proceeds to use various queries as proofs to validate that definition. The chapter then goes into the effects of NULLs on groups, aggregates, and partitions. Lastly, you'll find discussion on the more obscure and yet extremely powerful syntax of the window function's OVER clause (i.e., the "framing" or "windowing" clause).

Appendix B, *Rozenshtein Revisited*

Is a tribute to David Rozenshtein, to whom I owe my success in SQL development. Rozenshtein's book, *The Essence of SQL* (Coriolis Group Books) was the first book I purchased on SQL that was not required by a class. It was from that book that I learned how to "think in SQL." To this day I attribute much of my understanding of how SQL works to David's book. It truly is different from any other SQL book I've read, and I'm grateful that it was the first one I picked up on my own volition. Appendix B focuses on some of the queries presented in *The Essence of SQL*, and provides alternative solutions using window functions (which weren't available when *The Essence of SQL* was written) for those queries.

Platform and Version

SQL is a moving target. Vendors are constantly pumping new features and functionality into their products. Thus you should know up front which versions of the various platforms were used in the preparation of this text:

- DB2 v.8
- Oracle Database 10g (with the exception of a handful of recipes, the solutions will work for Oracle8i Database and Oracle9i Database as well)

- PostgreSQL 8
- SQL Server 2005
- MySQL 5

Tables Used in This Book

The majority of the examples in this book involve the use of two tables, EMP and DEPT. The EMP table is a simple 14-row table with only numeric, string, and date fields. The DEPT table is a simple four-row table with only numeric and string fields. These tables appear in many old database texts, and the many-to-one relationship between departments and employees is well understood.

While I'm on the topic of the example tables, I want to mention that all but a very few solutions in this book run against these tables. Nowhere do I tweak my example data to set up a solution that you would be unlikely to have a chance of implementing in the real world, as some books do.

And while I'm on the topic of solutions, let me just mention that whenever possible I've tried to provide a generic solution that will run on all five RDBMSs covered in this book. Often that's not possible. Even so, in many cases more than one vendor shares a solution. Because of their mutual support for window functions, for example, Oracle and DB2 often share solutions. Whenever solutions are shared, or at least are very similar, discussions are shared as well.

The contents of EMP and DEPT are shown below, respectively:

```
select * from emp;
```

EMPNO	ENAME	JOB	MGR	HIREDATE	SAL	COMM	DEPTNO
7369	SMITH	CLERK	7902	17-DEC-1980	800		20
7499	ALLEN	SALESMAN	7698	20-FEB-1981	1600	300	30
7521	WARD	SALESMAN	7698	22-FEB-1981	1250	500	30
7566	JONES	MANAGER	7839	02-APR-1981	2975		20
7654	MARTIN	SALESMAN	7698	28-SEP-1981	1250	1400	30
7698	BLAKE	MANAGER	7839	01-MAY-1981	2850		30
7782	CLARK	MANAGER	7839	09-JUN-1981	2450		10
7788	SCOTT	ANALYST	7566	09-DEC-1982	3000		20
7839	KING	PRESIDENT		17-NOV-1981	5000		10
7844	TURNER	SALESMAN	7698	08-SEP-1981	1500	0	30
7876	ADAMS	CLERK	7788	12-JAN-1983	1100		20
7900	JAMES	CLERK	7698	03-DEC-1981	950		30
7902	FORD	ANALYST	7566	03-DEC-1981	3000		20
7934	MILLER	CLERK	7782	23-JAN-1982	1300		10

```
select * from dept;
```

```
DEPTNO DNAME          LOC
------ -------------- ---------
    10 ACCOUNTING     NEW YORK
    20 RESEARCH       DALLAS
    30 SALES          CHICAGO
    40 OPERATIONS     BOSTON
```

Additionally, you will find four pivot tables used in this book; T1, T10, T100, and T500. Because these tables exist only to facilitate pivots, I did not find it necessary to give them clever names. The number following the "T" in each of the pivot tables signifies the number of rows in each table starting from 1. For example, the values for T1 and T10:

```
select id from t1;

        ID
----------
         1


select id from t10;

        ID
----------
         1
         2
         3
         4
         5
         6
         7
         8
         9
        10
```

As an aside, some vendors allow partial SELECT statements. For example, you can have SELECT without a FROM clause. I don't particularly like this, thus I select against a support table, T1, with a single row, rather than using partial queries.

Any other tables are specific to particular recipes and chapters, and will be introduced in the text when appropriate.

Conventions Used in This Book

I use a number of typographical and coding conventions in this book. Take time to become familiar with them. Doing so will enhance your understanding of the text. Coding conventions in particular are important, because I can't discuss them anew for each recipe in the book. Instead, I list the important conventions here.

Typographical Conventions

The following typographical conventions are used in this book:

UPPERCASE

> Used to indicate SQL keywords within text

lowercase

> Used for all queries in code examples. Other languages such as C and JAVA use lowercase for most keywords and I find it infinitely more readable than uppercase. Thus all queries will be lowercase.

`Constant width bold`

> Indicates user input in examples showing an interaction.

 Indicates a tip, suggestion, or general note.

 Indicates a warning or caution.

Coding Conventions

My preference for case in SQL statements is to always use lowercase, for both keywords and user-specified identifiers. For example:

```
select empno, ename
  from emp;
```

Your preference may be otherwise. For example, many prefer to uppercase SQL keywords. Use whatever coding style you prefer, or whatever your project requires.

Despite my use of lowercase in code examples, I consistently uppercase SQL keywords and identifiers in the text. I do this to make those items stand out as something other than regular prose. For example:

> The preceding query represents a SELECT against the EMP table.

While this book covers databases from five different vendors, I've decided to use one format for all the output:

```
EMPNO ENAME
----- ------
 7369 SMITH
 7499 ALLEN
 ...
```

Many solutions make use of *inline views*, or subqueries in the FROM clause. The ANSI SQL standard requires that such views be given table aliases. (Oracle is the only vendor that lets you get away without specifying such aliases.) Thus, my solutions use aliases such as x and y to identify the result sets from inline views:

```
select job, sal
  from (select job, max(sal) sal
          from emp
         group by job) x;
```

Notice the letter X following the final, closing parenthesis. That letter X becomes the name of the "table" returned by the subquery in the FROM clause. While column aliases are a valuable tool for writing self-documenting code, aliases on inline views (for most recipes in this book) are simply formalities. They are typically given trivial names such as X, Y, Z, TMP1, and TMP2. In cases where I feel a better alias will provide more understanding, I do so.

You will notice that the SQL in the Solution section of the recipes is typically numbered, for example:

```
1 select ename
2    from emp
3  where deptno = 10
```

The number is not part of the syntax; I have included it so I can reference parts of the query by number in the Discussion section.

Using Code Examples

This book is here to help you get your job done. In general, you may use the code in this book in your programs and documentation. You do not need to contact O'Reilly for permission unless you're reproducing a significant portion of the code. For example, writing a program that uses several chunks of code from this book does not require permission. Selling or distributing a CD-ROM of examples from O'Reilly books *does* require permission. Answering a question by citing this book and quoting example code does not require permission. Incorporating a significant amount of example code from this book into your product's documentation *does* require permission.

We appreciate, but do not require, attribution. An attribution usually includes the title, author, publisher, and ISBN. For example: *SQL Cookbook*, by Anthony Molinaro. Copyright 2006 O'Reilly Media, Inc., 978-0-596-00976-2.

If you feel your use of code examples falls outside fair use or the permission given above, feel free to contact us at *permissions@oreilly.com*.

Comments and Questions

We have tested and verified the information in this book to the best of our ability, but you may find that features have changed or that we have made mistakes. If so, please notify us by writing to:

O'Reilly Media, Inc.
1005 Gravenstein Highway North
Sebastopol, CA 95472
800-998-9938 (in the United States or Canada)
707-829-0515 (international or local)
707-829-0104 (fax)

You can also send messages electronically. To be put on the mailing list or request a catalog, send email to:

info@oreilly.com

To ask technical questions or comment on the book, or to suggest additional recipes for future editions, send email to:

bookquestions@oreilly.com

We have a web site for this book where you can find examples and errata (previously reported errors and corrections are available for public view there). You can access this page at:

http://www.oreilly.com/catalog/9780596009762

Safari® Enabled

 When you see a Safari® Enabled icon on the cover of your favorite technology book, that means the book is available online through the O'Reilly Network Safari Bookshelf.

Safari offers a solution that's better than e-Books. It's a virtual library that lets you easily search thousands of top tech books, cut and paste code samples, download chapters, and find quick answers when you need the most accurate, current information. Try it for free at *http://safari.oreilly.com*.

Acknowledgments

This book would not exist without all the support I've received from a great many people. I would like to thank my mother, Connie, to whom this book is dedicated. Without your hard work and sacrifice I would not be where I am today. Thank you for everything, Mom. I am thankful and appreciative of everything you've done for my brother and me. I have been blessed to have you as my mother.

To my brother, Joe: every time I came home from Baltimore to take a break from writing, you were there to remind me how great things are when we're not working, and how I should finish writing so I can get back to the more important things in life. You're a good man and I respect you. I am extremely proud of you, and proud to call you my brother.

To my wonderful fiancee, Georgia: Without your support I would not have made it through all 600-plus pages of this book. You were here sharing this experience with me, day after day. I know it was just as hard on you as it was on me. I spent all day working and all night writing, but you were great through it all. You were understanding and supportive and I am forever grateful. Thank you. I love you.

To my future in-laws: to my mother-in-law and father-in-law, Kiki and George. Thank you for your support throughout this whole experience. You always made me feel at home whenever I took a break and came to visit, and you made sure Georgia and I were always well fed. To my sisters-in-law, Anna and Kathy, it was always fun coming home and hanging out with you guys, giving Georgia and me a much needed break from the book and from Baltimore.

To my editor Jonathan Gennick, without whom this book would not exist. Jonathan, you deserve a tremendous amount of credit for this book. You went above and beyond what an editor would normally do and for that you deserve much thanks. From supplying recipes, to tons of rewrites, to keeping things humorous despite oncoming deadlines, I could not have done it without you. I am grateful to have had you as my editor and grateful for the opportunity you have given me. An experienced DBA and author yourself, it was a pleasure to work with someone of your technical level and expertise. I can't imagine there are too many editors out there that can, if they decided to, stop editing and work practically anywhere as a database administrator (DBA); Jonathan can. Being a DBA certainly gives you an edge as an editor as you usually know what I want to say even when I'm having trouble expressing it. O'Reilly is lucky to have you on staff and I am lucky to have you as an editor.

I would like to thank Ales Spetic and Jonathan Gennick for *Transact-SQL Cookbook*. Isaac Newton famously said, "If I have seen a little further it is by standing on the shoulders of giants." In the acknowledgments section of the *Transact-SQL Cookbook*, Ales Spetic wrote something that is a testament to this famous quote and I feel should be in every SQL book. I include it here:

> I hope that this book will complement the exiting opuses of outstanding authors like Joe Celko, David Rozenshtein, Anatoly Abramovich, Eugine Berger, Iztik Ben-Gan, Richard Snodgrass, and others. I spent many nights studying their work, and I learned almost everything I know from their books. As I am writing these lines, I'm aware that for every night I spent discovering their secrets, they must have spent 10 nights putting their knowledge into a consistent and readable form. It is an honor to be able to give something back to the SQL community.

I would like to thank Sanjay Mishra for his excellent *Mastering Oracle SQL* book, and also for putting me in touch with Jonathan. If not for Sanjay, I may have never been in touch with Jonathan and never would have written this book. Amazing how a simple email can change your life. I would like to thank David Rozenshtein, especially, for his *Essence of SQL* book, which provided me with a solid understanding of how to think and problem solve in sets/SQL. I would like to thank David Rozenshtein, Anatoly Abramovich, and Eugene Birger for their book *Optimizing Transact-SQL*, from which I learned many of the advanced SQL techniques I use today.

I would like to thank the whole team at Wireless Generation, a great company with great people. A big thank you to all of the people who took the time to review, critique, or offer advice to help me complete this book: Jesse Davis, Joel Patterson, Philip Zee, Kevin Marshall, Doug Daniels, Otis Gospodnetic, Ken Gunn, John Stewart, Jim Abramson, Adam Mayer, Susan Lau, Alexis Le-Quoc, and Paul Feuer. I would like to thank Maggie Ho for her careful review of my work and extremely useful feedback regarding the window function refresher. I would like to thank Chuck Van Buren and Gillian Gutenberg for their great advice about running. Early morning workouts helped me clear my mind and unwind. I don't think I would have been able to finish this book without getting out a bit. I would like to thank Steve Kang and Chad Levinson for putting up with all my incessant talk about different SQL techniques on the nights when all they wanted was to head to Union Square to get a beer and a burger at Heartland Brewery after a long day of work. I would like to thank Aaron Boyd for all his support, kind words, and, most importantly, good advice. Aaron is honest, hardworking, and a very straightforward guy; people like him make a company better. I would like to thank Olivier Pomel for his support and help in writing this book, in particular for the DB2 solution for creating delimited lists from rows. Olivier contributed that solution without even having a DB2 system to test it with! I explained to him how the WITH clause worked, and minutes later he came up with the solution you see in this book.

Jonah Harris and David Rozenshtein also provided helpful technical review feedback on the manuscript. And Arun Marathe, Nuno Pinto do Souto, and Andrew Odewahn weighed in on the outline and choice of recipes while this book was in its formative stages. Thanks, very much, to all of you.

I want to thank John Haydu and the MODEL clause development team at Oracle Corporation for taking the time to review the MODEL clause article I wrote for O'Reilly, and for ultimately giving me a better understanding of how that clause works. I would like to thank Tom Kyte of Oracle Corporation for allowing me to adapt his TO_BASE function into a SQL-only solution. Bruno Denuit of Microsoft answered questions I had regarding the functionality of the window functions introduced in SQL Server 2005. Simon Riggs of PostgreSQL kept me up to date about new SQL features in PostgreSQL (very big thanks: Simon, by knowing what was coming out and when, I was able to incorporate some new SQL features such as the ever-so-cool GENERATE_SERIES function, which I think made for more elegant solutions compared to pivot tables).

Last but certainly not least, I'd like to thank Kay Young. When you are talented and passionate about what you do, it is great to be able to work with people who are likewise as talented and passionate. Many of the recipes you see in this text have come from working with Kay and coming up with SQL solutions for everyday problems at Wireless Generation. I want to thank you and let you know I absolutely appreciate all the help you given me throughout all of this; from advice, to grammar corrections, to code, you played an integral role in the writing of this book. It's been great working with you, and Wireless Generation is a better company because you are there.

—Anthony Molinaro
September 2005

CHAPTER 1

Retrieving Records

This chapter focuses on very basic SELECT statements. It is important to have a solid understanding of the basics as many of the topics covered here are not only present in more difficult recipes but also are found in everyday SQL.

1.1   Retrieving All Rows and Columns from a Table

Problem

You have a table and want to see all of the data in it.

Solution

Use the special "*" character and issue a SELECT against the table:

```
1 select *
2   from emp
```

Discussion

The character "*" has special meaning in SQL. Using it will return every column for the table specified. Since there is no WHERE clause specified, every row will be returned as well. The alternative would be to list each column individually:

```
select empno,ename,job,sal,mgr,hiredate,comm,deptno
  from emp
```

In ad hoc queries that you execute interactively, it's easier to use SELECT *. However, when writing program code it's better to specify each column individually. The performance will be the same, but by being explicit you will always know what columns you are returning from the query. Likewise, such queries are easier to understand by people other than yourself (who may or may not know all the columns in the tables in the query).

1.2   Retrieving a Subset of Rows from a Table

Problem

You have a table and want to see only rows that satisfy a specific condition.

Solution

Use the WHERE clause to specify which rows to keep. For example, to view all employees assigned to department number 10:

```
1 select *
2   from emp
3  where deptno = 10
```

Discussion

The WHERE clause allows you to retrieve only rows you are interested in. If the expression in the WHERE clause is true for any row, then that row is returned.

Most vendors support common operators such as: =, <, >, <=, >=, !, <>. Additionally, you may want rows that satisfy multiple conditions; this can be done by specifying AND, OR, and parenthesis, as shown in the next recipe.

1.3   Finding Rows That Satisfy Multiple Conditions

Problem

You want to return rows that satisfy multiple conditions.

Solution

Use the WHERE clause along with the OR and AND clauses. For example, if you would like to find all the employees in department 10, along with any employees who earn a commission, along with any employees in department 20 who earn at most $2000:

```
1 select *
2   from emp
3  where deptno = 10
4     or comm is not null
5     or sal <= 2000 and deptno=20
```

Discussion

You can use a combination of AND, OR, and parenthesis to return rows that satisfy multiple conditions. In the solution example, the WHERE clause finds rows such that:

- The DEPTNO is 10.
- The COMM is not NULL
- The salary is $2000 or less for any employee in DEPTNO 20.

The presence of parentheses causes conditions within them to be evaluated together.

For example, consider how the result set changes if the query was written with the parentheses as shown below:

```
select *
 from emp
where (   deptno = 10
       or comm is not null
       or sal <= 2000
      )
  and deptno=20
```

```
EMPNO ENAME  JOB    MGR  HIREDATE      SAL    COMM DEPTNO
----- ------ ------ ---- ----------- ----- ---------- ------
 7369 SMITH  CLERK  7902 17-DEC-1980   800              20
 7876 ADAMS  CLERK  7788 12-JAN-1983  1100              20
```

1.4 Retrieving a Subset of Columns from a Table

Problem

You have a table and want to see values for specific columns rather than for all the columns.

Solution

Specify the columns you are interested in. For example, to see only name, department number, and salary for employees:

```
1 select ename,deptno,sal
2   from emp
```

Discussion

By specifying the columns in the SELECT clause, you ensure that no extraneous data is returned. This can be especially important when retrieving data across a network, as it avoids the waste of time inherent in retrieving data that you do not need.

1.5 Providing Meaningful Names for Columns

Problem

You would like to change the names of the columns that are returned by your query so they are more readable and understandable. Consider this query that returns the salaries and commissions for each employee:

```
1 select sal,comm
2   from emp
```

What's "sal"? Is it short for "sale"? Is it someone's name? What's "comm"? Is it communication? You want the results to have more meaningful labels.

Solution

To change the names of your query results use the AS keyword in the form: *original_name* AS *new_name*. Some databases do not require AS, but all accept it:

```
1 select sal as salary, comm as commission
2   from emp
```

```
SALARY COMMISSION
------- ----------
    800
   1600        300
   1250        500
   2975
   1250       1400
   2850
   2450
   3000
   5000
   1500          0
   1100
    950
   3000
   1300
```

Discussion

Using the AS keyword to give new names to columns returned by your query is known as *aliasing* those columns. The new names that you give are known as *aliases*. Creating good aliases can go a long way toward making a query and its results understandable to others.

1.6   Referencing an Aliased Column in the WHERE Clause

Problem

You have used aliases to provide more meaningful column names for your result set and would like to exclude some of the rows using the WHERE clause. However, your attempt to reference alias names in the WHERE clause fails:

```
select sal as salary, comm as commission
  from emp
 where salary < 5000
```

Solution

By wrapping your query as an inline view you can reference the aliased columns:

```
1 select *
2   from (
3 select sal as salary, comm as commission
4   from emp
5        ) x
6  where salary < 5000
```

Discussion

In this simple example, you can avoid the inline view and reference COMM or SAL directly in the WHERE clause to achieve the same result. This solution introduces you to what you would need to do when attempting to reference any of the following in a WHERE clause:

- Aggregate functions
- Scalar subqueries
- Windowing functions
- Aliases

Placing your query, the one giving aliases, in an inline view gives you the ability to reference the aliased columns in your outer query. Why do you need to do this? The WHERE clause is evaluated before the SELECT, thus, SALARY and COMMISSION do not yet exist when the Problem query's WHERE clause is evaluated. Those aliases are not applied until after the WHERE clause processing is complete. However, the FROM clause is evaluated before the WHERE. By placing the original query in a FROM clause, the results from that query are generated before the outermost WHERE clause, and your outermost WHERE clause "sees" the alias names. This technique is particularly useful when the columns in a table are not named particularly well.

The inline view in this solution is aliased X. Not all databases require an inline view to be explicitly aliased, but some do. All of them accept it.

1.7   Concatenating Column Values

Problem

You want to return values in multiple columns as one column. For example, you would like to produce this result set from a query against the EMP table:

```
CLARK WORKS AS A MANAGER
KING WORKS AS A PRESIDENT
MILLER WORKS AS A CLERK
```

However, the data that you need to generate this result set comes from two different columns, the ENAME and JOB columns in the EMP table:

```
select ename, job
  from emp
 where deptno = 10
```

```
ENAME       JOB
----------  ---------
CLARK       MANAGER
KING        PRESIDENT
MILLER      CLERK
```

Solution

Find and use the built-in function provided by your DBMS to concatenate values from multiple columns.

DB2, Oracle, PostgreSQL

These databases use the double vertical bar as the concatenation operator:

```
1 select ename||' WORKS AS A '||job as msg
2   from emp
3  where deptno=10
```

MySQL

This database supports a function called CONCAT:

```
1 select concat(ename, ' WORKS AS A ',job) as msg
2   from emp
3  where deptno=10
```

SQL Server

Use the "+" operator for concatenation:

```
1 select ename + ' WORKS AS A ' + job as msg
2   from emp
3  where deptno=10
```

Discussion

Use the CONCAT function to concatenate values from multiple columns. The || is a shortcut for the CONCAT function in DB2, Oracle, and PostgreSQL, while + is the shortcut for SQL Server.

1.8   Using Conditional Logic in a SELECT Statement

Problem

You want to perform IF-ELSE operations on values in your SELECT statement. For example, you would like to produce a result set such that, if an employee is paid $2000 or less, a message of "UNDERPAID" is returned, if an employee is paid $4000 or more, a message of "OVERPAID" is returned, if they make somewhere in between, then "OK" is returned. The result set should look like this:

```
ENAME           SAL STATUS
---------- ---------- ---------
SMITH           800 UNDERPAID
ALLEN          1600 UNDERPAID
WARD           1250 UNDERPAID
JONES          2975 OK
MARTIN         1250 UNDERPAID
BLAKE          2850 OK
CLARK          2450 OK
SCOTT          3000 OK
KING           5000 OVERPAID
TURNER         1500 UNDERPAID
ADAMS          1100 UNDERPAID
JAMES           950 UNDERPAID
FORD           3000 OK
MILLER         1300 UNDERPAID
```

Solution

Use the CASE expression to perform conditional logic directly in your SELECT statement:

```
1 select ename,sal,
2        case when sal <= 2000 then 'UNDERPAID'
3             when sal >= 4000 then 'OVERPAID'
4             else 'OK'
5        end as status
6   from emp
```

Discussion

The CASE expression allows you to perform condition logic on values returned by a query. You can provide an alias for a CASE expression to return a more readable result set. In the solution, you'll see the alias STATUS given to the result of the CASE expression. The ELSE clause is optional. Omit the ELSE, and the CASE expression will return NULL for any row that does not satisfy the test condition.

1.9   Limiting the Number of Rows Returned

Problem

You want to limit the number of rows returned in your query. You are not concerned with order; any *n* rows will do.

Solution

Use the built-in function provided by your database to control the number of rows returned.

DB2

In DB2 use the FETCH FIRST clause:

```
1 select *
2   from emp fetch first 5 rows only
```

MySQL and PostgreSQL

Do the same thing in MySQL and PostgreSQL using LIMIT:

```
1 select *
2   from emp limit 5
```

Oracle

In Oracle, place a restriction on the number of rows returned by restricting ROWNUM in the WHERE clause:

```
1 select *
2   from emp
3 where rownum <= 5
```

SQL Server

Use the TOP keyword to restrict the number of rows returned:

```
1 select top 5 *
2   from emp
```

Discussion

Many vendors provide clauses such as FETCH FIRST and LIMIT that let you specify the number of rows to be returned from a query. Oracle is different, in that you must make use of a function called ROWNUM that returns a number for each row returned (an increasing value starting from 1).

Here is what happens when you use ROWNUM <= 5 to return the first five rows:

1. Oracle executes your query.

2. Oracle fetches the first row and calls it row number 1.

3. Have we gotten past row number 5 yet? If no, then Oracle returns the row, because it meets the criteria of being numbered less than or equal to 5. If yes, then Oracle does not return the row.

4. Oracle fetches the next row and advances the row number (to 2, and then to 3, and then to 4, and so forth).

5. Go to step 3.

As this process shows, values from Oracle's ROWNUM are assigned *after* each row is fetched. This is a very important and key point. Many Oracle developers attempt to return only, say, the fifth row returned by a query by specifying ROWNUM = 5. Using an equality condition in conjunction with ROWNUM is a bad idea. Here is what happens when you try to return, say, the fifth row using ROWNUM = 5:

1. Oracle executes your query.

2. Oracle fetches the first row and calls it row number 1.

3. Have we gotten to row number 5 yet? If no, then Oracle discards the row, because it doesn't meet the criteria. If yes, then Oracle returns the row. But the answer will never be yes!

4. Oracle fetches the next row and calls it row number 1. This is because the first row to be returned from the query must be numbered as 1.

5. Go to step 3.

Study this process closely, and you can see why the use of ROWNUM = 5 to return the fifth row fails. You can't have a fifth row if you don't first return rows one through four!

You may notice that ROWNUM = 1 does, in fact, work to return the first row, which may seem to contradict the explanation thus far. The reason ROWNUM = 1 works to return the first row is that, to determine whether or not there are any rows in the table, Oracle has to attempt to fetch at least once. Read the preceding process carefully, substituting 1 for 5, and you'll understand why it's OK to specify ROWNUM = 1 as a condition (for returning one row).

1.10 Returning n Random Records from a Table

Problem

You want to return a specific number of random records from a table. You want to modify the following statement such that successive executions will produce a different set of five rows:

```
select ename, job
  from emp
```

Solution

Take any built-in function supported by your DBMS for returning random values.
Use that function in an ORDER BY clause to sort rows randomly. Then, use the previous recipe's technique to limit the number of randomly sorted rows to return.

DB2

Use the built-in function RAND in conjunction with ORDER BY and FETCH:

```
1 select ename,job
2   from emp
3  order by rand() fetch first 5 rows only
```

MySQL

Use the built-in RAND function in conjunction with LIMIT and ORDER BY:

```
1 select ename,job
2   from emp
3  order by rand() limit 5
```

PostgreSQL

Use the built-in RANDOM function in conjunction with LIMIT and ORDER BY:

```
1 select ename,job
2   from emp
3  order by random() limit 5
```

Oracle

Use the built-in function VALUE, found in the built-in package DBMS_RANDOM,
in conjunction with ORDER BY and the built-in function ROWNUM:

```
1 select *
2   from (
3  select ename, job
4    from emp
5   order by dbms_random.value()
6       )
7   where rownum <= 5
```

SQL Server

Use the built-in function NEWID in conjunction with TOP and ORDER BY to
return a random result set:

```
1  select top 5 ename,job
2    from emp
3   order by newid()
```

Discussion

The ORDER BY clause can accept a function's return value and use it to change the order of the result set. The solution queries all restrict the number of rows to return *after* the function in the ORDER BY clause is executed. Non-Oracle users may find it helpful to look at the Oracle solution as it shows (conceptually) what is happening under the covers of the other solutions.

It is important that you don't confuse using a function in the ORDER BY clause with using a numeric constant. When specifying a numeric constant in the ORDER BY clause, you are requesting that the sort be done according the column in that ordinal position in the SELECT list. When you specify a function in the ORDER BY clause, the sort is performed on the result from the function as it is evaluated for each row.

1.11   Finding Null Values

Problem

You want to find all rows that are null for a particular column.

Solution

To determine whether a value is null, you must use IS NULL:

```
1 select *
2   from emp
3  where comm is null
```

Discussion

NULL is never equal/not equal to anything, not even itself, therefore you cannot use = or != for testing whether a column is NULL. To determine whether or not a row has NULL values you must use IS NULL. You can also use IS NOT NULL to find rows without a null in a given column.

1.12   Transforming Nulls into Real Values

Problem

You have rows that contain nulls and would like to return non-null values in place of those nulls.

Solution

Use the function COALESCE to substitute real values for nulls:

```
1 select coalesce(comm,0)
2   from emp
```

Discussion

The COALESCE function takes one or more values as arguments. The function returns the first non-null value in the list. In the solution, the value of COMM is returned whenever COMM is not null. Otherwise, a zero is returned.

When working with nulls, it's best to take advantage of the built-in functionality provided by your DBMS; in many cases you'll find several functions work equally as well for this task. COALESCE happens to work for all DBMSs. Additionally, CASE can be used for all DBMSs as well:

```
select case
        when comm is not null then comm
        else 0
        end
    from emp
```

While you can use CASE to translate nulls into values, you can see that it's much easier and more succinct to use COALESCE.

1.13 Searching for Patterns

Problem

You want to return rows that match a particular substring or pattern. Consider the following query and result set:

```
select ename, job
  from emp
 where deptno in (10,20)
```

```
ENAME       JOB
----------  ---------
SMITH       CLERK
JONES       MANAGER
CLARK       MANAGER
SCOTT       ANALYST
KING        PRESIDENT
ADAMS       CLERK
FORD        ANALYST
MILLER      CLERK
```

Of the employees in departments 10 and 20, you want to return only those that have either an "I" somewhere in their name or a job title ending with "ER":

```
ENAME       JOB
----------  ---------
SMITH       CLERK
JONES       MANAGER
CLARK       MANAGER
KING        PRESIDENT
MILLER      CLERK
```

Solution

Use the LIKE operator in conjunction with the SQL wildcard operator ("%"):

```
1 select ename, job
2   from emp
3  where deptno in (10,20)
4    and (ename like '%I%' or job like '%ER')
```

Discussion

When used in a LIKE pattern-match operation, the percent ("%") operator matches any sequence of characters. Most SQL implementations also provide the underscore ("_") operator to match a single character. By enclosing the search pattern "I" with "%" operators, any string that contains an "I" (at any position) will be returned. If you do not enclose the search pattern with "%", then where you place the operator will affect the results of the query. For example, to find job titles that end in "ER", prefix the "%" operator to "ER"; if the requirement is to search for all job titles beginning with "ER", then append the "%" operator to "ER".

CHAPTER 2

Sorting Query Results

This chapter focuses on customizing how your query results look. By understanding how you can control and modify your result sets, you can provide more readable and meaningful data.

2.1 Returning Query Results in a Specified Order

Problem

You want to display the names, job, and salaries of employees in department 10 in order based on their salary (from lowest to highest). You want to return the following result set:

```
ENAME      JOB         SAL
---------- --------- ----------
MILLER     CLERK       1300
CLARK      MANAGER     2450
KING       PRESIDENT   5000
```

Solution

Use the ORDER BY clause:

```
1 select ename,job,sal
2   from emp
3  where deptno = 10
4  order by sal asc
```

Discussion

The ORDER BY clause allows you to order the rows of your result set. The solution sorts the rows based on SAL in ascending order. By default, ORDER BY will sort in ascending order, and the ASC clause is therefore optional. Alternatively, specify DESC to sort in descending order:

```
select ename,job,sal
  from emp
 where deptno = 10
 order by sal desc

ENAME        JOB              SAL
----------   ---------   ----------
KING         PRESIDENT       5000
CLARK        MANAGER         2450
MILLER       CLERK           1300
```

You need not specify the name of the column on which to sort. You can instead specify a number representing the column. The number starts at 1 and matches the items in the SELECT list from left to right. For example:

```
select ename,job,sal
  from emp
 where deptno = 10
 order by 3 desc

ENAME        JOB              SAL
----------   ---------   ----------
KING         PRESIDENT       5000
CLARK        MANAGER         2450
MILLER       CLERK           1300
```

The number 3 in this example's ORDER BY clause corresponds to the third column in the SELECT list, which is SAL.

2.2   Sorting by Multiple Fields

Problem

You want to sort the rows from EMP first by DEPTNO ascending, then by salary descending. You want to return the following result set:

```
EMPNO       DEPTNO         SAL ENAME        JOB
----------  ----------  ---------- ----------  ---------
  7839          10       5000 KING          PRESIDENT
  7782          10       2450 CLARK         MANAGER
  7934          10       1300 MILLER        CLERK
  7788          20       3000 SCOTT         ANALYST
  7902          20       3000 FORD          ANALYST
  7566          20       2975 JONES         MANAGER
  7876          20       1100 ADAMS         CLERK
  7369          20        800 SMITH         CLERK
  7698          30       2850 BLAKE         MANAGER
  7499          30       1600 ALLEN         SALESMAN
  7844          30       1500 TURNER        SALESMAN
  7521          30       1250 WARD          SALESMAN
  7654          30       1250 MARTIN        SALESMAN
  7900          30        950 JAMES         CLERK
```

Solution

List the different sort columns in the ORDER BY clause, separated by commas:

```
1 select empno,deptno,sal,ename,job
2   from emp
3  order by deptno, sal desc
```

Discussion

The order of precedence in ORDER BY is from left to right. If you are ordering using the numeric position of a column in the SELECT list, then that number must not be greater than the number of items in the SELECT list. You are generally permitted to order by a column not in the SELECT list, but to do so you must explicitly name the column. However, if you are using GROUP BY or DISTINCT in your query, you cannot order by columns that are not in the SELECT list.

2.3   Sorting by Substrings

Problem

You want to sort the results of a query by specific parts of a string. For example, you want to return employee names and jobs from table EMP and sort by the last two characters in the job field. The result set should look like the following:

```
ENAME       JOB
----------  ---------
KING        PRESIDENT
SMITH       CLERK
ADAMS       CLERK
JAMES       CLERK
MILLER      CLERK
JONES       MANAGER
CLARK       MANAGER
BLAKE       MANAGER
ALLEN       SALESMAN
MARTIN      SALESMAN
WARD        SALESMAN
TURNER      SALESMAN
SCOTT       ANALYST
FORD        ANALYST
```

Solution

DB2, MySQL, Oracle, and PostgreSQL

Use the SUBSTR function in the ORDER BY clause:

```
select ename,job
  from emp
 order by substr(job,length(job)-1)
```

SQL Server

Use the SUBSTRING function in the ORDER BY clause:

```
select ename,job
  from emp
 order by substring(job,len(job)-1,2)
```

Discussion

Using your DBMS's substring function, you can easily sort by any part of a string. To sort by the last two characters of a string, find the end of the string (which is the length of the string) and subtract 2. The start position will be the second to last character in the string. You then take all characters after that start position. Because SQL Server requires a third parameter in SUBSTRING to specify the number of characters to take. In this example, any number greater than or equal to 2 will work.

2.4   Sorting Mixed Alphanumeric Data

Problem

You have mixed alphanumeric data and want to sort by either the numeric or character portion of the data. Consider this view:

```
create view V
as
select ename||' '||deptno as data
  from emp

select * from V

DATA
-------------
SMITH 20
ALLEN 30
WARD 30
JONES 20
MARTIN 30
BLAKE 30
CLARK 10
SCOTT 20
KING 10
TURNER 30
ADAMS 20
JAMES 30
FORD 20
MILLER 10
```

You want to sort the results by DEPTNO or ENAME. Sorting by DEPTNO produces the following result set:

```
DATA
----------
CLARK 10
KING 10
MILLER 10
SMITH 20
ADAMS 20
FORD 20
SCOTT 20
JONES 20
ALLEN 30
BLAKE 30
MARTIN 30
JAMES 30
TURNER 30
WARD 30
```

Sorting by ENAME produces the following result set:

```
DATA
---------
ADAMS 20
ALLEN 30
BLAKE 30
CLARK 10
FORD 20
JAMES 30
JONES 20
KING 10
MARTIN 30
MILLER 10
SCOTT 20
SMITH 20
TURNER 30
WARD 30
```

Solution

Oracle and PostgreSQL

Use the functions REPLACE and TRANSLATE to modify the string for sorting:

```
/* ORDER BY DEPTNO */

1 select data
2   from V
3  order by replace(data,
4           replace(
5           translate(data,'0123456789','##########'),'#',''),'')

/* ORDER BY ENAME */
```

```
1 select data
2   from V
3  order by replace(
4             translate(data,'0123456789','##########'),'#','')
```

DB2

Implicit type conversion is more strict in DB2 than in Oracle or PostgreSQL, so you will need to cast DEPTNO to a CHAR for view V to be valid. Rather than recreate view V, this solution will simply use an inline view. The solution uses REPLACE and TRANSLATE in the same way as the Oracle and PostrgreSQL solution, but the order of arguments for TRANSLATE is slightly different for DB2:

```
/* ORDER BY DEPTNO */

1  select *
2    from (
3  select ename||' '||cast(deptno as char(2)) as data
4    from emp
5         ) v
6   order by replace(data,
7             replace(
8             translate(data,'##########','0123456789'),'#',''),'')

/* ORDER BY ENAME */

1  select *
2    from (
3  select ename||' '||cast(deptno as char(2)) as data
4    from emp
5         ) v
6   order by replace(
7             translate(data,'##########','0123456789'),'#','')
```

MySQL and SQL Server

The TRANSLATE function is not currently supported by these platforms, thus a solution for this problem will not be provided.

Discussion

The TRANSLATE and REPLACE functions remove either the numbers or characters from each row, allowing you to easily sort by one or the other. The values passed to ORDER BY are shown in the following query results (using the Oracle solution as the example, as the same technique applies to all three vendors; only the order of parameters passed to TRANSLATE is what sets DB2 apart):

```
select data,
       replace(data,
       replace(
       translate(data,'0123456789','##########'),'#',''),'') nums,
```

```
       replace(
         translate(data,'0123456789','##########'),'#','') chars
     from V

DATA          NUMS    CHARS
------------  ------  ----------
SMITH 20       20      SMITH
ALLEN 30       30      ALLEN
WARD 30        30      WARD
JONES 20       20      JONES
MARTIN 30      30      MARTIN
BLAKE 30       30      BLAKE
CLARK 10       10      CLARK
SCOTT 20       20      SCOTT
KING 10        10      KING
TURNER 30      30      TURNER
ADAMS 20       20      ADAMS
JAMES 30       30      JAMES
FORD 20        20      FORD
MILLER 10      10      MILLER
```

2.5   Dealing with Nulls When Sorting

Problem

You want to sort results from EMP by COMM, but the field is nullable. You need a way to specify whether nulls sort last:

```
ENAME          SAL        COMM
----------  ----------  ----------
TURNER         1500          0
ALLEN          1600        300
WARD           1250        500
MARTIN         1250       1400
SMITH           800
JONES          2975
JAMES           950
MILLER         1300
FORD           3000
ADAMS          1100
BLAKE          2850
CLARK          2450
SCOTT          3000
KING           5000
```

or whether they sort first:

```
ENAME          SAL        COMM
----------  ----------  ----------
SMITH           800
JONES          2975
CLARK          2450
```

BLAKE	2850	
SCOTT	3000	
KING	5000	
JAMES	950	
MILLER	1300	
FORD	3000	
ADAMS	1100	
MARTIN	1250	1400
WARD	1250	500
ALLEN	1600	300
TURNER	1500	0

Solution

Depending on how you want the data to look (and how your particular RDBMS sorts NULL values), you can sort the nullable column in ascending or descending order:

```
1 select ename,sal,comm
2   from emp
3 order by 3
```

```
1 select ename,sal,comm
2   from emp
3 order by 3 desc
```

This solution puts you in a position such that if the nullable column contains non-NULL values, they will be sorted in ascending or descending order as well, according to what you ask for; this may or may not what you have in mind. If instead you would like to sort NULL values differently than non-NULL values, for example, you want to sort non-NULL values in ascending or descending order and all NULL values last, you can use a CASE expression to conditionally sort the column.

DB2, MySQL, PostgreSQL, and SQL Server

Use a CASE expression to "flag" when a value is NULL. The idea is to have a flag with two values: one to represent NULLs, the other to represent non-NULLs. Once you have that, simply add this flag column to the ORDER BY clause. You'll easily be able to control whether NULL values are sorted first or last without interfering with non-NULL values:

```
/* NON-NULL COMM SORTED ASCENDING, ALL NULLS LAST */

1 select ename,sal,comm
2   from (
3 select ename,sal,comm,
4        case when comm is null then 0 else 1 end as is_null
5   from emp
6        ) x
7 order by is_null desc,comm
```

```
ENAME    SAL      COMM
------   -----    ----------
TURNER   1500            0
ALLEN    1600          300
WARD     1250          500
MARTIN   1250         1400
SMITH     800
JONES    2975
JAMES     950
MILLER   1300
FORD     3000
ADAMS    1100
BLAKE    2850
CLARK    2450
SCOTT    3000
KING     5000
```

```
/* NON-NULL COMM SORTED DESCENDING, ALL NULLS LAST */

1  select ename,sal,comm
2    from (
3  select ename,sal,comm,
4         case when comm is null then 0 else 1 end as is_null
5    from emp
6         ) x
7   order by is_null desc,comm desc
```

```
ENAME    SAL      COMM
------   -----    ----------
MARTIN   1250         1400
WARD     1250          500
ALLEN    1600          300
TURNER   1500            0
SMITH     800
JONES    2975
JAMES     950
MILLER   1300
FORD     3000
ADAMS    1100
BLAKE    2850
CLARK    2450
SCOTT    3000
KING     5000
```

```
/* NON-NULL COMM SORTED ASCENDING, ALL NULLS FIRST */

1  select ename,sal,comm
2    from (
3  select ename,sal,comm,
4         case when comm is null then 0 else 1 end as is_null
5    from emp
6         ) x
7   order by is_null,comm
```

```
ENAME    SAL     COMM
------  -----  ----------
SMITH    800
JONES   2975
CLARK   2450
BLAKE   2850
SCOTT   3000
KING    5000
JAMES    950
MILLER  1300
FORD    3000
ADAMS   1100
TURNER  1500        0
ALLEN   1600      300
WARD    1250      500
MARTIN  1250     1400
```

```
/* NON-NULL COMM SORTED DESCENDING, ALL NULLS FIRST */

1  select ename,sal,comm
2    from (
3  select ename,sal,comm,
4         case when comm is null then 0 else 1 end as is_null
5    from emp
6         ) x
7   order by is_null,comm desc
```

```
ENAME    SAL     COMM
------  -----  ----------
SMITH    800
JONES   2975
CLARK   2450
BLAKE   2850
SCOTT   3000
KING    5000
JAMES    950
MILLER  1300
FORD    3000
ADAMS   1100
MARTIN  1250     1400
WARD    1250      500
ALLEN   1600      300
TURNER  1500        0
```

Oracle

Users on Oracle8i Database and earlier can use the solution for the other platforms. Users on Oracle9i Database and later can use the NULLS FIRST and NULLS LAST extension to the ORDER BY clause to ensure NULLs are sorted first or last regardless of how non-NULL values are sorted:

```
/* NON-NULL COMM SORTED ASCENDING, ALL NULLS LAST */

1 select ename,sal,comm
2   from emp
3   order by comm nulls last

ENAME    SAL      COMM
------   -----    ----------
TURNER   1500            0
ALLEN    1600          300
WARD     1250          500
MARTIN   1250         1400
SMITH     800
JONES    2975
JAMES     950
MILLER   1300
FORD     3000
ADAMS    1100
BLAKE    2850
CLARK    2450
SCOTT    3000
KING     5000


/* NON-NULL COMM SORTED DESCENDING, ALL NULLS LAST */

1 select ename,sal,comm
2   from emp
3   order by comm desc nulls last

ENAME    SAL      COMM
------   -----    ----------
MARTIN   1250         1400
WARD     1250          500
ALLEN    1600          300
TURNER   1500            0
SMITH     800
JONES    2975
JAMES     950
MILLER   1300
FORD     3000
ADAMS    1100
BLAKE    2850
CLARK    2450
SCOTT    3000
KING     5000


/* NON-NULL COMM SORTED ASCENDING, ALL NULLS FIRST */

1 select ename,sal,comm
2   from emp
3   order by comm nulls first
```

```
ENAME    SAL    COMM
------  -----  ----------
SMITH    800
JONES   2975
CLARK   2450
BLAKE   2850
SCOTT   3000
KING    5000
JAMES    950
MILLER  1300
FORD    3000
ADAMS   1100
TURNER  1500         0
ALLEN   1600       300
WARD    1250       500
MARTIN  1250      1400


/* NON-NULL COMM SORTED DESCENDING, ALL NULLS FIRST */

1 select ename,sal,comm
2   from emp
3  order by comm desc nulls first

ENAME    SAL    COMM
------  -----  ----------
SMITH    800
JONES   2975
CLARK   2450
BLAKE   2850
SCOTT   3000
KING    5000
JAMES    950
MILLER  1300
FORD    3000
ADAMS   1100
MARTIN  1250      1400
WARD    1250       500
ALLEN   1600       300
TURNER  1500         0
```

Discussion

Unless your RDBMS provides you with a way to easily sort NULL values first or last without modifying non-NULL values in the same column (such as Oracle does), you'll need an auxiliary column.

> As of the time of this writing, DB2 users can use NULLS FIRST and NULLS LAST in the ORDER BY subclause of the OVER clause in window functions but not in the ORDER BY clause for the entire result set.

The purpose of this extra column (in the query only, not in the table) is to allow you to identify NULL values and sort them altogether, first or last. The following query returns the result set for inline view X for the non-Oracle solution:

```
select ename,sal,comm,
        case when comm is null then 0 else 1 end as is_null
    from emp
```

ENAME	SAL	COMM	IS_NULL
SMITH	800		0
ALLEN	1600	300	1
WARD	1250	500	1
JONES	2975		0
MARTIN	1250	1400	1
BLAKE	2850		0
CLARK	2450		0
SCOTT	3000		0
KING	5000		0
TURNER	1500	0	1
ADAMS	1100		0
JAMES	950		0
FORD	3000		0
MILLER	1300		0

By using the values returned by IS_NULL, you can easily sort NULLS first or last without interfering with the sorting of COMM.

2.6   Sorting on a Data Dependent Key

Problem

You want to sort based on some conditional logic. For example: if JOB is "SALES-MAN" you want to sort on COMM; otherwise, you want to sort by SAL. You want to return the following result set:

ENAME	SAL	JOB	COMM
TURNER	1500	SALESMAN	0
ALLEN	1600	SALESMAN	300
WARD	1250	SALESMAN	500
SMITH	800	CLERK	
JAMES	950	CLERK	
ADAMS	1100	CLERK	
MILLER	1300	CLERK	
MARTIN	1250	SALESMAN	1400
CLARK	2450	MANAGER	
BLAKE	2850	MANAGER	
JONES	2975	MANAGER	
SCOTT	3000	ANALYST	
FORD	3000	ANALYST	
KING	5000	PRESIDENT	

Solution

Use a CASE expression in the ORDER BY clause:

```
1 select ename,sal,job,comm
2   from emp
3  order by case when job = 'SALESMAN' then comm else sal end
```

Discussion

You can use the CASE expression to dynamically change how results are sorted. The values passed to the ORDER BY look as follows:

```
select ename,sal,job,comm,
       case when job = 'SALESMAN' then comm else sal end as ordered
  from emp
 order by 5
```

ENAME	SAL	JOB	COMM	ORDERED
TURNER	1500	SALESMAN	0	0
ALLEN	1600	SALESMAN	300	300
WARD	1250	SALESMAN	500	500
SMITH	800	CLERK		800
JAMES	950	CLERK		950
ADAMS	1100	CLERK		1100
MILLER	1300	CLERK		1300
MARTIN	1250	SALESMAN	1400	1400
CLARK	2450	MANAGER		2450
BLAKE	2850	MANAGER		2850
JONES	2975	MANAGER		2975
SCOTT	3000	ANALYST		3000
FORD	3000	ANALYST		3000
KING	5000	PRESIDENT		5000

CHAPTER 3

Working with Multiple Tables

This chapter introduces the use of joins and set operations to combine data from multiple tables. Joins are the foundation of SQL. Set operations are also very important. If you want to master the complex queries found in the later chapters of this book, you must start here, with joins and set operations.

3.1 Stacking One Rowset Atop Another

Problem

You want to return data stored in more than one table, conceptually stacking one result set atop the other. The tables do not necessarily have a common key, but their columns do have the same data types. For example, you want to display the name and department number of the employees in department 10 in table EMP, along with the name and department number of each department in table DEPT. You want the result set to look like the following:

```
ENAME_AND_DNAME    DEPTNO
---------------  ----------
CLARK                  10
KING                   10
MILLER                 10
----------
ACCOUNTING             10
RESEARCH               20
SALES                  30
OPERATIONS             40
```

Solution

Use the set operation UNION ALL to combine rows from multiple tables:

```
1  select ename as ename_and_dname, deptno
2    from emp
3   where deptno = 10
4   union all
```

```
5  select '----------', null
6    from t1
7  union all
8  select dname, deptno
9    from dept
```

Discussion

UNION ALL combines rows from multiple row sources into one result set. As with all set operations, the items in all the SELECT lists must match in number and data type. For example, both of the following queries will fail:

```
select deptno    |  select deptno, dname
  from dept      |    from dept
union all        |  union
select ename     |  select deptno
  from emp       |    from emp
```

It is important to note, UNION ALL will include duplicates if they exist. If you wish to filter out duplicates, use the UNION operator. For example, a UNION between EMP.DEPTNO and DEPT.DEPTNO returns only four rows:

```
select deptno
  from emp
union
select deptno
  from dept

    DEPTNO
----------
        10
        20
        30
        40
```

Specifying UNION rather than UNION ALL will most likely result in a sort operation in order to eliminate duplicates. Keep this in mind when working with large result sets. Using UNION is roughly equivalent to the following query, which applies DISTINCT to the output from a UNION ALL:

```
select distinct deptno
  from (
select deptno
  from emp
union all
select deptno
  from dept
      )

    DEPTNO
----------
        10
        20
        30
        40
```

You wouldn't use DISTINCT in a query unless you had to, and the same rule applies for UNION; don't use it instead of UNION ALL unless you have to.

3.2 Combining Related Rows

Problem

You want to return rows from multiple tables by joining on a known common column or joining on columns that share common values. For example, you want to display the names of all employees in department 10 along with the location of each employee's department, but that data is stored in two separate tables. You want the result set to be the following:

```
ENAME      LOC
---------- -------------
CLARK      NEW YORK
KING       NEW YORK
MILLER     NEW YORK
```

Solution

Join table EMP to table DEPT on DEPTNO:

```
1 select e.ename, d.loc
2   from emp e, dept d
3  where e.deptno = d.deptno
4    and e.deptno = 10
```

Discussion

The solution is an example of a *join*, or more accurately an *equi-join*, which is a type of *inner join*. A join is an operation that combines rows from two tables into one. An equi-join is one in which the join condition is based on an equality condition (e.g., where one department number equals another). An inner join is the original type of join; each row returned contains data from each table.

Conceptually, the result set from a join is produced by first creating a Cartesian product (all possible combinations of rows) from the tables listed in the FROM clause, as seen below:

```
select e.ename, d.loc,
       e.deptno as emp_deptno,
       d.deptno as dept_deptno
  from emp e, dept d
 where e.deptno = 10
```

```
ENAME      LOC           EMP_DEPTNO DEPT_DEPTNO
---------- ------------- ---------- -----------
CLARK      NEW YORK          10          10
KING       NEW YORK          10          10
MILLER     NEW YORK          10          10
CLARK      DALLAS            10          20
```

KING	DALLAS	10	20
MILLER	DALLAS	10	20
CLARK	CHICAGO	10	30
KING	CHICAGO	10	30
MILLER	CHICAGO	10	30
CLARK	BOSTON	10	40
KING	BOSTON	10	40
MILLER	BOSTON	10	40

Every employee in table EMP (in department 10) is returned along with every department in the table DEPT. Then, the expression in the WHERE clause involving e.deptno and d.deptno (the join) restricts the result set such that the only rows returned are the ones where EMP.DEPTNO and DEPT.DEPTNO are equal:

```
select e.ename, d.loc,
       e.deptno as emp_deptno,
       d.deptno as dept_deptno
  from emp e, dept d
 where e.deptno = d.deptno
   and e.deptno = 10
```

```
ENAME       LOC           EMP_DEPTNO DEPT_DEPTNO
----------  ------------- ---------- -----------
CLARK       NEW YORK            10          10
KING        NEW YORK            10          10
MILLER      NEW YORK            10          10
```

An alternative solution makes use of an explicit JOIN clause (the "INNER" keyword is optional):

```
select e.ename, d.loc
  from emp e inner join dept d
    on (e.deptno = d.deptno)
 where e.deptno = 10
```

Use the JOIN clause if you prefer to have the join logic in the FROM clause rather than the WHERE clause. Both styles are ANSI compliant and work on all the latest versions of the RDBMSs in this book.

3.3   Finding Rows in Common Between Two Tables

Problem

You want to find common rows between two tables but there are multiple columns on which you can join. For example, consider the following view V:

```
create view V
as
select ename,job,sal
  from emp
 where job = 'CLERK'

select * from V
```

ENAME	JOB	SAL
SMITH	CLERK	800
ADAMS	CLERK	1100
JAMES	CLERK	950
MILLER	CLERK	1300

Only clerks are returned from view V. However, the view does not show all possible EMP columns. You want to return the EMPNO, ENAME, JOB, SAL, and DEPTNO of all employees in EMP that match the rows from view V. You want the result set to be the following:

EMPNO	ENAME	JOB	SAL	DEPTNO
7369	SMITH	CLERK	800	20
7876	ADAMS	CLERK	1100	20
7900	JAMES	CLERK	950	30
7934	MILLER	CLERK	1300	10

Solution

Join the tables on all the columns necessary to return the correct result. Alternatively, use the set operation INTERSECT to avoid performing a join and instead return the intersection (common rows) of the two tables.

MySQL and SQL Server

Join table EMP to view V using multiple join conditions:

```
1  select e.empno,e.ename,e.job,e.sal,e.deptno
2    from emp e, V
3   where e.ename = v.ename
4     and e.job  = v.job
5     and e.sal  = v.sal
```

Alternatively, you can perform the same join via the JOIN clause:

```
1  select e.empno,e.ename,e.job,e.sal,e.deptno
2    from emp e join V
3      on (   e.ename = v.ename
4         and e.job  = v.job
5         and e.sal  = v.sal )
```

DB2, Oracle, and PostgreSQL

The MySQL and SQL Server solution also works for DB2, Oracle, and PostgreSQL. It's the solution you should use if you need to return values from view V.

If you do not actually need to return columns from view V, you may use the set operation INTERSECT along with an IN predicate:

```
1  select empno,ename,job,sal,deptno
2    from emp
3   where (ename,job,sal) in (
4    select ename,job,sal from emp
```

```
5    intersect
6    select ename,job,sal from V
7  )
```

Discussion

When performing joins, you must consider the proper columns to join on in order to return correct results. This is especially important when rows can have common values for some columns while having different values for others.

The set operation INTERSECT will return rows common to both row sources. When using INTERSECT, you are required to compare the same number of items, having the same data type, from two tables. When working with set operations keep in mind that, by default, duplicate rows will not be returned.

3.4   Retrieving Values from One Table That Do Not Exist in Another

Problem

You wish to find those values in one table, call it the source table, that do not also exist in some target table. For example, you want to find which departments (if any) in table DEPT do not exist in table EMP. In the example data, DEPTNO 40 from table DEPT does not exist in table EMP, so the result set should be the following:

```
DEPTNO
----------
        40
```

Solution

Having functions that perform set difference is particularly useful for this problem. DB2, PostgreSQL, and Oracle support set difference operations. If your DBMS does not support a set difference function, use a subquery as shown for MySQL and SQL Server.

DB2 and PostgreSQL

Use the set operation EXCEPT:

```
1 select deptno from dept
2 except
3 select deptno from emp
```

Oracle

Use the set operation MINUS:

```
1 select deptno from dept
2 minus
3 select deptno from emp
```

MySQL and SQL Server

Use a subquery to return all DEPTNOs from table EMP into an outer query that searches table DEPT for rows that are not amongst the rows returned from the subquery:

```
1 select deptno
2   from dept
3  where deptno not in (select deptno from emp)
```

Discussion

DB2 and PostgreSQL

The built-in functions provided by DB2 and PostgreSQL make this operation quite easy. The EXCEPT operator takes the first result set and removes from it all rows found in the second result set. The operation is very much like a subtraction.

There are restrictions on the use of set operators, including EXCEPT. Data types and number of values to compare must match in both SELECT lists. Additionally, EXCEPT will not return duplicates and, unlike a subquery using NOT IN, NULLs do not present a problem (see the discussion for MySQL and SQL Server). The EXCEPT operator will return rows from the upper query (the query before the EXCEPT) that do not exist in the lower query (the query after the EXCEPT).

Oracle

The Oracle solution is identical to that for DB2 and PostgreSQL, except that Oracle calls its set difference operator MINUS rather than EXCEPT. Otherwise, the preceding explanation applies to Oracle as well.

MySQL and SQL Server

The subquery will return all DEPTNOs from table EMP. The outer query returns all DEPTNOs from table DEPT that are "not in" or "not included in" the result set returned from the subquery.

Duplicate elimination is something you'll want to consider when using the MySQL and SQL Server solutions. The EXCEPT- and MINUS-based solutions used for the other platforms eliminate duplicate rows from the result set, ensuring that each DEPTNO is reported only one time. Of course, that can only be the case anyway, as DEPTNO is a key field in my example data. Were DEPTNO not a key field, you could use DISTINCT as follows to ensure that each DEPTNO value missing from EMP is reported only once:

```
select distinct deptno
  from dept
 where deptno not in (select deptno from emp)
```

Be mindful of NULLs when using NOT IN. Consider the following table, NEW_DEPT:

```
create table new_dept(deptno integer)
insert into new_dept values (10)
insert into new_dept values (50)
insert into new_dept values (null)
```

If you try to find the DEPTNOs in table DEPT that do not exist in table NEW_DEPT and use a subquery with NOT IN, you'll find that the query returns no rows:

```
select *
  from dept
 where deptno not in (select deptno from new_dept)
```

DEPTNOs 20, 30, and 40 are not in table NEW_DEPT, yet were not returned by the query. Why? The reason is the NULL value present in table NEW_DEPT. Three rows are returned by the subquery, with DEPTNOs of: 10, 50, and NULL. IN and NOT IN are essentially OR operations, and will yield different results because of how NULL values are treated by logical OR evaluations. To understand this, examine the truth tables below (Let T=True, F=False, N=Null):

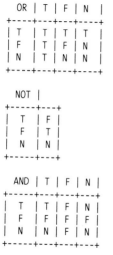

```
 OR | T | F | N |
+----+---+---+----+
| T  | T | T | T |
| F  | T | F | N |
| N  | T | N | N |
+----+---+---+----+

 NOT |
+-----+---+
|  T  | F |
|  F  | T |
|  N  | N |
+-----+---+

 AND | T | F | N |
+-----+---+---+---+
|  T  | T | F | N |
|  F  | F | F | F |
|  N  | N | F | N |
+-----+---+---+---+
```

Now consider the following example using IN and its equivalent using OR:

```
select deptno
  from dept
 where deptno in ( 10,50,null )

DEPTNO
-------
    10

select deptno
  from dept
 where (deptno=10 or deptno=50 or deptno=null)

DEPTNO
-------
10
```

Why was only DEPTNO 10 returned? There are four DEPTNOs in DEPT, (10,20,30,40), each one is evaluated against the predicate (deptno=10 or deptno=50 or deptno=null). According to the truth tables above, for each DEPTNO (10,20,30,40), the predicate yields:

```
DEPTNO=10
(deptno=10 or deptno=50 or deptno=null)
= (10=10 or 10=50 or 10=null)
= (T or F or N)
= (T or N)
= (T)

DEPTNO=20
(deptno=10 or deptno=50 or deptno=null)
= (20=10 or 20=50 or 20=null)
= (F or F or N)
= (F or N)
= (N)

DEPTNO=30
(deptno=10 or deptno=50 or deptno=null)
= (30=10 or 30=50 or 30=null)
= (F or F or N)
= (F or N)
= (N)

DEPTNO=40
(deptno=10 or deptno=50 or deptno=null)
= (40=10 or 40=50 or 40=null)
= (F or F or N)
= (F or N)
= (N)
```

Now it is obvious why only DEPTNO 10 was returned when using IN and OR. Now consider the same example using NOT IN and NOT OR:

```
select deptno
  from dept
 where deptno not in ( 10,50,null )

( no rows )

select deptno
  from dept
 where not (deptno=10 or deptno=50 or deptno=null)

( no rows )
```

Why are no rows returned? Let's check the truth tables:

```
DEPTNO=10
NOT (deptno=10 or deptno=50 or deptno=null)
= NOT (10=10 or 10=50 or 10=null)
= NOT (T or F or N)
= NOT (T or N)
= NOT (T)
= (F)
```

```
DEPTNO=20
NOT (deptno=10 or deptno=50 or deptno=null)
= NOT (20=10 or 20=50 or 20=null)
= NOT (F or F or N)
= NOT (F or N)
= NOT (N)
= (N)

DEPTNO=30
NOT (deptno=10 or deptno=50 or deptno=null)
= NOT (30=10 or 30=50 or 30=null)
= NOT (F or F or N)
= NOT (F or N)
= NOT (N)
= (N)

DEPTNO=40
NOT (deptno=10 or deptno=50 or deptno=null)
= NOT (40=10 or 40=50 or 40=null)
= NOT (F or F or N)
= NOT (F or N)
= NOT (N)
= (N)
```

In SQL, "TRUE or NULL" is TRUE, but "FALSE or NULL" is NULL! You must keep this in mind when using IN predicates and when performing logical OR evaluations when NULL values are involved.

To avoid the problem with NOT IN and NULLs, use a correlated subquery in conjunction with NOT EXISTS. The term "correlated subquery" is used because rows from the outer query are referenced in the subquery. The following example is an alternative solution that will not be affected by NULL rows (going back to the original query from the Problem section):

```
select d.deptno
  from dept d
 where not exists (
   select 1
     from emp e
    where d.deptno = e.deptno
)

DEPTNO
----------
40

select d.deptno
  from dept d
 where not exists (
   select 1
     from new_dept nd
    where d.deptno = nd.deptno
)

DEPTNO
----------
30
40
20
```

Conceptually, the outer query in this solution considers each row in the DEPT table. For each DEPT row, the following happens:

1. The subquery is executed to see whether the department number exists in the EMP table. Note the condition D.DEPTNO = E.DEPTNO, which brings together the department numbers from the two tables.

2. If the subquery returns results, then EXISTS (...) evaluates to true and NOT EXISTS (...) thus evaluates to FALSE, and the row being considered by the outer query is discarded.

3. If the subquery returns no results, then NOT EXISTS (...) evaluates to TRUE, and the row being considered by the outer query is returned (because it is for a department not represented in the EMP table).

The items in the SELECT list of the subquery are unimportant when using a correlated subquery with EXISTS/NOT EXISTS, which is why I chose to select NULL, to force you to focus on the join in the subquery rather than the items in the SELECT list.

3.5 Retrieving Rows from One Table That Do Not Correspond to Rows in Another

Problem

You want to find rows that are in one table that do not have a match in another table, for two tables that have common keys. For example, you want to find which departments have no employees. The result set should be the following:

```
DEPTNO DNAME          LOC
---------- -------------- --------------
    40 OPERATIONS     BOSTON
```

Finding the department each employee works in requires an equi-join on DEPTNO from EMP to DEPT. The DEPTNO column represents the common value between tables. Unfortunately, an equi-join will not show you which department has no employees. That's because by equi-joining EMP and DEPT you are returning all rows that satisfy the join condition. Instead you want only those rows from DEPT that do not satisfy the join condition.

This is a subtly different problem than in the preceding recipe, though at first glance they may seem the same. The difference is that the preceding recipe yields only a list of department numbers not represented in table EMP. Using this recipe, however, you can easily return other columns from the DEPT table; you can return more than just department numbers.

Solution

Return all rows from one table along with rows from another that may or may not have a match on the common column. Then, keep only those rows with no match.

DB2, MySQL, PostgreSQL, SQL Server

Use an outer join and filter for NULLs (keyword OUTER is optional):

```
1 select d.*
2   from dept d left outer join emp e
3     on (d.deptno = e.deptno)
4  where e.deptno is null
```

Oracle

For users on Oracle9i Database and later, the preceding solution will work. Alternatively, you can use the proprietary Oracle outer-join syntax:

```
1 select d.*
2   from dept d, emp e
3  where d.deptno = e.deptno (+)
4    and e.deptno is null
```

This proprietary syntax (note the use of the "+" in parens) is the only outer-join syntax available in Oracle8i Database and earlier.

Discussion

This solution works by outer joining and then keeping only rows that have no match. This sort of operation is sometimes called an *anti-join*. To get a better idea of how an anti-join works, first examine the result set without filtering for NULLs:

```
select e.ename, e.deptno as emp_deptno, d.*
  from dept d left join emp e
    on (d.deptno = e.deptno)
```

ENAME	EMP_DEPTNO	DEPTNO	DNAME	LOC
SMITH	20	20	RESEARCH	DALLAS
ALLEN	30	30	SALES	CHICAGO
WARD	30	30	SALES	CHICAGO
JONES	20	20	RESEARCH	DALLAS
MARTIN	30	30	SALES	CHICAGO
BLAKE	30	30	SALES	CHICAGO
CLARK	10	10	ACCOUNTING	NEW YORK
SCOTT	20	20	RESEARCH	DALLAS
KING	10	10	ACCOUNTING	NEW YORK
TURNER	30	30	SALES	CHICAGO
ADAMS	20	20	RESEARCH	DALLAS
JAMES	30	30	SALES	CHICAGO
FORD	20	20	RESEARCH	DALLAS
MILLER	10	10	ACCOUNTING	NEW YORK
		40	OPERATIONS	BOSTON

Notice, the last row has a NULL value for EMP.ENAME and EMP_DEPTNO. That's because no employees work in department 40. The solution uses the WHERE clause to keep only rows where EMP_DEPTNO is NULL (thus keeping only rows from DEPT that have no match in EMP).

3.6 Adding Joins to a Query Without Interfering with Other Joins

Problem

You have a query that returns the results you want. You need additional information, but when trying to get it, you lose data from the original result set. For example, you want to return all employees, the location of the department in which they work, and the date they received a bonus. For this problem, the EMP_BONUS table contains the following data:

```
select * from emp_bonus
```

```
    EMPNO RECEIVED         TYPE
---------- ----------- ----------
      7369 14-MAR-2005          1
      7900 14-MAR-2005          2
      7788 14-MAR-2005          3
```

The query you start with looks like this:

```
select e.ename, d.loc
  from emp e, dept d
 where e.deptno=d.deptno
```

```
ENAME      LOC
---------- -------------
SMITH      DALLAS
ALLEN      CHICAGO
WARD       CHICAGO
JONES      DALLAS
MARTIN     CHICAGO
BLAKE      CHICAGO
CLARK      NEW YORK
SCOTT      DALLAS
KING       NEW YORK
TURNER     CHICAGO
ADAMS      DALLAS
JAMES      CHICAGO
FORD       DALLAS
MILLER     NEW YORK
```

You want to add to these results the date a bonus was given to an employee, but joining to the EMP_BONUS table returns fewer rows than you wish because not every employee has a bonus:

```
select e.ename, d.loc,eb.received
  from emp e, dept d, emp_bonus eb
 where e.deptno=d.deptno
   and e.empno=eb.empno
```

ENAME	LOC	RECEIVED
SCOTT	DALLAS	14-MAR-2005
SMITH	DALLAS	14-MAR-2005
JAMES	CHICAGO	14-MAR-2005

Your desired result set is the following:

ENAME	LOC	RECEIVED
ALLEN	CHICAGO	
WARD	CHICAGO	
MARTIN	CHICAGO	
JAMES	CHICAGO	14-MAR-2005
TURNER	CHICAGO	
BLAKE	CHICAGO	
SMITH	DALLAS	14-MAR-2005
FORD	DALLAS	
ADAMS	DALLAS	
JONES	DALLAS	
SCOTT	DALLAS	14-MAR-2005
CLARK	NEW YORK	
KING	NEW YORK	
MILLER	NEW YORK	

Solution

You can use an outer join to obtain the additional information without losing the data from the original query. First join table EMP to table DEPT to get all employees and the location of the department they work, then outer join to table EMP_BONUS to return the date of the bonus if there is one. Following is the DB2, MySQL, PostgreSQL, and SQL Server syntax:

```
1 select e.ename, d.loc, eb.received
2   from emp e join dept d
3     on (e.deptno=d.deptno)
4   left join emp_bonus eb
5     on (e.empno=eb.empno)
6  order by 2
```

If you are using Oracle9i Database or later, the preceding solution will work for you. Alternatively, you can use Oracle's proprietary outer-join syntax, which is your only choice when using Oracle8i Database and earlier:

```
1 select e.ename, d.loc, eb.received
2   from emp e, dept d, emp_bonus eb
3  where e.deptno=d.deptno
4    and e.empno=eb.empno (+)
5  order by 2
```

You can also use a scalar subquery (a subquery placed in the SELECT list) to mimic an outer join:

```
1 select e.ename, d.loc,
2        (select eb.received from emp_bonus eb
3            where eb.empno=e.empno) as received
4   from emp e, dept d
5  where e.deptno=d.deptno
6  order by 2
```

The scalar subquery solution will work across all platforms.

Discussion

An outer join will return all rows from one table and matching rows from another. See the previous recipe for another example of such a join. The reason an outer join works to solve this problem is that it does not result in any rows being eliminated that would otherwise be returned. The query will return all the rows it would return without the outer join. And it also returns the received date, if one exists.

Use of a scalar subquery is also a convenient technique for this sort of problem, as it does not require you to modify already correct joins in your main query. Using a scalar subquery is an easy way to tack on extra data to a query without compromising the current result set. When working with scalar subqueries, you must ensure they return a scalar (single) value. If a subquery in the SELECT list returns more than one row, you will receive an error.

See Also

See Recipe 14.10 for a workaround to the problem of not being able to return multiple rows from a SELECT-list subquery.

3.7 Determining Whether Two Tables Have the Same Data

Problem

You want to know if two tables or views have the same data (cardinality and values). Consider the following view:

```
create view V
as
select * from emp where deptno != 10
 union all
select * from emp where ename = 'WARD'

select * from V
```

EMPNO	ENAME	JOB	MGR	HIREDATE	SAL	COMM	DEPTNO
7369	SMITH	CLERK	7902	17-DEC-1980	800		20
7499	ALLEN	SALESMAN	7698	20-FEB-1981	1600	300	30
7521	WARD	SALESMAN	7698	22-FEB-1981	1250	500	30
7566	JONES	MANAGER	7839	02-APR-1981	2975		20
7654	MARTIN	SALESMAN	7698	28-SEP-1981	1250	1400	30
7698	BLAKE	MANAGER	7839	01-MAY-1981	2850		30
7788	SCOTT	ANALYST	7566	09-DEC-1982	3000		20
7844	TURNER	SALESMAN	7698	08-SEP-1981	1500	0	30
7876	ADAMS	CLERK	7788	12-JAN-1983	1100		20
7900	JAMES	CLERK	7698	03-DEC-1981	950		30
7902	FORD	ANALYST	7566	03-DEC-1981	3000		20
7521	WARD	SALESMAN	7698	22-FEB-1981	1250	500	30

You want to determine whether or not this view has exactly the same data as table EMP. The row for employee "WARD" is duplicated to show that the solution will reveal not only different data but duplicates as well. Based on the rows in table EMP the difference will be the three rows for employees in department 10 and the two rows for employee "WARD". You want to return the following result set:

EMPNO	ENAME	JOB	MGR	HIREDATE	SAL	COMM	DEPTNO	CNT
7521	WARD	SALESMAN	7698	22-FEB-1981	1250	500	30	1
7521	WARD	SALESMAN	7698	22-FEB-1981	1250	500	30	2
7782	CLARK	MANAGER	7839	09-JUN-1981	2450		10	1
7839	KING	PRESIDENT		17-NOV-1981	5000		10	1
7934	MILLER	CLERK	7782	23-JAN-1982	1300		10	1

Solution

Functions that perform SET difference (MINUS or EXCEPT, depending on your DBMS) make the problem of comparing tables a relatively easy one to solve. If your DBMS does not offer such functions, you can use a correlated subquery.

DB2 and PostgreSQL

Use the set operations EXCEPT and UNION ALL to find the difference between view V and table EMP combined with the difference between table EMP and view V:

```
1  (
2   select empno,ename,job,mgr,hiredate,sal,comm,deptno,
3          count(*) as cnt
4     from V
5    group by empno,ename,job,mgr,hiredate,sal,comm,deptno
6   except
7   select empno,ename,job,mgr,hiredate,sal,comm,deptno,
8          count(*) as cnt
9     from emp
10   group by empno,ename,job,mgr,hiredate,sal,comm,deptno
11  )
```

```
12   union all
13   (
14    select empno,ename,job,mgr,hiredate,sal,comm,deptno,
15           count(*) as cnt
16      from emp
17      group by empno,ename,job,mgr,hiredate,sal,comm,deptno
18      except
19      select empno,ename,job,mgr,hiredate,sal,comm,deptno,
20           count(*) as cnt
21      from v
22      group by empno,ename,job,mgr,hiredate,sal,comm,deptno
23   )
```

Oracle

Use the set operations MINUS and UNION ALL to find the difference between view V and table EMP combined with the difference between table EMP and view V:

```
1   (
2    select empno,ename,job,mgr,hiredate,sal,comm,deptno,
3           count(*) as cnt
4      from V
5      group by empno,ename,job,mgr,hiredate,sal,comm,deptno
6      minus
7      select empno,ename,job,mgr,hiredate,sal,comm,deptno,
8           count(*) as cnt
9      from emp
10     group by empno,ename,job,mgr,hiredate,sal,comm,deptno
11   )
12   union all
13   (
14    select empno,ename,job,mgr,hiredate,sal,comm,deptno,
15           count(*) as cnt
16      from emp
17      group by empno,ename,job,mgr,hiredate,sal,comm,deptno
18      minus
19      select empno,ename,job,mgr,hiredate,sal,comm,deptno,
20           count(*) as cnt
21      from v
22      group by empno,ename,job,mgr,hiredate,sal,comm,deptno
23   )
```

MySQL and SQL Server

Use a correlated subquery and UNION ALL to find the rows in view V and not in table EMP combined with the rows in table EMP and not in view V:

```
1   select *
2     from (
3    select e.empno,e.ename,e.job,e.mgr,e.hiredate,
4           e.sal,e.comm,e.deptno, count(*) as cnt
5      from emp e
```

```
 6     group by empno,ename,job,mgr,hiredate,
 7            sal,comm,deptno
 8          ) e
 9    where not exists (
10    select null
11      from (
12    select v.empno,v.ename,v.job,v.mgr,v.hiredate,
13           v.sal,v.comm,v.deptno, count(*) as cnt
14      from v
15    group by empno,ename,job,mgr,hiredate,
16            sal,comm,deptno
17          ) v
18    where v.empno    = e.empno
19      and v.ename    = e.ename
20      and v.job      = e.job
21      and coalesce(v.mgr,0) = coalesce(e.mgr,0)
22      and v.hiredate = e.hiredate
23      and v.sal      = e.sal
24      and v.deptno   = e.deptno
25      and v.cnt      = e.cnt
26      and coalesce(v.comm,0) = coalesce(e.comm,0)
27    )
28    union all
29    select *
30      from (
31    select v.empno,v.ename,v.job,v.mgr,v.hiredate,
32           v.sal,v.comm,v.deptno, count(*) as cnt
33      from v
34    group by empno,ename,job,mgr,hiredate,
35            sal,comm,deptno
36          ) v
37    where not exists (
38    select null
39      from (
40    select e.empno,e.ename,e.job,e.mgr,e.hiredate,
41           e.sal,e.comm,e.deptno, count(*) as cnt
42      from emp e
43    group by empno,ename,job,mgr,hiredate,
44            sal,comm,deptno
45          ) e
46    where v.empno    = e.empno
47      and v.ename    = e.ename
48      and v.job      = e.job
49      and coalesce(v.mgr,0) = coalesce(e.mgr,0)
50      and v.hiredate = e.hiredate
51      and v.sal      = e.sal
52      and v.deptno   = e.deptno
53      and v.cnt      = e.cnt
54      and coalesce(v.comm,0) = coalesce(e.comm,0)
55    )
```

Discussion

Despite using different techniques, the concept is the same for all solutions:

1. First, find rows in table EMP that do not exist in view V.

2. Then combine (UNION ALL) those rows with rows from view V that do not exist in table EMP.

If the tables in question are equal, then no rows are returned. If the tables are different, the rows causing the difference are returned. As an easy first step when comparing tables, you can compare the cardinalities alone rather than including them with the data comparison. The following query is a simple example of this and will work on all DBMSs:

```
select count(*)
  from emp
 union
select count(*)
  from dept

COUNT(*)
--------
       4
      14
```

Because UNION will filter out duplicates, only one row will be returned if the tables' cardinalities are the same. Because two rows are returned in this example, you know that the tables do not contain identical rowsets.

DB2, Oracle, and PostgreSQL

MINUS and EXCEPT work in the same way, so I will use EXCEPT for this discussion. The queries before and after the UNION ALL are very similar. So, to understand how the solution works, simply execute the query prior to the UNION ALL by itself. The following result set is produced by executing lines 1–11 in the Solution section:

```
(
  select empno,ename,job,mgr,hiredate,sal,comm,deptno,
         count(*) as cnt
    from V
   group by empno,ename,job,mgr,hiredate,sal,comm,deptno
  except
  select empno,ename,job,mgr,hiredate,sal,comm,deptno,
         count(*) as cnt
    from emp
   group by empno,ename,job,mgr,hiredate,sal,comm,deptno
)

EMPNO ENAME        JOB         MGR HIREDATE      SAL  COMM DEPTNO CNT
----- ----------   ---------   ----- -----------  ----- ----- ------ ---
 7521 WARD         SALESMAN    7698 22-FEB-1981  1250   500     30   2
```

The result set represents a row found in view V that is either not in table EMP or has a different cardinality than that same row in table EMP. In this case, the duplicate row for employee "WARD" is found and returned. If you're still having trouble understanding how the result set is produced, run each query on either side of EXCEPT individually. You'll notice the only difference between the two result sets is the CNT for employee "WARD" returned by view V.

The portion of the query after the UNION ALL does the opposite of the query preceding UNION ALL. The query returns rows in table EMP not in view V:

```
(
  select empno,ename,job,mgr,hiredate,sal,comm,deptno,
         count(*) as cnt
    from emp
   group by empno,ename,job,mgr,hiredate,sal,comm,deptno
   minus
  select empno,ename,job,mgr,hiredate,sal,comm,deptno,
         count(*) as cnt
    from v
   group by empno,ename,job,mgr,hiredate,sal,comm,deptno
)
```

```
EMPNO ENAME      JOB        MGR  HIREDATE      SAL  COMM  DEPTNO CNT
----- ---------- ---------- ---- -----------  ----- ----- ------ ---
 7521 WARD       SALESMAN   7698 22-FEB-1981  1250   500     30   1
 7782 CLARK      MANAGER    7839 09-JUN-1981  2450            10   1
 7839 KING       PRESIDENT       17-NOV-1981  5000            10   1
 7934 MILLER     CLERK      7782 23-JAN-1982  1300            10   1
```

The results are then combined by UNION ALL to produce the final result set.

MySQL and SQL Server

The queries before and after the UNION ALL are very similar. To understand how the subquery-based solution works, simply execute the query prior to the UNION ALL by itself. The query below is from lines 1–27 in the Solution:

```
select *
  from (
select e.empno,e.ename,e.job,e.mgr,e.hiredate,
       e.sal,e.comm,e.deptno, count(*) as cnt
  from emp e
 group by empno,ename,job,mgr,hiredate,
          sal,comm,deptno
       ) e
 where not exists (
select null
  from (
select v.empno,v.ename,v.job,v.mgr,v.hiredate,
       v.sal,v.comm,v.deptno, count(*) as cnt
  from v
```

```
     group by empno,ename,job,mgr,hiredate,
             sal,comm,deptno
          ) v
    where v.empno    = e.empno
      and v.ename    = e.ename
      and v.job      = e.job
      and v.mgr      = e.mgr
      and v.hiredate = e.hiredate
      and v.sal      = e.sal
      and v.deptno   = e.deptno
      and v.cnt      = e.cnt
      and coalesce(v.comm,0) = coalesce(e.comm,0)
   )

EMPNO ENAME      JOB        MGR HIREDATE      SAL COMM DEPTNO CNT
----- ---------- ---------- ---- ----------- ----- ----- ------ ---
 7521 WARD       SALESMAN   7698 22-FEB-1981 1250  500      30  1
 7782 CLARK      MANAGER    7839 09-JUN-1981 2450           10  1
 7839 KING       PRESIDENT       17-NOV-1981 5000           10  1
 7934 MILLER     CLERK      7782 23-JAN-1982 1300           10  1
```

Notice that the comparison is not between table EMP and view V, but rather between inline view E and inline view V. The cardinality for each row is found and returned as an attribute for that row. You are comparing each row and its occurrence count. If you are having trouble understanding how the comparison works, run the subqueries independently. The next step is to find all rows (including CNT) in inline view E that do not exist in inline view V. The comparison uses a correlated subquery and NOT EXISTS. The joins will determine which rows are the same, and the result will be all rows from inline view E that are not the rows returned by the join. The query after the UNION ALL does the opposite; it finds all rows in inline view V that do not exist in inline view E:

```
select *
  from (
select v.empno,v.ename,v.job,v.mgr,v.hiredate,
       v.sal,v.comm,v.deptno, count(*) as cnt
  from v
 group by empno,ename,job,mgr,hiredate,
          sal,comm,deptno
       ) v
   where not exists (
select null
  from (
select e.empno,e.ename,e.job,e.mgr,e.hiredate,
       e.sal,e.comm,e.deptno, count(*) as cnt
  from emp e
 group by empno,ename,job,mgr,hiredate,
          sal,comm,deptno
       ) e
   where v.empno    = e.empno
     and v.ename    = e.ename
     and v.job      = e.job
```

```
    and v.mgr       = e.mgr
    and v.hiredate  = e.hiredate
    and v.sal       = e.sal
    and v.deptno    = e.deptno
    and v.cnt       = e.cnt
    and coalesce(v.comm,0) = coalesce(e.comm,0)
)
```

```
EMPNO ENAME      JOB        MGR HIREDATE      SAL COMM DEPTNO CNT
----- ---------- ---------- --- ----------- ----- ----- ------ ---
 7521 WARD       SALESMAN  7698 22-FEB-1981  1250   500     30   2
```

The results are then combined by UNION ALL to produce the final result set.

 Ales Spectic and Jonathan Gennick give an alternate solution in their book *Transact-SQL Cookbook* (O'Reilly). See the section "Comparing Two Sets for Equality" in Chapter 2.

3.8   Identifying and Avoiding Cartesian Products

Problem

You want to return the name of each employee in department 10 along with the location of the department. The following query is returning incorrect data:

```
select e.ename, d.loc
  from emp e, dept d
 where e.deptno = 10
```

```
ENAME      LOC
---------- -------------
CLARK      NEW YORK
CLARK      DALLAS
CLARK      CHICAGO
CLARK      BOSTON
KING       NEW YORK
KING       DALLAS
KING       CHICAGO
KING       BOSTON
MILLER     NEW YORK
MILLER     DALLAS
MILLER     CHICAGO
MILLER     BOSTON
```

The correct result set is the following:

```
ENAME      LOC
---------- -------------
CLARK      NEW YORK
KING       NEW YORK
MILLER     NEW YORK
```

Solution

Use a join between the tables in the FROM clause to return the correct result set:

```
1 select e.ename, d.loc
2   from emp e, dept d
3  where e.deptno = 10
4    and d.deptno = e.deptno
```

Discussion

Looking at the data in the DEPT table:

```
select * from dept
```

```
DEPTNO DNAME           LOC
---------- --------------- -------------
        10 ACCOUNTING      NEW YORK
        20 RESEARCH        DALLAS
        30 SALES           CHICAGO
        40 OPERATIONS      BOSTON
```

You can see that department 10 is in New York, and thus you can know that returning employees with any location other than New York is incorrect. The number of rows returned by the incorrect query is the product of the cardinalities of the two tables in the FROM clause. In the original query, the filter on EMP for department 10 will result in three rows. Because there is no filter for DEPT, all four rows from DEPT are returned. Three multiplied by four is twelve, so the incorrect query returns twelve rows. Generally, to avoid a Cartesian product you would apply the $n-1$ rule where n represents the number of tables in the FROM clause and $n-1$ represents the minimum number of joins necessary to avoid a Cartesian product. Depending on what the keys and join columns in your tables are, you may very well need more than $n-1$ joins, but $n-1$ is a good place to start when writing queries.

> When used properly, Cartesian products can be very useful. Recipe 6.1 uses a Cartesian product and is used by many other queries. Common uses of Cartesian products include transposing or pivoting (and unpivoting) a result set, generating a sequence of values, and mimicking a loop.

3.9 Performing Joins When Using Aggregates

Problem

You want to perform an aggregation but your query involves multiple tables. You want to ensure that joins do not disrupt the aggregation. For example, you want to find the sum of the salaries for employees in department 10 along with the sum of their bonuses. Some employees have more than one bonus and the join between table EMP and table EMP_BONUS is causing incorrect values to be returned by the aggregate function SUM. For this problem, table EMP_BONUS contains the following data:

```
select * from emp_bonus

EMPNO RECEIVED          TYPE
----- -----------  ----------
 7934 17-MAR-2005          1
 7934 15-FEB-2005          2
 7839 15-FEB-2005          3
 7782 15-FEB-2005          1
```

Now, consider the following query that returns the salary and bonus for all employees in department 10. Table BONUS.TYPE determines the amount of the bonus. A type 1 bonus is 10% of an employee's salary, type 2 is 20%, and type 3 is 30%.

```
select e.empno,
       e.ename,
       e.sal,
       e.deptno,
       e.sal*case when eb.type = 1 then .1
                  when eb.type = 2 then .2
                  else .3
             end as bonus
  from emp e, emp_bonus eb
 where e.empno  = eb.empno
   and e.deptno = 10

    EMPNO ENAME          SAL    DEPTNO      BONUS
-------- ----------  ---------- ---------- ----------
    7934 MILLER         1300        10        130
    7934 MILLER         1300        10        260
    7839 KING           5000        10       1500
    7782 CLARK          2450        10        245
```

So far, so good. However, things go awry when you attempt a join to the EMP_BONUS table in order to sum the bonus amounts:

```
select deptno,
       sum(sal) as total_sal,
       sum(bonus) as total_bonus
  from (
select e.empno,
       e.ename,
       e.sal,
       e.deptno,
       e.sal*case when eb.type = 1 then .1
                  when eb.type = 2 then .2
                  else .3
             end as bonus
  from emp e, emp_bonus eb
 where e.empno  = eb.empno
   and e.deptno = 10
       ) x
group by deptno
```

```
DEPTNO  TOTAL_SAL TOTAL_BONUS
------  ---------- -----------
    10       10050        2135
```

While the TOTAL_BONUS is correct, the TOTAL_SAL is incorrect. The sum of all salaries in department 10 is 8750, as the following query shows:

```
select sum(sal) from emp where deptno=10
```

```
SUM(SAL)
----------
    8750
```

Why is TOTAL_SAL incorrect? The reason is the duplicate rows in the SAL column created by the join. Consider the following query, which joins table EMP and EMP_BONUS:

```
select e.ename,
       e.sal
  from emp e, emp_bonus eb
 where e.empno  = eb.empno
   and e.deptno = 10
```

```
ENAME              SAL
----------  ----------
CLARK             2450
KING              5000
MILLER            1300
MILLER            1300
```

Now it is easy to see why the value for TOTAL_SAL is incorrect: MILLER's salary is counted twice. The final result set that you are really after is:

```
DEPTNO  TOTAL_SAL TOTAL_BONUS
------  ---------- -----------
    10        8750        2135
```

Solution

You have to be careful when computing aggregates across joins. Typically when duplicates are returned due to a join, you can avoid miscalculations by aggregate functions in two ways: you can simply use the keyword DISTINCT in the call to the aggregate function, so only unique instances of each value are used in the computation; or you can perform the aggregation first (in an inline view) prior to joining, thus avoiding the incorrect computation by the aggregate function because the aggregate will already be computed before you even join, thus avoiding the problem altogether. The solutions that follow use DISTINCT. The Discussion section will discuss the technique of using an inline view to perform the aggregation prior to joining.

MySQL and PostgreSQL

Perform a sum of only the DISTINCT salaries:

```
 1  select deptno,
 2         sum(distinct sal) as total_sal,
 3         sum(bonus) as total_bonus
 4    from (
 5  select e.empno,
 6         e.ename,
 7         e.sal,
 8         e.deptno,
 9         e.sal*case when eb.type = 1 then .1
10                    when eb.type = 2 then .2
11                    else .3
12              end  as bonus
13    from emp e, emp_bonus eb
14   where e.empno   = eb.empno
15     and e.deptno = 10
16         ) x
17   group by deptno
```

DB2, Oracle, and SQL Server

These platforms support the preceding solution, but they also support an alternative solution using the window function SUM OVER:

```
 1  select distinct deptno,total_sal,total_bonus
 2    from (
 3  select e.empno,
 4         e.ename,
 5         sum(distinct e.sal) over
 6         (partition by e.deptno) as total_sal,
 7         e.deptno,
 8         sum(e.sal*case when eb.type = 1 then .1
 9                        when eb.type = 2 then .2
10                        else .3 end) over
11         (partition by deptno) as total_bonus
12    from emp e, emp_bonus eb
13   where e.empno   = eb.empno
14     and e.deptno = 10
15         ) x
```

Discussion

MySQL and PostgreSQL

The second query in the Problem section of this recipe joins table EMP and table EMP_BONUS and returns two rows for employee "MILLER", which is what causes the error on the sum of EMP.SAL (the salary is added twice). The solution is to simply sum the distinct EMP.SAL values that are returned by the query. The following query is an alternative solution—necessary if there could be duplicate values in the column you are summing. The sum of all salaries in department 10 is computed first and that row is then joined to table EMP, which is then joined to table EMP_BONUS. The following query works for all DBMSs:

```
select d.deptno,
       d.total_sal,
       sum(e.sal*case when eb.type = 1 then .1
                      when eb.type = 2 then .2
                      else .3 end) as total_bonus
  from emp e,
       emp_bonus eb,
       (
select deptno, sum(sal) as total_sal
  from emp
 where deptno = 10
 group by deptno
       ) d
 where e.deptno = d.deptno
   and e.empno  = eb.empno
 group by d.deptno,d.total_sal

DEPTNO  TOTAL_SAL  TOTAL_BONUS
------- ---------- -----------
    10       8750         2135
```

DB2, Oracle, and SQL Server

This alternative solution takes advantage of the window function SUM OVER. The following query is taken from lines 3–14 in the Solution and returns the following result set:

```
select e.empno,
       e.ename,
       sum(distinct e.sal) over
       (partition by e.deptno) as total_sal,
       e.deptno,
       sum(e.sal*case when eb.type = 1 then .1
                      when eb.type = 2 then .2
                      else .3 end) over
       (partition by deptno) as total_bonus
  from emp e, emp_bonus eb
 where e.empno  = eb.empno
   and e.deptno = 10

EMPNO ENAME       TOTAL_SAL DEPTNO TOTAL_BONUS
----- ---------- ---------- ------ -----------
 7934 MILLER          8750     10        2135
 7934 MILLER          8750     10        2135
 7782 CLARK           8750     10        2135
 7839 KING            8750     10        2135
```

The windowing function, SUM OVER, is called twice, first to compute the sum of the distinct salaries for the defined partition or group. In this case, the partition is DEPTNO 10 and the sum of the distinct salaries for DEPTNO 10 is 8750. The next call to SUM OVER computes the sum of the bonuses for the same defined partition. The final result set is produced by taking the distinct values for TOTAL_SAL, DEPTNO, and TOTAL_BONUS.

3.10 Performing Outer Joins When Using Aggregates

Problem

Begin with the same problem as in Recipe 3.9, but modify table EMP_BONUS such that the difference in this case is not all employees in department 10 have been given bonuses. Consider the EMP_BONUS table and a query to (ostensibly) find both the sum of all salaries for department 10 and the sum of all bonuses for all employees in department 10:

```
select * from emp_bonus

    EMPNO RECEIVED        TYPE
---------- ----------- ----------
     7934 17-MAR-2005          1
     7934 15-FEB-2005          2

select deptno,
       sum(sal) as total_sal,
       sum(bonus) as total_bonus
  from (
select e.empno,
       e.ename,
       e.sal,
       e.deptno,
       e.sal*case when eb.type = 1 then .1
                  when eb.type = 2 then .2
                  else .3 end as bonus
  from emp e, emp_bonus eb
 where e.empno  = eb.empno
   and e.deptno = 10
       )
 group by deptno

DEPTNO  TOTAL_SAL TOTAL_BONUS
------  --------- -----------
    10       2600         390
```

The result for TOTAL_BONUS is correct, but the value returned for TOTAL_SAL does not represent the sum of all salaries in department 10. The following query shows why the TOTAL_SAL is incorrect:

```
select e.empno,
       e.ename,
       e.sal,
       e.deptno,
       e.sal*case when eb.type = 1 then .1
                  when eb.type = 2 then .2
              else .3 end as bonus
  from emp e, emp_bonus eb
 where e.empno  = eb.empno
   and e.deptno = 10
```

```
EMPNO ENAME           SAL   DEPTNO   BONUS
-------- ----------   ----- -------- ----------
    7934 MILLER       1300      10      130
    7934 MILLER       1300      10      260
```

Rather than sum all salaries in department 10, only the salary for "MILLER" is summed and it is erroneously summed twice. Ultimately, you would like to return the following result set:

```
DEPTNO  TOTAL_SAL TOTAL_BONUS
------  ---------- -----------
    10       8750         390
```

Solution

The solution is similar to that of Recipe 3.9, but here you outer join to EMP_BONUS to ensure all employees from department 10 are included.

DB2, MySQL, PostgreSQL, SQL Server

Outer join to EMP_BONUS, then perform the sum on only distinct salaries from department 10:

```
1  select deptno,
2         sum(distinct sal) as total_sal,
3         sum(bonus) as total_bonus
4    from (
5  select e.empno,
6         e.ename,
7         e.sal,
8         e.deptno,
9         e.sal*case when eb.type is null then 0
10                   when eb.type = 1 then .1
11                   when eb.type = 2 then .2
12                   else .3 end as bonus
13   from emp e left outer join emp_bonus eb
14     on (e.empno = eb.empno)
15  where e.deptno = 10
16        )
17  group by deptno
```

You can also use the window function SUM OVER:

```
1  select distinct deptno,total_sal,total_bonus
2    from (
3  select e.empno,
4         e.ename,
5         sum(distinct e.sal) over
6         (partition by e.deptno) as total_sal,
7         e.deptno,
8         sum(e.sal*case when eb.type is null then 0
9                   when eb.type = 1 then .1
10                  when eb.type = 2 then .2
11                  else .3
```

```
12                    end) over
13           (partition by deptno) as total_bonus
14      from emp e left outer join emp_bonus eb
15        on (e.empno = eb.empno)
16     where e.deptno = 10
17           ) x
```

Oracle

If you are using Oracle9i Database or later you can use the preceding solution. Alternatively, you can use the proprietary Oracle outer-join syntax, which is mandatory for users on Oracle8i Database and earlier:

```
1  select deptno,
2         sum(distinct sal) as total_sal,
3         sum(bonus) as total_bonus
4    from (
5  select e.empno,
6         e.ename,
7         e.sal,
8         e.deptno,
9         e.sal*case when eb.type is null then 0
10                    when eb.type = 1 then .1
11                    when eb.type = 2 then .2
12                    else .3 end as bonus
13    from emp e, emp_bonus eb
14   where e.empno  = eb.empno (+)
15     and e.deptno = 10
16         )
17   group by deptno
```

Oracle 8i Database users can also use the SUM OVER syntax shown for DB2 and the other databases, but must modify it to use the proprietary Oracle outer-join syntax shown in the preceding query.

Discussion

The second query in the Problem section of this recipe joins table EMP and table EMP_BONUS and returns only rows for employee "MILLER", which is what causes the error on the sum of EMP.SAL (the other employees in DEPTNO 10 do not have bonuses and their salaries are not included in the sum). The solution is to outer join table EMP to table EMP_BONUS so even employees without a bonus will be included in the result. If an employee does not have a bonus, NULL will be returned for EMP_BONUS.TYPE. It is important to keep this in mind as the CASE statement has been modified and is slightly different from the Solution in Recipe 3.9. If EMP_BONUS.TYPE is NULL, the CASE expression returns zero, which has no effect on the sum.

The following query is an alternative solution. The sum of all salaries in department 10 is computed first, then joined to table EMP, which is then joined to table EMP_BONUS (thus avoiding the outer join). The following query works for all DBMSs:

```
select d.deptno,
       d.total_sal,
       sum(e.sal*case when eb.type = 1 then .1
                      when eb.type = 2 then .2
                      else .3 end)  as total_bonus
  from emp e,
       emp_bonus eb,
       (
select deptno, sum(sal) as total_sal
  from emp
 where deptno = 10
 group by deptno
       ) d
 where e.deptno = d.deptno
   and e.empno  = eb.empno
 group by d.deptno,d.total_sal


DEPTNO  TOTAL_SAL TOTAL_BONUS
------- --------- -----------
    10       8750         390
```

3.11   Returning Missing Data from Multiple Tables

Problem

You want to return missing data from multiple tables simultaneously. Returning rows from table DEPT that do not exist in table EMP (any departments that have no employees) requires an outer join. Consider the following query, which returns all DEPTNOs and DNAMEs from DEPT along with the names of all the employees in each department (if there is an employee in a particular department):

```
select d.deptno,d.dname,e.ename
  from dept d left outer join emp e
    on (d.deptno=e.deptno)


DEPTNO DNAME           ENAME
------ --------------- ----------
    20 RESEARCH        SMITH
    30 SALES           ALLEN
    30 SALES           WARD
    20 RESEARCH        JONES
    30 SALES           MARTIN
    30 SALES           BLAKE
    10 ACCOUNTING      CLARK
    20 RESEARCH        SCOTT
    10 ACCOUNTING      KING
    30 SALES           TURNER
    20 RESEARCH        ADAMS
    30 SALES           JAMES
    20 RESEARCH        FORD
    10 ACCOUNTING      MILLER
    40 OPERATIONS
```

The last row, the OPERATIONS department, is returned despite that department not having any employees, because table EMP was outer joined to table DEPT. Now, suppose there was an employee without a department. How would you return the above result set along with a row for the employee having no department? In other words, you want to outer join to both table EMP and table DEPT, and in the same query. After creating the new employee, a first attempt may look like this:

```
insert into emp (empno,ename,job,mgr,hiredate,sal,comm,deptno)
select 1111,'YODA','JEDI',null,hiredate,sal,comm,null
  from emp
 where ename = 'KING'
```

```
select d.deptno,d.dname,e.ename
  from dept d right outer join emp e
    on (d.deptno=e.deptno)
```

```
DEPTNO DNAME          ENAME
------ -------------- ----------
    10 ACCOUNTING     MILLER
    10 ACCOUNTING     KING
    10 ACCOUNTING     CLARK
    20 RESEARCH       FORD
    20 RESEARCH       ADAMS
    20 RESEARCH       SCOTT
    20 RESEARCH       JONES
    20 RESEARCH       SMITH
    30 SALES          JAMES
    30 SALES          TURNER
    30 SALES          BLAKE
    30 SALES          MARTIN
    30 SALES          WARD
    30 SALES          ALLEN
                      YODA
```

This outer join manages to return the new employee but lost the OPERATIONS department from the original result set. The final result set should return a row for YODA as well as OPERATIONS, such as the following:

```
DEPTNO DNAME          ENAME
------ -------------- ----------
    10 ACCOUNTING     CLARK
    10 ACCOUNTING     KING
    10 ACCOUNTING     MILLER
    20 RESEARCH       ADAMS
    20 RESEARCH       FORD
    20 RESEARCH       JONES
    20 RESEARCH       SCOTT
    20 RESEARCH       SMITH
    30 SALES          ALLEN
    30 SALES          BLAKE
    30 SALES          JAMES
    30 SALES          MARTIN
    30 SALES          TURNER
```

```
30 SALES          WARD
40 OPERATIONS
                  YODA
```

Solution

Use a full outer join to return missing data from both tables based on a common value.

DB2, MySQL, PostgreSQL, SQL Server

Use the explicit FULL OUTER JOIN command to return missing rows from both tables along with matching rows:

```
1 select d.deptno,d.dname,e.ename
2   from dept d full outer join emp e
3     on (d.deptno=e.deptno)
```

Alternatively, since MySQL does not yet have a FULL OUTER JOIN, union the results of the two different outer joins:

```
1 select d.deptno,d.dname,e.ename
2   from dept d right outer join emp e
3     on (d.deptno=e.deptno)
4 union
5 select d.deptno,d.dname,e.ename
6   from dept d left outer join emp e
7     on (d.deptno=e.deptno)
```

Oracle

If you are on Oracle9i Database or later, you can use either of the preceding solutions. Alternatively, you can use Oracle's proprietary outer join syntax, which is the only choice for users on Oracle8i Database and earlier:

```
1 select d.deptno,d.dname,e.ename
2   from dept d, emp e
3   where d.deptno = e.deptno(+)
4 union
5 select d.deptno,d.dname,e.ename
6   from dept d, emp e
7   where d.deptno(+) = e.deptno
```

Discussion

The full outer join is simply the combination of outer joins on both tables. To see how a full outer join works "under the covers," simply run each outer join, then union the results. The following query returns rows from table DEPT and any matching rows from table EMP (if any).

```
select d.deptno,d.dname,e.ename
  from dept d left outer join emp e
    on (d.deptno = e.deptno)
```

```
DEPTNO DNAME          ENAME
------ -------------- ----------
    20 RESEARCH       SMITH
    30 SALES          ALLEN
    30 SALES          WARD
    20 RESEARCH       JONES
    30 SALES          MARTIN
    30 SALES          BLAKE
    10 ACCOUNTING     CLARK
    20 RESEARCH       SCOTT
    10 ACCOUNTING     KING
    30 SALES          TURNER
    20 RESEARCH       ADAMS
    30 SALES          JAMES
    20 RESEARCH       FORD
    10 ACCOUNTING     MILLER
    40 OPERATIONS
```

This next query returns rows from table EMP and any matching rows from table DEPT (if any):

```
select d.deptno,d.dname,e.ename
  from dept d right outer join emp e
    on (d.deptno = e.deptno)
```

```
DEPTNO DNAME          ENAME
------ -------------- ----------
    10 ACCOUNTING     MILLER
    10 ACCOUNTING     KING
    10 ACCOUNTING     CLARK
    20 RESEARCH       FORD
    20 RESEARCH       ADAMS
    20 RESEARCH       SCOTT
    20 RESEARCH       JONES
    20 RESEARCH       SMITH
    30 SALES          JAMES
    30 SALES          TURNER
    30 SALES          BLAKE
    30 SALES          MARTIN
    30 SALES          WARD
    30 SALES          ALLEN
                      YODA
```

The results from these two queries are unioned to provide the final result set.

3.12 Using NULLs in Operations and Comparisons

Problem

NULL is never equal to or not equal to any value, not even itself, but you want to evaluate values returned by a nullable column like you would evaluate real values. For example, you want to find all employees in EMP whose commission (COMM) is less than the commission of employee "WARD". Employees with a NULL commission should be included as well.

Solution

Use a function such as COALESCE to transform the NULL value into a real value that can be used in standard evaluation:

```
1 select ename,comm
2   from emp
3  where coalesce(comm,0) < ( select comm
4                               from emp
5                              where ename = 'WARD' )
```

Discussion

The COALESCE function will return the first non-NULL value from the list of values passed to it. When a NULL value is encountered it is replaced by zero, which is then compared with Ward's commission. This can be seen by putting the COALESCE function in the SELECT list:

```
select ename,comm,coalesce(comm,0)
  from emp
 where coalesce(comm,0) < ( select comm
                              from emp
                             where ename = 'WARD' )
```

ENAME	COMM	COALESCE(COMM,0)
SMITH		0
ALLEN	300	300
JONES		0
BLAKE		0
CLARK		0
SCOTT		0
KING		0
TURNER	0	0
ADAMS		0
JAMES		0
FORD		0
MILLER		0

CHAPTER 4

Inserting, Updating, Deleting

The past few chapters have focused on basic query techniques, all centered around the task of getting data out of a database. This chapter turns the tables, and focuses on the following three topic areas:

- Inserting new records into your database
- Updating existing records
- Deleting records that you no longer want

For ease in finding them when you need them, recipes in this chapter have been grouped by topic: all the insertion recipes come first, followed by the update recipes, and finally recipes for deleting data.

Inserting is usually a straightforward task. It begins with the simple problem of inserting a single row. Many times, however, it is more efficient to use a set-based approach to create new rows. To that end, you'll also find techniques for inserting many rows at a time.

Likewise, updating and deleting start out as simple tasks. You can update one record, and you can delete one record. But you can also update whole sets of records at once, and in very powerful ways. And there are many handy ways to delete records. For example, you can delete rows in one table depending on whether or not they exist in another table.

SQL even has a way, a relatively new addition to the standard, by which you can insert, update, and delete all at once. That may not sound like too useful a thing now, but the MERGE statement represents a very powerful way to bring a database table into sync with an external source of data (such as a flat file feed from a remote system). For details, check out Recipe 4.11 later in this chapter.

4.1   Inserting a New Record

Problem

You want to insert a new record into a table. For example, you want to insert a new record into the DEPT table. The value for DEPTNO should be 50, DNAME should be "PROGRAMMING", and LOC should be "BALTIMORE".

Solution

Use the INSERT statement with the VALUES clause to insert one row at a time:

```
insert into dept (deptno,dname,loc)
values (50,'PROGRAMMING','BALTIMORE')
```

For DB2 and MySQL you have the option of inserting one row at a time or multiple rows at a time by including multiple VALUES lists:

```
/* multi row insert */
insert into dept (deptno,dname,loc)
values (1,'A','B'),
       (2,'B','C')
```

Discussion

The INSERT statement allows you to create new rows in database tables. The syntax for inserting a single row is consistent across all database brands.

As a shortcut, you can omit the column list in an INSERT statement:

```
insert into dept
values (50,'PROGRAMMING','BALTIMORE')
```

However, if you do not list your target columns, you must insert into *all* of the columns in the table, and be mindful of the order of the values in the VALUES list; you must supply values in the same order in which the database displays columns in response to a SELECT * query.

4.2   Inserting Default Values

Problem

A table can be defined to take default values for specific columns. You want to insert a row of default values without having to specify those values. Consider the following table:

```
create table D (id integer default 0)
```

You want to insert zero without explicitly specifying zero in the values list of an INSERT statement. You want to explicitly insert the default, whatever that default is.

Solution

All brands support use of the DEFAULT keyword as a way of explicitly specifying the default value for a column. Some brands provide additional ways to solve the problem.

The following example illustrates the use of the DEFAULT keyword:

```
insert into D values (default)
```

You may also explicitly specify the column name, which you'll need to do anytime you are not inserting into all columns of a table:

```
insert into D (id) values (default)
```

Oracle8*i* Database and prior versions do not support the DEFAULT keyword. Prior to Oracle9*i* Database, there was no way to explicitly insert a default column value.

MySQL allows you to specify an empty values list if all columns have a default value defined:

```
insert into D values ()
```

In this case, all columns will be set to their default values.

PostgreSQL and SQL Server support a DEFAULT VALUES clause:

```
insert into D default values
```

The DEFAULT VALUES clause causes all columns to take on their default values.

Discussion

The DEFAULT keyword in the values list will insert the value that was specified as the default for a particular column during table creation. The keyword is available for all DBMSs.

MySQL, PostgreSQL, and SQL Server users have another option available if all columns in the table are defined with a default value (as table D is in this case). You may use an empty VALUES list (MySQL) or specify the DEFAULT VALUES clause (PostgreSQL and SQL Server) to create a new row with all default values; otherwise, you need to specify DEFAULT for each column in the table.

For tables with a mix of default and non-default columns, inserting default values for a column is as easy as excluding the column from the insert list; you do not need to use the DEFAULT keyword. Say that table D had an additional column that was not defined with a default value:

```
create table D (id integer default 0, foo varchar(10))
```

You can insert a default for ID by listing only FOO in the insert list:

```
insert into D (foo) values ('Bar')
```

This statement will result in a row in which ID is 0 and FOO is "Bar". ID takes on its default value because no other value is specified.

4.3   Overriding a Default Value with NULL

Problem

You are inserting into a column having a default value, and you wish to override that default value by setting the column to NULL. Consider the following table:

```
create table D (id integer default 0, foo VARCHAR(10))
```

You wish to insert a row with a NULL value for ID.

Solution

You can explicitly specify NULL in your values list:

```
insert into d (id, foo) values (null, 'Brighten')
```

Discussion

Not everyone realizes that you can explicitly specify NULL in the values list of an INSERT statement. Typically, when you do not wish to specify a value for a column, you leave that column out of your column and values lists:

```
insert into d (foo) values ('Brighten')
```

Here, no value for ID is specified. Many would expect the column to taken on the null value, but, alas, a default value was specified at table creation time, so the result of the preceding INSERT is that ID takes on the value 0 (the default). By specifying NULL as the value for a column, you can set the column to NULL despite any default value.

4.4   Copying Rows from One Table into Another

Problem

You want to copy rows from one table to another by using a query. The query may be complex or simple, but ultimately you want the result to be inserted into another table. For example, you want to copy rows from the DEPT table to the DEPT_EAST table. The DEPT_EAST table has already been created with the same structure (same columns and data types) as DEPT and is currently empty.

Solution

Use the INSERT statement followed by a query to produce the rows you want:

```
1 insert into dept_east (deptno,dname,loc)
2 select deptno,dname,loc
3   from dept
4  where loc in ( 'NEW YORK','BOSTON' )
```

Discussion

Simply follow the INSERT statement with a query that returns the desired rows. If you want to copy all rows from the source table, exclude the WHERE clause from the query. Like a regular insert, you do not have to explicitly specify which columns you are inserting into. But if you do not specify your target columns, you must insert into *all* of the table's columns, and you must be mindful of the order of the values in the SELECT list as described earlier in Recipe 4.1.

4.5   Copying a Table Definition

Problem

You want to create a new table having the same set of columns as an existing table. For example, you want to create a copy of the DEPT table and call it DEPT_2. You do not want to copy the rows, only the column structure of the table.

Solution

DB2

Use the LIKE clause with the CREATE TABLE command:

```
create table dept_2 like dept
```

Oracle, MySQL, and PostgreSQL

Use the CREATE TABLE command with a subquery that returns no rows:

```
1 create table dept_2
2 as
3 select *
4   from dept
5  where 1 = 0
```

SQL Server

Use the INTO clause with a subquery that returns no rows:

```
1 select *
2   into dept_2
3   from dept
4  where 1 = 0
```

Discussion

DB2

DB2's CREATE TABLE ... LIKE command allows you to easily use one table as the pattern for creating another. Simply specify your pattern table's name following the LIKE keyword.

Oracle, MySQL, and PostgreSQL

When using Create Table As Select (CTAS), all rows from your query will be used to populate the new table you are creating unless you specify a false condition in the WHERE clause. In the solution provided, the expression "1 = 0" in the WHERE clause of the query causes no rows to be returned. Thus the result of the CTAS statement is an empty table based on the columns in the SELECT clause of the query.

SQL Server

When using INTO to copy a table, all rows from your query will be used to populate the new table you are creating unless you specify a false condition in the WHERE clause of your query. In the solution provided, the expression "1 = 0" in the predicate of the query causes no rows to be returned. The result is an empty table based on the columns in the SELECT clause of the query.

4.6 Inserting into Multiple Tables at Once

Problem

You want to take rows returned by a query and insert those rows into multiple target tables. For example, you want to insert rows from DEPT into tables DEPT_EAST, DEPT_WEST, and DEPT_MID. All three tables have the same structure (same columns and data types) as DEPT and are currently empty.

Solution

The solution is to insert the result of a query into the target tables. The difference from Recipe 4.4 is that for this problem you have multiple target tables.

Oracle

Use either the INSERT ALL or INSERT FIRST statement. Both share the same syntax except for the choice between the ALL and FIRST keywords. The following statement uses INSERT ALL to cause all possible target tables to be considered:

```
1  insert all
2    when loc in ('NEW YORK','BOSTON') then
3      into dept_east (deptno,dname,loc) values (deptno,dname,loc)
4    when loc = 'CHICAGO' then
5      into dept_mid  (deptno,dname,loc) values (deptno,dname,loc)
6    else
7      into dept_west (deptno,dname,loc) values (deptno,dname,loc)
8  select deptno,dname,loc
9    from dept
```

DB2

Insert into an inline view that performs a UNION ALL on the tables to be inserted. You must also be sure to place constraints on the tables that will ensure each row goes into the correct table:

```
create table dept_east
( deptno integer,
  dname  varchar(10),
  loc    varchar(10) check (loc in ('NEW YORK','BOSTON')))

create table dept_mid
( deptno integer,
  dname  varchar(10),
  loc    varchar(10) check (loc = 'CHICAGO'))

create table dept_west
( deptno integer,
  dname  varchar(10),
  loc    varchar(10) check (loc = 'DALLAS'))
```

```
1  insert into (
2    select * from dept_west union all
3    select * from dept_east union all
4    select * from dept_mid
5  ) select * from dept
```

MySQL, PostgreSQL, and SQL Server

As of the time of this writing, these vendors do not support multi-table inserts.

Discussion

Oracle

Oracle's multi-table insert uses WHEN-THEN-ELSE clauses to evaluate the rows from the nested SELECT and insert them accordingly. In this recipe's example, INSERT ALL and INSERT FIRST would produce the same result, but there is a difference between the two. INSERT FIRST will break out of the WHEN-THEN-ELSE evaluation as soon as it encounters a condition evaluating to true; INSERT ALL will evaluate all conditions even if prior tests evaluate to true. Thus, you can use INSERT ALL to insert the same row into more than one table.

DB2

My DB2 solution is a bit of a hack. It requires that the tables to be inserted into have constraints defined to ensure that each row evaluated from the subquery will go into the correct table. The technique is to insert into a view that is defined as the UNION ALL of the tables. If the check constraints are not unique amongst the tables in the INSERT (i.e., multiple tables have the same check constraint), the INSERT statement will not know where to put the rows and it will fail.

MySQL, PostgreSQL, and SQL Server

As of the time of this writing, only Oracle and DB2 currently provide mechanisms to insert rows returned by a query into one or more of several tables within the same statement.

4.7 Blocking Inserts to Certain Columns

Problem

You wish to prevent users, or an errant software application, from inserting values into certain table columns. For example, you wish to allow a program to insert into EMP, but only into the EMPNO, ENAME, and JOB columns.

Solution

Create a view on the table exposing only those columns you wish to expose. Then force all inserts to go through that view.

For example, to create a view exposing the three columns in EMP:

```
create view new_emps as
select empno, ename, job
  from emp
```

Grant access to this view to those users and programs allowed to populate only the three fields in the view. Do not grant those users insert access to the EMP table. Users may then create new EMP records by inserting into the NEW_EMPS view, but they will not be able to provide values for columns other than the three that are specified in the view definition.

Discussion

When you insert into a simple view such as in the solution, your database server will translate that insert into the underlying table. For example, the following insert:

```
insert into new_emps
  (empno ename, job)
    values (1, 'Jonathan', 'Editor')
```

---

will be translated behind the scenes into:

```
insert into emp
   (empno ename, job)
   values (1, 'Jonathan', 'Editor')
```

It is also possible, but perhaps less useful, to insert into an inline view (currently only supported by Oracle):

```
insert into
   (select empno, ename, job
      from emp)
values (1, 'Jonathan', 'Editor')
```

View insertion is a complex topic. The rules become very complicated very quickly for all but the simplest of views. If you plan to make use of the ability to insert into views, it is imperative that you consult and fully understand your vendor documentation on the matter.

4.8 Modifying Records in a Table

Problem

You want to modify values for some or all rows in a table. For example, you might want to increase the salaries of everyone in department 20 by 10%. The following result set shows the DEPTNO, ENAME, and SAL for employees in that department:

```
select deptno,ename,sal
  from emp
 where deptno = 20
 order by 1,3

DEPTNO ENAME             SAL
------ ---------- ----------
    20 SMITH             800
    20 ADAMS            1100
    20 JONES            2975
    20 SCOTT            3000
    20 FORD             3000
```

You want to bump all the SAL values by 10%.

Solution

Use the UPDATE statement to modify existing rows in a database table. For example:

```
1 update emp
2    set sal = sal*1.10
3  where deptno = 20
```

Discussion

Use the UPDATE statement along with a WHERE clause to specify which rows to update; if you exclude a WHERE clause, then all rows are updated. The expression SAL*1.10 in this solution returns the salary increased by 10%.

When preparing for a mass update, you may wish to preview the results. You can do that by issuing a SELECT statement that includes the expressions you plan to put into your SET clauses. The following SELECT shows the result of a 10% salary increase:

```
select deptno,
       ename,
       sal       as orig_sal,
       sal*.10   as amt_to_add,
       sal*1.10 as new_sal
  from emp
 where deptno=20
 order by 1,5
```

```
DEPTNO ENAME  ORIG_SAL AMT_TO_ADD NEW_SAL
------ ------ -------- ---------- -------
    20 SMITH       800         80     880
    20 ADAMS      1100        110    1210
    20 JONES      2975        298    3273
    20 SCOTT      3000        300    3300
    20 FORD       3000        300    3300
```

The salary increase is broken down into two columns: one to show the increase over the old salary, and the other to show the new salary.

4.9   Updating When Corresponding Rows Exist

Problem

You want to update rows in one table when corresponding rows exist in another. For example, if an employee appears in table EMP_BONUS, you want to increase that employee's salary (in table EMP) by 20 percent. The following result set represents the data currently in table EMP_BONUS:

```
select empno, ename
  from emp_bonus

    EMPNO ENAME
---------- ----------
     7369 SMITH
     7900 JAMES
     7934 MILLER
```

Solution

Use a subquery in your UPDATE statement's WHERE clause to find employees in table EMP that are also in table EMP_BONUS. Your UPDATE will then act only on those rows, enabling you to increase their salary by 20 percent:

```
1 update emp
2    set sal=sal*1.20
3  where empno in ( select empno from emp_bonus )
```

Discussion

The results from the subquery represent the rows that will be updated in table EMP. The IN predicate tests values of EMPNO from the EMP table to see whether they are in the list of EMPNO values returned by the subquery. When they are, the corresponding SAL values are updated.

Alternatively, you can use EXISTS instead of IN:

```
update emp
   set sal = sal*1.20
 where exists ( select null
                 from emp_bonus
                where emp.empno=emp_bonus.empno )
```

You may be surprised to see NULL in the SELECT list of the EXISTS subquery. Fear not, that NULL does not have an adverse effect on the update. In my opinion it increases readability as it reinforces the fact that, unlike the solution using a subquery with an IN operator, what will drive the update (i.e., which rows will be updated) will be controlled by the WHERE clause of the subquery, not the values returned as a result of the subquery's SELECT list.

4.10 Updating with Values from Another Table

Problem

You wish to update rows in one table using values from another. For example, you have a table called NEW_SAL, which holds the new salaries for certain employees. The contents of table NEW_SAL are:

```
select *
  from new_sal

DEPTNO       SAL
------ ----------
    10      4000
```

Column DEPTNO is the primary key of table NEW_SAL. You want to update the salaries and commission of certain employees in table EMP using values table NEW_SAL if there is a match between EMP.DEPTNO and NEW_SAL.DEPTNO, update

EMP.SAL to NEW_SAL.SAL, and update EMP.COMM to 50% of NEW_SAL.SAL. The rows in EMP are as follows:

```
select deptno,ename,sal,comm
  from emp
 order by 1
```

```
DEPTNO ENAME           SAL        COMM
------ ---------- ---------- ----------
    10 CLARK          2450
    10 KING           5000
    10 MILLER         1300
    20 SMITH           800
    20 ADAMS          1100
    20 FORD           3000
    20 SCOTT          3000
    20 JONES          2975
    30 ALLEN          1600         300
    30 BLAKE          2850
    30 MARTIN         1250        1400
    30 JAMES           950
    30 TURNER         1500           0
    30 WARD           1250         500
```

Solution

Use a join between NEW_SAL and EMP to find and return the new COMM values to the UPDATE statement. It is quite common for updates such as this one to be performed via correlated subquery. Another technique involves creating a view (traditional or inline, depending on what your database supports), then updating that view.

DB2

Use a correlated subquery to set new SAL and COMM values in EMP. Also use a correlated subquery to identify which rows from EMP should be updated:

```
1  update emp e set (e.sal,e.comm) = (select ns.sal, ns.sal/2
2                                       from new_sal ns
3                                      where ns.deptno=e.deptno)
4   where exists ( select *
5                    from new_sal ns
6                   where ns.deptno = e.deptno )
```

MySQL

Include both EMP and NEW_SAL in the UPDATE clause of the UPDATE statement and join in the WHERE clause:

```
1  update emp e, new_sal ns
2     set e.sal = ns.sal,
3         e.comm = ns.sal/2
4   where e.deptno = ns.deptnoOracle
```

Oracle

The method for the DB2 solution will certainly work for Oracle, but as an alternative, you can update an inline view:

```
1 update (
2 select e.sal  as emp_sal, e.comm  as emp_comm,
3        ns.sal as ns_sal, ns.sal/2 as ns_comm
4   from emp e, new_sal ns
5  where e.deptno = ns.deptno
6 ) set emp_sal = ns_sal, emp_comm = ns_comm
```

PostgreSQL

The method used for the DB2 solution will work for PostgreSQL, but as an alternative you can (quite conveniently) join directly in the UPDATE statement:

```
1 update emp
2    set sal  = ns.sal,
3        comm = ns.sal/2
4   from new_sal ns
5  where ns.deptno = emp.deptno
```

SQL Server

The method used for the DB2 solution will work for SQL Server, but as an alternative you can (similarly to the PostgreSQL solution) join directly in the UPDATE statement:

```
1 update e
2    set e.sal  = ns.sal,
3        e.comm = ns.sal/2
4   from emp e,
5        new_sal ns
6  where ns.deptno = e.deptno
```

Discussion

Before discussing the different solutions, I'd like to mention something important regarding updates that use queries to supply new values. A WHERE clause in the subquery of a correlated update is not the same as the WHERE clause of the table being updated. If you look at the UPDATE statement in the Problem section, the join on DEPTNO between EMP and NEW_SAL is done and returns rows to the SET clause of the UPDATE statement. For employees in DEPTNO 10, valid values are returned because there is a match DEPTNO in table NEW_SAL. But what about employees in the other departments? NEW_SAL does not have any other departments, so the SAL and COMM for employees in DEPTNOs 20 and 30 are set to NULL. Unless you are doing so via LIMIT or TOP or whatever mechanism your vendor supplies for limiting the number of rows returned in a result set, the only way to restrict rows from a table in SQL is to use a WHERE clause. To correctly perform this UPDATE, use a WHERE clause on the table being updated along with a WHERE clause in the correlated subquery.

DB2

To ensure you do not update every row in table EMP, remember to include a correlated subquery in the WHERE clause of the UPDATE. Performing the join (the correlated subquery) in the SET clause is not enough. By using a WHERE clause in the UPDATE, you ensure that only rows in EMP that match on DEPTNO to table NEW_SAL are updated. This holds true for all RDBMSs.

Oracle

In the Oracle solution using the update join view, you are using equi-joins to determine which rows will be updated. You can confirm which rows are being updated by executing the query independently. To be able to successfully use this type of UPDATE, you must first understand the concept of key-preservation. The DEPTNO column of the table NEW_SAL is the primary key of that table, thus its values are unique within the table. When joining between EMP and NEW_SAL, however, NEW_SAL.DEPTNO is not unique in the result set, as can be seen below:

```
select e.empno, e.deptno e_dept, ns.sal, ns.deptno ns_deptno
  from emp e, new_sal ns
 where e.deptno = ns.deptno


EMPNO     E_DEPT       SAL  NS_DEPTNO
-----  ----------  ---------- ----------
 7782        10      4000        10
 7839        10      4000        10
 7934        10      4000        10
```

To enable Oracle to update this join, one of the tables must be key-preserved, meaning that if its values are not unique in the result set, it should at least be unique in the table it comes from. In this case NEW_SAL has a primary key on DEPTNO, which makes it unique in the table. Because it is unique in its table, it may appear multiple times in the result set and will still be considered key-preserved, thus allowing the update to complete successfully.

PostgreSQL, SQL Server, and MySQL

The syntax is a bit different among these platforms, but the technique is the same. Being able to join directly in the UPDATE statement is extremely convenient. Since you specify which table to update (the table listed after the UPDATE keyword) there's no confusion as to which table's rows are modified. Additionally, because you are using joins in the update (since there is an explicit WHERE clause), you can avoid some of the pitfalls when coding correlated subquery updates; in particular, if you missed a join here, it would be very obvious you'd have a problem.

4.11 Merging Records

Problem

You want to conditionally insert, update, or delete records in a table depending on whether or not corresponding records exist. (If a record exists, then update; if not, then insert; if after updating a row fails to meet a certain condition, delete it.) For example, you want to modify table EMP_COMMISSION such that:

- If any employee in EMP_COMMISSION also exists in table EMP, then update their commission (COMM) to 1000.

- For all employees who will potentially have their COMM updated to 1000, if their SAL is less than 2000, delete them (they should not be exist in EMP_COMMISSION).

- Otherwise, insert the EMPNO, ENAME, and DEPTNO values from table EMP into table EMP_COMMISSION.

Essentially, you wish to execute either an UPDATE or an INSERT depending on whether a given row from EMP has a match in EMP_COMMISSION. Then you wish to execute a DELETE if the result of an UPDATE causes a commission that's too high.

The following rows are currently in tables EMP and EMP_COMMISSION, respectively:

```
select deptno,empno,ename,comm
  from emp
 order by 1
```

DEPTNO	EMPNO	ENAME	COMM
10	7782	CLARK	
10	7839	KING	
10	7934	MILLER	
20	7369	SMITH	
20	7876	ADAMS	
20	7902	FORD	
20	7788	SCOTT	
20	7566	JONES	
30	7499	ALLEN	300
30	7698	BLAKE	
30	7654	MARTIN	1400
30	7900	JAMES	
30	7844	TURNER	0
30	7521	WARD	500

```
select deptno,empno,ename,comm
  from emp_commission
 order by 1
```

DEPTNO	EMPNO	ENAME	COMM
10	7782	CLARK	
10	7839	KING	
10	7934	MILLER	

Solution

Oracle is currently the only RDBMS with a statement designed to solve this problem. That statement is the MERGE statement, and it can perform either an UPDATE or an INSERT, as needed. For example:

```
1  merge into emp_commission ec
2  using (select * from emp) emp
3     on (ec.empno=emp.empno)
4  when matched then
5        update set ec.comm = 1000
6        delete where (sal < 2000)
7  when not matched then
8        insert (ec.empno,ec.ename,ec.deptno,ec.comm)
9        values (emp.empno,emp.ename,emp.deptno,emp.comm)
```

Discussion

The join on line 3 of the solution determines what rows already exist and will be updated. The join is between EMP_COMMISSION (aliased as EC) and the subquery (aliased as emp). When the join succeeds, the two rows are considered "matched" and the UPDATE specified in the WHEN MATCHED clause is executed. Otherwise, no match is found and the INSERT in WHEN NOT MATCHED is executed. Thus, rows from table EMP that do not have corresponding rows based on EMPNO in table EMP_COMMISSION will be inserted into EMP_COMMISSION. Of all the employees in table EMP only those in DEPTNO 10 should have their COMM updated in EMP_COMMISSION, while the rest of the employees are inserted. Additionally, since MILLER is in DEPTNO 10 he is a candidate to have his COMM updated, but because his SAL is less than 2000 it is deleted from EMP_COMMISSION.

4.12   Deleting All Records from a Table

Problem

You want to delete all the records from a table.

Solution

Use the DELETE command to delete records from a table. For example, to delete all records from EMP:

```
delete from emp
```

Discussion

When using the DELETE command without a WHERE clause, you will delete all rows from the table specified.

4.13 Deleting Specific Records

Problem

You wish to delete records meeting a specific criterion from a table.

Solution

Use the DELETE command with a WHERE clause specifying which rows to delete. For example, to delete all employees in department 10:

```
delete from emp where deptno = 10
```

Discussion

By using a WHERE clause with the DELETE command, you can delete a subset of rows in a table rather than all the rows.

4.14 Deleting a Single Record

Problem

You wish to delete a single record from a table.

Solution

This is a special case of Recipe 4.13. The key is to ensure that your selection criterion is narrow enough to specify only the one record that you wish to delete. Often you will want to delete based on the primary key. For example, to delete employee CLARK (EMPNO 7782):

```
delete from emp where empno = 7782
```

Discussion

Deleting is always about identifying the rows to be deleted, and the impact of a DELETE always comes down to its WHERE clause. Omit the WHERE clause and the scope of a DELETE is the entire table. By writing conditions in the WHERE clause, you can narrow the scope to a group of records, or to a single record. When deleting a single record, you should typically be identifying that record based on its primary key or on one of its unique keys.

If your deletion criterion is based on a primary or unique key, then you can be sure of deleting only one record. (This is because your RDBMS will not allow two rows to contain the same primary or unique key values.) Otherwise, you may want to check first, to be sure you aren't about to inadvertently delete more records than you intend.

4.15   Deleting Referential Integrity Violations

Problem

You wish to delete records from a table when those records refer to nonexistent records in some other table. Example: some employees are assigned to departments that do not exist. You wish to delete those employees.

Solution

Use the NOT EXISTS predicate with a subquery to test the validity of department numbers:

```
delete from emp
 where not exists (
   select * from dept
    where dept.deptno = emp.deptno
 )
```

Alternatively, you can write the query using a NOT IN predicate:

```
delete from emp
 where deptno not in (select deptno from dept)
```

Discussion

Deleting is really all about selecting: the real work lies in writing WHERE clause conditions to correctly describe those records that you wish to delete.

The NOT EXISTS solution uses a correlated subquery to test for the existence of a record in DEPT having a DEPTNO matching that in a given EMP record. If such a record exists, then the EMP record is retained. Otherwise, it is deleted. Each EMP record is checked in this manner.

The IN solution uses a subquery to retrieve a list of valid department numbers. DEPTNOs from each EMP record are then checked against that list. When an EMP record is found with a DEPTNO not in the list, the EMP record is deleted.

4.16   Deleting Duplicate Records

Problem

You want to delete duplicate records from a table. Consider the following table:

```
create table dupes (id integer, name varchar(10))

insert into dupes values (1, 'NAPOLEON')
insert into dupes values (2, 'DYNAMITE')
insert into dupes values (3, 'DYNAMITE')
insert into dupes values (4, 'SHE SELLS')
insert into dupes values (5, 'SEA SHELLS')
insert into dupes values (6, 'SEA SHELLS')
insert into dupes values (7, 'SEA SHELLS')

select * from dupes order by 1

        ID NAME
---------- ----------
         1 NAPOLEON
         2 DYNAMITE
         3 DYNAMITE
         4 SHE SELLS
         5 SEA SHELLS
         6 SEA SHELLS
         7 SEA SHELLS
```

For each group of duplicate names, such as "SEA SHELLS", you wish to arbitrarily retain one ID and delete the rest. In the case of "SEA SHELLS" you don't care whether you delete 5 and 6, or 5 and 7, or 6 and 7, but in the end you want just one record for "SEA SHELLS".

Solution

Use a subquery with an aggregate function such as MIN to arbitrarily choose the ID to retain (in this case only the NAME with the smallest value for ID is not deleted):

```
1 delete from dupes
2  where id not in ( select min(id)
3                      from dupes
4                     group by name )
```

For MySQL users you will need slightly different syntax because you cannot reference the same table twice in a delete (as of the time of this writing):

```
1 delete from dupes
2  where id not in
3        ( select min(id)
4     from ( select id,name from dupes ) tmp
5           group by name )
```

Discussion

The first thing to do when deleting duplicates is to define exactly what it means for two rows to be considered "duplicates" of each other. For my example in this recipe, the definition of "duplicate" is that two records contain the same value in their NAME column. Having that definition in place, you can look to some other column to discriminate among each set of duplicates, to identify those records to retain. It's best if this discriminating column (or columns) is a primary key. I used the ID column, which is a good choice because no two records have the same ID.

The key to the solution is that you group by the values that are duplicated (by NAME in this case), and then use an aggregate function to pick off just one key value to retain. The subquery in the Solution example will return the smallest ID for each NAME, which represents the row you will not delete:

```
select min(id)
  from dupes
 group by name


    MIN(ID)
 ----------
          2
          1
          5
          4
```

The DELETE then deletes any ID in the table that is not returned by the subquery (in this case IDs 3, 6, and 7). If you are having trouble seeing how this works, run the subquery first and include the NAME in the SELECT list:

```
select name, min(id)
  from dupes
 group by name


NAME          MIN(ID)
----------  ----------
DYNAMITE             2
NAPOLEON             1
SEA SHELLS           5
SHE SELLS            4
```

The rows returned by the subquery represent those to be retained. The NOT IN predicate in the DELETE statement causes all other rows to be deleted.

4.17 Deleting Records Referenced from Another Table

Problem

You want to delete records from one table when those records are referenced from some other table. Consider the following table, named DEPT_ACCIDENTS, which contains one row for each accident that occurs in a manufacturing business. Each row records the department in which an accident occurred and also the type of accident.

```
create table dept_accidents
( deptno         integer,
  accident_name  varchar(20) )
```

```
insert into dept_accidents values (10,'BROKEN FOOT')
insert into dept_accidents values (10,'FLESH WOUND')
insert into dept_accidents values (20,'FIRE')
insert into dept_accidents values (20,'FIRE')
insert into dept_accidents values (20,'FLOOD')
insert into dept_accidents values (30,'BRUISED GLUTE')

select * from dept_accidents

    DEPTNO ACCIDENT_NAME
---------- --------------------
        10 BROKEN FOOT
        10 FLESH WOUND
        20 FIRE
        20 FIRE
        20 FLOOD
        30 BRUISED GLUTE
```

You want to delete from EMP the records for those employees working at a department that has three or more accidents.

Solution

Use a subquery and the aggregate function COUNT to find the departments with three or more accidents. Then delete all employees working in those departments:

```
1 delete from emp
2  where deptno in ( select deptno
3                       from dept_accidents
4                      group by deptno
5                     having count(*) >= 3 )
```

Discussion

The subquery will identify which departments have three or more accidents:

```
select deptno
  from dept_accidents
 group by deptno
having count(*) >= 3

    DEPTNO
----------
        20
```

The DELETE will then delete any employees in the departments returned by the subquery (in this case, only in department 20).

CHAPTER 5

Metadata Queries

This chapter presents recipes that allow you to find information about a given schema. For example, you may wish to know what tables you've created or which foreign keys are not indexed. All of the RDBMSs in this book provide tables and views for obtaining such data. The recipes in this chapter will get you started on gleaning information from those tables and views. There is, however, far more information available than the recipes in this chapter can show. Consult your RDBMSs documentation for the complete list of catalog or data dictionary tables/views.

For purposes of demonstration, all the recipes in this chapter assume the schema name SMEAGOL.

5.1   Listing Tables in a Schema

Problem

You want to see a list of all the tables you've created in a given schema.

Solution

The solutions that follow all assume you are working with the SMEAGOL schema. The basic approach to a solution is the same for all RDBMSs: you query a system table (or view) containing a row for each table in the database.

DB2

Query SYSCAT.TABLES:

```
1 select tabname
2   from syscat.tables
3 where tabschema = 'SMEAGOL'
```

Oracle

Query SYS.ALL_TABLES:

```
select table_name
  from all_tables
 where owner = 'SMEAGOL'
```

PostgreSQL, MySQL, and SQL Server

Query INFORMATION_SCHEMA.TABLES:

```
1 select table_name
2   from information_schema.tables
3  where table_schema = 'SMEAGOL'
```

Discussion

In a delightfully circular manner, databases expose information about themselves through the very mechanisms that you create for your own applications: tables and views. Oracle, for example, maintains an extensive catalog of system views, such as ALL_TABLES, that you can query for information about tables, indexes, grants, and any other database object.

 Oracle's catalog views are just that, views. They are based on an underlying set of tables that contain the information in a very user-unfriendly form. The views put a very usable face on Oracle's catalog data.

Oracle's system views and DB2's system tables are each vendor-specific. PostgreSQL, MySQL, and SQL Server, on the other hand, support something called the *information schema*, which is a set of views defined by the ISO SQL standard. That's why the same query can work for all three of those databases.

5.2 Listing a Table's Columns

Problem

You want to list the columns in a table, along with their data types, and their position in the table they are in.

Solution

The following solutions assume that you wish to list columns, their data types, and their numeric position in the table named EMP in the schema SMEAGOL.

DB2

Query SYSCAT.COLUMNS:

```
1 select colname, typename, colno
2   from syscat.columns
3  where tabname   = 'EMP'
4    and tabschema = 'SMEAGOL'
```

Oracle

Query ALL_TAB_COLUMNS:

```
1  select column_name, data_type, column_id
2    from all_tab_columns
3   where owner      = 'SMEAGOL'
4     and table_name = 'EMP'
```

PostgreSQL, MySQL, and SQL Server

Query INFORMATION_SCHEMA.COLUMNS:

```
1 select column_name, data_type, ordinal_position
2   from information_schema.columns
3  where table_schema = 'SMEAGOL'
4    and table_name   = 'EMP'
```

Discussion

Each vendor provides ways for you to get detailed information about your column data. In the examples above only the column name, data type, and position are returned. Additional useful items of information include length, nullability, and default values.

5.3   Listing Indexed Columns for a Table

Problem

You want list indexes, their columns, and the column position (if available) in the index for a given table.

Solution

The vendor-specific solutions that follow all assume that you are listing indexes for the table EMP in the SMEAGOL schema.

DB2

Query SYSCAT.INDEXES:

```
1  select a.tabname, b.indname, b.colname, b.colseq
2    from syscat.indexes a,
3         syscat.indexcoluse b
```

```
4  where a.tabname    = 'EMP'
5    and a.tabschema = 'SMEAGOL'
6    and a.indschema = b.indschema
7    and a.indname   = b.indname
```

Oracle

Query SYS.ALL_IND_COLUMNS:

```
select table_name, index_name, column_name, column_position
  from sys.all_ind_columns
 where table_name  = 'EMP'
   and table_owner = 'SMEAGOL'
```

PostgreSQL

Query PG_CATALOG.PG_INDEXES and INFORMATION_SCHEMA.COLUMNS:

```
1  select a.tablename,a.indexname,b.column_name
2    from pg_catalog.pg_indexes a,
3         information_schema.columns b
4   where a.schemaname = 'SMEAGOL'
5     and a.tablename  = b.table_name
```

MySQL

Use the SHOW INDEX command:

```
show index from emp
```

SQL Server

Query SYS.TABLES, SYS.INDEXES, SYS.INDEX_COLUMNS, and SYS.COLUMNS:

```
1  select a.name table_name,
2         b.name index_name,
3         d.name column_name,
4         c.index_column_id
5    from sys.tables a,
6         sys.indexes b,
7         sys.index_columns c,
8         sys.columns d
9   where a.object_id = b.object_id
10    and b.object_id = c.object_id
11    and b.index_id  = c.index_id
12    and c.object_id = d.object_id
13    and c.column_id = d.column_id
14    and a.name      = 'EMP'
```

Discussion

When it comes to queries, it's important to know what columns are/aren't indexed. Indexes can provide good performance for queries against columns that are frequently used in filters and that are fairly selective. Indexes are also useful when joining between tables. By knowing what columns are indexed, you are already one step ahead of performance problems if they should occur. Additionally, you might want to find information about the indexes themselves: how many levels deep they are, how many distinct keys, how many leaf blocks, and so forth. Such information is also available from the views/tables queried in this recipe's solutions.

5.4   Listing Constraints on a Table

Problem

You want to list the constraints defined for a table in some schema and the columns they are defined on. For example, you want to find the constraints and the columns they are on for table EMP.

Solution

DB2

Query SYSCAT.TABCONST and SYSCAT.COLUMNS:

```
 1  select a.tabname, a.constname, a.colname,
 2         (select b.type from syscat.tabconst b
 3           where a.tabname    = b.tabname
 4             and a.tabschema  = b.tabschema
 5             and a.constname  = b.constname) as type
 6    from syscat.keycoluse a
 7   where a.tabname   = 'EMP'
 8     and a.tabschema = 'SMEAGOL'
 9   UNION
10  select tabname, constname, colname, usage
11    from syscat.colchecks
12   where tabname   = 'EMP'
13     and tabschema = 'SMEAGOL'
```

Oracle

Query SYS.ALL_CONSTRAINTS and SYS.ALL_CONS_COLUMNS:

```
 1  select a.table_name,
 2         a.constraint_name,
 3         b.column_name,
 4         a.constraint_type
 5    from all_constraints a,
 6         all_cons_columns b
 7   where a.table_name       = 'EMP'
 8     and a.owner            = 'SMEAGOL'
 9     and a.table_name       = b.table_name
10     and a.owner            = b.owner
11     and a.constraint_name  = b.constraint_name
```

PostgreSQL, MySQL, and SQL Server

Query INFORMATION_SCHEMA.TABLE_CONSTRAINTS and INFORMATION_SCHEMA.KEY_COLUMN_USAGE:

```
 1  select a.table_name,
 2         a.constraint_name,
 3         b.column_name,
 4         a.constraint_type
 5    from information_schema.table_constraints a,
 6         information_schema.key_column_usage b
 7   where a.table_name    = 'EMP'
 8     and a.table_schema  = 'SMEAGOL'
 9     and a.table_name    = b.table_name
10     and a.table_schema  = b.table_schema
11     and a.constraint_name = b.constraint_name
```

Discussion

Constraints are such a critical part of relational databases that it should go without saying why you need to know what constraints are on your tables. Listing the constraints on tables is useful for a variety of reasons: you may want to find tables missing a primary key, you may want to find which columns should be foreign keys but are not (i.e., child tables have data different from the parent tables and you want to know how that happened), or you may want to know about check constraints (are columns nullable? do they have to satisfy a specific condition? etc.).

5.5 Listing Foreign Keys Without Corresponding Indexes

Problem

You want to list tables that have foreign key columns that are not indexed. For example, you want to determine if the foreign keys on table EMP are indexed.

Solution

DB2

Query SYSCAT.TABCONST, SYSCAT.KEYCOLUSE, SYSCAT.INDEXES, and SYSCAT.INDEXCOLUSE:

```
 1  select fkeys.tabname,
 2         fkeys.constname,
 3         fkeys.colname,
 4         ind_cols.indname
```

```
 5    from (
 6  select a.tabschema, a.tabname, a.constname, b.colname
 7    from syscat.tabconst a,
 8         syscat.keycoluse b
 9   where a.tabname   = 'EMP'
10     and a.tabschema = 'SMEAGOL'
11     and a.type      = 'F'
12     and a.tabname   = b.tabname
13     and a.tabschema = b.tabschema
14         ) fkeys
15         left join
16         (
17  select a.tabschema,
18         a.tabname,
19         a.indname,
20         b.colname
21    from syscat.indexes a,
22         syscat.indexcoluse b
23   where a.indschema = b.indschema
24     and a.indname   = b.indname
25         ) ind_cols
26      on (     fkeys.tabschema = ind_cols.tabschema
27          and fkeys.tabname   = ind_cols.tabname
28          and fkeys.colname   = ind_cols.colname )
29   where ind_cols.indname is null
```

Oracle

Query SYS.ALL_CONS_COLUMNS, SYS.ALL_CONSTRAINTS, and SYS.ALL_
IND_COLUMNS:

```
 1  select a.table_name,
 2         a.constraint_name,
 3         a.column_name,
 4         c.index_name
 5    from all_cons_columns a,
 6         all_constraints b,
 7         all_ind_columns c
 8   where a.table_name      = 'EMP'
 9     and a.owner           = 'SMEAGOL'
10     and b.constraint_type = 'R'
11     and a.owner           = b.owner
12     and a.table_name      = b.table_name
13     and a.constraint_name = b.constraint_name
14     and a.owner           = c.table_owner  (+)
15     and a.table_name      = c.table_name   (+)
16     and a.column_name     = c.column_name  (+)
17     and c.index_name      is null
```

PostgreSQL

Query INFORMATION_SCHEMA.KEY_COLUMN_USAGE, INFORMATION_ SCHEMA.REFERENTIAL_CONSTRAINTS, INFORMATION_SCHEMA.COLUMNS, and PG_CATALOG.PG_INDEXES:

```
 1  select fkeys.table_name,
 2         fkeys.constraint_name,
 3         fkeys.column_name,
 4         ind_cols.indexname
 5    from (
 6  select a.constraint_schema,
 7         a.table_name,
 8         a.constraint_name,
 9         a.column_name
10    from information_schema.key_column_usage a,
11         information_schema.referential_constraints b
12   where a.constraint_name    = b.constraint_name
13     and a.constraint_schema  = b.constraint_schema
14     and a.constraint_schema  = 'SMEAGOL'
15     and a.table_name         = 'EMP'
16         ) fkeys
17         left join
18         (
19  select a.schemaname, a.tablename, a.indexname, b.column_name
20    from pg_catalog.pg_indexes a,
21         information_schema.columns b
22   where a.tablename  = b.table_name
23     and a.schemaname = b.table_schema
24         ) ind_cols
25      on (    fkeys.constraint_schema = ind_cols.schemaname
26         and fkeys.table_name        = ind_cols.tablename
27         and fkeys.column_name       = ind_cols.column_name )
28   where ind_cols.indexname is null
```

MySQL

You can use the SHOW INDEX command to retrieve index information such as index name, columns in the index, and ordinal position of the columns in the index. Additionally, you can query INFORMATION_SCHEMA.KEY_COLUMN_USAGE to list the foreign keys for a given table. In MySQL 5, foreign keys are said to be indexed automatically, but can in fact be dropped. To determine whether a foreign key column's index has been dropped you can execute SHOW INDEX for a particular table and compare the output with that of INFORMATION_SCHEMA.KEY_ COLUMN_USAGE.COLUMN_NAME for the same table. If the COLUMN_NAME is listed in KEY_COLUMN_USAGE but is not returned by SHOW INDEX, you know that column is not indexed.

SQL Server

Query SYS.TABLES, SYS.FOREIGN_KEYS, SYS.COLUMNS, SYS.INDEXES, and SYS.INDEX_COLUMNS:

```
1   select fkeys.table_name,
2          fkeys.constraint_name,
3          fkeys.column_name,
4          ind_cols.index_name
5    from (
6   select a.object_id,
7          d.column_id,
8          a.name table_name,
9          b.name constraint_name,
10         d.name column_name
11   from sys.tables a
12        join
13        sys.foreign_keys b
14     on (    a.name      = 'EMP'
15         and a.object_id = b.parent_object_id
16        )
17        join
18        sys.foreign_key_columns c
19     on ( b.object_id = c.constraint_object_id )
20        join
21        sys.columns d
22     on (    c.constraint_column_id = d.column_id
23         and a.object_id           = d.object_id
24        )
25        ) fkeys
26        left join
27        (
28   select a.name index_name,
29          b.object_id,
30          b.column_id
31    from sys.indexes a,
32         sys.index_columns b
33   where a.index_id = b.index_id
34        ) ind_cols
35     on (    fkeys.object_id = ind_cols.object_id
36         and fkeys.column_id = ind_cols.column_id )
37   where ind_cols.index_name is null
```

Discussion

Each vendor uses its own locking mechanism when modifying rows. In cases where there is a parent-child relationship enforced via foreign key, having indexes on the child column(s) can reducing locking (see your specific RDBMS documentation for details). In other cases, it is common that a child table is joined to a parent table on the foreign key column, so an index may help improve performance in that scenario as well.

5.6   Using SQL to Generate SQL

Problem

You want to create dynamic SQL statements, perhaps to automate maintenance tasks. You want to accomplish three tasks in particular: count the number of rows in your tables, disable foreign key constraints defined on your tables, and generate insert scripts from the data in your tables.

Solution

The concept is to use strings to build SQL statements, and the values that need to be filled in (such as the object name the command acts upon) will be supplied by data from the tables you are selecting from. Keep in mind, the queries only generate the statements; you must then run these statements via script, manually, or however you execute your SQL statements. The examples below are queries that would work on an Oracle system. For other RDBMSs the technique is exactly the same, the only difference being things like the names of the data dictionary tables and date formatting. The output shown from the queries below are a portion of the rows returned from an instance of Oracle on my laptop. Your result sets will of course vary.

```
/* generate SQL to count all the rows in all your tables */

select 'select count(*) from '||table_name||';' cnts
  from user_tables;

CNTS
-------------------------------------
select count(*) from ANT;
select count(*) from BONUS;
select count(*) from DEMO1;
select count(*) from DEMO2;
select count(*) from DEPT;
select count(*) from DUMMY;
select count(*) from EMP;
select count(*) from EMP_SALES;
select count(*) from EMP_SCORE;
select count(*) from PROFESSOR;
select count(*) from T;
select count(*) from T1;
select count(*) from T2;
select count(*) from T3;
select count(*) from TEACH;
select count(*) from TEST;
select count(*) from TRX_LOG;
select count(*) from X;


/* disable foreign keys from all tables */
```

```
select 'alter table '||table_name||
       ' disable constraint '||constraint_name||';' cons
  from user_constraints
 where constraint_type = 'R';

CONS
--------------------------------------------------------
alter table ANT disable constraint ANT_FK;
alter table BONUS disable constraint BONUS_FK;
alter table DEMO1 disable constraint DEMO1_FK;
alter table DEMO2 disable constraint DEMO2_FK;
alter table DEPT disable constraint DEPT_FK;
alter table DUMMY disable constraint DUMMY_FK;
alter table EMP disable constraint EMP_FK;
alter table EMP_SALES disable constraint EMP_SALES_FK;
alter table EMP_SCORE disable constraint EMP_SCORE_FK;
alter table PROFESSOR disable constraint PROFESSOR_FK;


/* generate an insert script from some columns in table EMP */

select 'insert into emp(empno,ename,hiredate) '||chr(10)||
       'values( '||empno||','||''''||ename
       ||''',to_date('||''''||hiredate||''') );' inserts
  from emp
 where deptno = 10;

INSERTS
--------------------------------------------------------
insert into emp(empno,ename,hiredate)
values( 7782,'CLARK',to_date('09-JUN-1981 00:00:00') );

insert into emp(empno,ename,hiredate)
values( 7839,'KING',to_date('17-NOV-1981 00:00:00') );

insert into emp(empno,ename,hiredate)
values( 7934,'MILLER',to_date('23-JAN-1982 00:00:00') );
```

Discussion

Using SQL to generate SQL is particularly useful for creating portable scripts such as you might use when testing on multiple environments. Additionally, as can be seen by the examples above, using SQL to generate SQL is useful for performing batch maintenance, and for easily finding out information about multiple objects in one go. Generating SQL with SQL is an extremely simple operation, and the more you experiment with it the easier it will become. The examples provided should give you a nice base on how to build your own "dynamic" SQL scripts because, quite frankly, there's not much to it. Work on it and you'll get it.

5.7 Describing the Data Dictionary Views in an Oracle Database

Problem

You are using Oracle. You can't remember what data dictionary views are available to you, nor can you remember their column definitions. Worse yet, you do not have convenient access to vendor documentation.

Solution

This is an Oracle-specific recipe. Oracle not only maintains a robust set of data dictionary views, but there are even data dictionary views to document the data dictionary views. It's all so wonderfully circular.

Query the view named DICTIONARY to list data dictionary views and their purposes:

```
select table_name, comments
  from dictionary
 order by table_name;
```

TABLE_NAME	COMMENTS
ALL_ALL_TABLES	Description of all object and relational tables accessible to the user
ALL_APPLY	Details about each apply process that dequeues from the queue visible to the current user
...	

Query DICT_COLUMNS to describe the columns in given a data dictionary view:

```
select column_name, comments
    from dict_columns
 where table_name = 'ALL_TAB_COLUMNS';
```

COLUMN_NAME	COMMENTS
OWNER	
TABLE_NAME	Table, view or cluster name
COLUMN_NAME	Column name
DATA_TYPE	Datatype of the column
DATA_TYPE_MOD	Datatype modifier of the column
DATA_TYPE_OWNER	Owner of the datatype of the column
DATA_LENGTH	Length of the column in bytes
DATA_PRECISION	Length: decimal digits (NUMBER) or binary digits (FLOAT)

Discussion

Back in the day when Oracle's documentation set wasn't so freely available on the Web, it was incredibly convenient that Oracle made the DICTIONARY and DICT_COLUMNS views available. Knowing just those two views, you could bootstrap to learning about all the other views, and from thence to learning about your entire database.

Even today, it's convenient to know about DICTIONARY and DICT_COLUMNS. Often, if you aren't quite certain which view describes a given object type, you can issue a wildcard query to find out. For example, to get a handle on what views might describe tables in your schema:

```
select table_name, comments
  from dictionary
 where table_name LIKE '%TABLE%'
 order by table_name;
```

This query returns all data dictionary view names that include the term "TABLE". This approach takes advantage of Oracle's fairly consistent data dictionary view naming conventions. Views describing tables are all likely to contain "TABLE" in their name. (Sometimes, as in the case of ALL_TAB_COLUMNS, TABLE is abbreviated TAB.)

CHAPTER 6

Working with Strings

This chapter focuses on string manipulation in SQL. Keep in mind that SQL is not designed to perform complex string manipulation and you can (and will) find working with strings in SQL to be very cumbersome and frustrating at times. Despite SQL's limitations, there are some very useful built-in functions provided by the different DBMSs, and I've tried to use them in creative ways. This chapter in particular is very representative of the message I tried to convey in the introduction; SQL is the good, the bad, and the ugly. I hope that you take away from this chapter a better appreciation for what can and can't be done in SQL when working with strings. In many cases you'll be surprised by how easy parsing and transforming of strings can be, while at other times you'll be aghast by the kind of SQL that is necessary to accomplish a particular task.

The first recipe in this chapter is critically important, as it is leveraged by several of the subsequent solutions. In many cases, you'd like to have the ability to traverse a string by moving through it a character at a time. Unfortunately, SQL does not make this easy. Because there is no loop functionality in SQL (Oracle's MODEL clause excluded), you need to mimic a loop to traverse a string. I call this operation "walking a string" or "walking through a string" and the very first recipe explains the technique. This is a fundamental operation in string parsing when using SQL, and is referenced and used by almost all recipes in this chapter. I strongly suggest becoming comfortable with how the technique works.

6.1 Walking a String

Problem

You want to traverse a string to return each character as a row, but SQL lacks a loop operation. For example, you want to display the ENAME "KING" from table EMP as four rows, where each row contains just characters from "KING".

Solution

Use a Cartesian product to generate the number of rows needed to return each character of a string on its own line. Then use your DBMS's built-in string parsing function to extract the characters you are interested in (SQL Server users will use SUBSTRING instead of SUBSTR, and DATALENGTH instead of LENGTH):

```
1 select substr(e.ename,iter.pos,1) as C
2   from (select ename from emp where ename = 'KING') e,
3        (select id as pos from t10) iter
4  where iter.pos <= length(e.ename)


C
-
K
I
N
G
```

Discussion

The key to iterating through a string's characters is to join against a table that has enough rows to produce the required number of iterations. This example uses table T10, which contains 10 rows (it has one column, ID, holding the values 1 through 10). The maximum number of rows that can be returned from this query is 10.

The following example shows the Cartesian product between E and ITER (i.e., between the specific name and the 10 rows from T10) without parsing ENAME:

```
select ename, iter.pos
  from (select ename from emp where ename = 'KING') e,
       (select id as pos from t10) iter
```

```
ENAME          POS
---------- ----------
KING            1
KING            2
KING            3
KING            4
KING            5
KING            6
KING            7
KING            8
KING            9
KING           10
```

The cardinality of inline view E is 1, and the cardinality of inline view ITER is 10. The Cartesian product is then 10 rows. Generating such a product is the first step in mimicking a loop in SQL.

It is common practice to refer to table T10 as a "pivot" table.

The solution uses a WHERE clause to break out of the loop after four rows have been returned. To restrict the result set to the same number of rows as there are characters in the name, that WHERE clause specifies ITER.POS <= LENGTH(E. ENAME) as the condition:

```
select ename, iter.pos
  from (select ename from emp where ename = 'KING') e,
       (select id as pos from t10) iter
 where iter.pos <= length(e.ename)
```

```
ENAME                POS
----------  ----------
KING                  1
KING                  2
KING                  3
KING                  4
```

Now that you have one row for each character in E.ENAME, you can use ITER.POS as a parameter to SUBSTR, allowing you to navigate through the characters in the string. ITER.POS increments with each row, and thus each row can be made to return a successive character from E.ENAME. This is how the solution example works.

Depending on what you are trying to accomplish you may or may not need to generate a row for every single character in a string. The following query is an example of walking E.ENAME and exposing different portions (more than a single character) of the string:

```
select substr(e.ename,iter.pos) a,
       substr(e.ename,length(e.ename)-iter.pos+1) b
  from (select ename from emp where ename = 'KING') e,
       (select id pos from t10) iter
 where iter.pos <= length(e.ename)
```

```
A           B
----------  ------
KING        G
ING         NG
NG          ING
G           KING
```

The most common scenarios for the recipes in this chapter involve walking the whole string to generate a row for each character in the string, or walking the string such that the number of rows generated reflects the number of particular characters or delimiters that are present in the string.

6.2 Embedding Quotes Within String Literals

Problem

You want to embed quote marks within string literals. You would like to produce results such as the following with SQL:

```
QMARKS
--------------
g'day mate
beavers' teeth
'
```

Solution

The following three SELECTs highlight different ways you can create quotes: in the middle of a string and by themselves:

```
1 select 'g''day mate' qmarks from t1 union all
2 select 'beavers'' teeth'    from t1 union all
3 select ''''                 from t1
```

Discussion

When working with quotes, it's often useful to think of them like parentheses. When you have an opening parenthesis, you must always have a closing parenthesis. The same goes for quotes. Keep in mind that you should always have an even number of quotes across any given string. To embed a single quote within a string you need to use two quotes:

```
select 'apples core', 'apple''s core',
       case when '' is null then 0 else 1 end
  from t1

 'APPLESCORE  'APPLE''SCOR  CASEWHEN''ISNULLTHENOELSE1END
 -----------  -----------  ----------------------------
 apples core  apple's core                            0
```

Following is the solution stripped down to its bare elements. You have two outer quotes defining a string literal, and, within that string literal you have two quotes that together represent just one quote in the string that you actually get:

```
select '''' as quote from t1

Q
-
'
```

When working with quotes, be sure to remember that a string literal comprising two quotes alone, with no intervening characters, is NULL.

6.3 Counting the Occurrences of a Character in a String

Problem

You want to count the number of times a character or substring occurs within a given string. Consider the following string:

    10,CLARK,MANAGER

You want to determine how many commas are in the string.

Solution

Subtract the length of the string without the commas from the original length of the string to determine the number of commas in the string. Each DBMS provides functions for obtaining the length of a string and removing characters from a string. In most cases, these functions are LENGTH and REPLACE, respectively (SQL Server users will use the built-in function LEN rather than LENGTH):

```
1 select (length('10,CLARK,MANAGER')-
2          length(replace('10,CLARK,MANAGER',',','')))/length(',')
3          as cnt
4    from t1
```

Discussion

You arrive at the solution by using simple subtraction. The call to LENGTH on line 1 returns the original size of the string, and the first call to LENGTH on line 2 returns the size of the string without the commas, which are removed by REPLACE.

By subtracting the two lengths you obtain the difference in terms of characters, which is the number of commas in the string. The last operation divides the difference by the length of your search string. This division is necessary if the string you are looking for has a length greater than 1. In the following example, counting the occurrence of "LL" in the string "HELLO HELLO" without dividing will return an incorrect result:

```
select
     (length('HELLO HELLO')-
     length(replace('HELLO HELLO','LL','')))/length('LL')
     as correct_cnt,
     (length('HELLO HELLO')-
     length(replace('HELLO HELLO','LL',''))) as incorrect_cnt
  from t1

CORRECT_CNT INCORRECT_CNT
----------- -------------
          2             4
```

6.4 Removing Unwanted Characters from a String

Problem

You want to remove specific characters from your data. Consider this result set:

```
ENAME          SAL
---------- ----------
SMITH          800
ALLEN         1600
WARD          1250
JONES         2975
MARTIN        1250
BLAKE         2850
CLARK         2450
SCOTT         3000
KING          5000
TURNER        1500
ADAMS         1100
JAMES          950
FORD          3000
MILLER        1300
```

You want to remove all zeros and vowels as shown by the following values in columns STRIPPED1 and STRIPPED2:

```
ENAME      STRIPPED1     SAL STRIPPED2
---------- ---------- ---------- ---------
SMITH      SMTH         800 8
ALLEN      LLN         1600 16
WARD       WRD         1250 125
JONES      JNS         2975 2975
MARTIN     MRTN        1250 125
BLAKE      BLK         2850 285
CLARK      CLRK        2450 245
SCOTT      SCTT        3000 3
KING       KNG         5000 5
TURNER     TRNR        1500 15
ADAMS      DMS         1100 11
JAMES      JMS          950 95
FORD       FRD         3000 3
MILLER     MLLR        1300 13
```

Solution

Each DBMS provides functions for removing unwanted characters from a string. The functions REPLACE and TRANSLATE are most useful for this problem.

DB2

Use the built-in functions TRANSLATE and REPLACE to remove unwanted characters and strings:

```
1 select ename,
2        replace(translate(ename,'aaaaa','AEIOU'),'a','') stripped1,
3        sal,
4        replace(cast(sal as char(4)),'0','') stripped2
5 from emp
```

MySQL and SQL Server

MySQL and SQL Server do not offer a TRANSLATE function, so several calls to REPLACE are needed:

```
1 select ename,
2        replace(
3        replace(
4        replace(
5        replace(
6        replace(ename,'A',''),'E',''),'I',''),'O',''),'U','')
7        as stripped1,
8        sal,
9        replace(sal,0,'') stripped2
10 from emp
```

Oracle and PostgreSQL

Use the built-in functions TRANSLATE and REPLACE to remove unwanted characters and strings:

```
1 select ename,
2        replace(translate(ename,'AEIOU','aaaaa'),'a')
3        as stripped1,
4        sal,
5        replace(sal,0,'') as stripped2
6 from emp
```

Discussion

The built-in function REPLACE removes all occurrences of zeros. To remove the vowels, use TRANSLATE to convert all vowels into one specific character (I used "a"; you can use any character), then use REPLACE to remove all occurrences of that character.

6.5   Separating Numeric and Character Data

Problem

You have (unfortunately) stored numeric data along with character data together in one column. You want to separate the character data from the numeric data. Consider the following result set:

```
DATA
---------------
SMITH800
ALLEN1600
WARD1250
JONES2975
MARTIN1250
BLAKE2850
CLARK2450
SCOTT3000
KING5000
TURNER1500
ADAMS1100
JAMES950
FORD3000
MILLER1300
```

You would like the result to be:

```
ENAME          SAL
----------  ----------
SMITH            800
ALLEN           1600
WARD            1250
JONES           2975
MARTIN          1250
BLAKE           2850
CLARK           2450
SCOTT           3000
KING            5000
TURNER          1500
ADAMS           1100
JAMES            950
FORD            3000
MILLER          1300
```

Solution

Use the built-in functions TRANSLATE and REPLACE to isolate the character from the numeric data. Like other recipes in this chapter, the trick is to use TRANSLATE to transform multiple characters into a single character you can reference. This way you are no longer searching for multiple numbers or characters, rather one character to represent all numbers or one character to represent all characters.

DB2

Use the functions TRANSLATE and REPLACE to isolate and separate the numeric from the character data:

```
1 select replace(
2      translate(data,'0000000000','0123456789'),'0','') ename,
3         cast(
4         replace(
5      translate(lower(data),repeat('z',26),
```

```
6                 'abcdefghijklmnopqrstuvwxyz'),'z','') as integer) sal
7     from (
8   select ename||cast(sal as char(4)) data
9     from emp
10         ) x
```

Oracle

Use the functions TRANSLATE and REPLACE to isolate and separate the numeric from the character data:

```
1  select replace(
2         translate(data,'0123456789','0000000000'),'0') ename,
3         to_number(
4           replace(
5           translate(lower(data),
6                     'abcdefghijklmnopqrstuvwxyz',
7                     rpad('z',26,'z')),'z')) sal
8     from (
9   select ename||sal data
10     from emp
11         )
```

PostgreSQL

Use the functions TRANSLATE and REPLACE to isolate and separate the numeric from the character data:

```
1 select replace(
2        translate(data,'0123456789','0000000000'),'0','') as ename,
3            cast(
4          replace(
5          translate(lower(data),
6                    'abcdefghijklmnopqrstuvwxyz',
7                    rpad('z',26,'z')),'z','') as integer) as sal
8    from (
9 select ename||sal as data
10    from emp
11        ) x
```

Discussion

The syntax is a bit different for each DBMS, but the technique is the same. I will use the solution for Oracle in the discussion section. The key to solving this problem is to isolate the numeric and character data. You can use TRANSLATE and REPLACE to do this. To extract the numeric data, first isolate all character data using TRANS-LATE:

```
select data,
       translate(lower(data),
                 'abcdefghijklmnopqrstuvwxyz',
                 rpad('z',26,'z')) sal
  from (select ename||sal data from emp)
```

```
DATA                   SAL
-------------------    --------------------
SMITH800               zzzzz800
ALLEN1600              zzzzz1600
WARD1250               zzzz1250
JONES2975              zzzzz2975
MARTIN1250             zzzzzz1250
BLAKE2850              zzzzz2850
CLARK2450              zzzzz2450
SCOTT3000              zzzzz3000
KING5000               zzzz5000
TURNER1500             zzzzzz1500
ADAMS1100              zzzzz1100
JAMES950               zzzzz950
FORD3000               zzzz3000
MILLER1300             zzzzzz1300
```

By using TRANSLATE you convert every non-numeric character into a lowercase Z. The next step is to remove all instances of lowercase Z from each record using REPLACE, leaving only numerical characters that can then be cast to a number:

```
select data,
       to_number(
         replace(
       translate(lower(data),
               'abcdefghijklmnopqrstuvwxyz',
               rpad('z',26,'z')),'z')) sal
  from (select ename||sal data from emp)
```

```
DATA                   SAL
-------------------    ----------
SMITH800                      800
ALLEN1600                    1600
WARD1250                     1250
JONES2975                    2975
MARTIN1250                   1250
BLAKE2850                    2850
CLARK2450                    2450
SCOTT3000                    3000
KING5000                     5000
TURNER1500                   1500
ADAMS1100                    1100
JAMES950                      950
FORD3000                     3000
MILLER1300                   1300
```

To extract the non-numeric characters, isolate the numeric characters using TRANSLATE:

```
select data,
       translate(data,'0123456789','0000000000') ename
  from (select ename||sal data from emp)
```

```
DATA                    ENAME
--------------------    ----------
SMITH800                SMITH000
ALLEN1600               ALLEN0000
WARD1250                WARD0000
JONES2975               JONES0000
MARTIN1250              MARTIN0000
BLAKE2850               BLAKE0000
CLARK2450               CLARK0000
SCOTT3000               SCOTT0000
KING5000                KING0000
TURNER1500              TURNER0000
ADAMS1100               ADAMS0000
JAMES950                JAMES000
FORD3000                FORD0000
MILLER1300              MILLER0000
```

By using TRANSLATE you convert every numeric character into a zero. The next step is to remove all instances of zero from each record using REPLACE, leaving only non-numeric characters:

```
select data,
       replace(translate(data,'0123456789','0000000000'),'0') ename
  from (select ename||sal data from emp)
```

```
DATA                    ENAME
--------------------    --------
SMITH800                SMITH
ALLEN1600               ALLEN
WARD1250                WARD
JONES2975               JONES
MARTIN1250              MARTIN
BLAKE2850               BLAKE
CLARK2450               CLARK
SCOTT3000               SCOTT
KING5000                KING
TURNER1500              TURNER
ADAMS1100               ADAMS
JAMES950                JAMES
FORD3000                FORD
MILLER1300              MILLER
```

Put the two techniques together and you have your solution.

6.6 Determining Whether a String Is Alphanumeric

Problem

You want to return rows from a table only when a column of interest contains no characters other than numbers and letters. Consider the following view V (SQL Server users will use the operator "+" for concatenation instead of "||"):

```
create view V as
select ename as data
  from emp
 where deptno=10
 union all
select ename||', $'|| cast(sal as char(4)) ||'.00' as data
  from emp
 where deptno=20
 union all
select ename|| cast(deptno as char(4)) as data
  from emp
 where deptno=30
```

The view V represents your table, and it returns the following:

```
DATA
--------------------
CLARK
KING
MILLER
SMITH, $800.00
JONES, $2975.00
SCOTT, $3000.00
ADAMS, $1100.00
FORD, $3000.00
ALLEN30
WARD30
MARTIN30
BLAKE30
TURNER30
JAMES30
```

However, from the view's data you want to return only the following records:

```
DATA
-------------
CLARK
KING
MILLER
ALLEN30
WARD30
MARTIN30
BLAKE30
TURNER30
JAMES30
```

In short, you wish to omit those rows containing data other than letters and digits.

Solution

It may seem intuitive at first to solve the problem by searching for all the possible non-alphanumeric characters that can be found in a string, but, on the contrary, you will find it easier to do the exact opposite: find all the alphanumeric characters. By doing so, you can treat all the alphanumeric characters as one by converting them to one single character. The reason you want to do this is so the alphanumeric characters can be manipulated together, as a whole. Once you've generated a copy of the string in which all alphanumeric characters are represented by a single character of your choosing, it is easy to isolate the alphanumeric characters from any other characters.

DB2

Use the function TRANSLATE to convert all alphanumeric characters to a single character, then identify any rows that have characters other than the converted alphanumeric character. For DB2 users, the CAST function calls in view V are necessary; otherwise, the view cannot be created due to type conversion errors. Take extra care when working with casts to CHAR as they are fixed length (padded):

```
1   select data
2     from V
3    where translate(lower(data),
4                     repeat('a',36),
5                     '0123456789abcdefghijklmnopqrstuvwxyz') =
6                     repeat('a',length(data))
```

MySQL

The syntax for view V is slightly different in MySQL:

```
create view V as
select ename as data
  from emp
 where deptno=10
 union all
select concat(ename,', $',sal,'.00') as data
  from emp
 where deptno=20
 union all
select concat(ename,deptno) as data
  from emp
 where deptno=30
```

Use a regular expression to easily find rows that contain non-alphanumeric data:

```
1 select data
2   from V
3  where data regexp '[^0-9a-zA-Z]' = 0
```

Oracle and PostgreSQL

Use the function TRANSLATE to convert all alphanumeric characters to a single character, then identify any rows that have characters other than the converted alphanumeric character. The CAST function calls in view V are not needed for Oracle and PostgreSQL. Take extra care when working with casts to CHAR as they are fixed length (padded). If you decide to cast, cast to VARCHAR or VARCHAR2:

```
1  select data
2    from V
3   where translate(lower(data),
4                 '0123456789abcdefghijklmnopqrstuvwxyz',
5                 rpad('a',36,'a')) = rpad('a',length(data),'a')
```

SQL Server

Because SQL Server does not support a TRANSLATE function, you must walk each row and find any that contains a character that contains a non-alphanumeric value. That can be done many ways, but the following solution uses an ASCII-value evaluation:

```
1  select data
2    from (
3  select v.data, iter.pos,
4         substring(v.data,iter.pos,1) c,
5         ascii(substring(v.data,iter.pos,1)) val
6    from v,
7         ( select id as pos from t100 ) iter
8   where iter.pos <= len(v.data)
9         ) x
10  group by data
11  having min(val) between 48 and 122
```

Discussion

The key to these solutions is being able to reference multiple characters concurrently. By using the function TRANSLATE you can easily manipulate all numbers or all characters without having to "iterate" and inspect each character one by one.

DB2, Oracle, and PostgreSQL

Only 9 of the 14 rows from view V are alphanumeric. To find the rows that are alphanumeric only, simply use the function TRANSLATE. In this example, TRANSLATE converts characters 0–9 and a–z to "a". Once the conversion is done, the converted row is then compared with a string of all "a" with the same length (as the row). If the length is the same, then you know all the characters are alphanumeric and nothing else.

By using the TRANSLATE function (using the Oracle syntax):

```
where translate(lower(data),
             '0123456789abcdefghijklmnopqrstuvwxyz',
             rpad('a',36,'a'))
```

you convert all numbers and letters into a distinct character (I chose "a"). Once the data is converted, all strings that are indeed alphanumeric can be identified as a string comprising only a single character (in this case, "a"). This can be seen by running TRANSLATE by itself:

```
select data, translate(lower(data),
                '0123456789abcdefghijklmnopqrstuvwxyz',
                rpad('a',36,'a'))
  from V

DATA                   TRANSLATE(LOWER(DATA)
-------------------    ---------------------
CLARK                  aaaaa
...
SMITH, $800.00         aaaaa, $aaa.aa
...
ALLEN30                aaaaaaa
...
```

The alphanumeric values are converted, but the string lengths have not been modified. Because the lengths are the same, the rows to keep are the ones for which the call to TRANSLATE returns all a's. You keep those rows, rejecting the others, by comparing each original string's length with the length of its corresponding string of a's:

```
select data, translate(lower(data),
                '0123456789abcdefghijklmnopqrstuvwxyz',
                rpad('a',36,'a')) translated,
        rpad('a',length(data),'a') fixed
  from V

DATA                   TRANSLATED              FIXED
-------------------    --------------------    ----------------
CLARK                  aaaaa                   aaaaa
...
SMITH, $800.00         aaaaa, $aaa.aa          aaaaaaaaaaaaaa
...
ALLEN30                aaaaaaa                 aaaaaaa
...
```

The last step is to keep only the strings where TRANSLATED equals FIXED.

MySQL

The expression in the WHERE clause:

```
where data regexp '[^0-9a-zA-Z]' = 0
```

causes rows that have only numbers or characters to be returned. The value ranges in the brackets, "0-9a-zA-Z", represent all possible numbers and letters. The character "^" is for negation, so the expression can be stated as "not numbers or letters." A return value of 1 is true and 0 is false, so the whole expression can be stated as "return rows where anything other than numbers and letters is false."

SQL Server

The first step is to walk each row returned by view V. Each character in the value returned for DATA will itself be returned as a row. The values returned by C represent each individual character for the values returned by DATA:

```
+------------------+------+------+------+
| data             | pos  | c    | val  |
+------------------+------+------+------+
| ADAMS, $1100.00  |    1 | A    |   65 |
| ADAMS, $1100.00  |    2 | D    |   68 |
| ADAMS, $1100.00  |    3 | A    |   65 |
| ADAMS, $1100.00  |    4 | M    |   77 |
| ADAMS, $1100.00  |    5 | S    |   83 |
| ADAMS, $1100.00  |    6 | ,    |   44 |
| ADAMS, $1100.00  |    7 |      |   32 |
| ADAMS, $1100.00  |    8 | $    |   36 |
| ADAMS, $1100.00  |    9 | 1    |   49 |
| ADAMS, $1100.00  |   10 | 1    |   49 |
| ADAMS, $1100.00  |   11 | 0    |   48 |
| ADAMS, $1100.00  |   12 | 0    |   48 |
| ADAMS, $1100.00  |   13 | .    |   46 |
| ADAMS, $1100.00  |   14 | 0    |   48 |
| ADAMS, $1100.00  |   15 | 0    |   48 |
```

Inline view Z not only returns each character in the column DATA row by row, it also provides the ASCII value for each character. For this particular implementation of SQL Server, the range 48–122 represents alphanumeric characters. With that knowledge, you can group each row in DATA and filter out any such that the minimum ASCII value is not in the 48–122 range.

6.7   Extracting Initials from a Name

Problem

You want convert a full name into initials. Consider the following name:

    Stewie Griffin

You would like to return:

    S.G.

Solution

It's important to keep in mind that SQL does not provide the flexibility of languages such as C or Python; therefore, creating a generic solution to deal with any name format is not something particularly easy to do in SQL. The solutions presented here expect the names to be either first and last name, or first, middle name/middle initial, and last name.

DB2

Use the built-in functions REPLACE, TRANSLATE, and REPEAT to extract the initials:

```
1 select replace(
2       replace(
3       translate(replace('Stewie Griffin', '.', ''),
4               repeat('#',26),
5               'abcdefghijklmnopqrstuvwxyz'),
6               '#','' ), ' ','.' )
7               ||'.'
8   from t1
```

MySQL

Use the built-in functions CONCAT, CONCAT_WS, SUBSTRING, and SUBSTRING_INDEX to extract the initials:

```
1   select case
2           when cnt = 2 then
3               trim(trailing '.' from
4                   concat_ws('.',
5                   substr(substring_index(name,' ',1),1,1),
6                   substr(name,
7                           length(substring_index(name,' ',1))+2,1),
8                   substr(substring_index(name,' ',-1),1,1),
9                   '.'))
10          else
11              trim(trailing '.' from
12                  concat_ws('.',
13                  substr(substring_index(name,' ',1),1,1),
14                  substr(substring_index(name,' ',-1),1,1)
15                  ))
16          end as initials
17      from (
18  select name,length(name)-length(replace(name,' ','')) as cnt
19      from (
20  select replace('Stewie Griffin','.','') as name from t1
21          )y
22          )x
```

Oracle and PostgreSQL

Use the built-in functions REPLACE, TRANSLATE, and RPAD to extract the initials:

```
1 select replace(
2       replace(
3       translate(replace('Stewie Griffin', '.', ''),
4               'abcdefghijklmnopqrstuvwxyz',
5               rpad('#',26,'#') ), '#','' ),' ','.' ) ||'.'
6   from t1
```

SQL Server

As of the time of this writing, neither TRANSLATE nor CONCAT_WS is supported in SQL Server.

Discussion

By isolating the capital letters you can extract the initials from a name. The following sections describe each vendor-specific solution in detail.

DB2

The REPLACE function will remove any periods in the name (to handle middle initials), and the TRANSLATE function will convert all non-uppercase letters to #.

```
select translate(replace('Stewie Griffin', '.', ''),
                 repeat('#',26),
                 'abcdefghijklmnopqrstuvwxyz')
  from t1

TRANSLATE('STE
--------------
S##### G######
```

At this point, the initials are the characters that are not #. The function REPLACE is then used to remove all the # characters:

```
select replace(
       translate(replace('Stewie Griffin', '.', ''),
                 repeat('#',26),
                 'abcdefghijklmnopqrstuvwxyz'),'#','')
  from t1

REP
---
S G
```

The next step is to replace the white space with a period by using REPLACE again:

```
select replace(
       replace(
       translate(replace('Stewie Griffin', '.', ''),
                 repeat('#',26),
                 'abcdefghijklmnopqrstuvwxyz'),'#',''),' ','.') || '.'
  from t1

REPLA
-----
S.G
```

The final step is to append a decimal to the end of the initials.

Oracle and PostgreSQL

The REPLACE function will remove any periods in the name (to handle middle initials), and the TRANSLATE function will convert all non-uppercase letters to '#'.

```
select translate(replace('Stewie Griffin','.',''),
                 'abcdefghijklmnopqrstuvwxyz',
                 rpad('#',26,'#'))
  from t1
```

```
TRANSLATE('STE
--------------
S##### G######
```

At this point, the initials are the characters that are not "#". The function REPLACE is then used to remove all the # characters:

```
select replace(
       translate(replace('Stewie Griffin','.',''),
                 'abcdefghijklmnopqrstuvwxyz',
                 rpad('#',26,'#')),'#','')
  from t1

REP
---
S G
```

The next step is to replace the white space with a period by using REPLACE again:

```
select replace(
       replace(
       translate(replace('Stewie Griffin','.',''),
                 'abcdefghijklmnopqrstuvwxyz',
                 rpad('#',26,'#') )),'#',''),' ','.') || '.'
  from t1

REPLA
-----
S.G
```

The final step is to append a decimal to the end of the initials.

MySQL

The inline view Y is used to remove any period from the name. The inline view X finds the number of white spaces in the name so the SUBSTR function can be called the correct number of times to extract the initials. The three calls to SUBSTRING_INDEX parse the string into individual names based on the location of the white space. Because there is only a first and last name, the code in the ELSE portion of the case statement is executed:

```
select substr(substring_index(name, ' ',1),1,1) as a,
       substr(substring_index(name,' ',-1),1,1) as b
  from (select 'Stewie Griffin' as name from t1) x

A B
- -
S G
```

If the name in question has a middle name or initial, the initial would be returned by executing:

```
substr(name,length(substring_index(name, ' ',1))+2,1)
```

which finds the end of the first name then moves two spaces to the beginning of the middle name or initial; that is, the start position for SUBSTR. Because only one character is kept, the middle name or initial is successfully returned. The initials are then passed to CONCAT_WS, which separates the initials by a period:

```
select concat_ws('.',
                  substr(substring_index(name, ' ',1),1,1),
                  substr(substring_index(name,' ',-1),1,1),
                  '.' ) a
  from (select 'Stewie Griffin' as name from t1) x


A
-----
S.G..
```

The last step is to trim the extraneous period from the initials.

6.8   Ordering by Parts of a String

Problem

You want to order your result set based on a substring. Consider the following records:

```
ENAME
----------
SMITH
ALLEN
WARD
JONES
MARTIN
BLAKE
CLARK
SCOTT
KING
TURNER
ADAMS
JAMES
FORD
MILLER
```

You want the records to be ordered based on the *last* two characters of each name:

```
ENAME
---------
ALLEN
TURNER
MILLER
JONES
JAMES
MARTIN
BLAKE
ADAMS
```

```
KING
WARD
FORD
CLARK
SMITH
SCOTT
```

Solution

The key to this solution is to find and use your DBMS's built-in function to extract the substring on which you wish to sort. This is typically done with the SUBSTR function.

DB2, Oracle, MySQL, and PostgreSQL

Use a combination of the built-in functions LENGTH and SUBSTR to order by a specific part of a string:

```
1 select ename
2   from emp
3 order by substr(ename,length(ename)-1,2)
```

SQL Server

Use functions SUBSTRING and LEN to order by a specific part of a string:

```
1 select ename
2   from emp
3 order by substring(ename,len(ename)-1,2)
```

Discussion

By using a SUBSTR expression in your ORDER BY clause, you can pick any part of a string to use in ordering a result set. You're not limited to SUBSTR either. You can order rows by the result of almost any expression.

6.9   Ordering by a Number in a String

Problem

You want order your result set based on a number within a string. Consider the following view:

```
create view V as
select e.ename ||' '||
       cast(e.empno as char(4))||' '||
       d.dname as data
  from emp e, dept d
 where e.deptno=d.deptno
```

This view returns the following data:

```
DATA
---------------------------
CLARK    7782 ACCOUNTING
KING     7839 ACCOUNTING
MILLER   7934 ACCOUNTING
SMITH    7369 RESEARCH
JONES    7566 RESEARCH
SCOTT    7788 RESEARCH
ADAMS    7876 RESEARCH
FORD     7902 RESEARCH
ALLEN    7499 SALES
WARD     7521 SALES
MARTIN   7654 SALES
BLAKE    7698 SALES
TURNER   7844 SALES
JAMES    7900 SALES
```

You want to order the results based on the employee number, which falls between the employee name and respective department:

```
DATA
---------------------------
SMITH    7369 RESEARCH
ALLEN    7499 SALES
WARD     7521 SALES
JONES    7566 RESEARCH
MARTIN   7654 SALES
BLAKE    7698 SALES
CLARK    7782 ACCOUNTING
SCOTT    7788 RESEARCH
KING     7839 ACCOUNTING
TURNER   7844 SALES
ADAMS    7876 RESEARCH
JAMES    7900 SALES
FORD     7902 RESEARCH
MILLER   7934 ACCOUNTING
```

Solution

Each solution uses functions and syntax specific to its DBMS, but the method (making use of the built-in functions REPLACE and TRANSLATE) is the same for each. The idea is to use REPLACE and TRANSLATE to remove non-digits from the strings, leaving only the numeric values upon which to sort.

DB2

Use the built-in functions REPLACE and TRANSLATE to order by numeric characters in a string:

```
1  select data
2    from V
3  order by
4        cast(
5       replace(
```

```
6      translate(data,repeat('#',length(data)),
7        replace(
8      translate(data,'##########','0123456789'),
9             '#','')),'#','') as integer)
```

Oracle

Use the built-in functions REPLACE and TRANSLATE to order by numeric characters in a string:

```
1  select data
2    from V
3   order by
4          to_number(
5            replace(
6          translate(data,
7            replace(
8          translate(data,'0123456789','##########'),
9               '#'),rpad('#',20,'#')),'#'))
```

PostgreSQL

Use the built-in functions REPLACE and TRANSLATE to order by numeric characters in a string:

```
1 select data
2   from V
3  order by
4          cast(
5        replace(
6      translate(data,
7        replace(
8      translate(data,'0123456789','##########'),
9             '#',''),rpad('#',20,'#')),'#','') as integer)
```

MySQL and SQL Server

As of the time of this writing, neither vendor supplies the TRANSLATE function.

Discussion

The purpose of view V is only to supply rows on which to demonstrate this recipe's
solution. The view simply concatenates several columns from the EMP table. The
solution shows how to take such concatenated text as input and sort it by the
employee number embedded within.

The ORDER BY clause in each solution may look a bit intimidating but performs quite
well and is pretty straightforward once you examine it piece by piece. To order by the
numbers in the string, it's easiest to remove any characters that are not numbers. Once
the non-numeric characters are removed all that is left to do is cast the string of
numerals into a number, then sort as you see fit. Before examining each function call it
is important to understand the order in which each function is called. Starting with the
innermost call, TRANSLATE (line 8 from each of the original solutions), you see that:

1. TRANSLATE (line 8) is called and the results are returned to

2. REPLACE (line 7) and those results are returned to

3. TRANSLATE (line 6) and those results are returned to

4. REPLACE (line 5) and those results are returned and finally

5. cast into a number

The first step is to convert the numbers into characters that do not exist in the rest of the string. For this example, I chose "#" and used TRANSLATE to convert all non-numeric characters into occurrences of "#". For example, the following query shows the original data on the left and the results from the first translation:

```
select data,
       translate(data,'0123456789','##########') as tmp
  from V
```

```
DATA                              TMP
--------------------------------  ----------------------
CLARK    7782 ACCOUNTING          CLARK    #### ACCOUNTING
KING     7839 ACCOUNTING          KING     #### ACCOUNTING
MILLER   7934 ACCOUNTING          MILLER   #### ACCOUNTING
SMITH    7369 RESEARCH            SMITH    #### RESEARCH
JONES    7566 RESEARCH            JONES    #### RESEARCH
SCOTT    7788 RESEARCH            SCOTT    #### RESEARCH
ADAMS    7876 RESEARCH            ADAMS    #### RESEARCH
FORD     7902 RESEARCH            FORD     #### RESEARCH
ALLEN    7499 SALES               ALLEN    #### SALES
WARD     7521 SALES               WARD     #### SALES
MARTIN   7654 SALES               MARTIN   #### SALES
BLAKE    7698 SALES               BLAKE    #### SALES
TURNER  7844 SALES                TURNER  #### SALES
JAMES   7900 SALES                JAMES   #### SALES
```

TRANSLATE finds the numerals in each string and converts each one to to the "#" character. The modified strings are then returned to REPLACE (line 11), which removes all occurrences of "#":

```
select data,
replace(
translate(data,'0123456789','##########'),'#') as tmp
  from V
```

```
DATA                              TMP
--------------------------------  --------------------
CLARK    7782 ACCOUNTING          CLARK    ACCOUNTING
KING     7839 ACCOUNTING          KING     ACCOUNTING
MILLER   7934 ACCOUNTING          MILLER   ACCOUNTING
SMITH    7369 RESEARCH            SMITH    RESEARCH
JONES    7566 RESEARCH            JONES    RESEARCH
SCOTT    7788 RESEARCH            SCOTT    RESEARCH
ADAMS    7876 RESEARCH            ADAMS    RESEARCH
FORD     7902 RESEARCH            FORD     RESEARCH
ALLEN    7499 SALES               ALLEN    SALES
```

```
WARD    7521 SALES          WARD     SALES
MARTIN  7654 SALES          MARTIN   SALES
BLAKE   7698 SALES          BLAKE    SALES
TURNER  7844 SALES          TURNER   SALES
JAMES   7900 SALES          JAMES    SALES
```

The strings are then returned to TRANSLATE once again, but this time it's the second (outermost) TRANSLATE in the solution. TRANSLATE searches the original string for any characters that match the characters in TMP. If any are found, they too are converted to "#"s. This conversion allows all non-numeric characters to be treated as a single character (because they are all transformed to the same character):

```
select data, translate(data,
             replace(
             translate(data,'0123456789','##########'),
                  '#'),
                  rpad('#',length(data),'#')) as tmp
   from V
```

```
DATA                        TMP
--------------------------- ---------------------------
CLARK   7782 ACCOUNTING     ########7782###########
KING    7839 ACCOUNTING     ########7839###########
MILLER  7934 ACCOUNTING     ########7934###########
SMITH   7369 RESEARCH       ########7369#########
JONES   7566 RESEARCH       ########7566#########
SCOTT   7788 RESEARCH       ########7788#########
ADAMS   7876 RESEARCH       ########7876#########
FORD    7902 RESEARCH       ########7902#########
ALLEN   7499 SALES          ########7499######
WARD    7521 SALES          ########7521######
MARTIN  7654 SALES          ########7654######
BLAKE   7698 SALES          ########7698######
TURNER  7844 SALES          ########7844######
JAMES   7900 SALES          ########7900#####
```

The next step is to remove all "#" characters through a call to REPLACE (line 8), leaving you with only numbers:

```
select data, replace(
             translate(data,
             replace(
             translate(data,'0123456789','##########'),
                  '#'),
                  rpad('#',length(data),'#')),'#') as tmp
   from V
```

```
DATA                        TMP
--------------------------- -----------
CLARK   7782 ACCOUNTING     7782
KING    7839 ACCOUNTING     7839
MILLER  7934 ACCOUNTING     7934
SMITH   7369 RESEARCH       7369
JONES   7566 RESEARCH       7566
```

```
SCOTT    7788 RESEARCH        7788
ADAMS    7876 RESEARCH        7876
FORD     7902 RESEARCH        7902
ALLEN    7499 SALES           7499
WARD     7521 SALES           7521
MARTIN   7654 SALES           7654
BLAKE    7698 SALES           7698
TURNER   7844 SALES           7844
JAMES    7900 SALES           7900
```

Finally, cast TMP to a number (line 4) using the appropriate DBMS function (often CAST) to accomplish this:

```
select data, to_number(
          replace(
          translate(data,
          replace(
    translate(data,'0123456789','##########'),
            '#'),
            rpad('#',length(data),'#')),'#')) as tmp
    from V
```

```
DATA                             TMP
------------------------------   ----------
CLARK    7782 ACCOUNTING         7782
KING     7839 ACCOUNTING         7839
MILLER   7934 ACCOUNTING         7934
SMITH    7369 RESEARCH           7369
JONES    7566 RESEARCH           7566
SCOTT    7788 RESEARCH           7788
ADAMS    7876 RESEARCH           7876
FORD     7902 RESEARCH           7902
ALLEN    7499 SALES              7499
WARD     7521 SALES              7521
MARTIN   7654 SALES              7654
BLAKE    7698 SALES              7698
TURNER   7844 SALES              7844
JAMES    7900 SALES              7900
```

When developing queries like this, it's helpful to work with your expressions in the SELECT list. That way, you can easily view the intermediate results as you work toward a final solution. However, because the point of this recipe is to order the results, ultimately you should place all the function calls into the ORDER BY clause:

```
select data
  from V
  order by
        to_number(
          replace(
        translate( data,
          replace(
        translate( data,'0123456789','##########'),
              '#'),rpad('#',length(data),'#')),'#'))
```

```
DATA
-------------------------
SMITH   7369  RESEARCH
ALLEN   7499  SALES
WARD    7521  SALES
JONES   7566  RESEARCH
MARTIN  7654  SALES
BLAKE   7698  SALES
CLARK   7782  ACCOUNTING
SCOTT   7788  RESEARCH
KING    7839  ACCOUNTING
TURNER  7844  SALES
ADAMS   7876  RESEARCH
JAMES   7900  SALES
FORD    7902  RESEARCH
MILLER  7934  ACCOUNTING
```

As a final note, the data in the view is comprised of three fields, only one being numeric. Keep in mind that if there had been multiple numeric fields, they would have all been concatenated into one number before the rows were sorted.

6.10   Creating a Delimited List from Table Rows

Problem

You want to return table rows as values in a delimited list, perhaps delimited by commas, rather than in vertical columns as they normally appear. You want to convert a result set from this:

```
DEPTNO EMPS
------ ----------
    10 CLARK
    10 KING
    10 MILLER
    20 SMITH
    20 ADAMS
    20 FORD
    20 SCOTT
    20 JONES
    30 ALLEN
    30 BLAKE
    30 MARTIN
    30 JAMES
    30 TURNER
    30 WARD
```

to this:

```
DEPTNO EMPS
------- ----------------------------------------
     10 CLARK,KING,MILLER
     20 SMITH,JONES,SCOTT,ADAMS,FORD
     30 ALLEN,WARD,MARTIN,BLAKE,TURNER,JAMES
```

Solution

Each DBMS requires a different approach to this problem. The key is to take advantage of the built-in functions provided by your DBMS. Understanding what is available to you will allow you to exploit your DBMS's functionality and come up with creative solutions for a problem that is typically not solved in SQL.

DB2

Use recursive WITH to build the delimited list:

```
1   with x (deptno, cnt, list, empno, len)
2      as (
3  select deptno, count(*) over (partition by deptno),
4          cast(ename as varchar(100)), empno, 1
5    from emp
6  union all
7   select x.deptno, x.cnt, x.list ||','|| e.ename, e.empno, x.len+1
8     from emp e, x
9    where e.deptno = x.deptno
10      and e.empno > x. empno
11         )
12   select deptno,list
13     from x
14    where len = cnt
```

MySQL

Use the built-in function GROUP_CONCAT to build the delimited list:

```
1 select deptno,
2          group_concat(ename order by empno separator ',') as emps
3    from emp
4   group by deptno
```

Oracle

Use the built-in function SYS_CONNECT_BY_PATH to build the delimited list:

```
1   select deptno,
2          ltrim(sys_connect_by_path(ename,','),',') emps
3     from (
4   select deptno,
5          ename,
6          row_number() over
7                 (partition by deptno order by empno) rn,
8          count(*) over
9                 (partition by deptno) cnt
10     from emp
11         )
12    where level   = cnt
13    start with rn = 1
14   connect by prior deptno = deptno and prior rn = rn-1
```

PostgreSQL

PostgreSQL does not offer a standard built-in function for creating a delimited list, so it is necessary to know how many values will be in the list in advance. Once you know the size of the largest list, you can determine the number of values to append to create your list by using standard transposition and concatenation:

```
 1 select deptno,
 2        rtrim(
 3             max(case when pos=1 then emps else '' end)||
 4             max(case when pos=2 then emps else '' end)||
 5             max(case when pos=3 then emps else '' end)||
 6             max(case when pos=4 then emps else '' end)||
 7             max(case when pos=5 then emps else '' end)||
 8             max(case when pos=6 then emps else '' end),','
 9          ) as emps
10    from (
11 select a.deptno,
12        a.ename||',' as emps,
13        d.cnt,
14        (select count(*) from emp b
15          where a.deptno=b.deptno and b.empno <= a.empno) as pos
16   from emp a,
17        (select deptno, count(ename) as cnt
18          from emp
19         group by deptno) d
20  where d.deptno=a.deptno
21        ) x
22  group by deptno
23  order by 1
```

SQL Server

Use recursive WITH to build the delimited list:

```
 1 with x (deptno, cnt, list, empno, len)
 2     as (
 3 select deptno, count(*) over (partition by deptno),
 4        cast(ename as varchar(100)),
 5        empno,
 6        1
 7   from emp
 8  union all
 9 select x.deptno, x.cnt,
10        cast(x.list + ',' + e.ename as varchar(100)),
11        e.empno, x.len+1
12   from emp e, x
13  where e.deptno = x.deptno
14    and e.empno > x. empno
15        )
16 select deptno,list
17   from x
18  where len = cnt
19  order by 1
```

Discussion

Being able to create delimited lists in SQL is useful because it is a common requirement. Yet each DBMS offers a unique method for building such a list in SQL. There's very little commonality between the vendor-specific solutions; the techniques vary from using recursion, to hierarchal functions, to classic transposition, to aggregation.

DB2 and SQL Server

The solution for these two databases differ slightly in syntax (the concatenation operators are "||" for DB2 and "+" for SQL Server), but the technique is the same. The first query in the WITH clause (upper portion of the UNION ALL) returns the following information about each employee: the department, the number of employees in that department, the name, the ID, and a constant 1 (which at this point doesn't do anything). Recursion takes place in the second query (lower half of the UNION ALL) to build the list. To understand how the list is built, examine the following excerpts from the Solution: first, the third SELECT-list item from the second query in the union:

```
x.list ||','|| e.ename
```

and then the WHERE clause from that same query:

```
where e.deptno = x.deptno
  and e.empno > x.empno
```

The solution works by first ensuring the employees are in the same department. Then, for every employee returned by the upper portion of the UNION ALL, append the name of the employees who have a greater EMPNO. By doing this, you ensure that no employee will have his own name appended. The expression

```
x.len+1
```

increments LEN (which starts at 1) every time an employee has been evaluated. When the incremented value equals the number of employees in the department:

```
where len = cnt
```

you know you have evaluated all the employees and have completed building the list. That is crucial to the query as it not only signals when the list is complete, but also stops the recursion from running longer than necessary.

MySQL

The function GROUP_CONCAT does all the work. It concatenates the values found in the column passed to it, in this case ENAME. It's an aggregate function, thus the need for GROUP BY in the query.

Oracle

The first step to understanding the Oracle query is to break it down. Running the inline view by itself (lines 4–10), you generate a result set that includes the following for each employee: her department, her name, a rank within her respective department that is derived by an ascending sort on EMPNO, and a count of all employees in her department. For example:

```
select deptno,
       ename,
       row_number() over
                   (partition by deptno order by empno) rn,
       count(*) over (partition by deptno) cnt
  from emp
```

```
DEPTNO ENAME       RN CNT
------ ----------  -- ---
    10 CLARK        1   3
    10 KING         2   3
    10 MILLER       3   3
    20 SMITH        1   5
    20 JONES        2   5
    20 SCOTT        3   5
    20 ADAMS        4   5
    20 FORD         5   5
    30 ALLEN        1   6
    30 WARD         2   6
    30 MARTIN       3   6
    30 BLAKE        4   6
    30 TURNER       5   6
    30 JAMES        6   6
```

The purpose of the rank (aliased RN in the query) is to allow you to walk the tree. Since the function ROW_NUMBER generates an enumeration starting from one with no duplicates or gaps, just subtract one (from the current value) to reference a prior (or parent) row. For example, the number prior to 3 is 3 minus 1, which equals 2. In this context, 2 is the parent of 3; you can observe this on line 12. Additionally, the lines

```
start with rn = 1
connect by prior deptno = deptno
```

identify the root for each DEPTNO as having RN equal to 1 and create a new list whenever a new department is encountered (whenever a new occurrence of 1 is found for RN).

At this point, it's important to stop and look at the ORDER BY portion of the ROW_NUMBER function. Keep in mind the names are ranked by EMPNO and the list will be created in that order. The number of employees per department is calculated (aliased CNT) and is used to ensure that the query returns only the list that has all the employee names for a department. This is done because SYS_CONNECT_BY_PATH builds the list iteratively, and you do not want to end up with partial lists. For hierarchical queries, the pseudocolumn LEVEL starts with 1 (for queries not using CONNECT BY, LEVEL is 0, unless you are on 10g and later when LEVEL is only available when using CONNECT BY) and increments by one after each employee in a department has been evaluated (for each level of depth in the hierarchy). Because of this, you know that once LEVEL reaches CNT, you have reached the last EMPNO and will have a complete list.

 The SYS_CONNECT_BY_PATH function prefixes the list with your chosen delimiter (in this case, a comma). You may or may not want that behavior. In this recipe's Solution, the call to the function LTRIM removes the leading comma from the list.

PostgreSQL

PostgreSQL's solution requires you to know in advance the maximum number of employees in any one department. Running the inline view by itself (lines 11–18) generates a result set that includes (for each employee) his department, his name with a comma appended, the number of employees in his department, and the number of employees who have an EMPNO that is less than his:

```
 deptno |  emps    | cnt | pos
--------+----------+-----+-----
     20 | SMITH,   |  5  |  1
     30 | ALLEN,   |  6  |  1
     30 | WARD,    |  6  |  2
     20 | JONES,   |  5  |  2
     30 | MARTIN,  |  6  |  3
     30 | BLAKE,   |  6  |  4
     10 | CLARK,   |  3  |  1
     20 | SCOTT,   |  5  |  3
     10 | KING,    |  3  |  2
     30 | TURNER,  |  6  |  5
     20 | ADAMS,   |  5  |  4
     30 | JAMES,   |  6  |  6
     20 | FORD,    |  5  |  5
     10 | MILLER,  |  3  |  3
```

The scalar subquery, POS (lines 14-15), is used to rank each employee by EMPNO. For example, the line:

```
max(case when pos = 1 then ename else '' end)||
```

evaluates whether or not POS equals 1. The CASE expression returns the employee name when POS is 1, and otherwise returns NULL.

You must query your table first to find the largest number of values that could be in any one list. Based on the EMP table, the largest number of employees in any one department is six, so the largest number of items in a list is six.

The next step is to begin creating the list. Do this by performing some conditional logic (in the form of CASE expressions) on the rows returned from the inline view. You must write as many CASE expressions as there are possible values to be concatenated together.

If POS equals one, the current name is added to the list. The second CASE expression evaluates whether or not POS equals two; if it does, then the second name is appended to the first. If there is no second name, then an additional comma is appended to the first name (this process is repeated for each distinct value of POS until the last one is reached).

The use of the MAX function is necessary because you want to build only one list per department (you can also use MIN; it makes no difference in this case, since POS returns only one value for each case evaluation). Whenever an aggregate function is used, any items in the SELECT list not acted upon by the aggregate must be specified in the GROUP BY clause. This guarantees you will have only one row per item in the SELECT list not acted upon by the aggregate function.

Notice that you also need the function RTRIM to remove trailing commas; the number of commas will always be equal to the maximum number of values that could potentially be in a list (in this case, six).

6.11 Converting Delimited Data into a Multi-Valued IN-List

Problem

You have delimited data that you want to pass to the IN-list iterator of a WHERE clause. Consider the following string:

```
7654,7698,7782,7788
```

You would like to use the string in a WHERE clause but the following SQL fails because EMPNO is a numeric column:

```
select ename,sal,deptno
  from emp
 where empno in ( '7654,7698,7782,7788' )
```

This SQL fails because, while EMPNO is a numeric column, the IN list is composed of a single string value. You want that string to be treated as a comma-delimited list of numeric values.

Solution

On the surface it may seem that SQL should do the work of treating a delimited string as a list of delimited values for you, but that is not the case. When a comma embedded within quotes is encountered, SQL can't possibly know that signals a multi-valued list. SQL must treat everything between the quotes as a single entity, as one string value. You must break the string up into individual EMPNOs. The key to this solution is to walk the string, but not into individual characters. You want to walk the string into valid EMPNO values.

DB2

By walking the string passed to the IN-list, you can easily convert it to rows. The functions ROW_NUMBER, LOCATE, and SUBSTR are particularly useful here:

```
1   select empno,ename,sal,deptno
2     from emp
3    where empno in (
4   select cast(substr(c,2,locate(',',c,2)-2) as integer) empno
5     from (
6   select substr(csv.emps,cast(iter.pos as integer)) as c
7     from (select ','||'7654,7698,7782,7788'||',' emps
8             from t1) csv,
9          (select id as pos
10             from t100 ) iter
11   where iter.pos <= length(csv.emps)
12         ) x
13   where length(c) > 1
14     and substr(c,1,1) = ','
15         )
```

MySQL

By walking the string passed to the IN-list, you can easily convert it to rows:

```
1 select empno, ename, sal, deptno
2   from emp
3  where empno in
4     (
5 select substring_index(
6        substring_index(list.vals,',',iter.pos),',',-1) empno
7   from (select id pos from t10) as iter,
8        (select '7654,7698,7782,7788' as vals
9           from t1) list
10  where iter.pos <=
11        (length(list.vals)-length(replace(list.vals,',','')))+1
12        )
```

Oracle

By walking the string passed to the IN-list, you can easily convert it to rows. The functions ROWNUM, SUBSTR, and INSTR are particularly useful here:

```
1 select empno,ename,sal,deptno
2   from emp
3  where empno in (
4         select to_number(
```

```
 5                    rtrim(
 6                      substr(emps,
 7                        instr(emps,',',1,iter.pos)+1,
 8                        instr(emps,',',1,iter.pos+1) -
 9                        instr(emps,',',1,iter.pos)),',')) emps
10              from (select ','||'7654,7698,7782,7788'||',' emps from t1) csv,
11                   (select rownum pos from emp) iter
12            where iter.pos <= ((length(csv.emps)-
13                      length(replace(csv.emps,',')))/length(','))-1
14    )
```

Postgres

By walking the string passed to the IN-list, you can easily convert it to rows. The function SPLIT_PART makes it easy to parse the string into individual numbers:

```
 1 select ename,sal,deptno
 2    from emp
 3  where empno in (
 4 select cast(empno as integer) as empno
 5    from (
 6 select split_part(list.vals,',',iter.pos) as empno
 7    from (select id as pos from t10) iter,
 8         (select ','||'7654,7698,7782,7788'||',' as vals
 9             from t1) list
10   where iter.pos <=
11         length(list.vals)-length(replace(list.vals,',',''))
12         ) z
13   where length(empno) > 0
14         )
```

SQL Server

By walking the string passed to the IN-list, you can easily convert it to rows. The functions ROW_NUMBER, CHARINDEX, and SUBSTRING are particularly useful here:

```
 1 select empno,ename,sal,deptno
 2    from emp
 3  where empno in (select substring(c,2,charindex(',',c,2)-2) as empno
 4    from (
 5 select substring(csv.emps,iter.pos,len(csv.emps)) as c
 6    from (select ','+'7654,7698,7782,7788'+',' as emps
 7             from t1) csv,
 8         (select id as pos
 9             from t100) iter
10   where iter.pos <= len(csv.emps)
11         ) x
12   where len(c) > 1
13     and substring(c,1,1) = ','
14         )
```

Discussion

The first and most important step in this solution is to walk the string. Once you've accomplished that, all that's left is to parse the string into individual, numeric values using your DBMS's provided functions.

DB2 and SQL Server

The inline view X (lines 6–11) walks the string. The idea in this solution is to "walk through" the string, so that each row has one less character than the one before it:

```
,7654,7698,7782,7788,
7654,7698,7782,7788,
654,7698,7782,7788,
54,7698,7782,7788,
4,7698,7782,7788,
,7698,7782,7788,
7698,7782,7788,
698,7782,7788,
98,7782,7788,
8,7782,7788,
,7782,7788,
7782,7788,
782,7788,
82,7788,
2,7788,
,7788,
7788,
788,
88,
8,
,
```

Notice that by enclosing the string in commas (the delimiter), there's no need to make special checks as to where the beginning or end of the string is.

The next step is to keep only the values you want to use in the IN-list. The values to keep are the ones with leading commas, with the exception of the last row with its lone comma. Use SUBSTR or SUBSTRING to identify which rows have a leading comma, then keep all characters found before the next comma in that row. Once that's done, cast the string to a number so it can be properly evaluated against the numeric column EMPNO (lines 4–14):

```
EMPNO
------
  7654
  7698
  7782
  7788
```

The final step is to use the results in a subquery to return the desired rows.

MySQL

The inline view (lines 5–9) walks the string. The expression on line 10 determines how many values are in the string by finding the number of commas (the delimiter) and adding one. The function SUBSTRING_INDEX (line 6) returns all characters in the string before (to the left of) the *n*th occurrence of a comma (the delimiter):

```
+-----------------------+
| empno                 |
+-----------------------+
| 7654                  |
| 7654,7698             |
| 7654,7698,7782        |
| 7654,7698,7782,7788   |
+-----------------------+
```

Those rows are then passed to another call to SUBSTRING_INDEX (line 5); this time the *n*th occurrence of the delimited is –1, which causes all values to the right of the *n*th occurrence of the delimiter to be kept:

```
+-------+
| empno |
+-------+
| 7654  |
| 7698  |
| 7782  |
| 7788  |
+-------+
```

The final step is to plug the results into a subquery.

Oracle

The first step is to walk the string:

```
select emps,pos
  from (select ','||'7654,7698,7782,7788'||',' emps
          from t1) csv,
       (select rownum pos from emp) iter
 where iter.pos <=
((length(csv.emps)-length(replace(csv.emps,',')))/length(','))-1

EMPS                           POS
---------------------- ----------
,7654,7698,7782,7788,           1
,7654,7698,7782,7788,           2
,7654,7698,7782,7788,           3
,7654,7698,7782,7788,           4
```

The number of rows returned represents the number of values in your list. The values for POS are crucial to the query as they are needed to parse the string into individual values. The strings are parsed using SUBSTR and INSTR. POS is used to locate the *n*th occurrence of the delimiter in each string. By enclosing the strings in commas, no special checks are necessary to determine the beginning or end of a string. The values passed to SUBSTR, INSTR (lines 7–9) locate the *n*th and *n*th+1 occurrence of the delimiter. By subtracting the value returned for the current comma (the location in the string where the current comma is) from the value returned by the next comma (the location in the string where the next comma is) you can extract each value from the string:

```
select substr(emps,
       instr(emps,',',1,iter.pos)+1,
       instr(emps,',',1,iter.pos+1) -
       instr(emps,',',1,iter.pos)) emps
  from (select ','||'7654,7698,7782,7788'||',' emps
          from t1) csv,
       (select rownum pos from emp) iter
 where iter.pos <=
   ((length(csv.emps)-length(replace(csv.emps,',')))/length(','))-1

EMPS
-----------
7654,
7698,
7782,
7788,
```

The final step is to remove the trailing comma from each value, cast it to a number, and plug it into a subquery.

PostgreSQL

The inline view Z (lines 6–9) walks the string. The number of rows returned is determined by how many values are in the string. To find the number of values in the string, subtract the size of the string without the delimiter from the size of the string with the delimiter (line 9). The function SPLIT_PART does the work of parsing the string. It looks for the value that comes before the *n*th occurrence of the delimiter:

```
select list.vals,
       split_part(list.vals,',',iter.pos) as empno,
       iter.pos
  from (select id as pos from t10) iter,
       (select ','||'7654,7698,7782,7788'||',' as vals
          from t1) list
 where iter.pos <=
       length(list.vals)-length(replace(list.vals,',',''))

          vals          | empno | pos
------------------------+-------+-----
 ,7654,7698,7782,7788,  |       |  1
 ,7654,7698,7782,7788,  |  7654 |  2
 ,7654,7698,7782,7788,  |  7698 |  3
 ,7654,7698,7782,7788,  |  7782 |  4
 ,7654,7698,7782,7788,  |  7788 |  5
```

The final step is to cast the values (EMPNO) to a number and plug it into a sub-query.

6.12   Alphabetizing a String

Problem

You want alphabetize the individual characters within strings in your tables. Consider the following result set:

```
ENAME
----------
ADAMS
ALLEN
BLAKE
CLARK
FORD
JAMES
JONES
KING
MARTIN
MILLER
SCOTT
SMITH
TURNER
WARD
```

You would like the result to be:

```
OLD_NAME    NEW_NAME
----------  --------
ADAMS       AADMS
ALLEN       AELLN
BLAKE       ABEKL
CLARK       ACKLR
FORD        DFOR
JAMES       AEJMS
JONES       EJNOS
KING        GIKN
MARTIN      AIMNRT
MILLER      EILLMR
SCOTT       COSTT
SMITH       HIMST
TURNER      ENRRTU
WARD        ADRW
```

Solution

This problem is a perfect example of why it is crucial to understand your DBMS and what functionality is available to you. In situations where your DBMS does not provide built-in functions to facilitate this solution, you need to come up with something creative. Compare the MySQL solution with the rest.

DB2

To alphabetize rows of strings it is necessary to walk each string then order its characters:

```
 1  select ename,
 2          max(case when pos=1 then c else '' end)||
 3          max(case when pos=2 then c else '' end)||
 4          max(case when pos=3 then c else '' end)||
 5          max(case when pos=4 then c else '' end)||
 6          max(case when pos=5 then c else '' end)||
 7          max(case when pos=6 then c else '' end)
 8     from (
 9   select e.ename,
10          cast(substr(e.ename,iter.pos,1) as varchar(100)) c,
11          cast(row_number()over(partition by e.ename
12                           order by substr(e.ename,iter.pos,1))
13            as integer) pos
14     from emp e,
15          (select cast(row_number()over() as integer) pos
16            from emp) iter
17    where iter.pos <= length(e.ename)
18          ) x
19    group by ename
```

MySQL

The key here is the GROUP_CONCAT function, which allows you to not only concatenate the characters that make up each name but also order them:

```
 1  select ename, group_concat(c order by c separator '')
 2     from (
 3   select ename, substr(a.ename,iter.pos,1) c
 4     from emp a,
 5          ( select id pos from t10 ) iter
 6    where iter.pos <= length(a.ename)
 7          ) x
 8    group by ename
```

Oracle

The function SYS_CONNECT_BY_PATH allows you to iteratively build a list:

```
 1  select old_name, new_name
 2     from (
 3   select old_name, replace(sys_connect_by_path(c,' '),' ') new_name
 4     from (
 5   select e.ename old_name,
 6          row_number() over(partition by e.ename
 7                           order by substr(e.ename,iter.pos,1)) rn,
 8          substr(e.ename,iter.pos,1) c
 9     from emp e,
10          ( select rownum pos from emp ) iter
11    where iter.pos <= length(e.ename)
```

```
12   order by 1
13      ) x
14   start with rn = 1
15 connect by prior rn = rn-1 and prior old_name = old_name
16      )
17   where length(old_name) = length(new_name)
```

PostgreSQL

PostgreSQL does not offer any built-in functions to easily sort characters in a string, so it is necessary not only to walk through each string but also to know in advance the largest length of any one name. View V is used in this solution for readability:

```
create or replace view V as
select x.*
  from (
select a.ename,
       substr(a.ename,iter.pos,1) as c
  from emp a,
       (select id as pos from t10) iter
 where iter.pos <= length(a.ename)
 order by 1,2
       ) x
```

The following select statement leverages the view:

```
 1 select ename,
 2       max(case when pos=1 then
 3                case when cnt=1 then c
 4                     else rpad(c,cast(cnt as integer),c)
 5                end
 6                else ''
 7           end)||
 8       max(case when pos=2 then
 9                case when cnt=1 then c
10                     else rpad(c,cast(cnt as integer),c)
11                end
12                else ''
13           end)||
14       max(case when pos=3 then
15                case when cnt=1 then c
16                     else rpad(c,cast(cnt as integer),c)
17                end
18                else ''
19           end)||
20       max(case when pos=4 then
21                case when cnt=1 then c
22                     else rpad(c,cast(cnt as integer),c)
23                end
24                else ''
25           end)||
26       max(case when pos=5 then
27                case when cnt=1 then c
28                     else rpad(c,cast(cnt as integer),c)
```

```
29              end
30              else ''
31          end)||
32      max(case when pos=6 then
33              case when cnt=1 then c
34                  else rpad(c,cast(cnt as integer),c)
35              end
36              else ''
37          end)
38  from (
39 select a.ename, a.c,
40      (select count(*)
41        from v b
42        where a.ename=b.ename and a.c=b.c ) as cnt,
43      (select count(*)+1
44        from v b
45        where a.ename=b.ename and b.c<a.c) as pos
46   from v a
47       ) x
48   group by ename
```

SQL Server

To alphabetize rows of strings it is necessary to walk each string, and then order their characters:

```
1  select ename,
2          max(case when pos=1 then c else '' end)+
3          max(case when pos=2 then c else '' end)+
4          max(case when pos=3 then c else '' end)+
5          max(case when pos=4 then c else '' end)+
6          max(case when pos=5 then c else '' end)+
7          max(case when pos=6 then c else '' end)
8      from (
9    select e.ename,
10          substring(e.ename,iter.pos,1) as c,
11          row_number() over (
12           partition by e.ename
13              order by substring(e.ename,iter.pos,1)) as pos
14    from emp e,
15         (select row_number()over(order by ename) as pos
16              from emp) iter
17    where iter.pos <= len(e.ename)
18          ) x
19      group by ename
```

Discussion

DB2 and SQL Server

The inline view X returns each character in each name as a row. The function SUB-STR or SUBSTRING extracts each character from each name, and the function ROW_NUMBER ranks each character alphabetically:

```
ENAME    C    POS
-----    -    ---
ADAMS    A    1
ADAMS    A    2
ADAMS    D    3
ADAMS    M    4
ADAMS    S    5
...
```

To return each letter of a string as a row, you must walk the string. This is accomplished with inline view ITER.

Now that the letters in each name have been alphabetized, the last step is to put those letters back together, into a string, in the order they are ranked. Each letter's position is evaluated by the CASE statements (lines 2–7). If a character is found at a particular position it is then concatenated to the result of the next evaluation (the following CASE statement). Because the aggregate function MAX is used as well, only one character per position POS is returned, so that only one row per name is returned. The CASE evaluation goes up to the number 6, which is the maximum number of characters in any name in table EMP.

MySQL

The inline view X (lines 3–6) returns each character in each name as a row. The function SUBSTR extracts each character from each name:

```
ENAME    C
-----    -
ADAMS    A
ADAMS    A
ADAMS    D
ADAMS    M
ADAMS    S
...
```

Inline view ITER is used to walk the string. From there, the rest of the work is done by the GROUP_CONCAT function. By specifying an order, the function not only concatenates each letter, it does so alphabetically.

Oracle

The real work is done by inline view X (lines 5–11), where the characters in each name are extracted and put into alphabetical order. This is accomplished by walking the string, then imposing order on those characters. The rest of the query merely glues the names back together.

The tearing apart of names can be seen by executing only inline view X:

```
OLD_NAME        RN C
----------  ---------- -
ADAMS            1 A
ADAMS            2 A
```

```
ADAMS                    3 D
ADAMS                    4 M
ADAMS                    5 S
...
```

The next step is to take the alphabetized characters and rebuild each name. This is done with the function SYS_CONNECT_BY_PATH by appending each character to the ones before it:

```
OLD_NAME    NEW_NAME
----------  ----------
ADAMS       A
ADAMS       AA
ADAMS       AAD
ADAMS       AADM
ADAMS       AADMS
...
```

The final step is to keep only the strings that have the same length as the names they were built from.

PostgreSQL

For readability, view V is used in this solution to walk the string. The function SUBSTR, in the view definition, extracts each character from each name so that the view returns:

```
ENAME    C
-----    -
ADAMS    A
ADAMS    A
ADAMS    D
ADAMS    M
ADAMS    S
...
```

The view also orders the results by ENAME and by each letter in each name. The inline view X (lines 15–18) returns the names and characters from view V, the number of times each character occurs in each name, and its position (alphabetically):

```
ename | c | cnt | pos
-------+---+-----+-----
ADAMS | A |  2  |  1
ADAMS | A |  2  |  1
ADAMS | D |  1  |  3
ADAMS | M |  1  |  4
ADAMS | S |  1  |  5
```

The extra columns CNT and POS, returned by the inline view X, are crucial to the solution. POS is used to rank each character and CNT is used to determine the number of times the character exists in each name. The final step is to evaluate the position of each character and rebuild the name. You'll notice that each case statement is actually two case statements. This is to determine whether or not a character occurs more than once in a name; if it does, then rather than return that character, what is returned is that character appended to itself CNT times. The aggregate function, MAX, is used to ensure there is only one row per name.

6.13 Identifying Strings That Can Be Treated As Numbers

Problem

You have a column that is defined to hold character data. Unfortunately, the rows contain mixed numeric and character data. Consider view V:

```
create view V as
select replace(mixed,' ','') as mixed
  from (
select substr(ename,1,2)||
       cast(deptno as char(4))||
       substr(ename,3,2) as mixed
  from emp
 where deptno = 10
 union all
select cast(empno as char(4)) as mixed
  from emp
 where deptno = 20
 union all
select ename as mixed
  from emp
 where deptno = 30
       ) x


select * from v

 MIXED
 ---------------
 CL10AR
 KI10NG
 MI10LL
 7369
 7566
 7788
 7876
 7902
 ALLEN
 WARD
 MARTIN
 BLAKE
 TURNER
 JAMES
```

You want to return rows that are numbers only, or that contain at least one number. If the numbers are mixed with character data, you want to remove the characters and return only the numbers. For the sample data above you want the following result set:

```
MIXED
--------
      10
      10
      10
    7369
    7566
    7788
    7876
    7902
```

Solution

The functions REPLACE and TRANSLATE are extremely useful for manipulating strings and individual characters. The key is to convert all numbers to a single character, which then makes it easy to isolate and identify any number by referring to a single character.

DB2

Use functions TRANSLATE, REPLACE, and POSSTR to isolate the numeric characters in each row. The calls to CAST are necessary in view V; otherwise, the view will fail to be created due to type conversion errors. You'll need the function REPLACE to remove extraneous white space due to casting to the fixed length CHAR:

```
 1 select mixed old,
 2        cast(
 3          case
 4          when
 5            replace(
 6             translate(mixed,'9999999999','0123456789'),'9','') = ''
 7          then
 8             mixed
 9          else replace(
10             translate(mixed,
11                repeat('#',length(mixed)),
12             replace(
13                translate(mixed,'9999999999','0123456789'),'9','')),
14                '#','')
15          end as integer ) mixed
16   from V
17  where posstr(translate(mixed,'9999999999','0123456789'),'9') > 0
```

MySQL

The syntax for MySQL is slightly different and will define view V as:

```
create view V as
select concat(
        substr(ename,1,2),
        replace(cast(deptno as char(4)),' ',''),
        substr(ename,3,2)
       ) as mixed
  from emp
 where deptno = 10
 union all
select replace(cast(empno as char(4)), ' ', '')
  from emp where deptno = 20
 union all
select ename from emp where deptno = 30
```

Because MySQL does not support the TRANSLATE function, you must walk each row and evaluate it on a character-by-character basis.

```
 1 select cast(group_concat(c order by pos separator '') as unsigned)
 2        as MIXED1
 3   from (
 4 select v.mixed, iter.pos, substr(v.mixed,iter.pos,1) as c
 5   from V,
 6        ( select id pos from t10 ) iter
 7  where iter.pos <= length(v.mixed)
 8    and ascii(substr(v.mixed,iter.pos,1)) between 48 and 57
 9        ) y
10  group by mixed
11  order by 1
```

Oracle

Use functions TRANSLATE, REPLACE, and INSTR to isolate the numeric characters in each row. The calls to CAST are not necessary in view V. Use the function REPLACE to remove extraneous white space due to casting to the fixed length CHAR. If you decide you would like to keep the explicit type conversion calls in the view definition, it is suggested you cast to VARCHAR2:

```
 1 select to_number (
 2        case
 3        when
 4          replace(translate(mixed,'0123456789','9999999999'),'9')
 5          is not null
 6        then
 7            replace(
 8          translate(mixed,
 9            replace(
10          translate(mixed,'0123456789','9999999999'),'9'),
11                  rpad('#',length(mixed),'#')),'#')
12        else
13            mixed
14        end
15        ) mixed
16   from V
17  where instr(translate(mixed,'0123456789','9999999999'),'9') > 0
```

PostgreSQL

Use functions TRANSLATE, REPLACE, and STRPOS to isolate the numeric characters in each row. The calls to CAST are not necessary in view V. Use the function REPLACE ito remove extraneous white space due to casting to the fixed length CHAR. If you decide you would like to keep the explicit type conversion calls in the view definition, it is suggested you cast to VARCHAR:

```
 1 select cast(
 2        case
 3        when
 4         replace(translate(mixed,'0123456789','9999999999'),'9','')
 5         is not null
 6        then
 7          replace(
 8        translate(mixed,
 9          replace(
10        translate(mixed,'0123456789','9999999999'),'9',''),
11                rpad('#',length(mixed),'#')),'#','')
12        else
13          mixed
14        end as integer ) as mixed
15     from V
16   where strpos(translate(mixed,'0123456789','9999999999'),'9') > 0
```

SQL Server

The built-in function ISNUMERIC along with a wildcard search allows you to easily identify strings that contains numbers, but getting numeric characters out of a string is not particularly efficient because the TRANSLATE function is not supported.

Discussion

The TRANSLATE function is very useful here as it allows you to easily isolate and identify numbers and characters. The trick is to convert all numbers to a single character; this way, rather than searching for different numbers you only search for one character.

DB2, Oracle, and PostgreSQL

The syntax differs slightly among these DBMSs, but the technique is the same. I'll use the solution for PostgreSQL for the discussion.

The real work is done by functions TRANSLATE and REPLACE. To get the final result set requires several function calls, each listed below in one query:

```
select mixed as orig,
translate(mixed,'0123456789','9999999999') as mixed1,
replace(translate(mixed,'0123456789','9999999999'),'9','') as mixed2,
 translate(mixed,
 replace(
translate(mixed,'0123456789','9999999999'),'9',''),
        rpad('#',length(mixed),'#')) as mixed3,
```

```
      replace(
      translate(mixed,
      replace(
      translate(mixed,'0123456789','9999999999'),'9',''),
            rpad('#',length(mixed),'#')),'#','') as mixed4
        from V
      where strpos(translate(mixed,'0123456789','9999999999'),'9') > 0
```

```
ORIG  | MIXED1 | MIXED2 | MIXED3 | MIXED4 | MIXED5
--------+--------+--------+--------+--------+--------
CL10AR | CL99AR | CLAR   | ##10## | 10     |     10
KI10NG | KI99NG | KING   | ##10## | 10     |     10
MI10LL | MI99LL | MILL   | ##10## | 10     |     10
7369   | 9999   |        | 7369   | 7369   |   7369
7566   | 9999   |        | 7566   | 7566   |   7566
7788   | 9999   |        | 7788   | 7788   |   7788
7876   | 9999   |        | 7876   | 7876   |   7876
7902   | 9999   |        | 7902   | 7902   |   7902
```

First, notice that any rows without at least one number are removed. How this is accomplished will become clear as you examine each of the columns in the above result set. The rows that are kept are the values in the ORIG column and are the rows that will eventually make up the result set. The first step to extracting the numbers is to use the function TRANSLATE to convert any number to a 9 (you can use any digit; 9 is arbitrary), this is represented by the values in MIXED1. Now that all numbers are 9's, they can be treating as a single unit. The next step is to remove all of the numbers by using the function REPLACE. Because all digits are now 9, REPLACE simply looks for any 9's and removes them. This is represented by the values in MIXED2. The next step, MIXED3, uses values that are returned by MIXED2. These values are then compared to the values in ORIG. If any characters from MIXED2 are found in ORIG, they are converted to the # character by TRANSLATE. The result set from MIXED3 shows that the letters, not the numbers, have now been singled out and converted to a single character. Now that all non-numeric characters are represented by #'s, they can be treated as a single unit. The next step, MIXED4, uses REPLACE to find and remove any # characters in each row; what's left are numbers only. The final step is to cast the numeric characters as numbers. Now that you've gone through the steps, you can see how the WHERE clause works. The results from MIXED1 are passed to STRPOS, and if a 9 is found (the position in the string where the first 9 is located) the result must be greater than 0. For rows that return a value greater than zero, it means there's at least one number in that row and it should be kept.

MySQL

The first step is to walk each string and evaluate each character and determine whether or not it's a number:

```
select v.mixed, iter.pos, substr(v.mixed,iter.pos,1) as c
  from V,
       ( select id pos from t10 ) iter
 where iter.pos <= length(v.mixed)
 order by 1,2
```

```
+--------+------+------+
| mixed  | pos  | c    |
+--------+------+------+
| 7369   |   1  | 7    |
| 7369   |   2  | 3    |
| 7369   |   3  | 6    |
| 7369   |   4  | 9    |

| ALLEN  |   1  | A    |
| ALLEN  |   2  | L    |
| ALLEN  |   3  | L    |
| ALLEN  |   4  | E    |
| ALLEN  |   5  | N    |

| CL10AR |   1  | C    |
| CL10AR |   2  | L    |
| CL10AR |   3  | 1    |
| CL10AR |   4  | 0    |
| CL10AR |   5  | A    |
| CL10AR |   6  | R    |
+--------+------+------+
```

Now that each character in each string can be evaluated individually, the next step is
to keep only the rows that have a number in the C column:

```
select v.mixed, iter.pos, substr(v.mixed,iter.pos,1) as c
  from V,
       ( select id pos from t10 ) iter
 where iter.pos <= length(v.mixed)
   and ascii(substr(v.mixed,iter.pos,1)) between 48 and 57
 order by 1,2
```

```
+--------+------+------+
| mixed  | pos  | c    |
+--------+------+------+
| 7369   |   1  | 7    |
| 7369   |   2  | 3    |
| 7369   |   3  | 6    |
| 7369   |   4  | 9    |

| CL10AR |   3  | 1    |
| CL10AR |   4  | 0    |

+--------+------+------+
```

At this point, all the rows in column C are numbers. The next step is to use
GROUP_CONCAT to concatenate the numbers to form their respective whole number in MIXED. The final result is then cast as a number:

```
  select cast(group_concat(c order by pos separator '') as unsigned)
          as MIXED1
    from (
  select v.mixed, iter.pos, substr(v.mixed,iter.pos,1) as c
    from V,
        ( select id pos from t10 ) iter
   where iter.pos <= length(v.mixed)
    and ascii(substr(x.mixed,iter.pos,1)) between 48 and 57
          ) y
    group by mixed
    order by 1

+--------+
| MIXED1 |
+--------+
|     10 |
|     10 |
|     10 |
|   7369 |
|   7566 |
|   7788 |
|   7876 |
|   7902 |
+--------+
```

As a final note, keep in mind that any digits in each string will be concatenated to form one numeric value. For example, an input value of, say, '99Gennick87' will result in the value 9987 being returned. This is something to keep in mind, particularly when working with serialized data.

6.14   Extracting the nth Delimited Substring

Problem

You want to extract a specified, delimited substring from a string. Consider the following view V, which generates source data for this problem:

```
create view V as
select 'mo,larry,curly' as name
  from t1
 union all
select 'tina,gina,jaunita,regina,leena' as name
  from t1
```

Output from the view is as follows:

```
select * from v

NAME
--------------------
mo,larry,curly
tina,gina,jaunita,regina,leena
```

You would like to extract the second name in each row, so the final result set would be:

```
SUB
-----
larry
gina
```

Solution

The key to solving this problem is to return each name as an individual row while preserving the order in which the name exists in the list. Exactly how you do these things depends on which DBMS you are using.

DB2

After walking the NAMEs returned by view V, use the function ROW_NUMBER to keep only the second name from each string:

```
 1 select substr(c,2,locate(',',c,2)-2)
 2   from (
 3 select pos, name, substr(name, pos) c,
 4        row_number() over(partition by name
 5                           order by length(substr(name,pos)) desc) rn
 6   from (
 7 select ',' ||csv.name|| ',' as name,
 8        cast(iter.pos as integer) as pos
 9   from V csv,
10        (select row_number() over() pos from t100 ) iter
11  where iter.pos <= length(csv.name)+2
12        ) x
13  where length(substr(name,pos)) > 1
14    and substr(substr(name,pos),1,1) = ','
15        ) y
16  where rn = 2
```

MySQL

After walking the NAMEs returned by view V, use the position of the commas to return only the second name in each string:

```
 1 select name
 2   from (
 3 select iter.pos,
 4        substring_index(
 5        substring_index(src.name,',',iter.pos),',',-1) name
 6   from V src,
 7        (select id pos from t10) iter,
 8  where iter.pos <=
 9        length(src.name)-length(replace(src.name,',',''))
10        ) x
11  where pos = 2
```

Oracle

After walking the NAMEs returned by view V, retrieve the second name in each list by using SUBSTR and INSTR:

```
 1 select sub
 2   from (
 3 select iter.pos,
 4        src.name,
 5        substr( src.name,
 6         instr( src.name,',',1,iter.pos )+1,
 7         instr( src.name,',',1,iter.pos+1 ) -
 8         instr( src.name,',',1,iter.pos )-1) sub
 9   from (select ','||name||',' as name from V) src,
10        (select rownum pos from emp) iter
11  where iter.pos < length(src.name)-length(replace(src.name,','))
12        )
13  where pos = 2
```

PostgreSQL

Use the function SPLIT_PART to help return each individual name as a row:

```
 1 select name
 2   from (
 3 select iter.pos, split_part(src.name,',',iter.pos) as name
 4   from (select id as pos from t10) iter,
 5        (select cast(name as text) as name from v) src
 6  where iter.pos <=
 7        length(src.name)-length(replace(src.name,',',''))+1
 9        ) x
10  where pos = 2
```

SQL Server

After walking the NAMEs returned by view V, use the function ROW_NUMBER to keep only the second name from each string:

```
 1  select substring(c,2,charindex(',',c,2)-2)
 2    from (
 3  select pos, name, substring(name, pos, len(name)) as c,
 4         row_number( ) over(
 5          partition by name
 6          order by len(substring(name,pos,len(name))) desc) rn
 7    from (
 8  select ',' + csv.name + ',' as name,
 9         iter.pos
10    from V csv,
11         (select id as pos from t100 ) iter
12   where iter.pos <= len(csv.name)+2
13         ) x
14   where len(substring(name,pos,len(name))) > 1
15     and substring(substring(name,pos,len(name)),1,1) = ','
16         ) y
17   where rn = 2
```

Discussion

DB2 and SQL Server

The syntax is slightly different between these two DBMSs, but the technique is the same. I will use the solution for DB2 for the discussion. The strings are walked and the results are represented by inline view X:

```
select ','||csv.name|| ',' as name,
       iter.pos
  from v csv,
       (select row_number() over() pos from t100 ) iter
 where iter.pos <= length(csv.name)+2
```

```
EMPS                                POS
----------------------------        ----
,tina,gina,jaunita,regina,leena,     1
,tina,gina,jaunita,regina,leena,     2
,tina,gina,jaunita,regina,leena,     3
...
```

The next step is to then step through each character in each string:

```
select pos, name, substr(name, pos) c,
       row_number() over(partition by name
                             order by length(substr(name, pos)) desc) rn
  from (
select ','||csv.name||',' as name,
       cast(iter.pos as integer) as pos
  from v csv,
       (select row_number() over() pos from t100 ) iter
 where iter.pos <= length(csv.name)+2
       ) x
 where length(substr(name,pos)) > 1
```

```
POS EMPS              C                 RN
--- ---------------   ---------------   --
  1 ,mo,larry,curly,  ,mo,larry,curly,   1
  2 ,mo,larry,curly,  mo,larry,curly,    2
  3 ,mo,larry,curly,  o,larry,curly,     3
  4 ,mo,larry,curly,  ,larry,curly,      4
...
```

Now that different portions of the string are available to you, simply identify which rows to keep. The rows you are interested in are the ones that begin with a comma; the rest can be discarded:

```
select pos, name, substr(name,pos) c,
       row_number() over(partition by name
                             order by length(substr(name, pos)) desc) rn
  from (
select ','||csv.name||',' as name,
       cast(iter.pos as integer) as pos
  from v csv,
```

```
           (select row_number() over() pos from t100 ) iter
      where iter.pos <= length(csv.name)+2
           )   x
      where length(substr(name,pos)) > 1
        and substr(substr(name,pos),1,1) = ','
```

```
POS    EMPS                                    C                                        RN
---    --------------                          ----------------                         --
  1    ,mo,larry,curly,                        ,mo,larry,curly,                          1
  4    ,mo,larry,curly,                        ,larry,curly,                             2
 10    ,mo,larry,curly,                        ,curly,                                   3
  1    ,tina,gina,jaunita,regina,leena,        ,tina,gina,jaunita,regina,leena,         1
  6    ,tina,gina,jaunita,regina,leena,        ,gina,jaunita,regina,leena,              2
 11    ,tina,gina,jaunita,regina,leena,        ,jaunita,regina,leena,                   3
 19    ,tina,gina,jaunita,regina,leena,        ,regina,leena,                           4
 26    ,tina,gina,jaunita,regina,leena,        ,leena,                                  5
```

This is an important step as it sets up how you will get the *n*th substring. Notice that many rows have been eliminated from this query because of the following condition in the WHERE clause:

```
substr(substr(name,pos),1,1) = ','
```

You'll notice that ,larry,curly, was ranked 4, but now is ranked 2. Remember, the WHERE clause is evaluated before the SELECT, so the rows with leading commas are kept, *then* ROW_NUMBER performs its ranking. At this point it's easy to see that, to get the *n*th substring you want rows where RN equals *n*. The last step is to keep only the rows you are interested in (in this case where RN equals 2) and use SUBSTR to extract the name from that row. The name to keep is the first name in the row: larry from ,larry,curly, and gina from ,gina,jaunita,regina,leena,.

MySQL

The inline view X walks each string. You can determine how many values are in each string by counting the delimiters in the string:

```
select iter.pos, src.name
  from (select id pos from t10) iter,
       V src
 where iter.pos <=
       length(src.name)-length(replace(src.name,',',''))
```

```
+------+-------------------------------+
| pos  | name                          |
+------+-------------------------------+
|    1 | mo,larry,curly                |
|    2 | mo,larry,curly                |
|    1 | tina,gina,jaunita,regina,leena |
|    2 | tina,gina,jaunita,regina,leena |
|    3 | tina,gina,jaunita,regina,leena |
|    4 | tina,gina,jaunita,regina,leena |
+------+-------------------------------+
```

In this case, there is one fewer row than values in each string because that's all that is needed. The function SUBSTRING_INDEX takes care of parsing the needed values:

```
select iter.pos,src.name name1,
       substring_index(src.name,',',iter.pos) name2,
       substring_index(
       substring_index(src.name,',',iter.pos),',',-1) name3
  from (select id pos from t10) iter,
       V src
 where iter.pos <=
       length(src.name)-length(replace(src.name,',',''))
```

```
+------+----------------------------------+--------------------------+---------+
| pos  | name1                            | name2                    | name3   |
+------+----------------------------------+--------------------------+---------+
|    1 | mo,larry,curly                   | mo                       | mo      |
|    2 | mo,larry,curly                   | mo,larry                 | larry   |
|    1 | tina,gina,jaunita,regina,leena   | tina                     | tina    |
|    2 | tina,gina,jaunita,regina,leena   | tina,gina                | gina    |
|    3 | tina,gina,jaunita,regina,leena   | tina,gina,jaunita        | jaunita |
|    4 | tina,gina,jaunita,regina,leena   | tina,gina,jaunita,regina | regina  |
+------+----------------------------------+--------------------------+---------+
```

I've shown three name fields, so you can see how the nested SUBSTRING_INDEX calls work. The inner call returns all characters to the left of the nth occurrence of a comma. The outer call returns everything to the right of the first comma it finds (starting from the end of the string). The final step is to keep the value for NAME3 where POS equals n, in this case 2.

Oracle

The inline view walks each string. The number of times each string is returned is determined by how many values are in each string. The solution finds the number of values in each string by counting the number of delimiters in it. Because each string is enclosed in commas, the number of values in a string is the number of commas minus one. The strings are then UNIONed and joined to a table with a cardinality that is at least the number of values in the largest string. The functions SUBSTR and INSTR use the value of POS to parse each string:

```
select iter.pos, src.name,
       substr( src.name,
       instr( src.name,',',1,iter.pos )+1,
       instr( src.name,',',1,iter.pos+1 ) -
       instr( src.name,',',1,iter.pos )-1) sub
  from (select ','||name||',' as name from v) src,
       (select rownum pos from emp) iter
 where iter.pos < length(src.name)-length(replace(src.name,','))
```

```
POS NAME                              SUB
--- ---------------------------------  -------------
  1 ,mo,larry,curly,                   mo
  1 , tina,gina,jaunita,regina,leena,  tina
  2 ,mo,larry,curly,                   larry
  2 , tina,gina,jaunita,regina,leena,  gina
  3 ,mo,larry,curly,                   curly
  3 , tina,gina,jaunita,regina,leena,  jaunita
  4 , tina,gina,jaunita,regina,leena,  regina
  5 , tina,gina,jaunita,regina,leena,  leena
```

The first call to INSTR within SUBSTR determines the start position of the substring to extract. The next call to INSTR within SUBSTR finds the position of the *n*th comma (same as the start position) as well the position of the *n*th + 1 comma. Subtracting the two values returns the length of the substring to extract. Because every value is parsed into its own row, simply specify WHERE POS = *n* to keep the *n*th substring (in this case, where POS = 2, so, the second substring in the list).

PostgreSQL

The inline view X walks each string. The number of rows returned is determined by how many values are in each string. To find the number of values in each string, find the number of delimiters in each string and add one. The function SPLIT_PART uses the values in POS to find the *n*th occurrence of the delimiter and parse the string into values:

```
select iter.pos, src.name as name1,
       split_part(src.name,',',iter.pos) as name2
  from (select id as pos from t10) iter,
       (select cast(name as text) as name from v) src
 where iter.pos <=
       length(src.name)-length(replace(src.name,',',''))+1
```

```
pos |            name1             |  name2
----+------------------------------+---------
  1 | mo,larry,curly               | mo
  2 | mo,larry,curly               | larry
  3 | mo,larry,curly               | curly
  1 | tina,gina,jaunita,regina,leena | tina
  2 | tina,gina,jaunita,regina,leena | gina
  3 | tina,gina,jaunita,regina,leena | jaunita
  4 | tina,gina,jaunita,regina,leena | regina
  5 | tina,gina,jaunita,regina,leena | leena
```

I've shown NAME twice so you can see how SPLIT_PART parses each string using POS. Once each string is parsed, the final step is the keep the rows where POS equals the *n*th substring you are interested in, in this case, 2.

6.15 Parsing an IP Address

Problem

You want to parse an IP address's fields into columns. Consider the following IP address:

```
111.22.3.4
```

You would like the result of your query to be:

```
A      B      C      D
-----  -----  -----  ---
111    22     3      4
```

Solution

The solution depends on the built-in functions provided by your DBMS. Regardless of your DBMS, being able to locate periods and the numbers immediately surrounding them are the keys to the solution.

DB2

Use the recursive WITH clause to simulate an iteration through the IP address while using SUBSTR to easily parse it. A leading period is added to the IP address so that every set of numbers has a period in front of it and can be treated the same way.

```
 1 with x (pos,ip) as (
 2   values (1,'.92.111.0.222')
 3   union all
 4  select pos+1,ip from x where pos+1 <= 20
 5 )
 6 select max(case when rn=1 then e end) a,
 7         max(case when rn=2 then e end) b,
 8         max(case when rn=3 then e end) c,
 9         max(case when rn=4 then e end) d
10    from (
11 select pos,c,d,
12         case when posstr(d,'.') > 0 then substr(d,1,posstr(d,'.')-1)
13             else d
14         end as e,
15         row_number() over(order by pos desc) rn
16    from (
17 select pos, ip,right(ip,pos) as c, substr(right(ip,pos),2) as d
18    from x
19 where pos <= length(ip)
20   and substr(right(ip,pos),1,1) = '.'
21      ) x
22      ) y
```

MySQL

The function SUBSTR_INDEX makes parsing an IP address an easy operation:

```
1 select substring_index(substring_index(y.ip,'.',1),'.',-1) a,
2        substring_index(substring_index(y.ip,'.',2),'.',-1) b,
3        substring_index(substring_index(y.ip,'.',3),'.',-1) c,
4        substring_index(substring_index(y.ip,'.',4),'.',-1) d
5   from (select '92.111.0.2' as ip from t1) y
```

Oracle

Use the built-in function SUBSTR and INSTR to parse and navigate through the IP address:

```
1 select ip,
2        substr(ip, 1, instr(ip,'.')-1 ) a,
3        substr(ip, instr(ip,'.')+1,
4                  instr(ip,'.',1,2)-instr(ip,'.')-1 ) b,
5        substr(ip, instr(ip,'.',1,2)+1,
6                  instr(ip,'.',1,3)-instr(ip,'.',1,2)-1 ) c,
7        substr(ip, instr(ip,'.',1,3)+1 ) d
8   from (select '92.111.0.2' as ip from t1)
```

PostgreSQL

Use the built-in function SPLIT_PART to parse an IP address:

```
1 select split_part(y.ip,'.',1) as a,
2        split_part(y.ip,'.',2) as b,
3        split_part(y.ip,'.',3) as c,
4        split_part(y.ip,'.',4) as d
5   from (select cast('92.111.0.2' as text) as ip from t1) as y
```

SQL Server

Use the recursive WITH clause to simulate an iteration through the IP address while using SUBSTR to easily parse it. A leading period is added to the IP address so that every set of numbers has a period in front of it and can be treated the same way:

```
 1    with x (pos,ip) as (
 2      select 1 as pos,'.92.111.0.222' as ip from t1
 3      union all
 4      select pos+1,ip from x where pos+1 <= 20
 5    )
 6    select max(case when rn=1 then e end) a,
 7           max(case when rn=2 then e end) b,
 8           max(case when rn=3 then e end) c,
 9           max(case when rn=4 then e end) d
10      from (
11    select pos,c,d,
12           case when charindex('.',d) > 0
13                then substring(d,1,charindex('.',d)-1)
```

```
14                  else d
15             end as e,
16             row_number() over(order by pos desc) rn
17      from (
18    select pos, ip,right(ip,pos) as c,
19             substring(right(ip,pos),2,len(ip)) as d
20       from x
21      where pos <= len(ip)
22        and substring(right(ip,pos),1,1) = '.'
23            ) x
24            ) y
```

Discussion

By using the built-in functions for your database, you can easily walk through parts of a string. The key is being able to locate each of the periods in the address. Then you can parse the numbers between each.

CHAPTER 7

Working with Numbers

This chapter focuses on common operations involving numbers, including numeric computations. While SQL is not typically considered the first choice for complex computations, it is very efficient for day-to-day numeric chores.

 Some recipes in this chapter make use of aggregate functions and the GROUP BY clause. If you are not familiar with grouping, please read at least the first major section, called "Grouping," in Appendix A.

7.1 Computing an Average

Problem

You want to compute the average value in a column, either for all rows in a table or for some subset of rows. For example, you might want to find the average salary for all employees as well as the average salary for each department.

Solution

When computing the average of all employee salaries, simply apply the AVG function to the column containing those salaries. By excluding a WHERE clause, the average is computed against all non-NULL values:

```
1 select avg(sal) as avg_sal
2   from emp

    AVG_SAL
 ----------
 2073.21429
```

To compute the average salary for each department, use the GROUP BY clause to create a group corresponding to each department:

```
1 select deptno, avg(sal) as avg_sal
2   from emp
3 group by deptno

    DEPTNO    AVG_SAL
---------- ----------
        10 2916.66667
        20       2175
        30 1566.66667
```

Discussion

When finding an average where the whole table is the group or window, simply apply the AVG function to the column you are interested in without using the GROUP BY clause. It is important to realize that the function AVG ignores NULLs. The effect of NULL values being ignored can be seen here:

```
create table t2(sal integer)
insert into t2 values (10)
insert into t2 values (20)
insert into t2 values (null)
```

```
select avg(sal)        select distinct 30/2
  from t2                 from t2

AVG(SAL)                      30/2
----------               ----------
       15                        15
```

```
select avg(coalesce(sal,0))    select distinct 30/3
  from t2                         from t2

AVG(COALESCE(SAL,0))                  30/3
--------------------             ----------
                  10                     10
```

The COALESCE function will return the first non-NULL value found in the list of values that you pass. When NULL SAL values are converted to zero, the average changes. When invoking aggregate functions, always give thought to how you want NULLs handled.

The second part of the solution uses GROUP BY (line 3) to divide employee records into groups based on department affiliation. GROUP BY automatically causes aggregate functions such as AVG to execute and return a result for each group. In this example, AVG would execute once for each department-based group of employee records.

It is not necessary, by the way, to include GROUP BY columns in your select list. For example:

```
select avg(sal)
  from emp
 group by deptno

 AVG(SAL)
----------
2916.66667
      2175
1566.66667
```

You are still grouping by DEPTNO even though it is not in the SELECT clause. Including the column you are grouping by in the SELECT clause often improves readability, but is not mandatory. It is mandatory, however, to avoid placing columns in your SELECT list that are not also in your GROUP BY clause.

See Also

Appendix A for a refresher on GROUP BY functionality.

7.2   Finding the Min/Max Value in a Column

Problem

You want to find the highest and lowest values in a given column. For example, you want to find the highest and lowest salaries for all employees, as well as the highest and lowest salaries for each department.

Solution

When searching for the lowest and highest salaries for all employees, simply use the functions MIN and MAX, respectively:

```
1 select min(sal) as min_sal, max(sal) as max_sal
2   from emp

   MIN_SAL    MAX_SAL
---------- ----------
       800       5000
```

When searching for the lowest and highest salaries for each department, use the functions MIN and MAX with the GROUP BY clause:

```
1 select deptno, min(sal) as min_sal, max(sal) as max_sal
2   from emp
3  group by deptno

    DEPTNO    MIN_SAL    MAX_SAL
---------- ---------- ----------
        10       1300       5000
        20        800       3000
        30        950       2850
```

Discussion

When searching for the highest or lowest values, and in cases where the whole table is the group or window, simply apply the MIN or MAX function to the column you are interested in without using the GROUP BY clause.

Remember that the MIN and MAX functions ignore NULLs, and that you can have NULL groups as well as NULL values for columns in a group. The following are examples that ultimately lead to a query using GROUP BY that returns NULL values for two groups (DEPTNO 10 and 20):

```
select deptno, comm
  from emp
 where deptno in (10,30)
 order by 1

    DEPTNO       COMM
---------- ----------
        10
        10
        10
        30        300
        30        500
        30
        30          0
        30       1300
        30

select min(comm), max(comm)
  from emp

 MIN(COMM)  MAX(COMM)
---------- ----------
         0       1300

select deptno, min(comm), max(comm)
  from emp
 group by deptno

    DEPTNO  MIN(COMM)  MAX(COMM)
---------- ---------- ----------
        10
        20
        30          0       1300
```

Remember, as Appendix A points out, even if nothing other than aggregate functions are listed in the SELECT clause, you can still group by other columns in the table; for example:

```
select min(comm), max(comm)
  from emp
 group by deptno
```

```
MIN(COMM)  MAX(COMM)
---------- ----------
        0       1300
```

Here you are still grouping by DEPTNO even though it is not in the SELECT clause. Including the column you are grouping by in the SELECT clause often improves readability, but is not mandatory. It is mandatory, however, that any column in the SELECT list of a GROUP BY query also be listed in the GROUP BY clause.

See Also

Appendix A for a refresher on GROUP BY functionality.

7.3   Summing the Values in a Column

Problem

You want to compute the sum of all values, such as all employee salaries, in a column.

Solution

When computing a sum where the whole table is the group or window, simply apply the SUM function to the columns you are interested in without using the GROUP BY clause:

```
1 select sum(sal)
2   from emp
```

```
SUM(SAL)
----------
   29025
```

When creating multiple groups or windows of data, use the SUM function with the GROUP BY clause. The following example sums employee salaries by department:

```
1 select deptno, sum(sal) as total_for_dept
2   from emp
3 group by deptno
```

```
DEPTNO TOTAL_FOR_DEPT
---------- --------------
    10           8750
    20          10875
    30           9400
```

Discussion

When searching for the sum of all salaries for each department, you are creating groups or "windows" of data. Each employee's salary is added together to produce a total for his respective department. This is an example of aggregation in SQL because detailed information, such as each individual employee's salary, is not the focus; the focus is the end result for each department. It is important to note that the SUM function will ignore NULLs, but you can have NULL groups, which can be seen here. DEPTNO 10 does not have any employees who earn a commission, thus grouping by DEPTNO 10 while attempting to SUM the values in COMM will result in a group with a NULL value returned by SUM:

```
select deptno, comm
  from emp
 where deptno in (10,30)
 order by 1

    DEPTNO       COMM
---------- ----------
        10
        10
        10
        30        300
        30        500
        30
        30          0
        30       1300
        30
```

```
select sum(comm)
  from emp

 SUM(COMM)
----------
      2100
```

```
select deptno, sum(comm)
  from emp
 where deptno in (10,30)
 group by deptno

    DEPTNO  SUM(COMM)
---------- ----------
        10
        30       2100
```

See Also

Appendix A for a refresher on GROUP BY functionality.

7.4   Counting Rows in a Table

Problem

You want to count the number of rows in a table, or you wish to count the number of values in a column. For example, you want to find the total number of employees as well as the number of employees in each department.

Solution

When counting rows where the whole table is the group or window, simply use the COUNT function along with the "*" character:

```
1 select count(*)
2   from emp

 COUNT(*)
----------
       14
```

When creating multiple groups, or windows of data, use the COUNT function with the GROUP BY clause:

```
1 select deptno, count(*)
2   from emp
3  group by deptno

 DEPTNO   COUNT(*)
---------- ----------
       10          3
       20          5
       30          6
```

Discussion

When counting the number of employees for each department, you are creating groups or "windows" of data. Each employee found increments the count by one to produce a total for her respective department. This is an example of aggregation in SQL because detailed information, such as each individual employee's salary or job, is not the focus; the focus is the end result for each department. It is important to note that the COUNT function will ignore NULLs when passed a column name as an argument, but will include NULLs when passed the "*" character or any constant; consider:

```
select deptno, comm
  from emp

 DEPTNO       COMM
---------- ----------
       20
       30        300
       30        500
       20
       30       1300
       30
       10
       20
       10
       30          0
```

```
20
30
20
10
```

```
select count(*), count(deptno), count(comm), count('hello')
  from emp
```

```
COUNT(*) COUNT(DEPTNO) COUNT(COMM) COUNT('HELLO')
-------- ------------- ----------- --------------
      14            14           4             14
```

```
select deptno, count(*), count(comm), count('hello')
  from emp
group by deptno
```

```
DEPTNO   COUNT(*) COUNT(COMM) COUNT('HELLO')
-------- -------- ----------- --------------
      10        3           0              3
      20        5           0              5
      30        6           4              6
```

If all rows are null for the column passed to COUNT or if the table is empty, COUNT will return zero. It should also be noted that, even if nothing other than aggregate functions are specified in the SELECT clause, you can still group by other columns in the table; for example:

```
select count(*)
  from emp
group by deptno
```

```
COUNT(*)
----------
        3
        5
        6
```

Notice that you are still grouping by DEPTNO even though it is not in the SELECT clause. Including the column you are grouping by in the SELECT clause often improves readability, but is not mandatory. If you do include it (in the SELECT list), it is mandatory that is it listed in the GROUP BY clause.

See Also

Appendix A for a refresher on GROUP BY functionality.

7.5   Counting Values in a Column

Problem

You wish to count the number of non-NULL values in a column. For example, you'd like to find out how many employees are on commission.

Solution

Count the number of non-NULL values in the EMP table's COMM column:

```
select count(comm)
  from emp

COUNT(COMM)
-----------
          4
```

Discussion

When you "count star," as in COUNT(*), what you are really counting is rows (regardless of actual value, which is why rows containing NULL and non-NULL values are counted). But when you COUNT a column, you are counting the number of non-NULL values in that column. The previous recipe's discussion touches on this distinction. In this solution, COUNT(COMM) returns the number of non-NULL values in the COMM column. Since only commissioned employees have commissions, the result of COUNT(COMM) is the number of such employees.

7.6   Generating a Running Total

Problem

You want to calculate a running total of values in a column.

Solution

As an example, the following solutions show how to compute a running total of salaries for all employees. For readability, results are ordered by SAL whenever possible so that you can easily eyeball the progression of the running total.

DB2 and Oracle

Use the windowing version of the function SUM to compute a running total:

```
1 select ename, sal,
2        sum(sal) over (order by sal,empno) as running_total
3   from emp
4  order by 2
```

```
ENAME          SAL  RUNNING_TOTAL
----------  -------  -------------
SMITH           800            800
JAMES           950           1750
ADAMS          1100           2850
WARD           1250           4100
MARTIN         1250           5350
MILLER         1300           6650
TURNER         1500           8150
ALLEN          1600           9750
CLARK          2450          12200
BLAKE          2850          15050
JONES          2975          18025
SCOTT          3000          21025
FORD           3000          24025
KING           5000          29025
```

MySQL, PostgreSQL, and SQL Server

Use a scalar subquery to compute a running total (without the use of a window function such as SUM OVER, you cannot easily order the result set by SAL as in the DB2 and Oracle solution). Ultimately, the running total is correct (the final value is the same as the above recipe), but the intermediate values differ due to the lack of ordering:

```
1 select e.ename, e.sal,
2        (select sum(d.sal) from emp d
3            where d.empno <= e.empno) as running_total
4    from emp e
5  order by 3
```

```
ENAME          SAL  RUNNING_TOTAL
----------  -------  -------------
SMITH           800            800
ALLEN          1600           2400
WARD           1250           3650
JONES          2975           6625
MARTIN         1250           7875
BLAKE          2850          10725
CLARK          2450          13175
SCOTT          3000          16175
KING           5000          21175
TURNER         1500          22675
ADAMS          1100          23775
JAMES           950          24725
FORD           3000          27725
MILLER         1300          29025
```

Discussion

Generating a running total is one of the tasks made simple by the new ANSI windowing functions. For DBMSs that do not yet support these windowing functions, a scalar subquery (joining on a field with unique values) is required.

DB2 and Oracle

The windowing function SUM OVER makes generating a running total a simple task. The ORDER BY clause in the solution includes not only the SAL column, but also the EMPNO column (which is the primary key) to avoid duplicate values in the running total. The column RUNNING_TOTAL2 in the following example illustrates the problem that you might otherwise have with duplicates:

```
select empno, sal,
       sum(sal)over(order by sal,empno) as running_total1,
       sum(sal)over(order by sal) as running_total2
  from emp
 order by 2
```

ENAME	SAL	RUNNING_TOTAL1	RUNNING_TOTAL2
SMITH	800	800	800
JAMES	950	1750	1750
ADAMS	1100	2850	2850
WARD	1250	4100	5350
MARTIN	1250	5350	5350
MILLER	1300	6650	6650
TURNER	1500	8150	8150
ALLEN	1600	9750	9750
CLARK	2450	12200	12200
BLAKE	2850	15050	15050
JONES	2975	18025	18025
SCOTT	3000	21025	24025
FORD	3000	24025	24025
KING	5000	29025	29025

The values in RUNNING_TOTAL2 for WARD, MARTIN, SCOTT, and FORD are incorrect. Their salaries occur more than once, and those duplicates are summed together and added to the running total. This is why EMPNO (which is unique) is needed to produce the (correct) results that you see in RUNNING_TOTAL1. Consider this: for ADAMS you see 2850 for RUNNING_TOTAL1 and RUNNING_TOTAL2. Add WARD's salary of 1250 to 2850 and you get 4100, yet RUNNING_TOTAL2 returns 5350. Why? Since WARD and MARTIN have the same SAL, their two 1250 salaries are added together to yield 2500, which is then added to 2850 to arrive at 5350 for both WARD and MARTIN. By specifying a combination of columns to order by that cannot result in duplicate values (e.g., any combination of SAL and EMPNO is unique), you ensure the correct progression of the running total.

MySQL, PostgreSQL, and SQL Server

Until windowing functions are fully supported for these DBMSs, you can use a scalar subquery to compute a running total. You must join on a column with unique values; otherwise the running total will have incorrect values in the event that duplicate salaries exist. The key to this recipe's Solution is the join on D.EMPNO to E.

EMPNO, which returns (sums) every D.SAL where D.EMPNO is less than or equal E.EMPNO. This can be understood easily by rewriting the scalar subquery as a join for a handful of the employees:

```
select e.ename as ename1, e.empno as empno1, e.sal as sal1,
       d.ename as ename2, d.empno as empno2, d.sal as sal2
  from emp e, emp d
 where d.empno <= e.empno
   and e.empno = 7566
```

ENAME	EMPNO1	SAL1	ENAME	EMPNO2	SAL2
JONES	7566	2975	SMITH	7369	800
JONES	7566	2975	ALLEN	7499	1600
JONES	7566	2975	WARD	7521	1250
JONES	7566	2975	JONES	7566	2975

Every value in EMPNO2 is compared against every value in EMPNO1. For every row where the value in EMPNO2 is less than or equal to the value in EMPNO1, the value in SAL2 is included in the sum. In this snippet, the EMPNO values for employees Smith, Allen, Ward, and Jones are compared against the EMPNO of Jones. Since all four employees' EMPNOs meet the condition of being less than or equal to Jones' EMPNO, those salaries are summed. Any employee whose EMPNO is greater than Jones' is not included in the SUM (in this snippet). The way the full query works is by summing all the salaries where the corresponding EMPNO is less than or equal to 7934 (Miller's EMPNO), which is the highest in the table.

7.7   Generating a Running Product

Problem

You want to compute a running product on a numeric column. The operation is similar to Recipe 7.6 but using multiplication instead of addition.

Solution

By way of example, the solutions all compute running products of employee salaries. While a running product of salaries may not be all that useful, the technique can easily be applied to other, more useful domains.

DB2 and Oracle

Use the windowing function SUM OVER and take advantage of the fact that you can simulate multiplication by adding logarithms:

```
1 select empno,ename,sal,
2        exp(sum(ln(sal))over(order by sal,empno)) as running_prod
3   from emp
4  where deptno = 10
```

EMPNO	ENAME	SAL	RUNNING_PROD
7934	MILLER	1300	1300
7782	CLARK	2450	3185000
7839	KING	5000	15925000000

It is not valid in SQL to compute logarithms of values less than or equal to zero. If you have such values in your tables you need to avoid passing those invalid values to SQL's LN function. Precautions against invalid values and NULLs are not provided in this solution for the sake of readability, but you should consider whether to place such precautions in production code that you write. If you absolutely must work with negative and zero values, then this solution may not work for you.

An alternative, Oracle-only solution is to use the MODEL clause that became available in Oracle Database 10g. In the following example, each SAL is returned as a negative number to show that negative values will not cause a problem for the running product:

```
1 select empno, ename, sal, tmp as running_prod
2  from (
3 select empno,ename,-sal as sal
4  from emp
5  where deptno=10
6        )
7 model
8   dimension by(row_number( )over(order by sal desc) rn )
9   measures(sal, 0 tmp, empno, ename)
10  rules (
11    tmp[any] = case when sal[cv( )-1] is null then sal[cv( )]
12                    else tmp[cv( )-1]*sal[cv( )]
13                end
14  )
```

EMPNO	ENAME	SAL	RUNNING_PROD
7934	MILLER	-1300	-1300
7782	CLARK	-2450	3185000
7839	KING	-5000	-15925000000

MySQL, PostgreSQL, and SQL Server

You still use the approach of summing logarithms, but these platforms do not support windowing functions, so use a scalar subquery instead:

```
1 select e.empno,e.ename,e.sal,
2        (select exp(sum(ln(d.sal)))
3           from emp d
4          where d.empno <= e.empno
5            and e.deptno=d.deptno) as running_prod
6  from emp e
7 where e.deptno=10
```

```
EMPNO ENAME        SAL      RUNNING_PROD
----- ---------- ----   ---------------------
 7782 CLARK       2450                    2450
 7839 KING        5000                12250000
 7934 MILLER      1300             15925000000
```

SQL Server users use LOG instead of LN.

Discussion

Except for the MODEL clause solution, which is only usable with Oracle Database 10g or later, all the solutions take advantage of the fact that you can multiply two numbers by:

1. Computing their respective natural logarithms

2. Summing those logarithms

3. Raising the result to the power of the mathematical constant *e* (using the EXP function)

The one caveat when using this approach is that it doesn't work for summing zero or negative values, because any value less than or equal to zero is out of range for an SQL logarithm.

DB2 and Oracle

For an explanation of how the window function SUM OVER works, see Recipe 7.6.

In Oracle Database 10g and later, you can generate running products via the MODEL clause. Using the MODEL clause along with the window function ROW_NUMBER allows you to easily access prior rows. Each item in the MEASURES list can be accessed like an array. The arrays can then be searched by using the items in the DIMENSIONS list (which are the values returned by ROW_NUMBER, alias RN):

```
select empno, ename, sal, tmp as running_prod,rn
  from (
select empno,ename,-sal as sal
  from emp
 where deptno=10
      )
  model
    dimension by(row_number()over(order by sal desc) rn )
    measures(sal, 0 tmp, empno, ename)
    rules ()

EMPNO ENAME            SAL RUNNING_PROD          RN
----- ---------- ---------- ------------ ----------
 7934 MILLER         -1300            0           1
 7782 CLARK          -2450            0           2
 7839 KING           -5000            0           3
```

Observe that SAL[1] has a value of −1300. Because the numbers are increasing by one with no gaps, you can reference prior rows by subtracting one. The RULES clause:

```
rules (
   tmp[any] = case when  sal[cv( )-1] is null then sal[cv( )]
                 else tmp[cv( )-1]*sal[cv( )]
              end
)
```

uses the built-in operator, ANY, to work through each row without hard-coding. ANY in this case will be the values 1, 2, and 3. TMP[*n*] is initialized to zero. A value is assigned to TMP[*n*] by evaluating the current value (the function CV returns the current value) of the corresponding SAL row. TMP[1] is initially zero and SAL[1] is −1300. There is no value for SAL[0] so TMP[1] is set to SAL[1]. After TMP[1] is set, the next row is TMP[2]. First SAL[1] is evaluated (SAL[CV( )−1] is SAL[1] because the current value of ANY is now 2). SAL[1] is not null, it is −1300, so TMP[2] is set to the product of TMP[1] and SAL[2]. This is continued for all the rows.

MySQL, PostgreSQL, and SQL Server

See Recipe 7.6 for an explanation of the subquery approach used for the MySQL, PostgreSQL, and SQL Server solutions.

Be aware that the output of the subquery-based solution is slightly different from that of the Oracle and DB2 solutions due to the EMPNO comparison (the running product is computed in a different order). Like a running total, the summation is driven by the predicate of the scalar subquery; the ordering of rows is by EMPNO for this solution whereas the Oracle/DB2 solution order is by SAL.

7.8   Calculating a Running Difference

Problem

You want to compute a running difference on values in a numeric column. For example, you want to compute a running difference on the salaries in DEPTNO 10. You would like to return the following result set:

```
ENAME          SAL RUNNING_DIFF
---------- ---------- ------------
MILLER         1300         1300
CLARK          2450        -1150
KING           5000        -6150
```

Solution

DB2 and Oracle

Use the window function SUM OVER to create a running difference:

```
1  select ename,sal,
2         sum(case when rn = 1 then sal else -sal end)
3          over(order by sal,empno) as running_diff
4    from (
5  select empno,ename,sal,
6         row_number( )over(order by sal,empno) as rn
7    from emp
8   where deptno = 10
9        ) x
```

MySQL, PostgreSQL, and SQL Server

Use a scalar subquery to compute a running difference:

```
1 select a.empno, a.ename, a.sal,
2        (select case when a.empno = min(b.empno) then sum(b.sal)
3                     else sum(-b.sal)
4               end
5          from emp b
6         where b.empno <= a.empno
7           and b.deptno = a.deptno ) as rnk
8    from emp a
9   where a.deptno = 10
```

Discussion

The solutions are identical to those of Recipe 7.6. The only difference is that all values for SAL are returned as negative values with the exception of the first (you want the starting point to be the first SAL in DEPTNO 10).

7.9   Calculating a Mode

Problem

You want to find the mode (for those of you who don't recall, the *mode* in mathematics is the element that appears most frequently for a given set of data) of the values in a column. For example, you wish to find mode of the salaries in DEPTNO 20. Based on the following salaries:

```
select sal
  from emp
 where deptno = 20
 order by sal
```

```
    SAL
----------
       800
      1100
      2975
      3000
      3000
```

the mode is 3000.

Solution

DB2 and SQL Server

Use the window function DENSE_RANK to rank the counts of the salaries to facilitate extracting the mode:

```
 1  select sal
 2    from (
 3  select sal,
 4         dense_rank( )over(order by cnt desc) as rnk
 5    from (
 6  select sal, count(*) as cnt
 8    from emp
 9   where deptno = 20
10   group by sal
11         ) x
12         ) y
13   where rnk = 1
```

Oracle

Users on Oracle8i Database can use the solution provided for DB2. If you are on Oracle9i Database and later, you can use the KEEP extension to the aggregate function MAX to find the mode SAL. One important note is that if there are ties, i.e., multiple rows that are the mode, the solution using KEEP will only keep one, and that is the one with the highest salary. If you want to see all modes (if more than one exists), you must modify this solution or simply use the DB2 solution presented above. In this case, since 3000 is the mode SAL in DEPTNO 20 and is also the highest SAL, this solution is sufficient:

```
 1  select max(sal)
 2         keep(dense_rank first order by cnt desc) sal
 3    from (
 4  select sal, count(*) cnt
 5    from emp
 6   where deptno=20
 7   group by sal
 8         )
```

MySQL and PostgreSQL

Use a subquery to find the mode:

```
1  select sal
2    from emp
3   where deptno = 20
4   group by sal
5  having count(*) >= all ( select count(*)
6                             from emp
7                            where deptno = 20
8                            group by sal )
```

Discussion

DB2 and SQL Server

The inline view X returns each SAL and the number of times it occurs. Inline view Y uses the window function DENSE_RANK (which allows for ties) to sort the results. The results are ranked based on the number of times each SAL occurs as is seen below:

```
1 select sal,
2        dense_rank( )over(order by cnt desc) as rnk
3   from (
4 select sal,count(*) as cnt
5   from emp
6  where deptno = 20
7  group by sal
8        ) x
```

SAL	RNK
3000	1
800	2
1100	2
2975	2

The outermost portion of query simply keeps the row(s) where RNK is 1.

Oracle

The inline view returns each SAL and the number of times it occurs and is shown below:

```
select sal, count(*) cnt
  from emp
 where deptno=20
 group by sal
```

SAL	CNT
800	1
1100	1
2975	1
3000	2

The next step is to use the KEEP extension of the aggregate function MAX to find the mode. If you analyze the KEEP clause shown below you will notice three subclauses, DENSE_RANK, FIRST, and ORDER BY CNT DESC:

```
keep(dense_rank first order by cnt desc)
```

What this does is extremely convenient for finding the mode. The KEEP clause determines which SAL will be returned by MAX by looking at the value of CNT returned by the inline view. Working from right to left, the values for CNT are ordered in descending order, then the first is kept of all the values for CNT returned in DENSE_RANK order. Looking at the result set from the inline view, you can see that 3000 has the highest CNT of 2. The MAX(SAL) returned is the greatest SAL that has the greatest CNT, in this case 3000.

See Also

Recipe 11.11 for a deeper discussion of Oracle's KEEP extension of aggregate functions.

MySQL and PostgreSQL

The subquery returns the number of times each SAL occurs. The outer query returns any SAL that has a number of occurrences greater than or equal to all of the counts returned by the subquery (or to put it another way, the outer query returns the most common salaries in DEPTNO 20).

7.10 Calculating a Median

Problem

You want to calculate the median (for those of who do not recall, the *median* is the value of the middle member of a set of ordered elements) value for a column of numeric values. For example, you want to find the median of the salaries in DEPTNO 20. Based on the following salaries:

```
select sal
  from emp
 where deptno = 20
 order by sal

       SAL
----------
       800
      1100
      2975
      3000
      3000
```

the median is 2975.

Solution

Other than the Oracle solution (which uses supplied functions to compute a median), all of the solutions are based on the method described by Rozenshtein, Abramovich, and Birger in *Optimizing Transact-SQL: Advanced Programming Techniques* (SQL Forum Press, 1997). The introduction of window functions allows for a more efficient solution compared to the traditional self join.

DB2

Use the window functions COUNT(*) OVER and ROW_NUMBER to find the median:

```
1   select avg(sal)
2     from (
3   select sal,
4          count(*) over() total,
5          cast(count(*) over() as decimal)/2 mid,
6          ceil(cast(count(*) over() as decimal)/2) next,
7          row_number() over (order by sal) rn
8      from emp
9     where deptno = 20
10        ) x
11   where ( mod(total,2) = 0
12           and rn in ( mid, mid+1 )
13         )
14      or ( mod(total,2) = 1
15           and rn = next
16         )
```

MySQL and PostgreSQL

Use a self join to find the median:

```
1   select avg(sal)
2     from (
3   select e.sal
4     from emp e, emp d
5    where e.deptno = d.deptno
6      and e.deptno = 20
7    group by e.sal
8   having sum(case when e.sal = d.sal then 1 else 0 end)
9                     >= abs(sum(sign(e.sal - d.sal)))
10        )
```

Oracle

Use the functions MEDIAN (Oracle Database 10g) or PERCENTILE_CONT (Oracle9i Database):

```
1 select median(sal)
2   from emp
3  where deptno=20
```

```
1 select percentile_cont(0.5)
2        within group(order by sal)
3   from emp
4  where deptno=20
```

Use the DB2 solution for Oracle8i Database. For versions prior to Oracle8i Database you can use the PostgreSQL/MySQL solution.

SQL Server

Use the window functions COUNT(*) OVER and ROW_NUMBER to find the median:

```
1   select avg(sal)
2     from (
3   select sal,
4          count(*)over( ) total,
5          cast(count(*)over( ) as decimal)/2 mid,
6          ceiling(cast(count(*)over( ) as decimal)/2) next,
7          row_number( )over(order by sal) rn
8     from emp
9    where deptno = 20
10          ) x
11    where ( total%2 = 0
12            and rn in ( mid, mid+1 )
13          )
14       or ( total%2 = 1
15            and rn = next
16          )
```

Discussion

DB2 and SQL Server

The only difference between the DB2 and SQL Server solutions is a small point of syntax: SQL Server uses "%" for modulo and DB2 uses the function MOD; otherwise they are the same. Inline view X returns three different counts, TOTAL, MID, and NEXT, along with RN, generated by ROW_NUMBER. These additional columns help determine how to find the median. Examine the result set for inline view X to see what these columns represent:

```
select sal,
       count(*)over( ) total,
       cast(count(*)over( ) as decimal)/2 mid,
       ceil(cast(count(*)over( ) as decimal)/2) next,
       row_number( )over(order by sal) rn
  from emp
 where deptno = 20
```

SAL	TOTAL	MID	NEXT	RN
800	5	2.5	3	1
1100	5	2.5	3	2
2975	5	2.5	3	3
3000	5	2.5	3	4
3000	5	2.5	3	5

To find the median, the values for SAL must be ordered from lowest to highest. Since DEPTNO 20 has an odd number of employees, the median is simply the SAL that is located in the position where RN equals NEXT (the position that represents the smallest whole number larger than the total number of employees divided by two).

The first part of the WHERE clause (lines 11–13) is not satisfied if there are an odd number of rows returned by the result set. If you know that the result set will always be odd, you can simplify to:

```
select avg(sal)
  from (
select sal,
       count(*)over( ) total,
       ceil(cast(count(*)over( ) as decimal)/2) next,
       row_number( )over(order by sal) rn
  from emp
 where deptno = 20
      ) x
 where rn = next
```

Unfortunately, if you have an even number of rows in the result set, the simplified solution will not work. The original solution handles even-numbered rows by using the values in the column MID. Consider what the results from inline view X would look like for DEPTNO 30, which has six employees:

```
select sal,
       count(*)over( ) total,
       cast(count(*)over( ) as decimal)/2 mid,
       ceil(cast(count(*)over( ) as decimal)/2) next,
       row_number( )over(order by sal) rn
  from emp
 where deptno = 30
```

SAL	TOTAL	MID	NEXT	RN
950	6	3	3	1
1250	6	3	3	2
1250	6	3	3	3
1500	6	3	3	4
1600	6	3	3	5
2850	6	3	3	6

Since there are an even number of rows returned, the median is computed by taking the average of two rows; the row where RN equals MID and the row where RN equals MID + 1.

MySQL and PostgreSQL

The median is computed by first self joining table EMP, which returns a Cartesian product for all the salaries (but the GROUP BY on E.SAL will prevent duplicates from being returned). The HAVING clause uses the function SUM to count the number of times E.SAL equals D.SAL; if this count is greater than or equal to the number of times E.SAL is greater than D.SAL then that row is the median. You can observe this by moving the SUM into the SELECT list:

```
select e.sal,
       sum(case when e.sal=d.sal
                then 1 else 0 end) as cnt1,
       abs(sum(sign(e.sal - d.sal))) as cnt2
  from emp e, emp d
 where e.deptno = d.deptno
   and e.deptno = 20
 group by e.sal


 SAL CNT1 CNT2
 ---- ---- ----
 800    1    4
1100    1    2
2975    1    0
3000    4    6
```

Oracle

If you are on Oracle Database 10g or Oracle9i Database, you can leave the work of computing a median to functions supplied by Oracle. If you are running Oracle8i Database, you can use the DB2 solution. Otherwise you must use the PostgreSQL solution. While the MEDIAN function obviously computes a median, it may not be at all obvious that PERCENTILE_CONT does so as well. The argument passed to PERCENTILE_CONT, 0.5, is a percentile value. The clause, WITHIN GROUP (ORDER BY SAL), determines which sorted rows PERCENTILE_CONT will search (remember, a median is the middle value from a set of ordered values). The value returned is the value from the sorted rows that falls into the given percentile (in this case, 0.5, which is the middle because the boundary values are 0 and 1).

7.11 Determining the Percentage of a Total

Problem

You want to determine the percentage that values in a specific column represent against a total. For example, you want to determine what percentage of all salaries are the salaries in DEPTNO 10 (the percentage that DEPTNO 10 salaries contribute to the total).

Solution

In general, computing a percentage against a total in SQL is no different than doing so on paper; simply divide, then multiply. In this example you want to find the percentage of total salaries in table EMP that come from DEPTNO 10. To do that, simply find the salaries for DEPTNO 10, and then divide by the total salary for the table. As the last step, multiply by 100 to return a value that represents a percent.

MySQL and PostgreSQL

Divide the sum of the salaries in DEPTNO 10 by the sum of all salaries:

```
1 select (sum(
2          case when deptno = 10 then sal end)/sum(sal)
3         )*100 as pct
4    from emp
```

DB2, Oracle, and SQL Server

Use an inline view with the window function SUM OVER to find the sum of all salaries along with the sum of all salaries in DEPTNO 10. Then do the division and multiplication in the outer query:

```
1  select distinct (d10/total)*100 as pct
2    from (
3  select deptno,
4         sum(sal)over() total,
5         sum(sal)over(partition by deptno) d10
6    from emp
7         ) x
8   where deptno=10
```

Discussion

MySQL and PostgreSQL

The CASE statement conveniently returns only the salaries from DEPTNO 10. They are then summed and divided by the sum of all the salaries. Because NULLs are ignored by aggregates, an ELSE clause is not needed in the CASE statement. To see exactly which values are divided, execute the query without the division:

```
select sum(case when deptno = 10 then sal end) as d10,
       sum(sal)
  from emp

D10   SUM(SAL)
----  ---------
8750     29025
```

Depending on how you define SAL, you may need to include explicit casts when performing division. For example, on DB2, SQL Server, and PostgreSQL, if SAL is stored as an integer, you can cast to decimal to get the correct answer, as seen below:

```
select (cast(
         sum(case when deptno = 10 then sal end)
            as decimal)/sum(sal)
        )*100 as pct
  from emp
```

DB2, Oracle, and SQL Server

As an alternative to the traditional solution, this solution uses window functions to compute a percentage relative to the total. For DB2 and SQL Server, if you've stored SAL as an integer, you'll need to cast before dividing:

```
select distinct
       cast(d10 as decimal)/total*100 as pct
  from (
select deptno,
       sum(sal)over() total,
       sum(sal)over(partition by deptno) d10
  from emp
       ) x
 where deptno=10
```

It is important to keep in mind that window functions are applied after the WHERE clause is evaluated. Thus, the filter on DEPTNO cannot be performed in inline view X. Consider the results of inline view X without and with the filter on DEPTNO. First without:

```
select deptno,
       sum(sal)over() total,
       sum(sal)over(partition by deptno) d10
  from emp
```

DEPTNO	TOTAL	D10
10	29025	8750
10	29025	8750
10	29025	8750
20	29025	10875
20	29025	10875
20	29025	10875
20	29025	10875
20	29025	10875
30	29025	9400
30	29025	9400
30	29025	9400
30	29025	9400
30	29025	9400
30	29025	9400

and now with:

```
select deptno,
       sum(sal)over( ) total,
       sum(sal)over(partition by deptno) d10
  from emp
 where deptno=10

DEPTNO    TOTAL      D10
------ --------- ---------
    10     8750      8750
    10     8750      8750
    10     8750      8750
```

Because window functions are applied after the WHERE clause, the value for TOTAL represents the sum of all salaries in DEPTNO 10 only. But to solve the problem you want the TOTAL to represent the sum of all salaries, period. That's why the filter on DEPTNO must happen outside of inline view X.

7.12 Aggregating Nullable Columns

Problem

You want to perform an aggregation on a column, but the column is nullable. You want the accuracy of your aggregation to be preserved, but are concerned because aggregate functions ignore NULLs. For example, you want to determine the average commission for employees in DEPTNO 30, but there are some employees who do not earn a commission (COMM is NULL for those employees). Because NULLs are ignored by aggregates, the accuracy of the output is compromised. You would like to somehow include NULL values in your aggregation.

Solution

Use the COALESCE function to convert NULLs to 0, so they will be included in the aggregation:

```
1  select avg(coalesce(comm,0)) as avg_comm
2    from emp
3   where deptno=30
```

Discussion

When working with aggregate functions, keep in mind that NULLs are ignored. Consider the output of the solution without using the COALESCE function:

```
select avg(comm)
  from emp
 where deptno=30
```

```
AVG(COMM)
---------
      550
```

This query shows an average commission of 550 for DEPTNO 30, but a quick examination of those rows:

```
select ename, comm
  from emp
 where deptno=30
order by comm desc

ENAME        COMM
---------- ---------
BLAKE
JAMES
MARTIN      1400
WARD         500
ALLEN        300
TURNER         0
```

shows that only four of the six employees can earn a commission. The sum of all commissions in DEPTNO 30 is 2200, and the average should be 2200/6, not 2200/4. By excluding the COALESCE function, you answer the question, "What is the average commission of employees in DEPTNO 30 *who can earn a commission?*" rather than "What is the average commission of all employees in DEPTNO 30?" When working with aggregates, remember to treat NULLs accordingly.

7.13 Computing Averages Without High and Low Values

Problem

You want to compute an average, but you wish to exclude the highest and lowest values in order to (hopefully) reduce the effect of skew. For example, you want to compute the average salary of all employees excluding the highest and lowest salaries.

Solution

MySQL and PostgreSQL

Use subqueries to exclude high and low values:

```
1 select avg(sal)
2   from emp
3  where sal not in (
4     (select min(sal) from emp),
5     (select max(sal) from emp)
6  )
```

DB2, Oracle, and SQL Server

Use an inline view with the windowing functions MAX OVER and MIN OVER to generate a result set from which you can easily eliminate the high and low values:

```
1   select avg(sal)
2     from (
3   select sal, min(sal)over() min_sal, max(sal)over() max_sal
4     from emp
5         ) x
6   where sal not in (min_sal,max_sal)
```

Discussion

MySQL and PostgreSQL

The subqueries return the highest and lowest salaries in the table. By using NOT IN against the values returned, you exclude the highest and lowest salaries from the average. Keep in mind that if there are duplicates (if multiple employees have the highest or lowest salaries), they will all be excluded from the average. If your goal is to exclude only a single instance of the high and low values, simply subtract them from the SUM and then divide:

```
select (sum(sal)-min(sal)-max(sal))/(count(*)-2)
  from emp
```

DB2, Oracle, and SQL Server

Inline view X returns each salary along with the highest and lowest salary:

```
select sal, min(sal)over() min_sal, max(sal)over() max_sal
  from emp
```

SAL	MIN_SAL	MAX_SAL
800	800	5000
1600	800	5000
1250	800	5000
2975	800	5000
1250	800	5000
2850	800	5000
2450	800	5000
3000	800	5000
5000	800	5000
1500	800	5000
1100	800	5000
950	800	5000
3000	800	5000
1300	800	5000

You can access the high and low salary at every row, so finding which salaries are highest and/or lowest is trivial. The outer query filters the rows returned from inline view X such that any salary that matches either MIN_SAL or MAX_SAL is excluded from the average.

7.14 Converting Alphanumeric Strings into Numbers

Problem

You have alphanumeric data and would like to return numbers only. You want to return the number 123321 from the string "paul123f321".

Solution

DB2

Use the functions TRANSLATE and REPLACE to extract numeric characters from an alphanumeric string:

```
1 select cast(
2        replace(
3        translate( 'paul123f321',
4                   repeat('#',26),
5                   'abcdefghijklmnopqrstuvwxyz'),'#','')
6        as integer ) as num
7   from t1
```

Oracle and PostgreSQL

Use the functions TRANSLATE and REPLACE to extract numeric characters from an alphanumeric string:

```
1 select cast(
2        replace(
3        translate( 'paul123f321',
4                   'abcdefghijklmnopqrstuvwxyz',
5                   rpad('#',26,'#')),'#','')
6        as integer ) as num
7   from t1
```

MySQL and SQL Server

As of the time of this writing, neither vendor supports the TRANSLATE function, thus a solution will not be provided.

Discussion

The only difference between the two solutions is syntax; DB2 uses the function REPEAT rather than RPAD and the parameter list for TRANSLATE is in a different order. The following explanation uses the Oracle/PostgreSQL solution but is relevant to DB2 as well. If you run query inside out (starting with TRANSLATE only), you'll see this is very simple. First, TRANSLATE converts any non-numeric character to an instance of "#":

```
select translate( 'paul123f321',
                  'abcdefghijklmnopqrstuvwxyz',
                  rpad('#',26,'#')) as num

   from t1


NUM
-----------
####123#321
```

Since all non-numeric characters are now represented by "#", simply use REPLACE to remove them, then cast the result to a number. This particular example is extremely simple because the data is alphanumeric. If additional characters can be stored, rather than fishing for those characters, it is easier to approach this problem differently: rather than finding non-numeric characters and then removing them, find all numeric characters and remove anything that is not amongst them. The following example will help clarify this technique:

```
select replace(
       translate('paul123f321',
            replace(translate( 'paul123f321',
                        '0123456789',
                        rpad('#',10,'#')),'#',''),
                  rpad('#',length('paul123f321'),'#')),'#','') as num

   from t1


NUM
------
123321
```

This solution looks a bit more convoluted than the original but is not so bad once you break it down. Observe the innermost call to TRANSLATE:

```
select translate( 'paul123f321',
                  '0123456789',
                  rpad('#',10,'#'))

   from t1


TRANSLATE('
-----------
paul###f###
```

So, the initial approach is different; rather than replacing each non-numeric character with an instance of "#", you replace each numeric character with an instance of "#". The next step removes all instances of "#", thus leaving only non-numeric characters:

```
select replace(translate( 'paul123f321',
                           '0123456789',
                           rpad('#',10,'#')),'#','')
  from t1

REPLA
-----
paulf
```

The next step is to call TRANSLATE again, this time to replace each of the non-numeric characters (from the query above) with an instance of "#" in the original string:

```
select translate('paul123f321',
       replace(translate( 'paul123f321',
                          '0123456789',
                          rpad('#',10,'#')),'#',''),
               rpad('#',length('paul123f321'),'#'))
  from t1

TRANSLATE('
-----------
####123#321
```

At this point, stop and examine the outermost call to TRANSLATE. The second parameter to RPAD (or the second parameter to REPEAT for DB2) is the length of the original string. This is convenient to use since no character can occur enough times to be greater than the string it is part of. Now that all non-numeric characters are replaced by instances of "#", the last step is to use REPLACE to remove all instances of "#". Now you are left with a number.

7.15 Changing Values in a Running Total

Problem

You want to modify the values in a running total depending on the values in another column. Consider a scenario where you want to display the transaction history of a credit card account along with the current balance after each transaction. The following view, V, will be used in this example:

```
create view V (id,amt,trx)
as
select 1, 100, 'PR' from t1 union all
select 2, 100, 'PR' from t1 union all
select 3, 50,  'PY' from t1 union all
```

```
select 4, 100, 'PR' from t1 union all
select 5, 200, 'PY' from t1 union all
select 6, 50,  'PY' from t1

select * from V
```

```
ID        AMT TR
--  ---------- --
 1        100 PR
 2        100 PR
 3         50 PY
 4        100 PR
 5        200 PY
 6         50 PY
```

The ID column uniquely identifies each transaction. The AMT column represents the amount of money involved in each transaction (either a purchase or a payment). The TRX column defines the type of transaction; a payment is "PY" and a purchase is "PR." If the value for TRX is PY, you want the current value for AMT subtracted from the running total; if the value for TRX is PR, you want the current value for AMT added to the running total. Ultimately you want to return the following result set:

```
TRX_TYPE        AMT    BALANCE
--------  ----------  ----------
PURCHASE        100        100
PURCHASE        100        200
PAYMENT          50        150
PURCHASE        100        250
PAYMENT         200         50
PAYMENT          50          0
```

Solution

DB2 and Oracle

Use the window function SUM OVER to create the running total along with a CASE expression to determine the type of transaction:

```
 1   select case when trx = 'PY'
 2               then 'PAYMENT'
 3               else 'PURCHASE'
 4          end trx_type,
 5          amt,
 6          sum(
 7            case when trx = 'PY'
 8                 then -amt else amt
 9            end
10          ) over (order by id,amt) as balance
11     from V
```

MySQL, PostgreSQL, and SQL Server

Use a scalar subquery to create the running total along with a CASE expression to determine the type of transaction:

```
1  select case when v1.trx = 'PY'
2              then 'PAYMENT'
3              else 'PURCHASE'
4         end as trx_type,
5         v1.amt,
6         (select sum(
7                     case when v2.trx = 'PY'
8                          then -v2.amt else v2.amt
9                     end
10                  )
11           from V v2
12          where v2.id <= v1.id) as balance
13    from V v1
```

Discussion

The CASE expression determines whether the current AMT is added or deducted from the running total. If the transaction is a payment, the AMT is changed to a negative value, thus reducing the amount of the running total. The result of the CASE expression is seen below:

```
select case when trx = 'PY'
            then 'PAYMENT'
            else 'PURCHASE'
       end trx_type,
       case when trx = 'PY'
            then -amt else amt
       end as amt
  from V

TRX_TYPE       AMT
--------   ---------
PURCHASE       100
PURCHASE       100
PAYMENT        -50
PURCHASE       100
PAYMENT       -200
PAYMENT        -50
```

After evaluating the transaction type, the values for AMT are then added to or subtracted from the running total. For an explanation on how the window function, SUM OVER, or the scalar subquery creates the running total, see Recipe 7.6.

CHAPTER 8

Date Arithmetic

This chapter introduces techniques for performing simple date arithmetic. Recipes cover common tasks like adding days to dates, finding the number of business days between dates, and finding the difference between dates in days.

Being able to successfully manipulate dates with your RDBMS's built-in functions can greatly improve your productivity. For all the recipes in this chapter, I try to take advantage of each RDBMS's built-in functions. In addition, I have chosen to use one date format for all the recipes, "DD-MON-YYYY". I chose to do this because I believe it will benefit those of you who work with one RDBMS and want to learn others. Seeing one standard format will help you focus on the different techniques and functions provided by each RDBMS without having to worry about default date formats.

 This chapter focuses on basic date arithmetic. You'll find more advanced date recipes in the following chapter. The recipes presented in this chapter use simple date data types. If you are using more complex date data types you will need to adjust the solutions accordingly.

8.1 Adding and Subtracting Days, Months, and Years

Problem

You need to add or subtract some number of days, months, or years from a date. For example, using the HIREDATE for employee CLARK you want to return six different dates: five days before and after CLARK was hired, five months before and after CLARK was hired, and, finally, five years before and after CLARK was hired. CLARK was hired on "09-JUN-1981", so you want to return the following result set:

```
HD_MINUS_5D HD_PLUS_5D  HD_MINUS_5M HD_PLUS_5M  HD_MINUS_5Y HD_PLUS_5Y
----------- ----------- ----------- ----------- ----------- -----------
04-JUN-1981 14-JUN-1981 09-JAN-1981 09-NOV-1981 09-JUN-1976 09-JUN-1986
12-NOV-1981 22-NOV-1981 17-JUN-1981 17-APR-1982 17-NOV-1976 17-NOV-1986
18-JAN-1982 28-JAN-1982 23-AUG-1981 23-JUN-1982 23-JAN-1977 23-JAN-1987
```

Solution

DB2

Standard addition and subtraction is allowed on date values, but any value that you add to or subtract from a date must be followed by the unit of time it represents:

```
1 select hiredate -5 day   as hd_minus_5D,
2        hiredate +5 day   as hd_plus_5D,
3        hiredate -5 month as hd_minus_5M,
4        hiredate +5 month as hd_plus_5M,
5        hiredate -5 year  as hd_minus_5Y,
6        hiredate +5 year  as hd_plus_5Y
7   from emp
8  where deptno = 10
```

Oracle

Use standard addition and subtraction for days, and use the ADD_MONTHS function to add and subtract months and years:

```
1 select hiredate-5               as hd_minus_5D,
2        hiredate+5               as hd_plus_5D,
3        add_months(hiredate,-5)   as hd_minus_5M,
4        add_months(hiredate,5)    as hd_plus_5M,
5        add_months(hiredate,-5*12) as hd_minus_5Y,
6        add_months(hiredate,5*12)  as hd_plus_5Y
7   from emp
8  where deptno = 10
```

PostgreSQL

Use standard addition and subtraction with the INTERVAL keyword specifying the unit of time to add or subtract. Single quotes are required when specifying an INTERVAL value:

```
1 select hiredate - interval '5 day'   as hd_minus_5D,
2        hiredate + interval '5 day'   as hd_plus_5D,
3        hiredate - interval '5 month' as hd_minus_5M,
4        hiredate + interval '5 month' as hd_plus_5M,
5        hiredate - interval '5 year'  as hd_minus_5Y,
6        hiredate + interval '5 year'  as hd_plus_5Y
7   from emp
8  where deptno=10
```

MySQL

Use standard addition and subtraction with the INTERVAL keyword specifying the unit of time to add or subtract. Unlike the PostgreSQL solution, you do not place single quotes around the INTERVAL value:

```
1 select hiredate - interval 5 day   as hd_minus_5D,
2        hiredate + interval 5 day   as hd_plus_5D,
3        hiredate - interval 5 month as hd_minus_5M,
4        hiredate + interval 5 month as hd_plus_5M,
5        hiredate - interval 5 year  as hd_minus_5Y,
6        hiredate + interval 5 year  as hd_plus_5Y
7   from emp
8  where deptno=10
```

Alternatively, you can use the DATE_ADD function, which is shown below:

```
1 select date_add(hiredate,interval -5 day)   as hd_minus_5D,
2        date_add(hiredate,interval  5 day)   as hd_plus_5D,
3        date_add(hiredate,interval -5 month) as hd_minus_5M,
4        date_add(hiredate,interval  5 month) as hd_plus_5M,
5        date_add(hiredate,interval -5 year)  as hd_minus_5Y,
6        date_add(hiredate,interval  5 year)  as hd_plus_5DY
7   from emp
8  where deptno=10
```

SQL Server

Use the DATEADD function to add or subtract different units of time to/from a date:

```
1 select dateadd(day,-5,hiredate)    as hd_minus_5D,
2        dateadd(day,5,hiredate)     as hd_plus_5D,
3        dateadd(month,-5,hiredate)  as hd_minus_5M,
4        dateadd(month,5,hiredate)   as hd_plus_5M,
5        dateadd(year,-5,hiredate)   as hd_minus_5Y,
6        dateadd(year,5,hiredate)    as hd_plus_5Y
7   from emp
8  where deptno = 10
```

Discussion

The Oracle solution takes advantage of the fact that integer values represent days when performing date arithmetic. However, that's true only of arithmetic with DATE types. Oracle9*i* Database introduced TIMESTAMP types. For those, you should use the INTERVAL solution shown for PostgreSQL. Beware too, of passing TIMESTAMPs to old-style date functions such as ADD_MONTHS. By doing so, you can lose any fractional seconds that such TIMESTAMP values may contain.

The INTERVAL keyword and the string literals that go with it represent ISO-standard SQL syntax. The standard requires that interval values be enclosed within single quotes. PostgreSQL (and Oracle9*i* Database and later) complies with the standard. MySQL deviates somewhat by omitting support for the quotes.

8.2 Determining the Number of Days Between Two Dates

Problem

You want to find the difference between two dates and represent the result in days. For example, you want to find the difference in days between the HIREDATEs of employee ALLEN and employee WARD.

Solution

DB2

Use two inline views to find the HIREDATEs for WARD and ALLEN. Then subtract one HIREDATE from the other using the DAYS function:

```
 1  select days(ward_hd) - days(allen_hd)
 2    from (
 3  select hiredate as ward_hd
 4    from emp
 5   where ename = 'WARD'
 6         ) x,
 7         (
 8  select hiredate as allen_hd
 9    from emp
10   where ename = 'ALLEN'
11         ) y
```

Oracle and PostgreSQL

Use two inline views to find the HIREDATEs for WARD and ALLEN, and then subtract one date from the other:

```
 1  select ward_hd - allen_hd
 2    from (
 3  select hiredate as ward_hd
 4    from emp
 5   where ename = 'WARD'
 6         ) x,
 7         (
 8  select hiredate as allen_hd
 9    from emp
10   where ename = 'ALLEN'
11         ) y
```

MySQL and SQL Server

Use the function DATEDIFF to find the number of days between two dates. MySQL's version of DATEDIFF requires only two parameters (the two dates you want to find the difference in days between), and the smaller of the two dates should be passed first to avoid negative values (opposite in SQL Server). SQL Server's version of the function allows you to specify what you want the return value to represent (in this example you want to return the difference in days). The solution following uses the SQL Server version:

```
 1  select datediff(day,allen_hd,ward_hd)
 2    from (
 3  select hiredate as ward_hd
 4    from emp
 5   where ename = 'WARD'
 6         ) x,
 7         (
 8  select hiredate as allen_hd
 9    from emp
10   where ename = 'ALLEN'
11         ) y
```

MySQL users can simply remove the first argument of the function and flip-flop the order in which ALLEN_HD and WARD_HD is passed.

Discussion

For all solutions, inline views X and Y return the HIREDATEs for employees WARD and ALLEN respectively. For example:

```
select ward_hd, allen_hd
    from (
select hiredate as ward_hd
  from emp
 where ename = 'WARD'
       ) y,
       (
select hiredate as allen_hd
  from emp
 where ename = 'ALLEN'
       ) x

WARD_HD     ALLEN_HD
----------- ---------
22-FEB-1981 20-FEB-1981
```

You'll notice a Cartesian product is created, because there is no join specified between X and Y. In this case, the lack of a join is harmless as the cardinalities for X and Y are both 1, thus the result set will ultimately have one row (obviously, because 1×1=1). To get the difference in days, simply subtract one of the two values returned from the other using methods appropriate for your database.

8.3 Determining the Number of Business Days Between Two Dates

Problem

Given two dates, you want to find how many "working" days are between them, including the two dates themselves. For example, if January 10th is a Monday and January 11th is a Tuesday, then the number of working days between these two dates is two, as both days are typical work days. For this recipe, "business days" is defined as any day that is not Saturday or Sunday.

Solution

The solution examples find the number of business days between the HIREDATEs of BLAKE and JONES. To determine the number of business days between two dates, you can use a pivot table to return a row for each day between the two dates (including the start and end dates). Having done that, finding the number of business days is simply counting the dates returned that are not Saturday or Sunday.

 If you want to exclude holidays as well, you can create a HOLIDAYS table. Then include a simple NOT IN predicate to exclude days listed in HOLIDAYS from the solution.

DB2

Use the pivot table T500 to generate the required number of rows (representing days) between the two dates. Then count each day that is not a weekend. Use the DAYNAME function to return the weekday name of each date. For example:

```
 1  select sum(case when dayname(jones_hd+t500.id day -1 day)
 2                  in ( 'Saturday','Sunday' )
 3                  then 0 else 1
 4              end) as days
 5    from (
 6  select max(case when ename = 'BLAKE'
 7                  then hiredate
 8              end) as blake_hd,
 9         max(case when ename = 'JONES'
10                  then hiredate
11              end) as jones_hd
12    from emp
13   where ename in ( 'BLAKE','JONES' )
14         ) x,
15         t500
16   where t500.id <= blake_hd-jones_hd+1
```

MySQL

Use the pivot table T500 to generate the required number of rows (days) between the two dates. Then count each day that is not a weekend. Use the DATE_ADD function to add days to each date. Use the DATE_FORMAT function to obtain the weekday name of each date:

```
1  select sum(case when date_format(
2                        date_add(jones_hd,
3                            interval t500.id-1 DAY),'%a')
4                  in ( 'Sat','Sun' )
5                  then 0 else 1
6             end) as days
7    from (
8  select max(case when ename = 'BLAKE'
9                  then hiredate
10             end) as blake_hd,
11         max(case when ename = 'JONES'
12                  then hiredate
13             end) as jones_hd
14    from emp
15   where ename in ( 'BLAKE','JONES' )
16         ) x,
17         t500
18   where t500.id <= datediff(blake_hd,jones_hd)+1
```

Oracle

Use the pivot table T500 to generate the required number of rows (days) between the two dates, and then count each day that is not a weekend. Use the TO_CHAR function to obtain the weekday name of each date:

```
1  select sum(case when to_char(jones_hd+t500.id-1,'DY')
2                  in ( 'SAT','SUN' )
3                  then 0 else 1
4             end) as days
5    from (
6  select max(case when ename = 'BLAKE'
7                  then hiredate
8             end) as blake_hd,
9         max(case when ename = 'JONES'
10                  then hiredate
11             end) as jones_hd
12    from emp
13   where ename in ( 'BLAKE','JONES' )
14         ) x,
15         t500
16   where t500.id <= blake_hd-jones_hd+1
```

PostgreSQL

Use the pivot table T500 to generate the required number of rows (days) between the two dates. Then count each day that is not a weekend. Use the TO_CHAR function to obtain the weekday name of each date:

```
 1  select sum(case when trim(to_char(jones_hd+t500.id-1,'DAY'))
 2                        in ( 'SATURDAY','SUNDAY' )
 3                     then 0 else 1
 4              end) as days
 5    from (
 6  select max(case when ename = 'BLAKE'
 7                    then hiredate
 8              end) as blake_hd,
 9         max(case when ename = 'JONES'
10                    then hiredate
11              end) as jones_hd
12    from emp
13   where ename in ( 'BLAKE','JONES' )
14         ) x,
15         t500
16   where t500.id <= blake_hd-jones_hd+1
```

SQL Server

Use the pivot table T500 to generate the required number of rows (days) between the two dates, and then count each day that is not a weekend. Use the DATENAME function to obtain the weekday name of each date:

```
 1  select sum(case when datename(dw,jones_hd+t500.id-1)
 2                        in ( 'SATURDAY','SUNDAY' )
 3                     then 0 else 1
 4              end) as days
 5    from (
 6  select max(case when ename = 'BLAKE'
 7                    then hiredate
 8              end) as blake_hd,
 9         max(case when ename = 'JONES'
10                    then hiredate
11              end) as jones_hd
12    from emp
13   where ename in ( 'BLAKE','JONES' )
14         ) x,
15         t500
16   where t500.id <= datediff(day,jones_hd-blake_hd)+1
```

Discussion

While each RDBMS requires the use of different built-in functions to determine the name of a day, the overall solution approach is the same for each. The solution can be broken into two steps:

1. Return the days between the start date and end date (inclusive).

2. Count how many days (i.e., rows) there are, excluding weekends.

Inline view X performs step 1. If you examine inline view X, you'll notice the use of the aggregate function MAX, which the recipe uses to remove NULLs. If the use of MAX is unclear, the following output might help you understand. The output shows the results from inline view X without MAX:

```
select case when ename = 'BLAKE'
            then hiredate
       end as blake_hd,
       case when ename = 'JONES'
            then hiredate
       end as jones_hd
  from emp
 where ename in ( 'BLAKE','JONES' )


BLAKE_HD    JONES_HD
----------- -----------
            02-APR-1981
01-MAY-1981
```

Without MAX, two rows are returned. By using MAX you return only one row instead of two, and the NULLs are eliminated:

```
select max(case when ename = 'BLAKE'
            then hiredate
       end) as blake_hd,
       max(case when ename = 'JONES'
            then hiredate
       end) as jones_hd
  from emp
 where ename in ( 'BLAKE','JONES' )


BLAKE_HD    JONES_HD
----------- -----------
01-MAY-1981 02-APR-1981
```

The number of days (inclusive) between the two dates here is 30. Now that the two dates are in one row, the next step is to generate one row for each of those 30 days. To return the 30 days (rows), use table T500. Since each value for ID in table T500 is simply 1 greater than the one before it, add each row returned by T500 to the earlier of the two dates (JONES_HD) to generate consecutive days starting from JONES_HD up to and including BLAKE_HD. The result of this addition is shown below (using Oracle syntax):

```
select x.*, t500.*, jones_hd+t500.id-1
  from (
select max(case when ename = 'BLAKE'
            then hiredate
       end) as blake_hd,
```

```
        max(case when ename = 'JONES'
                 then hiredate
             end) as jones_hd
   from emp
  where ename in ( 'BLAKE','JONES' )
        ) x,
        t500
  where t500.id <= blake_hd-jones_hd+1

BLAKE_HD     JONES_HD             ID JONES_HD+T5
-----------  -----------  -----------  -----------
01-MAY-1981 02-APR-1981      1 02-APR-1981
01-MAY-1981 02-APR-1981      2 03-APR-1981
01-MAY-1981 02-APR-1981      3 04-APR-1981
01-MAY-1981 02-APR-1981      4 05-APR-1981
01-MAY-1981 02-APR-1981      5 06-APR-1981
01-MAY-1981 02-APR-1981      6 07-APR-1981
01-MAY-1981 02-APR-1981      7 08-APR-1981
01-MAY-1981 02-APR-1981      8 09-APR-1981
01-MAY-1981 02-APR-1981      9 10-APR-1981
01-MAY-1981 02-APR-1981     10 11-APR-1981
01-MAY-1981 02-APR-1981     11 12-APR-1981
01-MAY-1981 02-APR-1981     12 13-APR-1981
01-MAY-1981 02-APR-1981     13 14-APR-1981
01-MAY-1981 02-APR-1981     14 15-APR-1981
01-MAY-1981 02-APR-1981     15 16-APR-1981
01-MAY-1981 02-APR-1981     16 17-APR-1981
01-MAY-1981 02-APR-1981     17 18-APR-1981
01-MAY-1981 02-APR-1981     18 19-APR-1981
01-MAY-1981 02-APR-1981     19 20-APR-1981
01-MAY-1981 02-APR-1981     20 21-APR-1981
01-MAY-1981 02-APR-1981     21 22-APR-1981
01-MAY-1981 02-APR-1981     22 23-APR-1981
01-MAY-1981 02-APR-1981     23 24-APR-1981
01-MAY-1981 02-APR-1981     24 25-APR-1981
01-MAY-1981 02-APR-1981     25 26-APR-1981
01-MAY-1981 02-APR-1981     26 27-APR-1981
01-MAY-1981 02-APR-1981     27 28-APR-1981
01-MAY-1981 02-APR-1981     28 29-APR-1981
01-MAY-1981 02-APR-1981     29 30-APR-1981
01-MAY-1981 02-APR-1981     30 01-MAY-1981
```

If you examine the WHERE clause, you'll notice that you add 1 to the difference between BLAKE_HD and JONES_HD to generate the required 30 rows (otherwise, you would get 29 rows). You'll also notice that you subtract 1 from T500.ID in the SELECT list of the outer query, since the values for ID start at 1 and adding 1 to JONES_HD would cause JONES_HD to be excluded from the final count.

Once you generate the number of rows required for the result set, use a CASE expression to "flag" whether or not each of the days returned are weekdays or weekends (return a 1 for a weekday and a 0 for a weekend). The final step is to use the aggregate function SUM to tally up the number of 1s to get the final answer.

8.4 Determining the Number of Months or Years Between Two Dates

Problem

You want to find the difference between two dates in terms of either months or years. For example, you want to find the number of months between the first and last employees hired, and you also wish to express that value as some number of years.

Solution

Since there are always 12 months in a year, you can find the number of months between two dates, and then divide by 12 to get the number of years. After getting comfortable with the solution, you'll want to round the results up or down depending on what you want for the year. For example, the first HIREDATE in table EMP is "17-DEC-1980" and the last is "12-JAN-1983". If you do the math on the years (1983 minus 1980) you get three years, yet the difference in months is approximately 25 (a little over two years). You should tweak the solution as you see fit. The solutions below will return 25 months and ~2 years.

DB2 and MySQL

Use the functions YEAR and MONTH to return the four-digit year and the two-digit month for the dates supplied:

```
1  select mnth, mnth/12
2    from (
3  select (year(max_hd) - year(min_hd))*12 +
4         (month(max_hd) - month(min_hd)) as mnth
5    from (
6  select min(hiredate) as min_hd, max(hiredate) as max_hd
7    from emp
8         ) x
9         ) y
```

Oracle

Use the function MONTHS_BETWEEN to find the difference between two dates in months (to get years, simply divide by 12):

```
1  select months_between(max_hd,min_hd),
2         months_between(max_hd,min_hd)/12
3    from (
4  select min(hiredate) min_hd, max(hiredate) max_hd
5    from emp
6         ) x
```

PostgreSQL

Use the function EXTRACT to return the four-digit year and two-digit month for the dates supplied:

```
1  select mnth, mnth/12
2    from (
3  select ( extract(year from max_hd) -
4           extract(year from min_hd) ) * 12
5         +
6         ( extract(month from max_hd) -
7           extract(month from min_hd) ) as mnth
8    from (
9  select min(hiredate) as min_hd, max(hiredate) as max_hd
10     from emp
11         ) x
12         ) y
```

SQL Server

Use the function DATEDIFF to find the difference between two dates in months (to get years, simply divide by 12):

```
1  select datediff(month,min_hd,max_hd),
2         datediff(month,min_hd,max_hd)/12
3    from (
4  select min(hiredate) min_hd, max(hiredate) max_hd
5    from emp
6         ) x
```

Discussion

DB2, MySQL, and PostgreSQL

Once you extract the year and month for MIN_HD and MAX_HD in the Post-greSQL solution, the method for finding the months and years between MIN_HD and MAX_HD is the same for all three RDBMs. This discussion will cover all three solutions. Inline view X returns the earliest and latest HIREDATEs in table EMP and can be seen below:

```
select min(hiredate) as min_hd,
       max(hiredate) as max_hd
  from emp

MIN_HD      MAX_HD
----------- -----------
17-DEC-1980 12-JAN-1983
```

To find the months between MAX_HD and MIN_HD, multiply the difference in years between MIN_HD and MAX_HD by 12, then add the difference in months between MAX_HD and MIN_HD. If you are having trouble seeing how this works, return the date component for each date. The numeric values for the years and months are show below:

```
select year(max_hd)  as max_yr,   year(min_hd) as min_yr,
       month(max_hd) as max_mon, month(min_hd) as min_mon
  from (
select min(hiredate) as min_hd, max(hiredate) as max_hd
  from emp
       ) x


MAX_YR     MIN_YR     MAX_MON     MIN_MON
------     ----------  ----------  ----------
  1983       1980          1          12
```

Looking at the results above, finding the months between MAX_HD and MIN_HD is simply (1983–1980)*12 + (1–12). To find the number of years between MIN_HD and MAX_HD, divide the number of months by 12. Again, depending on the results you are looking for you will want to round the values.

Oracle and SQL Server

Inline view X returns the earliest and latest HIREDATEs in table EMP and can be seen below:

```
select min(hiredate) as min_hd, max(hiredate) as max_hd
  from emp


MIN_HD        MAX_HD
-----------   -----------
17-DEC-1980  12-JAN-1983
```

The functions supplied by Oracle and SQL Server (MONTHS_BETWEEN and DATEDIFF, respectively) will return the number of months between two given dates. To find the year, divide the number of months by 12.

8.5   Determining the Number of Seconds, Minutes, or Hours Between Two Dates

Problem

You want to return the difference in seconds between two dates. For example, you want to return the difference between the HIREDATEs of ALLEN and WARD in seconds, minutes, and hours.

Solution

If you can find the number of days between two dates, you can find seconds, minutes, and hours as they are the units of time that make up a day.

DB2

Use the function DAYS to find the difference between ALLEN_HD and WARD_HD in days. Then multiply to find each unit of time:

```
1  select dy*24 hr, dy*24*60 min, dy*24*60*60 sec
2    from (
3  select ( days(max(case when ename = 'WARD'
4                    then hiredate
5            end)) -
6         days(max(case when ename = 'ALLEN'
7                    then hiredate
8            end))
9         ) as dy
10   from emp
11       ) x
```

MySQL and SQL Server

Use the DATEDIFF function to return the number of days between ALLEN_HD and WARD_HD. Then multiply to find each unit of time:

```
1  select datediff(day,allen_hd,ward_hd)*24 hr,
2         datediff(day,allen_hd,ward_hd)*24*60 min,
3         datediff(day,allen_hd,ward_hd)*24*60*60 sec
4    from (
5  select max(case when ename = 'WARD'
6                  then hiredate
7             end) as ward_hd,
8         max(case when ename = 'ALLEN'
9                  then hiredate
10            end) as allen_hd
11   from emp
12       ) x
```

Oracle and PostgreSQL

Use subtraction to return the number of days between ALLEN_HD and WARD_HD. Then multiply to find each unit of time:

```
1  select dy*24 as hr, dy*24*60 as min, dy*24*60*60 as sec
2    from (
3  select (max(case when ename = 'WARD'
4                   then hiredate
5              end) -
6         max(case when ename = 'ALLEN'
7                  then hiredate
8              end)) as dy
9    from emp
10       ) x
```

Discussion

Inline view X for all solutions returns the HIREDATEs for WARD and ALLEN, as can be seen below:

```
select max(case when ename = 'WARD'
                then hiredate
           end) as ward_hd,
       max(case when ename = 'ALLEN'
                then hiredate
           end) as allen_hd
  from emp


WARD_HD     ALLEN_HD
----------- -----------
22-FEB-1981 20-FEB-1981
```

Multiply the number of days between WARD_HD and ALLEN_HD by 24 (hours in a day), 1440 (minutes in a day), and 86400 (seconds in a day).

8.6   Counting the Occurrences of Weekdays in a Year

Problem

You want to count the number of times each weekday occurs in one year.

Solution

To find the number of occurrences of each weekday in a year, you must:

1. Generate all possible dates in the year.

2. Format the dates such that they resolve to the name of their respective weekdays.

3. Count the occurrence of each weekday name.

DB2

Use recursive WITH to avoid the need to SELECT against a table with at least 366 rows. Use the function DAYNAME to obtain the weekday name for each date, and then count the occurrence of each:

```
 1  with x (start_date,end_date)
 2  as (
 3  select start_date,
 4         start_date + 1 year end_date
 5    from (
 6  select (current_date -
 7         dayofyear(current_date) day)
 8         +1 day as start_date
 9    from t1
10         ) tmp
11    union all
```

```
12  select start_date + 1 day, end_date
13    from x
14   where start_date + 1 day < end_date
15  )
16  select dayname(start_date),count(*)
17    from x
18   group by dayname(start_date)
```

MySQL

Select against table T500 to generate enough rows to return every day in the year. Use the DATE_FORMAT function to obtain the weekday name of each date, and then count the occurrence of each name:

```
 1  select date_format(
 2            date_add(
 3               cast(
 4              concat(year(current_date),'-01-01')
 5                     as date),
 6                     interval t500.id-1 day),
 7                     '%W') day,
 8         count(*)
 9    from t500
10   where t500.id <= datediff(
11                     cast(
12                   concat(year(current_date)+1,'-01-01')
13                         as date),
14                   cast(
15                   concat(year(current_date),'-01-01')
16                         as date))
17   group by date_format(
18            date_add(
19               cast(
20              concat(year(current_date),'-01-01')
21                     as date),
22                     interval t500.id-1 day),
23                     '%W')
```

Oracle

If you are on Oracle9i Database or later, you can use the recursive CONNECT BY to return each day in a year. If you are on Oracle8i Database or earlier, select against table T500 to generate enough rows to return every day in a year. In either case, use the TO_CHAR function to obtain the weekday name of each date, and then count the occurrence of each name.

First, the CONNECT BY solution:

```
1 with x as (
2 select level lvl
3   from dual
4  connect by level <= (
5    add_months(trunc(sysdate,'y'),12)-trunc(sysdate,'y')
```

```
 6  )
 7  )
 8  select to_char(trunc(sysdate,'y')+lvl-1,'DAY'), count(*)
 9    from x
10   group by to_char(trunc(sysdate,'y')+lvl-1,'DAY')
```

and next, the solution for older releases of Oracle:

```
 1  select to_char(trunc(sysdate,'y')+rownum-1,'DAY'),
 2         count(*)
 3    from t500
 4   where rownum <= (add_months(trunc(sysdate,'y'),12)
 5                      - trunc(sysdate,'y'))
 6   group by to_char(trunc(sysdate,'y')+rownum-1,'DAY')
```

PostgreSQL

Use the built-in function GENERATE_SERIES to generate one rows for every day in
the year. Then use the TO_CHAR function to obtain the weekday name of each
date. Finally, count the occurrence of each weekday name. For example:

```
 1  select to_char(
 2            cast(
 3         date_trunc('year',current_date)
 4                  as date) + gs.id-1,'DAY'),
 5         count(*)
 6    from generate_series(1,366) gs(id)
 7   where gs.id <= (cast
 8                    ( date_trunc('year',current_date) +
 9                        interval '12 month' as date) -
10   cast(date_trunc('year',current_date)
11                      as date))
12   group by to_char(
13             cast(
14          date_trunc('year',current_date)
15             as date) + gs.id-1,'DAY')
```

SQL Server

Use the recursive WITH to avoid the need to SELECT against a table with at least
366 rows. If you are on a version of SQL Server that does not support the WITH
clause, see the alternative Oracle solution as a guideline for using a pivot table. Use
the DATENAME function to obtain the weekday name of each date, and then count
the occurrence of each name. For example:

```
 1  with x (start_date,end_date)
 2  as (
 3  select start_date,
 4         dateadd(year,1,start_date) end_date
 5    from (
 6  select cast(
 7         cast(year(getdate()) as varchar) + '-01-01'
 8               as datetime) start_date
```

```
 9    from t1
10         ) tmp
11  union all
12  select dateadd(day,1,start_date), end_date
13    from x
14    where dateadd(day,1,start_date) < end_date
15  )
16  select datename(dw,start_date),count(*)
17    from x
18    group by datename(dw,start_date)
19 OPTION (MAXRECURSION 366)
```

Discussion

DB2

Inline view TMP, in the recursive WITH view X, returns the first day of the current year and is shown below:

```
select (current_date -
        dayofyear(current_date) day)
       +1 day as start_date
  from t1
```

```
START_DATE
-----------
01-JAN-2005
```

The next step is to add one year to START_DATE, so that you have the beginning and end dates. You need to know both because you want to generate every day in a year. START_DATE and END_DATE are shown below:

```
select start_date,
       start_date + 1 year end_date
  from (
select (current_date -
        dayofyear(current_date) day)
       +1 day as start_date
  from t1
       ) tmp
```

```
START_DATE   END_DATE
-----------  -----------
01-JAN-2005  01-JAN-2006
```

The next step is to recursively increment START_DATE by one day, stopping before it equals END_DATE. A portion of the rows returned by the recursive view X is shown below:

```
with x (start_date,end_date)
as (
select start_date,
       start_date + 1 year end_date
  from (
```

```
select (current_date -
        dayofyear(current_date) day)
        +1 day as start_date
  from t1
        ) tmp
 union all
select start_date + 1 day, end_date
  from x
 where start_date + 1 day < end_date
 )
select * from x


START_DATE   END_DATE
-----------  -----------
01-JAN-2005  01-JAN-2006
02-JAN-2005  01-JAN-2006
03-JAN-2005  01-JAN-2006
...
29-JAN-2005  01-JAN-2006
30-JAN-2005  01-JAN-2006
31-JAN-2005  01-JAN-2006
...
01-DEC-2005  01-JAN-2006
02-DEC-2005  01-JAN-2006
03-DEC-2005  01-JAN-2006
...
29-DEC-2005  01-JAN-2006
30-DEC-2005  01-JAN-2006
31-DEC-2005  01-JAN-2006
```

The final step is to use the function DAYNAME on the rows returned by the recursive view X, and count how many times each weekday occurs. The final result is shown below:

```
with x (start_date,end_date)
as (
select start_date,
        start_date + 1 year end_date
  from (
select (current_date -
        dayofyear(current_date) day)
        +1 day as start_date
  from t1
        ) tmp
 union all
select start_date + 1 day, end_date
  from x
 where start_date + 1 day < end_date
 )
select dayname(start_date),count(*)
  from x
 group by dayname(start_date)
```

```
START_DATE    COUNT(*)
---------     ----------
FRIDAY        52
MONDAY        52
SATURDAY      53
SUNDAY        52
THURSDAY      52
TUESDAY       52
WEDNESDAY     52
```

MySQL

This solution selects against table T500 to generate one row for every day in the year. The command on line 4 returns the first day of the current year. It does this by returning the year of the date returned by the function CURRENT_DATE, and then appending a month and day (following MySQL's default date format). The result is shown below:

```
select concat(year(current_date),'-01-01')
  from t1

START_DATE
-----------
01-JAN-2005
```

Now that you have the first day in the current year, use the DATEADD function to add each value from T500.ID to generate each day in the year. Use the function DATE_FORMAT to return the weekday for each date. To generate the required number of rows from table T500, find the difference in days between the first day of the current year and the first day of the next year, and return that many rows (will be either 365 or 366). A portion of the results is shown below:

```
select date_format(
         date_add(
             cast(
           concat(year(current_date),'-01-01')
                  as date),
                  interval t500.id-1 day),
                  '%W') day
  from t500
 where t500.id <= datediff(
                    cast(
                  concat(year(current_date)+1,'-01-01')
                        as date),
                    cast(
                  concat(year(current_date),'-01-01')
                        as date))
```

```
DAY
-----------
01-JAN-2005
02-JAN-2005
03-JAN-2005
...
29-JAN-2005
30-JAN-2005
31-JAN-2005
...
01-DEC-2005
02-DEC-2005
03-DEC-2005
...
29-DEC-2005
30-DEC-2005
31-DEC-2005
```

Now that you can return every day in the current year, count the occurrences of each weekday returned by the function DAYNAME. The final results are shown below:

```
select date_format(
        date_add(
            cast(
          concat(year(current_date),'-01-01')
                as date),
                interval t500.id-1 day),
                '%W') day,
        count(*)
  from t500
  where t500.id <= datediff(
            cast(
          concat(year(current_date)+1,'-01-01')
                as date),
            cast(
          concat(year(current_date),'-01-01')
                as date))
  group by date_format(
        date_add(
            cast(
          concat(year(current_date),'-01-01')
                as date),
                interval t500.id-1 day),
                '%W')
```

```
DAY        COUNT(*)
---------  ----------
FRIDAY         52
MONDAY         52
SATURDAY       53
SUNDAY         52
THURSDAY       52
TUESDAY        52
WEDNESDAY      52
```

Oracle

The solutions provided either select against table T500 (a pivot table), or use the recursive CONNECT BY and WITH, to generate a row for every day in the current year. The call to the function TRUNC truncates the current date to the first day of the current year.

If you are using the CONNECT BY/WITH solution, you can use the pseudo-column LEVEL to generate sequential numbers beginning at 1. To generate the required number of rows needed for this solution, filter ROWNUM or LEVEL on the difference in days between the first day of the current year and the first day of the next year (will be 365 or 366 days). The next step is to increment each day by adding ROWNUM or LEVEL to the first day of the current year. Partial results are shown below:

```
/* Oracle 9i and later */
with x as (
select level lvl
  from dual
 connect by level <= (
   add_months(trunc(sysdate,'y'),12)-trunc(sysdate,'y')
 )
)
select trunc(sysdate,'y')+lvl-1
  from x
```

If you are using the pivot-table solution, you can use any table or view with at least 366 rows in it. And since Oracle has ROWNUM, there's no need for a table with incrementing values starting from 1. Consider the following example, which uses pivot table T500 to return every day in the current year:

```
/* Oracle 8i and earlier */
select trunc(sysdate,'y')+rownum-1 start_date
  from t500
 where rownum <= (add_months(trunc(sysdate,'y'),12)
                  - trunc(sysdate,'y'))

START_DATE
-----------
01-JAN-2005
02-JAN-2005
03-JAN-2005
...
29-JAN-2005
30-JAN-2005
31-JAN-2005
...
01-DEC-2005
02-DEC-2005
03-DEC-2005
...
```

```
29-DEC-2005
30-DEC-2005
31-DEC-2005
```

Regardless of which approach you take, you eventually must use the function TO_
CHAR to return the weekday name for each date, and then count the occurrence of
each name. The final results are shown below:

```
/* Oracle 9i and later */
with x as (
select level lvl
  from dual
 connect by level <= (
    add_months(trunc(sysdate,'y'),12)-trunc(sysdate,'y')
 )
)
select to_char(trunc(sysdate,'y')+lvl-1,'DAY'), count(*)
  from x
 group by to_char(trunc(sysdate,'y')+lvl-1,'DAY')

/* Oracle 8i and earlier */
select to_char(trunc(sysdate,'y')+rownum-1,'DAY') start_date,
       count(*)
  from t500
 where rownum <= (add_months(trunc(sysdate,'y'),12)
              - trunc(sysdate,'y'))
 group by to_char(trunc(sysdate,'y')+rownum-1,'DAY')

START_DATE   COUNT(*)
----------   ----------
FRIDAY            52
MONDAY           52
SATURDAY         53
SUNDAY           52
THURSDAY         52
TUESDAY          52
WEDNESDAY        52
```

PostgreSQL

The first step is to use the DATE_TRUNC function to return the year of the current
date (shown below, selecting against T1 so only one row is returned):

```
select cast(
        date_trunc('year',current_date)
       as date) as start_date
  from t1

START_DATE
----------
01-JAN-2005
```

The next step is to select against a row source (any table expression, really) with at least 366 rows. The solution uses the function GENERATE_SERIES as the row source. You can, of course, use table T500 instead. Then add one day to the first day of the current year until you return every day in the year (shown below):

```
select cast( date_trunc('year',current_date)
                as date) + gs.id-1 as start_date
  from generate_series (1,366) gs(id)
 where gs.id <= (cast
                    ( date_trunc('year',current_date) +
                        interval '12 month' as date) -
        cast(date_trunc('year',current_date)
                    as date))
```

```
START_DATE
-----------
01-JAN-2005
02-JAN-2005
03-JAN-2005
...
29-JAN-2005
30-JAN-2005
31-JAN-2005
...
01-DEC-2005
02-DEC-2005
03-DEC-2005
...
29-DEC-2005
30-DEC-2005
31-DEC-2005
```

The final step is to use the function TO_CHAR to return the weekday name for each date, and then count the occurrence of each name. The final results are shown below:

```
select to_char(
        cast(
    date_trunc('year',current_date)
            as date) + gs.id-1,'DAY') as start_dates,
        count(*)
  from generate_series(1,366) gs(id)
 where gs.id <= (cast
                    ( date_trunc('year',current_date) +
                        interval '12 month' as date) -
        cast(date_trunc('year',current_date)
                    as date))
 group by to_char(
            cast(
        date_trunc('year',current_date)
            as date) + gs.id-1,'DAY')
```

```
START_DATE   COUNT(*)
----------   ----------
FRIDAY            52
MONDAY            52
SATURDAY          53
SUNDAY            52
THURSDAY          52
TUESDAY           52
WEDNESDAY         52
```

SQL Server

Inline view TMP, in the recursive WITH view X, returns the first day of the current year and is shown below:

```
select cast(
        cast(year(getdate( )) as varchar) + '-01-01'
            as datetime) start_date
  from t1
```

```
START_DATE
-----------
01-JAN-2005
```

Once you return the first day of the current year, add one year to START_DATE so that you have the beginning and end dates. You need to know both because you want to generate every day in a year. START_DATE and END_DATE are shown below:

```
select start_date,
        dateadd(year,1,start_date) end_date
  from (
select cast(
        cast(year(getdate( )) as varchar) + '-01-01'
            as datetime) start_date
  from t1
        ) tmp
```

```
START_DATE   END_DATE
-----------  -----------
01-JAN-2005 01-JAN-2006
```

Next, recursively increment START_DATE by one day and stop before it equals END_DATE. A portion of the rows returned by the recursive view X is shown below:

```
with x (start_date,end_date)
  as (
select start_date,
        dateadd(year,1,start_date) end_date
  from (
select cast(
        cast(year(getdate( )) as varchar) + '-01-01'
            as datetime) start_date
```

```
      from t1
          ) tmp
  union all
  select dateadd(day,1,start_date), end_date
    from x
   where dateadd(day,1,start_date) < end_date
  )
  select * from x
  OPTION (MAXRECURSION 366)


START_DATE   END_DATE
----------   ----------
01-JAN-2005  01-JAN-2006
02-JAN-2005  01-JAN-2006
03-JAN-2005  01-JAN-2006
...
29-JAN-2005  01-JAN-2006
30-JAN-2005  01-JAN-2006
31-JAN-2005  01-JAN-2006
...
01-DEC-2005  01-JAN-2006
02-DEC-2005  01-JAN-2006
03-DEC-2005  01-JAN-2006
...
29-DEC-2005  01-JAN-2006
30-DEC-2005  01-JAN-2006
31-DEC-2005  01-JAN-2006
```

The final step is to use the function DATENAME on the rows returned by the recursive view X and count how many times each weekday occurs. The final result is shown below:

```
with x(start_date,end_date)
 as (
 select start_date,
        dateadd(year,1,start_date) end_date
   from (
 select cast(
        cast(year(getdate()) as varchar) + '-01-01'
             as datetime) start_date
   from t1
        ) tmp
union all
select dateadd(day,1,start_date), end_date
  from x
 where dateadd(day,1,start_date) < end_date
)
select datename(dw,start_date), count(*)
  from x
 group by datename(dw,start_date)
OPTION (MAXRECURSION 366)
```

```
START_DATE   COUNT(*)
---------    ----------
FRIDAY          52
MONDAY          52
SATURDAY        53
SUNDAY          52
THURSDAY        52
TUESDAY         52
WEDNESDAY       52
```

8.7 Determining the Date Difference Between the Current Record and the Next Record

Problem

You want to determine the difference in days between two dates (specifically dates stored in two different rows). For example, for every employee in DEPTNO 10, you want to determine the number of days between the day they were hired and the day the next employee (can be in another department) was hired.

Solution

The trick to this problem's solution is to find the earliest HIREDATE after the current employee was hired. After that, simply use the technique from Recipe 8.2 to find the difference in days.

DB2

Use a scalar subquery to find the next HIREDATE relative to the current HIRE-DATE. Then use the DAYS function to find the difference in days:

```
1  select x.*,
2        days(x.next_hd) - days(x.hiredate) diff
3    from (
4  select e.deptno, e.ename, e.hiredate,
5        (select min(d.hiredate) from emp d
6           where d.hiredate > e.hiredate) next_hd
7    from emp e
8   where e.deptno = 10
9        ) x
```

MySQL and SQL Server

Use a scalar subquery to find the next HIREDATE relative to the current HIRE-DATE. Then use the DATEDIFF function to find the difference in days. The SQL Server version of DATEDIFF is used below:

```
1  select x.*,
2         datediff(day,x.hiredate,x.next_hd) diff
3    from (
4  select e.deptno, e.ename, e.hiredate,
5         (select min(d.hiredate) from emp d
6           where d.hiredate > e.hiredate) next_hd
7    from emp e
8   where e.deptno = 10
9         ) x
```

MySQL users can exclude the first argument ("day") and switch the order of the two remaining arguments:

```
2         datediff(x.next_hd, x.hiredate) diff
```

Oracle

If you're on Oracle8i Database or later, use the window function LEAD OVER to access the next HIREDATE relative to the current row, thus facilitating subtraction:

```
1  select ename, hiredate, next_hd,
2         next_hd - hiredate diff
3    from (
4  select deptno, ename, hiredate,
5         lead(hiredate)over(order by hiredate) next_hd
6    from emp
7         )
8   where deptno=10
```

If you are on Oracle8 Database or earlier, you can use the PostgreSQL solution as an alternative.

PostgreSQL

Use a scalar subquery to find the next HIREDATE relative to the current HIRE-DATE. Then use simple subtraction to find the difference in days:

```
1  select x.*,
2         x.next_hd - x.hiredate as diff
3    from (
4  select e.deptno, e.ename, e.hiredate,
5         (select min(d.hiredate) from emp d
6           where d.hiredate > e.hiredate) as next_hd
7    from emp e
8   where e.deptno = 10
9         ) x
```

Discussion

DB2, MySQL, PostgreSQL, and SQL Server

Despite the differences in syntax, the approach is the same for all these solutions: use a scalar subquery to find the next HIREDATE relative to the current HIREDATE,

---

and then find the difference in days between the two using the technique described in Recipe 8.2.

Oracle

The window function LEAD OVER is extremely useful here as it allows you to access "future" rows ("future" determined by the ORDER BY clause, relative to the current row). The ability to access rows around your current row without additional joins provides for more readable and efficient code. When working with window functions, keep in mind that they are evaluated after the WHERE clause, hence the need for an inline view in the solution. If you were to move the filter on DEPTNO into the inline view, the results would change (only the HIREDATEs from DEPTNO 10 would be considered). One important note to mention about Oracle's LEAD and LAG functions is their behavior in the presence of duplicates. In the preface I mention that these recipes are not coded "defensively" because there are too many conditions that one can't possibly foresee that can break code. Or, even if one can foresee every problem, sometimes the resulting SQL becomes unreadable. So in most cases, the goal of a solution is to introduce a technique: one that you can use in your production system, but that must be tested and many times tweaked to work for your particular data. In this case, though, there is a situation that I will discuss simply because the workaround may not be all that obvious, particularly for those coming from non-Oracle systems. In this example there are no duplicate HIREDATEs in table EMP, but it is certainly possible (and probably likely) that there are duplicate date values in your tables. Consider the employees in DEPTNO 10 and their HIREDATEs:

```
select ename, hiredate
  from emp
 where deptno=10
 order by 2

ENAME   HIREDATE
------  -----------
CLARK   09-JUN-1981
KING    17-NOV-1981
MILLER  23-JAN-1982
```

For the sake of this example, let's insert four duplicates such that there are five employees (including KING) hired on November 17:

```
insert into emp (empno,ename,deptno,hiredate)
values (1,'ant',10,to_date('17-NOV-1981'))

insert into emp (empno,ename,deptno,hiredate)
values (2,'joe',10,to_date('17-NOV-1981'))

insert into emp (empno,ename,deptno,hiredate)
values (3,'jim',10,to_date('17-NOV-1981'))
```

```
insert into emp (empno,ename,deptno,hiredate)
values (4,'choi',10,to_date('17-NOV-1981'))

select ename, hiredate
  from emp
 where deptno=10
 order by 2

ENAME  HIREDATE
------ -----------
CLARK  09-JUN-1981
ant    17-NOV-1981
joe    17-NOV-1981
KING   17-NOV-1981
jim    17-NOV-1981
choi   17-NOV-1981
MILLER 23-JAN-1982
```

Now there are multiple employees in DEPTNO 10 hired on the same day. If you try to use the proposed solution (moving the filter into the inline view so you only are concerned with employees in DEPTNO 10 and their HIREDATEs) on this result set you get the following output:

```
select ename, hiredate, next_hd,
       next_hd - hiredate diff
  from (
select deptno, ename, hiredate,
       lead(hiredate)over(order by hiredate) next_hd
  from emp
 where deptno=10
       )

ENAME  HIREDATE    NEXT_HD          DIFF
------ ----------- ----------- ----------
CLARK  09-JUN-1981 17-NOV-1981        161
ant    17-NOV-1981 17-NOV-1981          0
joe    17-NOV-1981 17-NOV-1981          0
KING   17-NOV-1981 17-NOV-1981          0
jim    17-NOV-1981 17-NOV-1981          0
choi   17-NOV-1981 23-JAN-1982         67
MILLER 23-JAN-1982 (null)          (null)
```

Looking at the values of DIFF for four of the five employees hired on the same day, you can see that the value is zero. This is not correct. All employees hired on the same day should have their dates evaluated against the HIREDATE of the next date on which an employee was hired, i.e., all employees hired on November 17 should be evaluated against MILLER's HIREDATE. The problem here is that the LEAD function orders the rows by HIREDATE but does not skip duplicates. So, for example, when employee ANT's HIREDATE is evaluated against employee JOE's HIRE-DATE, the difference is zero, hence a DIFF value of zero for ANT. Fortunately, Oracle has provided an easy workaround for situations like this one. When invoking the

LEAD function, you can pass an argument to LEAD to specify exactly where the future row is (i.e., is it the next row, 10 rows later, etc.). So, looking at employee ANT, instead of looking ahead one row you need to look ahead five rows (you want to jump over all the other duplicates), because that's where MILLER is. If you look at employee JOE, he is four rows from MILLER, JIM is three rows from MILLER, KING is two rows from MILLER and, pretty boy CHOI is one row from MILLER. To get the correct answer, simply pass the distance from each employee to MILLER as an argument to LEAD. The solution is shown below:

```
select ename, hiredate, next_hd,
       next_hd - hiredate diff
  from (
select deptno, ename, hiredate,
       lead(hiredate,cnt-rn+1)over(order by hiredate) next_hd
  from (
select deptno,ename,hiredate,
       count(*)over(partition by hiredate) cnt,
       row_number()over(partition by hiredate order by empno) rn
  from emp
 where deptno=10
       )
       )

ENAME  HIREDATE    NEXT_HD         DIFF
------ ----------- ----------- ----------
CLARK  09-JUN-1981 17-NOV-1981        161
ant    17-NOV-1981 23-JAN-1982         67
joe    17-NOV-1981 23-JAN-1982         67
jim    17-NOV-1981 23-JAN-1982         67
choi   17-NOV-1981 23-JAN-1982         67
KING   17-NOV-1981 23-JAN-1982         67
MILLER 23-JAN-1982 (null)          (null)
```

Now the results are correct. All the employees hired on the same day have their HIREDATEs evaluated against the next HIREDATE, not a HIREDATE that matches their own. If the workaround isn't immediately obvious, simply break down the query. Start with the inline view:

```
select deptno,ename,hiredate,
       count(*)over(partition by hiredate) cnt,
       row_number()over(partition by hiredate order by empno) rn
  from emp
 where deptno=10

DEPTNO ENAME  HIREDATE            CNT          RN
------ ------ ----------- ----------- -----------
    10 CLARK  09-JUN-1981           1           1
    10 ant    17-NOV-1981           5           1
    10 joe    17-NOV-1981           5           2
    10 jim    17-NOV-1981           5           3
    10 choi   17-NOV-1981           5           4
    10 KING   17-NOV-1981           5           5
    10 MILLER 23-JAN-1982           1           1
```

The window function COUNT OVER counts the number of times each HIREDATE occurs and returns this value to each row. For the duplicate HIREDATEs, a value of 5 is returned for each row with that HIREDATE. The window function ROW_NUMBER OVER ranks each employee by EMPNO. The ranking is partitioned by HIREDATE, so unless there are duplicate HIREDATEs each employee will have a rank of 1. At this point, all the duplicates have been counted and ranked and the ranking can serve as the distance to the next HIREDATE (MILLER's HIREDATE). You can see this by subtracting RN from CNT and adding 1 for each row when calling LEAD:

```
select deptno, ename, hiredate,
       cnt-rn+1 distance_to_miller,
       lead(hiredate,cnt-rn+1)over(order by hiredate) next_hd
  from (
select deptno,ename,hiredate,
       count(*)over(partition by hiredate) cnt,
       row_number()over(partition by hiredate order by empno) rn
  from emp
 where deptno=10
       )

DEPTNO ENAME  HIREDATE    DISTANCE_TO_MILLER NEXT_HD
------ ------ ----------- ------------------ -----------
    10 CLARK  09-JUN-1981                  1 17-NOV-1981
    10 ant    17-NOV-1981                  5 23-JAN-1982
    10 joe    17-NOV-1981                  4 23-JAN-1982
    10 jim    17-NOV-1981                  3 23-JAN-1982
    10 choi   17-NOV-1981                  2 23-JAN-1982
    10 KING   17-NOV-1981                  1 23-JAN-1982
    10 MILLER 23-JAN-1982                  1 (null)
```

As you can see, by passing the appropriate distance to jump ahead to, the LEAD function performs the subtraction on the correct dates.

CHAPTER 9

Date Manipulation

This chapter introduces recipes for searching and modifying dates. Queries involving dates are very common. Thus, you need to know how to think when working with dates, and you need to have a good understanding of the functions that your RDBMS platform provides for manipulating them. The recipes in this chapter form an important foundation for future work as you move on to more complex queries involving not only dates, but times too.

Before getting into the recipes, I want to reinforce the concept (that I mentioned in the Preface) of using these solutions as guidelines to solving your specific problems. Try to think "big picture." For example, if a recipe solves a problem for the current month, keep in mind that you may be able to use the recipe for any month (with minor modifications), not just the month used in the recipe. Again, I want you to use these recipes as guidelines, not as the absolute final option. There's no possible way a book can contain an answer for all your problems, but if you understand what is presented here, modifying these solutions to fit your needs is trivial. I also urge you to consider alternative versions of the solutions I've provided. For instance, if I solve a problem using one particular function provided by your RDBMS, it is worth the time and effort to find out if there is an alternative—maybe one that is more or less efficient than what is presented here. Knowing what options you have will make you a better SQL programmer.

 The recipes presented in this chapter use simple date data types. If you are using more complex date data types you will need to adjust the solutions accordingly.

9.1 Determining If a Year Is a Leap Year

Problem

You want to determine whether the current year is a leap year.

Solution

If you've worked on SQL for some time, there's no doubt that you've come across several techniques for solving this problem. Just about all the solutions I've encountered work well, but the one presented in this recipe is probably the simplest. This solution simply checks the last day of February; if it is the 29th then the current year is a leap year.

DB2

Use the recursive WITH clause to return each day in February. Use the aggregate function MAX to determine the last day in February.

```
 1    with x (dy,mth)
 2       as (
 3  select dy, month(dy)
 4     from (
 5  select (current_date -
 6             dayofyear(current_date) days +1 days)
 7             +1 months as dy
 8     from t1
 9          ) tmp1
10   union all
11  select dy+1 days, mth
12     from x
13    where month(dy+1 day) = mth
14  )
15  select max(day(dy))
16     from x
```

Oracle

Use the function LAST_DAY to find the last day in February:

```
1 select to_char(
2            last_day(add_months(trunc(sysdate,'y'),1)),
3            'DD')
4     from t1
```

PostgreSQL

Use the function GENERATE_SERIES to return each day in February, then use the aggregate function MAX to find the last day in February:

```
 1  select max(to_char(tmp2.dy+x.id,'DD')) as dy
 2     from (
 3  select dy, to_char(dy,'MM') as mth
 4     from (
 5  select cast(cast(
 6             date_trunc('year',current_date) as date)
 7                   + interval '1 month' as date) as dy
 8     from t1
 9          ) tmp1
```

```
10         ) tmp2, generate_series (0,29) x(id)
11    where to_char(tmp2.dy+x.id,'MM') = tmp2.mth
```

MySQL

Use the function LAST_DAY to find the last day in February:

```
1   select day(
2          last_day(
3          date_add(
4          date_add(
5          date_add(current_date,
6                    interval -dayofyear(current_date) day),
7                    interval 1 day),
8                    interval 1 month))) dy
9     from t1
```

SQL Server

Use the recursive WITH clause to return each day in February. Use the aggregate function MAX to determine the last day in February:

```
1     with x (dy,mth)
2        as (
3   select dy, month(dy)
4     from (
5   select dateadd(mm,1,(getdate( )-datepart(dy,getdate( )))+1) dy
6     from t1
7          ) tmp1
8    union all
9   select dateadd(dd,1,dy), mth
10     from x
11    where month(dateadd(dd,1,dy)) = mth
12  )
13  select max(day(dy))
14     from x
```

Discussion

DB2

The inline view TMP1 in the recursive view X returns the first day in February by:

1. Starting with the current date

2. Using DAYOFYEAR to determine the number of days into the current year that the current date represents

3. Subtracting that number of days from the current date to get December 31 of the prior year, and then adding one to get to January 1 of the current year

4. Adding one month to get to February 1

The result of all this math is shown below:

```
select (current_date -
        dayofyear(current_date) days +1 days) +1 months as dy
  from t1

DY
-----------
01-FEB-2005
```

The next step is to return the month of the date returned by inline view TMP1 by using the MONTH function:

```
select dy, month(dy) as mth
  from (
select (current_date -
        dayofyear(current_date) days +1 days) +1 months as dy
  from t1
      ) tmp1

DY          MTH
----------- ---
01-FEB-2005   2
```

The results presented thus far provide the start point for the recursive operation that generates each day in February. To return each day in February, repeatedly add one day to DY until you are no longer in the month of February. A portion of the results of the WITH operation is shown below:

```
with x (dy,mth)
   as (
select dy, month(dy)
  from (
select (current_date -
        dayofyear(current_date) days +1 days) +1 months as dy
  from t1
      ) tmp1
union all
select dy+1 days, mth
  from x
 where month(dy+1 day) = mth
)
select dy,mth
  from x

DY          MTH
----------- ---
01-FEB-2005   2
...
10-FEB-2005   2
...
28-FEB-2005   2
```

The final step is to use the MAX function on the DY column to return the last day in February; if it is the 29th, you are in a leap year.

Oracle

The first step is to find the beginning of the year using the TRUNC function:

```
select trunc(sysdate,'y')
  from t1

DY
-----------
01-JAN-2005
```

Because the first day of the year is January 1st, the next step is to add one month to get to February 1st:

```
select add_months(trunc(sysdate,'y'),1) dy
  from t1

DY
-----------
01-FEB-2005
```

The next step is to use the LAST_DAY function to find the last day in February:

```
select last_day(add_months(trunc(sysdate,'y'),1)) dy
  from t1

DY
-----------
28-FEB-2005
```

The final step (which is optional) is to use TO_CHAR to return either 28 or 29.

PostgreSQL

The first step is to examine the results returned by inline view TMP1. Use the DATE_TRUNC function to find the beginning of the current year and cast that result as a DATE:

```
select cast(date_trunc('year',current_date) as date) as dy
  from t1

DY
-----------
01-JAN-2005
```

The next step is to add one month to the first day of the current year to get the first day in February, casting the result as a date:

```
select cast(cast(
            date_trunc('year',current_date) as date)
                    + interval '1 month' as date) as dy
  from t1

DY
-----------
01-FEB-2005
```

Next, return DY from inline view TMP1 along with the numeric month of DY. Return the numeric month by using the TO_CHAR function:

```
select dy, to_char(dy,'MM') as mth
  from (
 select cast(cast(
             date_trunc('year',current_date) as date)
                       + interval '1 month' as date) as dy
    from t1
        ) tmp1

DY           MTH
-----------  ---
01-FEB-2005   2
```

The results shown thus far comprise the result set of inline view TMP2. Your next step is to use the extremely useful function GENERATE_SERIES to return 29 rows (values 1 through 29). Every row returned by GENERATE_SERIES (aliased X) is added to DY from inline view TMP2. Partial results are shown below:

```
select tmp2.dy+x.id as dy, tmp2.mth
  from (
select dy, to_char(dy,'MM') as mth
  from (
select cast(cast(
            date_trunc('year',current_date) as date)
                      + interval '1 month' as date) as dy
  from t1
        ) tmp1
        ) tmp2, generate_series (0,29) x(id)
 where to_char(tmp2.dy+x.id,'MM') = tmp2.mth


DY           MTH
-----------  ---
01-FEB-2005   02
...
10-FEB-2005   02
...
28-FEB-2005   02
```

The final step is to use the MAX function to return the last day in February. The function TO_CHAR is applied to that value and will return either 28 or 29.

MySQL

The first step is to find the first day of the current year by subtracting from the current date the number of days it is into the year, and then adding one day. Do all of this with the DATE_ADD function:

```
select date_add(
        date_add(current_date,
                interval -dayofyear(current_date) day),
                interval 1 day) dy
```

```
    from t1

DY
-----------
01-JAN-2005
```

Then add one month again using the DATE_ADD function:

```
select date_add(
       date_add(
       date_add(current_date,
              interval -dayofyear(current_date) day),
              interval 1 day),
              interval 1 month) dy
    from t1

DY
-----------
01-FEB-2005
```

Now that you've made it to February, use the LAST_DAY function to find the last day of the month:

```
select last_day(
       date_add(
       date_add(
       date_add(current_date,
              interval -dayofyear(current_date) day),
              interval 1 day),
              interval 1 month)) dy
    from t1

DY
-----------
28-FEB-2005
```

The final step (which is optional) is to use the DAY function to return either a 28 or 29.

SQL Server

This solution uses the recursive WITH clause to generate each day in February. The first step is to find the first day of February. To do this, find the first day of the current year by subtracting from the current date the number of days it is into the year, and then adding one day. Once you have the first day of the current year, use the DATEADD function to add one month to advance to the first day of February:

```
select dateadd(mm,1,(getdate( )-datepart(dy,getdate( )))+1) dy
    from t1

DY
-----------
01-FEB-2005
```

Next, return the first day of February along with the numeric month for February:

```
select dy, month(dy) mth
  from (
select dateadd(mm,1,(getdate( )-datepart(dy,getdate( )))+1) dy
  from t1
      ) tmp1
```

```
DY            MTH
-----------   ---
01-FEB-2005    2
```

Then use the recursive capabilities of the WITH clause to repeatedly add one day to DY from inline view TMP1 until you are no longer in February (partial results shown below):

```
with x (dy,mth)
    as (
select dy, month(dy)
  from (
select dateadd(mm,1,(getdate( )-datepart(dy,getdate( )))+1) dy
  from t1
      ) tmp1
 union all
select dateadd(dd,1,dy), mth
  from x
 where month(dateadd(dd,1,dy)) = mth
)
select dy,mth from x
```

```
DY            MTH
-----------   ---
01-FEB-2005   02
...
10-FEB-2005   02
...
28-FEB-2005   02
```

Now that you can return each day in February, the final step is to use the MAX function to see if the last day is the 28th or 29th. As an optional last step, you can use the DAY function to return a 28 or 29, rather than a date.

9.2 Determining the Number of Days in a Year

Problem

You want to count the number of days in the current year.

Solution

The number of days in the current year is the difference between the first day of the next year and the first day of the current year (in days). For each solution the steps are:

1. Find the first day of the current year.
2. Add one year to that date (to get the first day of the next year).
3. Subtract the current year from the result of step 2.

The solutions differ only in the built-in functions that you use to perform these steps.

DB2

Use the function DAYOFYEAR to help find the first day of the current year, and use DAYS to find the number of days in the current year:

```
1 select days((curr_year + 1 year)) - days(curr_year)
2   from (
3 select (current_date -
4          dayofyear(current_date) day +
5          1 day) curr_year
6   from t1
7       ) x
```

Oracle

Use the function TRUNC to find the beginning of the current year, and use ADD_MONTHS to then find the beginning of next year:

```
1 select add_months(trunc(sysdate,'y'),12) - trunc(sysdate,'y')
2   from dual
```

PostgreSQL

Use the function DATE_TRUNC to find the beginning of the current year. Then use interval arithmetic to determine the beginning of next year:

```
1 select cast((curr_year + interval '1 year') as date) - curr_year
2   from (
3 select cast(date_trunc('year',current_date) as date) as curr_year
4   from t1
5       ) x
```

MySQL

Use ADDDATE to help find the beginning of the current year. Use DATEDIFF and interval arithmetic to determine the number of days in the year:

```
1 select datediff((curr_year + interval 1 year),curr_year)
2   from (
3 select adddate(current_date,-dayofyear(current_date)+1) curr_year
4   from t1
5       ) x
```

SQL Server

Use the function DATEADD to find the first day of the current year. Use DATED-
IFF to return the number of days in the current year:

```
1 select datediff(d,curr_year,dateadd(yy,1,curr_year))
2   from (
3 select dateadd(d,-datepart(dy,getdate())+1,getdate()) curr_year
4   from t1
5        ) x
```

Discussion

DB2

The first step is to find the first day of the current year. Use DAYOFYEAR to determine how many days you are into the current year. Subtract that value from the current date to get the last day of last year, and then add 1:

```
select (current_date -
        dayofyear(current_date) day +
        1 day) curr_year
  from t1

CURR_YEAR
-----------
01-JAN-2005
```

Now that you have the first day of the current year, just add one year to it; this gives
you the first day of next year. Then subtract the beginning of the current year from
the beginning of next year.

Oracle

The first step is to find the first day of the current year, which you can easily do by
invoking the built-in TRUNC function and passing 'Y' as the second argument
(thereby truncating the date to the beginning of the year):

```
select select trunc(sysdate,'y') curr_year
  from dual

CURR_YEAR
-----------
01-JAN-2005
```

Then add one year to arrive at the first day of the next year. Finally, subtract the two
dates to find the number of days in the current year.

PostgreSQL

Begin by finding the first day of the current year. To do that, invoke the DATE_
TRUNC function as follows:

```
select cast(date_trunc('year',current_date) as date) as curr_year
  from t1

CURR_YEAR
-----------
01-JAN-2005
```

You can then easily add a year to compute the first day of next year. Then all you need to do is to subtract the two dates. Be sure to subtract the earlier date from the later date. The result will be the number of days in the current year.

MySQL

Your first step is to find the first day of the current year. Use DAYOFYEAR to find how many days you are into the current year. Subtract that value from the current date, and add 1:

```
select adddate(current_date,-dayofyear(current_date)+1) curr_year
  from t1

CURR_YEAR
-----------
01-JAN-2005
```

Now that you have the first day of the current year, your next step is to add one year to it to get the first day of next year. Then subtract the beginning of the current year from the beginning of the next year. The result is the number of days in the current year.

SQL Server

Your first step is to find the first day of the current year. Use DATEADD and DATEPART to subtract from the current date the number of days into the year the current date is, and add 1:

```
select dateadd(d,-datepart(dy,getdate())+1,getdate()) curr_year
  from t1

CURR_YEAR
-----------
01-JAN-2005
```

Now that you have the first day of the current year, your next step is to add one year to it get the first day of the next year. Then subtract the beginning of the current year from the beginning of the next year. The result is the number of days in the current year.

9.3   Extracting Units of Time from a Date

Problem

You want to break the current date down into six parts: day, month, year, second, minute, and hour. You want the results to be returned as numbers.

Solution

My use of the current date is arbitrary. Feel free to use this recipe with other dates. In Chapter 1, I mention the importance of learning and taking advantage of the built-in functions provided by your RDBMS; this is especially true when it comes to working with dates. There are different ways of extracting units of time from a date than those presented in this recipe, and it would benefit you to experiment with different techniques and functions.

DB2

DB2 implements a set of built-in functions that make it easy for you to extract portions of a date. The function names HOUR, MINUTE, SECOND, DAY, MONTH, and YEAR conveniently correspond to the units of time you can return: if you want the day use DAY, hour use HOUR, etc. For example:

```
1  select   hour( current_timestamp ) hr,
2          minute( current_timestamp ) min,
3          second( current_timestamp ) sec,
4             day( current_timestamp ) dy,
5           month( current_timestamp ) mth,
6            year( current_timestamp ) yr
7    from t1

 HR   MIN   SEC   DY   MTH    YR
 ----  -----  -----  -----  -----  -----
  20   28   36   15    6   2005
```

Oracle

Use functions TO_CHAR and TO_NUMBER to return specific units of time from a date:

```
1  select to_number(to_char(sysdate,'hh24')) hour,
2         to_number(to_char(sysdate,'mi')) min,
3         to_number(to_char(sysdate,'ss')) sec,
4         to_number(to_char(sysdate,'dd')) day,
5         to_number(to_char(sysdate,'mm')) mth,
6         to_number(to_char(sysdate,'yyyy')) year
7    from dual

 HOUR   MIN   SEC   DAY   MTH  YEAR
 ----  -----  -----  -----  -----  -----
  20   28   36   15    6   2005
```

PostgreSQL

Use functions TO_CHAR and TO_NUMBER to return specific units of time from a date:

```
1 select to_number(to_char(current_timestamp,'hh24'),'99') as hr,
2        to_number(to_char(current_timestamp,'mi'),'99') as min,
3        to_number(to_char(current_timestamp,'ss'),'99') as sec,
4        to_number(to_char(current_timestamp,'dd'),'99') as day,
5        to_number(to_char(current_timestamp,'mm'),'99') as mth,
6        to_number(to_char(current_timestamp,'yyyy'),'9999') as yr
7   from t1

 HR   MIN   SEC   DAY   MTH    YR
 ----  ----- ----- ----- ----- -----
 20    28    36    15     6   2005
```

MySQL

Use the DATE_FORMAT function to return specific units of time from a date:

```
1 select date_format(current_timestamp,'%k') hr,
2        date_format(current_timestamp,'%i') min,
3        date_format(current_timestamp,'%s') sec,
4        date_format(current_timestamp,'%d') dy,
5        date_format(current_timestamp,'%m') mon,
6        date_format(current_timestamp,'%Y') yr
7   from t1

 HR   MIN   SEC    DY   MTH    YR
 ----  ----- ----- ----- ----- -----
 20    28    36    15     6   2005
```

SQL Server

Use the function DATEPART to return specific units of time from a date:

```
1 select datepart( hour,   getdate()) hr,
2        datepart( minute,getdate()) min,
3        datepart( second,getdate()) sec,
4        datepart( day,    getdate()) dy,
5        datepart( month, getdate()) mon,
6        datepart( year,  getdate()) yr
7   from t1

 HR   MIN   SEC    DY   MTH    YR
 ----  ----- ----- ----- ----- -----
 20    28    36    15     6   2005
```

Discussion

There's nothing fancy in these solutions; just take advantage of what you're already paying for. Take the time to learn the date functions available to you. This recipe only scratches the surface of the functions presented in each solution. You'll find that each of the functions takes many more arguments and can return more information than what this recipe provides you.

9.4 Determining the First and Last Day of a Month

Problem

You want to determine the first and last days for the current month.

Solution

The solutions presented here are for finding first and last days for the current month. Using the current month is arbitrary. With a bit of adjustment, you can make the solutions work for any month.

DB2

Use the DAY function to return the number of days into the current month the current date represents. Subtract this value from the current date, and then add 1 to get the first of the month. To get the last day of the month, add one month to the current date, then subtract from it the value returned by the DAY function as applied to the current date:

```
1 select (date(current_date) - day(date(current_date)) day +1 day) firstday,
2         (date(current_date)+1 month - day(date(current_date)+1 month) day) lastday
3   from t1
```

Oracle

Use the function TRUNC to find the first of the month, and the function LAST_DAY to find the last day of the month:

```
1 select trunc(sysdate,'mm') firstday,
2        last_day(sysdate) lastday
3   from dual
```

 Using TRUNC as decribed here will result in the loss of any time-of-day component, whereas LAST_DAY will preserve the time of day.

PostgreSQL

Use the DATE_TRUNC function to truncate the current date to the first of the current month. Once you have the first day of the month, add one month and subtract one day to find the end of the current month:

```
1 select firstday,
2        cast(firstday + interval '1 month'
3                      - interval '1 day' as date) as lastday
4   from (
5 select cast(date_trunc('month',current_date) as date) as firstday
6   from t1
7        ) x
```

MySQL

Use the DATE_ADD and DAY functions to find the number of days into the month the current date is. Then subtract that value from the current date and add 1 to find the first of the month. To find the last day of the current month, use the LAST_DAY function:

```
1 select date_add(current_date,
2                  interval -day(current_date)+1 day) firstday,
3          last_day(current_date) lastday
4    from t1
```

SQL Server

Use the DATEADD and DAY functions to find the number of days into the month represented by the current date. Then subtract that value from the current date and add 1 to find the first of the month. To get the last day of the month, add one month to the current date, and then subtract from that result the value returned by the DAY function applied to the current date plus 1 month, again using the functions DAY and DATEADD:

```
1 select dateadd(day,-day(getdate( ))+1,getdate( )) firstday,
2          dateadd(day,
3                   -day(dateadd(month,1,getdate( ))),
4                   dateadd(month,1,getdate( ))) lastday
5    from t1
```

Discussion

DB2

To find the first day of the month, simply find the numeric value of the current day of the month then subtract this from the current date. For example, if the date is March 14th, the numeric day value is 14. Subtracting 14 days from March 14th gives you the last day of the month in February. From there, simply add one day to get to the first of the current month. The technique to get the last day of the month is similar to that of the first; subtract the numeric day of the month from the current date to get the last day of the prior month. Since we want the last day of the current month (not the last day of the prior month), we need to add one month to the current date.

Oracle

To find the first day of the current month, use the TRUNC function with "mm" as the second argument to "truncate" the current date down to the first of the month. To find the last day of the current month, simply use the LAST_DAY function.

PostgreSQL

To find the first day of the current month, use the DATE_TRUNC function with "month" as the second argument to "truncate" the current date down to the first of the month. To find the last day of the current month, add one month to the first day of the month, and then subtract one day.

MySQL

To find the first day of the month, use the DAY function. The DAY function conveniently returns the day of the month for the date passed. If you subtract the value returned by DAY(CURRENT_DATE) from the current date, you get the last day of the prior month; add one day to get the first day of the current month. To find the last day of the current month, simply use the LAST_DAY function.

SQL Server

To find the first day of the month, use the DAY function. The DAY function conveniently returns the day of the month for the date passed. If you subtract the value returned by DAY(GETDATE()) from the current date, you get the last day of the prior month; add one day to get the first day of the current month. To find the last day of the current month, use the DATEADD function. Add one month to the current date, then subtract from it the value returned by DAY(DATEADD(MONTH,1,GETDATE())) to get the last day of the current month.

9.5 Determining All Dates for a Particular Weekday Throughout a Year

Problem

You want to find all the dates in a year that correspond to a given day of the week. For example, you may wish to generate a list of Fridays for the current year.

Solution

Regardless of vendor, the key to the solution is to return each day for the current year and keep only those dates corresponding to the day of the week that you care about. The solution examples retain all the Fridays.

DB2

Use the recursive WITH clause to return each day in the current year. Then use the function DAYNAME to keep only Fridays:

```
1    with x (dy,yr)
2       as (
3   select dy, year(dy) yr
4     from (
5   select (current_date -
6           dayofyear(current_date) days +1 days) as dy
7     from t1
8           ) tmp1
9    union all
10  select dy+1 days, yr
11    from x
12   where year(dy +1 day) = yr
13  )
14  select dy
15    from x
16   where dayname(dy) = 'Friday'
```

Oracle

Use the recursive CONNECT BY clause to return each day in the current year. Then use the function TO_CHAR to keep only Fridays:

```
1    with x
2       as (
3   select trunc(sysdate,'y')+level-1 dy
4     from t1
5     connect by level <=
6        add_months(trunc(sysdate,'y'),12)-trunc(sysdate,'y')
7   )
8   select *
9     from x
10   where to_char( dy, 'dy') = 'fri'
```

PostgreSQL

Use the function GENERATE_SERIES to return each day in the current year. Then use the function TO_CHAR to keep only Fridays:

```
1 select cast(date_trunc('year',current_date) as date)
2          + x.id as dy
3    from generate_series (
4          0,
5          ( select cast(
6                  cast(
7             date_trunc('year',current_date) as date)
8                        + interval '1 years' as date)
9                     - cast(
10                  date_trunc('year',current_date) as date) )-1
11          ) x(id)
12   where to_char(
13            cast(
14       date_trunc('year',current_date)
15                  as date)+x.id,'dy') = 'fri'
```

MySQL

Use the pivot table T500 to return each day in the current year. Then use the function DAYNAME to keep only Fridays:

```
1   select dy
2     from (
3   select adddate(x.dy,interval t500.id-1 day) dy
4     from (
5   select dy, year(dy) yr
6     from (
7   select adddate(
8          adddate(current_date,
9                  interval -dayofyear(current_date) day),
10                 interval 1 day ) dy
11    from t1
12         ) tmp1
13         ) x,
14         t500
15   where year(adddate(x.dy,interval t500.id-1 day)) = x.yr
16         ) tmp2
17   where dayname(dy) = 'Friday'
```

SQL Server

Use the recursive WITH clause to return each day in the current year. Then use the function DAYNAME to keep only Fridays:

```
1     with x (dy,yr)
2       as (
3   select dy, year(dy) yr
4     from (
5   select getdate( )-datepart(dy,getdate( ))+1 dy
6     from t1
7         ) tmp1
8    union all
9   select dateadd(dd,1,dy), yr
10    from x
11   where year(dateadd(dd,1,dy)) = yr
12  )
13  select x.dy
14    from x
15   where datename(dw,x.dy) = 'Friday'
16  option (maxrecursion 400)
```

Discussion

DB2

To find all the Fridays in the current year, you must be able to return every day in the current year. The first step is to find the first day of the year by using the DAYOF-YEAR function. Subtract the value returned by DAYOFYEAR(CURRENT_DATE) from the current date to get December 31 of the prior year, and then add 1 to get the first day of the current year:

```
select (current_date -
        dayofyear(current_date) days +1 days) as dy
  from t1

DY
-----------
01-JAN-2005
```

Now that you have the first day of the year, use the WITH clause to repeatedly add one day to the first day of the year until you are no longer in the current year. The result set will be every day in the current year (a portion of the rows returned by the recursive view X is shown below):

```
with x (dy,yr)
    as (
select dy, year(dy) yr
  from (
select (current_date -
        dayofyear(current_date) days +1 days) as dy
  from t1
        ) tmp1
union all
select dy+1 days, yr
  from x
 where year(dy +1 day) = yr
)
select dy
  from x

DY
-----------
01-JAN-2005
...
15-FEB-2005
...
22-NOV-2005
...
31-DEC-2005
```

The final step is to use the DAYNAME function to keep only rows that are Fridays.

Oracle

To find all the Fridays in the current year, you must be able to return every day in the current year. Begin by using the TRUNC function to find the first day of the year:

```
select trunc(sysdate,'y') dy
  from t1

DY
-----------
01-JAN-2005
```

Next, use the CONNECT BY clause to return every day in the current year (to understand how to use CONNECT BY to generate rows, see Recipe 10.5).

As an aside, this recipe uses the WITH clause, but you can also use an inline view.

At the time of this writing, Oracle's WITH clause is not meant for recursive operations (unlike the case with DB2 and SQL Server); recursive operations are done using CONNECT BY. A portion of the result set returned by view X is shown below:

```
with x
   as (
select trunc(sysdate,'y')+level-1 dy
  from t1
  connect by level <=
     add_months(trunc(sysdate,'y'),12)-trunc(sysdate,'y')
)
select *
  from x

DY
-----------
01-JAN-2005
...
15-FEB-2005
...
22-NOV-2005
...
31-DEC-2005
```

The final step is to use the TO_CHAR function to keep only Fridays.

PostgreSQL

To find all the Fridays in the current year, you must be able to return a row for every day in the current year. To do that, use the GENERATE_SERIES function. The start and end values to be returned by GENERATE_SERIES are 0 and the number of days in the current year minus 1. The first parameter passed to GENERATE_SERIES is 0, while the second is a query that determines the number of days in the current year (because you are adding to the first day of the current year, you actually want to add 1 less than the number of days in the current year, so as to not spill over into the next year). The result returned by the second parameter of the GENERATE_SERIES function is shown below:

```
select cast(
       cast(
date_trunc('year',current_date) as date)
          + interval '1 years' as date)
          - cast(
       date_trunc('year',current_date) as date)-1 as cnt
  from t1
```

```
CNT
---
364
```

Keeping in mind the result set above, the call to GENERATE_SERIES in the FROM clause will look like this: GENERATE_SERIES (0, 364). If you are in a leap year, such as 2004, the second parameter would be 365.

The next step after generating a list of dates in the year is to add the values returned by GENERATE_SERIES to the first day of the current year. A portion of the results is shown below:

```
select cast(date_trunc('year',current_date) as date)
        + x.id as dy
  from generate_series (
        0,
        ( select cast(
                cast(
            date_trunc('year',current_date) as date)
                      + interval '1 years' as date)
                    - cast(
                date_trunc('year',current_date) as date) )-1
        ) x(id)

DY
-----------
01-JAN-2005   ·
...
15-FEB-2005
...
22-NOV-2005
...
31-DEC-2005
```

The final step is to use the TO_CHAR function to keep only the Fridays.

MySQL

To find all the Fridays in the current year, you must be able to return every day in the current year. The first step is to find the first day of the year by using the DAYOF-YEAR function. Subtract the value returned by DAYOFYEAR(CURRENT_DATE) from the current date, and then add 1 to get the first day of the current year:

```
select adddate(
        adddate(current_date,
                interval -dayofyear(current_date) day),
                interval 1 day ) dy
   from t1

DY
-----------
01-JAN-2005
```

Then use table T500 to generate enough rows to return each day in the current year. You can do this by adding each value of T500.ID to the first day of the year until you break out of the current year. Partial results of this operation are shown below:

```
select adddate(x.dy,interval t500.id-1 day) dy
  from (
select dy, year(dy) yr
  from (
select adddate(
       adddate(current_date,
               interval -dayofyear(current_date) day),
               interval 1 day ) dy
  from t1
       ) tmp1
       ) x,
       t500
 where year(adddate(x.dy,interval t500.id-1 day)) = x.yr

DY
-----------
01-JAN-2005
...
15-FEB-2005
...
22-NOV-2005
...
31-DEC-2005
```

The final step is to use the DAYNAME function to keep only Fridays.

SQL Server

To find all the Fridays in the current year, you must be able to return every day in the current year. The first step is to find the first day of the year by using the DATEPART function. Subtract the value returned by DATEPART(DY,GETDATE()) from the current date, and then add 1 to get the first day of the current year:

```
select getdate( )-datepart(dy,getdate( ))+1 dy
  from t1

DY
-----------
01-JAN-2005
```

Now that you have the first day of the year, use the WITH clause and the DATEADD function to repeatedly add one day to the first day of the year until you are no longer in the current year. The result set will be every day in the current year (a portion of the rows returned by the recursive view X is shown below):

```
with x (dy,yr)
  as (
select dy, year(dy) yr
  from (
```

```
select getdate( )-datepart(dy,getdate( ))+1 dy
  from t1
        ) tmp1
 union all
select dateadd(dd,1,dy), yr
  from x
 where year(dateadd(dd,1,dy)) = yr
)
select x.dy
  from x
option (maxrecursion 400)

DY
-----------
01-JAN-2005
...
15-FEB-2005
...
22-NOV-2005
...
31-DEC-2005
```

Finally, use the DATENAME function to keep only rows that are Fridays. For this solution to work, you must set MAXRECURSION to at least 366 (the filter on the year portion of the current year, in recursive view X, guarantees you will never generate more than 366 rows).

9.6 Determining the Date of the First and Last Occurrence of a Specific Weekday in a Month

Problem

You want to find, for example, the first and last Mondays of the current month.

Solution

The choice to use Monday and the current month is arbitrary; you can use the solutions presented in this recipe for any weekday and any month. Because each weekday is seven days apart from itself, once you have the first instance of a weekday, you can add 7 days to get the second and 14 days to get the third. Likewise, if you have the last instance of a weekday in a month, you can subtract 7 days to get the third and subtract 14 days to get the second.

DB2

Use the recursive WITH clause to generate each day in the current month and use a CASE expression to flag all Mondays. The first and last Mondays will be the earliest and latest of the flagged dates:

```
1    with x (dy,mth,is_monday)
2        as (
3    select dy,month(dy),
4           case when dayname(dy)='Monday'
5                then 1 else 0
6           end
7     from (
8    select (current_date-day(current_date) day +1 day) dy
9       from t1
10           ) tmp1
11    union all
12    select (dy +1 day), mth,
13           case when dayname(dy +1 day)='Monday'
14                then 1 else 0
15           end
16     from x
17    where month(dy +1 day) = mth
18    )
19    select min(dy) first_monday, max(dy) last_monday
20      from x
21     where is_monday = 1
```

Oracle

Use the functions NEXT_DAY and LAST_DAY, together with a bit of clever date arithmetic, to find the first and last Mondays of the current month:

```
select next_day(trunc(sysdate,'mm')-1,'MONDAY') first_monday,
       next_day(last_day(trunc(sysdate,'mm'))-7,'MONDAY') last_monday
  from dual
```

PostgreSQL

Use the function DATE_TRUNC to find the first day of the month. Once you have the first day of the month, you can use simple arithmetic involving the numeric values of weekdays (Sun – Sat is 1 – 7) to find the first and last Mondays of the current month:

```
1    select first_monday,
2           case to_char(first_monday+28,'mm')
3                when mth then first_monday+28
4                          else first_monday+21
5           end as last_monday
6      from (
7    select case sign(cast(to_char(dy,'d') as integer)-2)
8                when  0
9                then dy
10               when -1
11               then dy+abs(cast(to_char(dy,'d') as integer)-2)
12               when  1
13               then (7-(cast(to_char(dy,'d') as integer)-2))+dy
14           end as first_monday,
15           mth
16     from (
```

```
17  select cast(date_trunc('month',current_date) as date) as dy,
18         to_char(current_date,'mm') as mth
19    from t1
20        ) x
21        ) y
```

MySQL

Use the ADDDATE function to find the first day of the month. Once you have the
first day of the month, you can use simple arithmetic on the numeric values of weekdays (Sun – Sat is 1 – 7) to find the first and last Mondays of the current month:

```
1   select first_monday,
2          case month(adddate(first_monday,28))
3               when mth then adddate(first_monday,28)
4                        else adddate(first_monday,21)
5          end last_monday
6     from (
7   select case sign(dayofweek(dy)-2)
8               when  0 then dy
9               when -1 then adddate(dy,abs(dayofweek(dy)-2))
10              when  1 then adddate(dy,(7-(dayofweek(dy)-2)))
11          end first_monday,
12          mth
13    from (
14  select adddate(adddate(current_date,-day(current_date)),1) dy,
15         month(current_date) mth
16    from t1
17        ) x
18        ) y
```

SQL Server

Use the recursive WITH clause to generate each day in the current month, and then
use a CASE expression to flag all Mondays. The first and last Mondays will be the
earliest and latest of the flagged dates:

```
1    with x (dy,mth,is_monday)
2       as (
3   select dy,mth,
4          case when datepart(dw,dy) = 2
5               then 1 else 0
6          end
7     from (
8   select dateadd(day,1,dateadd(day,-day(getdate()),getdate())) dy,
9          month(getdate()) mth
10    from t1
11        ) tmp1
12   union all
13  select dateadd(day,1,dy),
14         mth,
15         case when datepart(dw,dateadd(day,1,dy)) = 2
16              then 1 else 0
17         end
```

```
18    from x
19   where month(dateadd(day,1,dy)) = mth
20   )
21  select min(dy) first_monday,
22         max(dy) last_monday
23    from x
24   where is_monday = 1
```

Discussion

DB2 and SQL Server

DB2 and SQL Server use different functions to solve this problem, but the technique is exactly the same. If you eyeball both solutions you'll see the only difference between the two is the way dates are added. This discussion will cover both solutions, using the DB2 solution's code to show the results of intermediate steps.

 If you do not have access to the recursive WITH clause in the version of SQL Server or DB2 that you are running, you can use the PostgreSQL technique instead.

The first step in finding the first and last Mondays of the current month is to return the first day of the month. Inline view TMP1 in recursive view X finds the first day of the current month by first finding the current date, specifically, the day of the month for the current date. The day of the month for the current date represents how many days into the month you are (e.g., April 10th is the 10th day of the April). If you subtract this day of the month value from the current date, you end up at the last day of the previous month (e.g., subtracting 10 from April 10th puts you at the last day of March). After this subtraction, simply add one day to arrive at the first day of the current month:

```
select (current_date-day(current_date) day +1 day) dy
  from t1
```

```
DY
-----------
01-JUN-2005
```

Next, find the month for the current date using the MONTH function and a simple CASE expression to determine whether or not the first day of the month is a Monday:

```
select dy, month(dy) mth,
       case when dayname(dy)='Monday'
            then 1 else 0
       end is_monday
  from (
select (current_date-day(current_date) day +1 day) dy
  from t1
       ) tmp1
```

```
DY           MTH  IS_MONDAY
-----------  ---  ----------
01-JUN-2005   6            0
```

Then use the recursive capabilities of the WITH clause to repeatedly add one day to the first day of the month until you're no longer in the current month. Along the way, you will use a CASE expression to determine which days in the month are Mondays (Mondays will be flagged with "1"). A portion of the output from recursive view X is shown below:

```
with x (dy,mth,is_monday)
     as (
 select dy,month(dy) mth,
        case when dayname(dy)='Monday'
             then 1 else 0
        end is_monday
   from (
 select (current_date-day(current_date) day +1 day) dy
   from t1
        ) tmp1
  union all
 select (dy +1 day), mth,
        case when dayname(dy +1 day)='Monday'
             then 1 else 0
        end
   from x
  where month(dy +1 day) = mth
 )
 select *
   from x
```

```
DY           MTH  IS_MONDAY
-----------  ---  ----------
01-JUN-2005   6            0
02-JUN-2005   6            0
03-JUN-2005   6            0
04-JUN-2005   6            0
05-JUN-2005   6            0
06-JUN-2005   6            1
07-JUN-2005   6            0
08-JUN-2005   6            0
...
```

Only Mondays will have a value of 1 for IS_MONDAY, so the final step is to use the aggregate functions MIN and MAX on rows where IS_MONDAY is 1 to find the first and last Mondays of the month.

Oracle

The function NEXT_DAY makes this problem easy to solve. To find the first Monday of the current month, first return the last day of the prior month via some date arithmetic involving the TRUNC function:

```
select trunc(sysdate,'mm')-1 dy
  from dual
```

```
DY
-----------
31-MAY-2005
```

Then use the NEXT_DAY function to find the first Monday that comes after the last day of the previous month (i.e., the first Monday of the current month):

```
select next_day(trunc(sysdate,'mm')-1,'MONDAY') first_monday
  from dual
```

```
FIRST_MONDAY
------------
06-JUN-2005
```

To find the last Monday of the current month, start by returning the first day of the current month by using the TRUNC function:

```
select trunc(sysdate,'mm') dy
  from dual
```

```
DY
-----------
01-JUN-2005
```

The next step is to find the last week (the last seven days) of the month. Use the LAST_DAY function to find the last day of the month, and then subtract seven days:

```
select last_day(trunc(sysdate,'mm'))-7 dy
  from dual
```

```
DY
-----------
23-JUN-2005
```

If it isn't immediately obvious, you go back seven days from the last day of the month to ensure that you will have at least one of any weekday left in the month. The last step is to use the function NEXT_DAY to find the next (and last) Monday of the month:

```
select next_day(last_day(trunc(sysdate,'mm'))-7,'MONDAY') last_monday
  from dual
```

```
LAST_MONDAY
-----------
27-JUN-2005
```

PostgreSQL and MySQL

PostgreSQL and MySQL also share the same solution approach. The difference is in the functions that you invoke. Despite their lengths, the respective queries are extremely simple; little overhead is involved in finding the first and last Mondays of the current month.

The first step is to find the first day of the current month. The next step is to find the first Monday of the month. Since there is no function to find the next date for a given weekday, you need to use a little arithmetic. The CASE expression beginning on line 7 (of either solution) evaluates the difference between the numeric value for the weekday of the first day of the month and the numeric value corresponding to Monday. Given that the function TO_CHAR (PostgresSQL), when called with the 'D' or 'd' format, and the function DAYOFWEEK (MySQL) will return a numeric value from 1 to 7 representing days Sunday to Saturday; Monday is always represented by 2. The first test evaluated by CASE is the SIGN of the numeric value of the first day of the month (whatever it may be) minus the numeric value of Monday (2). If the result is 0, then the first day of the month falls on a Monday and that is the first Monday of the month. If the result is −1, then the first day of the month falls on a Sunday and to find the first Monday of the month simply add the difference in days between 2 and 1 (numeric values of Monday and Sunday, respectively) to the first day of the month.

If you are having trouble understanding how this works, forget the weekday names and just do the math. For example, say you happen to be starting on a Tuesday and you are looking for the next Friday. When using TO_CHAR with the 'd' format, or DAYOFWEEK, Friday is 6 and Tuesday is 3. To get to 6 from 3, simply take the difference (6–3 = 3) and add it to the smaller value ((6–3) + 3 = 6). So, regardless of the actual dates, if the numeric value of the day you are starting from is less than the numeric value of the day you are searching for, adding the difference between the two dates to the date you are starting from will get you to the date you are searching for.

If the result from SIGN is 1, then the first day of the month falls between Tuesday and Saturday (inclusive). When the first day of the month has a numeric value greater than 2 (Monday), subtract from 7 the difference between the numeric value of the first day of the month and the numeric value of Monday (2), and then add that value to the first day of the month. You will have arrived at the day of the week that you are after, in this case Monday.

Again, if you are having trouble understanding how this works, forget the weekday names and just do the math. For example, suppose you want to find the next Tuesday and you are starting from Friday. Tuesday (3) is less than Friday (6). To get to 3 from 6 subtract the difference between the two values from 7 (7 − (|3–6|) = 4) and add the result (4) to the start day Friday. (The vertical bars in |3-6| generate the absolute value of that difference.) Here, you're not adding 4 to 6 (which will give you 10), you are adding four days to Friday, which will give you the next Tuesday.

The idea behind the CASE expression is to create a sort of a "next day" function for PostgreSQL and MySQL. If you do not start with the first day of the month, the value for DY will be the value returned by CURRENT_DATE and the result of the CASE expression will return the date of the next Monday starting from the current date (unless CURRENT_DATE is a Monday, then that date will be returned).

Now that you have the first Monday of the month, add either 21 or 28 days to find the last Monday of the month. The CASE expression in lines 2–5 determines whether to add 21 or 28 days by checking to see whether 28 days takes you into the next month. The CASE expression does this through the following process:

1. It adds 28 to the value of FIRST_MONDAY.

2. Using either TO_CHAR (PostgreSQL) or MONTH, the CASE expression extracts the name of the current month from result of FIRST_MONDAY + 28.

3. The result from Step 2 is compared to the value MTH from the inline view. The value MTH is the name of the current month as derived from CURRENT_DATE. If the two month values match, then the month is large enough for you to need to add 28 days, and the CASE expression returns FIRST_MONDAY + 28. If the two month values do not match, then you do not have room to add 28 days, and the CASE expression returns FIRST_MONDAY + 21 days instead. It is convenient that our months are such that 28 and 21 are the only two possible values you need worry about adding.

You can extend the solution by adding 7 and 14 days to find the second and third Mondays of the month, respectively.

9.7   Creating a Calendar

Problem

You want to create a calendar for the current month. The calendar should be formatted like a calendar you might have on your desk seven columns across, (usually) five rows down.

Solution

Each solution will look a bit different, but they all solve the problem the same way: return each day for the current month, and then pivot on the day of the week for each week in the month to create a calendar.

There are different formats available for calendars. For example, the Unix *cal* command formats the days from Sunday to Saturday. The examples in this recipe are based on ISO weeks, so the Monday through Friday format is the most convenient to generate. Once you become comfortable with the solutions, you will see that reformatting however you like is simply a matter of modifying the values assigned by the ISO week before pivoting.

 As you begin to use different types of formatting with SQL to create readable output, you will notice your queries becoming longer. Don't let those long queries intimidate you; the queries presented for this recipe are extremely simple once broken down and run piece by piece.

DB2

Use the recursive WITH clause to return every day in the current month. Then pivot on the day of the week using CASE and MAX:

```
1   with x(dy,dm,mth,dw,wk)
2     as (
3 select (current_date -day(current_date) day +1 day) dy,
4         day((current_date -day(current_date) day +1 day)) dm,
5         month(current_date) mth,
6         dayofweek(current_date -day(current_date) day +1 day) dw,
7         week_iso(current_date -day(current_date) day +1 day) wk
8   from t1
9  union all
10 select dy+1 day, day(dy+1 day), mth,
11         dayofweek(dy+1 day), week_iso(dy+1 day)
12   from x
13  where month(dy+1 day) = mth
14   )
15 select max(case dw when 2 then dm end) as Mo,
16         max(case dw when 3 then dm end) as Tu,
17         max(case dw when 4 then dm end) as We,
18         max(case dw when 5 then dm end) as Th,
19         max(case dw when 6 then dm end) as Fr,
20         max(case dw when 7 then dm end) as Sa,
21         max(case dw when 1 then dm end) as Su
22   from x
23  group by wk
24  order by wk
```

Oracle

Use the recursive CONNECT BY clause to return each day in the current month. Then pivot on the day of the week using CASE and MAX:

```
1   with x
2     as (
3   select *
4     from (
5   select to_char(trunc(sysdate,'mm')+level-1,'iw') wk,
6          to_char(trunc(sysdate,'mm')+level-1,'dd') dm,
7          to_number(to_char(trunc(sysdate,'mm')+level-1,'d')) dw,
8          to_char(trunc(sysdate,'mm')+level-1,'mm') curr_mth,
9          to_char(sysdate,'mm') mth
10    from dual
```

```
11   connect by level <= 31
12         )
13   where curr_mth = mth
14   )
15   select max(case dw when 2 then dm end) Mo,
16          max(case dw when 3 then dm end) Tu,
17          max(case dw when 4 then dm end) We,
18          max(case dw when 5 then dm end) Th,
19          max(case dw when 6 then dm end) Fr,
20          max(case dw when 7 then dm end) Sa,
21          max(case dw when 1 then dm end) Su
22     from x
23    group by wk
24    order by wk
```

PostgreSQL

Use the function GENERATE_SERIES to return every day in the current month. Then pivot on the day of the week using MAX and CASE:

```
1   select max(case dw when 2 then dm end) as Mo,
2          max(case dw when 3 then dm end) as Tu,
3          max(case dw when 4 then dm end) as We,
4          max(case dw when 5 then dm end) as Th,
5          max(case dw when 6 then dm end) as Fr,
6          max(case dw when 7 then dm end) as Sa,
7          max(case dw when 1 then dm end) as Su
8     from (
9   select *
10    from (
11   select cast(date_trunc('month',current_date) as date)+x.id,
12          to_char(
13             cast(
14      date_trunc('month',current_date)
15                 as date)+x.id,'iw') as wk,
16          to_char(
17             cast(
18      date_trunc('month',current_date)
19                 as date)+x.id,'dd') as dm,
20          cast(
21        to_char(
22          cast(
23    date_trunc('month',current_date)
24                 as date)+x.id,'d') as integer) as dw,
25          to_char(
26             cast(
27      date_trunc('month',current_date)
28                 as date)+x.id,'mm') as curr_mth,
29          to_char(current_date,'mm') as mth
30     from generate_series (0,31) x(id)
31          ) x
32    where mth = curr_mth
33          ) y
34    group by wk
35    order by wk
```

MySQL

Use table T500 to return each day in the current month. Then pivot on the day of the week using MAX and CASE:

```
1  select max(case dw when 2 then dm end) as Mo,
2         max(case dw when 3 then dm end) as Tu,
3         max(case dw when 4 then dm end) as We,
4         max(case dw when 5 then dm end) as Th,
5         max(case dw when 6 then dm end) as Fr,
6         max(case dw when 7 then dm end) as Sa,
7         max(case dw when 1 then dm end) as Su
8    from (
9  select date_format(dy,'%u') wk,
10        date_format(dy,'%d') dm,
11        date_format(dy,'%w')+1 dw
12   from (
13 select adddate(x.dy,t500.id-1) dy,
14        x.mth
15   from (
16 select adddate(current_date,-dayofmonth(current_date)+1) dy,
17        date_format(
18            adddate(current_date,
19                    -dayofmonth(current_date)+1),
20                    '%m') mth
21   from t1
22         ) x,
23           t500
24   where t500.id <= 31
25     and date_format(adddate(x.dy,t500.id-1),'%m') = x.mth
26         ) y
27         ) z
28  group by wk
29  order by wk
```

SQL Server

Use the recursive WITH clause to return every day in the current month. Then pivot on the day of the week using CASE and MAX:

```
1   with x(dy,dm,mth,dw,wk)
2     as (
3  select dy,
4         day(dy) dm,
5         datepart(m,dy) mth,
6         datepart(dw,dy) dw,
7         case when datepart(dw,dy) = 1
8              then datepart(ww,dy)-1
9              else datepart(ww,dy)
10        end wk
11   from (
12 select dateadd(day,-day(getdate())+1,getdate()) dy
13   from t1
14         ) x
```

```
15    union all
16    select dateadd(d,1,dy), day(dateadd(d,1,dy)), mth,
17            datepart(dw,dateadd(d,1,dy)),
18            case when datepart(dw,dateadd(d,1,dy)) = 1
19                 then datepart(wk,dateadd(d,1,dy))-1
20                 else datepart(wk,dateadd(d,1,dy))
21            end
22      from x
23     where datepart(m,dateadd(d,1,dy)) = mth
24    )
25    select max(case dw when 2 then dm end) as Mo,
26           max(case dw when 3 then dm end) as Tu,
27           max(case dw when 4 then dm end) as We,
28           max(case dw when 5 then dm end) as Th,
29           max(case dw when 6 then dm end) as Fr,
30           max(case dw when 7 then dm end) as Sa,
31           max(case dw when 1 then dm end) as Su
32      from x
33    group by wk
34    order by wk
```

Discussion

DB2

The first step is to return each day in the month for which you want to create a calendar. Do that using the recursive WITH clause (if you don't have WITH available, you can use a pivot table, such as T500, as in the MySQL solution). Along with each day of the month (alias DM) you will need to return different parts of each date: the day of the week (alias DW), the current month you are working with (alias MTH), and the ISO week for each day of the month (alias WK). The results of the recursive view X prior to recursion taking place (the upper portion of the UNION ALL) are shown below:

```
select (current_date -day(current_date) day +1 day) dy,
       day((current_date -day(current_date) day +1 day)) dm,
       month(current_date) mth,
       dayofweek(current_date -day(current_date) day +1 day) dw,
       week_iso(current_date -day(current_date) day +1 day) wk
  from t1
```

```
DY          DM MTH     DW WK
----------- -- --- ----------- --
01-JUN-2005 01  06           4 22
```

The next step is to repeatedly increase the value for DM (move through the days of the month) until you are no longer in the current month. As you move through each day in the month, you will also return the day of the week that each day is, and which ISO week the current day of the month falls into. Partial results are shown below:

```
with x(dy,dm,mth,dw,wk)
  as (
select (current_date -day(current_date) day +1 day) dy,
       day((current_date -day(current_date) day +1 day)) dm,
       month(current_date) mth,
       dayofweek(current_date -day(current_date) day +1 day) dw,
       week_iso(current_date -day(current_date) day +1 day) wk
  from t1
 union all
 select dy+1 day, day(dy+1 day), mth,
        dayofweek(dy+1 day), week_iso(dy+1 day)
   from x
  where month(dy+1 day) = mth
)
select *
  from x


DY          DM MTH     DW WK
----------- -- --- ---------- --
01-JUN-2005 01  06          4 22
02-JUN-2005 02  06          5 22
...
21-JUN-2005 21  06          3 25
22-JUN-2005 22  06          4 25
...
30-JUN-2005 30  06          5 26
```

What you are returning at this point are: each day for the current month, the two-digit numeric day of the month, the two-digit numeric month, the one-digit day of the week (1–7 for Sun–Sat), and the two-digit ISO week each day falls into. With all this information available, you can use a CASE expression to determine which day of the week each value of DM (each day of the month) falls into. A portion of the results is shown below:

```
with x(dy,dm,mth,dw,wk)
  as (
select (current_date -day(current_date) day +1 day) dy,
       day((current_date -day(current_date) day +1 day)) dm,
       month(current_date) mth,
       dayofweek(current_date -day(current_date) day +1 day) dw,
       week_iso(current_date -day(current_date) day +1 day) wk
  from t1
 union all
 select dy+1 day, day(dy+1 day), mth,
        dayofweek(dy+1 day), week_iso(dy+1 day)
   from x
  where month(dy+1 day) = mth
)
select wk,
       case dw when 2 then dm end as Mo,
       case dw when 3 then dm end as Tu,
       case dw when 4 then dm end as We,
       case dw when 5 then dm end as Th,
```

```
        case dw when 6 then dm end as Fr,
        case dw when 7 then dm end as Sa,
        case dw when 1 then dm end as Su
   from x

WK MO TU WE TH FR SA SU
-- -- -- -- -- -- -- --
22       01
22          02
22             03
22                04
22                   05
23 06
23    07
23       08
23          09
23             10
23                11
23                   12
```

As you can see from the partial output, every day in each week is returned as a row. What you want to do now is to group the days by week, and then collapse all the days for each week into a single row. Use the aggregate function MAX, and group by WK (the ISO week) to return all the days for a week as one row. To properly format the calendar and ensure that the days are in the right order, order the results by WK. The final output is shown below:

```
with x(dy,dm,mth,dw,wk)
  as (
select (current_date -day(current_date) day +1 day) dy,
       day((current_date -day(current_date) day +1 day)) dm,
       month(current_date) mth,
       dayofweek(current_date -day(current_date) day +1 day) dw,
       week_iso(current_date -day(current_date) day +1 day) wk
  from t1
 union all
 select dy+1 day, day(dy+1 day), mth,
        dayofweek(dy+1 day), week_iso(dy+1 day)
   from x
  where month(dy+1 day) = mth
)
select max(case dw when 2 then dm end) as Mo,
       max(case dw when 3 then dm end) as Tu,
       max(case dw when 4 then dm end) as We,
       max(case dw when 5 then dm end) as Th,
       max(case dw when 6 then dm end) as Fr,
       max(case dw when 7 then dm end) as Sa,
       max(case dw when 1 then dm end) as Su
  from x
 group by wk
 order by wk
```

```
MO TU WE TH FR SA SU
-- -- -- -- -- -- --
      01 02 03 04 05
06 07 08 09 10 11 12
13 14 15 16 17 18 19
20 21 22 23 24 25 26
27 28 29 30
```

Oracle

Begin by using the recursive CONNECT BY clause to generate a row for each day in the month for which you wish to generate a calendar. If you aren't running at least Oracle9i Database, you can't use CONNECT BY this way. Instead, you can use a pivot table, such as T500 in the MySQL solution.

Along with each day of the month, you will need to return different bits of information for each day: the day of the month (alias DM), the day of the week (alias DW), the current month you are working with (alias MTH), and the ISO week for each day of the month (alias WK). The results of the WITH view X for the first day of the current month are shown below:

```
select trunc(sysdate,'mm') dy,
       to_char(trunc(sysdate,'mm'),'dd') dm,
       to_char(sysdate,'mm') mth,
       to_number(to_char(trunc(sysdate,'mm'),'d')) dw,
       to_char(trunc(sysdate,'mm'),'iw') wk
  from dual

DY          DM MT       DW WK
----------- -- -- ---------- --
01-JUN-2005 01 06          4 22
```

The next step is to repeatedly increase the value for DM (move through the days of the month) until you are no longer in the current month. As you move through each day in the month, you will also return the day of the week for each day and the ISO week into which the current day falls. Partial results are shown below (the full date for each day is added below for readability):

```
with x
  as (
select *
  from (
select trunc(sysdate,'mm')+level-1 dy,
       to_char(trunc(sysdate,'mm')+level-1,'iw') wk,
       to_char(trunc(sysdate,'mm')+level-1,'dd') dm,
       to_number(to_char(trunc(sysdate,'mm')+level-1,'d')) dw,
       to_char(trunc(sysdate,'mm')+level-1,'mm') curr_mth,
       to_char(sysdate,'mm') mth
  from dual
 connect by level <= 31
       )
```

```
  where curr_mth = mth
)
select *
  from x

DY              WK DM         DW CU MT
----------      -- -- ----------  -- --
01-JUN-2005 22 01             4 06 06
02-JUN-2005 22 02             5 06 06
...
21-JUN-2005 25 21             3 06 06
22-JUN-2005 25 22             4 06 06
...
30-JUN-2005 26 30             5 06 06
```

What you are returning at this point is one row for each day of the current month. In that row you have: the two-digit numeric day of the month, the two-digit numeric month, the one-digit day of the week (1–7 for Sun–Sat), and the two-digit ISO week number. With all this information available, you can use a CASE expression to determine which day of the week each value of DM (each day of the month) falls into. A portion of the results is shown below:

```
with x
  as (
select *
  from (
select trunc(sysdate,'mm')+level-1 dy,
       to_char(trunc(sysdate,'mm')+level-1,'iw') wk,
       to_char(trunc(sysdate,'mm')+level-1,'dd') dm,
       to_number(to_char(trunc(sysdate,'mm')+level-1,'d')) dw,
       to_char(trunc(sysdate,'mm')+level-1,'mm') curr_mth,
       to_char(sysdate,'mm') mth
  from dual
 connect by level <= 31
       )
 where curr_mth = mth
)
select wk,
       case dw when 2 then dm end as Mo,
       case dw when 3 then dm end as Tu,
       case dw when 4 then dm end as We,
       case dw when 5 then dm end as Th,
       case dw when 6 then dm end as Fr,
       case dw when 7 then dm end as Sa,
       case dw when 1 then dm end as Su
  from x

WK MO TU WE TH FR SA SU
-- -- -- -- -- -- -- --
22    01
22       02
22          03
```

```
22              04
22                 05
23 06
23    07
23       08
23          09
23             10
23          11
23             12
```

As you can see from the partial output, every day in each week is returned as a row, but the day number is in one of seven columns corresponding to the day of the week. Your task now is to consolidate the days into one row for each week. Use the aggregate function MAX and group by WK (the ISO week) to return all the days for a week as one row. To ensure the days are in the right order, order the results by WK. The final output is shown below:

```
with x
  as (
select *
  from (
select to_char(trunc(sysdate,'mm')+level-1,'iw') wk,
       to_char(trunc(sysdate,'mm')+level-1,'dd') dm,
       to_number(to_char(trunc(sysdate,'mm')+level-1,'d')) dw,
       to_char(trunc(sysdate,'mm')+level-1,'mm') curr_mth,
       to_char(sysdate,'mm') mth
  from dual
 connect by level <= 31
       )
 where curr_mth = mth
)
select max(case dw when 2 then dm end) Mo,
       max(case dw when 3 then dm end) Tu,
       max(case dw when 4 then dm end) We,
       max(case dw when 5 then dm end) Th,
       max(case dw when 6 then dm end) Fr,
       max(case dw when 7 then dm end) Sa,
       max(case dw when 1 then dm end) Su
  from x
 group by wk
 order by wk


MO TU WE TH FR SA SU
-- -- -- -- -- -- --
         01 02 03 04 05
06 07 08 09 10 11 12
13 14 15 16 17 18 19
20 21 22 23 24 25 26
27 28 29 30
```

PostgreSQL

Use the GENERATE_SERIES function to return one row for each day in the month. If your version of PostgreSQL doesn't support GENERATE_SERIES, then query a pivot table as shown in the MySQL solution.

For each day of the month, return the following information: the day of the month (alias DM), the day of the week (alias DW), the current month you are working with (alias MTH), and the ISO week for each day of the month (alias WK). The formatting and explicit casting makes this solution tough on the eyes, but it's really quite simple. Partial results from inline view X are shown below:

```
select cast(date_trunc('month',current_date) as date)+x.id as dy,
       to_char(
          cast(
       date_trunc('month',current_date)
               as date)+x.id,'iw') as wk,
          to_char(
             cast(
          date_trunc('month',current_date)
                  as date)+x.id,'dd') as dm,
          cast(
       to_char(
          cast(
       date_trunc('month',current_date)
               as date)+x.id,'d') as integer) as dw,
          to_char(
             cast(
          date_trunc('month',current_date)
                  as date)+x.id,'mm') as curr_mth,
          to_char(current_date,'mm') as mth
    from generate_series (0,31) x(id)


DY           WK DM          DW CU MT
----------- -- -- ----------- -- --
01-JUN-2005 22 01           4 06 06
02-JUN-2005 22 02           5 06 06
...
21-JUN-2005 25 21           3 06 06
22-JUN-2005 25 22           4 06 06
...
30-JUN-2005 26 30           5 06 06
```

Notice that as you move through each day in the month, you will also return the day of the week and the ISO week number. To ensure you return days only for the month you are interested in, return only rows where CURR_MTH = MTH (the month each day belongs to should be the month the current date belongs to). What you are returning at this point is, for each day for the current month: the two-digit numeric day of the month, the two-digit numeric month, the one-digit day of the week (1–7 for Sun – Sat), and the two-digit ISO week. Your next step is to use a CASE expression to determine which day of the week each value of DM (each day of the month) falls into. A portion of the results is shown below:

```
select case dw when 2 then dm end as Mo,
       case dw when 3 then dm end as Tu,
       case dw when 4 then dm end as We,
       case dw when 5 then dm end as Th,
       case dw when 6 then dm end as Fr,
       case dw when 7 then dm end as Sa,
       case dw when 1 then dm end as Su
  from (
select *
  from (
select cast(date_trunc('month',current_date) as date)+x.id,
       to_char(
         cast(
  date_trunc('month',current_date)
               as date)+x.id,'iw') as wk,
       to_char(
         cast(
  date_trunc('month',current_date)
               as date)+x.id,'dd') as dm,
       cast(
    to_char(
      cast(
  date_trunc('month',current_date)
               as date)+x.id,'d') as integer) as dw,
       to_char(
         cast(
  date_trunc('month',current_date)
               as date)+x.id,'mm') as curr_mth,
       to_char(current_date,'mm') as mth
  from generate_series (0,31) x(id)
       ) x
 where mth = curr_mth
       ) y

WK MO TU WE TH FR SA SU
-- -- -- -- -- -- -- --
22    01
22       02
22          03
22             04
22                05
23 06
23    07
23       08
23          09
23             10
23                11
23                   12
```

As you can see from the partial output, every day in each week is returned as a row, and each day number falls into the column corresponding to its day of the week. Your job now is to collapse the days into one row for each week. To that end, use the aggregate function MAX and group the rows by WK (the ISO week). The result will be all the days for each week returned as one row as you would see on a calendar. To ensure the days are in the right order, order the results by WK. The final output is shown below:

```
select max(case dw when 2 then dm end) as Mo,
       max(case dw when 3 then dm end) as Tu,
       max(case dw when 4 then dm end) as We,
       max(case dw when 5 then dm end) as Th,
       max(case dw when 6 then dm end) as Fr,
       max(case dw when 7 then dm end) as Sa,
       max(case dw when 1 then dm end) as Su
  from (
select *
  from (
select cast(date_trunc('month',current_date) as date)+x.id,
       to_char(
         cast(
date_trunc('month',current_date)
              as date)+x.id,'iw') as wk,
       to_char(
         cast(
date_trunc('month',current_date)
              as date)+x.id,'dd') as dm,
       cast(
       to_char(
         cast(
date_trunc('month',current_date)
              as date)+x.id,'d') as integer) as dw,
       to_char(
         cast(
date_trunc('month',current_date)
              as date)+x.id,'mm') as curr_mth,
       to_char(current_date,'mm') as mth
  from generate_series (0,31) x(id)
       ) x
 where mth = curr_mth
       ) y
 group by wk
 order by wk

MO TU WE TH FR SA SU
-- -- -- -- -- -- --
      01 02 03 04 05
06 07 08 09 10 11 12
13 14 15 16 17 18 19
20 21 22 23 24 25 26
27 28 29 30
```

MySQL

The first step is to return a row for each day in the month for which you want to create a calendar. To that end, query against table T500. By adding each value returned by T500 to the first day of the month, you can return each day in the month.

For each date, you will need to return the following bits of information: the day of the month (alias DM), the day of the week (alias DW), the current month you are working with (alias MTH), and the ISO week for each day of the month (alias WK). Inline view X returns the first day of the current month along with the two-digit numeric value for the current month. Results are shown below:

```
select adddate(current_date,-dayofmonth(current_date)+1) dy,
       date_format(
           adddate(current_date,
                   -dayofmonth(current_date)+1),
                   '%m') mth
  from t1


DY          MT
----------- --
01-JUN-2005 06
```

The next step is to move through the month, starting from the first day and returning each day in the month. Notice that as you move through each day in the month, you will also return the corresponding day of the week and ISO week number. To ensure you return days only for the month you are interested in, return only rows where the month of the day returned is equal to the current month (the month each day belongs to should be the month the current date belongs to). A portion of the rows from inline view Y is shown below:

```
select date_format(dy,'%u') wk,
       date_format(dy,'%d') dm,
       date_format(dy,'%w')+1 dw
  from (
select adddate(x.dy,t500.id-1) dy,
       x.mth
  from (
select adddate(current_date,-dayofmonth(current_date)+1) dy,
       date_format(
           adddate(current_date,
                   -dayofmonth(current_date)+1),
                   '%m') mth
  from t1
       ) x,
         t500
 where t500.id <= 31
   and date_format(adddate(x.dy,t500.id-1),'%m') = x.mth
       ) y


WK DM     DW
-- -- ----------
22 01          4
22 02          5
...
25 21          3
25 22          4
...
26 30          5
```

For each day for the current month you now have: the two-digit numeric day of the month (DM), the one-digit day of the week (DW), and the two-digit ISO week number (WK). Using this information, you can write a CASE expression to determine which day of the week each value of DM (each day of the month) falls into. A portion of the results is shown below:

```
select case dw when 2 then dm end as Mo,
       case dw when 3 then dm end as Tu,
       case dw when 4 then dm end as We,
       case dw when 5 then dm end as Th,
       case dw when 6 then dm end as Fr,
       case dw when 7 then dm end as Sa,
       case dw when 1 then dm end as Su
  from (
select date_format(dy,'%u') wk,
       date_format(dy,'%d') dm,
       date_format(dy,'%w')+1 dw
  from (
select adddate(x.dy,t500.id-1) dy,
       x.mth
  from (
select adddate(current_date,-dayofmonth(current_date)+1) dy,
       date_format(
           adddate(current_date,
                   -dayofmonth(current_date)+1),
                   '%m') mth
  from t1
       ) x,
          t500
  where t500.id <= 31
    and date_format(adddate(x.dy,t500.id-1),'%m') = x.mth
       ) y
       ) z
```

```
WK MO TU WE TH FR SA SU
-- -- -- -- -- -- -- --
22       01
22          02
22             03
22                04
22                   05
23 06
23    07
23       08
23          09
23             10
23                11
23                   12
```

As you can see from the partial output, every day in each week is returned as a row. Within each row, the day number falls into the column corresponding to the appropriate weekday. Now you need to consolidate the days into one row for each week.

To do that, use the aggregate function MAX, and group the rows by WK (the ISO week). To ensure the days are in the right order, order the results by WK. The final output is shown below:

```
select max(case dw when 2 then dm end) as Mo,
       max(case dw when 3 then dm end) as Tu,
       max(case dw when 4 then dm end) as We,
       max(case dw when 5 then dm end) as Th,
       max(case dw when 6 then dm end) as Fr,
       max(case dw when 7 then dm end) as Sa,
       max(case dw when 1 then dm end) as Su
  from (
select date_format(dy,'%u') wk,
       date_format(dy,'%d') dm,
       date_format(dy,'%w')+1 dw
  from (
select adddate(x.dy,t500.id-1) dy,
       x.mth
  from (
select adddate(current_date,-dayofmonth(current_date)+1) dy,
       date_format(
           adddate(current_date,
                   -dayofmonth(current_date)+1),
                   '%m') mth
  from t1
       ) x,
         t500
 where t500.id <= 31
   and date_format(adddate(x.dy,t500.id-1),'%m') = x.mth
       ) y
       ) z
 group by wk
 order by wk

MO TU WE TH FR SA SU
-- -- -- -- -- -- --
      01 02 03 04 05
06 07 08 09 10 11 12
13 14 15 16 17 18 19
20 21 22 23 24 25 26
27 28 29 30
```

SQL Server

Begin by returning one row for each day of the month. You can do that using the recursive WITH clause. Or, if your version of SQL Server doesn't support recursive WITH, you can use a pivot table in the same manner as the MySQL solution. For each row that you return, you will need the following items: the day of the month (alias DM), the day of the week (alias DW), the current month you are working with (alias MTH), and the ISO week for each day of the month (alias WK). The results of the recursive view X prior to recursion taking place (the upper portion of the UNION ALL) are shown below:

```
    select dy,
           day(dy) dm,
           datepart(m,dy) mth,
           datepart(dw,dy) dw,
           case when datepart(dw,dy) = 1
                then datepart(ww,dy)-1
                else datepart(ww,dy)
           end wk
      from (
    select dateadd(day,-day(getdate())+1,getdate()) dy
      from t1
           ) x


DY          DM MTH      DW WK
----------- -- --- ----------- --
01-JUN-2005  1   6           4 23
```

Your next step is to repeatedly increase the value for DM (move through the days of
the month) until you are no longer in the current month. As you move through each
day in the month, you will also return the day of the week and the ISO week number. Partial results are shown below:

```
    with x(dy,dm,mth,dw,wk)
      as (
    select dy,
           day(dy) dm,
           datepart(m,dy) mth,
           datepart(dw,dy) dw,
           case when datepart(dw,dy) = 1
                then datepart(ww,dy)-1
                else datepart(ww,dy)
           end wk
      from (
    select dateadd(day,-day(getdate())+1,getdate()) dy
      from t1
           ) x
    union all
    select dateadd(d,1,dy), day(dateadd(d,1,dy)), mth,
           datepart(dw,dateadd(d,1,dy)),
           case when datepart(dw,dateadd(d,1,dy)) = 1
                then datepart(wk,dateadd(d,1,dy))-1
                else datepart(wk,dateadd(d,1,dy))
           end
      from x
     where datepart(m,dateadd(d,1,dy)) = mth
    )
    select *
      from x


DY          DM MTH      DW WK
----------- -- --- ----------- --
01-JUN-2005 01  06          4 23
02-JUN-2005 02  06          5 23
...
```

```
21-JUN-2005 21  06       3 26
22-JUN-2005 22  06       4 26
...
30-JUN-2005 30  06       5 27
```

You now have, for each day in the current month: the two-digit numeric day of the month, the two-digit numeric month, the one-digit day of the week (1–7 for Sun–Sat), and the two-digit ISO week number.

Now, use a CASE expression to determine which day of the week each value of DM (each day of the month) falls into. A portion of the results is shown below:

```
with x(dy,dm,mth,dw,wk)
   as (
select dy,
       day(dy) dm,
       datepart(m,dy) mth,
       datepart(dw,dy) dw,
       case when datepart(dw,dy) = 1
            then datepart(ww,dy)-1
            else datepart(ww,dy)
       end wk
  from (
select dateadd(day,-day(getdate())+1,getdate()) dy
  from t1
       ) x
 union all
select dateadd(d,1,dy), day(dateadd(d,1,dy)), mth,
       datepart(dw,dateadd(d,1,dy)),
       case when datepart(dw,dateadd(d,1,dy)) = 1
            then datepart(wk,dateadd(d,1,dy))-1
            else datepart(wk,dateadd(d,1,dy))
       end
  from x
 where datepart(m,dateadd(d,1,dy)) = mth
)
select case dw when 2 then dm end as Mo,
       case dw when 3 then dm end as Tu,
       case dw when 4 then dm end as We,
       case dw when 5 then dm end as Th,
       case dw when 6 then dm end as Fr,
       case dw when 7 then dm end as Sa,
       case dw when 1 then dm end as Su
  from x

WK MO TU WE TH FR SA SU
-- -- -- -- -- -- -- --
22       01
22          02
22             03
22                04
22                   05
23 06
23    07
```

```
23       08
23          09
23             10
23                11
23                   12
```

Every day in each week is returned as a separate row. In each row, the column containing the day number corresponds to the day of the week. You now need to consolidate the days for each week into one row. Do that by grouping the rows by WK (the ISO week) and applying the MAX function to the different columns. The results will be in calendar format as shown below:

```
  with x(dy,dm,mth,dw,wk)
     as (
 select dy,
        day(dy) dm,
        datepart(m,dy) mth,
        datepart(dw,dy) dw,
        case when datepart(dw,dy) = 1
             then datepart(ww,dy)-1
             else datepart(ww,dy)
        end wk
   from (
 select dateadd(day,-day(getdate())+1,getdate()) dy
   from t1
        ) x
 union all
 select dateadd(d,1,dy), day(dateadd(d,1,dy)), mth,
        datepart(dw,dateadd(d,1,dy)),
         case when datepart(dw,dateadd(d,1,dy)) = 1
              then datepart(wk,dateadd(d,1,dy))-1
              else datepart(wk,dateadd(d,1,dy))
         end
   from x
  where datepart(m,dateadd(d,1,dy)) = mth
 )
 select max(case dw when 2 then dm end) as Mo,
        max(case dw when 3 then dm end) as Tu,
        max(case dw when 4 then dm end) as We,
        max(case dw when 5 then dm end) as Th,
        max(case dw when 6 then dm end) as Fr,
        max(case dw when 7 then dm end) as Sa,
        max(case dw when 1 then dm end) as Su
   from x
  group by wk
  order by wk

MO TU WE TH FR SA SU
-- -- -- -- -- -- --
         01 02 03 04 05
06 07 08 09 10 11 12
13 14 15 16 17 18 19
20 21 22 23 24 25 26
27 28 29 30
```

9.8 Listing Quarter Start and End Dates for the Year

Problem

You want to return the start and end dates for each of the four quarters of a given year.

Solution

There are four quarters to a year, so you know you will need to generate four rows. After generating the desired number of rows, simply use the date functions supplied by your RDBMS to return the quarter the start and end dates fall into. Your goal is to produce the following result set (one again, the choice to use the current year is arbitrary):

```
QTR Q_START      Q_END
--- ----------   ----------
  1 01-JAN-2005  31-MAR-2005
  2 01-APR-2005  30-JUN-2005
  3 01-JUL-2005  30-SEP-2005
  4 01-OCT-2005  31-DEC-2005
```

DB2

Use table EMP and the window function ROW_NUMBER OVER to generate four rows. Alternatively, you can use the WITH clause to generate rows (as many of the recipes do), or you can query against any table with at least four rows. The following solution uses the ROW_NUMBER OVER approach:

```
1  select quarter(dy-1 day) QTR,
2         dy-3 month Q_start,
3         dy-1 day Q_end
4    from (
5  select (current_date -
6            (dayofyear(current_date)-1) day
7              + (rn*3) month) dy
8    from (
9  select row_number()over() rn
10   from emp
11  fetch first 4 rows only
12       ) x
13       ) y
```

Oracle

Use the function ADD_MONTHS to find the start and end dates for each quarter. Use ROWNUM to represent the quarter the start and end dates belong to. The following solution uses table EMP to generate four rows.

```
1 select rownum qtr,
2        add_months(trunc(sysdate,'y'),(rownum-1)*3) q_start,
3        add_months(trunc(sysdate,'y'),rownum*3)-1 q_end
```

```
4    from emp
5   where rownum <= 4
```

PostgreSQL

Use the function GENERATE_SERIES to generate the required four quarters. Use the DATE_TRUNC function to truncate the dates generated for each quarter down to year and month. Use the TO_CHAR function to determine which quarter the start and end dates belong to:

```
1   select to_char(dy,'Q') as QTR,
2          date(
3            date_trunc('month',dy)-(2*interval '1 month')
4          ) as Q_start,
5          dy as Q_end
6     from (
7   select date(dy+((rn*3) * interval '1 month'))-1 as dy
8     from (
9   select rn, date(date_trunc('year',current_date)) as dy
10    from generate_series(1,4) gs(rn)
11        ) x
12        ) y
```

MySQL

Use table T500 to generate four rows (one for each quarter). Use functions DATE_ADD and ADDDATE to create the start and end dates for each quarter. Use the QUARTER function to determine which quarter the start and end dates belong to:

```
1   select quarter(adddate(dy,-1)) QTR,
2          date_add(dy,interval -3 month) Q_start,
3          adddate(dy,-1) Q_end
4     from (
5   select date_add(dy,interval (3*id) month) dy
6     from (
7   select id,
8          adddate(current_date,-dayofyear(current_date)+1) dy
9     from t500
10   where id <= 4
11        ) x
12        ) y
```

SQL Server

Use the recursive WITH clause to generate four rows. Use the function DATEADD to find the start and end dates. Use the function DATEPART to determine which quarter the start and end dates belong to:

```
1   with x (dy,cnt)
2     as (
3   select dateadd(d,-(datepart(dy,getdate())-1),getdate()),
4          1
5     from t1
```

```
 6    union all
 7   select dateadd(m,3,dy), cnt+1
 8     from x
 9    where cnt+1 <= 4
10   )
11   select datepart(q,dateadd(d,-1,dy)) QTR,
12          dateadd(m,-3,dy) Q_start,
13          dateadd(d,-1,dy) Q_end
14     from x
15    order by 1
```

Discussion

DB2

The first step is to generate four rows (with values 1 through 4) for each quarter in the year. Inline view X uses the window function ROW_NUMBER OVER and the FETCH FIRST clause to return only four rows from EMP. The results are shown below:

```
select row_number( )over( ) rn
  from emp
 fetch first 4 rows only


RN
--
 1
 2
 3
 4
```

The next step is to find the first day of the year, then add n months to it, where n is three times RN (you are adding 3, 6, 9, and 12 months to the first day of the year). The results are shown below:

```
select (current_date -
         (dayofyear(current_date)-1) day
           + (rn*3) month) dy
   from (
select row_number( )over( ) rn
  from emp
 fetch first 4 rows only
         ) x

DY
-----------
01-APR-2005
01-JUL-2005
01-OCT-2005
01-JAN-2005
```

At this point, the values for DY are one day after the end date for each quarter. The next step is to get the start and end dates for each quarter. Subtract one day from DY to get the end of each quarter, and subtract three months from DY to get the start of each quarter. Use the QUARTER function on DY-1 (the end date for each quarter) to determine which quarter the start and end dates belong to.

Oracle

The combination of ROWNUM, TRUNC, and ADD_MONTHS makes this solution very easy. To find the start of each quarter simply add *n* months to the first day of the year, where *n* is (ROWNUM-1)*3 (giving you 0,3,6,9). To find the end of each quarter add *n* months to the first day of the year, where *n* is ROWNUM*3, and subtract one day. As an aside, when working with quarters, you may also find it useful to use TO_CHAR and/or TRUNC with the 'q' formatting option.

PostgreSQL

The first step is to truncate the current date to the first day of the year using the DATE_TRUNC function. Next, add *n* months, where *n* is RN (the values returned by GENERATE_SERIES) times three, and subtract one day. The results are shown below:

```
select date(dy+((rn*3) * interval '1 month'))-1 as dy
  from (
select rn, date(date_trunc('year',current_date)) as dy
  from generate_series(1,4) gs(rn)
      ) x

DY
-----------
31-MAR-2005
30-JUN-2005
30-SEP-2005
31-DEC-2005
```

Now that you have the end dates for each quarter, the final step is to find the start date by subtracting two months from DY then truncating to the first day of the month by using the DATE_TRUNC function. Use the TO_CHAR function on the end date for each quarter (DY) to determine which quarter the start and end dates belong to.

MySQL

The first step is to find the first day of the year by using functions ADDDATE and DAYOFYEAR, then adding *n* months to the first day of the year, where *n* is T500.ID times three, by using the DATE_ADD function. The results are shown below:

```
select date_add(dy,interval (3*id) month) dy
  from (
select id,
       adddate(current_date,-dayofyear(current_date)+1) dy
  from t500
 where id <= 4
      ) x
```

```
DY
-----------
01-APR-2005
01-JUL-2005
01-OCT-2005
01-JAN-2005
```

At this point the dates are one day after the end of each quarter; to find the end of each quarter, simply subtract one day from DY. The next step is to find the start of each quarter by subtracting three months from DY. Use the QUARTER function on the end date of each quarter to determine which quarter the start and end dates belong to.

SQL Server

The first step is to find the first day of the year, then recursively add *n* months, where *n* is three times the current iteration (there are four iterations, therefore, you are adding 3*1 months, 3*2 months, etc.), using the DATEADD function. The results are shown below:

```
with x (dy,cnt)
   as (
select dateadd(d,-(datepart(dy,getdate( ))-1),getdate( )),
     1
  from t1
 union all
select dateadd(m,3,dy), cnt+1
  from x
 where cnt+1 <= 4
)
select dy
  from x

DY
-----------
01-APR-2005
01-JUL-2005
01-OCT-2005
01-JAN-2005
```

The values for DY are one day after the end of each quarter. To get the end of each quarter, simply subtract one day from DY by using the DATEADD function. To find the start of each quarter, use the DATEADD function to subtract three months from DY. Use the DATEPART function on the end date for each quarter to determine which quarter the start and end dates belong to.

9.9 Determining Quarter Start and End Dates for a Given Quarter

Problem

When given a year and quarter in the format of YYYYQ (four-digit year, one-digit quarter), you want to return the quarter's start and end dates.

Solution

The key to this solution is to find the quarter by using the modulus function on the YYYYQ value. (As an alternative to modulo, since the year format is four digits, you can simply substring out the last digit to get the quarter.) Once you have the quarter, simply multiply by 3 to get the ending month for the quarter. In the solutions that follow, inline view X will return all four year and quarter combinations. The result set for inline view X is as follows:

```
select 20051 as yrq from t1 union all
select 20052 as yrq from t1 union all
select 20053 as yrq from t1 union all
select 20054 as yrq from t1

   YRQ
------
 20051
 20052
 20053
 20054
```

DB2

Use the function SUBSTR to return the year from inline view X. Use the MOD function to determine which quarter you are looking for:

```
 1  select (q_end-2 month) q_start,
 2         (q_end+1 month)-1 day q_end
 3    from (
 4  select date(substr(cast(yrq as char(4)),1,4) ||'-'||
 5         rtrim(cast(mod(yrq,10)*3 as char(2))) ||'-1') q_end
 6    from (
 7  select 20051 yrq from t1 union all
 8  select 20052 yrq from t1 union all
 9  select 20053 yrq from t1 union all
10  select 20054 yrq from t1
11        ) x
12        ) y
```

Oracle

Use the function SUBSTR to return the year from inline view X. Use the MOD function to determine which quarter you are looking for:

```
1  select add_months(q_end,-2) q_start,
2         last_day(q_end) q_end
3    from (
4  select to_date(substr(yrq,1,4)||mod(yrq,10)*3,'yyyymm') q_end
5    from (
6  select 20051 yrq from dual union all
7  select 20052 yrq from dual union all
8  select 20053 yrq from dual union all
9  select 20054 yrq from dual
10        ) x
11        ) y
```

PostgreSQL

Use the function SUBSTR to return the year from the inline view X. Use the MOD function to determine which quarter you are looking for:

```
1  select date(q_end-(2*interval '1 month')) as q_start,
2         date(q_end+interval '1 month'-interval '1 day') as q_end
3    from (
4  select to_date(substr(yrq,1,4)||mod(yrq,10)*3,'yyyymm') as q_end
5    from (
6  select 20051 as yrq from t1 union all
7  select 20052 as yrq from t1 union all
8  select 20053 as yrq from t1 union all
9  select 20054 as yrq from t1
10        ) x
11        ) y
```

MySQL

Use the function SUBSTR to return the year from the inline view X. Use the MOD function to determine which quarter you are looking for:

```
1  select date_add(
2         adddate(q_end,-day(q_end)+1),
3             interval -2 month) q_start,
4         q_end
5    from (
6  select last_day(
7      str_to_date(
8          concat(
9          substr(yrq,1,4),mod(yrq,10)*3),'%Y%m')) q_end
10    from (
11  select 20051 as yrq from t1 union all
12  select 20052 as yrq from t1 union all
13  select 20053 as yrq from t1 union all
14  select 20054 as yrq from t1
15        ) x
16        ) y
```

SQL Server

Use the function SUBSTRING to return the year from the inline view X. Use the modulus function (%) to determine which quarter you are looking for:

```
1  select dateadd(m,-2,q_end) q_start,
2         dateadd(d,-1,dateadd(m,1,q_end)) q_end
3    from (
4  select cast(substring(cast(yrq as varchar),1,4)+'-'+
5         cast(yrq%10*3 as varchar)+'-1' as datetime) q_end
6    from (
7  select 20051 yrq from t1 union all
8  select 20052 yrq from t1 union all
9  select 20053 yrq from t1 union all
10 select 20054 yrq from t1
11       ) x
12       ) y
```

Discussion

DB2

The first step is to find the year and quarter you are working with. Substring out the year from inline view X (X.YRQ) using the SUBSTR function. To get the quarter, use modulus 10 on YRQ. Once you have the quarter, multiply by 3 to get the end month for the quarter. The results are shown below:

```
select substr(cast(yrq as char(4)),1,4) yr,
       mod(yrq,10)*3 mth
  from (
select 20051 yrq from t1 union all
select 20052 yrq from t1 union all
select 20053 yrq from t1 union all
select 20054 yrq from t1
       ) x

YR      MTH
----    ------
2005      3
2005      6
2005      9
2005     12
```

At this point you have the year and end month for each quarter. Use those values to construct a date, specifically, the first day of the last month for each quarter. Use the concatenation operator "||" to glue together the year and month, then use the DATE function to convert to a date:

```
select date(substr(cast(yrq as char(4)),1,4) ||'-'||
       rtrim(cast(mod(yrq,10)*3 as char(2))) ||'-1') q_end
  from (
select 20051 yrq from t1 union all
select 20052 yrq from t1 union all
```

```
select 20053 yrq from t1 union all
select 20054 yrq from t1
        ) x
```

```
Q_END
-----------
01-MAR-2005
01-JUN-2005
01-SEP-2005
01-DEC-2005
```

The values for Q_END are the first day of the last month of each quarter. To get to the last day of the month add one month to Q_END, then subtract one day. To find the start date for each quarter subtract two months from Q_END.

Oracle

The first step is to find the year and quarter you are working with. Substring out the year from inline view X (X.YRQ) using the SUBSTR function. To get the quarter, use modulus 10 on YRQ. Once you have the quarter, multiply by 3 to get the end month for the quarter. The results are shown below:

```
select substr(yrq,1,4) yr, mod(yrq,10)*3 mth
  from (
select 20051 yrq from dual union all
select 20052 yrq from dual union all
select 20053 yrq from dual union all
select 20054 yrq from dual
        ) x
```

```
YR      MTH
----  ------
2005      3
2005      6
2005      9
2005     12
```

At this point you have the year and end month for each quarter. Use those values to construct a date, specifically, the first day of the last month for each quarter. Use the concatenation operator "||" to glue together the year and month, then use the TO_DATE function to convert to a date:

```
select to_date(substr(yrq,1,4)||mod(yrq,10)*3,'yyyymm') q_end
  from (
select 20051 yrq from dual union all
select 20052 yrq from dual union all
select 20053 yrq from dual union all
select 20054 yrq from dual
        ) x
```

```
Q_END
-----------
01-MAR-2005
01-JUN-2005
01-SEP-2005
01-DEC-2005
```

The values for Q_END are the first day of the last month of each quarter. To get to the last day of the month use the LAST_DAY function on Q_END. To find the start date for each quarter subtract two months from Q_END using the ADD_MONTHS function.

PostgreSQL

The first step is to find the year and quarter you are working with. Substring out the year from inline view X (X.YRQ) using the SUBSTR function. To get the quarter, use modulus 10 on YRQ. Once you have the quarter, multiply by 3 to get the end month for the quarter. The results are shown below:

```
select substr(yrq,1,4) yr, mod(yrq,10)*3 mth
  from (
select 20051 yrq from dual union all
select 20052 yrq from dual union all
select 20053 yrq from dual union all
select 20054 yrq from dual
      ) x

YR      MTH
----  ------
2005     3
2005     6
2005     9
2005    12
```

At this point you have the year and end month for each quarter. Use those values to construct a date, specifically, the first day of the last month for each quarter. Use the concatenation operator "||" to glue together the year and month, then use the TO_DATE function to convert to a date:

```
select to_date(substr(yrq,1,4)||mod(yrq,10)*3,'yyyymm') q_end
  from (
select 20051 yrq from dual union all
select 20052 yrq from dual union all
select 20053 yrq from dual union all
select 20054 yrq from dual
      ) x

Q_END
-----------
01-MAR-2005
01-JUN-2005
01-SEP-2005
01-DEC-2005
```

The values for Q_END are the first day of the last month of each quarter. To get to the last day of the month add one month to Q_END and subtract one day. To find the start date for each quarter subtract two months from Q_END. Cast the final result as dates.

MySQL

The first step is to find the year and quarter you are working with. Substring out the year from inline view X (X.YRQ) using the SUBSTR function. To get the quarter, use modulus 10 on YRQ. Once you have the quarter, multiply by 3 to get the end month for the quarter. The results are shown below:

```
select substr(yrq,1,4) yr, mod(yrq,10)*3 mth
  from (
select 20051 yrq from dual union all
select 20052 yrq from dual union all
select 20053 yrq from dual union all
select 20054 yrq from dual
       ) x

YR      MTH
----    ------
2005     3
2005     6
2005     9
2005     12
```

At this point you have the year and end month for each quarter. Use those values to construct a date, specifically, the last day of each quarter. Use the CONCAT function to glue together the year and month, then use the STR_TO_DATE function to convert to a date. Use the LAST_DAY function to find the last day for each quarter:

```
select last_day(
     str_to_date(
          concat(
          substr(yrq,1,4),mod(yrq,10)*3),'%Y%m')) q_end
  from (
select 20051 as yrq from t1 union all
select 20052 as yrq from t1 union all
select 20053 as yrq from t1 union all
select 20054 as yrq from t1
       ) x

Q_END
-----------
31-MAR-2005
30-JUN-2005
30-SEP-2005
31-DEC-2005
```

Because you already have the end of each quarter, all that's left is to find the start date for each quarter. Use the DAY function to return the day of the month the end of each quarter falls on, and subtract that from Q_END using the ADDDATE function to give you the end of the prior month; add one day to bring you to the first day of the last month of each quarter. The last step is to use the DATE_ADD function to subtract two months from the first day of the last month of each quarter to get you to the start date for each quarter.

SQL Server

The first step is to find the year and quarter you are working with. Substring out the year from inline view X (X.YRQ) using the SUBSTRING function. To get the quarter, use modulus 10 on YRQ. Once you have the quarter, multiply by 3 to get the end month for the quarter. The results are shown below:

```
select substring(yrq,1,4) yr, yrq%10*3 mth
  from (
select 20051 yrq from dual union all
select 20052 yrq from dual union all
select 20053 yrq from dual union all
select 20054 yrq from dual
      ) x

YR      MTH
----  ------
2005      3
2005      6
2005      9
2005     12
```

At this point, you have the year and end month for each quarter. Use those values to construct a date, specifically, the first day of the last month for each quarter. Use the concatenation operator "+" to glue together the year and month, then use the CAST function to convert to a date:

```
select cast(substring(cast(yrq as varchar),1,4)+'-'+
         cast(yrq%10*3 as varchar)+'-1' as datetime) q_end
    from (
select 20051 yrq from t1 union all
select 20052 yrq from t1 union all
select 20053 yrq from t1 union all
select 20054 yrq from t1
        ) x

Q_END
-----------
01-MAR-2005
01-JUN-2005
01-SEP-2005
01-DEC-2005
```

The values for Q_END are the first day of the last month of each quarter. To get to the last day of the month add one month to Q_END and subtract one day using the DATEADD function. To find the start date for each quarter subtract two months from Q_END using the DATEADD function.

9.10   Filling in Missing Dates

Problem

You need to generate a row for every date (or every month, week, or year) within a given range. Such rowsets are often used to generate summary reports. For example, you want to count the number of employees hired every month of every year in which any employee has been hired. Examining the dates of all the employees hired, there have been hirings from 1980 to 1983:

```
select distinct
       extract(year from hiredate) as year
  from emp

YEAR
-----
 1980
 1981
 1982
 1983
```

You want to determine the number of employees hired each month from 1980 to 1983. A portion of the desired result set is shown below:

```
MTH           NUM_HIRED
-----------   ----------
01-JAN-1981        0
01-FEB-1981        2
01-MAR-1981        0
01-APR-1981        1
01-MAY-1981        1
01-JUN-1981        1
01-JUL-1981        0
01-AUG-1981        0
01-SEP-1981        2
01-OCT-1981        0
01-NOV-1981        1
01-DEC-1981        2
```

Solution

The trick here is that you want to return a row for each month even if no employee was hired (i.e., the count would be zero). Because there isn't an employee hired every month between 1980 and 1983, you must generate those months yourself, and then outer join to table EMP on HIREDATE (truncating the actual HIREDATE to its month, so it can match the generated months when possible).

DB2

Use the recursive WITH clause to generate every month (the first day of each month from January 1, 1980, to December 1, 1983). Once you have all the months for the

required range of dates, outer join to table EMP and use the aggregate function
COUNT to count the number of hires for each month:

```
1    with x (start_date,end_date)
2       as (
3    select (min(hiredate) -
4            dayofyear(min(hiredate)) day +1 day) start_date,
5            (max(hiredate) -
6            dayofyear(max(hiredate)) day +1 day) +1 year end_date
7      from emp
8     union all
9    select start_date +1 month, end_date
10     from x
11     where (start_date +1 month) < end_date
12   )
13   select x.start_date mth, count(e.hiredate) num_hired
14     from x left join emp e
15       on (x.start_date = (e.hiredate-(day(hiredate)-1) day))
16     group by x.start_date
17     order by 1
```

Oracle

Use the CONNECT BY clause to generate each month between 1980 and 1983.
Then outer join to table EMP and use the aggregate function COUNT to count the
number of employees hired in each month. If you are on Oracle8i Database and earlier, the ANSI outer join is not available to you, nor is the ability to use CONNECT
BY as a row generator; a simple workaround is to use a traditional pivot table (like
the one used in the MySQL solution). Following as an Oracle solution using Oracle's outer-join syntax:

```
1    with x
2       as (
3    select add_months(start_date,level-1) start_date
4      from (
5    select min(trunc(hiredate,'y')) start_date,
6           add_months(max(trunc(hiredate,'y')),12) end_date
7      from emp
8           )
9     connect by level <= months_between(end_date,start_date)
10   )
11   select x.start_date MTH, count(e.hiredate) num_hired
12     from x, emp e
13     where x.start_date = trunc(e.hiredate(+),'mm')
14     group by x.start_date
15     order by 1
```

and here is a second Oracle solution, this time using the ANSI syntax:

```
1    with x
2       as (
3    select add_months(start_date,level-1) start_date
4      from (
```

```
 5  select min(trunc(hiredate,'y')) start_date,
 6         add_months(max(trunc(hiredate,'y')),12) end_date
 7    from emp
 8         )
 9  connect by level <= months_between(end_date,start_date)
10  )
11  select x.start_date MTH, count(e.hiredate) num_hired
12    from x left join emp e
13      on (x.start_date = trunc(e.hiredate,'mm'))
14  group by x.start_date
15  order by 1
```

PostgreSQL

To improve readability, this solution uses a view, named V, to return the number of months between the first day of the first month of the year the first employee was hired and the first day of the last month of the year the most recent employee was hired. Use the value returned by view V as the second value passed to the function GENERATE_SERIES, so that the correct number of months (rows) are generated. Once you have all the months for the required range of dates, outer join to table EMP and use the aggregate function COUNT to count the number of hires for each month:

```
create view v
as
select cast(
         extract(year from age(last_month,first_month))*12-1
           as integer) as mths
  from (
select cast(date_trunc('year',min(hiredate)) as date) as first_month,
       cast(cast(date_trunc('year',max(hiredate))
             as date) + interval '1 year'
             as date) as last_month
  from emp
       ) x
```

```
 1  select y.mth, count(e.hiredate) as num_hired
 2    from (
 3  select cast(e.start_date + (x.id * interval '1 month')
 4           as date) as mth
 5    from generate_series (0,(select mths from v)) x(id),
 6         ( select cast(
 7                   date_trunc('year',min(hiredate))
 8                     as date) as start_date
 9             from emp ) e
10         ) y left join emp e
11      on (y.mth = date_trunc('month',e.hiredate))
12  group by y.mth
13  order by 1
```

MySQL

Use the pivot table T500 to generate each month between 1980 and 1983. Then outer join to table EMP and use the aggregate function COUNT to count the number of employees hired for each month:

```
1   select z.mth, count(e.hiredate) num_hired
2     from (
3   select date_add(min_hd,interval t500.id-1 month) mth
4     from (
5   select min_hd, date_add(max_hd,interval 11 month) max_hd
6     from (
7   select adddate(min(hiredate),-dayofyear(min(hiredate))+1) min_hd,
8          adddate(max(hiredate),-dayofyear(max(hiredate))+1) max_hd
9     from emp
10         ) x
11         ) y,
12         t500
13   where date_add(min_hd,interval t500.id-1 month) <= max_hd
14         ) z left join emp e
15     on (z.mth = adddate(
16               date_add(
17               last_day(e.hiredate),interval -1 month),1))
18   group by z.mth
19   order by 1
```

SQL Server

Use the recursive WITH clause to generate every month (the first day of each month from January 1, 1980, to December 1, 1983). Once you have all the months for the required range of dates, outer join to table EMP and use the aggregate function COUNT to count the number of hires for each month:

```
1   with x (start_date,end_date)
2      as (
3   select (min(hiredate) -
4           datepart(dy,min(hiredate))+1) start_date,
5          dateadd(yy,1,
6           (max(hiredate) -
7           datepart(dy,max(hiredate))+1)) end_date
8     from emp
9   union all
10  select dateadd(mm,1,start_date), end_date
11    from x
12   where dateadd(mm,1,start_date) < end_date
13  )
14  select x.start_date mth, count(e.hiredate) num_hired
15    from x left join emp e
16      on (x.start_date =
17             dateadd(dd,-day(e.hiredate)+1,e.hiredate))
18  group by x.start_date
19  order by 1
```

Discussion

DB2

The first step is to generate every month (actually the first day of each month) from 1980 to 1983. Start using the DAYOFYEAR function on the MIN and MAX HIRE-DATEs to find the boundary months:

```
select (min(hiredate) -
            dayofyear(min(hiredate)) day +1 day) start_date,
        (max(hiredate) -
            dayofyear(max(hiredate)) day +1 day) +1 year end_date
   from emp

START_DATE  END_DATE
----------- -----------
01-JAN-1980 01-JAN-1984
```

Your next step is to repeatedly add months to START_DATE to return all the months necessary for the final result set. The value for END_DATE is one day more than it should be. This is OK. As you recursively add months to START_DATE, you can stop before you hit END_DATE. A portion of the months created is shown below:

```
with x (start_date,end_date)
   as (
select (min(hiredate) -
            dayofyear(min(hiredate)) day +1 day) start_date,
        (max(hiredate) -
            dayofyear(max(hiredate)) day +1 day) +1 year end_date
   from emp
 union all
select start_date +1 month, end_date
   from x
  where (start_date +1 month) < end_date
)
select *
   from x

START_DATE  END_DATE
----------- -----------
01-JAN-1980 01-JAN-1984
01-FEB-1980 01-JAN-1984
01-MAR-1980 01-JAN-1984
...
01-OCT-1983 01-JAN-1984
01-NOV-1983 01-JAN-1984
01-DEC-1983 01-JAN-1984
```

At this point, you have all the months you need, and you can simply outer join to EMP.HIREDATE. Because the day for each START_DATE is the first of the month, truncate EMP.HIREDATE to the first day of its month. Finally, use the aggregate function COUNT on EMP.HIREDATE.

Oracle

The first step is to generate the first day of every for every month from 1980 to 1983. Start by using TRUNC and ADD_MONTHS together with the MIN and MAX HIREDATE values to find the boundary months:

```
select min(trunc(hiredate,'y')) start_date,
       add_months(max(trunc(hiredate,'y')),12) end_date
  from emp

START_DATE  END_DATE
----------- -----------
01-JAN-1980 01-JAN-1984
```

Then repeatedly add months to START_DATE to return all the months necessary for the final result set. The value for END_DATE is one day more than it should be, which is OK. As you recursively add months to START_DATE, you can stop before you hit END_DATE. A portion of the months created is shown below:

```
with x as (
select add_months(start_date,level-1) start_date
  from (
select min(trunc(hiredate,'y')) start_date,
       add_months(max(trunc(hiredate,'y')),12) end_date
  from emp
       )
 connect by level <= months_between(end_date,start_date)
)
select *
  from x

START_DATE
-----------
01-JAN-1980
01-FEB-1980
01-MAR-1980
...
01-OCT-1983
01-NOV-1983
01-DEC-1983
```

At this point, you have all the months you need; simply outer join to EMP.HIRE-DATE. Because the day for each START_DATE is the first of the month, truncate EMP.HIREDATE to the first day of the month it is in. The final step is to use the aggregate function COUNT on EMP.HIREDATE.

PostgreSQL

This solution uses the function GENERATE_SERIES to return the months you need. If you do not have the GENERATE_SERIES function available, you can use a pivot table as in the MySQL solution. The first step is to understand view V. View V simply finds the number of months you'll need to generate by finding the boundary dates for the range. Inline view X in view V uses the MIN and MAX HIREDATEs to find the start and end boundary dates and is shown below:

```
select cast(date_trunc('year',min(hiredate)) as date) as first_month,
       cast(cast(date_trunc('year',max(hiredate))
              as date) + interval '1 year'
              as date) as last_month
  from emp


FIRST_MONTH LAST_MONTH
----------- -----------
01-JAN-1980 01-JAN-1984
```

The value for LAST_MONTH is actually one day more than it should be. This is fine, as you can just subtract 1 when you calculate the months between these two dates. The next step is to use the AGE function to find the difference between the two dates in years, then multiply by 12 (and remember, subtract by 1!):

```
select cast(
          extract(year from age(last_month,first_month))*12-1
            as integer) as mths
  from (
select cast(date_trunc('year',min(hiredate)) as date) as first_month,
       cast(cast(date_trunc('year',max(hiredate))
              as date) + interval '1 year'
              as date) as last_month
  from emp
       ) x

MTHS
----
  47
```

Use the value returned by view V as the second parameter of GENERATE_SERIES to return the number of months you need. Your next step is then to find your start date. You'll repeatedly add months to your start date to create your range of months. Inline view Y uses the DATE_TRUNC function on the MIN(HIREDATE) to find the start date, and uses the values returned by GENERATE_SERIES to add months. Partial results are shown below:

```
select cast(e.start_date + (x.id * interval '1 month')
          as date) as mth
  from generate_series (0,(select mths from v)) x(id),
       ( select cast(
                 date_trunc('year',min(hiredate))
                   as date) as start_date
```

```
        from emp
    ) e

MTH
-----------
01-JAN-1980
01-FEB-1980
01-MAR-1980
...
01-OCT-1983
01-NOV-1983
01-DEC-1983
```

Now that you have each month you need for the final result set, outer join to EMP.
HIREDATE and use the aggregate function COUNT to count the number of hires
for each month.

MySQL

First, find the boundary dates by using the aggregate functions MIN and MAX along
with the DAYOFYEAR and ADDDATE functions. The result set shown below is
from inline view X:

```
select adddate(min(hiredate),-dayofyear(min(hiredate))+1) min_hd,
       adddate(max(hiredate),-dayofyear(max(hiredate))+1) max_hd
  from emp

MIN_HD      MAX_HD
----------- -----------
01-JAN-1980 01-JAN-1983
```

Next, increment MAX_HD to the last month of the year:

```
select min_hd, date_add(max_hd,interval 11 month) max_hd
  from (
select adddate(min(hiredate),-dayofyear(min(hiredate))+1) min_hd,
       adddate(max(hiredate),-dayofyear(max(hiredate))+1) max_hd
  from emp
    ) x

MIN_HD      MAX_HD
----------- -----------
01-JAN-1980 01-DEC-1983
```

Now that you have the boundary dates, add months to MIN_HD up to and including MAX_HD by using pivot table T500 to generate the rows you need. A portion of
the results is shown below:

```
select date_add(min_hd,interval t500.id-1 month) mth
  from (
select min_hd, date_add(max_hd,interval 11 month) max_hd
  from (
select adddate(min(hiredate),-dayofyear(min(hiredate))+1) min_hd,
       adddate(max(hiredate),-dayofyear(max(hiredate))+1) max_hd
```

```
    from emp
        ) x
        ) y,
        t500
    where date_add(min_hd,interval t500.id-1 month) <= max_hd
```

```
MTH
-----------
01-JAN-1980
01-FEB-1980
01-MAR-1980
...
01-OCT-1983
01-NOV-1983
01-DEC-1983
```

Now that you have all the months you need for the final result set, outer join to EMP.HIREDATE (be sure to truncate EMP.HIREDATE to the first day of the month) and use the aggregate function COUNT on EMP.HIREDATE to count the number of hires in each month.

SQL Server

Begin by generating every month (actually, the first day of each month) from 1980 to 1983. Then find the boundary months by applying the DAYOFYEAR function to the MIN and MAX HIREDATEs:

```
select (min(hiredate) -
        datepart(dy,min(hiredate))+1) start_date,
       dateadd(yy,1,
        (max(hiredate) -
        datepart(dy,max(hiredate))+1)) end_date
  from emp
```

```
START_DATE  END_DATE
----------- -----------
01-JAN-1980 01-JAN-1984
```

Your next step is to repeatedly add months to START_DATE to return all the months necessary for the final result set. The value for END_DATE is one day more than it should be, which is OK, as you can stop recursively adding months to START_DATE before you hit END_DATE. A portion of the months created is shown below:

```
with x (start_date,end_date)
  as (
select (min(hiredate) -
        datepart(dy,min(hiredate))+1) start_date,
       dateadd(yy,1,
        (max(hiredate) -
        datepart(dy,max(hiredate))+1)) end_date
  from emp
```

```
  union all
select dateadd(mm,1,start_date), end_date
  from x
 where dateadd(mm,1,start_date) < end_date
)
select *
  from x

START_DATE  END_DATE
----------- -----------
01-JAN-1980 01-JAN-1984
01-FEB-1980 01-JAN-1984
01-MAR-1980 01-JAN-1984
...
01-OCT-1983 01-JAN-1984
01-NOV-1983 01-JAN-1984
01-DEC-1983 01-JAN-1984
```

At this point, you have all the months you need. Simply outer join to EMP.HIRE-DATE. Because the day for each START_DATE is the first of the month, truncate EMP.HIREDATE to the first day of the month. The final step is to use the aggregate function COUNT on EMP.HIREDATE.

9.11   Searching on Specific Units of Time

Problem

You want to search for dates that match a given month, or day of the week, or some other unit of time. For example, you want to find all employees hired in February or December, as well as employees hired on a Tuesday.

Solution

Use the functions supplied by your RDBMS to find month and weekday names for dates. This particular recipe can be useful in various places. Consider, if you wanted to search HIREDATEs but wanted to ignore the year by extracting the month (or any other part of the HIREDATE you are interested in), you can do so. The example solutions to this problem search by month and weekday name. By studying the date formatting functions provided by your RDBMS, you can easily modify these solutions to search by year, quarter, combination of year and quarter, month and year combination, etc.

DB2 and MySQL

Use the functions MONTHNAME and DAYNAME to find the name of the month and weekday an employee was hired, respectively:

```
1 select ename
2   from emp
```

```
3  where monthname(hiredate) in ('February','December')
4     or dayname(hiredate) = 'Tuesday'
```

Oracle and PostgreSQL

Use the function TO_CHAR to find the names of the month and weekday an employee was hired. Use the function RTRIM to remove trailing whitespaces:

```
1 select ename
2   from emp
3  where rtrim(to_char(hiredate,'month')) in ('february','december')
4     or rtrim(to_char(hiredate,'day')) = 'tuesday'
```

SQL Server

Use the function DATENAME to find the names of the month and weekday an employee was hired:

```
1  select ename
2    from emp
3   where datename(m,hiredate) in ('February','December')
4      or datename(dw,hiredate) = 'Tuesday'
```

Discussion

The key to each solution is simply knowing which functions to use and how to use them. To verify what the return values are, put the functions in the SELECT clause and examine the output. Listed below is the result set for employees in DEPTNO 10 (using SQL Server syntax):

```
select ename,datename(m,hiredate) mth,datename(dw,hiredate) dw
  from emp
 where deptno = 10


ENAME   MTH        DW
------  ---------  ---------
CLARK   June       Tuesday
KING    November   Tuesday
MILLER  January    Saturday
```

Once you know what the function(s) return, finding rows using the functions shown in each of the solutions is easy.

9.12 Comparing Records Using Specific Parts of a Date

Problem

You want to find which employees have been hired on the same month and week-day. For example, if an employee was hired on Monday, March 10, 1988, and another employee was hired on Monday, March 2, 2001, you want those two to come up as a match since the day of week and month match. In table EMP, only three employees meet this requirement. You want to return the following result set:

```
MSG
--------------------------------------------------------
JAMES was hired on the same month and weekday as FORD
SCOTT was hired on the same month and weekday as JAMES
SCOTT was hired on the same month and weekday as FORD
```

Solution

Because you want to compare one employee's HIREDATE with the HIREDATE of the other employees, you will need to self join table EMP. That makes each possible combination of HIREDATEs available for you to compare. Then, simply extract the weekday and month from each HIREDATE and compare.

DB2

After self joining table EMP, use the function DAYOFWEEK to return the numeric day of the week. Use the function MONTHNAME to return the name of the month:

```
1 select a.ename ||
2        ' was hired on the same month and weekday as '||
3        b.ename msg
4   from emp a, emp b
5  where (dayofweek(a.hiredate),monthname(a.hiredate)) =
6        (dayofweek(b.hiredate),monthname(b.hiredate))
7    and a.empno < b.empno
8  order by a.ename
```

Oracle and PostgreSQL

After self joining table EMP, use the TO_CHAR function to format the HIREDATE into weekday and month for comparison:

```
1 select a.ename ||
2        ' was hired on the same month and weekday as '||
3        b.ename as msg
4   from emp a, emp b
5  where to_char(a.hiredate,'DMON') =
6        to_char(b.hiredate,'DMON')
7    and a.empno < b.empno
8  order by a.ename
```

MySQL

After self joining table EMP, use the DATE_FORMAT function to format the HIREDATE into weekday and month for comparison:

```
1 select concat(a.ename,
2        ' was hired on the same month and weekday as ',
3        b.ename) msg
4   from emp a, emp b
5  where date_format(a.hiredate,'%w%M') =
6        date_format(b.hiredate,'%w%M')
7    and a.empno < b.empno
8  order by a.ename
```

SQL Server

After self joining table EMP, use the DATENAME function to format the HIRE-DATE into weekday and month for comparison:

```
1 select a.ename +
2        ' was hired on the same month and weekday as '+
3        b.ename msg
4  from emp a, emp b
5  where datename(dw,a.hiredate) = datename(dw,b.hiredate)
6    and datename(m,a.hiredate)  = datename(m,b.hiredate)
7    and a.empno < b.empno
8  order by a.ename
```

Discussion

The only difference between the solutions is the date function used to format the HIREDATE. I'm going to use the Oracle/PostgreSQL solution in this discussion (because it's the shortest to type out), but the explanation holds true for the other solutions as well.

The first step is to self join EMP so that each employee has access to the other employees' HIREDATEs. Consider the results of the query below (filtered for SCOTT):

```
select a.ename as scott, a.hiredate as scott_hd,
       b.ename as other_emps, b.hiredate as other_hds
  from emp a, emp b
 where a.ename  = 'SCOTT'
   and a.empno != b.empno
```

SCOTT	SCOTT_HD	OTHER_EMPS	OTHER_HDS
SCOTT	09-DEC-1982	SMITH	17-DEC-1980
SCOTT	09-DEC-1982	ALLEN	20-FEB-1981
SCOTT	09-DEC-1982	WARD	22-FEB-1981
SCOTT	09-DEC-1982	JONES	02-APR-1981
SCOTT	09-DEC-1982	MARTIN	28-SEP-1981
SCOTT	09-DEC-1982	BLAKE	01-MAY-1981
SCOTT	09-DEC-1982	CLARK	09-JUN-1981
SCOTT	09-DEC-1982	KING	17-NOV-1981
SCOTT	09-DEC-1982	TURNER	08-SEP-1981
SCOTT	09-DEC-1982	ADAMS	12-JAN-1983
SCOTT	09-DEC-1982	JAMES	03-DEC-1981
SCOTT	09-DEC-1982	FORD	03-DEC-1981
SCOTT	09-DEC-1982	MILLER	23-JAN-1982

By self-joining table EMP, you can compare SCOTT's HIREDATE to the HIRE-DATE of all the other employees. The filter on EMPNO is so that SCOTT's HIRE-DATE is not returned as one of the OTHER_HDS. The next step is to use your RDBMS's supplied date formatting function(s) to compare the weekday and month of the HIREDATEs and keep only those that match:

```
select a.ename as emp1, a.hiredate as emp1_hd,
       b.ename as emp2, b.hiredate as emp2_hd
  from emp a, emp b
 where to_char(a.hiredate,'DMON') =
       to_char(b.hiredate,'DMON')
   and a.empno != b.empno
 order by 1
```

```
EMP1        EMP1_HD      EMP2        EMP2_HD
----------  -----------  ----------  -----------
FORD        03-DEC-1981  SCOTT       09-DEC-1982
FORD        03-DEC-1981  JAMES       03-DEC-1981
JAMES       03-DEC-1981  SCOTT       09-DEC-1982
JAMES       03-DEC-1981  FORD        03-DEC-1981
SCOTT       09-DEC-1982  JAMES       03-DEC-1981
SCOTT       09-DEC-1982  FORD        03-DEC-1981
```

At this point, the HIREDATEs are correctly matched, but there are six rows in the result set rather than the three in the Problem section of this recipe. The reason for the extra rows is the filter on EMPNO. By using "not equals" you do not filter out the reciprocals. For example, the first row matches FORD and SCOTT and the last row matches SCOTT and FORD. The six rows in the result set are technically accurate but redundant. To remove the redundancy use "less than" (the HIREDATEs are removed to bring the intermediate queries closer to the final result set):

```
select a.ename as emp1, b.ename as emp2
  from emp a, emp b
 where to_char(a.hiredate,'DMON') =
       to_char(b.hiredate,'DMON')
   and a.empno < b.empno
 order by 1
```

```
EMP1        EMP2
----------  ----------
JAMES       FORD
SCOTT       JAMES
SCOTT       FORD
```

The final step is to simply concatenate the result set to form the message.

9.13   Identifying Overlapping Date Ranges

Problem

You want to find all instances of an employee starting a new project before ending an existing project. Consider table EMP_PROJECT:

```
select *
  from emp_project
```

```
EMPNO ENAME       PROJ_ID PROJ_START  PROJ_END
----- ----------  ------- ----------- -----------
```

```
7782 CLARK          1 16-JUN-2005 18-JUN-2005
7782 CLARK          4 19-JUN-2005 24-JUN-2005
7782 CLARK          7 22-JUN-2005 25-JUN-2005
7782 CLARK         10 25-JUN-2005 28-JUN-2005
7782 CLARK         13 28-JUN-2005 02-JUL-2005
7839 KING           2 17-JUN-2005 21-JUN-2005
7839 KING           8 23-JUN-2005 25-JUN-2005
7839 KING          14 29-JUN-2005 30-JUN-2005
7839 KING          11 26-JUN-2005 27-JUN-2005
7839 KING           5 20-JUN-2005 24-JUN-2005
7934 MILLER         3 18-JUN-2005 22-JUN-2005
7934 MILLER        12 27-JUN-2005 28-JUN-2005
7934 MILLER        15 30-JUN-2005 03-JUL-2005
7934 MILLER         9 24-JUN-2005 27-JUN-2005
7934 MILLER         6 21-JUN-2005 23-JUN-2005
```

Looking at the results for employee KING, you see that KING began PROJ_ID 8 before finishing PROJ_ID 5 and began PROJ_ID 5 before finishing PROJ_ID 2. You want to return the following result set:

```
EMPNO ENAME      MSG
----- ---------- --------------------------------
 7782 CLARK      project 7 overlaps project 4
 7782 CLARK      project 10 overlaps project 7
 7782 CLARK      project 13 overlaps project 10
 7839 KING       project 8 overlaps project 5
 7839 KING       project 5 overlaps project 2
 7934 MILLER     project 12 overlaps project 9
 7934 MILLER     project 6 overlaps project 3
```

Solution

The key here is to find rows where PROJ_START (the date the new project starts) occurs on or after another project's PROJ_START date and on or before that other project's PROJ_END date. To begin, you need to be able to compare each project with each other project (for the same employee). By self joining EMP_PROJECT on employee, you generate every possible combination of two projects for each employee. To find the overlaps, simply find the rows where PROJ_START for any PROJ_ID falls between PROJ_START and PROJ_END for another PROJ_ID by the same employee.

DB2, PostgreSQL, and Oracle

Self join EMP_PROJECT. Then use the concatenation operator "||" to construct the message that explains which projects overlap:

```
1  select a.empno,a.ename,
2         'project '||b.proj_id||
3         ' overlaps project '||a.proj_id as msg
4    from emp_project a,
5         emp_project b
6   where a.empno = b.empno
```

```
7      and b.proj_start >= a.proj_start
8      and b.proj_start <= a.proj_end
9      and a.proj_id != b.proj_id
```

MySQL

Self join EMP_PROJECT. Then use the CONCAT function to construct the message that explains which projects overlap:

```
1  select a.empno,a.ename,
2         concat('project ',b.proj_id,
3          ' overlaps project ',a.proj_id) as msg
4    from emp_project a,
5         emp_project b
6   where a.empno = b.empno
7     and b.proj_start >= a.proj_start
8     and b.proj_start <= a.proj_end
9     and a.proj_id != b.proj_id
```

SQL Server

Self join EMP_PROJECT. Then use the concatenation operator "+" to construct the message that explains which projects overlap:

```
1  select a.empno,a.ename,
2         'project '+b.proj_id+
3          ' overlaps project '+a.proj_id as msg
4    from emp_project a,
5         emp_project b
6   where a.empno = b.empno
7     and b.proj_start >= a.proj_start
8     and b.proj_start <= a.proj_end
9     and a.proj_id != b.proj_id
```

Discussion

The only difference between the solutions lies in the string concatenation, so one discussion using the DB2 syntax will cover all three solutions. The first step is a self join of EMP_PROJECT so that the PROJ_START dates can be compared amongst the different projects. The output of the self join for employee KING is shown below. You can observe how each project can "see" the other projects:

```
select a.ename,
       a.proj_id as a_id,
       a.proj_start as a_start,
       a.proj_end as a_end,
       b.proj_id as b_id,
       b.proj_start as b_start
  from emp_project a,
       emp_project b
 where a.ename    = 'KING'
   and a.empno    = b.empno
   and a.proj_id != b.proj_id
 order by 2
```

```
ENAME   A_ID A_START     A_END        B_ID B_START
------  ----- ----------- ----------- ----- -----------
KING       2 17-JUN-2005 21-JUN-2005     8 23-JUN-2005
KING       2 17-JUN-2005 21-JUN-2005    14 29-JUN-2005
KING       2 17-JUN-2005 21-JUN-2005    11 26-JUN-2005
KING       2 17-JUN-2005 21-JUN-2005     5 20-JUN-2005
KING       5 20-JUN-2005 24-JUN-2005     2 17-JUN-2005
KING       5 20-JUN-2005 24-JUN-2005     8 23-JUN-2005
KING       5 20-JUN-2005 24-JUN-2005    11 26-JUN-2005
KING       5 20-JUN-2005 24-JUN-2005    14 29-JUN-2005
KING       8 23-JUN-2005 25-JUN-2005     2 17-JUN-2005
KING       8 23-JUN-2005 25-JUN-2005    14 29-JUN-2005
KING       8 23-JUN-2005 25-JUN-2005     5 20-JUN-2005
KING       8 23-JUN-2005 25-JUN-2005    11 26-JUN-2005
KING      11 26-JUN-2005 27-JUN-2005     2 17-JUN-2005
KING      11 26-JUN-2005 27-JUN-2005     8 23-JUN-2005
KING      11 26-JUN-2005 27-JUN-2005    14 29-JUN-2005
KING      11 26-JUN-2005 27-JUN-2005     5 20-JUN-2005
KING      14 29-JUN-2005 30-JUN-2005     2 17-JUN-2005
KING      14 29-JUN-2005 30-JUN-2005     8 23-JUN-2005
KING      14 29-JUN-2005 30-JUN-2005     5 20-JUN-2005
KING      14 29-JUN-2005 30-JUN-2005    11 26-JUN-2005
```

As you can see from the result set above, the self join makes finding overlapping dates easy; simply return each row where B_START occurs between A_START and A_END. If you look at the WHERE clause on lines 7 and 8 of the solution:

```
and b.proj_start >= a.proj_start
and b.proj_start <= a.proj_end
```

it is doing just that. Once you have the required rows, constructing the messages is just a matter of concatenating the return values.

Oracle users can use the window function LEAD OVER to avoid the self join, if the maximum number of projects per employee is fixed. This can come in handy if the self join is expensive for your particular results (if the self join requires more resources than the sorts needed for LEAD OVER). For example, consider the alternative for employee KING using LEAD OVER:

```
select empno,
       ename,
       proj_id,
       proj_start,
       proj_end,
       case
       when lead(proj_start,1)over(order by proj_start)
            between proj_start and proj_end
       then lead(proj_id)over(order by proj_start)
       when lead(proj_start,2)over(order by proj_start)
            between proj_start and proj_end
       then lead(proj_id)over(order by proj_start)
       when lead(proj_start,3)over(order by proj_start)
            between proj_start and proj_end
       then lead(proj_id)over(order by proj_start)
       when lead(proj_start,4)over(order by proj_start)
```

```
          between proj_start and proj_end
      then lead(proj_id)over(order by proj_start)
      end is_overlap
  from emp_project
 where ename = 'KING'
```

```
EMPNO ENAME  PROJ_ID PROJ_START  PROJ_END     IS_OVERLAP
----- ------ ------- ----------- ----------- ----------
 7839 KING         2 17-JUN-2005 21-JUN-2005          5
 7839 KING         5 20-JUN-2005 24-JUN-2005          8
 7839 KING         8 23-JUN-2005 25-JUN-2005
 7839 KING        11 26-JUN-2005 27-JUN-2005
 7839 KING        14 29-JUN-2005 30-JUN-2005
```

Because the number of projects is fixed at five for employee KING, you can use LEAD OVER to move examine the dates of all the projects without a self join. From here, producing the final result set is easy. Simply keep the rows where IS_OVER-LAP is not NULL:

```
select empno,ename,
       'project '||is_overlap||
       ' overlaps project '||proj_id msg
  from (
select empno,
       ename,
       proj_id,
       proj_start,
       proj_end,
       case
       when lead(proj_start,1)over(order by proj_start)
            between proj_start and proj_end
       then lead(proj_id)over(order by proj_start)
       when lead(proj_start,2)over(order by proj_start)
            between proj_start and proj_end
       then lead(proj_id)over(order by proj_start)
       when lead(proj_start,3)over(order by proj_start)
            between proj_start and proj_end
       then lead(proj_id)over(order by proj_start)
       when lead(proj_start,4)over(order by proj_start)
            between proj_start and proj_end
       then lead(proj_id)over(order by proj_start)
       end is_overlap
  from emp_project
 where ename = 'KING'
       )
 where is_overlap is not null
```

```
EMPNO ENAME  MSG
----- ------ -------------------------------
 7839 KING   project 5 overlaps project 2
 7839 KING   project 8 overlaps project 5
```

To allow the solution to work for all employees (not just KING), partition by ENAME in the LEAD OVER function:

```
select empno,ename,
       'project '||is_overlap||
       ' overlaps project '||proj_id msg
  from (
select empno,
       ename,
       proj_id,
       proj_start,
       proj_end,
       case
       when lead(proj_start,1)over(partition by ename
                                       order by proj_start)
            between proj_start and proj_end
       then lead(proj_id)over(partition by ename
                                  order by proj_start)
       when lead(proj_start,2)over(partition by ename
                                       order by proj_start)
            between proj_start and proj_end
       then lead(proj_id)over(partition by ename
                                  order by proj_start)
       when lead(proj_start,3)over(partition by ename
                                       order by proj_start)
            between proj_start and proj_end
       then lead(proj_id)over(partition by ename
                                  order by proj_start)
       when lead(proj_start,4)over(partition by ename
                                       order by proj_start)
            between proj_start and proj_end
       then lead(proj_id)over(partition by ename
                                  order by proj_start)
       end is_overlap
  from emp_project
       )
 where is_overlap is not null


EMPNO ENAME  MSG
----- ------ ------------------------------
 7782 CLARK  project 7 overlaps project 4
 7782 CLARK  project 10 overlaps project 7
 7782 CLARK  project 13 overlaps project 10
 7839 KING   project 5 overlaps project 2
 7839 KING   project 8 overlaps project 5
 7934 MILLER project 6 overlaps project 3
 7934 MILLER project 12 overlaps project 9
```

Working with Ranges

This chapter is about "everyday" queries that involve ranges. Ranges are common in everyday life. For example, projects that we work on range over consecutive periods of time. In SQL, it's often necessary to search for ranges, or to generate ranges, or to otherwise manipulate range-based data. The queries you'll read about here are slightly more involved than the queries found in the preceding chapters, but they are just as common, and they'll begin to give you a sense of what SQL can really do for you when you learn to take full advantage of it.

10.1 Locating a Range of Consecutive Values

Problem

You want to determine which rows represent a range of consecutive projects. Consider the following result set from view V, which contains data about a project and its start and end dates:

```
select *
  from V

PROJ_ID PROJ_START  PROJ_END
------- ----------- -----------
      1 01-JAN-2005 02-JAN-2005
      2 02-JAN-2005 03-JAN-2005
      3 03-JAN-2005 04-JAN-2005
      4 04-JAN-2005 05-JAN-2005
      5 06-JAN-2005 07-JAN-2005
      6 16-JAN-2005 17-JAN-2005
      7 17-JAN-2005 18-JAN-2005
      8 18-JAN-2005 19-JAN-2005
      9 19-JAN-2005 20-JAN-2005
     10 21-JAN-2005 22-JAN-2005
     11 26-JAN-2005 27-JAN-2005
     12 27-JAN-2005 28-JAN-2005
     13 28-JAN-2005 29-JAN-2005
     14 29-JAN-2005 30-JAN-2005
```

Excluding the first row, each row's PROJ_START should equal the PROJ_END of the row before it ("before" is defined as PROJ_ID − 1 for the current row). Examining the first five rows from view V, PROJ_IDs 1 through 3 are part of the same "group" as each PROJ_END equals the PROJ_START of the row after it. Because you want to find the range of dates for consecutive projects, you would like to return all rows where the current PROJ_END equals the next row's PROJ_START. If the first five rows comprised the entire result set, you would like to return only the first three rows. The final result set (using all 14 rows from view V) should be:

```
PROJ_ID PROJ_START  PROJ_END
------- ----------- -----------
      1 01-JAN-2005 02-JAN-2005
      2 02-JAN-2005 03-JAN-2005
      3 03-JAN-2005 04-JAN-2005
      6 16-JAN-2005 17-JAN-2005
      7 17-JAN-2005 18-JAN-2005
      8 18-JAN-2005 19-JAN-2005
     11 26-JAN-2005 27-JAN-2005
     12 27-JAN-2005 28-JAN-2005
     13 28-JAN-2005 29-JAN-2005
```

The rows with PROJ_IDs 4, 5, 9, 10, and 14 are excluded from this result set because the PROJ_END of each of these rows does not match the PROJ_START of the row following it.

Solution

DB2, MySQL, PostgreSQL, and SQL Server

Use a self join to find the rows with consecutive values:

```
1 select v1.proj_id,
2        v1.proj_start,
3        v1.proj_end
4   from V v1, V v2
5  where v1.proj_end = v2.proj_start
```

Oracle

The preceding solution will also work for Oracle. Alternatively, here is another solution that takes advantage of the window function LEAD OVER to look at the "next" row's BEGIN_DATE, thus avoiding the need to self join:

```
1 select proj_id,proj_start,proj_end
2   from (
3 select proj_id,proj_start,proj_end,
4        lead(proj_start)over(order by proj_id) next_proj_start
5   from V
6        )
7  where next_proj_start = proj_end
```

Discussion

DB2, MySQL, PostgreSQL, and SQL Server

By self joining the view to itself, each row can be compared to every other row returned. Consider a partial result set for IDs 1 and 4:

```
select v1.proj_id as v1_id,
       v1.proj_end as v1_end,
       v2.proj_start as v2_begin,
       v2.proj_id as v2_id
  from v v1, v v2
 where v1.proj_id in ( 1,4 )
```

```
V1_ID V1_END      V2_BEGIN        V2_ID
----- ----------- -----------  ----------
    1 02-JAN-2005 01-JAN-2005           1
    1 02-JAN-2005 02-JAN-2005           2
    1 02-JAN-2005 03-JAN-2005           3
    1 02-JAN-2005 04-JAN-2005           4
    1 02-JAN-2005 06-JAN-2005           5
    1 02-JAN-2005 16-JAN-2005           6
    1 02-JAN-2005 17-JAN-2005           7
    1 02-JAN-2005 18-JAN-2005           8
    1 02-JAN-2005 19-JAN-2005           9
    1 02-JAN-2005 21-JAN-2005          10
    1 02-JAN-2005 26-JAN-2005          11
    1 02-JAN-2005 27-JAN-2005          12
    1 02-JAN-2005 28-JAN-2005          13
    1 02-JAN-2005 29-JAN-2005          14
    4 05-JAN-2005 01-JAN-2005           1
    4 05-JAN-2005 02-JAN-2005           2
    4 05-JAN-2005 03-JAN-2005           3
    4 05-JAN-2005 04-JAN-2005           4
    4 05-JAN-2005 06-JAN-2005           5
    4 05-JAN-2005 16-JAN-2005           6
    4 05-JAN-2005 17-JAN-2005           7
    4 05-JAN-2005 18-JAN-2005           8
    4 05-JAN-2005 19-JAN-2005           9
    4 05-JAN-2005 21-JAN-2005          10
    4 05-JAN-2005 26-JAN-2005          11
    4 05-JAN-2005 27-JAN-2005          12
    4 05-JAN-2005 28-JAN-2005          13
    4 05-JAN-2005 29-JAN-2005          14
```

Examining this result set, you can see why PROJ_ID 1 is included in the final result set and PROJ_ID 4 is not: there is no corresponding V2_BEGIN value for the V1_END value returned for V1_ID 4.

Depending on how you view the data, PROJ_ID 4 can just as easily be considered contiguous. Consider the following result set:

```
select *
  from V
 where proj_id <= 5

PROJ_ID PROJ_START  PROJ_END
------- ----------- -----------
      1 01-JAN-2005 02-JAN-2005
      2 02-JAN-2005 03-JAN-2005
      3 03-JAN-2005 04-JAN-2005
      4 04-JAN-2005 05-JAN-2005
      5 06-JAN-2005 07-JAN-2005
```

If "contiguous" is defined as a project that starts the same day another project ends, then PROJ_ID 4 should be included in the result set. PROJ_ID 4 was originally eliminated because of the forward comparison (comparing its PROJ_END with the next PROJ_START), but if you do a backwards comparison (PROJ_START with the prior PROJ_END), then PROJ_ID 4 will be included in the result set.

Modifying the solution to include PROJ_ID 4 is trivial: simply add an additional predicate to ensure that both PROJ_START and PROJ_END are checked for being contiguous, not just PROJ_END. The modification shown in the following query produces a result set that includes PROJ_ID 4 (DISTINCT is necessary because some rows satisfy both predicate conditions):

```
select distinct
       v1.proj_id,
       v1.proj_start,
       v1.proj_end
  from V v1, V v2
 where v1.proj_end   = v2.proj_start
    or v1.proj_start = v2.proj_end

PROJ_ID PROJ_START  PROJ_END
------- ----------- -----------
      1 01-JAN-2005 02-JAN-2005
      2 02-JAN-2005 03-JAN-2005
      3 03-JAN-2005 04-JAN-2005
      4 04-JAN-2005 05-JAN-2005
```

Oracle

While the self-join solution certainly works, the window function LEAD OVER is perfect for this type of problem. The function LEAD OVER allows you to examine other rows without performing a self join (though the function must impose order on the result set to do so). Consider the results of the inline view (lines 3–5) for IDs 1 and 4:

```
select *
  from (
select proj_id,proj_start,proj_end,
       lead(proj_start)over(order by proj_id) next_proj_start
  from v
       )
 where proj_id in ( 1,4 )
```

```
PROJ_ID PROJ_START  PROJ_END    NEXT_PROJ_START
------- ----------- ----------- ----------------
      1 01-JAN-2005 02-JAN-2005 02-JAN-2005
      4 04-JAN-2005 05-JAN-2005 06-JAN-2005
```

Examining the above snippet of code and its result set, it is particularly easy to see why PROJ_ID 4 is excluded from the final result set of the complete solution. It's excluded because its PROJ_END date of 05-JAN-2005 does not match the "next" project's start date of 06-JAN-2005.

The function LEAD OVER is extremely handy when it comes to problems such as this one, particularly when examining partial results. When working with window functions, keep in mind that they are evaluated after the FROM and WHERE clauses, so the LEAD OVER function in the preceding query must be embedded within an inline view. Otherwise the LEAD OVER function is applied to the result set after the WHERE clause has filtered out all rows except for PROJ_ID's 1 and 4.

Now, depending on how you view the data, you may very well want to include PROJ_ID 4 in the final result set. Consider the first five rows from view V:

```
select *
  from V
 where proj_id <= 5

PROJ_ID PROJ_START  PROJ_END
------- ----------- -----------
      1 01-JAN-2005 02-JAN-2005
      2 02-JAN-2005 03-JAN-2005
      3 03-JAN-2005 04-JAN-2005
      4 04-JAN-2005 05-JAN-2005
      5 06-JAN-2005 07-JAN-2005
```

If your requirement is such that PROJ_ID 4 is in fact contiguous (because PROJ_START for PROJ_ID 4 matches PROJ_END for PROJ_ID 3), and that only PROJ_ID 5 should be discarded, the proposed solution for this recipe is incorrect (!), or at the very least, incomplete:

```
select proj_id,proj_start,proj_end
  from (
select proj_id,proj_start,proj_end,
       lead(proj_start)over(order by proj_id) next_start
  from V
 where proj_id <= 5
       )
 where proj_end = next_start

PROJ_ID PROJ_START  PROJ_END
------- ----------- -----------
      1 01-JAN-2005 02-JAN-2005
      2 02-JAN-2005 03-JAN-2005
      3 03-JAN-2005 04-JAN-2005
```

If you believe PROJ_ID 4 should be included, simply add LAG OVER to the query and use an additional filter in the WHERE clause:

```
select proj_id,proj_start,proj_end
  from (
select proj_id,proj_start,proj_end,
       lead(proj_start)over(order by proj_id) next_start,
       lag(proj_end)over(order by proj_id) last_end
  from V
 where proj_id <= 5
       )
 where proj_end   = next_start
    or proj_start = last_end


PROJ_ID PROJ_START  PROJ_END
------- ----------- -----------
      1 01-JAN-2005 02-JAN-2005
      2 02-JAN-2005 03-JAN-2005
      3 03-JAN-2005 04-JAN-2005
      4 04-JAN-2005 05-JAN-2005
```

Now PROJ_ID 4 is included in the final result set, and only the evil PROJ_ID 5 is excluded. Please consider your exact requirements when applying these recipes to your code.

10.2   Finding Differences Between Rows in the Same Group or Partition

Problem

You want to return the DEPTNO, ENAME, and SAL of each employee along with the difference in SAL between employees in the same department (i.e., having the same value for DEPTNO). The difference should be between each current employee and the employee hired immediately afterwards (you want to see if there is a correlation between seniority and salary on a "per department" basis). For each employee hired last in his department, return "N/A" for the difference. The result set should look like this:

```
DEPTNO ENAME          SAL HIREDATE    DIFF
------ ----------  ---------- ----------- ----------
    10 CLARK             2450 09-JUN-1981      -2550
    10 KING              5000 17-NOV-1981       3700
    10 MILLER            1300 23-JAN-1982        N/A
    20 SMITH              800 17-DEC-1980      -2175
    20 JONES             2975 02-APR-1981        -25
    20 FORD              3000 03-DEC-1981          0
    20 SCOTT             3000 09-DEC-1982       1900
    20 ADAMS             1100 12-JAN-1983        N/A
    30 ALLEN             1600 20-FEB-1981        350
```

```
30 WARD          1250 22-FEB-1981    -1600
30 BLAKE         2850 01-MAY-1981     1350
30 TURNER        1500 08-SEP-1981      250
30 MARTIN        1250 28-SEP-1981      300
30 JAMES          950 03-DEC-1981      N/A
```

Solution

The is another example of where the Oracle window functions LEAD OVER and LAG OVER come in handy. You can easily access next and prior rows without additional joins. For other RDBMSs, you can use scalar subqueries, though not as easily. This particular problem is not at all elegant when having to use scalar subqueries or self joins to solve it.

DB2, MySQL, PostgreSQL, and SQL Server

Use a scalar subquery to retrieve the HIREDATE of the employee hired immediately after each employee. Then use another scalar subquery to find the salary of said employee:

```
 1  select deptno,ename,hiredate,sal,
 2         coalesce(cast(sal-next_sal as char(10)),'N/A') as diff
 3    from (
 4  select e.deptno,
 5         e.ename,
 6         e.hiredate,
 7         e.sal,
 8         (select min(sal) from emp d
 9           where d.deptno=e.deptno
10             and d.hiredate =
11                (select min(hiredate) from emp d
12                  where e.deptno=d.deptno
13                    and d.hiredate > e.hiredate)) as next_sal
14    from emp e
15         ) x
```

Oracle

Use the window function LEAD OVER to access the "next" employee's salary relative to the current row:

```
1 select deptno,ename,sal,hiredate,
2        lpad(nvl(to_char(sal-next_sal),'N/A'),10) diff
3   from (
4 select deptno,ename,sal,hiredate,
5        lead(sal)over(partition by deptno
6                          order by hiredate) next_sal
7   from emp
8        )
```

Discussion

DB2, MySQL, PostgreSQL, and SQL Server

The first step is to use a scalar subquery to find the HIREDATE of the employee hired immediately after each employee in the same department. The solution uses MIN(HIREDATE) in the scalar subquery to ensure that only one value is returned even in the event of multiple people being hired on the same date:

```
select e.deptno,
       e.ename,
       e.hiredate,
       e.sal,
       (select min(hiredate) from emp d
          where e.deptno=d.deptno
            and d.hiredate > e.hiredate) as next_hire
  from emp e
 order by 1
```

```
DEPTNO ENAME      HIREDATE       SAL NEXT_HIRE
------ ---------- ----------- ------- -----------
    10 CLARK      09-JUN-1981    2450 17-NOV-1981
    10 KING       17-NOV-1981    5000 23-JAN-1982
    10 MILLER     23-JAN-1982    1300
    20 SMITH      17-DEC-1980     800 02-APR-1981
    20 ADAMS      12-JAN-1983    1100
    20 FORD       03-DEC-1981    3000 09-DEC-1982
    20 SCOTT      09-DEC-1982    3000 12-JAN-1983
    20 JONES      02-APR-1981    2975 03-DEC-1981
    30 ALLEN      20-FEB-1981    1600 22-FEB-1981
    30 BLAKE      01-MAY-1981    2850 08-SEP-1981
    30 MARTIN     28-SEP-1981    1250 03-DEC-1981
    30 JAMES      03-DEC-1981     950
    30 TURNER     08-SEP-1981    1500 28-SEP-1981
    30 WARD       22-FEB-1981    1250 01-MAY-1981
```

The next step is to use another scalar subquery to find the salary of the employee who was hired on the NEXT_HIRE date. Again, the solution uses MIN to ensure that just one value is always returned:

```
select e.deptno,
       e.ename,
       e.hiredate,
       e.sal,
       (select min(sal) from emp d
         where d.deptno=e.deptno
           and d.hiredate =
               (select min(hiredate) from emp d
                 where e.deptno=d.deptno
                   and d.hiredate > e.hiredate)) as next_sal
  from emp e
 order by 1
```

```
DEPTNO ENAME       HIREDATE         SAL   NEXT_SAL
------ ---------- ----------- ---------- ----------
    10 CLARK      09-JUN-1981       2450       5000
    10 KING       17-NOV-1981       5000       1300
    10 MILLER     23-JAN-1982       1300
    20 SMITH      17-DEC-1980        800       2975
    20 ADAMS      12-JAN-1983       1100
    20 FORD       03-DEC-1981       3000       3000
    20 SCOTT      09-DEC-1982       3000       1100
    20 JONES      02-APR-1981       2975       3000
    30 ALLEN      20-FEB-1981       1600       1250
    30 BLAKE      01-MAY-1981       2850       1500
    30 MARTIN     28-SEP-1981       1250        950
    30 JAMES      03-DEC-1981        950
    30 TURNER     08-SEP-1981       1500       1250
    30 WARD       22-FEB-1981       1250       2850
```

The final step is to find the difference between SAL and NEXT_SAL, and to use the function COALESCE to return "N/A" when applicable. Since the result of the subtraction is a number and can potentially be NULL, you must cast to a string for COALESCE to work:

```
select deptno,ename,hiredate,sal,
       coalesce(cast(sal-next_sal as char(10)),'N/A') as diff
  from (
select e.deptno,
       e.ename,
       e.hiredate,
       e.sal,
       (select min(sal) from emp d
         where d.deptno=e.deptno
           and d.hiredate =
               (select min(hiredate) from emp d
                 where e.deptno=d.deptno
                   and d.hiredate > e.hiredate)) as next_sal
  from emp e
       ) x
 order by 1
```

```
DEPTNO ENAME       HIREDATE           SAL DIFF
------ ---------- ----------- ---------- ---------
    10 CLARK      09-JUN-1981       2450 -2550
    10 KING       17-NOV-1981       5000 3700
    10 MILLER     23-JAN-1982       1300 N/A
    20 SMITH      17-DEC-1980        800 -2175
    20 ADAMS      12-JAN-1983       1100 N/A
    20 FORD       03-DEC-1981       3000 0
    20 SCOTT      09-DEC-1982       3000 1900
    20 JONES      02-APR-1981       2975 -25
    30 ALLEN      20-FEB-1981       1600 350
    30 BLAKE      01-MAY-1981       2850 1350
    30 MARTIN     28-SEP-1981       1250 300
    30 JAMES      03-DEC-1981        950 N/A
    30 TURNER     08-SEP-1981       1500 250
    30 WARD       22-FEB-1981       1250 -1600
```

The use of MIN(SAL) in this solution is an example of how, in some ways, you can unintentionally inject business logic into a query while making what appears to be a solely technical decision. If multiple salaries are available for a given date, should you take the least? the highest? the average? In my example, I choose to take the least. In real life, I might well punt that decision back to the business client who requested the report to begin with.

Oracle

The first step is to use the LEAD OVER window function to find the "next" salary for each employee within her department. The employees hired last in each department will have a NULL value for NEXT_SAL:

```
select deptno,ename,sal,hiredate,
       lead(sal)over(partition by deptno order by hiredate) next_sal
  from emp
```

DEPTNO	ENAME	SAL	HIREDATE	NEXT_SAL
10	CLARK	2450	09-JUN-1981	5000
10	KING	5000	17-NOV-1981	1300
10	MILLER	1300	23-JAN-1982	
20	SMITH	800	17-DEC-1980	2975
20	JONES	2975	02-APR-1981	3000
20	FORD	3000	03-DEC-1981	3000
20	SCOTT	3000	09-DEC-1982	1100
20	ADAMS	1100	12-JAN-1983	
30	ALLEN	1600	20-FEB-1981	1250
30	WARD	1250	22-FEB-1981	2850
30	BLAKE	2850	01-MAY-1981	1500
30	TURNER	1500	08-SEP-1981	1250
30	MARTIN	1250	28-SEP-1981	950
30	JAMES	950	03-DEC-1981	

The next step is to take the difference between each employee's salary and the salary of the employee hired immediately after her in the same department:

```
select deptno,ename,sal,hiredate, sal-next_sal diff
  from (
select deptno,ename,sal,hiredate,
       lead(sal)over(partition by deptno order by hiredate) next_sal
  from emp
       )
```

DEPTNO	ENAME	SAL	HIREDATE	DIFF
10	CLARK	2450	09-JUN-1981	-2550
10	KING	5000	17-NOV-1981	3700
10	MILLER	1300	23-JAN-1982	
20	SMITH	800	17-DEC-1980	-2175
20	JONES	2975	02-APR-1981	-25
20	FORD	3000	03-DEC-1981	0

```
20 SCOTT          3000 09-DEC-1982      1900
20 ADAMS          1100 12-JAN-1983
30 ALLEN          1600 20-FEB-1981       350
30 WARD           1250 22-FEB-1981     -1600
30 BLAKE          2850 01-MAY-1981      1350
30 TURNER         1500 08-SEP-1981       250
30 MARTIN         1250 28-SEP-1981       300
30 JAMES           950 03-DEC-1981
```

The next step is to use the function NVL to return "N/A" when DIFF is NULL. To be able to return "N/A" you must cast the value of DIFF to a string, otherwise NVL will fail:

```
select deptno,ename,sal,hiredate,
       nvl(to_char(sal-next_sal),'N/A') diff
  from (
select deptno,ename,sal,hiredate,
       lead(sal)over(partition by deptno order by hiredate) next_sal
  from emp
       )

DEPTNO ENAME          SAL HIREDATE    DIFF
------ ---------- ---------- ----------- ----------------
    10 CLARK          2450 09-JUN-1981 -2550
    10 KING           5000 17-NOV-1981 3700
    10 MILLER         1300 23-JAN-1982 N/A
    20 SMITH           800 17-DEC-1980 -2175
    20 JONES          2975 02-APR-1981 -25
    20 FORD           3000 03-DEC-1981 0
    20 SCOTT          3000 09-DEC-1982 1900
    20 ADAMS          1100 12-JAN-1983 N/A
    30 ALLEN          1600 20-FEB-1981 350
    30 WARD           1250 22-FEB-1981 -1600
    30 BLAKE          2850 01-MAY-1981 1350
    30 TURNER         1500 08-SEP-1981 250
    30 MARTIN         1250 28-SEP-1981 300
    30 JAMES           950 03-DEC-1981 N/A
```

The last step is to use the function LPAD to format the values for DIFF. This is because, by default, numbers are right justified while strings are left justified. Using LPAD, you can right justify all the results in the column:

```
select deptno,ename,sal,hiredate,
       lpad(nvl(to_char(sal-next_sal),'N/A'),10) diff
  from (
select deptno,ename,sal,hiredate,
       lead(sal)over(partition by deptno order by hiredate) next_sal
  from emp
       )

DEPTNO ENAME          SAL HIREDATE    DIFF
------ ---------- ---------- ----------- ----------
    10 CLARK          2450 09-JUN-1981      -2550
    10 KING           5000 17-NOV-1981       3700
    10 MILLER         1300 23-JAN-1982        N/A
```

20	SMITH	800	17-DEC-1980	-2175
20	JONES	2975	02-APR-1981	-25
20	FORD	3000	03-DEC-1981	0
20	SCOTT	3000	09-DEC-1982	1900
20	ADAMS	1100	12-JAN-1983	N/A
30	ALLEN	1600	20-FEB-1981	350
30	WARD	1250	22-FEB-1981	-1600
30	BLAKE	2850	01-MAY-1981	1350
30	TURNER	1500	08-SEP-1981	250
30	MARTIN	1250	28-SEP-1981	300
30	JAMES	950	03-DEC-1981	N/A

While the majority of the solutions provided in this book do not deal with "what if" scenarios (for the sake of readability and the author's sanity), the scenario involving duplicates when using Oracle's LEAD OVER function in this manner must be discussed. In the simple sample data in table EMP, no employees have duplicate HIREDATEs, yet this is a very likely situation. Normally, I would not discuss a "what if" situation such as duplicates (since there aren't any in table EMP), but the workaround involving LEAD (particularly to those of you with non-Oracle backgrounds) may not be immediately obvious. Consider the following query, which returns the difference in SAL between the employees in DEPTNO 10 (the difference is performed in the order in which they were hired):

```
select deptno,ename,sal,hiredate,
       lpad(nvl(to_char(sal-next_sal),'N/A'),10) diff
  from (
select deptno,ename,sal,hiredate,
       lead(sal)over(partition by deptno
                        order by hiredate) next_sal
  from emp
 where deptno=10 and empno > 10
       )
```

```
DEPTNO ENAME   SAL HIREDATE    DIFF
------ ------ ----- ----------- ----------
    10 CLARK  2450 09-JUN-1981      -2550
    10 KING   5000 17-NOV-1981       3700
    10 MILLER 1300 23-JAN-1982        N/A
```

This solution is correct considering the data in table EMP but, if there were duplicate rows, the solution would fail. Consider the example below, showing four more employees hired on the same day as KING:

```
insert into emp (empno,ename,deptno,sal,hiredate)
values (1,'ant',10,1000,to_date('17-NOV-1981'))

insert into emp (empno,ename,deptno,sal,hiredate)
values (2,'joe',10,1500,to_date('17-NOV-1981'))

insert into emp (empno,ename,deptno,sal,hiredate)
values (3,'jim',10,1600,to_date('17-NOV-1981'))
```

```
insert into emp (empno,ename,deptno,sal,hiredate)
values (4,'jon',10,1700,to_date('17-NOV-1981'))

select deptno,ename,sal,hiredate,
       lpad(nvl(to_char(sal-next_sal),'N/A'),10) diff
  from (
select deptno,ename,sal,hiredate,
       lead(sal)over(partition by deptno
                          order by hiredate) next_sal
  from emp
 where deptno=10
       )

DEPTNO ENAME   SAL HIREDATE    DIFF
------ ------ ----- ----------- ----------
    10 CLARK   2450 09-JUN-1981       1450
    10 ant     1000 17-NOV-1981       -500
    10 joe     1500 17-NOV-1981      -3500
    10 KING    5000 17-NOV-1981       3400
    10 jim     1600 17-NOV-1981       -100
    10 jon     1700 17-NOV-1981        400
    10 MILLER  1300 23-JAN-1982        N/A
```

You'll notice that with the exception of employee JON, all employees hired on the same date (November 17) evaluate their salary against another employee hired on the same date! This is incorrect. All employees hired on November 17 should have the difference of salary computed against MILLER's salary, not another employee hired on November 17. Take, for example, employee ANT. The value for DIFF for ANT is −500 because ANT's SAL is compared with JOE's SAL and is 500 less than JOE's SAL, hence the value of −500. The correct value for DIFF for employee ANT should be −300 because ANT makes 300 less than MILLER, who is the next employee hired by HIREDATE. The reason the solution seems to not work is due to the default behavior of Oracle's LEAD OVER function. By default, LEAD OVER only looks ahead one row. So, for employee ANT, the next SAL based on HIREDATE is JOE's SAL, because LEAD OVER simply looks one row ahead and doesn't skip duplicates. Fortunately, Oracle planned for such a situation and allows you to pass an additional parameter to LEAD OVER to determine how far ahead it should look. In the example above, the solution is simply a matter of counting: find the distance from each employee hired on November 17 to January 23 (MILLER's HIREDATE). The solution below shows how to accomplish this:

```
select deptno,ename,sal,hiredate,
       lpad(nvl(to_char(sal-next_sal),'N/A'),10) diff
  from (
select deptno,ename,sal,hiredate,
       lead(sal,cnt-rn+1)over(partition by deptno
                          order by hiredate) next_sal
  from (
select deptno,ename,sal,hiredate,
       count(*)over(partition by deptno,hiredate) cnt,
       row_number( )over(partition by deptno,hiredate order by sal) rn
```

```
     from emp
   where deptno=10
       )
       )

  DEPTNO ENAME     SAL HIREDATE     DIFF
  ------ ------   ----- ----------- ----------
      10 CLARK    2450 09-JUN-1981        1450
      10 ant      1000 17-NOV-1981        -300
      10 joe      1500 17-NOV-1981         200
      10 jim      1600 17-NOV-1981         300
      10 jon      1700 17-NOV-1981         400
      10 KING     5000 17-NOV-1981        3700
      10 MILLER   1300 23-JAN-1982         N/A
```

Now the solution is correct. As you can see, all the employees hired on November 17 now have their salaries compared with MILLER's salary. Inspecting the results, employee ANT now has a value of −300 for DIFF, which is what we were hoping for. If it isn't immediately obvious, the expression passed to LEAD OVER; CNT-RN+1 is simply the distance from each employee hired on November 17 to MILLER. Consider the inline view below, which shows the values for CNT and RN:

```
select deptno,ename,sal,hiredate,
       count(*)over(partition by deptno,hiredate) cnt,
       row_number( )over(partition by deptno,hiredate order by sal) rn
  from emp
 where deptno=10

  DEPTNO ENAME     SAL HIREDATE          CNT          RN
  ------ ------   ----- ----------- ---------- ----------
      10 CLARK    2450 09-JUN-1981          1           1
      10 ant      1000 17-NOV-1981          5           1
      10 joe      1500 17-NOV-1981          5           2
      10 jim      1600 17-NOV-1981          5           3
      10 jon      1700 17-NOV-1981          5           4
      10 KING     5000 17-NOV-1981          5           5
      10 MILLER   1300 23-JAN-1982          1           1
```

The value for CNT represents, for each employee with a duplicate HIREDATE, how many duplicates there are in total for their HIREDATE. The value for RN represents a ranking for the employees in DEPTNO 10. The rank is partitioned by DEPTNO and HIREDATE so only employees with a HIREDATE that another employee has will have a value greater than one. The ranking is sorted by SAL (this is arbitrary; SAL is convenient, but we could have just as easily chosen EMPNO). Now that you know how many total duplicates there are and you have a ranking of each duplicate, the distance to MILLER is simply the total number of duplicates minus the current rank plus one (CNT-RN+1). The results of the distance calculation and its effect on LEAD OVER are shown below:

```
select deptno,ename,sal,hiredate,
       lead(sal)over(partition by deptno
                        order by hiredate) incorrect,
```

```
        cnt-rn+1 distance,
        lead(sal,cnt-rn+1)over(partition by deptno
                        order by hiredate) correct
   from (
 select deptno,ename,sal,hiredate,
        count(*)over(partition by deptno,hiredate) cnt,
        row_number()over(partition by deptno,hiredate
                        order by sal) rn
   from emp
  where deptno=10
        )
```

DEPTNO	ENAME	SAL	HIREDATE	INCORRECT	DISTANCE	CORRECT
10	CLARK	2450	09-JUN-1981	1000	1	1000
10	ant	1000	17-NOV-1981	1500	5	1300
10	joe	1500	17-NOV-1981	1600	4	1300
10	jim	1600	17-NOV-1981	1700	3	1300
10	jon	1700	17-NOV-1981	5000	2	1300
10	KING	5000	17-NOV-1981	1300	1	1300
10	MILLER	1300	23-JAN-1982		1	

Now you can clearly see the effect that you have when you pass the correct distance to LEAD OVER. The rows for INCORRECT represent the values returned by LEAD OVER using a default distance of one. The rows for CORRECT represent the values returned by LEAD OVER using the proper distance for each employee with a duplicate HIREDATE to MILLER. At this point, all that is left is to find the difference between CORRECT and SAL for each row, which has already been shown.

10.3   Locating the Beginning and End of a Range of Consecutive Values

Problem

This recipe is an extension of Recipe 10.1, and it uses the same view V from the prior recipe. Now that you've located the ranges of consecutive values, you want to find just their start and end points. Unlike the prior recipe, if a row is not part of a set of consecutive values, you still want to return it. Why? Because such a row represents both the beginning and end of its range. Using the data from view V:

```
select *
  from V
```

PROJ_ID	PROJ_START	PROJ_END
1	01-JAN-2005	02-JAN-2005
2	02-JAN-2005	03-JAN-2005
3	03-JAN-2005	04-JAN-2005
4	04-JAN-2005	05-JAN-2005
5	06-JAN-2005	07-JAN-2005

```
 6 16-JAN-2005 17-JAN-2005
 7 17-JAN-2005 18-JAN-2005
 8 18-JAN-2005 19-JAN-2005
 9 19-JAN-2005 20-JAN-2005
10 21-JAN-2005 22-JAN-2005
11 26-JAN-2005 27-JAN-2005
12 27-JAN-2005 28-JAN-2005
13 28-JAN-2005 29-JAN-2005
14 29-JAN-2005 30-JAN-2005
```

you want the final result set to be:

```
PROJ_GRP PROJ_START  PROJ_END
-------- ----------- -----------
       1 01-JAN-2005 05-JAN-2005
       2 06-JAN-2005 07-JAN-2005
       3 16-JAN-2005 20-JAN-2005
       4 21-JAN-2005 22-JAN-2005
       5 26-JAN-2005 30-JAN-2005
```

Solution

This problem is a bit more involved than its predecessor. First, you must identify what the ranges are. A range of rows is defined by the values for PROJ_START and PROJ_END. For a row to be considered "consecutive" or part of a group, its PROJ_START value must equal the PROJ_END value of the row before it. In the case where a row's PROJ_START value does not equal the prior row's PROJ_END value and its PROJ_END value does not equal the next row's PROJ_START value, this is an instance of a single row group. Once you have identify the ranges, you need to be able to group the rows in these ranges together (into groups) and return only their start and end points.

Examine the first row of the desired result set. The PROJ_START is the PROJ_START for PROJ_ID 1 from view V and the PROJ_END is the PROJ_END for PROJ_ID 4 from view V. Despite the fact that PROJ_ID 4 does not have a consecutive value following it, it is the last of a range of consecutive values, and thus it is included in the first group.

DB2, MySQL, PostgreSQL, and SQL Server

The solution for these platforms will use use view V2 to help improve readability. View V2 is defined as follows:

```
create view v2
as
select a.*,
       case
         when (
           select b.proj_id
             from V b
            where a.proj_start = b.proj_end
            )
```

```
                    is not null then 0 else 1
            end as flag
        from V a
```

The result set from view V2 is:

```
select *
  from V2
```

```
PROJ_ID PROJ_START  PROJ_END            FLAG
------- ----------- ----------- ----------
      1 01-JAN-2005 02-JAN-2005          1
      2 02-JAN-2005 03-JAN-2005          0
      3 03-JAN-2005 04-JAN-2005          0
      4 04-JAN-2005 05-JAN-2005          0
      5 06-JAN-2005 07-JAN-2005          1
      6 16-JAN-2005 17-JAN-2005          1
      7 17-JAN-2005 18-JAN-2005          0
      8 18-JAN-2005 19-JAN-2005          0
      9 19-JAN-2005 20-JAN-2005          0
     10 21-JAN-2005 22-JAN-2005          1
     11 26-JAN-2005 27-JAN-2005          1
     12 27-JAN-2005 28-JAN-2005          0
     13 28-JAN-2005 29-JAN-2005          0
     14 29-JAN-2005 30-JAN-2005          0
```

Using V2, the solution is as follows. First, find the rows that are part of a set of consecutive values. Group those rows together. Then use the MIN and MAX functions to find their start and end points:

```
 1  select proj_grp,
 2         min(proj_start) as proj_start,
 3         max(proj_end) as proj_end
 4    from (
 5  select a.proj_id,a.proj_start,a.proj_end,
 6         (select sum(b.flag)
 7            from V2 b
 8           where b.proj_id <= a.proj_id) as proj_grp
 9    from V2 a
10         ) x
11   group by proj_grp
```

Oracle

While the solution for the other vendors will work for Oracle, there's no need to introduce additional views when you can take advantage of Oracle's LAG OVER window function. Use LAG OVER to determine whether or not each prior row's PROJ_END equals the current row's PROJ_START to help place the rows into groups. Once they are grouped, use the aggregate functions MIN and MAX to find their start and end points:

```
 1  select proj_grp, min(proj_start), max(proj_end)
 2    from (
 3  select proj_id,proj_start,proj_end,
```

```
 4        sum(flag)over(order by proj_id) proj_grp
 5    from (
 6   select proj_id,proj_start,proj_end,
 7        case when
 8            lag(proj_end)over(order by proj_id) = proj_start
 9            then 0 else 1
10        end flag
11    from V
12        )
13        )
14    group by proj_grp
```

Discussion

DB2, MySQL, PostgreSQL, and SQL Server

Using view V2 makes this problem relatively easy to solve. View V2 uses a scalar sub-query in a CASE expression to determine whether or not a particular row is part of a set of consecutive values. The CASE expression, aliased FLAG, returns a 0 if the current row is part of a consecutive set or a 1 if it is not (membership in a consecutive set is determined by whether or not there is a record with a PROJ_END value that matches the current row's PROJ_START value). The next step is to examine inline view X (lines 5–9). Inline view X returns all rows from view V2 along with a running total on FLAG; this running total is what creates our groups and can be seen below:

```
select a.proj_id,a.proj_start,a.proj_end,
       (select sum(b.flag)
          from v2 b
         where b.proj_id <= a.proj_id) as proj_grp
  from v2 a
```

PROJ_ID	PROJ_START	PROJ_END	PROJ_GRP
1	01-JAN-2005	02-JAN-2005	1
2	02-JAN-2005	03-JAN-2005	1
3	03-JAN-2005	04-JAN-2005	1
4	04-JAN-2005	05-JAN-2005	1
5	06-JAN-2005	07-JAN-2005	2
6	16-JAN-2005	17-JAN-2005	3
7	17-JAN-2005	18-JAN-2005	3
8	18-JAN-2005	19-JAN-2005	3
9	19-JAN-2005	20-JAN-2005	3
10	21-JAN-2005	22-JAN-2005	4
11	26-JAN-2005	27-JAN-2005	5
12	27-JAN-2005	28-JAN-2005	5
13	28-JAN-2005	29-JAN-2005	5
14	29-JAN-2005	30-JAN-2005	5

Now that the ranges have been grouped, find the start and end point for each by simply using the aggregate functions MIN and MAX on PROJ_START and PROJ_END respectively, and group by the values created by the running total.

Oracle

The window function LAG OVER is extremely useful in this situation. You can examine each prior row's PROJ_END value without a self join, without a scalar subquery, and without a view. The results of the LAG OVER function without the CASE expression are as follows:

```
select proj_id,proj_start,proj_end,
       lag(proj_end)over(order by proj_id) prior_proj_end
  from V


PROJ_ID PROJ_START  PROJ_END   PRIOR_PROJ_END
------- ----------- ---------- --------------
      1 01-JAN-2005 02-JAN-2005
      2 02-JAN-2005 03-JAN-2005 02-JAN-2005
      3 03-JAN-2005 04-JAN-2005 03-JAN-2005
      4 04-JAN-2005 05-JAN-2005 04-JAN-2005
      5 06-JAN-2005 07-JAN-2005 05-JAN-2005
      6 16-JAN-2005 17-JAN-2005 07-JAN-2005
      7 17-JAN-2005 18-JAN-2005 17-JAN-2005
      8 18-JAN-2005 19-JAN-2005 18-JAN-2005
      9 19-JAN-2005 20-JAN-2005 19-JAN-2005
     10 21-JAN-2005 22-JAN-2005 20-JAN-2005
     11 26-JAN-2005 27-JAN-2005 22-JAN-2005
     12 27-JAN-2005 28-JAN-2005 27-JAN-2005
     13 28-JAN-2005 29-JAN-2005 28-JAN-2005
     14 29-JAN-2005 30-JAN-2005 29-JAN-2005
```

The CASE expression in the complete solution simply compares the value returned by LAG OVER to the current row's PROJ_START value; if they are the same, return 0, else return 1. The next step is to create a running total on the 0's and 1's returned by the CASE expression to put each row into a group. The results of the running total can be seen below:

```
select proj_id,proj_start,proj_end,
       sum(flag)over(order by proj_id) proj_grp
  from (
select proj_id,proj_start,proj_end,
       case when
            lag(proj_end)over(order by proj_id) = proj_start
            then 0 else 1
       end flag
  from V
      )


PROJ_ID PROJ_START  PROJ_END    PROJ_GRP
------- ----------- ----------- ----------
      1 01-JAN-2005 02-JAN-2005          1
      2 02-JAN-2005 03-JAN-2005          1
      3 03-JAN-2005 04-JAN-2005          1
      4 04-JAN-2005 05-JAN-2005          1
      5 06-JAN-2005 07-JAN-2005          2
      6 16-JAN-2005 17-JAN-2005          3
      7 17-JAN-2005 18-JAN-2005          3
```

```
 8 18-JAN-2005 19-JAN-2005        3
 9 19-JAN-2005 20-JAN-2005        3
10 21-JAN-2005 22-JAN-2005        4
11 26-JAN-2005 27-JAN-2005        5
12 27-JAN-2005 28-JAN-2005        5
13 28-JAN-2005 29-JAN-2005        5
14 29-JAN-2005 30-JAN-2005        5
```

Now that each row has been placed into a group, simply use the aggregate functions MIN and MAX on PROJ_START and PROJ_END respectively, and group by the values created in the PROJ_GRP running total column.

10.4 Filling in Missing Values in a Range of Values

Problem

You want to return the number of employees hired each year for the entire decade of the 1980s, but there are some years in which no employees were hired. You would like to return the following result set:

```
YR       CNT
----  ----------
1980        1
1981       10
1982        2
1983        1
1984        0
1985        0
1986        0
1987        0
1988        0
1989        0
```

Solution

The trick to this solution is returning zeros for years that saw no employees hired. If no employee was hired in a given year, then no rows for that year will exist in table EMP. If the year does not exist in the table, how can you return a count, any count, even zero? The solution requires you to outer join. You must supply a result set that returns all the years you want to see, and then perform a count against table EMP to see if there were any employees hired in each of those years.

DB2

Use table EMP as a pivot table (because it has 14 rows) and the built-in function YEAR to generate one row for each year in the decade of 1980. Outer join to table EMP and count how many employees were hired each year:

```
1 select x.yr, coalesce(y.cnt,0) cnt
2   from (
3 select year(min(hiredate)over()) -
```

```
 4            mod(year(min(hiredate)over()),10) +
 5            row_number()over()-1 yr
 6    from emp fetch first 10 rows only
 7          ) x
 8    left join
 9          (
10 select year(hiredate) yr1, count(*) cnt
11    from emp
12   group by year(hiredate)
13          ) y
14      on ( x.yr = y.yr1 )
```

Oracle

Use table EMP as a pivot table (because it has 14 rows) and the built-in functions TO_NUMBER and TO_CHAR to generate one row for each year in the decade of 1980. Outer join to table EMP and count how many employees were hired each year:

```
 1  select x.yr, coalesce(cnt,0) cnt
 2     from (
 3  select extract(year from min(hiredate)over()) -
 4         mod(extract(year from min(hiredate)over()),10) +
 5         rownum-1 yr
 6    from emp
 7   where rownum <= 10
 8         ) x,
 9         (
10  select to_number(to_char(hiredate,'YYYY')) yr, count(*) cnt
11    from emp
12   group by to_number(to_char(hiredate,'YYYY'))
13         ) y
14   where x.yr = y.yr(+)
```

If you're using Oracle9i Database or later, you can implement the solution using the newly supported JOIN clause:

```
 1  select x.yr, coalesce(cnt,0) cnt
 2     from (
 3  select extract(year from min(hiredate)over()) -
 4         mod(extract(year from min(hiredate)over()),10) +
 5         rownum-1 yr
 6    from emp
 7   where rownum <= 10
 8         ) x
 9    left join
10         (
11  select to_number(to_char(hiredate,'YYYY')) yr, count(*) cnt
12    from emp
13   group by to_number(to_char(hiredate,'YYYY'))
14         ) y
15      on ( x.yr = y.yr )
```

PostgreSQL and MySQL

Use table T10 as a pivot table (because it has 10 rows) and the built-in function EXTRACT to generate one row for each year in the decade of 1980. Outer join to table EMP and count how many employees were hired each year:

```
 1  select y.yr, coalesce(x.cnt,0) as cnt
 2    from (
 3  select min_year-mod(cast(min_year as int),10)+rn as yr
 4    from (
 5  select (select min(extract(year from hiredate))
 6           from emp) as min_year,
 7          id-1 as rn
 8    from t10
 9         ) a
10         ) y
11    left join
12         (
13  select extract(year from hiredate) as yr, count(*) as cnt
14    from emp
15   group by extract(year from hiredate)
16         ) x
17      on ( y.yr = x.yr )
```

SQL Server

Use table EMP as a pivot table (because it has 14 rows) and the built-in function YEAR to generate one row for each year in the decade of 1980. Outer join to table EMP and count how many employees were hired each year:

```
 1  select x.yr, coalesce(y.cnt,0) cnt
 2    from (
 3  select top (10)
 4          (year(min(hiredate)over()) -
 5           year(min(hiredate)over())%10)+
 6           row_number()over(order by hiredate)-1 yr
 7    from emp
 8         ) x
 9    left join
10         (
11  select year(hiredate) yr, count(*) cnt
12    from emp
13   group by year(hiredate)
14         ) y
15      on ( x.yr = y.yr )
```

Discussion

Despite the difference in syntax, the approach is the same for all solutions. Inline view X returns each year in the decade of the '80s by first finding the year of the earliest HIREDATE. The next step is to add RN–1 to the difference between the earliest year and the earliest year modulus ten. To see how this works, simply execute inline view X and return each of the values involved separately. Listed below is the result set for inline view X using the window function MIN OVER (DB2, Oracle, SQL Server) and a scalar subquery (MySQL, PostgreSQL):

```
select year(min(hiredate)over()) -
       mod(year(min(hiredate)over()),10) +
       row_number()over()-1 yr,
       year(min(hiredate)over()) min_year,
       mod(year(min(hiredate)over()),10) mod_yr,
       row_number()over()-1 rn
  from emp fetch first 10 rows only
```

YR	MIN_YEAR	MOD_YR	RN
1980	1980	0	0
1981	1980	0	1
1982	1980	0	2
1983	1980	0	3
1984	1980	0	4
1985	1980	0	5
1986	1980	0	6
1987	1980	0	7
1988	1980	0	8
1989	1980	0	9

```
select min_year-mod(min_year,10)+rn as yr,
       min_year,
       mod(min_year,10) as mod_yr
       rn
  from (
select (select min(extract(year from hiredate))
          from emp) as min_year,
       id-1 as rn
  from t10
       ) x
```

YR	MIN_YEAR	MOD_YR	RN
1980	1980	0	0
1981	1980	0	1
1982	1980	0	2
1983	1980	0	3
1984	1980	0	4
1985	1980	0	5
1986	1980	0	6
1987	1980	0	7
1988	1980	0	8
1989	1980	0	9

Inline view Y returns the year for each HIREDATE and the number of employees hired during that year:

```
select year(hiredate) yr, count(*) cnt
  from emp
 group by year(hiredate)
```

```
  YR        CNT
-----  ----------
 1980          1
 1981         10
 1982          2
 1983          1
```

For the final solution, outer join inline view Y to inline view X so that every year is returned even if there are no employees hired.

10.5   Generating Consecutive Numeric Values

Problem

You would like to have a "row source generator" available to you in your queries. Row source generators are useful for queries that require pivoting. For example, you want to return a result set such as the following, up to any number of rows that you specify:

```
ID
---
 1
 2
 3
 4
 5
 6
 7
 8
 9
10
...
```

If your RDBMS provides built-in functions for returning rows dynamically, you do not need to create a pivot table in advance with a fixed number of rows. That's why a dynamic row generator can be so handy. Otherwise, you must use a traditional pivot table with a fixed number of rows (that may not always be enough) to generate rows when needed.

Solution

This solution shows how to return 10 rows of increasing numbers starting from 1. You can easily adapt the solution to return any number of rows.

The ability to return increasing values from 1 opens the door to many other solutions. For example, you can generate numbers to add to dates in order to generate sequences of days. You can also use such numbers to parse through strings.

DB2 and SQL Server

Use the recursive WITH clause to generate a sequence of rows with incrementing values. Use a one-row table such as T1 to kick off the row generation; the WITH clause does the rest:

```
 1  with x (id)
 2  as (
 3  select 1
 4    from t1
 5   union all
 6  select id+1
 7    from x
 8   where id+1 <= 10
 9  )
10  select * from x
```

Following is a second, alternative solution for DB2 only. Its advantage is that it does not require table T1:

```
1  with x (id)
2  as (
3  values (1)
4   union all
5  select id+1
6    from x
7   where id+1 <= 10
8  )
9  select * from x
```

Oracle

Use the recursive CONNECT BY clause (Oracle9i Database or later). In Oracle 9i Database, you must either wrap the CONNECT BY solution in an inline view or place it in the WITH clause:

```
1  with x
2  as (
3  select level id
4    from dual
5    connect by level <= 10
6  )
7  select * from x
```

In Oracle Database 10g or later, you can generate rows using the MODEL clause:

```
1  select array id
2    from dual
3    model
4     dimension by (0 idx)
5     measures(1 array)
6     rules iterate (10) (
7       array[iteration_number] = iteration_number+1
8     )
```

PostgreSQL

Use the very handy function GENERATE_SERIES, which is designed for the express purpose of generating rows:

```
1 select id
2   from generate_series (1,10) x(id)
```

Discussion

DB2 and SQL Server

The recursive WITH clause increments ID (which starts at 1) until the WHERE clause is satisfied. To kick things off you must generate one row having the value 1. You can do this by selecting 1 from a one-row table or, in the case of DB2, by using the VALUES clause to create a one-row result set.

Oracle

The solution places the CONNECT BY subquery into the WITH clause. Rows will continue to be returned unless short-circuited by the WHERE clause. Oracle will increment the pseudo-column LEVEL automatically, so there's no need for you to do so.

In the MODEL clause solution, there is an explicit ITERATE command that allows you to generate multiple rows. Without the ITERATE clause, only one row will be returned, since DUAL has only one row. For example:

```
select array id
  from dual
  model
    dimension by (0 idx)
    measures(1 array)
    rules ()

ID
--
 1
```

The MODEL clause not only allows you array access to rows, it allows you to easily "create" or return rows that are not in the table you are selecting against. In this solution, IDX is the array index (location of a specific value in the array) and ARRAY (aliased ID) is the "array" of rows. The first row defaults to 1 and can be referenced with ARRAY[0]. Oracle provides the function ITERATION_NUMBER so you can track the number of times you've iterated. The solution iterates 10 times, causing ITERATION_NUMBER to go from 0 to 9. Adding 1 to each of those values yields the results 1 through 10.

It may be easier to visualize what's happening with the model clause if you execute the following query:

```
select 'array['||idx||'] = '||array as output
  from dual
```

```
model
  dimension by (0 idx)
  measures(1 array)
  rules iterate (10) (
    array[iteration_number] = iteration_number+1
  )

OUTPUT
------------------
array[0] = 1
array[1] = 2
array[2] = 3
array[3] = 4
array[4] = 5
array[5] = 6
array[6] = 7
array[7] = 8
array[8] = 9
array[9] = 10
```

PostgreSQL

All the work is done by the function GENERATE_SERIES. The function accepts three parameters, all numeric values. The first parameter is the start value, the second parameter is the ending value, and the third parameter is an optional "step" value (how much each value is incremented by). If you do not pass a third parameter, the increment defaults to 1.

The GENERATE_SERIES function is flexible enough so that you do not have to hardcode parameters. For example, if you wanted to return five rows starting from value 10 and ending with value 30, incrementing by 5 such that the result set is the following:

```
ID
---
10
15
20
25
30
```

you can be creative and do something like this:

```
select id
  from generate_series(
         (select min(deptno) from emp),
         (select max(deptno) from emp),
         5
       ) x(id)
```

Notice here that the actual values passed to GENERATE_SERIES are not known when the query is written. Instead, they are generated by subqueries when the main query executes.

CHAPTER 11

Advanced Searching

In a very real sense, this entire book so far has been about searching. You've seen all sorts of queries that use joins and WHERE clauses and grouping techniques to search out and return the results that you need. Some types of searching operations, though, stand apart from others in that they represent a different way of thinking about searching. Perhaps you're displaying a result set one page at a time. Half of that problem is to identify (search for) the entire set of records that you want to display. The other half of that problem is to repeatedly search for the next page to display as a user cycles through the records on a display. Your first thought may not be to think of pagination as a searching problem, but it *can* be thought of that way, and it can be solved that way; that is the type of searching solution this chapter is all about.

11.1   Paginating Through a Result Set

Problem

You want to paginate or "scroll through" a result set. For example, you want to return the first five salaries from table EMP, then the next five, and so forth. Your goal is to allow a user to view five records at a time, scrolling forward with each click of a "Next" button.

Solution

Because there is no concept of first, last, or next in SQL, you must impose order on the rows you are working with. Only by imposing order can you accurately return ranges of records.

DB2, Oracle, and SQL Server

Use the window function ROW_NUMBER OVER to impose order, and specify the window of records that you want returned in your WHERE clause. For example, to return rows 1 through 5:

```
select sal
  from (
select row_number() over (order by sal) as rn,
       sal
  from emp
       ) x
 where rn between 1 and 5

SAL
----
 800
 950
1100
1250
1250
```

Then to return rows 6 through 10:

```
select sal
  from (
select row_number() over (order by sal) as rn,
       sal
  from emp
       ) x
 where rn between 6 and 10

 SAL
-----
1300
1500
1600
2450
2850
```

You can return any range of rows that you wish simply by changing the WHERE clause of your query.

MySQL and PostgreSQL

Scrolling through a result set is particularly easy due to the LIMIT and OFFSET clauses that these products support. Use LIMIT to specify the number of rows to return, and use OFFSET to specify the number of rows to skip. For example, to return the first five rows in order of salary:

```
select sal
  from emp
 order by sal limit 5 offset 0
```

```
SAL
------
 800
 950
1100
1250
1250
```

To return the next group of five rows:

```
select sal
  from emp
 order by sal limit 5 offset 5
```

```
SAL
-----
1300
1500
1600
2450
2850
```

LIMIT and OFFSET not only make the MySQL and PostgreSQL solutions easy to write, but they are quite readable, too.

Discussion

DB2, Oracle, and SQL Server

The window function ROW_NUMBER OVER in inline view X will assign a unique number to each salary (in increasing order starting from 1). Listed below is the result set for inline view X:

```
select row_number( ) over (order by sal) as rn,
       sal
  from emp
```

```
RN      SAL
--  ----------
 1      800
 2      950
 3     1100
 4     1250
 5     1250
 6     1300
 7     1500
 8     1600
 9     2450
10     2850
11     2975
12     3000
13     3000
14     5000
```

Once a number has been assigned to a salary, simply pick the range you want to return by specifying values for RN.

For Oracle users, an alternative: you can use ROWNUM instead of ROW NUMBER OVER to generate sequence numbers for the rows:

```
select sal
  from (
select sal, rownum rn
  from (
select sal
  from emp
 order by sal
       )
       )
 where rn between 6 and 10

 SAL
-----
1300
1500
1600
2450
2850
```

Using ROWNUM forces you into writing an extra level of subquery. The innermost subquery sorts rows by salary. The next outermost subquery applies row numbers to those rows, and, finally, the very outermost SELECT returns the data you are after.

MySQL and PostgreSQL

The OFFSET clause added to the SELECT clause makes scrolling through results intuitive and easy. Specifying OFFSET 0 will start you at the first row, OFFSET 5 at the sixth row, and OFFSET 10 at the eleventh row. The LIMIT clause restricts the number of rows returned. By combining the two clauses you can easily specify where in a result set to start returning rows and how many to return.

11.2   Skipping n Rows from a Table

Problem

You want a query to return every other employee in table EMP; you want the first employee, third employee, and so forth. For example, from the following result set:

```
ENAME
--------
ADAMS
ALLEN
BLAKE
CLARK
FORD
```

```
JAMES
JONES
KING
MARTIN
MILLER
SCOTT
SMITH
TURNER
WARD
```

you want to return:

```
ENAME
----------
ADAMS
BLAKE
FORD
JONES
MARTIN
SCOTT
TURNER
```

Solution

To skip the second or fourth or *n*th row from a result set, you must impose order on the result set, otherwise there is no concept of first or next, second, or fourth.

DB2, Oracle, and SQL Server

Use the window function ROW_NUMBER OVER to assign a number to each row, which you can then use in conjunction with the modulo function to skip unwanted rows. The modulo function is MOD for DB2 and Oracle. In SQL Server, use the percent (%) operator. The following example uses MOD to skip even-numbered rows:

```
1  select ename
2    from (
3  select row_number() over (order by ename) rn,
4           ename
5    from emp
6         ) x
7   where mod(rn,2) = 1
```

MySQL and PostgreSQL

Because there are no built-in functions for ranking or numbering rows, you need to use a scalar subquery to rank the rows (by name in this example). Then use modulus to skip rows:

```
1  select x.ename
2    from (
3  select a.ename,
4         (select count(*)
```

```
5            from emp b
6          where b.ename <= a.ename) as rn
7    from emp a
8          ) x
9   where mod(x.rn,2) = 1
```

Discussion

DB2, Oracle, and SQL Server

The call to the window function ROW_NUMBER OVER in inline view X will assign a rank to each row (no ties, even with duplicate names). The results are shown below:

```
select row_number() over (order by ename) rn, ename
  from emp

RN ENAME
-- --------
 1 ADAMS
 2 ALLEN
 3 BLAKE
 4 CLARK
 5 FORD
 6 JAMES
 7 JONES
 8 KING
 9 MARTIN
10 MILLER
11 SCOTT
12 SMITH
13 TURNER
14 WARD
```

The last step is to simply use modulus to skip every other row.

MySQL and PostgreSQL

With a function to rank or number rows, you can use a scalar subquery to first rank the employee names. Inline view X ranks each name and is shown below:

```
select a.ename,
       (select count(*)
          from emp b
         where b.ename <= a.ename) as rn
  from emp a

ENAME          RN
---------- ----------
ADAMS           1
ALLEN           2
BLAKE           3
CLARK           4
```

FORD	5
JAMES	6
JONES	7
KING	8
MARTIN	9
MILLER	10
SCOTT	11
SMITH	12
TURNER	13
WARD	14

The final step is to use the modulo function on the generated rank to skip rows.

11.3   Incorporating OR Logic When Using Outer Joins

Problem

You want to return the name and department information for all employees in departments 10 and 20 along with department information for departments 30 and 40 (but no employee information). Your first attempt looks like this:

```
select e.ename, d.deptno, d.dname, d.loc
  from dept d, emp e
 where d.deptno = e.deptno
   and (e.deptno = 10 or e.deptno = 20)
 order by 2
```

ENAME	DEPTNO	DNAME	LOC
CLARK	10	ACCOUNTING	NEW YORK
KING	10	ACCOUNTING	NEW YORK
MILLER	10	ACCOUNTING	NEW YORK
SMITH	20	RESEARCH	DALLAS
ADAMS	20	RESEARCH	DALLAS
FORD	20	RESEARCH	DALLAS
SCOTT	20	RESEARCH	DALLAS
JONES	20	RESEARCH	DALLAS

Because the join in this query is an inner join, the result set does not include department information for DEPTNOs 30 and 40.

You attempt to outer join EMP to DEPT with the following query, but you still do not get the correct results:

```
select e.ename, d.deptno, d.dname, d.loc
  from dept d left join emp e
    on (d.deptno = e.deptno)
 where e.deptno = 10
    or e.deptno = 20
 order by 2
```

ENAME	DEPTNO	DNAME	LOC
CLARK	10	ACCOUNTING	NEW YORK
KING	10	ACCOUNTING	NEW YORK
MILLER	10	ACCOUNTING	NEW YORK
SMITH	20	RESEARCH	DALLAS
ADAMS	20	RESEARCH	DALLAS
FORD	20	RESEARCH	DALLAS
SCOTT	20	RESEARCH	DALLAS
JONES	20	RESEARCH	DALLAS

Ultimately, you would like the result set to be:

ENAME	DEPTNO	DNAME	LOC
CLARK	10	ACCOUNTING	NEW YORK
KING	10	ACCOUNTING	NEW YORK
MILLER	10	ACCOUNTING	NEW YORK
SMITH	20	RESEARCH	DALLAS
JONES	20	RESEARCH	DALLAS
SCOTT	20	RESEARCH	DALLAS
ADAMS	20	RESEARCH	DALLAS
FORD	20	RESEARCH	DALLAS
	30	SALES	CHICAGO
	40	OPERATIONS	BOSTON

Solution

DB2, MySQL, PostgreSQL, and SQL Server

Move the OR condition into the JOIN clause:

```
1  select e.ename, d.deptno, d.dname, d.loc
2    from dept d left join emp e
3      on (d.deptno = e.deptno
4          and (e.deptno=10 or e.deptno=20))
5   order by 2
```

Alternatively, you can filter on EMP.DEPTNO first in an inline view and then outer join:

```
1  select e.ename, d.deptno, d.dname, d.loc
2    from dept d
3    left join
4        (select ename, deptno
5           from emp
6          where deptno in ( 10, 20 )
7        ) e on ( e.deptno = d.deptno )
8   order by 2
```

Oracle

If you are on Oracle9i Database or later, you can use either of the solutions for the other products. Otherwise, you need to use CASE or DECODE in a workaround. Following is a solution using CASE:

```
select e.ename, d.deptno, d.dname, d.loc
  from dept d, emp e
 where d.deptno = e.deptno (+)
   and d.deptno = case when e.deptno(+) = 10 then e.deptno(+)
                       when e.deptno(+) = 20 then e.deptno(+)
                  end
 order by 2
```

And next is the same solution, but this time using DECODE:

```
select e.ename, d.deptno, d.dname, d.loc
  from dept d, emp e
 where d.deptno = e.deptno (+)
   and d.deptno = decode(e.deptno(+),10,e.deptno(+),
                                      20,e.deptno(+))
 order by 2
```

When using the proprietary Oracle outer join syntax (+) along with an IN or OR predicate on an outer joined column, the query will return an error. The solution is to move the IN or OR predicate to an inline view:

```
select e.ename, d.deptno, d.dname, d.loc
  from dept d,
       ( select ename, deptno
           from emp
          where deptno in ( 10, 20 )
       ) e
 where d.deptno = e.deptno (+)
 order by 2
```

Discussion

DB2, MySQL, PostgreSQL, and SQL Server

Two solutions are given for these products. The first moves the OR condition into the JOIN clause, making it part of the join condition. By doing that, you can filter the rows returned from EMP without losing DEPTNOs 30 and 40 from DEPT.

The second solution moves the filtering into an inline view. Inline view E filters on EMP.DEPTNO and returns EMP rows of interest. These are then outer joined to DEPT. Because DEPT is the anchor table in the outer join, all departments, including 30 and 40, are returned.

Oracle

Use the CASE and DECODE functions as a workaround for what seems to be a bug in the older outer-join syntax. The solution using inline view E works by first finding the rows of interest in table EMP, and then outer joining to DEPT.

11.4 Determining Which Rows Are Reciprocals

Problem

You have a table containing the results of two tests, and you want to determine which pair of scores are reciprocals. Consider the result set below from view V:

```
select *
  from V

 TEST1     TEST2
 -----  ----------
    20         20
    50         25
    20         20
    60         30
    70         90
    80        130
    90         70
   100         50
   110         55
   120         60
   130         80
   140         70
```

Examining these results, you see that a test score for TEST1 of 70 and TEST2 of 90 is a reciprocal (there exists a score of 90 for TEST1 and a score of 70 for TEST2). Likewise, the scores of 80 for TEST1 and 130 for TEST2 are reciprocals of 130 for TEST1 and 80 for TEST2. Additionally, the scores of 20 for TEST1 and 20 for TEST2 are reciprocals of 20 for TEST2 and 20 for TEST1. You want to identify only one set of reciprocals. You want your result set to be this:

```
 TEST1     TEST2
 -----  ----------
    20         20
    70         90
    80        130
```

not this:

```
 TEST1     TEST2
 -----  ----------
    20         20
    20         20
    70         90
    80        130
    90         70
   130         80
```

Solution

Use a self join to identify rows where TEST1 equals TEST2 and vice versa:

```
   select distinct v1.*
     from V v1, V v2
    where v1.test1  = v2.test2
      and v1.test2  = v2.test1
      and v1.test1 <= v1.test2
```

Discussion

The self-join results in a Cartesian product in which every TEST1 score can be compared against every TEST2 score and vice versa. The query below will identify the reciprocals:

```
   select v1.*
     from V v1, V v2
    where v1.test1 = v2.test2
      and v1.test2 = v2.test1
```

```
TEST1      TEST2
-----  ----------
   20         20
   20         20
   20         20
   20         20
   90         70
  130         80
   70         90
   80        130
```

The use of DISTINCT ensures that duplicate rows are removed from the final result set. The final filter in the WHERE clause (and V1.TEST1 <= V1.TEST2) will ensure that only one pair of reciprocals (where TEST1 is the smaller or equal value) is returned.

11.5   Selecting the Top n Records

Problem

You want to limit a result set to a specific number of records based on a ranking of some sort. For example, you want to return the names and salaries of the employees with the top five salaries.

Solution

The key to this solution is to make two passes: first rank the rows on whatever value you want to rank on; then limit the result set to the number of rows you are interested in.

DB2, Oracle, and SQL Server

The solution to this problem depends on the use of a window function. Which window function you will use depends on how you want to deal with ties. The following solution uses DENSE_RANK, so that each tie in salary will count as only one against the total:

```
1  select ename,sal
2    from (
3  select ename, sal,
4         dense_rank() over (order by sal desc) dr
5    from emp
6         ) x
7   where dr <= 5
```

The total number of rows returned may exceed five, but there will be only five distinct salaries. Use ROW_NUMBER OVER if you wish to return five rows regardless of ties (as no ties are allowed with this function).

MySQL and PostgreSQL

Use a scalar subquery to create a rank for each salary. Then restrict the results of that subquery by rank:

```
1  select ename,sal
2    from (
3  select (select count(distinct b.sal)
4            from emp b
5           where a.sal <= b.sal) as rnk,
6         a.sal,
7         a.ename
8    from emp a
9         )
10  where rnk <= 5
```

Discussion

DB2, Oracle, and SQL Server

The window function DENSE_RANK OVER in inline view X does all the work. The following example shows the entire table after applying that function:

```
select ename, sal,
       dense_rank() over (order by sal desc) dr
  from emp
```

ENAME	SAL	DR
KING	5000	1
SCOTT	3000	2
FORD	3000	2

```
JONES      2975         3
BLAKE      2850         4
CLARK      2450         5
ALLEN      1600         6
TURNER     1500         7
MILLER     1300         8
WARD       1250         9
MARTIN     1250         9
ADAMS      1100        10
JAMES       950        11
SMITH       800        12
```

Now it's just a matter of returning rows where DR is less than or equal to five.

MySQL and PostgreSQL

The scalar subquery in inline view X ranks the salaries as follows:

```
select (select count(distinct b.sal)
          from emp b
         where a.sal <= b.sal) as rnk,
       a.sal,
       a.ename
  from emp a

RNK    SAL ENAME
--- ------ -------
  1   5000 KING
  2   3000 SCOTT
  2   3000 FORD
  3   2975 JONES
  4   2850 BLAKE
  5   2450 CLARK
  6   1600 ALLEN
  7   1500 TURNER
  8   1300 MILLER
  9   1250 WARD
  9   1250 MARTIN
 10   1100 ADAMS
 11    950 JAMES
 12    800 SMITH
```

The final step is to return only rows where RNK is less than or equal to five.

11.6 Finding Records with the Highest and Lowest Values

Problem

You want to find "extreme" values in your table. For example, you want to find the employees with the highest and lowest salaries in table EMP.

Solution

DB2, Oracle, and SQL Server

Use the window functions MIN OVER and MAX OVER to find the lowest and highest salaries, respectively:

```
1  select ename
2    from (
3  select ename, sal,
4         min(sal)over( ) min_sal,
5         max(sal)over( ) max_sal
6    from emp
7         ) x
8   where sal in (min_sal,max_sal)
```

MySQL and PostgreSQL

Write two subqueries, one each to return the MIN and MAX values of SAL:

```
1  select ename
2    from emp
3   where sal in ( (select min(sal) from emp),
4                  (select max(sal) from emp) )
```

Discussion

DB2, Oracle, and SQL Server

The window functions MIN OVER and MAX OVER allow each row to have access to the lowest and highest salaries. The result set from inline view X is as follows:

```
select ename, sal,
       min(sal)over( ) min_sal,
       max(sal)over( ) max_sal
  from emp
```

ENAME	SAL	MIN_SAL	MAX_SAL
SMITH	800	800	5000
ALLEN	1600	800	5000
WARD	1250	800	5000
JONES	2975	800	5000
MARTIN	1250	800	5000
BLAKE	2850	800	5000
CLARK	2450	800	5000
SCOTT	3000	800	5000
KING	5000	800	5000
TURNER	1500	800	5000
ADAMS	1100	800	5000
JAMES	950	800	5000
FORD	3000	800	5000
MILLER	1300	800	5000

Given this result set, all that's left is to return rows where SAL equals MIN_SAL or MAX_SAL.

MySQL and PostgreSQL

This solution uses two subqueries in one IN list to find the lowest and highest salaries from EMP. The rows returned by the outer query are the ones having salaries that match the values returned by either subquery.

11.7 Investigating Future Rows

Problem

You want to find any employees who earn less than the employee hired immediately after them. Based on the following result set:

```
ENAME           SAL HIREDATE
----------  ---------- ---------
SMITH           800 17-DEC-80
ALLEN          1600 20-FEB-81
WARD           1250 22-FEB-81
JONES          2975 02-APR-81
BLAKE          2850 01-MAY-81
CLARK          2450 09-JUN-81
TURNER         1500 08-SEP-81
MARTIN         1250 28-SEP-81
KING           5000 17-NOV-81
JAMES           950 03-DEC-81
FORD           3000 03-DEC-81
MILLER         1300 23-JAN-82
SCOTT          3000 09-DEC-82
ADAMS          1100 12-JAN-83
```

SMITH, WARD, MARTIN, JAMES, and MILLER earn less than the person hired immediately after they were hired, so those are the employees you wish to find with a query.

Solution

The first step is to define what "future" means. You must impose order on your result set to be able to define a row as having a value that is "later" than another.

DB2, MySQL, PostgreSQL, and SQL Server

Use subqueries to determine the following for each employee:

- The date of the first person subsequently hired with a greater salary
- The date of the next person to be hired

When the two dates match, you have what you are looking for:

```
1  select ename, sal, hiredate
2    from (
3  select a.ename, a.sal, a.hiredate,
4         (select min(hiredate) from emp b
5           where b.hiredate > a.hiredate
6             and b.sal      > a.sal ) as next_sal_grtr,
7         (select min(hiredate) from emp b
8           where b.hiredate > a.hiredate) as next_hire
9    from emp a
10        ) x
11   where next_sal_grtr = next_hire
```

Oracle

You can use the LEAD OVER window function to access the salary of the next employee that was hired. It's then a simple matter to check whether that salary is larger:

```
1  select ename, sal, hiredate
2    from (
3  select ename, sal, hiredate,
4         lead(sal)over(order by hiredate) next_sal
5    from emp
6         )
7   where sal < next_sal
```

Discussion

DB2, MySQL, PostgreSQL, and SQL Server

The scalar subqueries return, for each employee, the HIREDATE of the very next employee hired and the HIREDATE of the first, subsequently hired employee who earns more than the current employee. Here's a look at the raw data:

```
select a.ename, a.sal, a.hiredate,
       (select min(hiredate) from emp b
         where b.hiredate > a.hiredate
           and b.sal      > a.sal ) as next_sal_grtr,
       (select min(hiredate) from emp b
         where b.hiredate > a.hiredate) as next_hire
  from emp a
```

ENAME	SAL	HIREDATE	NEXT_SAL_GRTR	NEXT_HIRE
SMITH	800	17-DEC-80	20-FEB-81	20-FEB-81
ALLEN	1600	20-FEB-81	02-APR-81	22-FEB-81
WARD	1250	22-FEB-81	02-APR-81	02-APR-81
JONES	2975	02-APR-81	17-NOV-81	01-MAY-81
MARTIN	1250	28-SEP-81	17-NOV-81	17-NOV-81
BLAKE	2850	01-MAY-81	17-NOV-81	09-JUN-81
CLARK	2450	09-JUN-81	17-NOV-81	08-SEP-81
SCOTT	3000	09-DEC-82		12-JAN-83

KING	5000	17-NOV-81		03-DEC-81
TURNER	1500	08-SEP-81	17-NOV-81	28-SEP-81
ADAMS	1100	12-JAN-83		
JAMES	950	03-DEC-81	23-JAN-82	23-JAN-82
FORD	3000	03-DEC-81		23-JAN-82
MILLER	1300	23-JAN-82	09-DEC-82	09-DEC-82

Someone hired subsequently may or may not have been hired immediately after the current employee was hired. The next (and last) step then is to return only rows where NEXT_SAL_GRTR (the earliest HIREDATE of an employee who earns more than the current employee) equals NEXT_HIRE (the HIREDATE of the very next employee relative to the current employee's HIREDATE).

Oracle

The window function LEAD OVER is perfect for a problem such as this one. It not only makes for a more readable query than the solution for the other products, LEAD OVER also leads to a more flexible solution because an argument can be passed to it that will determine how many rows ahead it should look (by default 1). Being able to leap ahead more than one row is important in the case of duplicates in the column you are ordering by.

The following example shows how easy it is to use LEAD OVER to look at the salary of the "next" employee hired:

```
select ename, sal, hiredate,
       lead(sal)over(order by hiredate) next_sal
  from emp

ENAME     SAL HIREDATE   NEXT_SAL
-------  ----- ---------  ----------
SMITH      800 17-DEC-80        1600
ALLEN     1600 20-FEB-81        1250
WARD      1250 22-FEB-81        2975
JONES     2975 02-APR-81        2850
BLAKE     2850 01-MAY-81        2450
CLARK     2450 09-JUN-81        1500
TURNER    1500 08-SEP-81        1250
MARTIN    1250 28-SEP-81        5000
KING      5000 17-NOV-81         950
JAMES      950 03-DEC-81        3000
FORD      3000 03-DEC-81        1300
MILLER    1300 23-JAN-82        3000
SCOTT     3000 09-DEC-82        1100
ADAMS     1100 12-JAN-83
```

The final step is to return only rows where SAL is less than NEXT_SAL. Because of LEAD OVER's default range of one row, if there had been duplicates in table EMP, in particular, multiple employees hired on the same date, their SAL would be compared. This may or may not have been what you intended. If your goal is to compare the SAL of each employee with SAL of the next employee hired, excluding other employees hired on the same day, you can use the following solution as an alternative:

```
select ename, sal, hiredate
  from (
select ename, sal, hiredate,
       lead(sal,cnt-rn+1)over(order by hiredate) next_sal
  from (
select ename,sal,hiredate,
       count(*)over(partition by hiredate) cnt,
       row_number()over(partition by hiredate order by empno) rn
  from emp
       )
       )
 where sal < next_sal
```

The idea behind this solution is to find the distance from the current row to the row it should be compared with. For example, if there are five duplicates, the first of the five needs to leap five rows to get to its correct LEAD OVER row. The value for CNT represents, for each employee with a duplicate HIREDATE, how many duplicates there are in total for their HIREDATE. The value for RN represents a ranking for the employees in DEPTNO 10. The rank is partitioned by HIREDATE so only employees with a HIREDATE that another employee has will have a value greater than one. The ranking is sorted by EMPNO (this is arbitrary). Now that you now how many total duplicates there are and you have a ranking of each duplicate, the distance to the next HIREDATE is simply the total number of duplicates minus the current rank plus one (CNT-RN+1).

See Also

For additional examples of using LEAD OVER in the presence of duplicates (and a more thorough discussion of the technique above), see Recipe 8.7 and Recipe 10.2.

11.8 Shifting Row Values

Problem

You want to return each employee's name and salary along with the next highest and lowest salaries. If there are no higher or lower salaries, you want the results to wrap (first SAL shows last SAL and vice versa). You want to return the following result set:

ENAME	SAL	FORWARD	REWIND
SMITH	800	950	5000
JAMES	950	1100	800
ADAMS	1100	1250	950
WARD	1250	1250	1100
MARTIN	1250	1300	1250
MILLER	1300	1500	1250
TURNER	1500	1600	1300
ALLEN	1600	2450	1500
CLARK	2450	2850	1600

BLAKE	2850	2975	2450
JONES	2975	3000	2850
SCOTT	3000	3000	2975
FORD	3000	5000	3000
KING	5000	800	3000

Solution

For Oracle users, the window functions LEAD OVER and LAG OVER make this problem easy to solve and the resulting queries very readable. With other RDBMSs you can use scalar subqueries, though ties will present a problem. Because of the problem with ties, the RDBMSs without support for window functions enable only an approximate solution to this problem.

DB2, SQL Server, MySQL, and PostgreSQL

Use a scalar subquery to find next and prior salaries relative to each salary:

```
1  select e.ename, e.sal,
2         coalesce(
3           (select min(sal) from emp d where d.sal > e.sal),
4           (select min(sal) from emp)
5         ) as forward,
6         coalesce(
7           (select max(sal) from emp d where d.sal < e.sal),
8           (select max(sal) from emp)
9         ) as rewind
10    from emp e
11   order by 2
```

Oracle

Use the window functions LAG OVER and LEAD OVER to access prior and next rows relative to the current row:

```
1 select ename,sal,
2        nvl(lead(sal)over(order by sal),min(sal)over()) forward,
3        nvl(lag(sal)over(order by sal),max(sal)over()) rewind
4   from emp
```

Discussion

DB2, SQL Server, MySQL, and PostgreSQL

The scalar subquery solution is not a true solution to the problem. It's an approximation that will fail in the event any two records contain the same value for SAL. It's the best you can do without having window functions available.

Oracle

The window functions LAG OVER and LEAD OVER will (by default and unless otherwise specified) return values from the row before and after the current row, respectively. You define what "before" or "after" means in the ORDER BY portion of the OVER clause. If you examine the solution, the first step is to return the next and prior rows relative to the current row, ordered by SAL:

```
select ename,sal,
       lead(sal)over(order by sal) forward,
       lag(sal)over(order by sal) rewind
  from emp
```

ENAME	SAL	FORWARD	REWIND
SMITH	800	950	
JAMES	950	1100	800
ADAMS	1100	1250	950
WARD	1250	1250	1100
MARTIN	1250	1300	1250
MILLER	1300	1500	1250
TURNER	1500	1600	1300
ALLEN	1600	2450	1500
CLARK	2450	2850	1600
BLAKE	2850	2975	2450
JONES	2975	3000	2850
SCOTT	3000	3000	2975
FORD	3000	5000	3000
KING	5000		3000

Notice that REWIND is NULL for employee SMITH and FORWARD is NULL for employee KING; that is because those two employees have the lowest and highest salaries, respectively. The requirement in the problem section should NULL values exist in FORWARD or REWIND is to "wrap" the results meaning that, for the highest SAL, FORWARD should be the value of the lowest SAL in the table, and for the lowest SAL, REWIND should be the value of the highest SAL in the table. The window functions MIN OVER and MAX OVER with no partition or window specified (i.e., an empty parenthesis after the OVER clause) will return the lowest and highest salaries in the table, respectively. The results are shown below:

```
select ename,sal,
       nvl(lead(sal)over(order by sal),min(sal)over()) forward,
       nvl(lag(sal)over(order by sal),max(sal)over()) rewind
  from emp
```

ENAME	SAL	FORWARD	REWIND
SMITH	800	950	5000
JAMES	950	1100	800
ADAMS	1100	1250	950

WARD	1250	1250	1100
MARTIN	1250	1300	1250
MILLER	1300	1500	1250
TURNER	1500	1600	1300
ALLEN	1600	2450	1500
CLARK	2450	2850	1600
BLAKE	2850	2975	2450
JONES	2975	3000	2850
SCOTT	3000	3000	2975
FORD	3000	5000	3000
KING	5000	800	3000

Another useful feature of LAG OVER and LEAD OVER is the ability to define how far forward or back you would like to go. In the example for this recipe, you go only one row forward or back. If want to move three rows forward and five rows back, doing so is simple. Just specify the values 3 and 5 as shown below:

```
select ename,sal,
       lead(sal,3)over(order by sal) forward,
       lag(sal,5)over(order by sal) rewind
  from emp
```

ENAME	SAL	FORWARD	REWIND
SMITH	800	1250	
JAMES	950	1250	
ADAMS	1100	1300	
WARD	1250	1500	
MARTIN	1250	1600	
MILLER	1300	2450	800
TURNER	1500	2850	950
ALLEN	1600	2975	1100
CLARK	2450	3000	1250
BLAKE	2850	3000	1250
JONES	2975	5000	1300
SCOTT	3000		1500
FORD	3000		1600
KING	5000		2450

11.9   Ranking Results

Problem

You want to rank the salaries in table EMP while allowing for ties. You want to return the following result set:

RNK	SAL
1	800
2	950
3	1100

4	1250
4	1250
5	1300
6	1500
7	1600
8	2450
9	2850
10	2975
11	3000
11	3000
12	5000

Solution

Window functions make ranking queries extremely simple. Three window functions are particularly useful for ranking: DENSE_RANK OVER, ROW_NUMBER OVER, and RANK OVER.

DB2, Oracle, and SQL Server

Because you want to allow for ties, use the window function DENSE_RANK OVER:

```
1 select dense_rank() over(order by sal) rnk, sal
2   from emp
```

MySQL and PostgreSQL

Until window functions are introduced, use a scalar subquery to rank the salaries:

```
1  select (select count(distinct b.sal)
2            from emp b
3           where b.sal <= a.sal) as rnk,
4         a.sal
5    from emp a
```

Discussion

DB2, Oracle, and SQL Server

The window function DENSE_RANK OVER does all the legwork here. In parentheses following the OVER keyword you place an ORDER BY clause to specify the order in which rows are ranked. The solution uses ORDER BY SAL, so rows from EMP are ranked in ascending order of salary.

MySQL and PostgreSQL

The output from the scalar subquery solution is similar to that of DENSE_RANK because the driving predicate in the scalar subquery is on SAL.

11.10 Suppressing Duplicates

Problem

You want to find the different job types in table EMP but do not want to see duplicates. The result set should be:

```
JOB
---------
ANALYST
CLERK
MANAGER
PRESIDENT
SALESMAN
```

Solution

All of the RDBMSs support the keyword DISTINCT, and it arguably is the easiest mechanism for suppressing duplicates from the result set. However, this recipe will also cover two additional methods for suppressing duplicates.

DB2, Oracle, and SQL Server

The traditional method of using DISTINCT and sometimes GROUP BY (as seen next in the MySQL/PostgreSQL solution) certainly works for these RDBMSs. The solution below is an alternative that makes use of the window function ROW_NUMBER OVER:

```
1  select job
2    from (
3  select job,
4         row_number()over(partition by job order by job) rn
5    from emp
6         ) x
7   where rn = 1
```

MySQL and PostgreSQL

Use the DISTINCT keyword to suppress duplicates from the result set:

```
select distinct job
  from emp
```

Additionally, it is also possible to use GROUP BY to suppress duplicates:

```
select job
  from emp
 group by job
```

Discussion

DB2, Oracle, and SQL Server

This solution depends on some outside-the-box thinking about partitioned window functions. By using PARTITION BY in the OVER clause of ROW_NUMBER, you can reset the value returned by ROW_NUMBER to 1 whenever a new job is encountered. The results below are from inline view X:

```
select job,
       row_number( )over(partition by job order by job) rn
  from emp
```

JOB	RN
ANALYST	1
ANALYST	2
CLERK	1
CLERK	2
CLERK	3
CLERK	4
MANAGER	1
MANAGER	2
MANAGER	3
PRESIDENT	1
SALESMAN	1
SALESMAN	2
SALESMAN	3
SALESMAN	4

Each row is given an increasing, sequential number, and that number is reset to 1 whenever the job changes. To filter out the duplicates, all you must do is keep the rows where RN is 1.

An ORDER BY clause is mandatory when using ROW_NUMBER OVER (except in DB2) but doesn't affect the result. Which job is returned is irrelevant so long as you return one of each job.

MySQL and PostgreSQL

The first solution shows how to use the keyword DISTINCT to suppress duplicates from a result set. Keep in mind that DISTINCT is applied to the whole SELECT list; additional columns can and will change the result set. Consider the difference between the two queries below:

```
select distinct job
  from emp
```

JOB
ANALYST
CLERK
MANAGER
PRESIDENT
SALESMAN

```
select distinct job, deptno
  from emp
```

JOB	DEPTNO
ANALYST	20
CLERK	10
CLERK	20
CLERK	30
MANAGER	10
MANAGER	20
MANAGER	30
PRESIDENT	10
SALESMAN	30

By adding DEPTNO to the SELECT list, what you return is each DISTINCT pair of JOB/DEPTNO values from table EMP.

The second solution uses GROUP BY to suppress duplicates. While using GROUP BY this way is not uncommon, keep in mind that GROUP BY and DISTINCT are two very different clauses that are not interchangeable. I've included GROUP BY in this solution for completeness, as you will no doubt come across it at some point.

11.11 Finding Knight Values

Problem

You want return a result set that contains each employee's name, the department they work in, their salary, the date they were hired, and the salary of the last employee hired, in each department. You want to return the following result set:

```
DEPTNO ENAME        SAL HIREDATE     LATEST_SAL
------ ---------- ----- -----------  ----------
    10 MILLER      1300 23-JAN-1982       1300
    10 KING        5000 17-NOV-1981       1300
    10 CLARK       2450 09-JUN-1981       1300
    20 ADAMS       1100 12-JAN-1983       1100
    20 SCOTT       3000 09-DEC-1982       1100
    20 FORD        3000 03-DEC-1981       1100
    20 JONES       2975 02-APR-1981       1100
    20 SMITH        800 17-DEC-1980       1100
    30 JAMES        950 03-DEC-1981        950
    30 MARTIN      1250 28-SEP-1981        950
    30 TURNER      1500 08-SEP-1981        950
    30 BLAKE       2850 01-MAY-1981        950
    30 WARD        1250 22-FEB-1981        950
    30 ALLEN       1600 20-FEB-1981        950
```

The values in LATEST_SAL are the "Knight values" because the path to find them is analogous to a knight's path in the game of chess. You determine the result the way a knight determines a new location: by jumping to a row then turning and jumping to a different column (see Figure 11-1). To find the correct values for LATEST_SAL, you must first locate (jump to) the row with the latest HIREDATE in each DEPTNO, and then you select (jump to) the SAL column of that row.

 The term "Knight value" was coined by a very clever coworker of mine, Kay Young. After having him review the recipes for correctness I admitted to him that I was stumped and could not come up with a good title. Because you need to initially evaluate one row then "jump" and take a value from another, he came up with the term "Knight value."

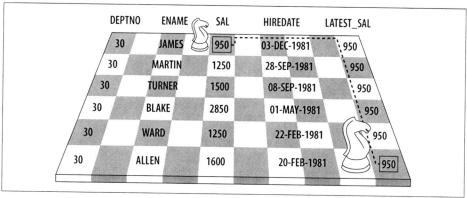

Figure 11-1. A knight value comes from "up and over"

Solution

DB2 and SQL Server

Use a CASE expression in a subquery to return the SAL of the last employee hired in each DEPTNO; for all other salaries, return zero. Use the window function MAX OVER in the outer query to return the non-zero SAL for each employee's department:

```
 1 select deptno,
 2        ename,
 3        sal,
 4        hiredate,
 5        max(latest_sal)over(partition by deptno) latest_sal
 6   from (
 7 select deptno,
 8        ename,
 9        sal,
10        hiredate,
11        case
12          when hiredate = max(hiredate)over(partition by deptno)
13          then sal else 0
14        end latest_sal
15   from emp
16        ) x
17  order by 1, 4 desc
```

MySQL and PostgreSQL

Use a scalar subquery nested two levels deep. First, find the HIREDATE of the last employee in each DEPTO. Then use the aggregate function MAX (in case there are duplicates) to find the SAL of the last employee hired in each DEPTNO:

```
1   select e.deptno,
2          e.ename,
3          e.sal,
4          e.hiredate,
5          (select max(d.sal)
6             from emp d
7            where d.deptno   = e.deptno
8              and d.hiredate =
9                  (select max(f.hiredate)
10                    from emp f
11                   where f.deptno = e.deptno)) as latest_sal
12     from emp e
13    order by 1, 4 desc
```

Oracle

Use the window function MAX OVER to return the highest SAL for each DEPTNO.
Use the functions DENSE_RANK and LAST, while ordering by HIREDATE, in the
KEEP clause to return the highest SAL for the latest HIREDATE in a given
DEPTNO:

```
1   select deptno,
2          ename,
3          sal,
4          hiredate,
5          max(sal)
6             keep(dense_rank last order by hiredate)
7             over(partition by deptno) latest_sal
8     from emp
9    order by 1, 4 desc
```

Discussion

DB2 and SQL Server

The first step is to use the window function MAX OVER in a CASE expression to
find the employee hired last, or most recently, in each DEPTNO. If an employee's
HIREDATE matches the value returned by MAX OVER, then use a CASE expression to return that employee's SAL; otherwise return 0. The results of this are shown
below:

```
select deptno,
       ename,
       sal,
       hiredate,
       case
           when hiredate = max(hiredate)over(partition by deptno)
           then sal else 0
       end latest_sal
  from emp

DEPTNO ENAME              SAL HIREDATE     LATEST_SAL
------ ---------- ---------- ----------- ----------
```

```
10 CLARK      2450 09-JUN-1981        0
10 KING       5000 17-NOV-1981        0
10 MILLER     1300 23-JAN-1982     1300
20 SMITH       800 17-DEC-1980        0
20 ADAMS      1100 12-JAN-1983     1100
20 FORD       3000 03-DEC-1981        0
20 SCOTT      3000 09-DEC-1982        0
20 JONES      2975 02-APR-1981        0
30 ALLEN      1600 20-FEB-1981        0
30 BLAKE      2850 01-MAY-1981        0
30 MARTIN     1250 28-SEP-1981        0
30 JAMES       950 03-DEC-1981      950
30 TURNER     1500 08-SEP-1981        0
30 WARD       1250 22-FEB-1981        0
```

Because the value for LATEST_SAL will be either 0 or the SAL of the employee(s) hired most recently, you can wrap the above query in an inline view and use MAX OVER again, but this time to return the greatest non-zero LATEST_SAL for each DEPTNO:

```
select deptno,
       ename,
       sal,
       hiredate,
       max(latest_sal)over(partition by deptno) latest_sal
  from (
select deptno,
       ename,
       sal,
       hiredate,
       case
          when hiredate = max(hiredate)over(partition by deptno)
          then sal else 0
       end latest_sal
  from emp
       ) x
 order by 1, 4 desc

DEPTNO ENAME          SAL HIREDATE     LATEST_SAL
------ ---------- ------- -----------  ----------
    10 MILLER        1300 23-JAN-1982        1300
    10 KING          5000 17-NOV-1981        1300
    10 CLARK         2450 09-JUN-1981        1300
    20 ADAMS         1100 12-JAN-1983        1100
    20 SCOTT         3000 09-DEC-1982        1100
    20 FORD          3000 03-DEC-1981        1100
    20 JONES         2975 02-APR-1981        1100
    20 SMITH          800 17-DEC-1980        1100
    30 JAMES          950 03-DEC-1981         950
    30 MARTIN        1250 28-SEP-1981         950
    30 TURNER        1500 08-SEP-1981         950
    30 BLAKE         2850 01-MAY-1981         950
    30 WARD          1250 22-FEB-1981         950
    30 ALLEN         1600 20-FEB-1981         950
```

MySQL and PostgreSQL

The first step is to use a scalar subquery to find the HIREDATE of the last employee hired in each DEPTNO:

```
select e.deptno,
       e.ename,
       e.sal,
       e.hiredate,
       (select max(f.hiredate)
          from emp f
         where f.deptno = e.deptno) as last_hire
  from emp e
 order by 1, 4 desc

DEPTNO ENAME            SAL HIREDATE    LAST_HIRE
------ ----------  ---------- ----------- -----------
    10 MILLER          1300 23-JAN-1982 23-JAN-1982
    10 KING            5000 17-NOV-1981 23-JAN-1982
    10 CLARK           2450 09-JUN-1981 23-JAN-1982
    20 ADAMS           1100 12-JAN-1983 12-JAN-1983
    20 SCOTT           3000 09-DEC-1982 12-JAN-1983
    20 FORD            3000 03-DEC-1981 12-JAN-1983
    20 JONES           2975 02-APR-1981 12-JAN-1983
    20 SMITH            800 17-DEC-1980 12-JAN-1983
    30 JAMES            950 03-DEC-1981 03-DEC-1981
    30 MARTIN          1250 28-SEP-1981 03-DEC-1981
    30 TURNER          1500 08-SEP-1981 03-DEC-1981
    30 BLAKE           2850 01-MAY-1981 03-DEC-1981
    30 WARD            1250 22-FEB-1981 03-DEC-1981
    30 ALLEN           1600 20-FEB-1981 03-DEC-1981
```

The next step is to find the SAL for the employee(s) in each DEPTNO hired on LAST_HIRE. Use the aggregate function MAX to keep the highest (if there are multiple employees hired on the same day):

```
select e.deptno,
       e.ename,
       e.sal,
       e.hiredate,
       (select max(d.sal)
          from emp d
         where d.deptno   = e.deptno
           and d.hiredate =
              (select max(f.hiredate)
                 from emp f
                where f.deptno = e.deptno)) as latest_sal
  from emp e
 order by 1, 4 desc

DEPTNO ENAME            SAL HIREDATE    LATEST_SAL
------ ----------  ---------- ----------- ----------
    10 MILLER          1300 23-JAN-1982       1300
    10 KING            5000 17-NOV-1981       1300
    10 CLARK           2450 09-JUN-1981       1300
```

20 ADAMS	1100 12-JAN-1983	1100
20 SCOTT	3000 09-DEC-1982	1100
20 FORD	3000 03-DEC-1981	1100
20 JONES	2975 02-APR-1981	1100
20 SMITH	800 17-DEC-1980	1100
30 JAMES	950 03-DEC-1981	950
30 MARTIN	1250 28-SEP-1981	950
30 TURNER	1500 08-SEP-1981	950
30 BLAKE	2850 01-MAY-1981	950
30 WARD	1250 22-FEB-1981	950
30 ALLEN	1600 20-FEB-1981	950

Oracle

Users on Oracle8*i* Database can use the DB2 solution. For users on Oracle9*i* Database and later, you can use the solution presented below. The key to the Oracle solution is to take advantage of the KEEP clause. The KEEP clause allows you to rank the rows returned by a group/partition and work with the first or last row in the group. Consider what the solution looks like without KEEP:

```
select deptno,
       ename,
       sal,
       hiredate,
       max(sal) over(partition by deptno) latest_sal
  from emp
 order by 1, 4 desc
```

DEPTNO	ENAME	SAL	HIREDATE	LATEST_SAL
10	MILLER	1300	23-JAN-1982	5000
10	KING	5000	17-NOV-1981	5000
10	CLARK	2450	09-JUN-1981	5000
20	ADAMS	1100	12-JAN-1983	3000
20	SCOTT	3000	09-DEC-1982	3000
20	FORD	3000	03-DEC-1981	3000
20	JONES	2975	02-APR-1981	3000
20	SMITH	800	17-DEC-1980	3000
30	JAMES	950	03-DEC-1981	2850
30	MARTIN	1250	28-SEP-1981	2850
30	TURNER	1500	08-SEP-1981	2850
30	BLAKE	2850	01-MAY-1981	2850
30	WARD	1250	22-FEB-1981	2850
30	ALLEN	1600	20-FEB-1981	2850

Rather than returning the SAL of the latest employee hired, MAX OVER without KEEP simply returns the highest salary in each DEPTNO. KEEP, in this recipe, allows you to order the salaries by HIREDATE in each DEPTNO by specifying ORDER BY HIREDATE. Then, the function DENSE_RANK assigns a rank to each HIREDATE in ascending order. Finally, the function LAST determines which row to apply the aggregate function to: the "last" row based on the ranking of DENSE_RANK. In this case, the aggregate function MAX is applied to the SAL column for the row with the "last" HIREDATE. In essence, keep the SAL of the HIREDATE ranked last in each DEPTNO.

You are ranking the rows in each DEPTNO based on one column (HIREDATE), but then applying the aggregation (MAX) on another column (SAL). This ability to rank in one dimension and aggregate over another is convenient as it allows you to avoid extra joins and inline views as are used in the other solutions. Finally, by adding the OVER clause after the KEEP clause you can return the SAL "kept" by KEEP for each row in the partition.

Alternatively, you can order by HIREDATE in descending order and "keep" the first SAL. Compare the two queries below, which return the same result set:

```
select deptno,
       ename,
       sal,
       hiredate,
       max(sal)
         keep(dense_rank last order by hiredate)
         over(partition by deptno) latest_sal
  from emp
 order by 1, 4 desc
```

DEPTNO	ENAME	SAL	HIREDATE	LATEST_SAL
10	MILLER	1300	23-JAN-1982	1300
10	KING	5000	17-NOV-1981	1300
10	CLARK	2450	09-JUN-1981	1300
20	ADAMS	1100	12-JAN-1983	1100
20	SCOTT	3000	09-DEC-1982	1100
20	FORD	3000	03-DEC-1981	1100
20	JONES	2975	02-APR-1981	1100
20	SMITH	800	17-DEC-1980	1100
30	JAMES	950	03-DEC-1981	950
30	MARTIN	1250	28-SEP-1981	950
30	TURNER	1500	08-SEP-1981	950
30	BLAKE	2850	01-MAY-1981	950
30	WARD	1250	22-FEB-1981	950
30	ALLEN	1600	20-FEB-1981	950

```
select deptno,
       ename,
       sal,
       hiredate,
       max(sal)
         keep(dense_rank first order by hiredate desc)
         over(partition by deptno) latest_sal
  from emp
 order by 1, 4 desc
```

DEPTNO	ENAME	SAL	HIREDATE	LATEST_SAL

```
10 MILLER     1300 23-JAN-1982    1300
10 KING       5000 17-NOV-1981    1300
10 CLARK      2450 09-JUN-1981    1300
20 ADAMS      1100 12-JAN-1983    1100
20 SCOTT      3000 09-DEC-1982    1100
20 FORD       3000 03-DEC-1981    1100
20 JONES      2975 02-APR-1981    1100
20 SMITH       800 17-DEC-1980    1100
30 JAMES       950 03-DEC-1981     950
30 MARTIN     1250 28-SEP-1981     950
30 TURNER     1500 08-SEP-1981     950
30 BLAKE      2850 01-MAY-1981     950
30 WARD       1250 22-FEB-1981     950
30 ALLEN      1600 20-FEB-1981     950
```

11.12 Generating Simple Forecasts

Problem

Based on current data, you want to return addition rows and columns representing future actions. For example, consider the following result set:

```
ID ORDER_DATE  PROCESS_DATE
-- ----------- ------------
 1 25-SEP-2005 27-SEP-2005
 2 26-SEP-2005 28-SEP-2005
 3 27-SEP-2005 29-SEP-2005
```

You want to return three rows per row returned in your result set (each row plus two additional rows for each order). Along with the extra rows you would like to return two additional columns providing dates for expected order processing.

From the result set above you can see that an order takes two days to process. For the purposes of this example, let's say the next step after processing is verification, and the last step is shipment. Verification occurs one day after processing and shipment occurs one day after verification. You want to return a result set expressing the whole procedure. Ultimately you want to transform the result set above to the following result set:

```
ID ORDER_DATE  PROCESS_DATE VERIFIED    SHIPPED
-- ----------- ------------ ----------- -----------
 1 25-SEP-2005 27-SEP-2005
 1 25-SEP-2005 27-SEP-2005  28-SEP-2005
 1 25-SEP-2005 27-SEP-2005  28-SEP-2005 29-SEP-2005
 2 26-SEP-2005 28-SEP-2005
 2 26-SEP-2005 28-SEP-2005  29-SEP-2005
 2 26-SEP-2005 28-SEP-2005  29-SEP-2005 30-SEP-2005
 3 27-SEP-2005 29-SEP-2005
 3 27-SEP-2005 29-SEP-2005  30-SEP-2005
 3 27-SEP-2005 29-SEP-2005  30-SEP-2005 01-OCT-2005
```

Solution

The key is to use a Cartesian product to generate two additional rows for each order then simply use CASE expressions to create the required column values.

DB2 and SQL Server

Use the recursive WITH clause to generate rows needed for your Cartesian product. The DB2 and SQL Server solutions are identical except for the function used to retrieve the current date. DB2 uses CURRENT_DATE and SQL Server uses GET-DATE. The SQL Server solution is shown below:

```
 1  with nrows(n) as (
 2  select 1 from t1 union all
 3  select n+1 from nrows where n+1 <= 3
 4  )
 5  select id,
 6         order_date,
 7         process_date,
 8         case when nrows.n >= 2
 9              then process_date+1
10              else null
11         end as verified,
12         case when nrows.n = 3
13              then process_date+2
14              else null
15         end  as shipped
16    from (
17  select nrows.n id,
18         getdate()+nrows.n   as order_date,
19         getdate()+nrows.n+2 as process_date
20    from nrows
21         ) orders, nrows
22    order by 1
```

Oracle

Use the hierarchical CONNECT BY clause to generate the three rows needed for the Cartesian product. Use the WITH clause to allow you to reuse the results returned by CONNECT BY without having to call it again:

```
 1  with nrows as (
 2  select level n
 3    from dual
 4 connect by level <= 3
 5  )
 6  select id,
 7         order_date,
 8         process_date,
 9         case when nrows.n >= 2
10              then process_date+1
11              else null
```

```
12              end as verified,
13              case when nrows.n = 3
14                    then process_date+2
15                    else null
16              end  as shipped
17      from (
18  select nrows.n id,
19              sysdate+nrows.n   as order_date,
20              sysdate+nrows.n+2 as process_date
21      from nrows
22              ) orders, nrows
```

PostgreSQL

You can create a Cartesian product many different ways; this solution uses the Post-greSQL function GENERATE_SERIES:

```
1   select id,
2              order_date,
3              process_date,
4              case when gs.n >= 2
5                    then process_date+1
6                    else null
7              end as verified,
8              case when gs.n = 3
9                    then process_date+2
10                   else null
11             end  as shipped
12      from (
13  select gs.id,
14              current_date+gs.id   as order_date,
15              current_date+gs.id+2 as process_date
16      from generate_series(1,3) gs (id)
17              ) orders,
18                generate_series(1,3)gs(n)
```

MySQL

MySQL does not support a function for automatic row generation.

Discussion

DB2 and SQL Server

The result set presented in the problem section is returned via inline view ORDERS and is shown below:

```
with nrows(n) as (
select 1 from t1 union all
select n+1 from nrows where n+1 <= 3
)
select nrows.n id,
```

```
        getdate()+nrows.n    as order_date,
        getdate()+nrows.n+2 as process_date
   from nrows
```

```
ID ORDER_DATE  PROCESS_DATE
-- -----------  ------------
 1 25-SEP-2005  27-SEP-2005
 2 26-SEP-2005  28-SEP-2005
 3 27-SEP-2005  29-SEP-2005
```

The query above simply uses the WITH clause to make up three rows representing the orders you must process. NROWS returns the values 1, 2, and 3, and those numbers are added to GETDATE (CURRENT_DATE for DB2) to represent the dates of the orders. Because the problem section states that processing time takes two days, the query above also adds two days to the ORDER_DATE (adds the value returned by NROWS to GETDATE, then adds two more days).

Now that you have your base result set, the next step is to create a Cartesian product because the requirement is to return three rows for each order. Use NROWS to create a Cartesian product to return three rows for each order:

```
with nrows(n) as (
select 1 from t1 union all
select n+1 from nrows where n+1 <= 3
)
select nrows.n,
       orders.*
  from (
select nrows.n id,
       getdate()+nrows.n    as order_date,
       getdate()+nrows.n+2 as process_date
  from nrows
       ) orders, nrows
 order by 2,1
```

```
 N  ID ORDER_DATE  PROCESS_DATE
--- --- -----------  ------------
 1   1 25-SEP-2005  27-SEP-2005
 2   1 25-SEP-2005  27-SEP-2005
 3   1 25-SEP-2005  27-SEP-2005
 1   2 26-SEP-2005  28-SEP-2005
 2   2 26-SEP-2005  28-SEP-2005
 3   2 26-SEP-2005  28-SEP-2005
 1   3 27-SEP-2005  29-SEP-2005
 2   3 27-SEP-2005  29-SEP-2005
 3   3 27-SEP-2005  29-SEP-2005
```

Now that you have three rows for each order, simply use a CASE expression to create the addition column values to represent the status of verification and shipment.

The first row for each order should have a NULL value for VERIFIED and SHIPPED. The second row for each order should have a NULL value for SHIPPED. The third row for each order should have non-NULL values for each column. The final result set is shown below:

```
with nrows(n) as (
select 1 from t1 union all
select n+1 from nrows where n+1 <= 3
)
select id,
       order_date,
       process_date,
       case when nrows.n >= 2
            then process_date+1
            else null
       end as verified,
       case when nrows.n = 3
            then process_date+2
            else null
       end  as shipped
  from (
select nrows.n id,
       getdate()+nrows.n   as order_date,
       getdate()+nrows.n+2 as process_date
  from nrows
       ) orders, nrows
 order by 1
```

```
ID ORDER_DATE  PROCESS_DATE VERIFIED    SHIPPED
-- ----------- ------------ ----------- -----------
 1 25-SEP-2005  27-SEP-2005
 1 25-SEP-2005  27-SEP-2005 28-SEP-2005
 1 25-SEP-2005  27-SEP-2005 28-SEP-2005 29-SEP-2005
 2 26-SEP-2005  28-SEP-2005
 2 26-SEP-2005  28-SEP-2005 29-SEP-2005
 2 26-SEP-2005  28-SEP-2005 29-SEP-2005 30-SEP-2005
 3 27-SEP-2005  29-SEP-2005
 3 27-SEP-2005  29-SEP-2005 30-SEP-2005
 3 27-SEP-2005  29-SEP-2005 30-SEP-2005 01-OCT-2005
```

The final result set expresses the complete order process from the day the order was received to the day it should be shipped.

Oracle

The result set presented in the problem section is returned via inline view ORDERS and is shown below:

```
with nrows as (
select level n
  from dual
connect by level <= 3
)
```

```
select nrows.n id,
       sysdate+nrows.n    order_date,
       sysdate+nrows.n+2 process_date
  from nrows
```

```
ID ORDER_DATE  PROCESS_DATE
-- ----------- ------------
 1 25-SEP-2005  27-SEP-2005
 2 26-SEP-2005  28-SEP-2005
 3 27-SEP-2005  29-SEP-2005
```

The query above simply uses CONNECT BY to make up three rows representing the orders you must process. Use the WITH clause to refer to the rows returned by CONNECT BY as NROWS.N. CONNECT BY returns the values 1, 2, and 3, and those numbers are added to SYSDATE to represent the dates of the orders. Since the problem section states that processing time takes two days, the query above also adds two days to the ORDER_DATE (adds the value returned by GENERATE_SERIES to SYSDATE, then adds two more days).

Now that you have your base result set, the next step is to create a Cartesian product because the requirement is to return three rows for each order. Use NROWS to create a Cartesian product to return three rows for each order:

```
with nrows as (
select level n
  from dual
connect by level <= 3
)
select nrows.n,
       orders.*
  from (
select nrows.n id,
       sysdate+nrows.n    order_date,
       sysdate+nrows.n+2 process_date
  from nrows
       ) orders, nrows
```

```
N  ID ORDER_DATE  PROCESS_DATE
--- --- ----------- ------------
 1   1 25-SEP-2005  27-SEP-2005
 2   1 25-SEP-2005  27-SEP-2005
 3   1 25-SEP-2005  27-SEP-2005
 1   2 26-SEP-2005  28-SEP-2005
 2   2 26-SEP-2005  28-SEP-2005
 3   2 26-SEP-2005  28-SEP-2005
 1   3 27-SEP-2005  29-SEP-2005
 2   3 27-SEP-2005  29-SEP-2005
 3   3 27-SEP-2005  29-SEP-2005
```

Now that you have three rows for each order, simply use a CASE expression to create the addition column values to represent the status of verification and shipment.

The first row for each order should have a NULL value for VERIFIED and SHIPPED. The second row for each order should have a NULL value for SHIPPED. The third row for each order should have non-NULL values for each column. The final result set is shown below:

```
with nrows as (
select level n
  from dual
connect by level <= 3
)
select id,
       order_date,
       process_date,
       case when nrows.n >= 2
            then process_date+1
            else null
       end as verified,
       case when nrows.n = 3
            then process_date+2
            else null
       end  as shipped
  from (
select nrows.n id,
       sysdate+nrows.n    order_date,
       sysdate+nrows.n+2 process_date
  from nrows
       ) orders, nrows
```

```
ID ORDER_DATE  PROCESS_DATE VERIFIED    SHIPPED
-- ----------- ------------ ----------- -----------
 1 25-SEP-2005  27-SEP-2005
 1 25-SEP-2005  27-SEP-2005 28-SEP-2005
 1 25-SEP-2005  27-SEP-2005 28-SEP-2005 29-SEP-2005
 2 26-SEP-2005  28-SEP-2005
 2 26-SEP-2005  28-SEP-2005 29-SEP-2005
 2 26-SEP-2005  28-SEP-2005 29-SEP-2005 30-SEP-2005
 3 27-SEP-2005  29-SEP-2005
 3 27-SEP-2005  29-SEP-2005 30-SEP-2005
 3 27-SEP-2005  29-SEP-2005 30-SEP-2005 01-OCT-2005
```

The final result set expresses the complete order process from the day the order was received to the day it should be shipped.

PostgreSQL

The result set presented in the problem section is returned via inline view ORDERS and is shown below:

```
select gs.id,
       current_date+gs.id   as order_date,
       current_date+gs.id+2 as process_date
  from generate_series(1,3) gs (id)
```

```
ID ORDER_DATE  PROCESS_DATE
-- ----------  ------------
 1 25-SEP-2005  27-SEP-2005
 2 26-SEP-2005  28-SEP-2005
 3 27-SEP-2005  29-SEP-2005
```

The query above simply uses the GENERATE_SERIES function to make up three rows representing the orders you must process. GENERATE_SERIES returns the values 1, 2, and 3, and those numbers are added to CURRENT_DATE to represent the dates of the orders. Since the problem section states that processing time takes two days, the query above also adds two days to the ORDER_DATE (adds the value returned by GENERATE_SERIES to CURRENT_DATE, then adds two more days).

Now that you have your base result set, the next step is to create a Cartesian product because the requirement is to return three rows for each order. Use the GENERATE_SERIES function to create a Cartesian product to return three rows for each order:

```
select gs.n,
       orders.*
  from (
select gs.id,
       current_date+gs.id   as order_date,
       current_date+gs.id+2 as process_date
  from generate_series(1,3) gs (id)
       ) orders,
        generate_series(1,3)gs(n)
```

```
 N  ID ORDER_DATE  PROCESS_DATE
--- --- ----------  ------------
  1   1 25-SEP-2005  27-SEP-2005
  2   1 25-SEP-2005  27-SEP-2005
  3   1 25-SEP-2005  27-SEP-2005
  1   2 26-SEP-2005  28-SEP-2005
  2   2 26-SEP-2005  28-SEP-2005
  3   2 26-SEP-2005  28-SEP-2005
  1   3 27-SEP-2005  29-SEP-2005
  2   3 27-SEP-2005  29-SEP-2005
  3   3 27-SEP-2005  29-SEP-2005
```

Now that you have three rows for each order, simply use a CASE expression to create the addition column values to represent the status of verification and shipment.

The first row for each order should have a NULL value for VERIFIED and SHIPPED. The second row for each order should have a NULL value for SHIPPED. The third row for each order should have non-NULL values for each column. The final result set is shown below:

```
select id,
       order_date,
       process_date,
       case when gs.n >= 2
            then process_date+1
            else null
       end as verified,
       case when gs.n = 3
            then process_date+2
            else null
       end  as shipped
  from (
select gs.id,
       current_date+gs.id   as order_date,
       current_date+gs.id+2 as process_date
  from generate_series(1,3) gs(id)
       ) orders,
         generate_series(1,3)gs(n)


ID ORDER_DATE  PROCESS_DATE VERIFIED     SHIPPED
-- ----------- ------------ -----------  -----------
 1 25-SEP-2005  27-SEP-2005
 1 25-SEP-2005  27-SEP-2005 28-SEP-2005
 1 25-SEP-2005  27-SEP-2005 28-SEP-2005 29-SEP-2005
 2 26-SEP-2005  28-SEP-2005
 2 26-SEP-2005  28-SEP-2005 29-SEP-2005
 2 26-SEP-2005  28-SEP-2005 29-SEP-2005 30-SEP-2005
 3 27-SEP-2005  29-SEP-2005
 3 27-SEP-2005  29-SEP-2005 30-SEP-2005
 3 27-SEP-2005  29-SEP-2005 30-SEP-2005 01-OCT-2005
```

The final result set expresses the complete order process from the day the order was received to the day it should be shipped.

CHAPTER 12

Reporting and Warehousing

This chapter introduces queries you may find helpful for creating reports. These typically involve reporting-specific formatting considerations along with different levels of aggregation. Another focus of this chapter is on transposing or pivoting result sets, converting rows into columns. Pivoting is an extremely useful technique for solving a variety of problems. As your comfort level increases with pivoting, you'll undoubtedly find uses for it outside of what are presented in this chapter.

12.1 Pivoting a Result Set into One Row

Problem

You wish to take values from groups of rows and turn those values into columns in a single row per group. For example, you have a result set displaying the number of employees in each department:

```
DEPTNO        CNT
------ ----------
    10          3
    20          5
    30          6
```

You would like to reformat the output such the result set looks as follows:

```
DEPTNO_10  DEPTNO_20  DEPTNO_30
---------- ---------- ----------
        3          5          6
```

Solution

Transpose the result set using a CASE expression and the aggregate function SUM:

```
1  select sum(case when deptno=10 then 1 else 0 end) as deptno_10,
2         sum(case when deptno=20 then 1 else 0 end) as deptno_20,
3         sum(case when deptno=30 then 1 else 0 end) as deptno_30
4    from emp
```

Discussion

This example is an excellent introduction to pivoting. The concept is simple: for each row returned by the unpivoted query, use a CASE expression to separate the rows into columns. Then, because this particular problem is to count the number of employees per department, use the aggregate function SUM to count the occurrence of each DEPTNO. If you're having trouble understanding how this works exactly, execute the query with the aggregate function SUM and include DEPTNO for readability:

```
select deptno,
       case when deptno=10 then 1 else 0 end as deptno_10,
       case when deptno=20 then 1 else 0 end as deptno_20,
       case when deptno=30 then 1 else 0 end as deptno_30
  from emp
 order by 1
```

DEPTNO	DEPTNO_10	DEPTNO_20	DEPTNO_30
10	1	0	0
10	1	0	0
10	1	0	0
20	0	1	0
20	0	1	0
20	0	1	0
20	0	1	0
20	0	1	0
30	0	0	1
30	0	0	1
30	0	0	1
30	0	0	1
30	0	0	1
30	0	0	1

You can think of each CASE expression as a flag to determine which DEPTNO a row belongs to. At this point, the "rows to columns" transformation is already done; the next step is to simply sum the values returned by DEPTNO_10, DEPTNO_20, and DEPTNO_30, and then to group by DEPTNO. Following are the results:

```
select deptno,
       sum(case when deptno=10 then 1 else 0 end) as deptno_10,
       sum(case when deptno=20 then 1 else 0 end) as deptno_20,
       sum(case when deptno=30 then 1 else 0 end) as deptno_30
  from emp
 group by deptno
```

DEPTNO	DEPTNO_10	DEPTNO_20	DEPTNO_30
10	3	0	0
20	0	5	0
30	0	0	6

If you eyeball this result set, you see that logically the output makes sense; for example, DEPTNO 10 has 3 employees in DEPTNO_10 and zero in the other departments. Since the goal is to return one row, the last step is to lose the DEPTNO and GROUP BY, and simply sum the CASE expressions:

```
select sum(case when deptno=10 then 1 else 0 end) as deptno_10,
       sum(case when deptno=20 then 1 else 0 end) as deptno_20,
       sum(case when deptno=30 then 1 else 0 end) as deptno_30
  from emp
```

```
DEPTNO_10  DEPTNO_20  DEPTNO_30
---------  ---------  ---------
        3          5          6
```

Following is another approach that you may sometimes see applied to this same sort of problem:

```
select max(case when deptno=10 then empcount else null end) as deptno_10
       max(case when deptno=20 then empcount else null end) as deptno_20,
       max(case when deptno=30 then empcount else null end) as deptno_30
  from (
select deptno, count(*) as empcount
  from emp
 group by deptno
       ) x
```

This approach uses an inline view to generate the employee counts per department. CASE expressions in the main query translate rows to columns, getting you to the following results:

```
DEPTNO_10  DEPTNO_20  DEPTNO_30
---------  ---------  ---------
        3       NULL       NULL
     NULL          5       NULL
     NULL       NULL          6
```

Then the MAX functions collapses the columns into one row:

```
DEPTNO_10  DEPTNO_20  DEPTNO_30
---------  ---------  ---------
        3          5          6
```

12.2   Pivoting a Result Set into Multiple Rows

Problem

You want to turn rows into columns by creating a column corresponding to each of the values in a single given column. However, unlike in the previous recipe, you need multiple rows of output.

For example, you want to return each employee and their position (JOB), and you currently use a query that returns the following result set:

```
JOB        ENAME
---------  ----------
ANALYST    SCOTT
ANALYST    FORD
CLERK      SMITH
CLERK      ADAMS
CLERK      MILLER
CLERK      JAMES
MANAGER    JONES
MANAGER    CLARK
MANAGER    BLAKE
PRESIDENT  KING
SALESMAN   ALLEN
SALESMAN   MARTIN
SALESMAN   TURNER
SALESMAN   WARD
```

You would like to format the result set such that each job gets its own column:

```
CLERKS ANALYSTS MGRS   PREZ SALES
------ -------- -----  ---- ------
MILLER FORD     CLARK  KING TURNER
JAMES  SCOTT    BLAKE       MARTIN
ADAMS           JONES       WARD
SMITH                       ALLEN
```

Solution

Unlike the first recipe in this chapter, the result set for this recipe consists of more than one row. Using the previous recipe's technique will not work for this recipe, as the MAX(ENAME) for each JOB would be returned, which would result in one ENAME for each JOB (i.e., one row will be returned as in Recipe 12.1). To solve this problem, you must make each JOB/ENAME combination unique. Then, when you apply an aggregate function to remove NULLs, you don't lose any ENAMEs.

DB2, Oracle, and SQL Server

Use the window function ROW_NUMBER OVER to make each JOB/ENAME combination unique. Pivot the result set using a CASE expression and the aggregate function MAX while grouping on the value returned by the window function:

```
 1  select max(case when job='CLERK'
 2                   then ename else null end) as clerks,
 3         max(case when job='ANALYST'
 4                   then ename else null end) as analysts,
 5         max(case when job='MANAGER'
 6                   then ename else null end) as mgrs,
 7         max(case when job='PRESIDENT'
 8                   then ename else null end) as prez,
 9         max(case when job='SALESMAN'
10                   then ename else null end) as sales
11    from (
```

```
12    select job,
13          ename,
14          row_number( )over(partition by job order by ename) rn
15       from emp
16          ) x
17    group by rn
```

PostgreSQL and MySQL

Use a scalar subquery to rank each employee by EMPNO. Pivot the result set using a CASE expression and the aggregate function MAX while grouping on the value returned by the scalar subquery:

```
1   select max(case when job='CLERK'
2                   then ename else null end) as clerks,
3          max(case when job='ANALYST'
4                   then ename else null end) as analysts,
5          max(case when job='MANAGER'
6                   then ename else null end) as mgrs,
7          max(case when job='PRESIDENT'
8                   then ename else null end) as prez,
9          max(case when job='SALESMAN'
10                  then ename else null end) as sales
11      from (
12   select e.job,
13          e.ename,
14          (select count(*) from emp d
15             where e.job=d.job and e.empno < d.empno) as rnk
16      from emp e
17          ) x
18   group by rnk
```

Discussion

DB2, Oracle, and SQL Server

The first step is to use the window function ROW_NUMBER OVER to help make each JOB/ENAME combination unique:

```
select job,
       ename,
       row_number( )over(partition by job order by ename) rn
   from emp

JOB        ENAME        RN
---------  ----------  ----------
ANALYST    FORD          1
ANALYST    SCOTT         2
CLERK      ADAMS         1
CLERK      JAMES         2
CLERK      MILLER        3
CLERK      SMITH         4
MANAGER    BLAKE         1
MANAGER    CLARK         2
```

```
MANAGER    JONES          3
PRESIDENT  KING           1
SALESMAN   ALLEN          1
SALESMAN   MARTIN         2
SALESMAN   TURNER         3
SALESMAN   WARD           4
```

Giving each ENAME a unique "row number" within a given job prevents any problems that might otherwise result from two employees having the same name and job. The goal here is to be able to group on row number (on RN) without dropping any employees from the result set due to the use of MAX. This step is the most important step in solving the problem. Without this first step, the aggregation in the outer query will remove necessary rows. Consider what the result set would look like without using ROW_NUMBER OVER, using the same technique as seen in Recipe 12.1:

```
select max(case when job='CLERK'
                then ename else null end) as clerks,
       max(case when job='ANALYST'
                then ename else null end) as analysts,
       max(case when job='MANAGER'
                then ename else null end) as mgrs,
       max(case when job='PRESIDENT'
                then ename else null end) as prez,
       max(case when job='SALESMAN'
                then ename else null end) as sales
  from emp


CLERKS     ANALYSTS    MGRS       PREZ        SALES
---------- ----------  ---------- ----------  ----------
SMITH      SCOTT       JONES      KING        WARD
```

Unfortunately, only one row is returned for each JOB: the employee with the MAX ENAME. When it comes time to pivot the result set, using MIN or MAX should serve as a means to remove NULLs from the result set, not restrict the ENAMEs returned. How this works will be come clearer as you continue through the explanation.

The next step uses a CASE expression to organize the ENAMEs into their proper column (JOB):

```
select rn,
       case when job='CLERK'
            then ename else null end as clerks,
       case when job='ANALYST'
            then ename else null end as analysts,
       case when job='MANAGER'
            then ename else null end as mgrs,
       case when job='PRESIDENT'
            then ename else null end as prez,
       case when job='SALESMAN'
            then ename else null end as sales
  from (
select job,
       ename,
       row_number()over(partition by job order by ename) rn
```

```
    from emp
        ) x

RN CLERKS      ANALYSTS    MGRS        PREZ        SALES
-- ----------  ----------  ----------  ----------  ----------
 1             FORD
 2             SCOTT
 1 ADAMS
 2 JAMES
 3 MILLER
 4 SMITH
 1                         BLAKE
 2                         CLARK
 3                         JONES
 1                                     KING
 1                                                 ALLEN
 1                                                 MARTIN
 2                                                 TURNER
 3                                                 WARD
 4
```

At this point, the rows are transposed into columns and the last step is to remove the
NULLs to make the result set more readable. To remove the NULLs use the aggregate function MAX and group by RN. (You can use the function MIN as well. The
choice to use MAX is arbitrary, as you will only ever be aggregating one value per
group.) There is only one value for each RN/JOB/ENAME combination. Grouping
by RN in conjunction with the CASE expressions embedded within the calls to MAX
ensures that each call to MAX results in picking only one name from a group of otherwise NULL values:

```
select max(case when job='CLERK'
                then ename else null end) as clerks,
       max(case when job='ANALYST'
                then ename else null end) as analysts,
       max(case when job='MANAGER'
                then ename else null end) as mgrs,
       max(case when job='PRESIDENT'
                then ename else null end) as prez,
       max(case when job='SALESMAN'
                then ename else null end) as sales
  from (
select job,
       ename,
       row_number()over(partition by job order by ename) rn
  from emp
        ) x
 group by rn

CLERKS ANALYSTS MGRS  PREZ SALES
------ -------- ----- ---- ------
MILLER FORD     CLARK KING TURNER
JAMES  SCOTT    BLAKE      MARTIN
ADAMS           JONES      WARD
SMITH                      ALLEN
```

The technique of using ROW_NUMBER OVER to create unique combinations of rows is extremely useful for formatting query results. Consider the query below that creates a sparse report showing employees by DEPTNO and JOB:

```
select deptno dno, job,
       max(case when deptno=10
               then ename else null end) as d10,
       max(case when deptno=20
               then ename else null end) as d20,
       max(case when deptno=30
               then ename else null end) as d30,
       max(case when job='CLERK'
               then ename else null end) as clerks,
       max(case when job='ANALYST'
               then ename else null end) as anals,
       max(case when job='MANAGER'
               then ename else null end) as mgrs,
       max(case when job='PRESIDENT'
               then ename else null end) as prez,
       max(case when job='SALESMAN'
               then ename else null end) as sales
  from (
select deptno,
       job,
       ename,
       row_number()over(partition by job    order by ename) rn_job,
       row_number()over(partition by deptno order by ename) rn_deptno
  from emp
       ) x
 group by deptno, job, rn_deptno, rn_job
 order by 1
```

```
DNO JOB        D10    D20    D30    CLERKS ANALS MGRS  PREZ SALES
--- ---------- ------ ------ ------ ------ ----- ----- ---- ------
 10 CLERK      MILLER               MILLER
 10 MANAGER    CLARK                              CLARK
 10 PRESIDENT  KING                                    KING
 20 ANALYST           FORD                 FORD
 20 ANALYST           SCOTT                SCOTT
 20 CLERK             ADAMS         ADAMS
 20 CLERK             SMITH         SMITH
 20 MANAGER           JONES                      JONES
 30 CLERK                    JAMES  JAMES
 30 MANAGER                  BLAKE                BLAKE
 30 SALESMAN                 ALLEN                      ALLEN
 30 SALESMAN                 MARTIN                     MARTIN
 30 SALESMAN                 TURNER                     TURNER
 30 SALESMAN                 WARD                       WARD
```

By simply modifying what you group by (hence the nonaggregate items in the SELECT list above), you can produce reports with different formats. It is worth the time of changing things around to understand how these formats change based on what you include in your GROUP BY clause.

PostgreSQL and MySQL

The technique for these RDBMSs is the same as for the others once a method of creating unique JOB/ENAME combinations is established. The first step is to use a scalar subquery to provide a "row number" or "rank" for each JOB/ENAME combination:

```
select e.job,
       e.ename,
       (select count(*) from emp d
         where e.job=d.job and e.empno < d.empno) as rnk
  from emp e
```

JOB	ENAME	RNK
CLERK	SMITH	3
SALESMAN	ALLEN	3
SALESMAN	WARD	2
MANAGER	JONES	2
SALESMAN	MARTIN	1
MANAGER	BLAKE	1
MANAGER	CLARK	0
ANALYST	SCOTT	1
PRESIDENT	KING	0
SALESMAN	TURNER	0
CLERK	ADAMS	2
CLERK	JAMES	1
ANALYST	FORD	0
CLERK	MILLER	0

Giving each JOB/ENAME combination a unique "rank" makes each row unique. Even if there are employees with the same name working the same job, no two employees will share the same rank within a job. This step is the most important step in solving the problem. Without this first step, the aggregation in the outer query will remove necessary rows. Consider what the result set would look like without applying a rank to each JOB/ENAME combination, using the same technique as seen in Recipe 12.1:

```
select max(case when job='CLERK'
                then ename else null end) as clerks,
       max(case when job='ANALYST'
                then ename else null end) as analysts,
       max(case when job='MANAGER'
                then ename else null end) as mgrs,
       max(case when job='PRESIDENT'
                then ename else null end) as prez,
       max(case when job='SALESMAN'
                then ename else null end) as sales
  from emp
```

CLERKS	ANALYSTS	MGRS	PREZ	SALES
SMITH	SCOTT	JONES	KING	WARD

Unfortunately, only one row is returned for each JOB: the employee with the MAX ENAME. When it comes time to pivot the result set, using MIN or MAX should serve as a means to remove NULLs from the result set, not to restrict the ENAMEs returned.

Now, that you see the purpose of applying a rank, you can move on to the next step. The next step uses a CASE expression to organize the ENAMEs into their proper column (JOB):

```
select rnk,
       case when job='CLERK'
            then ename else null end as clerks,
       case when job='ANALYST'
            then ename else null end as analysts,
       case when job='MANAGER'
            then ename else null end as mgrs,
       case when job='PRESIDENT'
            then ename else null end as prez,
       case when job='SALESMAN'
            then ename else null end as sales
  from (
select e.job,
       e.ename,
       (select count(*) from emp d
         where e.job=d.job and e.empno < d.empno) as rnk
  from emp e
       ) x

RNK CLERKS ANALYSTS MGRS  PREZ SALES
--- ------ -------- ----- ---- ----------
  3 SMITH
  3                              ALLEN
  2                              WARD
  2             JONES
  1                              MARTIN
  1             BLAKE
  0             CLARK
  1     SCOTT
  0                        KING
  0                              TURNER
  2 ADAMS
  1 JAMES
  0       FORD
  0 MILLER
```

At this point, the rows are transposed into columns and the last step is to remove the NULLs to make the result set more readable. To remove the NULLs use the aggregate function MAX and group by RNK. (MAX is an arbitrary choice. You can use the function MIN as well.) There is only one value for each RN/JOB/ENAME combination, so the application of the aggregate function is simply to remove NULLs:

```
    select max(case when job='CLERK'
                   then ename else null end) as clerks,
           max(case when job='ANALYST'
                   then ename else null end) as analysts,
           max(case when job='MANAGER'
                   then ename else null end) as mgrs,
           max(case when job='PRESIDENT'
                   then ename else null end) as prez,
           max(case when job='SALESMAN'
                   then ename else null end) as sales
      from (
    select e.job,
           e.ename,
           (select count(*) from emp d
              where e.job=d.job and e.empno < d.empno) as rnk
      from emp e
          ) x
     group by rnk

    CLERKS ANALYSTS MGRS  PREZ SALES
    ------ -------- ----- ---- ------
    MILLER FORD     CLARK KING TURNER
    JAMES  SCOTT    BLAKE      MARTIN
    ADAMS           JONES      WARD
    SMITH                      ALLEN
```

12.3   Reverse Pivoting a Result Set

Problem

You want to transform columns to rows. Consider the following result set:

```
    DEPTNO_10  DEPTNO_20  DEPTNO_30
    ---------- ---------- ----------
            3          5          6
```

You would like to convert that to:

```
    DEPTNO COUNTS_BY_DEPT
    ------ --------------
        10              3
        20              5
        30              6
```

Solution

Examining the desired result set, it's easy to see that you can execute a simple COUNT and GROUP BY on table EMP to produce the desired result. The object here, though, is to imagine that the data is not stored as rows; perhaps the data is denormalized and aggregated values are stored as multiple columns.

To convert columns to rows, use a Cartesian product. You'll need to know in advance how many columns you want to convert to rows because the table expression you use to create the Cartesian product must have a cardinality of at least the number of columns you want to transpose.

Rather than create a denormalized table of data, the solution for this recipe will use the solution from Recipe 12.1 to create a "wide" result set. The full solution is as follows:

```
 1  select dept.deptno,
 2         case dept.deptno
 3             when 10 then emp_cnts.deptno_10
 4             when 20 then emp_cnts.deptno_20
 5             when 30 then emp_cnts.deptno_30
 6         end as counts_by_dept
 7    from (
 8  select sum(case when deptno=10 then 1 else 0 end) as deptno_10,
 9         sum(case when deptno=20 then 1 else 0 end) as deptno_20,
10         sum(case when deptno=30 then 1 else 0 end) as deptno_30
11    from emp
12         ) emp_cnts,
13         (select deptno from dept where deptno <= 30) dept
```

Discussion

The inline view EMP_CNTS represents the denormalized view, or "wide" result set that you want to convert to rows, and is shown below:

```
select sum(case when deptno=10 then 1 else 0 end) as deptno_10,
       sum(case when deptno=20 then 1 else 0 end) as deptno_20,
       sum(case when deptno=30 then 1 else 0 end) as deptno_30
  from emp


DEPTNO_10  DEPTNO_20  DEPTNO_30
---------  ---------  ---------
        3          5          6
```

Because there are three columns, you will create three rows. Begin by creating a Cartesian product between inline view EMP_CNTS and some table expression that has at least three rows. The following code uses table DEPT to create the Cartesian product; DEPT has four rows:

```
select dept.deptno,
       emp_cnts.deptno_10,
       emp_cnts.deptno_20,
       emp_cnts.deptno_30
  from (
select sum(case when deptno=10 then 1 else 0 end) as deptno_10,
       sum(case when deptno=20 then 1 else 0 end) as deptno_20,
       sum(case when deptno=30 then 1 else 0 end) as deptno_30
  from emp
       ) emp_cnts,
       (select deptno from dept where deptno <= 30) dept
```

```
DEPTNO  DEPTNO_10  DEPTNO_20  DEPTNO_30
------  ---------  ---------  ---------
    10          3          5          6
    20          3          5          6
    30          3          5          6
```

The Cartesian product enables you to return a row for each column in inline view EMP_CNTS. Since the final result set should have only the DEPTNO and the number of employees in said DEPTNO, use a CASE expression to transform the three columns into one:

```
select dept.deptno,
       case dept.deptno
            when 10 then emp_cnts.deptno_10
            when 20 then emp_cnts.deptno_20
            when 30 then emp_cnts.deptno_30
       end as counts_by_dept
  from (
select sum(case when deptno=10 then 1 else 0 end) as deptno_10,
       sum(case when deptno=20 then 1 else 0 end) as deptno_20,
       sum(case when deptno=30 then 1 else 0 end) as deptno_30
  from emp
       ) emp_cnts,
       (select deptno from dept where deptno <= 30) dept

DEPTNO COUNTS_BY_DEPT
------ --------------
    10              3
    20              5
    30              6
```

12.4   Reverse Pivoting a Result Set into One Column

Problem

You want to return all columns from a query as just one column. For example, you want to return the ENAME, JOB, and SAL of all employees in DEPTNO 10, and you want to return all three values in one column. You want to return three rows for each employee and one row of white space between employees. You want to return the following result set:

```
EMPS
----------
CLARK
MANAGER
2450

KING
PRESIDENT
5000
```

```
MILLER
CLERK
1300
```

Solution

The key is to use a Cartesian product to return four rows for each employee. This lets you return one column value per row and have an extra row for spacing between employees.

DB2, Oracle, and SQL Server

Use the window function ROW_NUMBER OVER to rank each row based on EMPNO (1–4). Then use a CASE expression to transform three columns into one:

```
 1  select case rn
 2             when 1 then ename
 3             when 2 then job
 4             when 3 then cast(sal as char(4))
 5         end emps
 6    from (
 7  select e.ename,e.job,e.sal,
 8         row_number()over(partition by e.empno
 9                              order by e.empno) rn
10    from emp e,
11        (select *
12           from emp where job='CLERK') four_rows
13   where e.deptno=10
14        ) x
```

PostgreSQL and MySQL

This recipe is meant to highlight the use of window functions to provide a ranking for your rows, which then comes into play later when pivoting. At the time of this writing, neither PostgreSQL nor MySQL support window functions.

Discussion

DB2, Oracle, and SQL Server

The first step is to use the window function ROW_NUMBER OVER to create a ranking for each employee in DEPTNO 10:

```
select e.ename,e.job,e.sal,
       row_number()over(partition by e.empno
                            order by e.empno) rn
  from emp e
 where e.deptno=10
```

ENAME	JOB	SAL	RN
CLARK	MANAGER	2450	1
KING	PRESIDENT	5000	1
MILLER	CLERK	1300	1

At this point the ranking doesn't mean much. You are partitioning by EMPNO, so the rank is 1 for all three rows in DEPTNO 10. Once you add the Cartesian product, the rank will begin to take shape, as can be seen in the following results:

```
select e.ename,e.job,e.sal,
       row_number( )over(partition by e.empno
                         order by e.empno) rn
  from emp e,
       (select *
          from emp where job='CLERK') four_rows
 where e.deptno=10
```

ENAME	JOB	SAL	RN
CLARK	MANAGER	2450	1
CLARK	MANAGER	2450	2
CLARK	MANAGER	2450	3
CLARK	MANAGER	2450	4
KING	PRESIDENT	5000	1
KING	PRESIDENT	5000	2
KING	PRESIDENT	5000	3
KING	PRESIDENT	5000	4
MILLER	CLERK	1300	1
MILLER	CLERK	1300	2
MILLER	CLERK	1300	3
MILLER	CLERK	1300	4

You should stop at this point and understand two key points:

- RN is no longer 1 for each employee; it is now a repeating sequence of values from 1 to 4, the reason being, window functions are applied after the FROM and WHERE clauses are evaluated. So, partitioning by EMPNO causes the RN to reset to 1 when a new employee is encountered.

- The inline view FOUR_ROWS is simply that a SQL statement exists simply to return four rows. That is all it does. You want to return a row for every column (ENAME, JOB, SAL) plus an additional row for whitespace.

At this point, the hard work is done and all that is left is to use a CASE expression to put ENAME, JOB, and SAL into one column for each employee (you need to cast SAL to a string to make CASE happy):

```
select case rn
            when 1 then ename
            when 2 then job
            when 3 then cast(sal as char(4))
       end emps
  from (
```

```
select e.ename,e.job,e.sal,
       row_number()over(partition by e.empno
                             order by e.empno) rn
  from emp e,
       (select *
          from emp where job='CLERK') four_rows
 where e.deptno=10
       ) x

EMPS
----------
CLARK
MANAGER
2450

KING
PRESIDENT
5000

MILLER
CLERK
1300
```

12.5 Suppressing Repeating Values from a Result Set

Problem

You are generating a report, and, when two rows have the same value in a column, you wish to display that value only once. For example, you want to return DEPTNO and ENAME from table EMP, you wish to group all rows for each DEPTNO, and you wish to display each DEPTNO only one time. You want to return the following result set:

```
DEPTNO ENAME
------ ---------
    10 CLARK
       KING
       MILLER
    20 SMITH
       ADAMS
       FORD
       SCOTT
       JONES
    30 ALLEN
       BLAKE
       MARTIN
       JAMES
       TURNER
       WARD
```

Solution

This is a simple formatting problem that is easily solved by the window function LAG OVER provided by Oracle. There are other methods such as scalar subqueries and other window functions that you can use (and that you'll have to use for non-Oracle platforms), but LAG OVER is most convenient and appropriate here.

DB2 and SQL Server

You can use the window function MIN OVER to find the smallest EMPNO for each DEPTNO. Then use a CASE expression to "white out" the rows that do not have this EMPNO:

```
 1  select case when empno=min_empno
 2               then deptno else null
 3          end deptno,
 4          ename
 5    from (
 6  select deptno,
 7         min(empno)over(partition by deptno) min_empno,
 8         empno,
 9         ename
10    from emp
11         ) x
```

Oracle

Use the window function LAG OVER to access prior rows relative to the current row, to find the first DEPTNO for each partition:

```
1 select to_number(
2          decode(lag(deptno)over(order by deptno),
3                 deptno,null,deptno)
4          ) deptno, ename
5    from emp
```

PostgreSQL and MySQL

This recipe highlights the use of window functions for easily accessing rows around your current row. At the time of this writing, these vendors do not support window functions.

Discussion

DB2 and SQL Server

The first step is to use the window function MIN OVER to find the lowest EMPNO in each DEPTNO:

```
select deptno,
       min(empno)over(partition by deptno) min_empno,
       empno,
```

```
        ename
   from emp

 DEPTNO  MIN_EMPNO      EMPNO ENAME
 ------  ---------- ---------- ----------
     10       7782       7782 CLARK
     10       7782       7839 KING
     10       7782       7934 MILLER
     20       7369       7369 SMITH
     20       7369       7876 ADAMS
     20       7369       7902 FORD
     20       7369       7788 SCOTT
     20       7369       7566 JONES
     30       7499       7499 ALLEN
     30       7499       7698 BLAKE
     30       7499       7654 MARTIN
     30       7499       7900 JAMES
     30       7499       7844 TURNER
     30       7499       7521 WARD
```

The next and last step is to use a CASE expression to suppress the repeated display of DEPTNO. If an employee's EMPNO matches MIN_EMPNO, return DEPTNO, otherwise return NULL:

```
select case when empno=min_empno
            then deptno else null
       end deptno,
       ename
  from (
select deptno,
       min(empno)over(partition by deptno) min_empno,
       empno,
       ename
  from emp
       ) x

DEPTNO ENAME
------ ----------
    10 CLARK
       KING
       MILLER
    20 SMITH
       ADAMS
       FORD
       SCOTT
       JONES
    30 ALLEN
       BLAKE
       MARTIN
       JAMES
       TURNER
       WARD
```

Oracle

The first step is to use the window function LAG OVER to return the prior DEPTNO
for each row:

```
select lag(deptno)over(order by deptno) lag_deptno,
       deptno,
       ename
  from emp

LAG_DEPTNO    DEPTNO ENAME
----------  ---------- ----------
                   10 CLARK
        10         10 KING
        10         10 MILLER
        10         20 SMITH
        20         20 ADAMS
        20         20 FORD
        20         20 SCOTT
        20         20 JONES
        20         30 ALLEN
        30         30 BLAKE
        30         30 MARTIN
        30         30 JAMES
        30         30 TURNER
        30         30 WARD
```

If you eyeball the result set above, you can easily see where DEPTNO matches LAG_
DEPTNO. For those rows, you want to set DEPTNO to NULL. Do that by using
DECODE (TO_NUMBER is included to cast DEPTNO as a number):

```
select to_number(
            decode(lag(deptno)over(order by deptno),
                   deptno,null,deptno)
          ) deptno, ename
  from emp

DEPTNO ENAME
------ ----------
    10 CLARK
       KING
       MILLER
    20 SMITH
       ADAMS
       FORD
       SCOTT
       JONES
    30 ALLEN
       BLAKE
       MARTIN
       JAMES
       TURNER
       WARD
```

12.6 Pivoting a Result Set to Facilitate Inter-Row Calculations

Problem

You wish to make calculations involving data from multiple rows. To make your job easier, you wish to pivot those rows into columns such that all values you need are then in a single row.

In this book's example data, DEPTNO 20 is the department with the highest combined salary, which you can confirm by executing the following query:

```
select deptno, sum(sal) as sal
  from emp
 group by deptno

DEPTNO      SAL
------  ----------
    10     8750
    20    10875
    30     9400
```

You want to calculate the difference between the salaries of DEPTNO 20 and DEPTNO 10 and between DEPTNO 20 and DEPTNO 30.

Solution

Transpose the totals using the aggregate function SUM and a CASE expression. Then code your expressions in the select list:

```
1  select d20_sal - d10_sal as d20_10_diff,
2         d20_sal - d30_sal as d20_30_diff
3    from (
4  select sum(case when deptno=10 then sal end) as d10_sal,
5         sum(case when deptno=20 then sal end) as d20_sal,
6         sum(case when deptno=30 then sal end) as d30_sal
7    from emp
8         ) totals_by_dept
```

Discussion

The first step is to pivot the salaries for each DEPTNO from rows to columns by using a CASE expression:

```
select case when deptno=10 then sal end as d10_sal,
       case when deptno=20 then sal end as d20_sal,
       case when deptno=30 then sal end as d30_sal
  from emp
```

D10_SAL	D20_SAL	D30_SAL
	800	
		1600
		1250
	2975	
		1250
		2850
2450		
	3000	
5000		
		1500
	1100	
		950
	3000	
1300		

The next step is to sum all the salaries for each DEPTNO by applying the aggregate function SUM to each CASE expression:

```
select sum(case when deptno=10 then sal end) as d10_sal,
       sum(case when deptno=20 then sal end) as d20_sal,
       sum(case when deptno=30 then sal end) as d30_sal
  from emp
```

D10_SAL	D20_SAL	D30_SAL
8750	10875	9400

The final step is to simply wrap the above SQL in an inline view and perform the subtractions.

12.7 Creating Buckets of Data, of a Fixed Size

Problem

You wish to organized data into evenly sized buckets, with a predetermined number of elements in each bucket. The total number of buckets may be unknown, but you want to ensure that each bucket has five elements. For example, you want to organize the employees in table EMP into groups of five based on the value of EMPNO, as shown in the following results:

GRP	EMPNO	ENAME
1	7369	SMITH
1	7499	ALLEN
1	7521	WARD
1	7566	JONES
1	7654	MARTIN
2	7698	BLAKE
2	7782	CLARK
2	7788	SCOTT

```
2      7839 KING
2      7844 TURNER
3      7876 ADAMS
3      7900 JAMES
3      7902 FORD
3      7934 MILLER
```

Solution

The solution to this problem is greatly simplified if your RDBMS provides functions for ranking rows. Once rows are ranked, creating buckets of five is simply a matter of dividing and then taking the mathematical ceiling of the quotient.

DB2, Oracle, and SQL Server

Use the window function ROW_NUMBER OVER to rank each employee by EMPNO. Then divide by 5 to create the groups (SQL Server users will use CEIL-ING, not CEIL):

```
1 select ceil(row_number( )over(order by empno)/5.0) grp,
2        empno,
3        ename
4   from emp
```

PostgreSQL and MySQL

Use a scalar subquery to rank each EMPNO. Then divide by 5 to create the groups:

```
1  select ceil(rnk/5.0) as grp,
2         empno, ename
3    from (
4  select e.empno, e.ename,
5         (select count(*) from emp d
6           where e.empno < d.empno)+1 as rnk
7    from emp e
8         ) x
9   order by grp
```

Discussion

DB2, Oracle, and SQL Server

The window function ROW_NUMBER OVER assigns a rank or "row number" to each row sorted by EMPNO:

```
select row_number( )over(order by empno) rn,
       empno,
       ename
  from emp
```

```
RN      EMPNO ENAME
--  ---------- ----------
 1       7369 SMITH
 2       7499 ALLEN
 3       7521 WARD
 4       7566 JONES
 5       7654 MARTIN
 6       7698 BLAKE
 7       7782 CLARK
 8       7788 SCOTT
 9       7839 KING
10       7844 TURNER
11       7876 ADAMS
12       7900 JAMES
13       7902 FORD
14       7934 MILLER
```

The next step is to apply the function CEIL (or CEILING) after dividing ROW_NUMBER OVER by five. Dividing by five logically organizes the rows into groups of five, i.e., five values less than or equal to 1, five values greater than 1 but less than or equal to 2, the remaining group (composed of the last four rows since 14, the number of rows in table EMP, is not a multiple of 5) has a value greater than 2 but less than or equal to 3.

The CEIL function will return the smallest whole number greater than the value passed to it; this will create whole number groups. The results of the division and application of the CEIL are shown below. You can follow the order of operation from left to right, from RN to DIVISION to GRP:

```
select row_number()over(order by empno) rn,
       row_number()over(order by empno)/5.0 division,
       ceil(row_number()over(order by empno)/5.0) grp,
       empno,
       ename
  from emp

RN   DIVISION GRP EMPNO ENAME
--  ---------- --- ----- ----------
 1         .2   1  7369 SMITH
 2         .4   1  7499 ALLEN
 3         .6   1  7521 WARD
 4         .8   1  7566 JONES
 5          1   1  7654 MARTIN
 6        1.2   2  7698 BLAKE
 7        1.4   2  7782 CLARK
 8        1.6   2  7788 SCOTT
 9        1.8   2  7839 KING
10          2   2  7844 TURNER
11        2.2   3  7876 ADAMS
12        2.4   3  7900 JAMES
13        2.6   3  7902 FORD
14        2.8   3  7934 MILLER
```

PostgreSQL and MySQL

The first step is to use a scalar subquery to rank each row by EMPNO:

```
select (select count(*) from emp d
          where e.empno < d.empno)+1 as rnk,
        e.empno, e.ename
  from emp e
 order by 1
```

```
RNK      EMPNO ENAME
---  ---------- ----------
  1      7934 MILLER
  2      7902 FORD
  3      7900 JAMES
  4      7876 ADAMS
  5      7844 TURNER
  6      7839 KING
  7      7788 SCOTT
  8      7782 CLARK
  9      7698 BLAKE
 10      7654 MARTIN
 11      7566 JONES
 12      7521 WARD
 13      7499 ALLEN
 14      7369 SMITH
```

The next step is to apply the function CEIL after dividing RNK by 5. Dividing by 5 logically organizes the rows into groups of five, i.e., five values less than or equal to 1, five values greater than one but less than or equal to 2, the remaining group (composed of the last four rows since 14, the number of rows in table EMP, is not a multiple of 5) has a value greater than 2 but less than or equal to 3. The results of the division and application of the CEIL are shown below. You can follow the order of operation from left to right as you work your way from RNK over to GRP:

```
select rnk,
       rnk/5.0 as division,
       ceil(rnk/5.0) as grp,
       empno, ename
  from (
select e.empno, e.ename,
       (select count(*) from emp d
         where e.empno < d.empno)+1 as rnk
  from emp e
       ) x
 order by 1
```

```
RNK   DIVISION GRP EMPNO ENAME
---  ---------- --- ----- -------
  1         .2   1  7934 MILLER
  2         .4   1  7902 FORD
  3         .6   1  7900 JAMES
  4         .8   1  7876 ADAMS
```

5	1	1	7844	TURNER
6	1.2	2	7839	KING
7	1.4	2	7788	SCOTT
8	1.6	2	7782	CLARK
9	1.8	2	7698	BLAKE
10	2	2	7654	MARTIN
11	2.2	3	7566	JONES
12	2.4	3	7521	WARD
13	2.6	3	7499	ALLEN
14	2.8	3	7369	SMITH

12.8 Creating a Predefined Number of Buckets

Problem

You want to organize your data into a fixed number of buckets. For example, you want to organize the employees in table EMP into four buckets. The result set should look similar to the following:

```
GRP EMPNO ENAME
--- ----- ---------
  1  7369 SMITH
  1  7499 ALLEN
  1  7521 WARD
  1  7566 JONES
  2  7654 MARTIN
  2  7698 BLAKE
  2  7782 CLARK
  2  7788 SCOTT
  3  7839 KING
  3  7844 TURNER
  3  7876 ADAMS
  4  7900 JAMES
  4  7902 FORD
  4  7934 MILLER
```

This problem is the opposite of the previous recipe, where you had an unknown number of buckets but a predetermined number of elements in each bucket. In this recipe, the goal is such that you may not necessarily know how many elements are in each bucket, but you are defining a fixed (known) number of buckets to be created.

Solution

The solution to this problem is trivial if your RDBMS provides functions for creating "buckets" of rows. If your RDBMS provides no such functions, you can simply rank each row, and then use the modulus of said rank and n, where n is the number of buckets you wish to create, in an expression to determine into which bucket the row falls. Where available, this solution will make use of the NTILE window function for creating a fixed number of buckets. NTILE organizes an ordered set into the number

---

of buckets you specify, with any stragglers distributed into the available buckets starting from the first bucket. The desired result set for this recipe reflects this: buckets 1 and 2 have four rows while buckets 3 and 4 have three rows. If your RDBMS does not support NTILE, don't worry about which rows are in which buckets; the main goal of this recipe is to create the fixed number of buckets you are requesting.

DB2

Use the window function ROW_NUMBER OVER window function to rank the rows by EMPNO, then use the modulus of the rank and 4 to create four buckets:

```
1  select mod(row_number( )over(order by empno),4)+1 grp,
2         empno,
3         ename
4    from emp
5   order by 1
```

Oracle and SQL Server

The DB2 solution will work for these vendors but alternatively (conveniently) you may use the NTILE window function to create four buckets:

```
1  select ntile(4)over(order by empno) grp,
2         empno,
3         ename
4    from emp
```

MySQL, and PostgreSQL

Use a self join to rank the rows by EMPNO, then use the modulus of the rank and 4 to create your buckets:

```
1  select mod(count(*),4)+1 as grp,
2         e.empno,
3         e.ename
4    from emp e, emp d
5   where e.empno >= d.empno
6   group by e.empno,e.ename
7   order by 1
```

Discussion

DB2

The first step is to use the window function ROW_NUMBER OVER to rank each row by EMPNO:

```
select row_number( )over(order by empno) grp,
       empno,
       ename
  from emp
```

```
GRP EMPNO ENAME
--- ----- ------
  1  7369 SMITH
  2  7499 ALLEN
  3  7521 WARD
  4  7566 JONES
  5  7654 MARTIN
  6  7698 BLAKE
  7  7782 CLARK
  8  7788 SCOTT
  9  7839 KING
 10  7844 TURNER
 11  7876 ADAMS
 12  7900 JAMES
 13  7902 FORD
 14  7934 MILLER
```

Now that the rows are ranked, use the modulo function, MOD, to create four buckets:

```
select mod(row_number( )over(order by empno),4) grp,
       empno,
       ename
  from emp

GRP EMPNO ENAME
--- ----- ------
  1  7369 SMITH
  2  7499 ALLEN
  3  7521 WARD
  0  7566 JONES
  1  7654 MARTIN
  2  7698 BLAKE
  3  7782 CLARK
  0  7788 SCOTT
  1  7839 KING
  2  7844 TURNER
  3  7876 ADAMS
  0  7900 JAMES
  1  7902 FORD
  2  7934 MILLER
```

The last step is to add one GRP so the buckets start at 1, not 0, and use ORDER BY on GRP to order the rows by bucket.

Oracle and SQL Server

All the work is done by the NTILE function. Simply pass it a number representing the number of buckets you want, and watch the magic unfold right in front of your eyes.

MySQL and PostgreSQL

The fist step is to generate a Cartesian product with table EMP so that each EMPNO can be compared with every other EMPNO [only a snippet of the Cartesian is shown below because there would be 196 rows returned (14×14)]:

```
select e.empno,
       e.ename,
       d.empno,
       d.ename
  from emp e, emp d
```

```
EMPNO ENAME            EMPNO ENAME
----- ----------  ----------  ---------
 7369 SMITH             7369 SMITH
 7369 SMITH             7499 ALLEN
 7369 SMITH             7521 WARD
 7369 SMITH             7566 JONES
 7369 SMITH             7654 MARTIN
 7369 SMITH             7698 BLAKE
 7369 SMITH             7782 CLARK
 7369 SMITH             7788 SCOTT
 7369 SMITH             7839 KING
 7369 SMITH             7844 TURNER
 7369 SMITH             7876 ADAMS
 7369 SMITH             7900 JAMES
 7369 SMITH             7902 FORD
 7369 SMITH             7934 MILLER
 ...
```

As you can see from this result set, you can compare SMITH's EMPNO to the EMPNO of all the other employees in EMP (you can compare each employee's EMPNO with all the other employees' EMPNOs). The next step is to restrict the Cartesian product to only those EMPNOs that are greater than or equal to another EMPNO. A portion of the result set (as there are 105 rows) is shown below:

```
select e.empno,
       e.ename,
       d.empno,
       d.ename
  from emp e, emp d
 where e.empno >= d.empno
```

```
EMPNO ENAME            EMPNO ENAME
----- ----------  ----------  ----------
 7934 MILLER            7934 MILLER
 7934 MILLER            7902 FORD
 7934 MILLER            7900 JAMES
 7934 MILLER            7876 ADAMS
 7934 MILLER            7844 TURNER
 7934 MILLER            7839 KING
 7934 MILLER            7788 SCOTT
```

```
7934 MILLER          7782 CLARK
7934 MILLER          7698 BLAKE
7934 MILLER          7654 MARTIN
7934 MILLER          7566 JONES
7934 MILLER          7521 WARD
7934 MILLER          7499 ALLEN
7934 MILLER          7369 SMITH
...
7499 ALLEN           7499 ALLEN
7499 ALLEN           7369 SMITH
7369 SMITH           7369 SMITH
```

Of the entire result set, I've included only rows (from EMP E) for MILLER, ALLEN, and SMITH in this output. The reason is to show you how the Cartesian product has been restricted by the WHERE clause. Because the filter on EMPNO in the WHERE clause uses "greater than or equal to," you know you will get at least one row for each employee because each EMPNO is equal to itself. But why is there only one row for SMITH (on the left-hand side of the result set) when there are two rows for ALLEN and 14 rows for MILLER? The reason is the compound evaluation on EMPNO in the WHERE clause: "greater than or equal to". In SMITH's case, there is no EMPNO that 7369 is greater than, so only one row is returned for SMITH. In ALLEN's case, ALLEN's EMPNO is obviously equal to itself (so that row is returned), but 7499 is also greater than 7369 (SMITH's EMPNO) so two rows are returned for ALLEN. In the case of MILLER's EMPNO 7934, it is greater than all the other EMPNOs in table EMP (and obviously equal to itself) so there are 14 MILLER rows returned.

Now you can compare each EMPNO and determine which ones are greater than others. Use the aggregate function COUNT to return the self join as a more expressive result set:

```
select count(*) as grp,
       e.empno,
       e.ename
  from emp e, emp d
 where e.empno >= d.empno
 group by e.empno,e.ename
 order by 1

GRP     EMPNO ENAME
---  --------- ----------
  1       7369 SMITH
  2       7499 ALLEN
  3       7521 WARD
  4       7566 JONES
  5       7654 MARTIN
  6       7698 BLAKE
  7       7782 CLARK
  8       7788 SCOTT
```

```
9        7839 KING
10        7844 TURNER
11        7876 ADAMS
12        7900 JAMES
13        7902 FORD
14        7934 MILLER
```

Now that the rows are ranked, simply add 1 to the modulus of GRP and 4 to create
four buckets (adding 1 so the buckets start at 1, not 0). Use the ORDER BY clause
on GRP to order the buckets appropriately:

```
select mod(count(*),4)+1 as grp,
       e.empno,
       e.ename
  from emp e, emp d
 where e.empno >= d.empno
 group by e.empno,e.ename
 order by 1

GRP    EMPNO ENAME
--- ---------- ---------
  1     7900 JAMES
  1     7566 JONES
  1     7788 SCOTT
  2     7369 SMITH
  2     7902 FORD
  2     7654 MARTIN
  2     7839 KING
  3     7499 ALLEN
  3     7698 BLAKE
  3     7934 MILLER
  3     7844 TURNER
  4     7521 WARD
  4     7782 CLARK
  4     7876 ADAMS
```

12.9   Creating Horizontal Histograms

Problem

You want to use SQL to generate histograms that extend horizontally. For example,
you want to display the number of employees in each department as a horizontal histogram with each employee represented by an instance of "*". You want to return the
following result set:

```
DEPTNO CNT
------ ----------
    10 ***
    20 *****
    30 ******
```

Solution

The key to this solution is to use the aggregate function COUNT, and use GROUP BY DEPTNO to determine the number of employees in each DEPTNO. The value returned by COUNT is then passed to a string function that generates a series of "*" characters.

DB2

Use the REPEAT function to generate the histogram:

```
1 select deptno,
2        repeat('*',count(*)) cnt
3   from emp
4 group by deptno
```

Oracle, PostgreSQL, and MySQL

Use the LPAD function to generate the needed strings of "*" characters:

```
1 select deptno,
2        lpad('*',count(*),'*') as cnt
3   from emp
4 group by deptno
```

SQL Server

Generate the histogram using the REPLICATE function:

```
1 select deptno,
2        replicate('*',count(*)) cnt
3   from emp
4 group by deptno
```

Discussion

The technique is the same for all vendors. The only difference lies in the string function used to return a "*" for each employee. The Oracle solution will be used for this discussion, but the explanation is relevant for all the solutions.

The first step is to count the number of employees in each department:

```
select deptno,
       count(*)
  from emp
 group by deptno

DEPTNO    COUNT(*)
------  ----------
    10           3
    20           5
    30           6
```

The next step is to use the value returned by COUNT(*) to control the number of "*"characters to return for each department. Simply pass COUNT(*) as an argument to the string function LPAD to return the desired number of "*"s:

```
select deptno,
       lpad('*',count(*),'*') as cnt
  from emp
 group by deptno

DEPTNO CNT
------ ----------
    10 ***
    20 *****
    30 ******
```

For PostgreSQL users, you may need to explicitly cast the value returned by COUNT(*) to an integer as can be seen below:

```
select deptno,
       lpad('*',count(*)::integer,'*') as cnt
  from emp
 group by deptno

DEPTNO CNT
------ ----------
    10 ***
    20 *****
    30 ******
```

This CAST is necessary because PostgreSQL requires the numeric argument to LPAD to be an integer.

12.10 Creating Vertical Histograms

Problem

You want to generate a histogram that grows from the bottom up. For example, you want to display the number of employees in each department as a vertical histogram with each employee represented by an instance of "*". You want to return the following result set:

```
D10 D20 D30
--- --- ---
         *
     *   *
     *   *
 *   *   *
 *   *   *
 *   *   *
```

Solution

The technique used to solve this problem is built upon Recipe 12.2.

DB2, Oracle, and SQL Server

Use the ROW_NUMBER OVER function to uniquely identify each instance of "*"
for each DEPTNO. Use the aggregate function MAX to pivot the result set and group
by the values returned by ROW_NUMBER OVER (SQL Server users should not use
DESC in the ORDER BY clause):

```
 1  select max(deptno_10) d10,
 2         max(deptno_20) d20,
 3         max(deptno_30) d30
 4    from (
 5  select row_number()over(partition by deptno order by empno) rn,
 6         case when deptno=10 then '*' else null end deptno_10,
 7         case when deptno=20 then '*' else null end deptno_20,
 8         case when deptno=30 then '*' else null end deptno_30
 9    from emp
10         ) x
11   group by rn
12   order by 1 desc, 2 desc, 3 desc
```

PostgreSQL and MySQL

Use a scalar subquery to uniquely identify each instance of "*" for each DEPTNO.
Use the aggregate function MAX on the values returned by inline view X, while also
grouping by RNK to pivot the result set. MySQL users should not use DESC in the
ORDER BY clause:

```
 1  select max(deptno_10) as d10,
 2         max(deptno_20) as d20,
 3         max(deptno_30) as d30
 4    from (
 5  select case when e.deptno=10 then '*' else null end deptno_10,
 6         case when e.deptno=20 then '*' else null end deptno_20,
 7         case when e.deptno=30 then '*' else null end deptno_30,
 8         (select count(*) from emp d
 9            where e.deptno=d.deptno and e.empno < d.empno ) as rnk
10    from emp e
11         ) x
12   group by rnk
13   order by 1 desc, 2 desc, 3 desc
```

Discussion

DB2, Oracle, and SQL Server

The first step is to use the window function ROW_NUMBER to uniquely identify
each instance of "*" in each department. Use a CASE expression to return a "*" for
each employee in each department:

```
select row_number()over(partition by deptno order by empno) rn,
       case when deptno=10 then '*' else null end deptno_10,
       case when deptno=20 then '*' else null end deptno_20,
```

```
            case when deptno=30 then '*' else null end deptno_30
    from emp


RN DEPTNO_10  DEPTNO_20  DEPTNO_30
-- ----------  ----------  ---------
 1 *
 2 *
 3 *
 1                *
 2                *
 3                *
 4                *
 5                *
 1                           *
 2                           *
 3                           *
 4                           *
 5                           *
 6                           *
```

The next and last step is to use the aggregate function MAX on each CASE expression, grouping by RN to remove the NULLs from the result set. Order the results ASC or DESC depending on how your RDBMS sorts NULLs:

```
select max(deptno_10) d10,
       max(deptno_20) d20,
       max(deptno_30) d30
  from (
select row_number()over(partition by deptno order by empno) rn,
       case when deptno=10 then '*' else null end deptno_10,
       case when deptno=20 then '*' else null end deptno_20,
       case when deptno=30 then '*' else null end deptno_30
  from emp
       ) x
 group by rn
 order by 1 desc, 2 desc, 3 desc

D10 D20 D30
--- --- ---
         *
     *   *
     *   *
 *   *   *
 *   *   *
 *   *   *
```

PostgreSQL and MySQL

The first step is to use a scalar subquery to uniquely identify each instance of "*" in each department. The scalar subquery ranks the employees by EMPNO in each DEPTNO, so there can be no duplicates. Use a CASE expression to generate a "*" for each employee in each department:

```
select case when e.deptno=10 then '*' else null end deptno_10,
       case when e.deptno=20 then '*' else null end deptno_20,
       case when e.deptno=30 then '*' else null end deptno_30,
       (select count(*) from emp d
          where e.deptno=d.deptno and e.empno < d.empno ) as rnk
  from emp e
```

DEPTNO_10	DEPTNO_20	DEPTNO_30	RNK
	*		4
		*	5
		*	4
	*		3
		*	3
		*	2
*			2
	*		2
*			1
		*	1
	*		1
		*	0
	*		0
*			0

Then use the aggregate function MAX on each CASE expression, being sure to group by RNK to remove the NULLs from the result set. Order the results ASC or DESC depending on how your RDBMS sorts NULLs:

```
select max(deptno_10) as d10,
       max(deptno_20) as d20,
       max(deptno_30) as d30
  from (
select case when e.deptno=10 then '*' else null end deptno_10,
       case when e.deptno=20 then '*' else null end deptno_20,
       case when e.deptno=30 then '*' else null end deptno_30,
       (select count(*) from emp d
          where e.deptno=d.deptno and e.empno < d.empno ) as rnk
  from emp e
       ) x
 group by rnk
 order by 1 desc, 2 desc, 3 desc
```

D10	D20	D30
		*
	*	*
	*	*
*	*	*
*	*	*
*	*	*

12.11 Returning Non-GROUP BY Columns

Problem

You are executing a GROUP BY query, and you wish to return columns in your select list that are not also listed in your GROUP BY clause. This is not normally possible, as such ungrouped columns would not represent a single value per row.

Say that you want to find the employees who earn the highest and lowest salaries in each department, as well as the employees who earn the highest and lowest salaries in each job. You want to see each employee's name, the department he works in, his job title, and his salary. You want to return the following result set:

```
DEPTNO ENAME  JOB         SAL DEPT_STATUS      JOB_STATUS
------ ------ --------- ----- ---------------- ---------------
    10 MILLER CLERK      1300 LOW SAL IN DEPT  TOP SAL IN JOB
    10 CLARK  MANAGER    2450                  LOW SAL IN JOB
    10 KING   PRESIDENT  5000 TOP SAL IN DEPT  TOP SAL IN JOB
    20 SCOTT  ANALYST    3000 TOP SAL IN DEPT  TOP SAL IN JOB
    20 FORD   ANALYST    3000 TOP SAL IN DEPT  TOP SAL IN JOB
    20 SMITH  CLERK       800 LOW SAL IN DEPT  LOW SAL IN JOB
    20 JONES  MANAGER    2975                  TOP SAL IN JOB
    30 JAMES  CLERK       950 LOW SAL IN DEPT
    30 MARTIN SALESMAN   1250                  LOW SAL IN JOB
    30 WARD   SALESMAN   1250                  LOW SAL IN JOB
    30 ALLEN  SALESMAN   1600                  TOP SAL IN JOB
    30 BLAKE  MANAGER    2850 TOP SAL IN DEPT
```

Unfortunately, including all these columns in the SELECT clause will ruin the grouping. Consider the following example. Employee "KING" earns the highest salary. You want to verify this with the following query:

```
select ename,max(sal)
  from emp
 group by ename
```

Instead of seeing "KING" and KING's salary, the above query will return all 14 rows from table EMP. The reason is because of the grouping: the MAX(SAL) is applied to each ENAME. So, it would seem the above query can be stated as "find the employee with the highest salary" but in fact what it is doing is "find the highest salary for each ENAME in table EMP." This recipe explains a technique for including ENAME without the need to GROUP BY that column.

Solution

Use an inline view to find the high and low salaries by DEPTNO and JOB. Then keep only the employees who make those salaries.

DB2, Oracle, and SQL Server

Use the window functions MAX OVER and MIN OVER to find the highest and lowest salaries by DEPTNO and JOB. Then keep the rows where the salaries are those that are highest or lowest by DEPTNO or JOB:

```
1   select deptno,ename,job,sal,
2          case when sal = max_by_dept
3               then 'TOP SAL IN DEPT'
4               when sal = min_by_dept
5               then 'LOW SAL IN DEPT'
6          end dept_status,
7          case when sal = max_by_job
8               then 'TOP SAL IN JOB'
9               when sal = min_by_job
10              then 'LOW SAL IN JOB'
11         end job_status
12    from (
13  select deptno,ename,job,sal,
14         max(sal)over(partition by deptno) max_by_dept,
15         max(sal)over(partition by job)    max_by_job,
16         min(sal)over(partition by deptno) min_by_dept,
17         min(sal)over(partition by job)    min_by_job
18    from emp
19         ) emp_sals
20   where sal in (max_by_dept,max_by_job,
21                 min_by_dept,min_by_job)
```

PostgreSQL and MySQL

Use scalar subqueries to find the highest and lowest salaries by DEPTNO and JOB. Then keep only those employees who match those salaries:

```
1   select deptno,ename,job,sal,
2          case when sal = max_by_dept
3               then 'TOP SAL IN DEPT'
4               when sal = min_by_dept
5               then 'LOW SAL IN DEPT'
6          end as dept_status,
7          case when sal = max_by_job
8               then 'TOP SAL IN JOB'
9               when sal = min_by_job
10              then 'LOW SAL IN JOB'
11         end as job_status
12    from (
13  select e.deptno,e.ename,e.job,e.sal,
14         (select max(sal) from  emp d
15           where d.deptno = e.deptno) as max_by_dept,
16         (select max(sal) from  emp d
17           where d.job = e.job) as max_by_job,
18         (select min(sal) from  emp d
19           where d.deptno = e.deptno) as min_by_dept,
20         (select min(sal) from  emp d
21           where d.job = e.job) as min_by_job
```

```
22    from emp e
23         ) x
24   where sal in (max_by_dept,max_by_job,
25                 min_by_dept,min_by_job)
```

Discussion

DB2, Oracle, and SQL Server

The first step is to use the window functions MAX OVER and MIN OVER to find the highest and lowest salaries by DEPTNO and JOB:

```
select deptno,ename,job,sal,
       max(sal)over(partition by deptno) maxDEPT,
       max(sal)over(partition by job)    maxJOB,
       min(sal)over(partition by deptno) minDEPT,
       min(sal)over(partition by job)    minJOB
  from emp
```

DEPTNO	ENAME	JOB	SAL	MAXDEPT	MAXJOB	MINDEPT	MINJOB
10	MILLER	CLERK	1300	5000	1300	1300	800
10	CLARK	MANAGER	2450	5000	2975	1300	2450
10	KING	PRESIDENT	5000	5000	5000	1300	5000
20	SCOTT	ANALYST	3000	3000	3000	800	3000
20	FORD	ANALYST	3000	3000	3000	800	3000
20	SMITH	CLERK	800	3000	1300	800	800
20	JONES	MANAGER	2975	3000	2975	800	2450
20	ADAMS	CLERK	1100	3000	1300	800	800
30	JAMES	CLERK	950	2850	1300	950	800
30	MARTIN	SALESMAN	1250	2850	1600	950	1250
30	TURNER	SALESMAN	1500	2850	1600	950	1250
30	WARD	SALESMAN	1250	2850	1600	950	1250
30	ALLEN	SALESMAN	1600	2850	1600	950	1250
30	BLAKE	MANAGER	2850	2850	2975	950	2450

At this point, every salary can be compared with the highest and lowest salaries by DEPTNO and JOB. Notice that the grouping (the inclusion of multiple columns in the SELECT clause) does not affect the values returned by MIN OVER and MAX OVER. This is the beauty of window functions: the aggregate is computed over a defined "group" or partition and returns multiple rows for each group. The last step is to simply wrap the window functions in an inline view and keep only those rows that match the values returned by the window functions. Use a simple CASE expression to display the "status" of each employee in the final result set:

```
select deptno,ename,job,sal,
       case when sal = max_by_dept
            then 'TOP SAL IN DEPT'
            when sal = min_by_dept
            then 'LOW SAL IN DEPT'
       end dept_status,
       case when sal = max_by_job
```

```
                then 'TOP SAL IN JOB'
                when sal = min_by_job
                then 'LOW SAL IN JOB'
          end job_status
     from (
select deptno,ename,job,sal,
          max(sal)over(partition by deptno) max_by_dept,
          max(sal)over(partition by job) max_by_job,
          min(sal)over(partition by deptno) min_by_dept,
          min(sal)over(partition by job) min_by_job
     from emp
          ) x
     where sal in (max_by_dept,max_by_job,
                   min_by_dept,min_by_job)


DEPTNO ENAME  JOB           SAL DEPT_STATUS      JOB_STATUS
------ ------ --------- ------- ---------------- ---------------
    10 MILLER CLERK        1300 LOW SAL IN DEPT  TOP SAL IN JOB
    10 CLARK  MANAGER      2450                  LOW SAL IN JOB
    10 KING   PRESIDENT    5000 TOP SAL IN DEPT  TOP SAL IN JOB
    20 SCOTT  ANALYST      3000 TOP SAL IN DEPT  TOP SAL IN JOB
    20 FORD   ANALYST      3000 TOP SAL IN DEPT  TOP SAL IN JOB
    20 SMITH  CLERK         800 LOW SAL IN DEPT  LOW SAL IN JOB
    20 JONES  MANAGER      2975                  TOP SAL IN JOB
    30 JAMES  CLERK         950 LOW SAL IN DEPT
    30 MARTIN SALESMAN     1250                  LOW SAL IN JOB
    30 WARD   SALESMAN     1250                  LOW SAL IN JOB
    30 ALLEN  SALESMAN     1600                  TOP SAL IN JOB
    30 BLAKE  MANAGER      2850 TOP SAL IN DEPT
```

PostgreSQL and MySQL

The first step is to use scalar subqueries to find the highest and lowest salaries by
DEPTNO and JOB:

```
select e.deptno,e.ename,e.job,e.sal,
          (select max(sal) from  emp d
            where d.deptno = e.deptno) as maxDEPT,
          (select max(sal) from  emp d
            where d.job = e.job) as maxJOB,
          (select min(sal) from  emp d
            where d.deptno = e.deptno) as minDEPT,
          (select min(sal) from  emp d
            where d.job = e.job) as minJOB
     from emp e


DEPTNO ENAME  JOB          SAL MAXDEPT MAXJOB MINDEPT MINJOB
------ ------ --------- ------ ------- ------ ------- ------
    20 SMITH  CLERK        800    3000   1300     800    800
    30 ALLEN  SALESMAN    1600    2850   1600     950   1250
    30 WARD   SALESMAN    1250    2850   1600     950   1250
    20 JONES  MANAGER     2975    3000   2975     800   2450
    30 MARTIN SALESMAN    1250    2850   1600     950   1250
    30 BLAKE  MANAGER     2850    2850   2975     950   2450
    10 CLARK  MANAGER     2450    5000   2975    1300   2450
```

20	SCOTT	ANALYST	3000	3000	3000	800	3000
10	KING	PRESIDENT	5000	5000	5000	1300	5000
30	TURNER	SALESMAN	1500	2850	1600	950	1250
20	ADAMS	CLERK	1100	3000	1300	800	800
30	JAMES	CLERK	950	2850	1300	950	800
20	FORD	ANALYST	3000	3000	3000	800	3000
10	MILLER	CLERK	1300	5000	1300	1300	800

The highest and lowest salaries by DEPTNO and JOB can now be compared with all other salaries in table EMP. The final step is to wrap the scalar subqueries in an inline view and simply keep the employees whose salaries match one of the scalar subqueries. Use a CASE expression to display each employee's status in the final result set:

```
select deptno,ename,job,sal,
       case when sal = max_by_dept
            then 'TOP SAL IN DEPT'
            when sal = min_by_dept
            then 'LOW SAL IN DEPT'
       end as dept_status,
       case when sal = max_by_job
            then 'TOP SAL IN JOB'
            when sal = min_by_job
            then 'LOW SAL IN JOB'
       end as job_status
  from (
select e.deptno,e.ename,e.job,e.sal,
       (select max(sal) from  emp d
         where d.deptno = e.deptno) as max_by_dept,
       (select max(sal) from  emp d
         where d.job = e.job) as max_by_job,
       (select min(sal) from  emp d
         where d.deptno = e.deptno) as min_by_dept,
       (select min(sal) from  emp d
         where d.job = e.job) as min_by_job
  from emp e
       ) x
 where sal in (max_by_dept,max_by_job,
               min_by_dept,min_by_job)
```

DEPTNO	ENAME	JOB	SAL	DEPT_STATUS	JOB_STATUS
10	CLARK	MANAGER	2450		LOW SAL IN JOB
10	KING	PRESIDENT	5000	TOP SAL IN DEPT	TOP SAL IN JOB
10	MILLER	CLERK	1300	LOW SAL IN DEPT	TOP SAL IN JOB
20	SMITH	CLERK	800	LOW SAL IN DEPT	LOW SAL IN JOB
20	FORD	ANALYST	3000	TOP SAL IN DEPT	TOP SAL IN JOB
20	SCOTT	ANALYST	3000	TOP SAL IN DEPT	TOP SAL IN JOB
20	JONES	MANAGER	2975		TOP SAL IN JOB
30	ALLEN	SALESMAN	1600		TOP SAL IN JOB
30	BLAKE	MANAGER	2850	TOP SAL IN DEPT	
30	MARTIN	SALESMAN	1250		LOW SAL IN JOB
30	JAMES	CLERK	950	LOW SAL IN DEPT	
30	WARD	SALESMAN	1250		LOW SAL IN JOB

12.12 Calculating Simple Subtotals

Problem

For the purposes of this recipe, a "simple subtotal" is defined as a result set that contains values from the aggregation of one column along with a grand total value for the table. An example would be a result set that sums the salaries in table EMP by JOB, and that also includes the sum of all salaries in table EMP. The summed salaries by JOB are the subtotals, and the sum of all salaries in table EMP is the grand total. Such a result set should look as follows:

```
JOB            SAL
---------  ----------
ANALYST        6000
CLERK          4150
MANAGER        8275
PRESIDENT      5000
SALESMAN       5600
TOTAL         29025
```

Solution

The ROLLUP extension to the GROUP BY clause solves this problem perfectly. If ROLLUP is not available for your RDBMS, you can solve the problem, albeit with more difficulty, using a scalar subquery or a UNION query.

DB2 and Oracle

Use the aggregate function SUM to sum the salaries, and use the ROLLUP extension of GROUP BY to organize the results into subtotals (by JOB) and a grand total (for the whole table):

```
1 select case grouping(job)
2             when 0 then job
3             else 'TOTAL'
4        end job,
5        sum(sal) sal
6   from emp
7  group by rollup(job)
```

SQL Server and MySQL

Use the aggregate function SUM to sum the salaries, and use WITH ROLLUP to organize the results into subtotals (by JOB) and a grand total (for the whole table). Then use COALESCE to supply the label 'TOTAL' for the grand total row (which will otherwise have a NULL in the job column):

```
1 select coalesce(job,'TOTAL') job,
2        sum(sal) sal
3   from emp
4  group by job with rollup
```

With SQL Server, you also have the option to use the GROUPING function shown in the Oracle/DB2 recipe rather than COALESCE to determine the level of aggregation.

PostgreSQL

Use the aggregate function SUM to sum the salaries by DEPTNO. Then UNION ALL with a query generating the sum of all the salaries in the table:

```
1 select job, sum(sal) as sal
2   from emp
3  group by job
4  union all
5 select 'TOTAL', sum(sal)
6   from emp
```

Discussion

DB2 and Oracle

The first step is to use the aggregate function SUM, grouping by JOB in order to sum the salaries by JOB:

```
select job, sum(sal) sal
  from emp
 group by job
```

JOB	SAL
ANALYST	6000
CLERK	4150
MANAGER	8275
PRESIDENT	5000
SALESMAN	5600

The next step is to use the ROLLUP extension to GROUP BY to produce a grand total for all salaries along with the subtotals for each JOB:

```
select job, sum(sal) sal
  from emp
 group by rollup(job)
```

JOB	SAL
ANALYST	6000
CLERK	4150
MANAGER	8275
PRESIDENT	5000
SALESMAN	5600
	29025

The last step is to use the GROUPING function in the JOB column to display a label for the grand total. If the value of JOB is NULL, the GROUPING function will return 1, which signifies that the value for SAL is the grand total created by ROLLUP. If the value of JOB is not NULL, the GROUPING function will return 0, which signifies the value for SAL is the result of the GROUP BY, not the ROLLUP. Wrap the call to GROUPING(JOB) in a CASE expression that returns either the job name or the label 'TOTAL', as appropriate:

```
select case grouping(job)
            when 0 then job
            else 'TOTAL'
       end job,
       sum(sal) sal
  from emp
 group by rollup(job)
```

```
JOB               SAL
---------  ----------
ANALYST          6000
CLERK            4150
MANAGER          8275
PRESIDENT        5000
SALESMAN         5600
TOTAL           29025
```

SQL Server and MySQL

The first step is to use the aggregate function SUM, grouping the results by JOB to generate salary sums by JOB:

```
select job, sum(sal) sal
  from emp
 group by job
```

```
JOB        SAL
---------  -----
ANALYST    6000
CLERK      4150
MANAGER    8275
PRESIDENT  5000
SALESMAN   5600
```

The next step is to use GROUP BY's ROLLUP extension to produce a grand total for all salaries along with the subtotals for each JOB:

```
select job, sum(sal) sal
  from emp
 group by job with rollup
```

```
JOB        SAL
---------  -------
ANALYST    6000
CLERK      4150
MANAGER    8275
PRESIDENT  5000
SALESMAN   5600
           29025
```

The last step is to use the COEALESCE function against the JOB column. If the value of JOB is NULL, the value for SAL is the grand total created by ROLLUP. If the value of JOB is not NULL, the value for SAL is the result of the "regular" GROUP BY, not the ROLLUP:

```
select coalesce(job,'TOTAL') job,
       sum(sal) sal
  from emp
 group by job with rollup
```

```
JOB              SAL
---------   ----------
ANALYST          6000
CLERK            4150
MANAGER          8275
PRESIDENT        5000
SALESMAN         5600
TOTAL           29025
```

PostgreSQL

The first step is to group the results by job, using the aggregate function SUM to return salary totals by JOB:

```
select job, sum(sal) sal
  from emp
 group by job
```

```
JOB         SAL
---------   -----
ANALYST     6000
CLERK       4150
MANAGER     8275
PRESIDENT   5000
SALESMAN    5600
```

The last step is to use a UNION ALL to supply the grand total to the above query:

```
select job, sum(sal) as sal
  from emp
 group by job
 union all
select 'TOTAL', sum(sal)
  from emp
```

```
JOB         SAL
---------   -------
ANALYST     6000
CLERK       4150
MANAGER     8275
PRESIDENT   5000
SALESMAN    5600
TOTAL       29025
```

12.13 Calculating Subtotals for All Possible Expression Combinations

Problem

You want to find the sum of all salaries by DEPTNO, and by JOB, for every JOB/DEPTNO combination. You also want a grand total for all salaries in table EMP. You want to return the following result set:

```
DEPTNO JOB       CATEGORY                  SAL
------ --------- --------------------- -------
    10 CLERK     TOTAL BY DEPT AND JOB    1300
    10 MANAGER   TOTAL BY DEPT AND JOB    2450
    10 PRESIDENT TOTAL BY DEPT AND JOB    5000
    20 CLERK     TOTAL BY DEPT AND JOB    1900
    30 CLERK     TOTAL BY DEPT AND JOB     950
    30 SALESMAN  TOTAL BY DEPT AND JOB    5600
    30 MANAGER   TOTAL BY DEPT AND JOB    2850
    20 MANAGER   TOTAL BY DEPT AND JOB    2975
    20 ANALYST   TOTAL BY DEPT AND JOB    6000
       CLERK     TOTAL BY JOB             4150
       ANALYST   TOTAL BY JOB             6000
       MANAGER   TOTAL BY JOB             8275
       PRESIDENT TOTAL BY JOB             5000
       SALESMAN  TOTAL BY JOB             5600
    10           TOTAL BY DEPT            8750
    30           TOTAL BY DEPT            9400
    20           TOTAL BY DEPT           10875
                 GRAND TOTAL FOR TABLE   29025
```

Solution

Extensions added to GROUP BY in recent years make this a fairly easy problem to solve. If your platform does not supply such extensions for computing various levels of subtotals, then you must compute them manually (via self joins or scalar subqueries).

DB2

For DB2, you will need to CAST the results from GROUPING to the CHAR(1) data type:

```
1  select deptno,
2         job,
3         case cast(grouping(deptno) as char(1))||
4              cast(grouping(job) as char(1))
5              when '00' then 'TOTAL BY DEPT AND JOB'
6              when '10' then 'TOTAL BY JOB'
7              when '01' then 'TOTAL BY DEPT'
8              when '11' then 'TOTAL FOR TABLE'
9         end category,
10        sum(sal)
```

```
11    from emp
12   group by cube(deptno,job)
13   order by grouping(job),grouping(deptno)
```

Oracle

Use the CUBE extension to the GROUP BY clause with the concatenation operator ||:

```
1  select deptno,
2         job,
3         case grouping(deptno)||grouping(job)
4              when '00' then 'TOTAL BY DEPT AND JOB'
5              when '10' then 'TOTAL BY JOB'
6              when '01' then 'TOTAL BY DEPT'
7              when '11' then 'GRAND TOTAL FOR TABLE'
8         end category,
9         sum(sal) sal
10   from emp
11  group by cube(deptno,job)
12  order by grouping(job),grouping(deptno)
```

SQL Server

Use the CUBE extension to the GROUP BY clause. For SQL Server, you will need to CAST the results from GROUPING to CHAR(1), and you will need to use the + operator for concatenation (as opposed to Oracle's || operator):

```
1  select deptno,
2         job,
3         case cast(grouping(deptno)as char(1))+
4              cast(grouping(job)as char(1))
5              when '00' then 'TOTAL BY DEPT AND JOB'
6              when '10' then 'TOTAL BY JOB'
7              when '01' then 'TOTAL BY DEPT'
8              when '11' then 'GRAND TOTAL FOR TABLE'
9         end category,
10         sum(sal) sal
11   from emp
12  group by deptno,job with cube
13  order by grouping(job),grouping(deptno)
```

PostgreSQL and MySQL

Use multiple UNION ALLs, creating different sums for each:

```
1  select deptno, job,
2         'TOTAL BY DEPT AND JOB' as category,
3         sum(sal) as sal
4    from emp
5   group by deptno, job
6   union all
7  select null, job, 'TOTAL BY JOB', sum(sal)
8    from emp
9   group by job
```

```
10   union all
11   select deptno, null, 'TOTAL BY DEPT', sum(sal)
12     from emp
13     group by deptno
14   union all
15   select null,null,'GRAND TOTAL FOR TABLE', sum(sal)
16     from emp
```

Discussion

Oracle, DB2, and SQL Server

The solutions for all three are essentially the same. The first step is to use the aggregate function SUM and group by both DEPTNO and JOB to find the total salaries for each JOB and DEPTNO combination:

```
select deptno, job, sum(sal) sal
  from emp
 group by deptno, job

DEPTNO JOB            SAL
------ ---------  -------
    10 CLERK         1300
    10 MANAGER       2450
    10 PRESIDENT     5000
    20 CLERK         1900
    20 ANALYST       6000
    20 MANAGER       2975
    30 CLERK          950
    30 MANAGER       2850
    30 SALESMAN      5600
```

The next step is to create subtotals by JOB and DEPTNO along with the grand total for the whole table. Use the CUBE extension to the GROUP BY clause to perform aggregations on SAL by DEPTNO, JOB, and for the whole table:

```
select deptno,
       job,
       sum(sal) sal
  from emp
 group by cube(deptno,job)

DEPTNO JOB            SAL
------ ---------  -------
                    29025
       CLERK         4150
       ANALYST       6000
       MANAGER       8275
       SALESMAN      5600
       PRESIDENT     5000
    10                8750
    10 CLERK         1300
    10 MANAGER       2450
    10 PRESIDENT     5000
```

```
20              10875
   20 CLERK       1900
   20 ANALYST     6000
   20 MANAGER     2975
30               9400
   30 CLERK        950
   30 MANAGER     2850
   30 SALESMAN    5600
```

Next, use the GROUPING function in conjunction with CASE to format the results into more meaningful output. The value from GROUPING(JOB) will be 1 or 0 depending on whether or not the values for SAL are due to the GROUP BY or the CUBE. If the results are due to the CUBE, the value will be 1, otherwise it will be 0. The same goes for GROUPING(DEPTNO). Looking at the first step of the solution, you should see that grouping is done by DEPTNO and JOB. Thus, the expected values from the calls to GROUPING when a row represents a combination of both DEPTNO and JOB is 0. The query below confirms this:

```
select deptno,
       job,
       grouping(deptno) is_deptno_subtotal,
       grouping(job) is_job_subtotal,
       sum(sal) sal
  from emp
 group by cube(deptno,job)
 order by 3,4
```

DEPTNO	JOB	IS_DEPTNO_SUBTOTAL	IS_JOB_SUBTOTAL	SAL
10	CLERK	0	0	1300
10	MANAGER	0	0	2450
10	PRESIDENT	0	0	5000
20	CLERK	0	0	1900
30	CLERK	0	0	950
30	SALESMAN	0	0	5600
30	MANAGER	0	0	2850
20	MANAGER	0	0	2975
20	ANALYST	0	0	6000
10		0	1	8750
20		0	1	10875
30		0	1	9400
	CLERK	1	0	4150
	ANALYST	1	0	6000
	MANAGER	1	0	8275
	PRESIDENT	1	0	5000
	SALESMAN	1	0	5600
		1	1	29025

The final step is to use a CASE expression to determine which category each row belongs to based on the values returned by GROUPING(JOB) and GROUPING(DEPTNO) concatenated:

```
select deptno,
       job,
       case grouping(deptno)||grouping(job)
            when '00' then 'TOTAL BY DEPT AND JOB'
            when '10' then 'TOTAL BY JOB'
            when '01' then 'TOTAL BY DEPT'
            when '11' then 'GRAND TOTAL FOR TABLE'
       end category,
       sum(sal) sal
  from emp
 group by cube(deptno,job)
 order by grouping(job),grouping(deptno)

DEPTNO JOB        CATEGORY                    SAL
------ ---------  ---------------------  -------
    10 CLERK      TOTAL BY DEPT AND JOB     1300
    10 MANAGER    TOTAL BY DEPT AND JOB     2450
    10 PRESIDENT  TOTAL BY DEPT AND JOB     5000
    20 CLERK      TOTAL BY DEPT AND JOB     1900
    30 CLERK      TOTAL BY DEPT AND JOB      950
    30 SALESMAN   TOTAL BY DEPT AND JOB     5600
    30 MANAGER    TOTAL BY DEPT AND JOB     2850
    20 MANAGER    TOTAL BY DEPT AND JOB     2975
    20 ANALYST    TOTAL BY DEPT AND JOB     6000
       CLERK      TOTAL BY JOB              4150
       ANALYST    TOTAL BY JOB              6000
       MANAGER    TOTAL BY JOB              8275
       PRESIDENT  TOTAL BY JOB              5000
       SALESMAN   TOTAL BY JOB              5600
    10            TOTAL BY DEPT             8750
    30            TOTAL BY DEPT             9400
    20            TOTAL BY DEPT            10875
                  GRAND TOTAL FOR TABLE    29025
```

This Oracle solution implicitly converts the results from the GROUPING functions to a character type in preparation for concatenating the two values. DB2 and SQL Server users will need to explicitly CAST the results of the GROUPING functions to CHAR(1) as shown in the solution. In addition, SQL Server users must use the + operator, and not the || operator, to concatenate the results from the two GROUPING calls into one string.

For Oracle and DB2 users, there is an additional extension to GROUP BY called GROUPING SETS; this extension is extremely useful. For example, you can use GROUPING SETS to mimic the output created by CUBE as is done below (DB2 and SQL Server users will need to add explicit CASTS to the values returned by the GROUPING function just as in the CUBE solution):

```
select deptno,
       job,
       case grouping(deptno)||grouping(job)
            when '00' then 'TOTAL BY DEPT AND JOB'
            when '10' then 'TOTAL BY JOB'
            when '01' then 'TOTAL BY DEPT'
```

```
              when '11' then 'GRAND TOTAL FOR TABLE'
         end category,
         sum(sal) sal
    from emp
 group by grouping sets ((deptno),(job),(deptno,job),())

DEPTNO JOB       CATEGORY                   SAL
------ --------- -------------------- -------
    10 CLERK     TOTAL BY DEPT AND JOB   1300
    20 CLERK     TOTAL BY DEPT AND JOB   1900
    30 CLERK     TOTAL BY DEPT AND JOB    950
    20 ANALYST   TOTAL BY DEPT AND JOB   6000
    10 MANAGER   TOTAL BY DEPT AND JOB   2450
    20 MANAGER   TOTAL BY DEPT AND JOB   2975
    30 MANAGER   TOTAL BY DEPT AND JOB   2850
    30 SALESMAN  TOTAL BY DEPT AND JOB   5600
    10 PRESIDENT TOTAL BY DEPT AND JOB   5000
       CLERK     TOTAL BY JOB            4150
       ANALYST   TOTAL BY JOB            6000
       MANAGER   TOTAL BY JOB            8275
       SALESMAN  TOTAL BY JOB            5600
       PRESIDENT TOTAL BY JOB            5000
    10           TOTAL BY DEPT           8750
    20           TOTAL BY DEPT          10875
    30           TOTAL BY DEPT           9400
                 GRAND TOTAL FOR TABLE  29025
```

What's great about GROUPING SETS is that it allows you to define the groups. The GROUPING SETS clause in the preceding query causes groups to be created by DEPTNO, by JOB, by the combination of DEPTNO and JOB, and finally the empty parenthesis requests a grand total. GROUPING SETS gives you enormous flexibility for creating reports with different levels of aggregation; for example, if you wanted to modify the preceding example to exclude the GRAND TOTAL, simply modify the GROUPING SETS clause by excluding the empty parentheses:

```
/* no grand total */

select deptno,
       job,
       case grouping(deptno)||grouping(job)
            when '00' then 'TOTAL BY DEPT AND JOB'
            when '10' then 'TOTAL BY JOB'
            when '01' then 'TOTAL BY DEPT'
            when '11' then 'GRAND TOTAL FOR TABLE'
       end category,
       sum(sal) sal
  from emp
 group by grouping sets ((deptno),(job),(deptno,job))

DEPTNO JOB       CATEGORY                    SAL
------ --------- -------------------- ----------
    10 CLERK     TOTAL BY DEPT AND JOB      1300
    20 CLERK     TOTAL BY DEPT AND JOB      1900
```

```
30 CLERK     TOTAL BY DEPT AND JOB     950
20 ANALYST   TOTAL BY DEPT AND JOB    6000
10 MANAGER   TOTAL BY DEPT AND JOB    2450
20 MANAGER   TOTAL BY DEPT AND JOB    2975
30 MANAGER   TOTAL BY DEPT AND JOB    2850
30 SALESMAN  TOTAL BY DEPT AND JOB    5600
10 PRESIDENT TOTAL BY DEPT AND JOB    5000
   CLERK     TOTAL BY JOB             4150
   ANALYST   TOTAL BY JOB             6000
   MANAGER   TOTAL BY JOB             8275
   SALESMAN  TOTAL BY JOB             5600
   PRESIDENT TOTAL BY JOB             5000
10           TOTAL BY DEPT            8750
20           TOTAL BY DEPT           10875
30           TOTAL BY DEPT            9400
```

You can also eliminate a subtotal, such as the one on DEPTNO, simply by omitting (DEPTNO) from the GROUPING SETS clause:

```
/* no subtotals by DEPTNO */

select deptno,
       job,
       case grouping(deptno)||grouping(job)
            when '00' then 'TOTAL BY DEPT AND JOB'
            when '10' then 'TOTAL BY JOB'
            when '01' then 'TOTAL BY DEPT'
            when '11' then 'GRAND TOTAL FOR TABLE'
       end category,
       sum(sal) sal
  from emp
group by grouping sets ((job),(deptno,job),())
order by 3
```

```
DEPTNO JOB        CATEGORY                      SAL
------ ---------- --------------------- ----------
                  GRAND TOTAL FOR TABLE       29025
    10 CLERK      TOTAL BY DEPT AND JOB        1300
    20 CLERK      TOTAL BY DEPT AND JOB        1900
    30 CLERK      TOTAL BY DEPT AND JOB         950
    20 ANALYST    TOTAL BY DEPT AND JOB        6000
    20 MANAGER    TOTAL BY DEPT AND JOB        2975
    30 MANAGER    TOTAL BY DEPT AND JOB        2850
    30 SALESMAN   TOTAL BY DEPT AND JOB        5600
    10 PRESIDENT  TOTAL BY DEPT AND JOB        5000
    10 MANAGER    TOTAL BY DEPT AND JOB        2450
       CLERK      TOTAL BY JOB                 4150
       SALESMAN   TOTAL BY JOB                 5600
       PRESIDENT  TOTAL BY JOB                 5000
       MANAGER    TOTAL BY JOB                 8275
       ANALYST    TOTAL BY JOB                 6000
```

As you can see, GROUPING SETS makes it very easy indeed to play around with totals and subtotals in order to look at your data from different angles.

PostgreSQL and MySQL

The first step is to use the aggregate function SUM and group by both DEPTNO and JOB:

```
select deptno, job,
       'TOTAL BY DEPT AND JOB' as category,
       sum(sal) as sal
  from emp
group by deptno, job
```

```
DEPTNO JOB        CATEGORY                    SAL
------ ---------- --------------------- -------
    10 CLERK      TOTAL BY DEPT AND JOB   1300
    10 MANAGER    TOTAL BY DEPT AND JOB   2450
    10 PRESIDENT  TOTAL BY DEPT AND JOB   5000
    20 CLERK      TOTAL BY DEPT AND JOB   1900
    20 ANALYST    TOTAL BY DEPT AND JOB   6000
    20 MANAGER    TOTAL BY DEPT AND JOB   2975
    30 CLERK      TOTAL BY DEPT AND JOB    950
    30 MANAGER    TOTAL BY DEPT AND JOB   2850
    30 SALESMAN   TOTAL BY DEPT AND JOB   5600
```

The next step is to UNION ALL the sum of all the salaries by JOB:

```
select deptno, job,
       'TOTAL BY DEPT AND JOB' as category,
       sum(sal) as sal
  from emp
group by deptno, job
union all
select null, job, 'TOTAL BY JOB', sum(sal)
  from emp
group by job
```

```
DEPTNO JOB        CATEGORY                    SAL
------ ---------- --------------------- -------
    10 CLERK      TOTAL BY DEPT AND JOB   1300
    10 MANAGER    TOTAL BY DEPT AND JOB   2450
    10 PRESIDENT  TOTAL BY DEPT AND JOB   5000
    20 CLERK      TOTAL BY DEPT AND JOB   1900
    20 ANALYST    TOTAL BY DEPT AND JOB   6000
    20 MANAGER    TOTAL BY DEPT AND JOB   2975
    30 CLERK      TOTAL BY DEPT AND JOB    950
    30 MANAGER    TOTAL BY DEPT AND JOB   2850
    30 SALESMAN   TOTAL BY DEPT AND JOB   5600
       ANALYST    TOTAL BY JOB            6000
       CLERK      TOTAL BY JOB            4150
       MANAGER    TOTAL BY JOB            8275
       PRESIDENT  TOTAL BY JOB            5000
       SALESMAN   TOTAL BY JOB            5600
```

The next step is to UNION ALL the sum of all the salaries by DEPTNO:

```
select deptno, job,
       'TOTAL BY DEPT AND JOB' as category,
       sum(sal) as sal
  from emp
 group by deptno, job
 union all
select null, job, 'TOTAL BY JOB', sum(sal)
  from emp
 group by job
 union all
select deptno, null, 'TOTAL BY DEPT', sum(sal)
  from emp
 group by deptno
```

```
DEPTNO JOB        CATEGORY                   SAL
------ --------- --------------------- -------
    10 CLERK      TOTAL BY DEPT AND JOB  1300
    10 MANAGER    TOTAL BY DEPT AND JOB  2450
    10 PRESIDENT  TOTAL BY DEPT AND JOB  5000
    20 CLERK      TOTAL BY DEPT AND JOB  1900
    20 ANALYST    TOTAL BY DEPT AND JOB  6000
    20 MANAGER    TOTAL BY DEPT AND JOB  2975
    30 CLERK      TOTAL BY DEPT AND JOB   950
    30 MANAGER    TOTAL BY DEPT AND JOB  2850
    30 SALESMAN   TOTAL BY DEPT AND JOB  5600
       ANALYST    TOTAL BY JOB           6000
       CLERK      TOTAL BY JOB           4150
       MANAGER    TOTAL BY JOB           8275
       PRESIDENT  TOTAL BY JOB           5000
       SALESMAN   TOTAL BY JOB           5600
    10            TOTAL BY DEPT          8750
    20            TOTAL BY DEPT         10875
    30            TOTAL BY DEPT          9400
```

The final step is to UNION ALL the sum of all salaries in table EMP:

```
select deptno, job,
       'TOTAL BY DEPT AND JOB' as category,
       sum(sal) as sal
  from emp
 group by deptno, job
 union all
select null, job, 'TOTAL BY JOB', sum(sal)
  from emp
 group by job
 union all
select deptno, null, 'TOTAL BY DEPT', sum(sal)
  from emp
 group by deptno
 union all
select null,null, 'GRAND TOTAL FOR TABLE', sum(sal)
  from emp
```

```
DEPTNO JOB        CATEGORY                   SAL
------ --------- --------------------- -------
```

```
10 CLERK     TOTAL BY DEPT AND JOB   1300
10 MANAGER   TOTAL BY DEPT AND JOB   2450
10 PRESIDENT TOTAL BY DEPT AND JOB   5000
20 CLERK     TOTAL BY DEPT AND JOB   1900
20 ANALYST   TOTAL BY DEPT AND JOB   6000
20 MANAGER   TOTAL BY DEPT AND JOB   2975
30 CLERK     TOTAL BY DEPT AND JOB    950
30 MANAGER   TOTAL BY DEPT AND JOB   2850
30 SALESMAN  TOTAL BY DEPT AND JOB   5600
   ANALYST   TOTAL BY JOB            6000
   CLERK     TOTAL BY JOB            4150
   MANAGER   TOTAL BY JOB            8275
   PRESIDENT TOTAL BY JOB            5000
   SALESMAN  TOTAL BY JOB            5600
10           TOTAL BY DEPT           8750
20           TOTAL BY DEPT          10875
30           TOTAL BY DEPT           9400
             GRAND TOTAL FOR TABLE  29025
```

12.14 Identifying Rows That Are Not Subtotals

Problem

You've used the CUBE extension of the GROUP BY clause to create a report, and you need a way to differentiate between rows that would be generated by a normal GROUP BY clause and those rows that have been generated as a result of using CUBE or ROLLUP.

Following is the result set from a query using the CUBE extension to GROUP BY to create a breakdown of the salaries in table EMP:

```
DEPTNO JOB           SAL
------ ---------  -------
                    29025
       CLERK         4150
       ANALYST       6000
       MANAGER       8275
       SALESMAN      5600
       PRESIDENT     5000
   10                8750
   10  CLERK         1300
   10  MANAGER       2450
   10  PRESIDENT     5000
   20               10875
   20  CLERK         1900
   20  ANALYST       6000
   20  MANAGER       2975
   30                9400
   30  CLERK          950
   30  MANAGER       2850
   30  SALESMAN      5600
```

This report includes the sum of all salaries by DEPTNO and JOB (for each JOB per DEPTNO), the sum of all salaries by DEPTNO, the sum of all salaries by JOB, and finally a grand total (the sum of all salaries in table EMP). You want to clearly identify the different levels of aggregation. You want to be able to identify which category an aggregated value belongs to (i.e., does a given value in the SAL column represent a total by DEPTNO? By JOB? The grand total?). You would like to return the following result set:

```
DEPTNO JOB            SAL DEPTNO_SUBTOTALS  JOB_SUBTOTALS
------ ---------  -------  ----------------- -------------
                    29025                  1             1
       CLERK         4150                  1             0
       ANALYST       6000                  1             0
       MANAGER       8275                  1             0
       SALESMAN      5600                  1             0
       PRESIDENT     5000                  1             0
    10               8750                  0             1
    10 CLERK         1300                  0             0
    10 MANAGER       2450                  0             0
    10 PRESIDENT     5000                  0             0
    20              10875                  0             1
    20 CLERK         1900                  0             0
    20 ANALYST       6000                  0             0
    20 MANAGER       2975                  0             0
    30               9400                  0             1
    30 CLERK          950                  0             0
    30 MANAGER       2850                  0             0
    30 SALESMAN      5600                  0             0
```

Solution

Use the GROUPING function to identify which values exist due to CUBE's or ROLLUP's creation of subtotals, or *superaggregate* values. The following is an example for DB2 and Oracle:

```
1  select deptno, job, sum(sal) sal,
2         grouping(deptno) deptno_subtotals,
3         grouping(job) job_subtotals
4    from emp
5   group by cube(deptno,job)
```

The only difference between the SQL Server solution and that for DB2 and Oracle lies in how the CUBE/ROLLUP clauses are written:

```
1  select deptno, job, sum(sal) sal,
2         grouping(deptno) deptno_subtotals,
3         grouping(job) job_subtotals
4    from emp
5   group by deptno,job with cube
```

This recipe is meant to highlight the use of CUBE and GROUPING when working with subtotals. As of the time of this writing, PostgreSQL and MySQL support neither CUBE nor GROUPING.

Discussion

If DEPTNO_SUBTOTALS is 0 and JOB_SUBTOTALS is 1 (in which case JOB is NULL), the value of SAL represents a subtotal of salaries by DEPTNO created by CUBE. If JOB_SUBTOTALS is 0 and DEPTNO_SUBTOTALS is 1 (in which case DEPTNO is NULL), the value of SAL represents a subtotal of salaries by JOB created by CUBE. Rows with 0 for both DEPTNO_SUBTOTALS and JOB_SUBTOTALS represent rows created by regular aggregation (the sum of SAL for each DEPTNO/JOB combination).

12.15 Using Case Expressions to Flag Rows

Problem

You want to map the values in a column, say, the EMP table's JOB column, into a series of "Boolean" flags. For example, you wish to return the following result set:

```
ENAME   IS_CLERK IS_SALES IS_MGR IS_ANALYST IS_PREZ
------  -------- -------- ------ ---------- -------
KING           0        0      0          0       1
SCOTT          0        0      0          1       0
FORD           0        0      0          1       0
JONES          0        0      1          0       0
BLAKE          0        0      1          0       0
CLARK          0        0      1          0       0
ALLEN          0        1      0          0       0
WARD           0        1      0          0       0
MARTIN         0        1      0          0       0
TURNER         0        1      0          0       0
SMITH          1        0      0          0       0
MILLER         1        0      0          0       0
ADAMS          1        0      0          0       0
JAMES          1        0      0          0       0
```

Such a result set can be useful for debugging and to provide yourself a view of the data different from what you'd see in a more typical result set.

Solution

Use a CASE expression to evaluate each employee's JOB, and return a 1 or 0 to signify her JOB. You'll need to write one CASE expression, and thus create one column for each possible job:

```
1  select ename,
2         case when job = 'CLERK'
3              then 1 else 0
4         end as is_clerk,
5         case when job = 'SALESMAN'
6              then 1 else 0
7         end as is_sales,
```

```
 8          case when job = 'MANAGER'
 9               then 1 else 0
10          end as is_mgr,
11          case when job = 'ANALYST'
12               then 1 else 0
13          end as is_analyst,
14          case when job = 'PRESIDENT'
15               then 1 else 0
16          end as is_prez
17   from emp
18   order by 2,3,4,5,6
```

Discussion

The solution code is pretty much self-explanatory. If you are having trouble understanding it, simply add JOB to the SELECT clause:

```
select ename,
       job,
       case when job = 'CLERK'
            then 1 else 0
       end as is_clerk,
       case when job = 'SALESMAN'
            then 1 else 0
       end as is_sales,
       case when job = 'MANAGER'
            then 1 else 0
       end as is_mgr,
       case when job = 'ANALYST'
            then 1 else 0
       end as is_analyst,
       case when job = 'PRESIDENT'
            then 1 else 0
       end as is_prez
  from emp
 order by 2
```

ENAME	JOB	IS_CLERK	IS_SALES	IS_MGR	IS_ANALYST	IS_PREZ
SCOTT	ANALYST	0	0	0	1	0
FORD	ANALYST	0	0	0	1	0
SMITH	CLERK	1	0	0	0	0
ADAMS	CLERK	1	0	0	0	0
MILLER	CLERK	1	0	0	0	0
JAMES	CLERK	1	0	0	0	0
JONES	MANAGER	0	0	1	0	0
CLARK	MANAGER	0	0	1	0	0
BLAKE	MANAGER	0	0	1	0	1
KING	PRESIDENT	0	0	0	0	1
ALLEN	SALESMAN	0	1	0	0	0
MARTIN	SALESMAN	0	1	0	0	0
TURNER	SALESMAN	0	1	0	0	0
WARD	SALESMAN	0	1	0	0	0

12.16 Creating a Sparse Matrix

Problem

You want to create a sparse matrix, such as the following one transposing the DEPTNO and JOB columns of table EMP:

D10	D20	D30	CLERKS	MGRS	PREZ	ANALS	SALES
	SMITH		SMITH				
		ALLEN					ALLEN
		WARD					WARD
	JONES			JONES			
		MARTIN					MARTIN
		BLAKE		BLAKE			
CLARK				CLARK			
	SCOTT					SCOTT	
KING					KING		
		TURNER					TURNER
	ADAMS		ADAMS				
		JAMES	JAMES				
	FORD					FORD	
MILLER			MILLER				

Solution

Use CASE expressions to create a sparse row-to-column transformation:

```
1  select case deptno when 10 then ename end as d10,
2         case deptno when 20 then ename end as d20,
3         case deptno when 30 then ename end as d30,
4         case job when 'CLERK'     then ename end as clerks,
5         case job when 'MANAGER'   then ename end as mgrs,
6         case job when 'PRESIDENT' then ename end as prez,
7         case job when 'ANALYST'   then ename end as anals,
8         case job when 'SALESMAN'  then ename end as sales
9    from emp
```

Discussion

To transform the DEPTNO and JOB rows to columns, simply use a CASE expression to evaluate the possible values returned by those rows. That's all there is to it. As an aside, if you want to "densify" the report and get rid of some of those NULL rows, you would need to find something to group by. For example, use the window function ROW_NUMBER OVER to assign a ranking for each employee per DEPTNO, and then use the aggregate function MAX to rub out some of the NULLs:

```
select max(case deptno when 10 then ename end) d10,
       max(case deptno when 20 then ename end) d20,
       max(case deptno when 30 then ename end) d30,
       max(case job when 'CLERK'     then ename end) clerks,
       max(case job when 'MANAGER'   then ename end) mgrs,
```

```
        max(case job when 'PRESIDENT' then ename end) prez,
        max(case job when 'ANALYST'   then ename end) anals,
        max(case job when 'SALESMAN'  then ename end) sales
   from (
select deptno, job, ename,
       row_number()over(partition by deptno order by empno) rn
   from emp
       ) x
 group by rn
```

```
D10         D20         D30         CLERKS MGRS  PREZ ANALS SALES
----------  ----------  ----------  ------ ----- ---- ----- ------
CLARK       SMITH       ALLEN       SMITH  CLARK            ALLEN
KING        JONES       WARD               JONES KING       WARD
MILLER      SCOTT       MARTIN      MILLER            SCOTT MARTIN
            ADAMS       BLAKE       ADAMS  BLAKE
            FORD        TURNER                        FORD  TURNER
                        JAMES       JAMES
```

12.17 Grouping Rows by Units of Time

Problem

You want to summarize data by some interval of time. For example, you have a transaction log and want to summarize transactions by 5-second intervals. The rows in table TRX_LOG are shown below:

```
select trx_id,
       trx_date,
       trx_cnt
  from trx_log
```

```
TRX_ID TRX_DATE                TRX_CNT
------ -------------------- ----------
     1 28-JUL-2005 19:03:07      44
     2 28-JUL-2005 19:03:08      18
     3 28-JUL-2005 19:03:09      23
     4 28-JUL-2005 19:03:10      29
     5 28-JUL-2005 19:03:11      27
     6 28-JUL-2005 19:03:12      45
     7 28-JUL-2005 19:03:13      45
     8 28-JUL-2005 19:03:14      32
     9 28-JUL-2005 19:03:15      41
    10 28-JUL-2005 19:03:16      15
    11 28-JUL-2005 19:03:17      24
    12 28-JUL-2005 19:03:18      47
    13 28-JUL-2005 19:03:19      37
    14 28-JUL-2005 19:03:20      48
    15 28-JUL-2005 19:03:21      46
    16 28-JUL-2005 19:03:22      44
    17 28-JUL-2005 19:03:23      36
```

```
18  28-JUL-2005  19:03:24        41
19  28-JUL-2005  19:03:25        33
20  28-JUL-2005  19:03:26        19
```

You want to return the following result set:

```
GRP  TRX_START             TRX_END                 TOTAL
---  --------------------  --------------------  ----------
  1  28-JUL-2005 19:03:07  28-JUL-2005 19:03:11      141
  2  28-JUL-2005 19:03:12  28-JUL-2005 19:03:16      178
  3  28-JUL-2005 19:03:17  28-JUL-2005 19:03:21      202
  4  28-JUL-2005 19:03:22  28-JUL-2005 19:03:26      173
```

Solution

Group the entries into five row buckets. There are several ways to accomplish that logical grouping; this recipe does so by dividing the TRX_ID values by 5, using a technique shown in Recipe 12.7.

Once you've created the "groups," use the aggregate functions MIN, MAX, and SUM to find the start time, end time, and total number of transactions for each "group" (SQL Server users should use CEILING instead of CEIL):

```
1  select ceil(trx_id/5.0) as grp,
2         min(trx_date)   as trx_start,
3         max(trx_date)   as trx_end,
4         sum(trx_cnt)    as total
5    from trx_log
6   group by ceil(trx_id/5.0)
```

Discussion

The first step, and the key to the whole solution, is to logically group the rows together. By dividing by 5 and taking the smallest whole number greater than the quotient, you can create logical groups. For example:

```
select trx_id,
       trx_date,
       trx_cnt,
       trx_id/5.0      as val,
       ceil(trx_id/5.0) as grp
  from trx_log
```

```
TRX_ID TRX_DATE             TRX_CNT   VAL  GRP
------ --------------------  ------- ------ ---
     1 28-JUL-2005 19:03:07      44   .20   1
     2 28-JUL-2005 19:03:08      18   .40   1
     3 28-JUL-2005 19:03:09      23   .60   1
     4 28-JUL-2005 19:03:10      29   .80   1
     5 28-JUL-2005 19:03:11      27  1.00   1
     6 28-JUL-2005 19:03:12      45  1.20   2
     7 28-JUL-2005 19:03:13      45  1.40   2
     8 28-JUL-2005 19:03:14      32  1.60   2
     9 28-JUL-2005 19:03:15      41  1.80   2
```

```
10 28-JUL-2005 19:03:16      15    2.00    2
11 28-JUL-2005 19:03:17      24    2.20    3
12 28-JUL-2005 19:03:18      47    2.40    3
13 28-JUL-2005 19:03:19      37    2.60    3
14 28-JUL-2005 19:03:20      48    2.80    3
15 28-JUL-2005 19:03:21      46    3.00    3
16 28-JUL-2005 19:03:22      44    3.20    4
17 28-JUL-2005 19:03:23      36    3.40    4
18 28-JUL-2005 19:03:24      41    3.60    4
19 28-JUL-2005 19:03:25      33    3.80    4
20 28-JUL-2005 19:03:26      19    4.00    4
```

The last step is to apply the appropriate aggregate functions to find the total number of transactions per 5 seconds along with the start and end times for each transaction:

```
select ceil(trx_id/5.0) as grp,
       min(trx_date)    as trx_start,
       max(trx_date)    as trx_end,
       sum(trx_cnt)     as total
  from trx_log
 group by ceil(trx_id/5.0)
```

```
GRP TRX_START              TRX_END                   TOTAL
--- --------------------   --------------------   ----------
  1 28-JUL-2005 19:03:07   28-JUL-2005 19:03:11      141
  2 28-JUL-2005 19:03:12   28-JUL-2005 19:03:16      178
  3 28-JUL-2005 19:03:17   28-JUL-2005 19:03:21      202
  4 28-JUL-2005 19:03:22   28-JUL-2005 19:03:26      173
```

If your data is slightly different (perhaps you don't have an ID for each row), you can always "group" by dividing the seconds of each TRX_DATE row by 5 to create a similar grouping. Then you can include the hour for each TRX_DATE and group by the actual hour and logical "grouping," GRP. Following is an example of this technique (using Oracle's TO_CHAR and TO_NUMBER functions, you would use the appropriate date and character formatting functions for your platform):

```
select trx_date,trx_cnt,
       to_number(to_char(trx_date,'hh24')) hr,
       ceil(to_number(to_char(trx_date-1/24/60/60,'miss'))/5.0) grp
  from trx_log
```

```
TRX_DATE                   TRX_CNT      HR      GRP
--------------------    ----------  ----------  ----------
28-JUL-2005 19:03:07        44         19        62
28-JUL-2005 19:03:08        18         19        62
28-JUL-2005 19:03:09        23         19        62
28-JUL-2005 19:03:10        29         19        62
28-JUL-2005 19:03:11        27         19        62
28-JUL-2005 19:03:12        45         19        63
28-JUL-2005 19:03:13        45         19        63
28-JUL-2005 19:03:14        32         19        63
28-JUL-2005 19:03:15        41         19        63
28-JUL-2005 19:03:16        15         19        63
28-JUL-2005 19:03:17        24         19        64
```

```
28-JUL-2005 19:03:18      47      19      64
28-JUL-2005 19:03:19      37      19      64
28-JUL-2005 19:03:20      48      19      64
28-JUL-2005 19:03:21      46      19      64
28-JUL-2005 19:03:22      44      19      65
28-JUL-2005 19:03:23      36      19      65
28-JUL-2005 19:03:24      41      19      65
28-JUL-2005 19:03:25      33      19      65
28-JUL-2005 19:03:26      19      19      65
```

Regardless of the actual values for GRP, the key here is that you are grouping for every 5 seconds. From there you can apply the aggregate functions in the same way as in the original solution:

```
select hr,grp,sum(trx_cnt) total
  from (
select trx_date,trx_cnt,
       to_number(to_char(trx_date,'hh24')) hr,
       ceil(to_number(to_char(trx_date-1/24/60/60,'miss'))/5.0) grp
  from trx_log
       ) x
 group by hr,grp


HR       GRP       TOTAL
--  ----------  ----------
19        62         141
19        63         178
19        64         202
19        65         173
```

Including the hour in the grouping is useful if your transaction log spans hours. In DB2 and Oracle, you can also use the window function SUM OVER to produce the same result. The following query returns all rows from TRX_LOG along with a running total for TRX_CNT by logical "group," and the TOTAL for TRX_CNT for each row in the "group":

```
select trx_id, trx_date, trx_cnt,
       sum(trx_cnt)over(partition by ceil(trx_id/5.0)
                        order by trx_date
                        range between unbounded preceding
                            and current row) runing_total,
       sum(trx_cnt)over(partition by ceil(trx_id/5.0)) total,
       case when mod(trx_id,5.0) = 0 then 'X' end grp_end
  from trx_log


TRX_ID TRX_DATE              TRX_CNT RUNING_TOTAL      TOTAL GRP_END
------ --------------------  ------- ------------  ---------- -------
     1 28-JUL-2005 19:03:07      44           44         141
     2 28-JUL-2005 19:03:08      18           62         141
     3 28-JUL-2005 19:03:09      23           85         141
     4 28-JUL-2005 19:03:10      29          114         141
     5 28-JUL-2005 19:03:11      27          141         141 X
     6 28-JUL-2005 19:03:12      45           45         178
     7 28-JUL-2005 19:03:13      45           90         178
```

8	28-JUL-2005 19:03:14	32	122	178	
9	28-JUL-2005 19:03:15	41	163	178	
10	28-JUL-2005 19:03:16	15	178	178	X
11	28-JUL-2005 19:03:17	24	24	202	
12	28-JUL-2005 19:03:18	47	71	202	
13	28-JUL-2005 19:03:19	37	108	202	
14	28-JUL-2005 19:03:20	48	156	202	
15	28-JUL-2005 19:03:21	46	202	202	X
16	28-JUL-2005 19:03:22	44	44	173	
17	28-JUL-2005 19:03:23	36	80	173	
18	28-JUL-2005 19:03:24	41	121	173	
19	28-JUL-2005 19:03:25	33	154	173	
20	28-JUL-2005 19:03:26	19	173	173	X

12.18 Performing Aggregations over Different Groups/ Partitions Simultaneously

Problem

You want to aggregate over different dimensions at the same time. For example, you want to return a result set that lists each employee's name, his department, the number of employees in his department (himself included), the number of employees that have the same job as he does (himself included in this count as well), and the total number of employees in the EMP table. The result set should look like the following:

ENAME	DEPTNO	DEPTNO_CNT	JOB	JOB_CNT	TOTAL
MILLER	10	3	CLERK	4	14
CLARK	10	3	MANAGER	3	14
KING	10	3	PRESIDENT	1	14
SCOTT	20	5	ANALYST	2	14
FORD	20	5	ANALYST	2	14
SMITH	20	5	CLERK	4	14
JONES	20	5	MANAGER	3	14
ADAMS	20	5	CLERK	4	14
JAMES	30	6	CLERK	4	14
MARTIN	30	6	SALESMAN	4	14
TURNER	30	6	SALESMAN	4	14
WARD	30	6	SALESMAN	4	14
ALLEN	30	6	SALESMAN	4	14
BLAKE	30	6	MANAGER	3	14

Solution

Window functions make this problem quite easy to solve. If you do not have window functions available to you, you can use scalar subqueries.

DB2, Oracle, and SQL Server

Use the COUNT OVER window function while specifying different *partitions*, or groups of data on which to perform aggregation:

```
select ename,
       deptno,
       count(*)over(partition by deptno) deptno_cnt,
       job,
       count(*)over(partition by job) job_cnt,
       count(*)over( ) total
  from emp
```

PostgreSQL and MySQL

Use scalar subqueries in your SELECT list to perform the aggregate count operations on different groups of rows:

```
1   select e.ename,
2          e.deptno,
3          (select count(*) from emp d
4            where d.deptno = e.deptno) as deptno_cnt,
5          job,
6          (select count(*) from emp d
7            where d.job = e.job) as job_cnt,
8          (select count(*) from emp) as total
9     from emp e
```

Discussion

DB2, Oracle, and SQL Server

This example really shows off the power and convenience of window functions. By simply specifying different partitions or groups of data to aggregate, you can create immensely detailed reports without having to self join over and over, and without having to write cumbersome and perhaps poorly performing subqueries in your SELECT list. All the work is done by the window function COUNT OVER. To understand the output, focus on the OVER clause for a moment for each COUNT operation:

```
count(*)over(partition by deptno)
```

```
count(*)over(partition by job)
```

```
count(*)over( )
```

Remember the main parts of the OVER clause: the partition, specified by PARTITION BY: and the frame or window, specified by ORDER BY. Look at the first COUNT, which partitions by DEPTNO. The rows in table EMP will be grouped by DEPTNO and the COUNT operation will be performed on all the rows in each group. Since there is no frame or window clause specified (no ORDER BY), all the rows in the group are counted. The PARTITION BY clause finds all the unique DEPTNO values, and then the COUNT function counts the number of rows having each value. In the specific example of COUNT(*)OVER(PARTITION BY DEPTNO), The PARTITION BY clause identifies the partitions or groups to be values 10, 20, and 30.

The same processing is applied to the second COUNT, which partitions by JOB. The last count does not partition by anything, and simply has an empty parenthesis. An empty parenthesis implies "the whole table." So, whereas the two prior COUNTs aggregate values based on the defined groups or partitions, the final COUNT counts all rows in table EMP.

Keep in mind that window functions are applied after the WHERE clause. If you were to filter the result set in some way, for example, excluding all employees in DEPTNO 10, the value for TOTAL would not be 14, it would be 11. To filter results after window functions have been evaluated, you must make your windowing query into an inline view and then filter on the results from that view.

PostgreSQL and MySQL

For every row returned by the main query (rows from EMP E), use multiple scalar subqueries in the SELECT list to perform different counts for each DEPTNO and JOB. To get the TOTAL, simply use another scalar subquery to get the count of all employees in table EMP.

12.19 Performing Aggregations over a Moving Range of Values

Problem

You want to compute a moving aggregation, such as a moving sum on the salaries in table EMP. You want to compute a sum for every 90 days, starting with the HIRE-DATE of the first employee. You want to see how spending has fluctuated for every 90-day period between the first and last employee hired. You want to return the following result set:

```
HIREDATE       SAL SPENDING_PATTERN
-----------   ----- ----------------
17-DEC-1980    800              800
20-FEB-1981   1600             2400
22-FEB-1981   1250             3650
02-APR-1981   2975             5825
01-MAY-1981   2850             8675
09-JUN-1981   2450             8275
```

08-SEP-1981	1500	1500
28-SEP-1981	1250	2750
17-NOV-1981	5000	7750
03-DEC-1981	950	11700
03-DEC-1981	3000	11700
23-JAN-1982	1300	10250
09-DEC-1982	3000	3000
12-JAN-1983	1100	4100

Solution

Being able to specify a moving window in the framing or windowing clause of window functions makes this problem very easy to solve, if your RDBMS supports such functions. The key is to order by HIREDATE in your window function and then specify a window of 90 days starting from the earliest employee hired. The sum will be computed using the salaries of employees hired up to 90 days prior to the current employee's HIREDATE (the current employee is included in the sum). If you do not have window functions available, you can use scalar subqueries, but the solution will be more complex.

DB2 and Oracle

For DB2 and Oracle, use the window function SUM OVER and order by HIREDATE. Specify a range of 90 days in the window or "framing" clause to allow the sum to be computed for each employee's salary and to include the salaries of all employees hired up to 90 days earlier. Because DB2 does not allow you to specify HIREDATE in the ORDER BY clause of a window function (line 3 below), you can order by DAYS(HIREDATE) instead:

```
1  select hiredate,
2         sal,
3         sum(sal)over(order by days(hiredate)
4                       range between 90 preceding
5                        and current row) spending_pattern
6    from emp e
```

The Oracle solution is more straightforward than DB2's, because Oracle allows window functions to order by datetime types:

```
1  select hiredate,
2         sal,
3         sum(sal)over(order by hiredate
4                       range between 90 preceding
5                        and current row) spending_pattern
6    from emp e
```

MySQL, PostgreSQL, and SQL Server

Use a scalar subquery to sum the salaries of all employees hired up to 90 days prior to the day each employee was hired:

```
1 select e.hiredate,
2        e.sal,
3        (select sum(sal) from emp d
4           where d.hiredate between e.hiredate-90
5                               and e.hiredate) as spending_pattern
6   from emp e
7 order by 1
```

Discussion

DB2 and Oracle

DB2 and Oracle share the same solution. The only difference, and it's minor between the two solutions, lies in how you specify HIREDATE in the ORDER BY clause of the window function. At the time of this book's writing, DB2 doesn't allow a DATE value in such an ORDER BY clause if you are using a numeric value to set the window's range. (For example, RANGE BETWEEN UNBOUNDED PRECEDING AND CURRENT ROW allows you to order by a date, but RANGE BETWEEN 90 PRECEDING AND CURRENT ROW does not.)

To understand what the solution query is doing, you simply need to understand what the window clause is doing. The window you are defining orders the salaries for all employees by HIREDATE. Then the function computes a sum. The sum is not computed for all salaries. Instead, the processing is as follows:

1. The salary of the first employee hired is evaluated. Since no employees were hired before the first employee, the sum at this point is simply the first employee's salary.

2. The salary of the next employee (by HIREDATE) is evaluated. This employee's salary is included in the moving sum along with any other employees who were hired up to 90 days prior.

The HIREDATE of the first employee is December 17, 1980, and the HIREDATE of the next hired employee is February 20, 1981. The second employee was hired less than 90 days after the first employee, and thus the moving sum for the second employee is 2400 (1600 + 800). If you are having trouble understanding where the values in SPENDING_PATTERN come from, examine the following query and result set:

```
select distinct
       dense_rank( )over(order by e.hiredate) window,
       e.hiredate current_hiredate,
       d.hiredate hiredate_within_90_days,
       d.sal sals_used_for_sum
  from emp e,
       emp d
 where d.hiredate between e.hiredate-90 and e.hiredate
```

WINDOW	CURRENT_HIREDATE	HIREDATE_WITHIN_90_DAYS	SALS_USED_FOR_SUM
1	17-DEC-1980	17-DEC-1980	800
2	20-FEB-1981	17-DEC-1980	800
2	20-FEB-1981	20-FEB-1981	1600
3	22-FEB-1981	17-DEC-1980	800
3	22-FEB-1981	20-FEB-1981	1600
3	22-FEB-1981	22-FEB-1981	1250
4	02-APR-1981	20-FEB-1981	1600
4	02-APR-1981	22-FEB-1981	1250
4	02-APR-1981	02-APR-1981	2975
5	01-MAY-1981	20-FEB-1981	1600
5	01-MAY-1981	22-FEB-1981	1250
5	01-MAY-1981	02-APR-1981	2975
5	01-MAY-1981	01-MAY-1981	2850
6	09-JUN-1981	02-APR-1981	2975
6	09-JUN-1981	01-MAY-1981	2850
6	09-JUN-1981	09-JUN-1981	2450
7	08-SEP-1981	08-SEP-1981	1500
8	28-SEP-1981	08-SEP-1981	1500
8	28-SEP-1981	28-SEP-1981	1250
9	17-NOV-1981	08-SEP-1981	1500
9	17-NOV-1981	28-SEP-1981	1250
9	17-NOV-1981	17-NOV-1981	5000
10	03-DEC-1981	08-SEP-1981	1500
10	03-DEC-1981	28-SEP-1981	1250
10	03-DEC-1981	17-NOV-1981	5000
10	03-DEC-1981	03-DEC-1981	950
10	03-DEC-1981	03-DEC-1981	3000
11	23-JAN-1982	17-NOV-1981	5000
11	23-JAN-1982	03-DEC-1981	950
11	23-JAN-1982	03-DEC-1981	3000
11	23-JAN-1982	23-JAN-1982	1300
12	09-DEC-1982	09-DEC-1982	3000
13	12-JAN-1983	09-DEC-1982	3000
13	12-JAN-1983	12-JAN-1983	1100

If you look at the WINDOW column, only those rows with the same WINDOW value will be considered for each sum. Take for example, WINDOW 3. The salaries used for the sum for that window are 800, 1600, and 1250, which total 3650. If you look at the final result set in the Problem section, you'll see the SPENDING_PAT-TERN for February 22, 1981 (WINDOW 3) is 3650. As proof, to verify that the above self join includes the correct salaries for the windows defined, simply sum the values in SALS_USED_FOR_SUM and group by CURRENT_DATE. The result should be the same as the result set shown in the Problem section (with the dupli-cate row for December 3, 1981, filtered out):

```
select current_hiredate,
       sum(sals_used_for_sum) spending_pattern
  from (
select distinct
       dense_rank( )over(order by e.hiredate) window,
       e.hiredate current_hiredate,
```

```
        d.hiredate hiredate_within_90_days,
        d.sal sals_used_for_sum
  from emp e,
       emp d
 where d.hiredate between e.hiredate-90 and e.hiredate
       ) x
 group by current_hiredate

CURRENT_HIREDATE SPENDING_PATTERN
---------------- ----------------
 17-DEC-1980                  800
 20-FEB-1981                 2400
 22-FEB-1981                 3650
 02-APR-1981                 5825
 01-MAY-1981                 8675
 09-JUN-1981                 8275
 08-SEP-1981                 1500
 28-SEP-1981                 2750
 17-NOV-1981                 7750
 03-DEC-1981                11700
 23-JAN-1982                10250
 09-DEC-1982                 3000
 12-JAN-1983                 4100
```

MySQL, PostgreSQL, and SQL Server

The key to this solution is to use a scalar subquery (a self join will work as well) while using the aggregate function SUM to compute a sum for every 90 days based on HIREDATE. If you are having trouble seeing how this works, simply convert the solution to a self join and examine which rows are included in the computations. Consider the result set below, which returns the same result set as that in the solution:

```
select e.hiredate,
       e.sal,
       sum(d.sal) as spending_pattern
  from emp e, emp d
 where d.hiredate
       between e.hiredate-90 and e.hiredate
 group by e.hiredate,e.sal
 order by 1

HIREDATE      SAL SPENDING_PATTERN
----------- ----- ----------------
 17-DEC-1980   800              800
 20-FEB-1981  1600             2400
 22-FEB-1981  1250             3650
 02-APR-1981  2975             5825
 01-MAY-1981  2850             8675
 09-JUN-1981  2450             8275
 08-SEP-1981  1500             1500
 28-SEP-1981  1250             2750
 17-NOV-1981  5000             7750
 03-DEC-1981   950            11700
```

03-DEC-1981	3000	11700
23-JAN-1982	1300	10250
09-DEC-1982	3000	3000
12-JAN-1983	1100	4100

If it is still unclear, simply remove the aggregation and start with the Cartesian product. The first step is to generate a Cartesian product using table EMP so that each HIREDATE can be compared with all the other HIREDATEs. (Only a snippet of the result set is shown below because there are 196 rows [14×14] returned by a Cartesian of EMP.)

```
select e.hiredate,
       e.sal,
       d.sal,
       d.hiredate
  from emp e, emp d
```

```
HIREDATE       SAL   SAL HIREDATE
-----------  -----  ----- -----------
17-DEC-1980    800    800 17-DEC-1980
17-DEC-1980    800   1600 20-FEB-1981
17-DEC-1980    800   1250 22-FEB-1981
17-DEC-1980    800   2975 02-APR-1981
17-DEC-1980    800   1250 28-SEP-1981
17-DEC-1980    800   2850 01-MAY-1981
17-DEC-1980    800   2450 09-JUN-1981
17-DEC-1980    800   3000 09-DEC-1982
17-DEC-1980    800   5000 17-NOV-1981
17-DEC-1980    800   1500 08-SEP-1981
17-DEC-1980    800   1100 12-JAN-1983
17-DEC-1980    800    950 03-DEC-1981
17-DEC-1980    800   3000 03-DEC-1981
17-DEC-1980    800   1300 23-JAN-1982
20-FEB-1981   1600    800 17-DEC-1980
20-FEB-1981   1600   1600 20-FEB-1981
20-FEB-1981   1600   1250 22-FEB-1981
20-FEB-1981   1600   2975 02-APR-1981
20-FEB-1981   1600   1250 28-SEP-1981
20-FEB-1981   1600   2850 01-MAY-1981
20-FEB-1981   1600   2450 09-JUN-1981
20-FEB-1981   1600   3000 09-DEC-1982
20-FEB-1981   1600   5000 17-NOV-1981
20-FEB-1981   1600   1500 08-SEP-1981
20-FEB-1981   1600   1100 12-JAN-1983
20-FEB-1981   1600    950 03-DEC-1981
20-FEB-1981   1600   3000 03-DEC-1981
20-FEB-1981   1600   1300 23-JAN-1982
```

If you examine the result set above, you'll notice that there is no HIREDATE 90 days earlier or equal to December 17, except for December 17. So, the sum for that row should be only 800. If you examine the next HIREDATE, February 20, you'll notice that there is one HIREDATE that falls within the 90-day window (within 90 days prior), and that is December 17. If you sum the SAL from December 17 with the SAL from February 20 (because we are looking for HIREDATEs equal to each HIRE-DATE or within 90 days earlier) you get 2400, which happens to be the final result for that HIREDATE.

Now that you know how it works, use a filter in the WHERE clause to return for each HIREDATE and HIREDATE that is equal to it or is no more than 90 days earlier:

```
select e.hiredate,
       e.sal,
       d.sal sal_to_sum,
       d.hiredate within_90_days
  from emp e, emp d
 where d.hiredate
       between e.hiredate-90 and e.hiredate
 order by 1
```

HIREDATE	SAL	SAL_TO_SUM	WITHIN_90_DAYS
17-DEC-1980	800	800	17-DEC-1980
20-FEB-1981	1600	800	17-DEC-1980
20-FEB-1981	1600	1600	20-FEB-1981
22-FEB-1981	1250	800	17-DEC-1980
22-FEB-1981	1250	1600	20-FEB-1981
22-FEB-1981	1250	1250	22-FEB-1981
02-APR-1981	2975	1600	20-FEB-1981
02-APR-1981	2975	1250	22-FEB-1981
02-APR-1981	2975	2975	02-APR-1981
01-MAY-1981	2850	1600	20-FEB-1981
01-MAY-1981	2850	1250	22-FEB-1981
01-MAY-1981	2850	2975	02-APR-1981
01-MAY-1981	2850	2850	01-MAY-1981
09-JUN-1981	2450	2975	02-APR-1981
09-JUN-1981	2450	2850	01-MAY-1981
09-JUN-1981	2450	2450	09-JUN-1981
08-SEP-1981	1500	1500	08-SEP-1981
28-SEP-1981	1250	1500	08-SEP-1981
28-SEP-1981	1250	1250	28-SEP-1981
17-NOV-1981	5000	1500	08-SEP-1981
17-NOV-1981	5000	1250	28-SEP-1981
17-NOV-1981	5000	5000	17-NOV-1981
03-DEC-1981	950	1500	08-SEP-1981
03-DEC-1981	950	1250	28-SEP-1981
03-DEC-1981	950	5000	17-NOV-1981
03-DEC-1981	950	950	03-DEC-1981
03-DEC-1981	950	3000	03-DEC-1981
03-DEC-1981	3000	1500	08-SEP-1981
03-DEC-1981	3000	1250	28-SEP-1981
03-DEC-1981	3000	5000	17-NOV-1981
03-DEC-1981	3000	950	03-DEC-1981
03-DEC-1981	3000	3000	03-DEC-1981
23-JAN-1982	1300	5000	17-NOV-1981
23-JAN-1982	1300	950	03-DEC-1981
23-JAN-1982	1300	3000	03-DEC-1981
23-JAN-1982	1300	1300	23-JAN-1982

```
09-DEC-1982  3000        3000  09-DEC-1982
12-JAN-1983  1100        3000  09-DEC-1982
12-JAN-1983  1100        1100  12-JAN-1983
```

Now that you know which SALs are to be included in the moving window of summation, simply use the aggregate function SUM to produce a more expressive result set:

```
select e.hiredate,
       e.sal,
       sum(d.sal) as spending_pattern
  from emp e, emp d
 where d.hiredate
       between e.hiredate-90 and e.hiredate
 group by e.hiredate,e.sal
 order by 1
```

If you compare the result set for the query above and the result set for the query below (which is the original solution presented), you will see they are the same:

```
select e.hiredate,
       e.sal,
       (select sum(sal) from emp d
         where d.hiredate between e.hiredate-90
                           and e.hiredate) as spending_pattern
  from emp e
 order by 1


HIREDATE      SAL SPENDING_PATTERN
----------- ----- ----------------
17-DEC-1980   800              800
20-FEB-1981  1600             2400
22-FEB-1981  1250             3650
02-APR-1981  2975             5825
01-MAY-1981  2850             8675
09-JUN-1981  2450             8275
08-SEP-1981  1500             1500
28-SEP-1981  1250             2750
17-NOV-1981  5000             7750
03-DEC-1981   950            11700
03-DEC-1981  3000            11700
23-JAN-1982  1300            10250
09-DEC-1982  3000             3000
12-JAN-1983  1100             4100
```

12.20 Pivoting a Result Set with Subtotals

Problem

You want to create a report containing subtotals, then transpose the results to provide a more readable report. For example, you've been asked to create a report that displays for each department, the managers in the department along with a sum of the salaries of the employees who work for those managers. Additionally, you want to return two subtotals: the sum of all salaries in each department for those employees who have managers, and a sum of all salaries in the result set (the sum of the department subtotals). You currently have the following report:

```
DEPTNO      MGR       SAL
------  ----------  ----------
    10      7782        1300
    10      7839        2450
    10                  3750
    20      7566        6000
    20      7788        1100
    20      7839        2975
    20      7902         800
    20                 10875
    30      7698        6550
    30      7839        2850
    30                  9400
                       24025
```

You want to provide a more readable report and wish to transform the above result set to the following, which makes the meaning of the report much more clear:

```
MGR      DEPT10      DEPT20      DEPT30      TOTAL
----  ----------  ----------  ----------  ----------
7566           0        6000           0
7698           0           0        6550
7782        1300           0           0
7788           0        1100           0
7839        2450        2975        2850
7902           0         800           0
            3750       10875        9400       24025
```

Solution

The first step is to generate subtotals using the ROLLUP extension to GROUP BY. The next step is to perform a classic pivot (aggregate and CASE expression) to create the desired columns for your report. The GROUPING function allows you to easily determine which values are subtotals (that is, exist because of ROLLUP and otherwise would not normally be there). Depending on how your RDBMS sorts NULL values, you may need to add an ORDER BY to the solution to allow it to look like the target result set above.

DB2 and Oracle

Use the ROLLUP extension to GROUP BY then use a CASE expression to format the data into a more readable report:

```
1  select mgr,
2         sum(case deptno when 10 then sal else 0 end) dept10,
3         sum(case deptno when 20 then sal else 0 end) dept20,
4         sum(case deptno when 30 then sal else 0 end) dept30,
5         sum(case flag   when '11' then sal else null end) total
```

```
 6    from (
 7  select deptno,mgr,sum(sal) sal,
 8         cast(grouping(deptno) as char(1))||
 9         cast(grouping(mgr)    as char(1)) flag
10    from emp
11   where mgr is not null
12   group by rollup(deptno,mgr)
13         ) x
14   group by mgr
```

SQL Server

Use the ROLLUP extension to GROUP BY then use a CASE expression to format the data into a more readable report:

```
 1  select mgr,
 2         sum(case deptno when 10 then sal else 0 end) dept10,
 3         sum(case deptno when 20 then sal else 0 end) dept20,
 4         sum(case deptno when 30 then sal else 0 end) dept30,
 5         sum(case flag   when '11' then sal else null end) total
 6    from (
 7  select deptno,mgr,sum(sal) sal,
 8         cast(grouping(deptno) as char(1))+
 9         cast(grouping(mgr)    as char(1)) flag
10    from emp
11   where mgr is not null
12   group by deptno,mgr with rollup
13         ) x
14   group by mgr
```

MySQL and PostgreSQL

The GROUPING function is not supported by either RDBMS.

Discussion

The solutions provided above are identical except for the string concatenation and how GROUPING is specified. Because the solutions are so similar, the discussion below will refer to the SQL Server solution to highlight the intermediate result sets (the discussion is relevant to DB2 and Oracle as well).

The first step is to generate a result set that sums the SAL for the employees in each DEPTNO per MGR. The idea is to show how much the employees make under a particular manager in a particular department. For example, this query below will allow you to compare the salaries of employees who work for KING in DEPTNO 10 compared with those who work for KING in DEPTNO 30:

```
select deptno,mgr,sum(sal) sal
  from emp
 where mgr is not null
 group by mgr,deptno
 order by 1,2
```

DEPTNO	MGR	SAL
10	7782	1300
10	7839	2450
20	7566	6000
20	7788	1100
20	7839	2975
20	7902	800
30	7698	6550
30	7839	2850

The next step is to use the ROLLUP extension to GROUP BY to create subtotals for each DEPTNO and across all employees (who have a manager):

```
select deptno,mgr,sum(sal) sal
  from emp
 where mgr is not null
 group by deptno,mgr with rollup
```

DEPTNO	MGR	SAL
10	7782	1300
10	7839	2450
10		3750
20	7566	6000
20	7788	1100
20	7839	2975
20	7902	800
20		10875
30	7698	6550
30	7839	2850
30		9400
		24025

With the subtotals created, you need a way to determine which values are in fact subtotals (created by ROLLUP) and which are results of the regular GROUP BY. Use the GROUPING function to create bitmaps to help identify the subtotal values from the regular aggregate values:

```
select deptno,mgr,sum(sal) sal,
       cast(grouping(deptno) as char(1))+
       cast(grouping(mgr)    as char(1)) flag
  from emp
 where mgr is not null
 group by deptno,mgr with rollup
```

DEPTNO	MGR	SAL	FLAG
10	7782	1300	00
10	7839	2450	00
10		3750	01
20	7566	6000	00
20	7788	1100	00

```
20        7839        2975  00
20        7902         800  00
20                   10875  01
30        7698        6550  00
30        7839        2850  00
30                    9400  01
                     24025  11
```

If it isn't immediately obvious, the rows with a value of 00 for FLAG are the results of regular aggregation. The rows with a value of 01 for FLAG are the results of ROL-LUP aggregating SAL by DEPTNO (since DEPTNO is listed first in the ROLLUP; if you switch the order, for example, "GROUP BY MGR, DEPTNO WITH ROLLUP", you'd see quite different results). The row with a value of 11 for FLAG is the result of ROLLUP aggregating SAL over all rows.

At this point you have everything you need to create a beautified report by simply using CASE expressions. The goal is to provide a report that shows employee salaries for each manager across departments. If a manager does not have any subordinates in a particular department, a zero should be returned; otherwise, you want to return the sum of all salaries for that manager's subordinates in that department. Additionally, you want to add a final column, TOTAL, representing a sum of all the salaries in the report. The solution satisfying all these requirements is shown below:

```
select mgr,
       sum(case deptno when 10 then sal else 0 end) dept10,
       sum(case deptno when 20 then sal else 0 end) dept20,
       sum(case deptno when 30 then sal else 0 end) dept30,
       sum(case flag   when '11' then sal else null end) total
  from (
select deptno,mgr,sum(sal) sal,
       cast(grouping(deptno) as char(1))+
       cast(grouping(mgr)    as char(1)) flag
  from emp
 where mgr is not null
 group by deptno,mgr with rollup
       ) x
 group by mgr
 order by coalesce(mgr,9999)
```

MGR	DEPT10	DEPT20	DEPT30	TOTAL
7566	0	6000	0	
7698	0	0	6550	
7782	1300	0	0	
7788	0	1100	0	
7839	2450	2975	2850	
7902	0	800	0	
	3750	10875	9400	24025

CHAPTER 13

Hierarchical Queries

This chapter introduces recipes for expressing hierarchical relationships that you may have in your data. It is typical when working with hierarchical data to have more difficulty retrieving and displaying the data (as a hierarchy) than storing it. This is particularly true because of the inflexibility of SQL (SQL's nonrecursive nature). When working with hierarchical queries, it is absolutely crucial that you take advantage of what your RDBMS supplies you to facilitate these operations; otherwise you will end up writing potentially less efficient queries and constructing convoluted data models to deal with the hierarchical data. For PostgreSQL users, the recursive WITH clause will most likely be added to later versions PostgreSQL, so it would behoove you to pay attention to the DB2 solutions to these queries.

This chapter will provide recipes to help you unravel the hierarchical structure of your data by taking advantage of the functions supplied by each of the RDBMSs. Before starting, examine table EMP and the hierarchical relationship between EMPNO and MGR:

```
select empno,mgr
  from emp
 order by 2
```

EMPNO	MGR
7788	7566
7902	7566
7499	7698
7521	7698
7900	7698
7844	7698
7654	7698
7934	7782
7876	7788
7566	7839
7782	7839
7698	7839
7369	7902
7839	

If you look carefully, you will see that each value for MGR is also an EMPNO, meaning the manager of each employee in table EMP is also an employee in table EMP and not stored somewhere else. The relationship between MGR and EMPNO is a parent–child relationship in that the value for MGR is the most immediate parent for a given EMPNO (it is also possible that the manager for a specific employee can have a manager herself, and those managers can in turn have managers, and so on, creating an *n*-tier hierarchy). If an employee has no manager, then MGR is NULL.

13.1   Expressing a Parent-Child Relationship

Problem

You want to include parent information along with data from child records. For example, you want to display each employee's name along with the name of his manager. You want to return the following result set:

```
EMPS_AND_MGRS
-----------------------------
FORD works for JONES
SCOTT works for JONES
JAMES works for BLAKE
TURNER works for BLAKE
MARTIN works for BLAKE
WARD works for BLAKE
ALLEN works for BLAKE
MILLER works for CLARK
ADAMS works for SCOTT
CLARK works for KING
BLAKE works for KING
JONES works for KING
SMITH works for FORD
```

Solution

Self join EMP on MGR and EMPNO to find the name of each employee's manager. Then use your RDBMS's supplied function(s) for string concatenation to generate the strings in the desired result set.

DB2, Oracle, and PostgreSQL

Self join on EMP. Then use the double vertical-bar (||) concatenation operator:

```
1 select a.ename || ' works for ' || b.ename as emps_and_mgrs
2   from emp a, emp b
3  where a.mgr = b.empno
```

MySQL

Self join on EMP. Then use the concatenation function CONCAT:

```
1 select concat(a.ename, ' works for ',b.ename) as emps_and_mgrs
2   from emp a, emp b
3  where a.mgr = b.empno
```

SQL Server

Self join on EMP. Then use the plus sign (+) as the concatenation operator:

```
1 select a.ename + ' works for ' + b.ename as emps_and_mgrs
2   from emp a, emp b
3  where a.mgr = b.empno
```

Discussion

The implementation is essentially the same for all the solutions. The difference lies only in the method of string concatenation, and thus one discussion will cover all of the solutions.

The key is the join between MGR and EMPNO. The fist step is to build a Cartesian product by joining EMP to itself (only a portion of the rows returned by the Cartesian product is shown below):

```
select a.empno, b.empno
  from emp a, emp b
```

EMPNO	MGR
7369	7369
7369	7499
7369	7521
7369	7566
7369	7654
7369	7698
7369	7782
7369	7788
7369	7839
7369	7844
7369	7876
7369	7900
7369	7902
7369	7934
7499	7369
7499	7499
7499	7521
7499	7566
7499	7654
7499	7698
7499	7782
7499	7788
7499	7839
7499	7844
7499	7876
7499	7900
7499	7902
7499	7934

As you can see, by using a Cartesian product you are returning every possible EMPNO/EMPNO combination (such that it looks like the manager for EMPNO 7369 is all the other employees in the table, including EMPNO 7369).

The next step is to filter the results such that you return only each employee and his manager's EMPNO. Accomplish this by joining on MGR and EMPNO:

```
1  select a.empno, b.empno mgr
2    from emp a, emp b
3   where a.mgr = b.empno
```

```
    EMPNO        MGR
---------- ----------
      7902       7566
      7788       7566
      7900       7698
      7844       7698
      7654       7698
      7521       7698
      7499       7698
      7934       7782
      7876       7788
      7782       7839
      7698       7839
      7566       7839
      7369       7902
```

Now that you have each employee and the EMPNO of his manager, you can return the name of each manager by simply selecting B.ENAME rather than B.EMPNO. If after some practice you have difficulty grasping how this works, you can use a scalar subquery rather than a self join to get the answer:

```
select a.ename,
       (select b.ename
          from emp b
         where b.empno = a.mgr) as mgr
  from emp a
```

```
ENAME      MGR
---------- ----------
SMITH      FORD
ALLEN      BLAKE
WARD       BLAKE
JONES      KING
MARTIN     BLAKE
BLAKE      KING
CLARK      KING
SCOTT      JONES
KING
TURNER     BLAKE
ADAMS      SCOTT
JAMES      BLAKE
FORD       JONES
MILLER     CLARK
```

The scalar subquery version is equivalent to the self join, except for one row: employee KING is in the result set, but that is not the case with the self join. "Why not?" you might ask. Remember, NULL is never equal to anything, not even itself. In the self-join solution, you use an equi-join between EMPNO and MGR, thus filtering out any employees who have NULL for MGR. To see employee KING when using the self-join method, you must outer join as shown in the following two queries. The first solution uses the ANSI outer join while the second uses the Oracle outer-join syntax. The output is the same for both and is shown following the second query:

```
/* ANSI */
select a.ename, b.ename mgr
   from emp a left join emp b
     on (a.mgr = b.empno)

/* Oracle */
select a.ename, b.ename mgr
   from emp a, emp b
  where a.mgr = b.empno (+)
```

```
ENAME       MGR
----------  ----------
FORD        JONES
SCOTT       JONES
JAMES       BLAKE
TURNER      BLAKE
MARTIN      BLAKE
WARD        BLAKE
ALLEN       BLAKE
MILLER      CLARK
ADAMS       SCOTT
CLARK       KING
BLAKE       KING
JONES       KING
SMITH       FORD
KING
```

13.2 Expressing a Child-Parent-Grandparent Relationship

Problem

Employee CLARK works for KING and to express that relationship you can use the first recipe in this chapter. What if employee CLARK was in turn a manager for another employee? Consider the following query:

```
select ename,empno,mgr
   from emp
  where ename in ('KING','CLARK','MILLER')
```

```
ENAME           EMPNO       MGR
----------   ----------  ----------
CLARK           7782       7839
KING            7839
MILLER          7934       7782
```

As you can see, employee MILLER works for CLARK who in turn works for KING. You want to express the full hierarchy from MILLER to KING. You want to return the following result set:

```
LEAF___BRANCH___ROOT
----------------------
MILLER-->CLARK-->KING
```

However, the single self-join approach from the previous recipe will not suffice to show the entire relationship from top to bottom. You could write a query that does two self joins, but what you really need is a general approach for traversing such hierarchies.

Solution

This recipe differs from the first recipe because there is now a three-tier relationship, as the title suggests. If your RDBMS does not supply functionality for traversing tree-structured data, then you can solve this problem using the techniques described for PostgreSQL and MySQL, but you must add an additional self join. DB2, SQL Server, and Oracle offer functions for expressing hierarchies. Thus self joins on those RDBMSs aren't necessary, though they certainly work.

DB2 and SQL Server

Use the recursive WITH clause to find MILLER's manager, CLARK, then CLARK's manager, KING. The SQL Server string concatenation operator + is used in this solution:

```
1     with x (tree,mgr,depth)
2         as (
3     select cast(ename as varchar(100)),
4            mgr, 0
5       from emp
6      where ename = 'MILLER'
7      union all
8     select cast(x.tree+'-->'+e.ename as varchar(100)),
9            e.mgr, x.depth+1
10      from emp e, x
11     where x.mgr = e.empno
12    )
13    select tree leaf___branch___root
14      from x
15     where depth = 2
```

The only modification necessary for this solution to work on DB2 is to use DB2's concatenation operator, ||. Otherwise, the solution will work as is, on DB2 as well as SQL Server.

Oracle

Use the function SYS_CONNECT_BY_PATH to return MILLER, MILLER's manager, CLARK, then CLARK's manager, KING. Use the CONNECT BY clause to walk the tree:

```
1  select ltrim(
2           sys_connect_by_path(ename,'-->'),
3           '-->') leaf___branch___root
4    from emp
5   where level = 3
6   start with ename = 'MILLER'
7 connect by prior mgr = empno
```

PostgreSQL and MySQL

Self join on table EMP twice to return MILLER, MILLER's manager, CLARK, then CLARK's manager, KING. The following solution uses PostgreSQL's concatenation operator, the double vertical-bar (||):

```
1  select a.ename||'-->'||b.ename
2              ||'-->'||c.ename as leaf___branch___root
3    from emp a, emp b, emp c
4   where a.ename = 'MILLER'
5     and a.mgr = b.empno
6     and b.mgr = c.empno
```

For MySQL users, simply use the CONCAT function; this solution will work for PostgreSQL as well.

Discussion

DB2 and SQL Server

The approach here is to start at the leaf node and walk your way up to the root (as useful practice, try walking in the other direction). The upper part of the UNION ALL simply finds the row for employee MILLER (the leaf node). The lower part of the UNION ALL finds the employee who is MILLER's manager, then finds that person's manager, and this process of finding the "manager's manager" repeats until processing stops at the highest-level manager (the root node). The value for DEPTH starts at 0 and increments automatically by 1 each time a manager is found. DEPTH is a value that DB2 maintains for you when you execute a recursive query.

 For an interesting and in-depth introduction to the WITH clause with focus on its use recursively, see Jonathan Gennick's article "Understanding the WITH Clause" at *http://gennick.com/with.htm*.

Next, the second query of the UNION ALL joins the recursive view X to table EMP, to define the parent–child relationship. The query at this point, using SQL Server's concatenation operator, is as follows:

```
    with x (tree,mgr,depth)
      as (
  select cast(ename as varchar(100)),
         mgr, 0
    from emp
   where ename = 'MILLER'
   union all
  select cast(e.ename as varchar(100)),
         e.mgr, x.depth+1
    from emp e, x
   where x.mgr = e.empno
  )
  select tree leaf__branch___root, depth
    from x
```

```
TREE              DEPTH
----------  ----------
MILLER               0
CLARK                1
KING                 2
```

At this point, the heart of the problem has been solved; starting from MILLER, return the full hierarchical relationship from bottom to top. What's left then is merely formatting. Since the tree traversal is recursive, simply concatenate the current ENAME from EMP to the one before it, which gives you the following result set:

```
    with x (tree,mgr,depth)
      as (
  select cast(ename as varchar(100)),
         mgr, 0
    from emp
   where ename = 'MILLER'
   union all
  select cast(x.tree+'-->'+e.ename as varchar(100)),
         e.mgr, x.depth+1
    from emp e, x
   where x.mgr = e.empno
  )
  select depth, tree
    from x
```

```
DEPTH TREE
----- ----------------------
    0 MILLER
    1 MILLER-->CLARK
    2 MILLER-->CLARK-->KING
```

The final step is to keep only the last row in the hierarchy. There are several ways to do this, but the solution uses DEPTH to determine when the root is reached (obviously, if CLARK has a manager other than KING, the filter on DEPTH would have to change; for a more generic solution that requires no such filter, see Recipe 13.3).

Oracle

The CONNECT BY clause does all the work in the Oracle solution. Starting with MILLER, you walk all the way to KING without the need for any joins. The expression in the CONNECT BY clause defines the relationship of the data and how the tree will be walked:

```
select ename
  from emp
 start with ename = 'MILLER'
connect by prior mgr = empno

ENAME
----------
MILLER
CLARK
KING
```

The keyword PRIOR lets you access values from the previous record in the hierarchy. Thus, for any given EMPNO you can use PRIOR MGR to access that employee's manager number. When you see a clause such as CONNECT BY PRIOR MGR = EMPNO, think of that clause as expressing a join between, in this case, parent and child.

 For more on CONNECT BY and related features, see the following Oracle Technology Network articles: "Querying Hierarchies: Top-of-the-Line Support" at *http://www.oracle.com/technology/oramag/webcolumns/2003/techarticles/gennick_connectby.html*, and "New CONNECT BY Features in Oracle Database 10g" at *http://www.oracle.com/technology/oramag/webcolumns/2003/techarticles/gennick_connectby_10g.html*.

At this point you have successfully displayed the full hierarchy starting from MILLER and ending at KING. The problem is for the most part solved. All that remains is the formatting. Use the function SYS_CONNECT_BY_PATH to append each ENAME to the one before it:

```
select sys_connect_by_path(ename,'-->') tree
  from emp
 start with ename = 'MILLER'
connect by prior mgr = empno
```

```
TREE
---------------------------
-->MILLER
-->MILLER-->CLARK
-->MILLER-->CLARK-->KING
```

Because you are interested in only the complete hierarchy, you can filter on the pseudo-column LEVEL (a more generic approach is shown in the next recipe):

```
select sys_connect_by_path(ename,'-->') tree
  from emp
 where level = 3
 start with ename = 'MILLER'
connect by prior mgr = empno


TREE
---------------------------
-->MILLER-->CLARK-->KING
```

The final step is to use the LTRIM function to remove the leading "-->" from the result set.

PostgreSQL and MySQL

Without built-in support for hierarchical queries, you must self join *n* times to return the whole tree (where *n* is the number of nodes between the leaf and the root, including the root itself; in this example, relative to MILLER, CLARK is a branch node and KING is the root node, so the distance is two nodes, and *n* = 2). This solution simply uses the technique from the previous recipe and adds one more self join:

```
select a.ename as leaf,
       b.ename as branch,
       c.ename as root
  from emp a, emp b, emp c
 where a.ename = 'MILLER'
   and a.mgr = b.empno
   and b.mgr = c.empno


LEAF        BRANCH      ROOT
----------  ----------  -----
MILLER      CLARK       KING
```

The next and last step is to format the output using the || concatenation operator for PostgreSQL or the CONCAT function for MySQL. The drawback to this kind of query is that if the hierarchy changes—for example, if there is another node between CLARK and KING—the query would need to have yet another join to return the whole tree. This is why it is such an advantage to have and use built-in functions for hierarchies.

13.3 Creating a Hierarchical View of a Table

Problem

You want to return a result set that describes the hierarchy of an entire table. In the case of the EMP table, employee KING has no manager, so KING is the root node. You want to display, starting from KING, all employees under KING and all employees (if any) under KING's subordinates. Ultimately, you want to return the following result set:

```
EMP_TREE
----------------------------
KING
KING - BLAKE
KING - BLAKE - ALLEN
KING - BLAKE - JAMES
KING - BLAKE - MARTIN
KING - BLAKE - TURNER
KING - BLAKE - WARD
KING - CLARK
KING - CLARK - MILLER
KING - JONES
KING - JONES - FORD
KING - JONES - FORD - SMITH
KING - JONES - SCOTT
KING - JONES - SCOTT - ADAMS
```

Solution

DB2 and SQL Server

Use the recursive WITH clause to start building the hierarchy at KING and then ultimately display all the employees. The solution following uses the DB2 concatenation operator "||". SQL Server users use the concatenation operator +. Other than the concatenation operators, the solution will work as-is on both RDBMSs:

```
1   with x (ename,empno)
2       as (
3   select cast(ename as varchar(100)),empno
4     from emp
5    where mgr is null
6    union all
7   select cast(x.ename||' - '||e.ename as varchar(100)),
8          e.empno
9     from emp e, x
10   where e.mgr = x.empno
11  )
12  select ename as emp_tree
13    from x
14   order by 1
```

Oracle

Use the CONNECT BY function to define the hierarchy. Use SYS_CONNECT_BY_PATH function to format the output accordingly:

```
1  select ltrim(
2         sys_connect_by_path(ename,' - '),
3         ' - ') emp_tree
4    from emp
5   start with mgr is null
6  connect by prior empno=mgr
7   order by 1
```

This solution differs from that in the previous recipe in that it includes no filter on the LEVEL pseudo-column. Without the filter, all possible trees (where PRIOR EMPNO=MGR) are displayed.

PostgreSQL

Use three UNIONs and multiple self joins:

```
1  select emp_tree
2    from (
3  select ename as emp_tree
4    from emp
5   where mgr is null
6  union
7  select a.ename||' - '||b.ename
8    from emp a
9         join
10        emp b on (a.empno=b.mgr)
11   where a.mgr is null
12  union
13  select rtrim(a.ename||' - '||b.ename
14                ||' - '||c.ename,' - ')
15    from emp a
16        join
17        emp b on (a.empno=b.mgr)
18        left join
19        emp c on (b.empno=c.mgr)
20   where a.ename = 'KING'
21  union
22  select rtrim(a.ename||' - '||b.ename||' - '||
23            c.ename||' - '||d.ename,' - ')
24    from emp a
25        join
26        emp b on (a.empno=b.mgr)
27        join
28        emp c on (b.empno=c.mgr)
29        left join
30        emp d on (c.empno=d.mgr)
31   where a.ename = 'KING'
32        ) x
33   where tree is not null
34   order by 1
```

MySQL

Use three UNIONs and multiple self joins:

```
1   select emp_tree
2     from (
3   select ename as emp_tree
4     from emp
5    where mgr is null
6   union
7   select concat(a.ename,' - ',b.ename)
8     from emp a
9          join
10         emp b on (a.empno=b.mgr)
11    where a.mgr is null
12  union
13  select concat(a.ename,' - ',
14                b.ename,' - ',c.ename)
15    from emp a
16         join
17         emp b on (a.empno=b.mgr)
18         left join
19         emp c on (b.empno=c.mgr)
20   where a.ename = 'KING'
21  union
22  select concat(a.ename,' - ',b.ename,' - ',
23                c.ename,' - ',d.ename)
24    from emp a
25         join
26         emp b on (a.empno=b.mgr)
27         join
28         emp c on (b.empno=c.mgr)
29         left join
30         emp d on (c.empno=d.mgr)
31   where a.ename = 'KING'
32         ) x
33   where tree is not null
34   order by 1
```

Discussion

DB2 and SQL Server

The first step is to identify the root row (employee KING) in the upper part of the UNION ALL in the recursive view X. The next step is to find KING's subordinates, and their subordinates if there are any, by joining recursive view X to table EMP. Recursion will continue until you've returned all employees. Without the formatting you see in the final result set, the result set returned by the recursive view X is shown below:

```
with x (ename,empno)
    as (
select cast(ename as varchar(100)),empno
```

```
   from emp
 where mgr is null
 union all
select cast(e.ename as varchar(100)),e.empno
   from emp e, x
  where e.mgr = x.empno
)
select ename emp_tree
   from x

EMP_TREE
-----------------
KING
JONES
SCOTT
ADAMS
FORD
SMITH
BLAKE
ALLEN
WARD
MARTIN
TURNER
JAMES
CLARK
MILLER
```

All the rows in the hierarchy are returned (which can be useful), but without the formatting you cannot tell who the managers are. By concatenating each employee to her manager, you return more meaningful output. Produce the desired output simply by using

```
cast(x.ename+','+e.ename as varchar(100))
```

in the SELECT clause of the lower portion of the UNION ALL in recursive view X.

The WITH clause is extremely useful in solving this type of problem, because the hierarchy can change (for example, leaf nodes become branch nodes) without any need to modify the query.

Oracle

The CONNECT BY clause returns the rows in the hierarchy. The START WITH clause defines the root row. If you run the solution without SYS_CONNECT_BY_PATH, you can see that the correct rows are returned (which can be useful), but not formatted to express the relationship of the rows:

```
select ename emp_tree
  from emp
 start with mgr is null
connect by prior empno = mgr
```

```
EMP_TREE
-----------------
KING
JONES
SCOTT
ADAMS
FORD
SMITH
BLAKE
ALLEN
WARD
MARTIN
TURNER
JAMES
CLARK
MILLER
```

By using the pseudo-column LEVEL and the function LPAD, you can see the hierarchy more clearly, and you can ultimately see why SYS_CONNECT_BY_PATH returns the results that you see in the desired output shown earlier:

```
select lpad('.',2*level,'.')||ename emp_tree
    from emp
  start with mgr is null
connect by prior empno = mgr


EMP_TREE
-----------------
..KING
....JONES
......SCOTT
........ADAMS
......FORD
........SMITH
....BLAKE
......ALLEN
......WARD
......MARTIN
......TURNER
......JAMES
....CLARK
......MILLER
```

The indentation in this output indicates who the managers are by nesting subordinates under their superiors. For example, KING works for no one. JONES works for KING. SCOTT works for JONES. ADAMS works for SCOTT.

If you look at the corresponding rows from the solution when using SYS_CONNECT_BY_PATH, you will see that SYS_CONNECT_BY_PATH rolls up the hierarchy for you. When you get to a new node, you see all the prior nodes as well:

```
KING
KING - JONES
KING - JONES - SCOTT
KING - JONES - SCOTT - ADAMS
```

If you are on Oracle8i Database or earlier, you can use the PostgreSQL solution to this problem. Alternatively, because CONNECT BY is available on older versions of Oracle, you can simply use LEVEL and RPAD/ LPAD for formatting (although to reproduce the output created by SYS_ CONNECT_BY_PATH would require a bit more work).

PostgreSQL and MySQL

With the exception of string concatenation in the SELECT clauses, the solutions are the same for both PostgreSQL and MySQL. The first step is to determine the maximum number of nodes for any one branch. You have to do this manually, before you write the query. If you examine the data in the EMP table, you will see that employees ADAM and SMITH are the leaf nodes at the greatest depth (you may wish to look at the Oracle discussion where you'll find a nicely formatted tree of the EMP hierarchy). If you look at employee ADAMS, you see that ADAMS works for SCOTT who in turn works for JONES who in turn works for KING, so the depth is 4. To be able to express a hierarchy with a depth of four, you must self join four instances of table EMP, and you must write a four-part UNION query. The results of the four-way self join (which is the lower part of the last UNION, from top to bottom) is shown below (using PostgreSQL syntax; MySQL users, simply substitute "||" for the CONCAT function call):

```
select rtrim(a.ename||' - '||b.ename||' - '||
             c.ename||' - '||d.ename,' - ') as max_depth_4
   from emp a
        join
        emp b on (a.empno=b.mgr)
        join
        emp c on (b.empno=c.mgr)
        left join
        emp d on (c.empno=d.mgr)
  where a.ename = 'KING'

MAX_DEPTH_4
----------------------------
KING - JONES - FORD  - SMITH
KING - JONES - SCOTT - ADAMS
KING - BLAKE - TURNER
KING - BLAKE - ALLEN
KING - BLAKE - WARD
KING - CLARK - MILLER
KING - BLAKE - MARTIN
KING - BLAKE - JAMES
```

The filter on A.ENAME is necessary to ensure that the root row is KING and no other employee. If you look at the result set above and compare it with the final result set, you'll see that there are some three-deep hierarchies not returned: KING - JONES - FORD and KING - JONES - SCOTT. To include those rows in the final result set, you need to write another query similar to the one above, but with one less join (self joining only three instances of table EMP rather than four). The result set of this query is shown below:

```
select rtrim(a.ename||' - '||b.ename
             ||' - '||c.ename,' - ') as max_depth_3
  from emp a
       join
       emp b on (a.empno=b.mgr)
       left join
       emp c on (b.empno=c.mgr)
 where a.ename = 'KING'


MAX_DEPTH_3
--------------------------
KING - BLAKE - ALLEN
KING - BLAKE - WARD
KING - BLAKE - MARTIN
KING - JONES - SCOTT
KING - BLAKE - TURNER
KING - BLAKE - JAMES
KING - JONES - FORD
KING - CLARK - MILLER
```

Like the query before it, the filter on A.ENAME is necessary to ensure the root row node is KING. You'll notice some overlapping rows between the query above and the four-way EMP join. To get rid of the redundant rows, simply UNION the two queries:

```
select rtrim(a.ename||' - '||b.ename
             ||' - '||c.ename,' - ') as partial_tree
  from emp a
       join
       emp b on (a.empno=b.mgr)
       left join
       emp c on (b.empno=c.mgr)
 where a.ename = 'KING'
union
select rtrim(a.ename||' - '||b.ename||' - '||
            c.ename||' - '||d.ename,' - ')
  from emp a
       join
       emp b on (a.empno=b.mgr)
       join
       emp c on (b.empno=c.mgr)
       left join
       emp d on (c.empno=d.mgr)
 where a.ename = 'KING'


PARTIAL_TREE
--------------------------
KING - BLAKE - ALLEN
KING - BLAKE - JAMES
KING - BLAKE - MARTIN
KING - BLAKE - TURNER
KING - BLAKE - WARD
```

```
KING - CLARK - MILLER
KING - JONES - FORD
KING - JONES - FORD - SMITH
KING - JONES - SCOTT
KING - JONES - SCOTT - ADAMS
```

At this point the tree is almost complete. The next step is to return rows that represent a two-deep hierarchy with KING as the root node (i.e., employees who work
directly for KING). The query to return those rows is shown below:

```
select a.ename||' - '||b.ename as max_depth_2
  from emp a
       join
       emp b on (a.empno=b.mgr)
 where a.mgr is null


MAX_DEPTH_2
---------------
KING - JONES
KING - BLAKE
KING - CLARK
```

The next step is to UNION the above query, to the PARTIAL_TREE union:

```
select a.ename||' - '||b.ename as partial_tree
  from emp a
       join
       emp b on (a.empno=b.mgr)
 where a.mgr is null
union
select rtrim(a.ename||' - '||b.ename
                   ||' - '||c.ename,' - ')
  from emp a
       join
       emp b on (a.empno=b.mgr)
       left join
       emp c on (b.empno=c.mgr)
 where a.ename = 'KING'
union
select rtrim(a.ename||' - '||b.ename||' - '||
            c.ename||' - '||d.ename,' - ')
  from emp a
       join
       emp b on (a.empno=b.mgr)
       join
       emp c on (b.empno=c.mgr)
       left join
       emp d on (c.empno=d.mgr)
 where a.ename = 'KING'


PARTIAL_TREE
----------------------------------
KING - BLAKE
KING - BLAKE - ALLEN
KING - BLAKE - JAMES
```

```
KING - BLAKE - MARTIN
KING - BLAKE - TURNER
KING - BLAKE - WARD
KING - CLARK
KING - CLARK - MILLER
KING - JONES
KING - JONES - FORD
KING - JONES - FORD - SMITH
KING - JONES - SCOTT
KING - JONES - SCOTT - ADAMS
```

The final step is to UNION KING to the top of PARTIAL_TREE to return the desired result set.

13.4   Finding All Child Rows for a Given Parent Row

Problem

You want to find all the employees who work for JONES, either directly or indirectly (i.e., they work for someone who works for JONES). The list of employees under JONES is shown below (JONES is included in the result set):

```
ENAME
---------
JONES
SCOTT
ADAMS
FORD
SMITH
```

Solution

Being able to move to the absolute top or bottom of a tree is extremely useful. For this solution there is no special formatting necessary. The goal is to simply return all employees who work under employee JONES, including JONES himself. This type of query really shows the usefulness of recursive SQL extensions like Oracle's CONNECT BY and SQL Server's/DB2's WITH clause.

DB2 and SQL Server

Use the recursive WITH clause to find all employees under JONES. Begin with JONES by specifying WHERE ENAME = 'JONES' in the first of the two union queries:

```
1    with x (ename,empno)
2       as (
3    select ename,empno
4      from emp
5     where ename = 'JONES'
6     union all
7    select e.ename, e.empno
8      from emp e, x
```

```
 9    where x.empno = e.mgr
10  )
11  select ename
12    from x
```

Oracle

Use the CONNECT BY clause and specify START WITH ENAME = 'JONES' to find all the employees under JONES:

```
1  select ename
2    from emp
3    start with ename = 'JONES'
4  connect by prior empno = mgr
```

PostgreSQL and MySQL

You must know in advance how many nodes there are in the tree. The following queries show how to determine the depth of the hierarchy:

```
/* find JONES' EMPNO */
select ename,empno,mgr
  from emp
 where ename = 'JONES'


ENAME         EMPNO      MGR
----------  ----------  ----------
JONES          7566        7839


/* are there any employees who work directly under JONES? */
select count(*)
  from emp
 where mgr = 7566


 COUNT(*)
----------
       2


/* there are two employees under JONES, find their EMPNOs */
select ename,empno,mgr
  from emp
 where mgr = 7566


ENAME         EMPNO      MGR
----------  ----------  ----------
SCOTT          7788       7566
FORD           7902       7566


/* are there any employees under SCOTT or FORD? */
select count(*)
  from emp
 where mgr in (7788,7902)
```

```
COUNT(*)
----------
         2

/* there are two employees under SCOTT or FORD, find their EMPNOs */
select ename,empno,mgr
  from emp
 where mgr in (7788,7902)

ENAME          EMPNO        MGR
----------  ----------  ----------
SMITH           7369       7902
ADAMS           7876       7788

/* are there any employees under SMITH or ADAMS? */
select count(*)
  from emp
 where mgr in (7369,7876)

COUNT(*)
----------
         0
```

The hierarchy starting from JONES ends with employees SMITH and ADAMS. That makes the hierarchy three levels deep. Now that you know the depth, you can begin to traverse the hierarchy from top to bottom.

First, self join table EMP twice. Then unpivot inline view X to transform three columns with two rows into one column with six rows (in PostgreSQL, you can use GENERATE_SERIES(1,6) as an alternative to querying the T100 pivot table):

```
1   select distinct
2          case t100.id
3               when 1 then root
4               when 2 then branch
5               else       leaf
6          end as JONES_SUBORDINATES
7     from (
8   select a.ename as root,
9          b.ename as branch,
10         c.ename as leaf
11    from emp a, emp b, emp c
12   where a.ename = 'JONES'
13     and a.empno = b.mgr
14     and b.empno = c.mgr
15         ) x,
16         t100
17   where t100.id <= 6
```

As an alternative, you can use views and UNION the results. If you create the following views:

```
create view v1
as
select ename,mgr,empno
  from emp
 where ename = 'JONES'


create view v2
as
select ename,mgr,empno
  from emp
 where mgr = (select empno from v1)


create view v3
as
select ename,mgr,empno
  from emp
 where mgr in (select empno from v2)
```

the solution then becomes:

```
select ename from v1
 union
select ename from v2
 union
select ename from v3
```

Discussion

DB2 and SQL Server

The recursive WITH clause makes this a relatively easy problem to solve. The first part of the WITH clause, the upper part of the UNION ALL, returns the row for employee JONES. You need to return ENAME to see the name and EMPNO so you can use it to join on. The lower part of the UNION ALL recursively joins EMP.MGR to X.EMPNO. The join condition will be applied until the result set is exhausted.

Oracle

The START WTH clause tells the query to make JONES the root node. The condition in the CONNECT BY clause drives the tree walk and will run until the condition is no longer true.

PostgreSQL and MySQL

The technique used here is the same as in Recipe 13.2. A major drawback is that you must know in advance the depth of the hierarchy.

13.5   Determining Which Rows Are Leaf, Branch, or Root Nodes

Problem

You want to determine what type of node a given row is: a leaf, branch, or root. For this example, a leaf node is an employee who is not a manager. A branch node is an employee who is both a manager and also has a manager. A root node is an employee without a manager. You want to return 1 (TRUE) or 0 (FALSE) to reflect the status of each row in the hierarchy. You want to return the following result set:

ENAME	IS_LEAF	IS_BRANCH	IS_ROOT
KING	0	0	1
JONES	0	1	0
SCOTT	0	1	0
FORD	0	1	0
CLARK	0	1	0
BLAKE	0	1	0
ADAMS	1	0	0
MILLER	1	0	0
JAMES	1	0	0
TURNER	1	0	0
ALLEN	1	0	0
WARD	1	0	0
MARTIN	1	0	0
SMITH	1	0	0

Solution

It is important to realize that the EMP table is modeled in a tree hierarchy, not a recursive hierarchy, the value for MGR for root nodes is NULL. If EMP was modeled to use a recursive hierarchy, root nodes would be self-referencing (i.e., the value for MGR for employee KING would be KING's EMPNO). I find self-referencing to be counterintuitive and thus am using NULL values for root nodes' MGR. For Oracle users using CONNECT BY and DB2/SQL Server users using WITH, you'll find tree hierarchies easier to work with and potentially more efficient than recursive hierarchies. If you are in a situation where you have a recursive hierarchy and are using CONNECT BY or WITH, watch out: you can end up with a loop in your SQL. You need to code around such loops if you are stuck with recursive hierarchies.

DB2, PostgreSQL, MySQL, and SQL Server

Use three scalar subqueries to determine the correct "Boolean" value (either a 1 or a 0) to return for each node type:

```
1  select e.ename,
2        (select sign(count(*)) from emp d
3          where 0 =
```

```
4              (select count(*) from emp f
5                where f.mgr = e.empno)) as is_leaf,
6           (select sign(count(*)) from emp d
7             where d.mgr = e.empno
8               and e.mgr is not null) as is_branch,
9           (select sign(count(*)) from emp d
10            where d.empno = e.empno
11              and d.mgr is null) as is_root
12     from emp e
13   order by 4 desc,3 desc
```

Oracle

The scalar subquery solution will work for Oracle as well, and should be used if you are on a version of Oracle prior to Oracle Database 10g. The following solution high-lights built-in functions provided by Oracle (that were introduced in Oracle Database 10g) to identify root and leaf rows. The functions are CONNECT_BY_ROOT and CONNECT_BY_ISLEAF, respectively:

```
1    select ename,
2           connect_by_isleaf is_leaf,
3           (select count(*) from emp e
4             where e.mgr = emp.empno
5               and emp.mgr is not null
6               and rownum = 1) is_branch,
7           decode(ename,connect_by_root(ename),1,0) is_root
8      from emp
9     start with mgr is null
10   connect by prior empno = mgr
11   order by 4 desc, 3 desc
```

Discussion

DB2, PostgreSQL, MySQL, and SQL Server

This solution simply applies the rules defined in the Problem section to determine leaves, branches, and roots. The first step is to find determine whether an employee is a leaf node. If the employee is not a manager (no one works under her), then she is a leaf node. The first scalar subquery, IS_LEAF, is shown below:

```
select e.ename,
       (select sign(count(*)) from emp d
         where 0 =
           (select count(*) from emp f
             where f.mgr = e.empno)) as is_leaf
  from emp e
order by 2 desc

ENAME        IS_LEAF
---------- ----------
SMITH              1
ALLEN              1
WARD               1
```

ADAMS	1
TURNER	1
MARTIN	1
JAMES	1
MILLER	1
JONES	0
BLAKE	0
CLARK	0
FORD	0
SCOTT	0
KING	0

Because the output for IS_LEAF should be a 0 or 1, it is necessary to take the SIGN of the COUNT(*) operation. Otherwise you would get 14 instead of 1 for leaf rows. As an alternative, you can use a table with only one row to count against, because you only want to return 0 or 1. For example:

```
select e.ename,
       (select count(*) from t1 d
         where not exists
           (select null from emp f
             where f.mgr = e.empno)) as is_leaf
    from emp e
order by 2 desc

ENAME       IS_LEAF
---------- ----------
SMITH          1
ALLEN          1
WARD           1
ADAMS          1
TURNER         1
MARTIN         1
JAMES          1
MILLER         1
JONES          0
BLAKE          0
CLARK          0
FORD           0
SCOTT          0
KING           0
```

The next step is to find branch nodes. If an employee is a manager (someone works for them), and they also happen to work for someone else, then the employee is a branch node. The results of the scalar subquery IS_BRANCH are shown below:

```
select e.ename,
       (select sign(count(*)) from emp d
         where d.mgr = e.empno
           and e.mgr is not null) as is_branch
    from emp e
order by 2 desc
```

ENAME	IS_BRANCH
JONES	1
BLAKE	1
SCOTT	1
CLARK	1
FORD	1
SMITH	0
TURNER	0
MILLER	0
JAMES	0
ADAMS	0
KING	0
ALLEN	0
MARTIN	0
WARD	0

Again, it is necessary to take the SIGN of the COUNT(*) operation. Otherwise you will get (potentially) values greater than 1 when a node is a branch. Like scalar subquery IS_LEAF, you can use a table with one row to avoid using SIGN. The following solution uses a one-row table named dual:

```
select e.ename,
       (select count(*) from t1 t
         where exists (
          select null from emp f
          where f.mgr = e.empno
            and e.mgr is not null)) as is_branch
  from emp e
order by 2 desc
```

ENAME	IS_BRANCH
JONES	1
BLAKE	1
SCOTT	1
CLARK	1
FORD	1
SMITH	0
TURNER	0
MILLER	0
JAMES	0
ADAMS	0
KING	0
ALLEN	0
MARTIN	0
WARD	0

The last step is to find the root nodes. A root node is defined as an employee who is a manager but who does not work for anyone else. In table EMP, only KING is a root node. Scalar subquery IS_ROOT is shown below:

```
select e.ename,
       (select sign(count(*)) from emp d
          where d.empno = e.empno
            and d.mgr is null) as is_root
  from emp e
order by 2 desc

ENAME        IS_ROOT
----------   ----------
KING             1
SMITH            0
ALLEN            0
WARD             0
JONES            0
TURNER           0
JAMES            0
MILLER           0
FORD             0
ADAMS            0
MARTIN           0
BLAKE            0
CLARK            0
SCOTT            0
```

Because EMP is a small 14-row table, it is easy to see that employee KING is the only root node, so in this case taking the SIGN of the COUNT(*) operation is not strictly necessary. If there can be multiple root nodes, then you can use SIGN, or you can use a one-row table in the scalar subquery as is shown earlier for IS_BRANCH and IS_LEAF.

Oracle

For those of you on versions of Oracle prior to Oracle Database 10g, you can follow the discussion for the other RDBMSs, as that solution will work (without modifications) in Oracle. If you are on Oracle Database 10g or later, you may want to take advantage of two functions to make identifying root and leaf nodes a simple task: they are CONNECT_BY_ROOT and CONNECT_BY_ISLEAF, respectively. As of the time of this writing, it is necessary to use CONNECT BY in your SQL statement in order for you to be able to use CONNECT_BY_ROOT and CONNECT_BY_ISLEAF. The first step is to find the leaf nodes by using CONNECT_BY_ISLEAF as follows:

```
select ename,
       connect_by_isleaf is_leaf
  from emp
 start with mgr is null
connect by prior empno = mgr
 order by 2 desc

ENAME        IS_LEAF
----------   ----------
```

```
     ADAMS                 1
     SMITH                 1
     ALLEN                 1
     TURNER                1
     MARTIN                1
     WARD                  1
     JAMES                 1
     MILLER                1
     KING                  0
     JONES                 0
     BLAKE                 0
     CLARK                 0
     FORD                  0
     SCOTT                 0
```

The next step is to use a scalar subquery to find the branch nodes. Branch nodes are employees who are managers but who also work for someone else:

```
select ename,
       (select count(*) from emp e
         where e.mgr = emp.empno
           and emp.mgr is not null
           and rownum = 1) is_branch
  from emp
 start with mgr is null
connect by prior empno = mgr
order by 2 desc

ENAME        IS_BRANCH
----------   ----------
JONES                1
SCOTT                1
BLAKE                1
FORD                 1
CLARK                1
KING                 0
MARTIN               0
MILLER               0
JAMES                0
TURNER               0
WARD                 0
ADAMS                0
ALLEN                0
SMITH                0
```

The filter on ROWNUM is necessary to ensure that you return a count of 1 or 0, and nothing else.

The last step is to identify the root nodes by using the function CONNECT_BY_ROOT. The solution finds the ENAME for the root node and compares it with all the rows returned by the query. If there is a match, that row is the root node:

```
select ename,
       decode(ename,connect_by_root(ename),1,0) is_root
```

```
  from emp
 start with mgr is null
 connect by prior empno = mgr
 order by 2 desc

 ENAME         IS_ROOT
 ----------    ----------
 KING                  1
 JONES                 0
 SCOTT                 0
 ADAMS                 0
 FORD                  0
 SMITH                 0
 BLAKE                 0
 ALLEN                 0
 WARD                  0
 MARTIN                0
 TURNER                0
 JAMES                 0
 CLARK                 0
 MILLER                0
```

If using Oracle9*i* Database or later, you can use the SYS_CONNECT_BY_PATH function as an alternative to CONNECT_BY_ROOT. The Oracle9*i* Database version of the preceding would be:

```
select ename,
       decode(substr(root,1,instr(root,',')-1),NULL,1,0) root
  from (
select ename,
       ltrim(sys_connect_by_path(ename,','),',') root
  from emp
start with mgr is null
connect by prior empno=mgr
       )

 ENAME        ROOT
 ----------   ----
 KING            1
 JONES           0
 SCOTT           0
 ADAMS           0
 FORD            0
 SMITH           0
 BLAKE           0
 ALLEN           0
 WARD            0
 MARTIN          0
 TURNER          0
 JAMES           0
 CLARK           0
 MILLER          0
```

The SYS_CONNECT_BY_PATH function rolls up a hierarchy starting from the root value as is shown below:

```
select ename,
       ltrim(sys_connect_by_path(ename,','),',') path
  from emp
start with mgr is null
connect by prior empno=mgr

ENAME      PATH
---------- ---------------------------
KING       KING
JONES      KING,JONES
SCOTT      KING,JONES,SCOTT
ADAMS      KING,JONES,SCOTT,ADAMS
FORD       KING,JONES,FORD
SMITH      KING,JONES,FORD,SMITH
BLAKE      KING,BLAKE
ALLEN      KING,BLAKE,ALLEN
WARD       KING,BLAKE,WARD
MARTIN     KING,BLAKE,MARTIN
TURNER     KING,BLAKE,TURNER
JAMES      KING,BLAKE,JAMES
CLARK      KING,CLARK
MILLER     KING,CLARK,MILLER
```

To get the root row, simply substring out the first ENAME in PATH:

```
select ename,
       substr(root,1,instr(root,',')-1) root
  from (
select ename,
       ltrim(sys_connect_by_path(ename,','),',') root
  from emp
start with mgr is null
connect by prior empno=mgr
       )

ENAME      ROOT
---------- ---------
KING
JONES      KING
SCOTT      KING
ADAMS      KING
FORD       KING
SMITH      KING
BLAKE      KING
ALLEN      KING
WARD       KING
MARTIN     KING
TURNER     KING
JAMES      KING
CLARK      KING
MILLER     KING
```

The last step is to flag the result from the ROOT column if it is NULL; that is your root row.

CHAPTER 14

Odds 'n' Ends

This chapter contains queries that didn't fit in any other chapter either because the chapter they would belong to is already long enough, or because the problems they solve are more fun than realistic. This chapter is meant to be a "fun" chapter, in that the recipes here may or may not be recipes that you would actually use; nevertheless, I consider the queries interesting and wanted to include them somewhere in this book.

14.1 Creating Cross-Tab Reports Using SQL Server's PIVOT Operator

Problem

You want to create a cross-tab report, to transform your result set's rows into columns. You are aware of traditional methods of pivoting but would like to try something different. In particular, you want to return the following result set without using CASE expressions or joins:

```
DEPT_10    DEPT_20    DEPT_30    DEPT_40
-------  ---------- ---------- ----------
      3          5          6          0
```

Solution

Use the PIVOT operator to create the required result set without CASE expressions or additional joins:

```
1  select [10] as dept_10,
2         [20] as dept_20,
3         [30] as dept_30,
4         [40] as dept_40
5    from (select deptno, empno from emp) driver
6    pivot (
7       count(driver.empno)
8       for driver.deptno in ( [10],[20],[30],[40] )
9    ) as empPivot
```

Discussion

The PIVOT operator may seem strange at first, but the operation it performs in the solution is technically the same as the more familiar transposition query shown below:

```
select sum(case deptno when 10 then 1 else 0 end) as dept_10,
       sum(case deptno when 20 then 1 else 0 end) as dept_20,
       sum(case deptno when 30 then 1 else 0 end) as dept_30,
       sum(case deptno when 40 then 1 else 0 end) as dept_40
  from emp


DEPT_10    DEPT_20    DEPT_30    DEPT_40
-------    -------    -------    -------
      3          5          6          0
```

Now that you know what is essentially happening, let's break down what the PIVOT operator is doing. Line 5 of the solution shows an inline view named DRIVER:

```
from (select deptno, empno from emp) driver
```

I've chosen the alias "driver" because the rows from this inline view (or table expression) feed directly into the PIVOT operation. The PIVOT operator rotates the rows to columns by evaluating the items listed on line 8 in the FOR list (shown below):

```
for driver.deptno in ( [10],[20],[30],[40] )
```

The evaluation goes something like this:

1. If there are any DEPTNOs with a value of 10, perform the aggregate operation defined (COUNT(DRIVER.EMPNO)) for those rows.
2. Repeat for DEPTNOs 20, 30, and 40.

The items listed in the brackets on line 8 serve not only to define values for which aggregation is performed; the items also become the column names in the result set (without the square brackets). In the SELECT clause of the solution, the items in the FOR list are referenced and aliased. If you do not alias the items in the FOR list, the column names become the items in the FOR list sans brackets.

Interestingly enough, since inline view DRIVER is just that, an inline view, you may put more complex SQL in there. For example, consider the situation where you want to modify the result set such that the actual department name is the name of the column. Listed below are the rows in table DEPT:

```
select * from dept


DEPTNO DNAME          LOC
------ -------------- -------------
    10 ACCOUNTING     NEW YORK
    20 RESEARCH       DALLAS
    30 SALES          CHICAGO
    40 OPERATIONS     BOSTON
```

You would like to use PIVOT to return the following result set:

```
ACCOUNTING   RESEARCH    SALES OPERATIONS
----------  ----------  ---------- ----------
        3           5           6          0
```

Because inline view DRIVER can be practically any valid table expression, you can perform the join from table EMP to table DEPT, and then have PIVOT evaluate those rows. The following query will return the desired result set:

```
select [ACCOUNTING] as ACCOUNTING,
       [SALES]      as SALES,
       [RESEARCH]   as RESEARCH,
       [OPERATIONS] as OPERATIONS
  from (
          select d.dname, e.empno
            from emp e,dept d
           where e.deptno=d.deptno

       ) driver
  pivot (
    count(driver.empno)
    for driver.dname in ([ACCOUNTING],[SALES],[RESEARCH],[OPERATIONS])
  ) as empPivot
```

As you can see, PIVOT provides an interesting spin on pivoting result sets. Regardless of whether or not you prefer using it to the traditional methods of pivoting, it's nice to have another tool in your toolbox.

14.2 Unpivoting a Cross-Tab Report Using SQL Server's UNPIVOT Operator

Problem

You have a pivoted result set (or simply a fat table) and you wish to unpivot the result set. For example, instead of having a result set with one row and four columns you want to return a result set with two columns and four rows. Using the result set from the previous recipe, you want to convert it from this:

```
ACCOUNTING   RESEARCH    SALES OPERATIONS
----------  ----------  ---------- ----------
        3           5           6          0
```

to this:

```
DNAME              CNT
--------------  ----------
ACCOUNTING            3
RESEARCH             5
SALES                6
OPERATIONS           0
```

Solution

You didn't think SQL Server would give you the ability to PIVOT without being able to UNPIVOT, did you? To unpivot the result set just use it as the driver and let the UNPIVOT operator do all the work. All you need to do is specify the column names:

```
1   select DNAME, CNT
2     from (
3       select [ACCOUNTING] as ACCOUNTING,
4               [SALES]      as SALES,
5               [RESEARCH]   as RESEARCH,
6               [OPERATIONS] as OPERATIONS
7         from (
8               select d.dname, e.empno
9                 from emp e,dept d
10                where e.deptno=d.deptno
11
12             ) driver
13          pivot (
14            count(driver.empno)
15            for driver.dname in ([ACCOUNTING],[SALES],[RESEARCH],[OPERATIONS])
16          ) as empPivot
17   ) new_driver
18   unpivot (cnt for dname in (ACCOUNTING,SALES,RESEARCH,OPERATIONS)
19   ) as un_pivot
```

Hopefully, before reading this recipe you've read the one prior to it, because the inline view NEW_DRIVER is simply the code from Recipe 14.1 (if you don't understand it, please refer to the previous recipe before looking at this one). Since lines 3–16 consist of code you've already seen, the only new syntax is on line 18, where you use UNPIVOT.

The UNPIVOT command simply looks at the result set from NEW_DRIVER and evaluates each column and row. For example, the UNPIVOT operator evaluates the column names from NEW_DRIVER. When it encounters ACCOUNTING, it transforms the column name ACCOUNTING into a row value (under the column DNAME). It also takes the value for ACCOUNTING from NEW_DRIVER (which is 3) and returns that as part of the ACCOUNTING row as well (under the column CNT). UNPIVOT does this for each of the items specified in the FOR list and simply returns each one as a row.

The new result set is now skinny and has two columns, DNAME and CNT, with four rows:

```
select DNAME, CNT
  from (
    select [ACCOUNTING] as ACCOUNTING,
            [SALES]      as SALES,
            [RESEARCH]   as RESEARCH,
            [OPERATIONS] as OPERATIONS
      from (
```

```
        select d.dname, e.empno
          from emp e,dept d
          where e.deptno=d.deptno

         ) driver
   pivot (
       count(driver.empno)
       for driver.dname in ( [ACCOUNTING],[SALES],[RESEARCH],[OPERATIONS] )
   ) as empPivot
) new_driver
unpivot (cnt for dname in (ACCOUNTING,SALES,RESEARCH,OPERATIONS)
) as un_pivot

DNAME              CNT
-------------- ----------
ACCOUNTING           3
RESEARCH             5
SALES                6
OPERATIONS           0
```

14.3 Transposing a Result Set Using Oracle's MODEL Clause

Problem

Like the fist recipe in this chapter, you wish to find an alternative to the traditional pivoting techniques you've seen already. You want to try your hand at Oracle's MODEL clause. Unlike SQL Server's PIVOT operator, Oracle's MODEL clause does not exist to transpose result sets; as a matter of fact, it would be quite accurate to say the application of the MODEL clause for pivoting would be a misuse and clearly not what the MODEL clause was intended for. Nevertheless, the MODEL clause provides for an interesting approach to a common problem. For this particular problem, you want to transform the following result set from this:

```
select deptno, count(*) cnt
  from emp
  group by deptno

DEPTNO      CNT
------ ----------
    10        3
    20        5
    30        6
```

to this:

```
      D10        D20        D30
---------- ---------- ----------
       3          5          6
```

Solution

Use aggregation and CASE expressions in the MODEL clause just as you would use them if pivoting with traditional techniques. The main difference in this case is that you use arrays to store the values of the aggregation and return the arrays in the result set:

```
select max(d10) d10,
       max(d20) d20,
       max(d30) d30
  from (
select d10,d20,d30
  from ( select deptno, count(*) cnt from emp group by deptno )
 model
  dimension by(deptno d)
   measures(deptno, cnt d10, cnt d20, cnt d30)
   rules(
     d10[any] = case when deptno[cv( )]=10 then d10[cv( )] else 0 end,
     d20[any] = case when deptno[cv( )]=20 then d20[cv( )] else 0 end,
     d30[any] = case when deptno[cv( )]=30 then d30[cv( )] else 0 end
 )
 )
```

Discussion

The MODEL clause is an extremely useful and powerful addition to the Oracle SQL toolbox. Once you begin working with MODEL you'll notice helpful features such as iteration, array access to row values, the ability to "upsert" rows into a result set, and the ability to build reference models. You'll quickly see that this recipe doesn't take advantage of any of the cool features the MODEL clause offers, but it's nice to be able to look at a problem from multiple angles and use different features in unexpected ways (if for no other reason than to learn where certain features are more useful than others).

The first step to understanding the solution is to examine the inline view in the FROM clause. The inline view simply counts the number of employees in each DEPTNO in table EMP. The results are shown below:

```
select deptno, count(*) cnt
  from emp
 group by deptno

DEPTNO      CNT
------ ----------
    10        3
    20        5
    30        6
```

This result set is what is given to MODEL to work with. Examining the MODEL clause, you see three subclauses that stand out: DIMENSION BY, MEASURES, and RULES. Let's start with MEASURES.

The items in the MEASURES list are simply the arrays you are declaring for this query. The query uses four arrays: DEPTNO, D10, D20, and D30. Like columns in a SELECT list, arrays in the MEASURES list can have aliases. As you can see, three of the four arrays are actually CNT from the inline view.

If the MEASURES list contains our arrays, then the items in the DIMENSION BY subclause are the array indices. Consider this: array D10 is simply an alias for CNT. If you look at the result set for the inline view above, you'll see that CNT has three values: 3, 5, and 6. When you create an array of CNT, you are creating an array with three elements, namely, the three integers 3, 5, and 6. Now, how do you access these values from the array individually? You use the array index. The index, defined in the DIMENSION BY subclause, has the values of 10, 20, and 30 (from the result set above). So, for example, the following expression:

    d10[10]

would evaluate to 3, as you are accessing the value for CNT in array D10 for DEPTNO 10 (which is 3).

Because each of the three arrays (D10, D20, D30) contain the values from CNT, all three of them have the same results. How then do we get the proper count into the correct array? Enter the RULES subclause. If you look at the result set for the inline view shown earlier, you'll see that the values for DEPTNO are 10, 20, and 30. The expressions involving CASE in the RULES clause simply evaluate each value in the DEPTNO array:

- If the value is 10, store the CNT for DEPTNO 10 in D10[10] else store 0.
- If the value is 20, store the CNT for DEPTNO 20 in D20[20] else store 0.
- If the value is 30, store the CNT for DEPTNO 30 in D30[30] else store 0.

If you find yourself feeling a bit like Alice tumbling down the rabbit hole, don't worry; just stop and execute what's been discussed thus far. The following result set represents what has been discussed. Sometimes it's easier to read a bit, look at the code that actually performs what you just read, then go back and read it again. The following is quite simple once you see it in action:

```
select deptno, d10,d20,d30
  from ( select deptno, count(*) cnt from emp group by deptno )
model
  dimension by(deptno d)
  measures(deptno, cnt d10, cnt d20, cnt d30)
  rules(
      d10[any] = case when deptno[cv( )]=10 then d10[cv( )] else 0 end,
      d20[any] = case when deptno[cv( )]=20 then d20[cv( )] else 0 end,
      d30[any] = case when deptno[cv( )]=30 then d30[cv( )] else 0 end
  )
```

```
DEPTNO        D10       D20       D30
------  ----------  ----------  ----------
    10          3         0          0
    20          0         5          0
    30          0         0          6
```

As you can see, the RULES subclause is what changed the values in each array. If you are still not catching on, simply execute the same query but comment out the expressions in the RULES subclase:

```
select deptno, d10,d20,d30
  from ( select deptno, count(*) cnt from emp group by deptno )
 model
  dimension by(deptno d)
  measures(deptno, cnt d10, cnt d20, cnt d30)
  rules(
   /*
    d10[any] = case when deptno[cv( )]=10 then d10[cv( )] else 0 end,
    d20[any] = case when deptno[cv( )]=20 then d20[cv( )] else 0 end,
    d30[any] = case when deptno[cv( )]=30 then d30[cv( )] else 0 end
   */
  )
```

```
DEPTNO        D10       D20       D30
------  ----------  ----------  ----------
    10          3         3          3
    20          5         5          5
    30          6         6          6
```

It should be clear now that the result set from the MODEL clause is the same as the inline view, except that the COUNT operation is aliased D10, D20, and D30. The query below proves this:

```
select deptno, count(*) d10, count(*) d20, count(*) d30
  from emp
 group by deptno
```

```
DEPTNO        D10       D20       D30
------  ----------  ----------  ----------
    10          3   .      3          3
    20          5         5          5
    30          6         6          6
```

So, all the MODEL clause did was to take the values for DEPTNO and CNT, put them into arrays, and then make sure that each array represents a single DEPTNO. At this point, arrays D10, D20, and D30 each have a single non-zero value representing the CNT for a given DEPTNO. The result set is already transposed, and all that is left is to use the aggregate function MAX (you could have used MIN or SUM; it would make no difference in this case) to return only one row:

```
select max(d10) d10,
       max(d20) d20,
       max(d30) d30
  from (
select d10,d20,d30
  from ( select deptno, count(*) cnt from emp group by deptno )
 model
  dimension by(deptno d)
   measures(deptno, cnt d10, cnt d20, cnt d30)
   rules(
     d10[any] = case when deptno[cv()]=10 then d10[cv()] else 0 end,
     d20[any] = case when deptno[cv()]=20 then d20[cv()] else 0 end,
     d30[any] = case when deptno[cv()]=30 then d30[cv()] else 0 end
 )
 )

     D10        D20        D30
---------- ---------- ----------
      3          5          6
```

14.4   Extracting Elements of a String from Unfixed Locations

Problem

You have a string field that contains serialized log data. You want to parse through the string and extract the relevant information. Unfortunately, the relevant information is not at fixed points in the string. Instead, you must use the fact that certain characters exist around the information you need, to extract said information. For example, consider the following strings:

```
xxxxxabc[867]xxx[-]xxxx[5309]xxxxx
xxxxxtime:[11271978]favnum:[4]id:[Joe]xxxxx
call:[F_GET_ROWS()]b1:[ROSEWOOD...SIR]b2:[44400002]77.90xxxxx
film:[non_marked]qq:[unit]tailpipe:[withabanana?]80sxxxxx
```

You want to extract the values between the square brackets, returning the following result set:

```
FIRST_VAL         SECOND_VAL        LAST_VAL
---------------   ---------------   ---------------
867               -                 5309
11271978          4                 Joe
F_GET_ROWS()      ROSEWOOD...SIR    44400002
non_marked        unit              withabanana?
```

Solution

Despite not knowing the exact locations within the string of the interesting values, you do know that they are located between square brackets [], and you know there are three of them. Use Oracle's built-in function INSTR to find the locations to of the brackets. Use the built-in function SUBSTR to extract the values from the string. View V will contain the strings to parse and is defined as follows (its use is strictly for readability):

```
create view V
as
select 'xxxxxabc[867]xxx[-]xxxx[5309]xxxxx' msg
    from dual
  union all
  select 'xxxxxtime:[11271978]favnum:[4]id:[Joe]xxxxx' msg
    from dual
  union all
  select 'call:[F_GET_ROWS()]b1:[ROSEWOOD...SIR]b2:[44400002]77.90xxxxx' msg
    from dual
  union all
  select 'film:[non_marked]qq:[unit]tailpipe:[withabanana?]80sxxxxx' msg
    from dual
```

```
1   select substr(msg,
2          instr(msg,'[',1,1)+1,
3          instr(msg,']',1,1)-instr(msg,'[',1,1)-1) first_val,
4        substr(msg,
5          instr(msg,'[',1,2)+1,
6          instr(msg,']',1,2)-instr(msg,'[',1,2)-1) second_val,
7        substr(msg,
8          instr(msg,'[',-1,1)+1,
9          instr(msg,']',-1,1)-instr(msg,'[',-1,1)-1) last_val
10    from V
```

Discussion

Using Oracle's built-in function INSTR makes this problem fairly simple to solve. Since you know the values you are after are enclosed in [], and that there are three sets of [], the first step to this solution is to simply use INSTR to find the numeric positions of [] in each string. The following example returns the numeric position of the opening and closing brackets in each row:

```
select instr(msg,'[',1,1) "1st_[",
       instr(msg,']',1,1) "]_1st",
       instr(msg,'[',1,2) "2nd_[",
       instr(msg,']',1,2) "]_2nd",
       instr(msg,'[',-1,1) "3rd_[",
       instr(msg,']',-1,1) "]_3rd"
  from V
```

1st_[	]_1st	2nd_[	]_2nd	3rd_[	]_3rd
9	13	17	19	24	29
11	20	28	30	34	38
6	19	23	38	42	51
6	17	21	26	36	49

At this point, the hard work is done. All that is left is to plug the numeric positions into SUBSTR to parse MSG at those locations. You'll notice that in the complete solution there's some simple arithmetic on the values returned by INSTR, particularly, +1 and −1; this is necessary to ensure the opening square bracket, [, is not returned in the final result set. Listed below is the solution less addition and subtraction of 1 on the return values from INSTR; notice how each value has a leading square bracket:

```
select substr(msg,
       instr(msg,'[',1,1),
       instr(msg,']',1,1)-instr(msg,'[',1,1)) first_val,
       substr(msg,
       instr(msg,'[',1,2),
       instr(msg,']',1,2)-instr(msg,'[',1,2)) second_val,
       substr(msg,
       instr(msg,'[',-1,1),
       instr(msg,']',-1,1)-instr(msg,'[',-1,1)) last_val
  from V
```

FIRST_VAL	SECOND_VAL	LAST_VAL
[867	[-	[5309
[11271978	[4	[Joe
[F_GET_ROWS( )	[ROSEWOOD...SIR	[44400002
[non_marked	[unit	[withabanana?

From the result set above, you can see that the open bracket is there. You may be thinking: "OK, put the addition of 1 to INSTR back and the leading square bracket goes away. Why do we need to subtract 1?" The reason is this: if you put the addition back but leave out the subtraction, you end up including the closing square bracket, as can be seen below:

```
select substr(msg,
       instr(msg,'[',1,1)+1,
       instr(msg,']',1,1)-instr(msg,'[',1,1)) first_val,
       substr(msg,
       instr(msg,'[',1,2)+1,
       instr(msg,']',1,2)-instr(msg,'[',1,2)) second_val,
       substr(msg,
       instr(msg,'[',-1,1)+1,
       instr(msg,']',-1,1)-instr(msg,'[',-1,1)) last_val
  from V
```

```
FIRST_VAL        SECOND_VAL        LAST_VAL
---------------  ---------------   --------------
867]             -]                5309]
11271978]        4]                Joe]
F_GET_ROWS()]    ROSEWOOD...SIR]   44400002]
non_marked]      unit]             withabanana?]
```

At this point it should be clear: to ensure you include neither of the square brackets, you must add 1 to the beginning index and subtract one from the ending index.

14.5 Finding the Number of Days in a Year (an Alternate Solution for Oracle)

Problem

You want to find the number of days in a year.

 This recipe presents an alternative solution to Recipe 9.2. This solution is specific to Oracle.

Solution

Use the TO_CHAR function to format the last date of the year into a three-digit day-of-the-year number:

```
1  select 'Days in 2005: '||
2         to_char(add_months(trunc(sysdate,'y'),12)-1,'DDD')
3         as report
4    from dual
5  union all
6  select 'Days in 2004: '||
7         to_char(add_months(trunc(
8                      to_date('01-SEP-2004'),'y'),12)-1,'DDD')
9    from dual
```

```
REPORT
-----------------
Days in 2005: 365
Days in 2004: 366
```

Discussion

Begin by using the TRUNC function to return the first day of the year for the given date, as follows:

```
select trunc(to_date('01-SEP-2004'),'y')
  from dual
```

```
TRUNC(TO_DA
-----------
01-JAN-2004
```

Next, use ADD_MONTHS to add one year (12 months) to the truncated date. Then subtract one day, bringing you to the end of the year in which your original date falls:

```
select add_months(
        trunc(to_date('01-SEP-2004'),'y'),
        12) before_subtraction,
      add_months(
        trunc(to_date('01-SEP-2004'),'y'),
        12)-1 after_subtraction
  from dual

BEFORE_SUBT AFTER_SUBTR
----------- -----------
01-JAN-2005 31-DEC-2004
```

Now that you have found the last day in the year you are working with, simply use TO_CHAR to return a three-digit number representing on which day (1st, 50th, etc.) of the year the last day is:

```
select to_char(
        add_months(
          trunc(to_date('01-SEP-2004'),'y'),
          12)-1,'DDD') num_days_in_2004
  from dual

NUM
---
366
```

14.6   Searching for Mixed Alphanumeric Strings

Problem

You have a column with mixed alphanumeric data. You want to return those rows that have both alphabetical and numeric characters; in other words, if a string has only number or only letters, do not return it. The return values should have a mix of both letters and numbers. Consider the following data:

```
STRINGS
-----------
1010 switch
333
3453430278
ClassSummary
findRow 55
threes
```

The final result set should contain only those rows that have both letters and numbers:

```
STRINGS
------------
1010 switch
findRow 55
```

Solution

Use the built-in function TRANSLATE to convert each occurrence of a letter or digit into a specific character. Then keep only those strings that have at least one occurrence of both. The solution uses Oracle syntax, but both DB2 and PostgreSQL support TRANSLATE, so modifying the solution to work on those platforms should be trivial:

```
with v as (
select 'ClassSummary' strings from dual union
select '3453430278'         from dual union
select 'findRow 55'         from dual union
select '1010 switch'        from dual union
select '333'                from dual union
select 'threes'             from dual
)
select strings
  from (
select strings,
       translate(
         strings,
         'abcdefghijklmnopqrstuvwxyz0123456789',
         rpad('#',26,'#')||rpad('*',10,'*')) translated
  from v
     ) x
where instr(translated,'#') > 0
  and instr(translated,'*') > 0
```

 As an alternative to the WITH clause, you may use an inline view or simply create a view.

Discussion

The TRANSLATE function makes this problem extremely easy to solve. The first step is to use TRANSLATE to identify all letters and all digits by pound (#) and asterisk (*) characters, respectively. The intermediate results (from inline view X) are as follows:

```
with v as (
select 'ClassSummary' strings from dual union
select '3453430278'         from dual union
select 'findRow 55'         from dual union
```

```
select '1010 switch'        from dual union
select '333'                from dual union
select 'threes'             from dual
)
select strings,
       translate(
         strings,
         'abcdefghijklmnopqrstuvwxyz0123456789',
         rpad('#',26,'#')||rpad('*',10,'*')) translated
  from v

STRINGS       TRANSLATED
------------  ------------
1010 switch   **** ######
333           ***
3453430278    *********
ClassSummary  C####S######
findRow 55    ####R## **
threes        ######
```

At this point, it is only a matter of keeping those rows that have at least one instance each of "#" and "*". Use the function INSTR to determine whether "#" and "*" are in a string. If those two characters are, in fact, present, then the value returned will be greater than zero. The final strings to return, along with their translated values, are shown next for clarity:

```
with v as (
select 'ClassSummary' strings from dual union
select '3453430278'           from dual union
select 'findRow 55'           from dual union
select '1010 switch'          from dual union
select '333'                  from dual union
select 'threes'               from dual
)
select strings, translated
  from (
select strings,
       translate(
         strings,
         'abcdefghijklmnopqrstuvwxyz0123456789',
         rpad('#',26,'#')||rpad('*',10,'*')) translated
  from v
       )
 where instr(translated,'#') > 0
   and instr(translated,'*') > 0

STRINGS       TRANSLATED
------------  ------------
1010 switch   **** ######
findRow 55    ####R## **
```

14.7 Converting Whole Numbers to Binary Using Oracle

Problem

You want to convert a whole number to its binary representation on an Oracle system. For example, you would like to return all the salaries in table EMP in binary as part of the following result set:

```
ENAME           SAL SAL_BINARY
----------   ----- --------------------
SMITH          800 1100100000
ALLEN         1600 11001000000
WARD          1250 10011100010
JONES         2975 101110011111
MARTIN        1250 10011100010
BLAKE         2850 101100100010
CLARK         2450 100110010010
SCOTT         3000 101110111000
KING          5000 1001110001000
TURNER        1500 10111011100
ADAMS         1100 10001001100
JAMES          950 1110110110
FORD          3000 101110111000
MILLER        1300 10100010100
```

Solution

This solution makes use of the MODEL clause, so you'll need to be running Oracle Database 10g or later for it to work. Because of MODEL's ability to iterate and provide array access to row values, it is a natural choice for this operation (assuming you are forced to solve the problem in SQL, as a stored function is more appropriate here). Like the rest of the solutions in this book, even if you don't find a practical application for this code, focus on the technique. It is useful to know that the MODEL clause can perform procedural tasks while still keeping SQL's set-based nature and power. So, even if you find yourself saying: "I'd never do this in SQL," that's fine. I'm in no way suggesting you should or shouldn't. I only remind you to focus on the technique, so you can apply it to whatever you consider a more "practical" application.

The following solution returns all ENAME and SAL from table EMP, while calling the MODEL clause in a scalar subquery (this way it serves as sort of a standalone function from table EMP that simply receives an input, processes it, and returns a value, much like a function would):

```
1  select ename,
2         sal,
3         (
4         select bin
5           from dual
```

```
 6        model
 7        dimension by ( 0 attr )
 8        measures ( sal num,
 9                    cast(null as varchar2(30)) bin,
10                    '0123456789ABCDEF' hex
11                  )
12        rules iterate (10000) until (num[0] <= 0) (
13          bin[0] = substr(hex[cv()],mod(num[cv()],2)+1,1)||bin[cv()],
14          num[0] = trunc(num[cv()]/2)
15        )
16      ) sal_binary
17   from emp
```

Discussion

I mentioned in the Solution section that this problem is most likely better solved via a stored function. Indeed, the idea for this recipe came from a function. As a matter of fact, this recipe is an adaptation of a function called TO_BASE, written by Tom Kyte of Oracle Corporation. Like other recipes in this book that you may decide not to use, even if you do not use this recipe it does a nice job of showing of some of the features of the MODEL clause such as iteration and array access of rows.

To make the explanation easier, I am going to focus on a slight variation of the sub-query containing the MODEL clause. The code that follows is essentially the sub-query from the solution, except that it's been hard-wired to return the value 2 in binary:

```
select bin
  from dual
model
dimension by ( 0 attr )
measures ( 2 num,
            cast(null as varchar2(30)) bin,
            '0123456789ABCDEF' hex
          )
rules iterate (10000) until (num[0] <= 0) (
  bin[0] = substr (hex[cv()],mod(num[cv()],2)+1,1)||bin[cv()],
  num[0] = trunc(num[cv()]/2)
)

BIN
----------
10
```

The following query outputs the values returned from one iteration of the RULES defined in the query above:

```
select 2 start_val,
       '0123456789ABCDEF' hex,
       substr('0123456789ABCDEF',mod(2,2)+1,1) ||
       cast(null as varchar2(30)) bin,
       trunc(2/2) num
  from dual
```

```
START_VAL HEX                BIN        NUM
--------- ----------------- ---------- ---
        2 0123456789ABCDEF  0               1
```

START_VAL represents the number you want to convert to binary, which in this case is 2. The value for BIN is the result of a substring operation on '0123456789ABCDEF' (HEX, in the original solution). The value for NUM is the test that will determine when you exit the loop.

As you can see from the preceding result set, the first time through the loop BIN is 0 and NUM is 1. Because NUM is not less than or equal to 0, another loop iteration occurs. The following SQL statement shows the results of the next iteration:

```
select num start_val,
       substr('0123456789ABCDEF',mod(1,2)+1,1) || bin bin,
       trunc(1/2) num
  from (
select 2 start_val,
       '0123456789ABCDEF' hex,
       substr('0123456789ABCDEF',mod(2,2)+1,1) ||
       cast(null as varchar2(30)) bin,
       trunc(2/2) num
  from dual
       )
```

```
START_VAL BIN        NUM
--------- ---------- ---
        1 10           0
```

The next time through the loop, the result of the substring operation on HEX returns 1 and the prior value of BIN, 0, is appended to it. The test, NUM, is now 0, thus this is the last iteration and the return value "10" is the binary representation of the number 2. Once you're comfortable with what's going on, you can remove the iteration from the MODEL clause and step through it row by row to follow how the rules are applied to come to the final result set, as is shown below:

```
select 2 orig_val, num, bin
  from dual
model
dimension by ( 0 attr )
measures ( 2 num,
           cast(null as varchar2(30)) bin,
           '0123456789ABCDEF' hex
         )
rules (
  bin[0] = substr (hex[cv()],mod(num[cv()],2)+1,1)||bin[cv()],
  num[0] = trunc(num[cv()]/2),
  bin[1] = substr (hex[0],mod(num[0],2)+1,1)||bin[0],
  num[1] = trunc(num[0]/2)
)
```

```
ORIG_VAL NUM BIN
-------- --- ---------
       2   1 0
       2   0 10
```

14.8 Pivoting a Ranked Result Set

Problem

You want to rank the values in a table, then pivot the result set into three columns. The idea is to show the top three, the next three, then all the rest. For example, you want to rank the employees in table EMP by SAL, and then pivot the results into three columns. The desired result set is as follows:

```
TOP_3             NEXT_3           REST
--------------- ---------------- --------------
KING   (5000)   BLAKE  (2850)    TURNER (1500)
FORD   (3000)   CLARK  (2450)    MILLER (1300)
SCOTT  (3000)   ALLEN  (1600)    MARTIN (1250)
JONES  (2975)                    WARD   (1250)
                                 ADAMS  (1100)
                                 JAMES  (950)
                                 SMITH  (800)
```

Solution

The key to this solution is to first use the window function DENSE_RANK OVER to rank the employees by SAL while allowing for ties. By using DENSE_RANK OVER, you can easily see the top three salaries, the next three salaries, and then all the rest. Next, use the window function ROW_NUMBER OVER to rank each employee within his group (the top three, next three, or last group). From there, simply perform a classic transpose, while using the built-in string functions available on your platform to beautify the results. The following solution uses Oracle syntax. Since both DB2 and SQL Server 2005 support window functions, converting the solution to work for those platforms is trivial:

```
 1  select max(case grp when 1 then rpad(ename,6) ||
 2                  ' ('|| sal ||')' end) top_3,
 3         max(case grp when 2 then rpad(ename,6) ||
 4                  ' ('|| sal ||')' end) next_3,
 5         max(case grp when 3 then rpad(ename,6) ||
 6                  ' ('|| sal ||')' end) rest
 7    from (
 8  select ename,
 9         sal,
10         rnk,
11         case when rnk <= 3 then 1
12              when rnk <= 6 then 2
13              else          3
14         end grp,
15         row_number( )over (
```

```
16              partition by case when rnk <= 3 then 1
17                             when rnk <= 6 then 2
18                             else          3
19                        end
20              order by sal desc, ename
21         ) grp_rnk
22   from (
23  select ename,
24         sal,
25         dense_rank( )over(order by sal desc) rnk
26    from emp
27         ) x
28         ) y
29   group by grp_rnk
```

Discussion

This recipe is a perfect example of how much you can accomplish with so little, with the help of window functions. The solution may look involved, but as you break it down from inside out you will be surprised how simple it is. Let's begin by executing inline view X first:

```
select ename,
       sal,
       dense_rank( )over(order by sal desc) rnk
  from emp


ENAME        SAL        RNK
----------  -----  ----------
KING         5000          1
SCOTT        3000          2
FORD         3000          2
JONES        2975          3
BLAKE        2850          4
CLARK        2450          5
ALLEN        1600          6
TURNER       1500          7
MILLER       1300          8
WARD         1250          9
MARTIN       1250          9
ADAMS        1100         10
JAMES         950         11
SMITH         800         12
```

As you can see from the result set above, inline view X simply ranks the employees by SAL, while allowing for ties (because the solution uses DENSE_RANK instead of RANK, there are ties without gaps). The next step is to take the rows from inline view X and create groups by using a CASE expression to evaluate the ranking from DENSE_RANK. Additionally, use the window function ROW_NUMBER OVER to rank the employees by SAL within their group (within the group you are creating with the CASE expression). All of this happens in inline view Y and is shown below:

```
select ename,
       sal,
       rnk,
       case when rnk <= 3 then 1
            when rnk <= 6 then 2
            else              3
       end grp,
       row_number( )over (
          partition by case when rnk <= 3 then 1
                            when rnk <= 6 then 2
                            else              3
                       end
                  order by sal desc, ename
       ) grp_rnk
  from (
select ename,
       sal,
       dense_rank( )over(order by sal desc) rnk
  from emp
       ) x


ENAME        SAL  RNK  GRP GRP_RNK
----------  ----- ---- ---- -------
KING         5000   1    1      1
FORD         3000   2    1      2
SCOTT        3000   2    1      3
JONES        2975   3    1      4
BLAKE        2850   4    2      1
CLARK        2450   5    2      2
ALLEN        1600   6    2      3
TURNER       1500   7    3      1
MILLER       1300   8    3      2
MARTIN       1250   9    3      3
WARD         1250   9    3      4
ADAMS        1100  10    3      5
JAMES         950  11    3      6
SMITH         800  12    3      7
```

Now the query is starting to take shape and, if you followed it from the beginning (from inline view X), you can see that it's not that complicated. The query so far returns each employee, her SAL, her RNK, which represents where her SAL ranks amongst all employees, her GRP, which indicates the group each employee is in (based on SAL), and finally GRP_RANK, which is a ranking (based on SAL) within her GRP.

At this point, perform a traditional pivot on ENAME while using the Oracle concatenation operator || to append the SAL. The function RPAD ensures that the numeric values in parentheses line up nicely. Finally, use GROUP BY on GRP_RNK to ensure you show each employee in the result set. The final result set is shown below:

```
  select max(case grp when 1 then rpad(ename,6) ||
                          ' ('|| sal ||')' end) top_3,
         max(case grp when 2 then rpad(ename,6) ||
                          ' ('|| sal ||')' end) next_3,
         max(case grp when 3 then rpad(ename,6) ||
                          ' ('|| sal ||')' end) rest
    from (
  select ename,
         sal,
         rnk,
         case when rnk <= 3 then 1
              when rnk <= 6 then 2
              else            3
         end grp,
         row_number( )over (
           partition by case when rnk <= 3 then 1
                             when rnk <= 6 then 2
                             else            3
                        end
                 order by sal desc, ename
         ) grp_rnk
    from (
  select ename,
         sal,
         dense_rank( )over(order by sal desc) rnk
    from emp
         ) x
         ) y
   group by grp_rnk


TOP_3            NEXT_3           REST
---------------  ---------------  ---------------
KING   (5000)    BLAKE  (2850)    TURNER (1500)
FORD   (3000)    CLARK  (2450)    MILLER (1300)
SCOTT  (3000)    ALLEN  (1600)    MARTIN (1250)
JONES  (2975)                     WARD   (1250)
                                  ADAMS  (1100)
                                  JAMES  (950)
                                  SMITH  (800)
```

If you examine the queries in all of the steps you'll notice that table EMP is accessed exactly once. One of the remarkable things about window functions is how much work you can do in just one pass through your data. No need for self joins or temp tables; just get the rows you need, then let the window functions do the rest. Only in inline view X do you need to access EMP. From there, it's simply a matter of massaging the result set to look the way you want. Consider what all this means for performance if you can create this type of report with a single table access. Pretty cool.

14.9   Adding a Column Header into a Double Pivoted Result Set

Problem

You want to stack two result sets, and then pivot them into two columns. Additionally, you want to add a "header" for each group of rows in each column. For example, you have two tables containing information about employees working in different areas of development in your company (say, in research and applications):

```
select * from it_research

DEPTNO ENAME
------ --------------------
   100 HOPKINS
   100 JONES
   100 TONEY
   200 MORALES
   200 P.WHITAKER
   200 MARCIANO
   200 ROBINSON
   300 LACY
   300 WRIGHT
   300 J.TAYLOR


select * from it_apps

DEPTNO ENAME
------ -----------------
   400 CORRALES
   400 MAYWEATHER
   400 CASTILLO
   400 MARQUEZ
   400 MOSLEY
   500 GATTI
   500 CALZAGHE
   600 LAMOTTA
   600 HAGLER
   600 HEARNS
   600 FRAZIER
   700 GUINN
   700 JUDAH
   700 MARGARITO
```

You would like to create a report listing the employees from each table in two columns. You want to return the DEPTNO followed by ENAME for each. Ultimately you want to return the following result set:

```
RESEARCH              APPS
------------------    ----------------
100                   400
  JONES                 MAYWEATHER
  TONEY                 CASTILLO
  HOPKINS               MARQUEZ
200                     MOSLEY
  P.WHITAKER            CORRALES
  MARCIANO            500
  ROBINSON              CALZAGHE
  MORALES              GATTI
300                   600
  WRIGHT                HAGLER
  J.TAYLOR              HEARNS
  LACY                  FRAZIER
                        LAMOTTA
                      700
                        JUDAH
                        MARGARITO
                        GUINN
```

Solution

For the most part, this solution requires nothing more than a simple stack-n-pivot (union then pivot) with an added twist: the DEPTNO must precede the ENAME for each employee returned. The technique here uses a Cartesian product to generate an extra row for each DEPTNO, so you have the required rows necessary to show all employees, plus room for the DEPTNO. The solution uses Oracle syntax, but since DB2 supports window functions that can compute moving windows (the framing clause), converting this solution to work for DB2 is trivial. Because the IT_RESEARCH and IT_APPS tables exist only for this recipe, their table creation statements are shown along with this solution:

```
create table IT_research (deptno number, ename varchar2(20))

insert into IT_research values (100,'HOPKINS')
insert into IT_research values (100,'JONES')
insert into IT_research values (100,'TONEY')
insert into IT_research values (200,'MORALES')
insert into IT_research values (200,'P.WHITAKER')
insert into IT_research values (200,'MARCIANO')
insert into IT_research values (200,'ROBINSON')
insert into IT_research values (300,'LACY')
insert into IT_research values (300,'WRIGHT')
insert into IT_research values (300,'J.TAYLOR')


create table IT_apps (deptno number, ename varchar2(20))
```

```
insert into IT_apps values (400,'CORRALES')
insert into IT_apps values (400,'MAYWEATHER')
insert into IT_apps values (400,'CASTILLO')
insert into IT_apps values (400,'MARQUEZ')
insert into IT_apps values (400,'MOSLEY')
insert into IT_apps values (500,'GATTI')
insert into IT_apps values (500,'CALZAGHE')
insert into IT_apps values (600,'LAMOTTA')
insert into IT_apps values (600,'HAGLER')
insert into IT_apps values (600,'HEARNS')
insert into IT_apps values (600,'FRAZIER')
insert into IT_apps values (700,'GUINN')
insert into IT_apps values (700,'JUDAH')
insert into IT_apps values (700,'MARGARITO')
```

```
 1  select max(decode(flag2,0,it_dept)) research,
 2         max(decode(flag2,1,it_dept)) apps
 3    from (
 4  select sum(flag1)over(partition by flag2
 5                              order by flag1,rownum) flag,
 6         it_dept, flag2
 7    from (
 8  select 1 flag1, 0 flag2,
 9         decode(rn,1,to_char(deptno),'  '||ename) it_dept
10    from (
11  select x.*, y.id,
12         row_number( )over(partition by x.deptno order by y.id) rn
13    from (
14  select deptno,
15         ename,
16         count(*)over(partition by deptno) cnt
17    from it_research
18         ) x,
19         (select level id from dual connect by level <= 2) y
20         )
21   where rn <= cnt+1
22  union all
23  select 1 flag1, 1 flag2,
24         decode(rn,1,to_char(deptno),'  '||ename) it_dept
25    from (
26  select x.*, y.id,
27         row_number( )over(partition by x.deptno order by y.id) rn
28    from (
29  select deptno,
30         ename,
31         count(*)over(partition by deptno) cnt
32    from it_apps
33         ) x,
34         (select level id from dual connect by level <= 2) y
35         )
36   where rn <= cnt+1
37         ) tmp1
38         ) tmp2
39   group by flag
```

Discussion

Like many of the other warehousing/report type queries, the solution presented looks quite convoluted but once broken down you'll seen it's nothing more than a stack-n-pivot with a Cartesian twist (on the rocks, with a little umbrella). The way to break this query down is to work on each part of the UNION ALL first, then bring it together for the pivot. Let's start with the lower portion of the UNION ALL:

```
select 1 flag1, 1 flag2,
       decode(rn,1,to_char(deptno),'  '||ename) it_dept
  from (
select x.*, y.id,
       row_number()over(partition by x.deptno order by y.id) rn
  from (
select deptno,
       ename,
       count(*)over(partition by deptno) cnt
  from it_apps
       ) x,
       (select level id from dual connect by level <= 2) y
       ) z
 where rn <= cnt+1
```

```
FLAG1    FLAG2 IT_DEPT
-----  ----------  -------------------------
    1          1 400
    1          1    MAYWEATHER
    1          1    CASTILLO
    1          1    MARQUEZ
    1          1    MOSLEY
    1          1    CORRALES
    1          1 500
    1          1    CALZAGHE
    1          1    GATTI
    1          1 600
    1          1    HAGLER
    1          1    HEARNS
    1          1    FRAZIER
    1          1    LAMOTTA
    1          1 700
    1          1    JUDAH
    1          1    MARGARITO
    1          1    GUINN
```

Let's examine exactly how that result set is put together. Breaking down the above query to its simplest components, you have inline view X, which simply returns each ENAME and DEPTNO and the number of employees in each DEPTNO from table IT_APPS. The results are as follows:

```
select deptno deptno,
       ename,
       count(*)over(partition by deptno) cnt
  from it_apps
```

```
DEPTNO ENAME                    CNT
------ -------------------- ----------
   400 CORRALES                   5
   400 MAYWEATHER                 5
   400 CASTILLO                   5
   400 MARQUEZ                    5
   400 MOSLEY                     5
   500 GATTI                      2
   500 CALZAGHE                   2
   600 LAMOTTA                    4
   600 HAGLER                     4
   600 HEARNS                     4
   600 FRAZIER                    4
   700 GUINN                      3
   700 JUDAH                      3
   700 MARGARITO                  3
```

The next step is to create a Cartesian product between the rows returned from inline view X and two rows generated from DUAL using CONNECT BY. The results of this operation are as follows:

```
select *
  from (
select deptno deptno,
       ename,
       count(*)over(partition by deptno) cnt
  from it_apps
       ) x,
       (select level id from dual connect by level <= 2) y
 order by 2
```

```
DEPTNO ENAME       CNT  ID
------ ----------  ---  ---
   500 CALZAGHE      2    1
   500 CALZAGHE      2    2
   400 CASTILLO      5    1
   400 CASTILLO      5    2
   400 CORRALES      5    1
   400 CORRALES      5    2
   600 FRAZIER       4    1
   600 FRAZIER       4    2
   500 GATTI         2    1
   500 GATTI         2    2
   700 GUINN         3    1
   700 GUINN         3    2
   600 HAGLER        4    1
   600 HAGLER        4    2
   600 HEARNS        4    1
   600 HEARNS        4    2
   700 JUDAH         3    1
   700 JUDAH         3    2
   600 LAMOTTA       4    1
   600 LAMOTTA       4    2
   700 MARGARITO     3    1
   700 MARGARITO     3    2
```

```
400 MARQUEZ        5    1
400 MARQUEZ        5    2
400 MAYWEATHER     5    1
400 MAYWEATHER     5    2
400 MOSLEY         5    1
400 MOSLEY         5    2
```

As you can see from these results, each row from inline view X is now returned twice due to the Cartesian product with inline view Y. The reason a Cartesian is needed will become clear shortly. The next step is to take the current result set and rank each employee within his DEPTNO by ID (ID has a value of 1 or 2 as was returned by the Cartesian product). The result of this ranking is shown in the output from the following query:

```
select x.*, y.id,
       row_number( )over(partition by x.deptno order by y.id) rn
  from (
select deptno deptno,
       ename,
       count(*)over(partition by deptno) cnt
  from it_apps
       ) x,
       (select level id from dual connect by level <= 2) y
```

```
DEPTNO ENAME         CNT  ID        RN
------ ----------    ---  ---   ----------
   400 CORRALES        5    1         1
   400 MAYWEATHER      5    1         2
   400 CASTILLO        5    1         3
   400 MARQUEZ         5    1         4
   400 MOSLEY          5    1         5
   400 CORRALES        5    2         6
   400 MOSLEY          5    2         7
   400 MAYWEATHER      5    2         8
   400 CASTILLO        5    2         9
   400 MARQUEZ         5    2        10
   500 GATTI           2    1         1
   500 CALZAGHE        2    1         2
   500 GATTI           2    2         3
   500 CALZAGHE        2    2         4
   600 LAMOTTA         4    1         1
   600 HAGLER          4    1         2
   600 HEARNS          4    1         3
   600 FRAZIER         4    1         4
   600 LAMOTTA         4    2         5
   600 HAGLER          4    2         6
   600 FRAZIER         4    2         7
   600 HEARNS          4    2         8
   700 GUINN           3    1         1
   700 JUDAH           3    1         2
   700 MARGARITO       3    1         3
   700 GUINN           3    2         4
   700 JUDAH           3    2         5
   700 MARGARITO       3    2         6
```

Each employee is ranked; then his duplicate is ranked. The result set contains duplicates for all employees in table IT_APP, along with their ranking within their DEPTNO. The reason you need to generate these extra rows is because you need a slot in the result set to slip in the DEPTNO in the ENAME column. If you Cartesian-join IT_APPS with a one-row table, you get no extra rows (because cardinality of any table ×1 = cardinality of that table).

The next step is to take the results returned thus far and pivot the result set such that all the ENAMES are returned in one column but are preceded by the DEPTNO they are in. The following query shows how this happens:

```
select 1 flag1, 1 flag2,
       decode(rn,1,to_char(deptno),'  '||ename) it_dept
  from (
select x.*, y.id,
       row_number()over(partition by x.deptno order by y.id) rn
  from (
select deptno deptno,
       ename,
       count(*)over(partition by deptno) cnt
  from it_apps
       ) x,
       (select level id from dual connect by level <= 2) y
       ) z
 where rn <= cnt+1

FLAG1     FLAG2 IT_DEPT
----- ---------- -------------------------
    1          1 400
    1          1   MAYWEATHER
    1          1   CASTILLO
    1          1   MARQUEZ
    1          1   MOSLEY
    1          1   CORRALES
    1          1 500
    1          1   CALZAGHE
    1          1   GATTI
    1          1 600
    1          1   HAGLER
    1          1   HEARNS
    1          1   FRAZIER
    1          1   LAMOTTA
    1          1 700
    1          1   JUDAH
    1          1   MARGARITO
    1          1   GUINN
```

FLAG1 and FLAG2 come into play later and can be ignored for the moment. Focus your attention on the rows in IT_DEPT. The number of rows returned for each DEPTNO is CNT*2, but all that is needed is CNT+1, which is the filter in the WHERE clause. RN is the ranking for each employee. The rows kept are all those ranked less than or equal to CNT+1; i.e., all employees in each DEPTNO plus one more (this extra employee is the employee who is ranked first in their DEPTNO). This extra row is where the DEPTNO will slide in. By using DECODE (an older Oracle function that gives more or less the equivalent of a CASE expression) to evaluate the value of RN, you can slide the value of DEPTNO into the result set. The employee who was at position 1 (based on the value of RN) is still shown in the result set, but is now last in each DEPTNO (because the order is irrelevant, this is not a problem). That pretty much covers the lower part of the UNION ALL.

The upper part of the UNION ALL is processed in the same way as the lower part so there's no need to explain how that works. Instead, let's examine the result set returned when stacking the queries:

```
select 1 flag1, 0 flag2,
       decode(rn,1,to_char(deptno),'  '||ename) it_dept
  from (
select x.*, y.id,
       row_number( )over(partition by x.deptno order by y.id) rn
  from (
select deptno,
       ename,
       count(*)over(partition by deptno) cnt
  from it_research
       ) x,
       (select level id from dual connect by level <= 2) y
       )
 where rn <= cnt+1
union all
select 1 flag1, 1 flag2,
       decode(rn,1,to_char(deptno),'  '||ename) it_dept
  from (
select x.*, y.id,
       row_number( )over(partition by x.deptno order by y.id) rn
  from (
select deptno deptno,
       ename,
       count(*)over(partition by deptno) cnt
  from it_apps
       ) x,
       (select level id from dual connect by level <= 2) y
       )
 where rn <= cnt+1


FLAG1     FLAG2 IT_DEPT
-----  ----------  -----------------------
    1         0 100
    1         0    JONES
    1         0    TONEY
    1         0    HOPKINS
    1         0 200
    1         0    P.WHITAKER
    1         0    MARCIANO
    1         0    ROBINSON
```

```
1          0   MORALES
1          0 300
1          0   WRIGHT
1          0   J.TAYLOR
1          0   LACY
1          1 400
1          1   MAYWEATHER
1          1   CASTILLO
1          1   MARQUEZ
1          1   MOSLEY
1          1   CORRALES
1          1 500
1          1   CALZAGHE
1          1   GATTI
1          1 600
1          1   HAGLER
1          1   HEARNS
1          1   FRAZIER
1          1   LAMOTTA
1          1 700
1          1   JUDAH
1          1   MARGARITO
1          1   GUINN
```

At this point, it isn't clear what FLAG1's purpose is, but you can see that FLAG2 identifies which rows come from which part of the UNION ALL (0 for the upper part, 1 for the lower part).

The next step is to wrap the stacked result set in an inline view and create a running total on FLAG1 (finally, its purpose is revealed!), which will act as a ranking for each row in each stack. The results of the ranking (running total) are shown below:

```
select sum(flag1)over(partition by flag2
                            order by flag1,rownum) flag,
        it_dept, flag2
  from (
select 1 flag1, 0 flag2,
        decode(rn,1,to_char(deptno),'  '||ename) it_dept
  from (
select x.*, y.id,
        row_number()over(partition by x.deptno order by y.id) rn
  from (
select deptno,
        ename,
        count(*)over(partition by deptno) cnt
  from it_research
        ) x,
        (select level id from dual connect by level <= 2) y
        )
  where rn <= cnt+1
union all
select 1 flag1, 1 flag2,
        decode(rn,1,to_char(deptno),'  '||ename) it_dept
```

```
      from (
select x.*, y.id,
       row_number( )over(partition by x.deptno order by y.id) rn
   from (
select deptno deptno,
       ename,
       count(*)over(partition by deptno) cnt
   from it_apps
       ) x,
       (select level id from dual connect by level <= 2) y
       )
  where rn <= cnt+1
       ) tmp1
```

```
FLAG IT_DEPT              FLAG2
---- ---------------   ----------
   1 100                     0
   2    JONES                0
   3    TONEY                0
   4    HOPKINS              0
   5 200                     0
   6    P.WHITAKER           0
   7    MARCIANO             0
   8    ROBINSON             0
   9    MORALES              0
  10 300                     0
  11    WRIGHT               0
  12    J.TAYLOR             0
  13    LACY                 0
   1 400                     1
   2    MAYWEATHER           1
   3    CASTILLO             1
   4    MARQUEZ              1
   5    MOSLEY               1
   6    CORRALES             1
   7 500                     1
   8    CALZAGHE             1
   9    GATTI                1
  10 600                     1
  11    HAGLER               1
  12    HEARNS               1
  13    FRAZIER              1
  14    LAMOTTA              1
  15 700                     1
  16    JUDAH                1
  17    MARGARITO            1
  18    GUINN                1
```

The last remaining step (finally!) is to pivot the value returned by TMP1 on FLAG2 while grouping by FLAG (the running total generated in TMP1). The results from TMP1 are wrapped in an inline view and pivoted (wrapped in a final inline view called TMP2). The final solution and result set is shown below:

```
select max(decode(flag2,0,it_dept)) research,
       max(decode(flag2,1,it_dept)) apps
  from (
select sum(flag1)over(partition by flag2
                            order by flag1,rownum) flag,
       it_dept, flag2
  from (
select 1 flag1, 0 flag2,
       decode(rn,1,to_char(deptno),'  '||ename) it_dept
  from (
select x.*, y.id,
       row_number()over(partition by x.deptno order by y.id) rn
  from (
select deptno,
       ename,
       count(*)over(partition by deptno) cnt
  from it_research
       ) x,
       (select level id from dual connect by level <= 2) y
       )
  where rn <= cnt+1
union all
select 1 flag1, 1 flag2,
       decode(rn,1,to_char(deptno),'  '||ename) it_dept
  from (
select x.*, y.id,
       row_number()over(partition by x.deptno order by y.id) rn
  from (
select deptno deptno,
       ename,
       count(*)over(partition by deptno) cnt
  from it_apps
       ) x,
       (select level id from dual connect by level <= 2) y
       )
  where rn <= cnt+1
       ) tmp1
       ) tmp2
  group by flag

RESEARCH              APPS
-------------------- ---------------
100                  400
  JONES                MAYWEATHER
  TONEY                CASTILLO
  HOPKINS              MARQUEZ
200                  MOSLEY
  P.WHITAKER           CORRALES
  MARCIANO           500
  ROBINSON             CALZAGHE
  MORALES              GATTI
300                  600
  WRIGHT               HAGLER
  J.TAYLOR             HEARNS
  LACY                 FRAZIER
```

```
LAMOTTA
700
  JUDAH
  MARGARITO
  GUINN
```

14.10 Converting a Scalar Subquery to a Composite Subquery in Oracle

Problem

You would like to bypass the restriction of returning exactly one value from a scalar subquery. For example, you attempt to execute the following query:

```
select e.deptno,
       e.ename,
       e.sal,
       (select d.dname,d.loc,sysdate today
          from dept d
         where e.deptno=d.deptno)
  from emp e
```

but receive an error because subqueries in the SELECT list are allowed to return only a single value.

Solution

Admittedly, this problem is quite unrealistic, because a simple join between tables EMP and DEPT would allow you to return as many values you want from DEPT. Nevertheless, the key is to focus on the technique and understand how to apply it to a scenario that you find useful. The key to bypassing the requirement to return a single value when placing a SELECT within SELECT (scalar subquery) is to take advantage of Oracle's object types. You can define an object to have several attributes, and then you can work with it as a single entity or reference each element individually. In effect, you don't really bypass the rule at all. You simply return one value, an object, that in turn contains many attributes.

This solution makes use of the following object type:

```
create type generic_obj
    as object (
    val1 varchar2(10),
    val2 varchar2(10),
    val3 date
  );
```

With this type in place, you can execute the following query:

```
1  select x.deptno,
2         x.ename,
3         x.multival.val1 dname,
```

```
 4          x.multival.val2 loc,
 5          x.multival.val3 today
 6    from (
 7  select e.deptno,
 8         e.ename,
 9         e.sal,
10         (select generic_obj(d.dname,d.loc,sysdate+1)
11            from dept d
12          where e.deptno=d.deptno) multival
13    from emp e
14         ) x

DEPTNO ENAME      DNAME      LOC        TODAY
------ ---------- ---------- ---------- -----------
    20 SMITH      RESEARCH   DALLAS     12-SEP-2005
    30 ALLEN      SALES      CHICAGO    12-SEP-2005
    30 WARD       SALES      CHICAGO    12-SEP-2005
    20 JONES      RESEARCH   DALLAS     12-SEP-2005
    30 MARTIN     SALES      CHICAGO    12-SEP-2005
    30 BLAKE      SALES      CHICAGO    12-SEP-2005
    10 CLARK      ACCOUNTING NEW YORK   12-SEP-2005
    20 SCOTT      RESEARCH   DALLAS     12-SEP-2005
    10 KING       ACCOUNTING NEW YORK   12-SEP-2005
    30 TURNER     SALES      CHICAGO    12-SEP-2005
    20 ADAMS      RESEARCH   DALLAS     12-SEP-2005
    30 JAMES      SALES      CHICAGO    12-SEP-2005
    20 FORD       RESEARCH   DALLAS     12-SEP-2005
    10 MILLER     ACCOUNTING NEW YORK   12-SEP-2005
```

Discussion

The key to the solution is to use the object's constructor function (by default the constructor function has the same name as the object). Because the object itself is a single scalar value, it does not violate the scalar subquery rule, as you can see from the following:

```
select e.deptno,
       e.ename,
       e.sal,
       (select generic_obj(d.dname,d.loc,sysdate-1)
          from dept d
        where e.deptno=d.deptno) multival
  from emp e

DEPTNO ENAME    SAL MULTIVAL(VAL1, VAL2, VAL3)
------ ------ ----- ----------------------------------------------------
    20 SMITH    800 GENERIC_OBJ('RESEARCH', 'DALLAS', '12-SEP-2005')
    30 ALLEN   1600 GENERIC_OBJ('SALES', 'CHICAGO', '12-SEP-2005')
    30 WARD    1250 GENERIC_OBJ('SALES', 'CHICAGO', '12-SEP-2005')
    20 JONES   2975 GENERIC_OBJ('RESEARCH', 'DALLAS', '12-SEP-2005')
    30 MARTIN  1250 GENERIC_OBJ('SALES', 'CHICAGO', '12-SEP-2005')
    30 BLAKE   2850 GENERIC_OBJ('SALES', 'CHICAGO', '12-SEP-2005')
    10 CLARK   2450 GENERIC_OBJ('ACCOUNTING', 'NEW YORK', '12-SEP-2005')
```

```
20 SCOTT   3000 GENERIC_OBJ('RESEARCH', 'DALLAS', '12-SEP-2005')
10 KING    5000 GENERIC_OBJ('ACCOUNTING', 'NEW YORK', '12-SEP-2005')
30 TURNER  1500 GENERIC_OBJ('SALES', 'CHICAGO', '12-SEP-2005')
20 ADAMS   1100 GENERIC_OBJ('RESEARCH', 'DALLAS', '12-SEP-2005')
30 JAMES    950 GENERIC_OBJ('SALES', 'CHICAGO', '12-SEP-2005')
20 FORD    3000 GENERIC_OBJ('RESEARCH', 'DALLAS', '12-SEP-2005')
10 MILLER  1300 GENERIC_OBJ('ACCOUNTING', 'NEW YORK', '12-SEP-2005')
```

The next step is to simply wrap the query in an inline view and extract the attributes.

 One important note: In Oracle, unlike the case with other vendors, you do not generally need to name your inline views. In this particular case, however, you do need to name your inline view. Otherwise you will not be able to reference the object's attributes.

14.11 Parsing Serialized Data into Rows

Problem

You have serialized data (stored in strings) that you want to parse and return as rows. For example, you store the following data:

```
STRINGS
-----------------------------------
entry:stewiegriffin:lois:brian:
entry:moe::sizlack:
entry:petergriffin:meg:chris:
entry:willie:
entry:quagmire:mayorwest:cleveland:
entry:::flanders:
entry:robo:tchi:ken:
```

You want to convert these serialized strings into the following result set:

```
VAL1            VAL2             VAL3
--------------  ---------------  ---------------
moe                              sizlack
petergriffin    meg              chris
quagmire        mayorwest        cleveland
robo            tchi             ken
stewiegriffin   lois             brian
willie

                                 flanders
```

Solution

Each serialized string in this example can store up to three values. The values are delimited by colons, and a string may or may not have all three entries. If a string does not have all three entries, you must be careful to place the entries that are available into the correct column in the result set. For example, consider the following row:

```
entry:::flanders:
```

This row represents an entry with the first two values missing and only the third value available. Hence, if you examine the target result set in the "Problem" section, you will notice that for the row "flanders" is in, both VAL1 and VAL2 are NULL.

The key to this solution is nothing more than a string walk with some string parsing, following by a simple pivot. This solution uses rows from view V, which is defined as follows. The example uses Oracle syntax, but since nothing more than string parsing functions are needed for this recipe, converting to other platforms is trivial:

```
create view V
     as
select 'entry:stewiegriffin:lois:brian:' strings
  from dual
 union all
select 'entry:moe::sizlack:'
  from dual
 union all
select 'entry:petergriffin:meg:chris:'
  from dual
 union all
select 'entry:willie:'
  from dual
 union all
select 'entry:quagmire:mayorwest:cleveland:'
  from dual
 union all
select 'entry:::flanders:'
  from dual
 union all
select 'entry:robo:tchi:ken:'
  from dual
```

Using view V to supply the example data to parse, the solution is as follows:

```
 1  with cartesian as (
 2  select level id
 3    from dual
 4   connect by level <= 100
 5  )
 6  select max(decode(id,1,substr(strings,p1+1,p2-1))) val1,
 7         max(decode(id,2,substr(strings,p1+1,p2-1))) val2,
 8         max(decode(id,3,substr(strings,p1+1,p2-1))) val3
 9    from (
10  select v.strings,
11         c.id,
12         instr(v.strings,':',1,c.id) p1,
13         instr(v.strings,':',1,c.id+1)-instr(v.strings,':',1,c.id) p2
14    from v, cartesian c
15   where c.id <= (length(v.strings)-length(replace(v.strings,':')))-1
16         )
17   group by strings
18   order by 1
```

Discussion

The first step is to walk the serialized strings:

```
with cartesian as (
select level id
  from dual
 connect by level <= 100
)
select v.strings,
       c.id
  from v,cartesian c
 where c.id <= (length(v.strings)-length(replace(v.strings,':')))-1
```

```
STRINGS                                 ID
--------------------------------------- ---
entry:::flanders:                         1
entry:::flanders:                         2
entry:::flanders:                         3
entry:moe::sizlack:                       1
entry:moe::sizlack:                       2
entry:moe::sizlack:                       3
entry:petergriffin:meg:chris:             1
entry:petergriffin:meg:chris:             3
entry:petergriffin:meg:chris:             2
entry:quagmire:mayorwest:cleveland:       1
entry:quagmire:mayorwest:cleveland:       3
entry:quagmire:mayorwest:cleveland:       2
entry:robo:tchi:ken:                      1
entry:robo:tchi:ken:                      2
entry:robo:tchi:ken:                      3
entry:stewiegriffin:lois:brian:           1
entry:stewiegriffin:lois:brian:           3
entry:stewiegriffin:lois:brian:           2
entry:willie:                             1
```

The next step is to use the function INSTR to find the numeric position of each colon in each string. Since each value you need to extract is enclosed by two colons, the numeric values are aliased P1 and P2, for "position 1" and "position 2":

```
with cartesian as (
select level id
  from dual
 connect by level <= 100
)
select v.strings,
       c.id,
       instr(v.strings,':',1,c.id) p1,
       instr(v.strings,':',1,c.id+1)-instr(v.strings,':',1,c.id) p2
  from v,cartesian c
 where c.id <= (length(v.strings)-length(replace(v.strings,':')))-1
 order by 1
```

```
STRINGS                                      ID    P1      P2
-------------------------------------------  ---  ------  ------
entry:::flanders:                             1     6       1
entry:::flanders:                             2     7       1
entry:::flanders:                             3     8       9
entry:moe::sizlack:                           1     6       4
entry:moe::sizlack:                           2    10       1
entry:moe::sizlack:                           3    11       8
entry:petergriffin:meg:chris:                 1     6      13
entry:petergriffin:meg:chris:                 3    23       6
entry:petergriffin:meg:chris:                 2    19       4
entry:quagmire:mayorwest:cleveland:           1     6       9
entry:quagmire:mayorwest:cleveland:           3    25      10
entry:quagmire:mayorwest:cleveland:           2    15      10
entry:robo:tchi:ken:                          1     6       5
entry:robo:tchi:ken:                          2    11       5
entry:robo:tchi:ken:                          3    16       4
entry:stewiegriffin:lois:brian:               1     6      14
entry:stewiegriffin:lois:brian:               3    25       6
entry:stewiegriffin:lois:brian:               2    20       5
entry:willie:                                 1     6       7
```

Now that you know the numeric positions for each pair of colons in each string, simply pass the information to the function SUBSTR to extract values. Since you want to create a result set with three columns, use DECODE to evaluate the ID from the Cartesian product:

```
with cartesian as (
select level id
  from dual
 connect by level <= 100
)
select decode(id,1,substr(strings,p1+1,p2-1)) val1,
       decode(id,2,substr(strings,p1+1,p2-1)) val2,
       decode(id,3,substr(strings,p1+1,p2-1)) val3
  from (
select v.strings,
       c.id,
       instr(v.strings,':',1,c.id) p1,
       instr(v.strings,':',1,c.id+1)-instr(v.strings,':',1,c.id) p2
  from v,cartesian c
 where c.id <= (length(v.strings)-length(replace(v.strings,':')))-1
       )
 order by 1

VAL1              VAL2              VAL3
---------------   ---------------   --------------
moe
petergriffin
quagmire
robo
stewiegriffin
willie

                  lois
```

```
        meg
        mayorwest

        tchi
                      brian
                      sizlack
                      chris
                      cleveland
                      flanders
                      ken
```

The last step is to apply an aggregate function to the values returned by SUBSTR while grouping by ID, to make a human-readable result set:

```
with cartesian as (
select level id
  from dual
 connect by level <= 100
)
select max(decode(id,1,substr(strings,p1+1,p2-1))) val1,
       max(decode(id,2,substr(strings,p1+1,p2-1))) val2,
       max(decode(id,3,substr(strings,p1+1,p2-1))) val3
  from (
select v.strings,
       c.id,
       instr(v.strings,':',1,c.id) p1,
       instr(v.strings,':',1,c.id+1)-instr(v.strings,':',1,c.id) p2
  from v,cartesian c
 where c.id <= (length(v.strings)-length(replace(v.strings,':')))-1
       )
 group by strings
 order by 1


VAL1              VAL2              VAL3
---------------   ---------------   -----------
moe                                 sizlack
petergriffin      meg               chris
quagmire          mayorwest         cleveland
robo              tchi              ken
stewiegriffin     lois              brian
willie
                                    flanders
```

14.12 Calculating Percent Relative to Total

Problem

You want to report a set of numeric values, and you want to show each value as a percentage of the whole. For example, you are on an Oracle system and you want to return a result set that shows the breakdown of salaries by JOB so that you can determine which JOB position costs the company the most money. You also want to include the number of employees per JOB to prevent the results from being misleading. You want to produce the following report:

JOB	NUM_EMPS	PCT_OF_ALL_SALARIES
CLERK	4	14
ANALYST	2	20
MANAGER	3	28
SALESMAN	4	19
PRESIDENT	1	17

As you can see, if the number of employees is not included in the report, it would look as if the president position takes very little of the overall salary. Seeing that there is only one president helps put into perspective what that 17% means.

Solution

Only Oracle enables a decent solution to this problem, which involves using the built-in function RATIO_TO_REPORT. To calculate percentages of the whole for other databases, you can use division as shown in Recipe 7.11.

```
1  select job,num_emps,sum(round(pct)) pct_of_all_salaries
2    from (
3  select job,
4         count(*)over(partition by job) num_emps,
5         ratio_to_report(sal)over( )*100 pct
6    from emp
7         )
8   group by job,num_emps
```

Discussion

The first step is to use the window function COUNT OVER to return the number of employees per JOB. Then use RATIO_TO_REPORT to return the percentage each salary counts against the total (the value is returned in decimal):

```
select job,
       count(*)over(partition by job) num_emps,
       ratio_to_report(sal)over( )*100 pct
  from emp
```

JOB	NUM_EMPS	PCT
ANALYST	2	10.3359173
ANALYST	2	10.3359173
CLERK	4	2.75624462
CLERK	4	3.78983635
CLERK	4	4.4788975
CLERK	4	3.27304048
MANAGER	3	10.2497847
MANAGER	3	8.44099914
MANAGER	3	9.81912145
PRESIDENT	1	17.2265289
SALESMAN	4	5.51248923
SALESMAN	4	4.30663221
SALESMAN	4	5.16795866
SALESMAN	4	4.30663221

The last step is to use the aggregate function SUM to sum the values returned by
RATIO_TO_REPORT. Be sure to group by JOB and NUM_EMPS. Multiply by 100
to return a whole number that represents a percentage (e.g., to return 25 rather than
0.25 for 25%):

```
select job,num_emps,sum(round(pct)) pct_of_all_salaries
  from (
select job,
       count(*)over(partition by job) num_emps,
       ratio_to_report(sal)over( )*100 pct
  from emp
       )
 group by job,num_emps
```

```
JOB         NUM_EMPS PCT_OF_ALL_SALARIES
---------   ---------- --------------------
CLERK              4                  14
ANALYST            2                  20
MANAGER            3                  28
SALESMAN           4                  19
PRESIDENT          1                  17
```

14.13 Creating CSV Output from Oracle

Problem

You want to create a delimited list (perhaps comma delimited) from rows in a table.
For example, using table EMP, you want to return the following result set:

```
DEPTNO LIST
------ ------------------------------------
    10 MILLER,KING,CLARK
    20 FORD,ADAMS,SCOTT,JONES,SMITH
    30 JAMES,TURNER,BLAKE,MARTIN,WARD,ALLEN
```

You are on an Oracle system (Oracle Database 10g or later) and want to use the
MODEL clause.

Solution

This solution takes advantage of the iteration capabilities of Oracle's MODEL clause.
The technique is to use the window function ROW_NUMBER OVER to rank each
employee (by EMPNO, which is arbitrary) in each DEPTNO. Because MODEL provides array access, you can access prior array elements by subtracting from the rank.
So, for each row, create a list that includes each employee's name, plus the name of
the employee ranked before the current employee:

```
1  select deptno,
2         list
3    from (
4  select *
```

```
 5    from (
 6  select deptno,empno,ename,
 7          lag(deptno)over(partition by deptno
 8                               order by empno) prior_deptno
 9    from emp
10         )
11  model
12    dimension by
13    (
14      deptno,
15      row_number()over(partition by deptno order by empno) rn
16    )
17    measures
18    (
19      ename,
20      prior_deptno,cast(null as varchar2(60)) list,
21      count(*)over(partition by deptno) cnt,
22      row_number()over(partition by deptno order by empno) rnk
23    )
24    rules
25    (
26      list[any,any]
27      order by deptno,rn = case when prior_deptno[cv(),cv()] is null
28                            then ename[cv(),cv()]
29                            else ename[cv(),cv()]||','||
30                                 list[cv(),rnk[cv(),cv()]-1]
31                       end
32    )
33    )
34  where cnt = rn
```

Discussion

The first step is to use the window function LAG OVER to return the DEPTNO of the previous employee (sorted by EMPNO). The results are partitioned by DEPTNO, so the return value will be NULL for the first employee (by EMPNO) in the department and DEPTNO for the rest. The results are as follows:

```
select deptno,empno,ename,
       lag(deptno)over(partition by deptno
                       order by empno) prior_deptno
  from emp
```

DEPTNO	EMPNO	ENAME	PRIOR_DEPTNO
10	7782	CLARK	
10	7839	KING	10
10	7934	MILLER	10
20	7369	SMITH	
20	7566	JONES	20
20	7788	SCOTT	20
20	7876	ADAMS	20
20	7902	FORD	20
30	7499	ALLEN	

30	7521 WARD	30
30	7654 MARTIN	30
30	7698 BLAKE	30
30	7844 TURNER	30
30	7900 JAMES	30

The next step is to examine the MEASURES subclause of the MODEL clause. The items in the MEASURES list are the arrays:

ENAME

> An array of all the ENAMEs in EMP

PRIOR_DEPTNO

> An array of the values returned by the LAG OVER window function

CNT

> An array of the number of employees in each DEPTNO

RNK

> An array of rankings (by EMPNO) for each employee in each DEPTNO

The array indices are DEPTNO and RN (the value returned by the ROW_NUMBER OVER window function in the DIMENSION BY subclause). To see what all these arrays contain, simply comment out the code listed in the RULES subclause of the MODEL clause and execute the query, as follows:

```
select *
  from (
select deptno,empno,ename,
       lag(deptno)over(partition by deptno
                               order by empno) prior_deptno
  from emp
       )
 model
  dimension by
  (
    deptno,
    row_number( )over(partition by deptno order by empno) rn
  )
  measures
  (
    ename,
    prior_deptno,cast(null as varchar2(60)) list,
    count(*)over(partition by deptno) cnt,
    row_number( )over(partition by deptno order by empno) rnk
  )
  rules
  (
/*
    list[any,any]
    order by deptno,rn = case when prior_deptno[cv( ),cv( )] is null
                              then ename[cv( ),cv( )]
                              else ename[cv( ),cv( )]||','||
                                   list[cv( ),rnk[cv( ),cv( )]-1]
                         end
```

```
*/
  )
order by 1
```

```
DEPTNO  RN ENAME  PRIOR_DEPTNO LIST        CNT  RNK
------  --- ------ ------------ ----------  ---  ----
    10   1 CLARK                             3    1
    10   2 KING         10                   3    2
    10   3 MILLER       10                   3    3
    20   1 SMITH                             5    1
    20   2 JONES        20                   5    2
    20   4 ADAMS        20                   5    4
    20   5 FORD         20                   5    5
    20   3 SCOTT        20                   5    3
    30   1 ALLEN                             6    1
    30   6 JAMES        30                   6    6
    30   4 BLAKE        30                   6    4
    30   3 MARTIN       30                   6    3
    30   5 TURNER       30                   6    5
    30   2 WARD         30                   6    2
```

Now that you know exactly what each item declared in the MODEL clause does, continue on to the RULES subclause. If you look at the CASE expression, you'll see that the current value for PRIOR_DEPTNO is being evaluated. If that value is NULL, it signifies that the first employee in each DEPTNO and ENAME should be returned to that employee's LIST array. If the value for PRIOR_DEPTNO is not NULL, then append the value of the prior employee's LIST to the current employee's name (ENAME array), and then return that result as the current employee's LIST. This CASE expression operation, when performed for each row in DEPTNO, results in an iteratively built comma-separated values (CSV) list. You can see the intermediate results in the following example:

```
select deptno,
       list
  from (
select *
  from (
select deptno,empno,ename,
       lag(deptno)over(partition by deptno
                         order by empno) prior_deptno
  from emp
       )
 model
   dimension by
   (
     deptno,
     row_number()over(partition by deptno order by empno) rn
   )
   measures
   (
     ename,
     prior_deptno,cast(null as varchar2(60)) list,
```

```
     count(*)over(partition by deptno) cnt,
     row_number( )over(partition by deptno order by empno) rnk
  )
  rules
  (
    list[any,any]
    order by deptno,rn = case when prior_deptno[cv( ),cv( )] is null
                              then ename[cv( ),cv( )]
                              else ename[cv( ),cv( )]||','||
                                   list[cv(),rnk[cv(),cv()]-1]
                         end
  )
  )

DEPTNO LIST
------ ---------------------------------------
    10 CLARK
    10 KING,CLARK
    10 MILLER,KING,CLARK
    20 SMITH
    20 JONES,SMITH
    20 SCOTT,JONES,SMITH
    20 ADAMS,SCOTT,JONES,SMITH
    20 FORD,ADAMS,SCOTT,JONES,SMITH
    30 ALLEN
    30 WARD,ALLEN
    30 MARTIN,WARD,ALLEN
    30 BLAKE,MARTIN,WARD,ALLEN
    30 TURNER,BLAKE,MARTIN,WARD,ALLEN
    30 JAMES,TURNER,BLAKE,MARTIN,WARD,ALLEN
```

The last step is to keep only the last employee in each DEPTNO to ensure that you have a complete CSV list for each DEPTNO. Use the values stored in the CNT array and the values stored in the RN array to keep only the completed CSV for each DEPTNO. Because RN represents a ranking of employees in each DEPTNO by EMPNO, the last employee in each DEPTNO will be the one where CNT = RN, as the following example shows:

```
select deptno,
       list
  from (
select *
  from (
select deptno,empno,ename,
       lag(deptno)over(partition by deptno
                            order by empno) prior_deptno
  from emp
       )
model
  dimension by
  (
    deptno,
    row_number( )over(partition by deptno order by empno) rn
```

```
    )
    measures
    (
      ename,
      prior_deptno,cast(null as varchar2(60)) list,
      count(*)over(partition by deptno) cnt,
      row_number( )over(partition by deptno order by empno) rnk
    )
    rules
    (
      list[any,any]
      order by deptno,rn = case when prior_deptno[cv( ),cv( )] is null
                           then ename[cv( ),cv( )]
                           else ename[cv( ),cv( )]||','||
                                list[cv( ),rnk[cv( ),cv( )]-1]
                           end
    )
    )
    where cnt = rn

DEPTNO LIST
------ ----------------------------------------
    10 MILLER,KING,CLARK
    20 FORD,ADAMS,SCOTT,JONES,SMITH
    30 JAMES,TURNER,BLAKE,MARTIN,WARD,ALLEN
```

14.14 Finding Text Not Matching a Pattern (Oracle)

Problem

You have a text field that contains some structured text values (e.g., phone numbers), and you wish to find occurrences where those values are structured incorrectly. For example, you have data like the following:

```
select emp_id, text
  from employee_comment

EMP_ID     TEXT
---------- -----------------------------------------------------------
7369       126 Varnum, Edmore MI 48829, 989 313-5351
7499       1105 McConnell Court
           Cedar Lake MI 48812
           Home: 989-387-4321
           Cell: (237) 438-3333
```

and you wish to list rows having invalidly formatted phone numbers. For example, you wish to list the following row because its phone number uses two different separator characters:

```
7369       126 Varnum, Edmore MI 48829, 989 313-5351
```

You wish to consider valid only those phone numbers that use the same character for both delimiters.

Solution

This problem has a multi-part solution:

1. Find a way to describe the universe of apparent phone numbers that you wish to consider.

2. Remove any validly formatted phone numbers from consideration.

3. See whether you still have any apparent phone numbers left. If you do, you know those are invalidly formatted.

The following solution makes good use of the regular expression functionality introduced in Oracle Database 10g:

```
select emp_id, text
from employee_comment
where regexp_like(text, '[0-9]{3}[-. ][0-9]{3}[-. ][0-9]{4}')
  and regexp_like(
        regexp_replace(text,
           '[0-9]{3}([-. ])[0-9]{3}\1[0-9]{4}','***'),
        '[0-9]{3}[-. ][0-9]{3}[-. ][0-9]{4}')

    EMP_ID TEXT
---------- ------------------------------------------------------------
      7369 126 Varnum, Edmore MI 48829, 989 313-5351
      7844 989-387.5359
      9999 906-387-1698, 313-535.8886
```

Each of these rows contains at least one apparent phone number that is not correctly formatted.

Discussion

The key to this solution lies in the detection of an "apparent phone number." Given that the phone numbers are stored in a comment field, any text at all in the field could be construed to be an invalid phone number. You need a way to narrow the field to a more reasonable set of values to consider. You don't, for example, want to see the following row in your output:

```
    EMP_ID TEXT
---------- ------------------------------------------------------------
      7900 Cares for 100-year-old aunt during the day. Schedule only
           for evening and night shifts.
```

Clearly there's no phone number at all in this row, much less one that is invalid. You and I can see that. The question is, how do you get the RDBMS to "see" it. I think you'll enjoy the answer. Please read on.

 This recipe comes (with permission) from an article by Jonathan Gennick called "Regular Expression Anti-Patterns," which you can read at: *http://gennick.com/antiregex.htm.*

The solution uses Pattern A to define the set of "apparent" phone numbers to consider:

```
Pattern A: [0-9]{3}[-. ][0-9]{3}[-. ][0-9]{4}
```

Pattern A checks for two groups of three digits followed by one group of four digits. Any one of a dash (-), a period (.), or a space are accepted as delimiters between groups. You could come up with a more complex pattern. For example, you could decide that you also wish to consider seven-digit phone numbers. But don't get sidetracked. The point now is that somehow you do need to define the universe of possible phone number strings to consider, and for this problem that universe is defined by Pattern A. You can define a different Pattern A, and the general solution still applies.

The solution uses Pattern A in the WHERE clause to ensure that only rows having potential phone numbers (as defined by the pattern!) are considered:

```
select emp_id, text
  from employee_comment
 where regexp_like(text, '[0-9]{3}[-. ][0-9]{3}[-. ][0-9]{4}')
```

Next, you need to define what a "good" phone number looks like. The solution does this using Pattern B:

```
Pattern B: [0-9]{3}([-. ])[0-9]{3}\1[0-9]{4}
```

This time, the pattern uses \1 to reference the first subexpression. Whichever character is matched by ([-.]) must also be matched by \1. Pattern B describes good phone numbers, which must be eliminated from consideration (as they are not bad). The solution eliminates the well-formatted phone numbers through a call to REGEXP_REPLACE:

```
regexp_replace(text,
   '[0-9]{3}([-. ])[0-9]{3}\1[0-9]{4}','***'),
```

This call to REGEXP_REPLACE occurs in the WHERE clause. Any well-formatted phone numbers are replaced by a string of three asterisks. Again, Pattern B can be any pattern that you desire. The point is that Pattern B describes the acceptable pattern that you are after.

Having replaced well-formatted phone numbers with strings of three asterisks (***), any "apparent" phone numbers that remain must, by definition, be poorly formatted. The solution applies REGEXP_LIKE to the output from REGEXP_LIKE to see whether any poorly formatted phone numbers remain:

```
and regexp_like(
      regexp_replace(text,
         '[0-9]{3}([-. ])[0-9]{3}\1[0-9]{4}','***'),
      '[0-9]{3}[-. ][0-9]{3}[-. ][0-9]{4}')
```

This recipe would be difficult to implement without the pattern matching capabilities inherent in Oracle's relatively new regular expression features. In particular, this recipe depends on REGEXP_REPLACE. Other databases (notably PostgreSQL) implement support for regular expressions. But to my knowledge, only Oracle supports the regular expression search and replace functionality on which this recipe depends.

14.15 Transforming Data with an Inline View

Problem

You have a table in a column that sometimes contains numeric data and sometimes character data. Another column in the same table indicates which is the case. You wish to use a subquery to isolate only the numeric data:

```
select *
  from ( select flag, to_number(num) num
         from subtest
         where flag in ('A', 'C') )
         where num > 0
```

Unfortunately, this query against an inline view often (but perhaps not always!) results in the following error message;

```
ERROR:
ORA-01722: invalid number
```

Solution

One solution is to force the inline view to completely execute prior to the outer SELECT statement. You can do that, in Oracle at least, by including the row number pseudo-column in your inner SELECT list:

```
select *
  from ( select rownum, flag, to_number(num) num
         from subtest
         where flag in ('A', 'C') )
         where num > 0
```

See the Discussion section for an explanation of why this solution works.

Discussion

The reason for the invalid number error in the problem query is that some optimizers will merge the inner and outer queries. While it looks like you are executing an inner query first to remove all non-numeric NUM values, you might really be executing:

```
select flag, to_number(num) num
from subtest
where to_number(num) > 0 and flag in ('A', 'C');
```

And now you can probably clearly see the reason for the error: rows with non-numeric NUM values are *not* filtered out before the TO_NUMBER function is applied.

Should a database merge sub and main queries? The answer depends on whether you are thinking in terms of relational theory, in terms of the SQL standard, or in terms of how your particular database vendor chooses to implement his brand of SQL. You can learn more by visiting *http://gennick.com/madness.html*.

The solution solves the problem, in Oracle at least, because it adds ROWNUM to the inner query's SELECT list. ROWNUM is a function that returns a sequentially increasing number for each row *returned by a query.* Those last words are important. The sequentially increasing number, termed a *row number,* cannot be computed outside the context of returning a row from a query. Thus, Oracle is forced to materialize the result of the subquery, which means that Oracle is forced to execute the subquery first in order to return rows from that subquery in order to properly assign row numbers. Thus, querying for ROWNUM is one mechanism that you can use to force Oracle to fully execute a subquery prior to the main query (i.e., no merging of queries allowed). If you are not using Oracle, and you need to force the order of execution of a subquery, check to see whether your database supports something analogous to Oracle's ROWNUM function.

14.16 Testing for Existence of a Value Within a Group

Problem

You want to create a Boolean flag for a row depending on whether or not any row in its group contains a specific value. Consider an example of a student who has taken a certain number of exams during a period of time. A student will take three exams over three months. If a student passes one of these exams, the requirement is satisfied and a flag should be returned to express that fact. If a student did not pass any of the three tests in the three month period, then an additional flag should be returned to express that fact as well. Consider the following example (using Oracle syntax to make up rows for this example; minor modifications are necessary for DB2 and SQL Server, because both support window functions):

```
create view V
as
select 1 student_id,
       1 test_id,
       2 grade_id,
       1 period_id,
       to_date('02/01/2005','MM/DD/YYYY') test_date,
       0 pass_fail
  from dual union all
select 1, 2, 2, 1, to_date('03/01/2005','MM/DD/YYYY'), 1 from dual union all
select 1, 3, 2, 1, to_date('04/01/2005','MM/DD/YYYY'), 0 from dual union all
select 1, 4, 2, 2, to_date('05/01/2005','MM/DD/YYYY'), 0 from dual union all
select 1, 5, 2, 2, to_date('06/01/2005','MM/DD/YYYY'), 0 from dual union all
```

```
select 1, 6, 2, 2, to_date('07/01/2005','MM/DD/YYYY'),  0 from dual

select *
  from V


STUDENT_ID TEST_ID GRADE_ID PERIOD_ID TEST_DATE   PASS_FAIL
---------- ------- -------- --------- ----------- ---------
        1       1        2         1 01-FEB-2005          0
        1       2        2         1 01-MAR-2005          1
        1       3        2         1 01-APR-2005          0
        1       4        2         2 01-MAY-2005          0
        1       5        2         2 01-JUN-2005          0
        1       6        2         2 01-JUL-2005          0
```

Examining the result set above, you see that the student has taken six tests over two, three-month periods. The student has passed one test (1 means "pass"; 0 means "fail"), thus the requirement is satisfied for the entire first period. Because the student did not pass any exams during the second period (the next three months), PASS_FAIL is 0 for all three exams. You want to return a result set that highlights whether or not a student has passed a test for a given period. Ultimately you want to return the following result set:

```
STUDENT_ID TEST_ID GRADE_ID PERIOD_ID TEST_DATE   METREQ IN_PROGRESS
---------- ------- -------- --------- ----------- ------ -----------
        1       1        2         1 01-FEB-2005     +             0
        1       2        2         1 01-MAR-2005     +             0
        1       3        2         1 01-APR-2005     +             0
        1       4        2         2 01-MAY-2005     -             0
        1       5        2         2 01-JUN-2005     -             0
        1       6        2         2 01-JUL-2005     -             1
```

The values for METREQ ("met requirement") are + and -, signifying the student either has or has not satisfied the requirement of passing at least one test in a period (three-month span), respectively. The value for IN_PROGRESS should be 0 if a student has already passed a test in a given period. If a student has not passed a test for a given period, then the row that has the latest exam date for that student will have a value of 1 for IN_PROGRESS.

Solution

What makes this problem a bit tricky is the fact that you have to treat rows in a group as a group and not as individuals. Consider the values for PASS_FAIL in the problem section. If you evaluate row by row, it would seem that the value for METREQ for each row except TEST_ID 2 should be "-", when in fact that is not the case. You must ensure you evaluate the rows as a group. By using the window function MAX OVER you can easily determine whether or not a student passed at least one test during a particular period. Once you have that information, the "Boolean" values are a simple matter of using CASE expressions:

```
 1  select student_id,
 2         test_id,
 3         grade_id,
 4         period_id,
 5         test_date,
 6         decode( grp_p_f,1,lpad('+',6),lpad('-',6) ) metreq,
 7         decode( grp_p_f,1,0,
 8                     decode( test_date,last_test,1,0 ) ) in_progress
 9    from (
10  select V.*,
11         max(pass_fail)over(partition by
12                    student_id,grade_id,period_id) grp_p_f,
13         max(test_date)over(partition by
14                    student_id,grade_id,period_id) last_test
15    from V
16          ) x
```

Discussion

The key to the solution is using the window function MAX OVER to return the greatest value of PASS_FAIL for each group. Because the values for PASS_FAIL are only 1 or 0, if a student passed at least one exam, then MAX OVER would return 1 for the entire group. How this works is shown below:

```
select V.*,
       max(pass_fail)over(partition by
                  student_id,grade_id,period_id) grp_pass_fail
  from V
```

STUDENT_ID	TEST_ID	GRADE_ID	PERIOD_ID	TEST_DATE	PASS_FAIL	GRP_PASS_FAIL
1	1	2	1	01-FEB-2005	0	1
1	2	2	1	01-MAR-2005	1	1
1	3	2	1	01-APR-2005	0	1
1	4	2	2	01-MAY-2005	0	0
1	5	2	2	01-JUN-2005	0	0
1	6	2	2	01-JUL-2005	0	0

The result set above shows that the student passed at least one test during the first period, thus the entire group has a value of 1 or "pass." The next requirement is that if the student has not passed any tests in a period, return a value of 1 for he IN_PROGRESS flag for the latest test date in that group. You can use the window function MAX OVER to do this as well:

```
select V.*,
       max(pass_fail)over(partition by
                  student_id,grade_id,period_id) grp_p_f,
       max(test_date)over(partition by
                  student_id,grade_id,period_id) last_test
  from V
```

```
STUDENT_ID TEST_ID GRADE_ID PERIOD_ID TEST_DATE    PASS_FAIL GRP_P_F LAST_TEST
---------- ------- -------- --------- ----------- --------- ------- -----------
         1       1        2         1 01-FEB-2005          0       1 01-APR-2005
         1       2        2         1 01-MAR-2005          1       1 01-APR-2005
         1       3        2         1 01-APR-2005          0       1 01-APR-2005
         1       4        2         2 01-MAY-2005          0       0 01-JUL-2005
         1       5        2         2 01-JUN-2005          0       0 01-JUL-2005
         1       6        2         2 01-JUL-2005          0       0 01-JUL-2005
```

Now that you have determined for which period the student has passed a test and what the latest test date for each period is, the last step is simply a matter of applying some formatting magic to make the result set look nice. The final solution uses Oracle's DECODE function (CASE supporters eat your hearts out) to create the METREQ and IN_PROGRESS columns. Use the LPAD function to right justify the values for METREQ:

```
select student_id,
       test_id,
       grade_id,
       period_id,
       test_date,
       decode( grp_p_f,1,lpad('+',6),lpad('-',6) ) metreq,
       decode( grp_p_f,1,0,
               decode( test_date,last_test,1,0 ) ) in_progress
  from (
select V.*,
       max(pass_fail)over(partition by
                    student_id,grade_id,period_id) grp_p_f,
       max(test_date)over(partition by
                    student_id,grade_id,period_id) last_test
  from V
       ) x
```

```
STUDENT_ID TEST_ID GRADE_ID PERIOD_ID TEST_DATE   METREQ IN_PROGRESS
---------- ------- -------- --------- ----------- ------ -----------
         1       1        2         1 01-FEB-2005      +           0
         1       2        2         1 01-MAR-2005      +           0
         1       3        2         1 01-APR-2005      +           0
         1       4        2         2 01-MAY-2005      -           0
         1       5        2         2 01-JUN-2005      -           0
         1       6        2         2 01-JUL-2005      -           1
```

Window Function Refresher

The recipes in this book take full advantage of the window functions added to the ISO SQL standard in 2003, as well as vendor-specific window functions. This appendix is meant to serve as a brief overview of how window functions work. Window functions make many typically difficult tasks (difficult to solve using standard SQL, that is) quite easy. For a complete list of window functions available, full syntax, and in-depth coverage of how they work, please consult your vendor's documentation.

Grouping

Before moving on to window functions, it is crucial that you understand how grouping works in SQL. In my experience, the concept of grouping results in SQL has been a stumbling block for many. The problems stem from not fully understanding how the GROUP BY clause works and why certain queries return certain results when using GROUP BY.

Simply stated, grouping is a way to organize like rows together. When you use GROUP BY in a query, each row in the result set is a group and represents one or more rows with the same values in one or more columns that you specify. That's the gist of it.

If a group is simply a unique instance of a row that represents one or more rows with the same value for a particular column (or columns), then practical examples of groups from table EMP include *all employees in department 10* (the common value for these employees that enable them to be in the same group is DEPTNO=10) or *all clerks* (the common value for these employees that enable them to be in the same group is JOB='CLERK'). Consider the following queries. The first shows all employees in department 10; the second query groups the employees in department 10 and returns the following information about the group: the number of rows (members) in the group, the highest salary, and the lowest salary:

```
select deptno,ename
  from emp
 where deptno=10

DEPTNO ENAME
------ ----------
    10 CLARK
    10 KING
    10 MILLER

select deptno,
       count(*) as cnt,
       max(sal) as hi_sal,
       min(sal) as lo_sal
  from emp
 where deptno=10
 group by deptno

DEPTNO      CNT    HI_SAL    LO_SAL
------ ---------- ---------- ----------
    10          3      5000      1300
```

If you were not able to group the employees in department 10 together, to get the information in the second query above you would have to manually inspect the rows for that department (trivial if there are only three rows, but what if there were three million rows?). So, why would anyone want to group? Reasons for doing so vary; perhaps you want to see how many different groups exist or how many members (rows) are in each group. As you can see from the simple example above, grouping allows you to get information about many rows in a table without having to inspect them one by one.

Definition of an SQL Group

In mathematics, a group is defined, for the most part, as $(G, \bullet, e)$, where G is a set, $\bullet$ is a binary operation in G, and e is a member of G. We will use this definition as the foundation for what a SQL group is. A SQL group will be defined as (G, e), where G is a result set of a single or self-contained query that uses GROUP BY, e is a member of G, and the following axioms are satisfied:

- For each e in G, e is distinct and represents one or more instances of e.
- For each e in G, the aggregate function COUNT returns a value > 0.

 The result set is included in the definition of a SQL group to reinforce the fact that we are defining what groups are when working with queries only. Thus, it would be accurate to replace "e" in each axiom with the word "row" because the rows in the result set are technically the groups.

Because these properties are fundamental to what we consider a group, it is important that we prove they are true (and we will proceed to do so through the use of some example SQL queries).

Groups are non-empty

By its very definition, a group must have at least one member (or row). If we accept this as a truth, then it can be said that a group cannot be created from an empty table. To prove that proposition true, simply try to prove it is false. The following example creates an empty table, and then attempts to create groups via three different queries against that empty table:

```
create table fruits (name varchar(10))

select name
  from fruits
 group by name

(no rows selected)


select count(*) as cnt
  from fruits
 group by name

(no rows selected)


select name, count(*) as cnt
  from fruits
 group by name

(no rows selected)
```

As you can see from these queries, it is impossible to create what SQL considers a group from an empty table.

Groups are distinct

Now let's prove that the groups created via queries with a GROUP BY clause are distinct. The following example inserts five rows into table FRUITS, and then creates groups from those rows:

```
insert into fruits values ('Oranges')
insert into fruits values ('Oranges')
insert into fruits values ('Oranges')
insert into fruits values ('Apple')
insert into fruits values ('Peach')

select *
  from fruits
```

```
NAME
----------
Oranges
Oranges
Oranges
Apple
Peach


select name
  from fruits
 group by name

NAME
----------
Apple
Oranges
Peach


select name, count(*) as cnt
  from fruits
 group by name

NAME             CNT
---------- ----------
Apple              1
Oranges            3
Peach              1
```

The first query shows that "Oranges" occurs three times in table FRUITS. However, the second and third queries (using GROUP BY) return only one instance of "Oranges." Taken together, these queries prove that the rows in the result set (*e* in G, from our definition) are distinct, and each value of NAME represents one or more instances of itself in table FRUITS.

Knowing that groups are distinct is important because it means, typically, you would not use the DISTINCT keyword in your SELECT list when using a GROUP BY in your queries.

 I am in no way suggesting GROUP BY and DISTINCT are the same. They represent two completely different concepts. I am merely stating that the items listed in the GROUP BY clause will be distinct in the result set and that using DISTINCT as well as GROUP BY is redundant.

Frege's Axiom and Russell's Paradox

For those of you who are interested, Frege's *axiom of abstraction*, based on Cantor's solution for defining set membership for infinite or uncountable sets, states that, given a specific identifying property, there exists a set whose members are only those items having that property. The source of trouble, as put by Robert Stoll, "is the unrestrictd use of the principal of abstraction." Bertrand Russell asked Gottlob Frege to consider a set whose members are sets and have the defining property of not being members of themselves.

As Russell pointed out, the axiom of abstraction gives too much freedom because you are simply specifiying a condition or property to define set membership, thus a contradiction can be found. To better explain how a contradiction can be found, he devised the "Barber Puzzle." The Barber Puzzle states:

> In a certain town there is a male barber who shaves all those men, and only those men, who do not shave themselves. If this is true, who, then, shaves the barber?

For a more concrete example, consider the set that can be described as:

For all members x in y that satisfy a specific condition (P)

The mathematical notation for this description is:

{x ε y | P(x)}

Because the above set considers *only those x in y that satisfy a condition (P)* you may find it more intuitive to describe the set as *x is a member of y if and only if x satisfies a condition (P)*.

At this point let us define this condition $P(x)$ as *x is not a member of x*:

(x ε x)

The set is now defined as *x is a member of y if and only if x is not a member of x*:

{x ε y | (x ε x)}

Russell's paradox may not be clear to you yet, but ask yourself this: can the set above be a member of itself? Let's assume that $x = y$ and look at the above set again. The following set can be defined as *y is a member of y if and only if y is not a member of y*:

{y ε y | (y ε y)}

—continued—

Simply put, Russell's paradox leaves us in a position to have a set that is concurrently a member of itself and not a member of itself, which is a contradiction. Intuitive thinking would lead one to believe this isn't a problem at all; indeed, how can a set be a member of itself? The set of all books, after all, is not a book. So why does this paradox exist and how can it be an issue? It becomes an issue when you consider more abstract applications of set theory. For example, a "practical" application of Russell's paradox can be demonstrated by considering the set of all sets. If we allow such a concept to exist, then by its very definition, it must be a member of itself (it is, after all, the set of all sets). What then happens when you apply $P(x)$ above to the set of all sets? Simply stated, Russell's paradox would state that the set of all sets is a member of itself if and only if it is not a member of itself—clearly a contradiction.

For those of you who are interested, Ernst Zermelo developed the axiom schema of separation (also referred to as the axiom schema of subsets or the axiom of specification) to elegantly sidestep Russell's paradox in axiomatic set theory.

COUNT is never zero

The queries and results in the preceding section also prove the final axiom that the aggregate function COUNT will never return zero when used in a query with GROUP BY on a nonempty table. It should not be surprising that you cannot return a count of zero for a group. We have already proved that a group cannot be created from an empty table, thus a group must have at least one row. If at least one row exists, then the count will always be at least 1.

 Remember, we are talking about using COUNT with GROUP BY, not COUNT by itself. A query using COUNT without a GROUP BY on an empty table will of course return zero.

Paradoxes

"Hardly anything more unfortunate can befall a scientific writer than to have one of the foundations of his edifice shaken after the work is finished.... This was the position I was placed in by a letter of Mr. Bertrand Russell, just when the printing of this volume was nearing its completion."

The preceding quote is from Gottlob Frege in response to Bertrand Russell's discovery of a contradiction to Frege's axiom of abstraction in set theory.

Paradoxes many times provide scenarios that would seem to contradict established theories or ideas. In many cases these contradictions are localized and can be "worked around," or they are applicable to such small test cases that they can be safely ignored.

You may have guessed by now that the point to all this discussion of paradoxes is that there exists a paradox concerning our definition of an SQL group, and that paradox must be addressed. Although our focus right now is on groups, ultimately we are discussing SQL queries. In its GROUP BY clause, a query may have a wide range of values such as constants, expressions, or, most commonly, columns from a table. We pay a price for this flexibility, because NULL is a valid "value" in SQL. NULLs present problems because they are effectively ignored by aggregate functions. With that said, if a table consists of a single row and its value is NULL, what would the aggregate function COUNT return when used in a GROUP BY query? By our very definition, when using GROUP BY and the aggregate function COUNT, a value >= 1 must be returned. What happens, then, in the case of values ignored by functions such as COUNT, and what does this mean to our definition of a GROUP? Consider the following example, which reveals the NULL group paradox (using the function COALESCE when necessary for readability):

```
select *
  from fruits

NAME
----------
Oranges
Oranges
Oranges
Apple
Peach


insert into fruits values (null)
insert into fruits values (null)
insert into fruits values (null)
insert into fruits values (null)
insert into fruits values (null)

select coalesce(name,'NULL') as name
  from fruits

NAME
----------
Oranges
Oranges
Oranges
Apple
Peach
NULL
NULL
NULL
NULL
NULL


select coalesce(name,'NULL') as name,
       count(name) as cnt
  from fruits
 group by name
```

NAME	CNT
Apple	1
NULL	0
Oranges	3
Peach	1

It would seem that the presence of NULL values in our table introduces a contradiction, or paradox, to our definition of a SQL group. Fortunately, this contradiction is not a real cause for concern, because the paradox has more to do with the implementation of aggregate functions than our definition. Consider the final query in the preceding set; a general problem statement for that query would be:

Count the number of times each name occurs in table FRUITS or count the number of members in each group.

Examining the INSERT statements above, it's clear that there are five rows with NULL values, which means there exists a NULL group with five members.

 While NULL certainly has properties that differentiate it from other values, it is nevertheless a value, and can in fact be a group.

How, then, can we write the query to return a count of 5 instead of 0, thus returning the information we are looking for while conforming to our definition of a group? The example below shows a workaround to deal with the NULL group paradox:

```
select coalesce(name,'NULL') as name,
       count(*) as cnt
  from fruits
 group by name
```

NAME	CNT
Apple	1
Oranges	3
Peach	1
NULL	5

The workaround is to use COUNT(*) rather than COUNT(NAME) to avoid the NULL group paradox. Aggregate functions will ignore NULL values if any exist in the column passed to them. Thus, to avoid a zero when using COUNT do not pass the column name; instead, pass in an asterisk (*). The * causes the COUNT function to count rows rather than the actual column values, so whether or not the actual values are NULL or not NULL is irrelevant.

One more paradox has to do with the axiom that each group in a result set (for each *e* in *G*) is distinct. Because of the nature of SQL result sets and tables, which are more accurately defined as multisets or "bags," not sets (because duplicate rows are allowed), it is possible to return a result set with duplicate groups. Consider the following queries:

```
select coalesce(name,'NULL') as name,
       count(*) as cnt
  from fruits
 group by name
 union all
select coalesce(name,'NULL') as name,
       count(*) as cnt
  from fruits
 group by name
```

```
NAME                CNT
----------   ----------
Apple                 1
Oranges               3
Peach                 1
NULL                  5
Apple                 1
Oranges               3
Peach                 1
NULL                  5
```

```
select x.*
  from (
select coalesce(name,'NULL') as name,
       count(*) as cnt
  from fruits
 group by name
       ) x,
       (select deptno from dept) y
```

```
NAME                CNT
----------   ----------
Apple                 1
Apple                 1
Apple                 1
Apple                 1
Oranges               3
Oranges               3
Oranges               3
Oranges               3
Peach                 1
Peach                 1
Peach                 1
Peach                 1
NULL                  5
NULL                  5
NULL                  5
NULL                  5
```

As you can see in these queries, the groups are in fact repeated in the final results. Fortunately, this is not much to worry about because it represents only a partial paradox. The first property of a group states that for (G,e), G is a result set from a single or self-contained query that uses GROUP BY. Simply put, the result set from any

GROUP BY query itself conforms to our definition of a group. It is only when you combine the result sets from two GROUP BY queries to create a multiset that groups may repeat. The first query in the preceding example uses UNION ALL, which is not a set operation but a multiset operation, and invokes GROUP BY twice, effectively executing two queries.

 If you use UNION, which is a set operation, you will not see repeating groups.

The second query in the preceding set uses a Cartesian product, which only works if you materialize the group first and then perform the Cartesian. Thus the GROUP BY query when self-contained conforms to our definition. Neither of the two examples takes anything away from the definition of a SQL group. They are shown for completeness, and so that you can be aware that almost anything is possible in SQL.

Relationship Between SELECT and GROUP BY

With the concept of a group defined and proved, it is now time to move on to more practical matters concerning queries using GROUP BY. It is important to understand the relationship between the SELECT clause and the GROUP BY clause when grouping in SQL. It is important to keep in mind when using aggregate functions such as COUNT that any item in your SELECT list that is not used as an argument to an aggregate function must be part of your group. For example, if you write a SELECT clause such as:

```
select deptno, count(*) as cnt
  from emp
```

then you must list DEPTNO in your GROUP BY clause:

```
select deptno, count(*) as cnt
  from emp
 group by deptno

DEPTNO    CNT
------ ------
    10      3
    20      5
    30      6
```

Constants, scalar values returned by user-defined functions, window functions, and non-correlated scalar subqueries are exceptions to this rule. Since the SELECT clause is evaluated after the GROUP BY clause, these constructs are allowed in the SELECT list and do not have to (and in some cases cannot) be specified in the GROUP BY clause. For example:

```
select 'hello' as msg,
        1 as num,
        deptno,
```

```
        (select count(*) from emp) as total,
        count(*) as cnt
  from emp
 group by deptno

 MSG   NUM DEPTNO TOTAL CNT
 ----- --- ------ ----- ---
 hello  1    10    14    3
 hello  1    20    14    5
 hello  1    30    14    6
```

Don't let this query confuse you. The items in the SELECT list not listed in the GROUP BY clause do not change the value of CNT for each DEPTNO, nor do the values for DEPTNO change. Based on the results of the preceding query, we can define the rule about matching items in the SELECT list and the GROUP BY clause when using aggregates a bit more precisely:

> Items in a SELECT list that can potentially change the group or change the value returned by an aggregate function must be included in the GROUP BY clause.

The additional items in the preceding SELECT list did not change the value of CNT for any group (each DEPTNO), nor did they change the groups themselves.

Now it's fair to ask: exactly what items in a SELECT list can change a grouping or the value returned by an aggregate function? The answer is simple: other columns from the table(s) you are selecting from. Consider the prospect of adding the JOB column to the query we've been looking at:

```
select deptno, job, count(*) as cnt
  from emp
 group by deptno, job

DEPTNO JOB         CNT
------ ---------- ---
    10 CLERK        1
    10 MANAGER      1
    10 PRESIDENT    1
    20 CLERK        2
    20 ANALYST      2
    20 MANAGER      1
    30 CLERK        1
    30 MANAGER      1
    30 SALESMAN     4
```

By listing another column, JOB, from table EMP, we are changing the group and changing the result set; thus we must now include JOB in the GROUP BY clause along with DEPTNO, otherwise the query will fail. The inclusion of JOB in the SELECT/GROUP BY clauses changes the query from "How many employees are in each department?" to "How many different types of employees are in each department?" Notice again that the groups are distinct; the values for DEPTNO and JOB *individually* are not distinct, but the combination of the two (which is what is in the GROUP BY and SELECT list, and thus is the group) are distinct (e.g., 10 and CLERK appear only once).

If you choose not to put items other than aggregate functions in the SELECT list, then you may list any valid column you wish, in the GROUP BY clause. Consider the following two queries, which highlight this fact:

```
select count(*)
  from emp
 group by deptno

   COUNT(*)
 ----------
          3
          5
          6

select count(*)
  from emp
 group by deptno,job

   COUNT(*)
 ----------
          1
          1
          1
          2
          2
          1
          1
          1
          4
```

Including items other than aggregate functions in the SELECT list is not mandatory, but often improves readability and usability of the results.

 As a rule, when using GROUP BY and aggregate functions, any items in the SELECT list [from the table(s) in the FROM clause] not used as an argument to an aggregate function must be included in the GROUP BY clause. However, MySQL has a "feature" that allows you to deviate from this rule, allowing you to place items in your SELECT list [that are columns in the table(s) you are selecting from] that are not used as arguments to an aggregate function and that are not present in your GROUP BY clause. I use the term "feature" very loosely here as its use is a bug waiting to happen and I urge you to avoid it. As a matter of fact, if you use MySQL and care at all about the accuracy of your queries I suggest you urge them to remove this, ahem, "feature."

Windowing

Once you understand the concept of grouping and using aggregates in SQL, understanding *window functions* is easy. Window functions, like aggregate functions, perform an aggregation on a defined set (a group) of rows, but rather than returning one value per group, window functions can return multiple values for each group. The group of rows to perform the aggregation on is the *window* (hence the name "window functions"). DB2 actually calls such functions *online analytic processing (OLAP) functions*, and Oracle calls them *analytic functions*, but the ISO SQL standard calls them window functions, so that's the term I use in this book.

A Simple Example

Let's say that you wish to count the total number of employees across all departments. The traditional method for doing that is to issue a COUNT(*) query against the entire EMP table:

```
select count(*) as cnt
  from emp

   CNT
------
   14
```

This is easy enough, but often you will find yourself wanting to access such aggregate data from rows that do not represent an aggregation, or that represent a different aggregation. Window functions make light work of such problems. For example, the following query shows how you can use a window function to access aggregate data (the total count of employees) from detail rows (one per employee):

```
select ename,
       deptno,
       count(*) over() as cnt
  from emp
 order by 2

ENAME      DEPTNO   CNT
---------- ------ ------
CLARK          10     14
KING           10     14
MILLER         10     14
SMITH          20     14
ADAMS          20     14
FORD           20     14
SCOTT          20     14
JONES          20     14
ALLEN          30     14
BLAKE          30     14
MARTIN         30     14
JAMES          30     14
TURNER         30     14
WARD           30     14
```

The window function invocation in this example is COUNT(*) OVER(). The presence of the OVER keyword indicates that the invocation of COUNT will be treated as a window function, not as an aggregate function. In general, the SQL standard allows for all aggregate functions to also be window functions, and the keyword OVER is how the language distinguishes between the two uses.

So, what did the window function COUNT(*) OVER () do exactly? For every row being returned in the query, it returned the count of *all the rows* in the table. As the empty parentheses suggest, the OVER keyword accepts additional clauses to affect the range of rows that a given window function considers. Absent any such clauses, the window function looks at all rows in the result set, which is why you see the value 14 repeated in each row of output.

Hopefully you begin to see the great utility of window functions, which is that they allow you to work with multiple levels of aggregation in one row. As you continue through this appendix, you'll begin to see even more just how incredibly useful that ability can be.

Order of Evaluation

Before digging deeper into the OVER clause, it is important to note that window functions are performed as the last step in SQL processing prior to the ORDER BY clause. As an example of how window functions are processed last, let's take the query from the preceding section and use a WHERE clause to filter out employees from DEPTNO 20 and 30:

```
select ename,
       deptno,
       count(*) over() as cnt
  from emp
 where deptno = 10
 order by 2

ENAME       DEPTNO   CNT
----------  ------  ------
CLARK          10     3
KING           10     3
MILLER         10     3
```

The value for CNT for each row is no longer 14, it is now 3. In this example, it is the WHERE clause that restricts the result set to three rows, hence the window function will count only three rows (there are only three rows available to the window function by the time processing reaches the SELECT portion of the query). From this example you can see that window functions perform their computations after clauses such as WHERE and GROUP BY are evaluated.

Partitions

Use the PARTITION BY clause to define a *partition* or group of rows to perform an aggregation over. As we've seen already, if you use empty parentheses then the entire result set is the partition that a window function aggregation will be computed over. You can think of the PARTITION BY clause as a "moving GROUP BY" because unlike a traditional GROUP BY, a group created by PARTITION BY is not distinct in a result set. You can use PARTITION BY to compute an aggregation over a defined group of rows (resetting when a new group is encountered) and rather than having one group represent all instances of that value in the table, each value (each member in each group) is returned. Consider the following query:

```
select ename,
       deptno,
       count(*) over(partition by deptno) as cnt
  from emp
 order by 2
```

```
ENAME       DEPTNO   CNT
----------  ------  ------
CLARK          10      3
KING           10      3
MILLER         10      3
SMITH          20      5
ADAMS          20      5
FORD           20      5
SCOTT          20      5
JONES          20      5
ALLEN          30      6
BLAKE          30      6
MARTIN         30      6
JAMES          30      6
TURNER         30      6
WARD           30      6
```

This query still returns 14 rows, but now the COUNT is performed for each department as a result of the PARTITION BY DEPTNO clause. Each employee in the same department (in the same partition) will have the same value for CNT, because the aggregation will not reset (recompute) until a new department is encountered. Also note that you are returning information about each group, along with the members of each group. You can think of the preceding query as a more efficient version of the following:

```
select e.ename,
       e.deptno,
       (select count(*) from emp d
         where e.deptno=d.deptno) as cnt
  from emp e
 order by 2
```

```
ENAME       DEPTNO   CNT
----------  ------  ------
CLARK          10      3
KING           10      3
MILLER         10      3
SMITH          20      5
ADAMS          20      5
FORD           20      5
SCOTT          20      5
JONES          20      5
ALLEN          30      6
BLAKE          30      6
```

```
MARTIN      30      6
JAMES       30      6
TURNER      30      6
WARD        30      6
```

Additionally, what's nice about the PARTITION BY clause is that it performs its computations independently of other window functions, partitioning by different columns in the same SELECT statement. Consider the following query, which returns each employee, her department, the number of employees in her respective department, her job, and the number of employees with the same job:

```
select ename,
       deptno,
       count(*) over(partition by deptno) as dept_cnt,
       job,
       count(*) over(partition by job)     as job_cnt
  from emp
 order by 2
```

```
ENAME     DEPTNO DEPT_CNT JOB          JOB_CNT
--------- ------ -------- ----------   -------
MILLER       10        3 CLERK            4
CLARK        10        3 MANAGER          3
KING         10        3 PRESIDENT        1
SCOTT        20        5 ANALYST          2
FORD         20        5 ANALYST          2
SMITH        20        5 CLERK            4
JONES        20        5 MANAGER          3
ADAMS        20        5 CLERK            4
JAMES        30        6 CLERK            4
MARTIN       30        6 SALESMAN         4
TURNER       30        6 SALESMAN         4
WARD         30        6 SALESMAN         4
ALLEN        30        6 SALESMAN         4
BLAKE        30        6 MANAGER          3
```

In this result set, you can see that employees in the same department have the same value for DEPT_CNT, and that employees who have the same job position have the same value for JOB_CNT.

By now it should be clear that the PARTITION BY clause works like a GROUP BY clause, but it does so without being affected by the other items in the SELECT clause and without requiring you to write a GROUP BY clause.

Effect of NULLs

Like the GROUP BY clause, the PARTITION BY clause lumps all the NULLs into one group or partition. Thus, the effect from NULLs when using PARTITION BY is similar to that from using GROUP BY. The following query uses a window function to count the number of employees with each distinct commission (returning −1 in place of NULL for readability):

```
select coalesce(comm,-1) as comm,
       count(*)over(partition by comm) as cnt
  from emp
```

```
COMM        CNT
------  ----------
     0         1
   300         1
   500         1
  1400         1
    -1        10
    -1        10
    -1        10
    -1        10
    -1        10
    -1        10
    -1        10
    -1        10
    -1        10
    -1        10
```

Because COUNT(*) is used, the function counts rows. You can see that there are 10 employees having NULL commissions. Use COMM instead of *, however, and you get quite different results:

```
select coalesce(comm,-1) as comm,
       count(comm)over(partition by comm) as cnt
  from emp
```

```
COMM        CNT
----   ----------
    0         1
  300         1
  500         1
 1400         1
   -1         0
   -1         0
   -1         0
   -1         0
   -1         0
   -1         0
   -1         0
   -1         0
   -1         0
   -1         0
```

This query uses COUNT(COMM), which means that only the non-NULL values in the COMM column are counted. There is one employee with a commission of 0, one employee with a commission of 300, and so forth. But notice the counts for those with NULL commissions! Those counts are 0. Why? Because aggregate functions ignore NULL values, or more accurately, aggregate functions count only non-NULL values.

When using COUNT, consider whether you wish to include NULLs. Use COUNT(column) to avoid counting NULLs. Use COUNT(*) if you do wish to include NULLs (since you are no longer counting actual column values, you are counting rows).

When Order Matters

Sometimes the order in which rows are treated by a window function is material to the results that you wish to obtain from a query. For this reason, window function syntax includes an ORDER BY subclause that you can place within an OVER clause. Use the ORDER BY clause to specify how the rows are ordered with a partition (remember, "partition" in the absence of a PARTITION BY clause means the entire result set).

Some window functions *require* you to impose order on the partitions of rows being affected. Thus, for some window functions an ORDER BY clause is mandatory. At the time of this writing, SQL Server does not allow ORDER BY in the OVER clause when used with aggregate window functions. SQL Server does permit ORDER BY in the OVER clause when used with window ranking functions.

When you use an ORDER BY clause in the OVER clause of a window function you are specifying two things:

1. How the rows in the partition are ordered
2. What rows are included in the computation

Consider the following query, which sums and computes a running total of salaries for employees in DEPTNO 10:

```
select deptno,
       ename,
       hiredate,
       sal,
       sum(sal)over(partition by deptno) as total1,
       sum(sal)over() as total2,
       sum(sal)over(order by hiredate) as running_total
  from emp
 where deptno=10

DEPTNO ENAME  HIREDATE     SAL TOTAL1 TOTAL2 RUNNING_TOTAL
------ ------ ----------- ----- ------ ------ -------------
    10 CLARK  09-JUN-1981  2450   8750   8750          2450
    10 KING   17-NOV-1981  5000   8750   8750          7450
    10 MILLER 23-JAN-1982  1300   8750   8750          8750
```

Just to keep you on your toes, I've included a sum with empty parentheses. Notice how TOTAL1 and TOTAL2 have the same values. Why? Once again, the order in which window functions are evaluated answers the question. The WHERE clause filters the result set such that only salaries from DEPTNO 10 are considered for summation. In this case there is only one partition—the entire result set, which consists of only salaries from DEPTNO 10. Thus TOTAL1 and TOTAL2 are the same.

Looking at the values returned by column SAL, you can easily see where the values for RUNNING_TOTAL come from. You can eyeball the values and add them yourself to compute the running total. But more importantly, why did including an ORDER BY in the OVER clause create a running total in the first place? The reason is, when you use ORDER BY in the OVER clause you are specify a default "moving" or "sliding" window within the partition even though you don't see it. The ORDER BY HIREDATE clause terminates summation at the HIREDATE in the current row.

The following query is the same as the previous one, but uses the RANGE BETWEEN clause (which you'll learn more about later) to explicitly specify the default behavior that results from ORDER BY HIREDATE:

```
select deptno,
       ename,
       hiredate,
       sal,
       sum(sal)over(partition by deptno) as total1,
       sum(sal)over( ) as total2,
       sum(sal)over(order by hiredate
                 range between unbounded preceding
                     and current row) as running_total
  from emp
 where deptno=10

DEPTNO ENAME  HIREDATE     SAL TOTAL1 TOTAL2 RUNNING_TOTAL
------ ------ ----------- ----- ------ ------ -------------
    10 CLARK  09-JUN-1981  2450   8750   8750          2450
    10 KING   17-NOV-1981  5000   8750   8750          7450
    10 MILLER 23-JAN-1982  1300   8750   8750          8750
```

The RANGE BETWEEN clause that you see in this query is termed the *framing clause* by ANSI and I'll use that term here. Now, it should be easy to see why specifying an ORDER BY in the OVER clause created a running total; we've (by default) told the query to sum all rows starting from the current row and include all prior rows ("prior" as defined in the ORDER BY, in this case ordering the rows by HIREDATE).

The Framing Clause

Let's apply the framing clause from the preceding query to the result set, starting with the first employee hired, who is named CLARK.

1. Starting with CLARK's salary, 2450, and including all employees hired before CLARK, compute a sum. Since CLARK was the first employee hired in DEPTNO 10, the sum is simply CLARK's salary, 2450, which is the first value returned by RUNNING_TOTAL.

2. Let's move to the next employee based on HIREDATE, named KING, and apply the framing clause once again. Compute a sum on SAL starting with the current row, 5000 (KING's salary), and include all prior rows (all employees hired before KING). CLARK is the only one hired before KING so the sum is 5000 + 2450, which is 7450, the second value returned by RUNNING_TOTAL.

3. Moving on to MILLER, the last employee in the partition based on HIREDATE, let's one more time apply the framing clause. Compute a sum on SAL starting with the current row, 1300 (MILLER's salary), and include all prior rows (all employees hired before MILLER). CLARK and KING were both hired before MILLER, and thus their salaries are included in MILLER's RUNNING_TOTAL: 2450 + 5000 + 1300 is 8750, which is the value for RUNNING_TOTAL for MILLER.

As you can see, it is really the framing clause that produces the running total. The ORDER BY defines the order of evaluation and happens to also imply a default framing.

In general, the framing clause allows you to define different "sub-windows" of data to include in your computations. There are many ways to specify such sub-windows. Consider the following query:

```
select deptno,
       ename,
       sal,
       sum(sal)over(order by hiredate
                    range between unbounded preceding
                      and current row) as run_total1,
       sum(sal)over(order by hiredate
                    rows between 1 preceding
                      and current row) as run_total2,
       sum(sal)over(order by hiredate
                    range between current row
                      and unbounded following) as run_total3,
       sum(sal)over(order by hiredate
                    rows between current row
                      and 1 following) as run_total4
  from emp
 where deptno=10
```

DEPTNO	ENAME	SAL	RUN_TOTAL1	RUN_TOTAL2	RUN_TOTAL3	RUN_TOTAL4
10	CLARK	2450	2450	2450	8750	7450
10	KING	5000	7450	7450	6300	6300
10	MILLER	1300	8750	6300	1300	1300

Don't be intimidated here; this query is not as bad as it looks. You've already seen RUN_TOTAL1 and the effects of the framing clause "UNBOUNDED PRECEDING AND CURRENT ROW". Here's a quick description of what's happening in the other examples:

RUN_TOTAL2

Rather than the keyword RANGE, this framing clause specifies ROWS, which means the *frame*, or window, is going to be constructed by counting some number of rows. The 1 PRECEDING means that the frame will begin with the row immediately preceding the current row. The range continues through the CURRENT ROW. So what you get in RUN_TOTAL2 is the sum of the current employee's salary and that of the preceding employee, based on HIREDATE.

 It so happens that RUN_TOTAL1 and RUN_TOTAL2 are the same for both CLARK and KING. Why? Think about which values are being summed for each of those employees, for each of the two window functions. Think carefully, and you'll get the answer.

RUN_TOTAL3

The window function for RUN_TOTAL3 works just the opposite of that for RUN_TOTAL1; rather than starting with the current row and including all prior rows in the summation, summation begins with the current row and includes all subsequent rows in the summation.

RUN_TOTAL4

Is inverse of RUN_TOTAL2; rather than starting from the current row and including one prior row in the summation, start with the current row and include one subsequent row in the summation.

 If you can understand what's been explained thus far, you will have no problem with any of the recipes in this book. If you're not catching on, though, try practicing with your own examples and your own data. I personally find learning easier by actually coding new features rather than just reading about them.

A Framing Finale

As a final example of the effect of the framing clause on query output, consider the following query:

```
select ename,
       sal,
       min(sal)over(order by sal) min1,
       max(sal)over(order by sal) max1,
       min(sal)over(order by sal
                    range between unbounded preceding
                        and unbounded following) min2,
       max(sal)over(order by sal
                    range between unbounded preceding
                        and unbounded following) max2,
       min(sal)over(order by sal
                    range between current row
                        and current row) min3,
       max(sal)over(order by sal
                    range between current row
                        and current row) max3,
       max(sal)over(order by sal
                    rows between 3 preceding
                        and 3 following) max4
  from emp

ENAME    SAL   MIN1   MAX1   MIN2   MAX2   MIN3   MAX3   MAX4
------  -----  -----  -----  -----  -----  -----  -----  -----
SMITH    800    800    800    800   5000    800    800   1250
JAMES    950    800    950    800   5000    950    950   1250
ADAMS   1100    800   1100    800   5000   1100   1100   1300
WARD    1250    800   1250    800   5000   1250   1250   1500
MARTIN  1250    800   1250    800   5000   1250   1250   1600
MILLER  1300    800   1300    800   5000   1300   1300   2450
TURNER  1500    800   1500    800   5000   1500   1500   2850
ALLEN   1600    800   1600    800   5000   1600   1600   2975
CLARK   2450    800   2450    800   5000   2450   2450   3000
BLAKE   2850    800   2850    800   5000   2850   2850   3000
JONES   2975    800   2975    800   5000   2975   2975   5000
SCOTT   3000    800   3000    800   5000   3000   3000   5000
FORD    3000    800   3000    800   5000   3000   3000   5000
KING    5000    800   5000    800   5000   5000   5000   5000
```

OK, let's break this query down:

MIN1

The window function generating this column does not specify a framing clause, so the default framing clause of UNBOUNDED PRECEDING AND CURRENT ROW kicks in. Why is MIN1 800 for all rows? It's because the lowest salary comes first (ORDER BY SAL), and it remains the lowest, or minimum, salary forever after.

MAX1

The values for MAX1 are much different from those for MIN1. Why? The answer (again) is the default framing clause UNBOUNDED PRECEDING AND CURRENT ROW. In conjunction with ORDER BY SAL, this framing clause ensures that the maximum salary will also correspond to that of the current row.

Consider the first row, for SMITH. When evaluating SMITH's salary and all prior salaries, MAX1 for SMITH is SMITH's salary, because there are no prior salaries. Moving on to the next row, JAMES, when comparing JAMES' salary to all prior salaries, in this case comparing to the salary of SMITH, JAMES' salary is the higher of the two, and thus it is the maximum. If you apply this logic to all rows, you will see that the value of MAX1 for each row is the current employee's salary.

MIN2 and MAX2

The framing clause given for these is UNBOUNDED PRECEDING AND UNBOUNDED FOLLOWING, which is the same as specifying empty parentheses. Thus, all rows in the result set are considered when computing MIN and MAX. As you might expect, the MIN and MAX values for the entire result set are constant, and thus the value of these columns is constant as well.

MIN3 and MAX3

The framing clause for these is CURRENT ROW AND CURRENT ROW, which simply means use only the current employee's salary when looking for the MIN and MAX salary. Thus both MIN3 and MAX3 are the same as SAL for each row. That was easy, wasn't it?

MAX4

The framing clause defined for MAX4 is 3 PRECEDING AND 3 FOLLOWING, which means, for every row, consider the three rows prior and the three rows after the current row, as well as the current row itself. This particular invocation of MAX(SAL) will return from those rows the highest salary value.

If you look at the value of MAX4 for employee MARTIN you can see how the framing clause is applied. MARTIN's salary is 1250 and the three employee salaries prior to MARTIN's are WARD's (1250), ADAMS' (1100) and JAMES' (950). The three employee salaries after MARTIN's are MILLER's (1300), TURNER's (1500), and ALLEN's (1600). Out of all those salaries, including MARTIN's, the highest is ALLEN's, and thus the value of MAX4 for MARTIN is 1600.

Readability + Performance = Power

As you can see, window functions are extremely powerful as they allow you to write queries that contain both detailed and aggregate information. Using window functions allows you to write smaller, more efficient queries as compared to using multiple self join and/or scalar subqueries. Consider the following query, which easily answers all of the following questions: "What is the number of employees in each department? How many different types of employees are in each department (e.g., how many clerks are in department 10)? How many total employees are in table EMP?"

```
select deptno,
       job,
       count(*) over (partition by deptno) as emp_cnt,
       count(job) over (partition by deptno,job) as job_cnt,
       count(*) over () as total
  from emp

DEPTNO JOB          EMP_CNT    JOB_CNT     TOTAL
------ ---------  ----------  ---------- ----------
    10 CLERK            3          1          14
    10 MANAGER          3          1          14
    10 PRESIDENT        3          1          14
    20 ANALYST          5          2          14
    20 ANALYST          5          2          14
    20 CLERK            5          2          14
    20 CLERK            5          2          14
    20 MANAGER          5          1          14
    30 CLERK            6          1          14
    30 MANAGER          6          1          14
    30 SALESMAN         6          4          14
    30 SALESMAN         6          4          14
    30 SALESMAN         6          4          14
    30 SALESMAN         6          4          14
```

To return the same result set without using window functions would require a bit more work:

```
select a.deptno, a.job,
       (select count(*) from emp b
         where b.deptno = a.deptno) as emp_cnt,
       (select count(*) from emp b
         where b.deptno = a.deptno and b.job = a.job) as job_cnt,
       (select count(*) from emp) as total
  from emp a
 order by 1,2

DEPTNO JOB          EMP_CNT    JOB_CNT     TOTAL
------ ---------  ----------  ---------- ----------
    10 CLERK            3          1          14
    10 MANAGER          3          1          14
    10 PRESIDENT        3          1          14
    20 ANALYST          5          2          14
    20 ANALYST          5          2          14
    20 CLERK            5          2          14
    20 CLERK            5          2          14
    20 MANAGER          5          1          14
    30 CLERK            6          1          14
    30 MANAGER          6          1          14
    30 SALESMAN         6          4          14
    30 SALESMAN         6          4          14
    30 SALESMAN         6          4          14
    30 SALESMAN         6          4          14
```

The non-window solution is obviously not difficult to write, yet it certainly is not as clean or efficient (you won't see performance differences with a 14-row table, but try these queries with, say, a 1,000- or 10,000-row table and then you'll see the benefit of using window functions over multiple self joins and scalar subqueries).

Providing a Base

Besides readability and performance, window functions are useful for providing a "base" for more complex "report style" queries. For example, consider the following "report style" query that uses window functions in an inline view and then aggregates the results in an outer query. Using window functions allows you to return detailed as well as aggregate data, which is useful for reports. The query below uses window functions to find counts using different partitions. Because the aggregation is applied to multiple rows, the inline view returns all rows from EMP, which the outer CASE expressions can use to transpose and create a formatted report:

```
select deptno,
       emp_cnt as dept_total,
       total,
       max(case when job = 'CLERK'
               then job_cnt else 0 end)  as clerks,
       max(case when job = 'MANAGER'
               then job_cnt else 0  end) as mgrs,
       max(case when job = 'PRESIDENT'
               then job_cnt else 0  end) as prez,
       max(case when job = 'ANALYST'
               then job_cnt else 0  end) as anals,
       max(case when job = 'SALESMAN'
               then job_cnt else 0  end) as smen
  from (
select deptno,
       job,
       count(*) over (partition by deptno) as emp_cnt,
       count(job) over (partition by deptno,job) as job_cnt,
       count(*) over () as total
  from emp
       ) x
 group by deptno, emp_cnt, total

DEPTNO DEPT_TOTAL TOTAL CLERKS MGRS PREZ ANALS SMEN
------ ---------- ----- ------ ---- ---- ----- ----
    10          3    14      1    1    1     0    0
    20          5    14      2    1    0     2    0
    30          6    14      1    1    0     0    4
```

The query above returns each department, the total number of employees in each department, the total number of employees in table EMP, and a breakdown of the number of different job types in each department. All this is done in one query, without additional joins or temp tables!

As a final example of how easily multiple questions can be answered using window functions, consider the following query:

```
select ename as name,
       sal,
       max(sal)over(partition by deptno) as hiDpt,
       min(sal)over(partition by deptno) as loDpt,
       max(sal)over(partition by job) as hiJob,
       min(sal)over(partition by job) as loJob,
       max(sal)over() as hi,
       min(sal)over() as lo,
       sum(sal)over(partition by deptno
                        order by sal,empno) as dptRT,
       sum(sal)over(partition by deptno) as dptSum,
       sum(sal)over() as ttl
  from emp
 order by deptno,dptRT
```

NAME	SAL	HIDPT	LODPT	HIJOB	LOJOB	HI	LO	DPTRT	DPTSUM	TTL
MILLER	1300	5000	1300	1300	800	5000	800	1300	8750	29025
CLARK	2450	5000	1300	2975	2450	5000	800	3750	8750	29025
KING	5000	5000	1300	5000	5000	5000	800	8750	8750	29025
SMITH	800	3000	800	1300	800	5000	800	800	10875	29025
ADAMS	1100	3000	800	1300	800	5000	800	1900	10875	29025
JONES	2975	3000	800	2975	2450	5000	800	4875	10875	29025
SCOTT	3000	3000	800	3000	3000	5000	800	7875	10875	29025
FORD	3000	3000	800	3000	3000	5000	800	10875	10875	29025
JAMES	950	2850	950	1300	800	5000	800	950	9400	29025
WARD	1250	2850	950	1600	1250	5000	800	2200	9400	29025
MARTIN	1250	2850	950	1600	1250	5000	800	3450	9400	29025
TURNER	1500	2850	950	1600	1250	5000	800	4950	9400	29025
ALLEN	1600	2850	950	1600	1250	5000	800	6550	9400	29025
BLAKE	2850	2850	950	2975	2450	5000	800	9400	9400	29025

This query answers the following questions easily, efficiently, and readably (and without additional joins to EMP!). Simply match the employee and her salary with the different rows in the result set to determine:

1. who makes the highest salary of all employees (HI)

2. who makes the lowest salary of all employees (LO)

3. who makes the highest salary in her department (HIDPT)

4. who makes the lowest salary in her department (LODPT)

5. who makes the highest salary in her job (HIJOB)

6. who makes the lowest salary in her job (LOJOB)

7. what is the sum of all salaries (TTL)

8. what is the sum of salaries per department (DPTSUM)

9. what is the running total of all salaries per department (DPTRT)

Rozenshtein Revisited

This appendix is a tribute to David Rozenshtein. As I mentioned in the introduction, I feel his book *The Essence of SQL* is (even today) the best book ever written on SQL. Although only 119 pages long, the book covers what I consider to be crucial topics for any SQL programmer. In particular, David shows how to think through a problem and arrive at an answer. The solutions provided by Rozenshtein are very set oriented. Even if the size of your tables do not permit you to use his solutions in a practical environment, his approach is excellent as it forces you to stop searching for a procedural solution to a problem and start thinking in sets.

The Essence of SQL was published long before window functions and MODEL clauses. In this appendix I provide alternative solutions to some of the questions in Rozenshtein's book using some of the newer functions available in standard SQL. (Whether these new solutions are "better" than Rozenshtein's depends on the circumstances.) At the end of each discussion, I present a solution based on the original solution from Rozenshtein's book. For the examples in which I present a variation of a problem found in Rozenshtein's text, I will also present a variation of a solution (a solution that may not necessarily exist in Rozenshtein's book, but that uses a similar technique).

Rozenshtein's Example Tables

The following tables are based on Rozenshtein's book and will be used in this appendix:

```
/* table of students */
create table student
( sno    integer,
  sname  varchar(10),
  age    integer
)
```

```
/* table of courses */
create table courses
( cno      varchar(5),
  title    varchar(10),
  credits  integer
)

/* table of professors */
create table professor
( lname    varchar(10),
  dept     varchar(10),
  salary   integer,
  age      integer
)

/* table of students and the courses they take */
create table take
( sno      integer,
  cno      varchar(5)
)


/* table of professors and the courses they teach */
create table teach
( lname    varchar(10),
  cno      varchar(5)
)

insert into student values (1,'AARON',20)
insert into student values (2,'CHUCK',21)
insert into student values (3,'DOUG',20)
insert into student values (4,'MAGGIE',19)
insert into student values (5,'STEVE',22)
insert into student values (6,'JING',18)
insert into student values (7,'BRIAN',21)
insert into student values (8,'KAY',20)
insert into student values (9,'GILLIAN',20)
insert into student values (10,'CHAD',21)

insert into courses values ('CS112','PHYSICS',4)
insert into courses values ('CS113','CALCULUS',4)
insert into courses values ('CS114','HISTORY',4)

insert into professor values ('CHOI','SCIENCE',400,45)
insert into professor values ('GUNN','HISTORY',300,60)
insert into professor values ('MAYER','MATH',400,55)
insert into professor values ('POMEL','SCIENCE',500,65)
insert into professor values ('FEUER','MATH',400,40)

insert into take values (1,'CS112')
insert into take values (1,'CS113')
insert into take values (1,'CS114')
insert into take values (2,'CS112')
```

```
insert into take values (3,'CS112')
insert into take values (3,'CS114')
insert into take values (4,'CS112')
insert into take values (4,'CS113')
insert into take values (5,'CS113')
insert into take values (6,'CS113')
insert into take values (6,'CS114')

insert into teach values ('CHOI','CS112')
insert into teach values ('CHOI','CS113')
insert into teach values ('CHOI','CS114')
insert into teach values ('POMEL','CS113')
insert into teach values ('MAYER','CS112')
insert into teach values ('MAYER','CS114')
```

Answering Questions Involving Negation

In his book, Rozenshtein approached the teaching of SQL through an examination of the different types of fundamental problems that you are often called upon to solve, in one form or another. Negation is one such type. It is often necessary to find rows for which some condition is not true. Simple conditions are easy but, as the following questions show, some negation problems require a bit of creativity and thought to solve.

Question 1

You want to find students who do not take CS112, but the following query is returning the wrong results:

```
select *
  from student
 where sno in ( select sno
                  from take
                 where cno != 'CS112' )
```

Because a student may take several courses, this query can (and does) return students who take CS112. The query is incorrect because it does not answer the question: "Who does not take CS112?" Instead, it answers the question "Who takes a course that is not CS112?" The correct result set should include students who take no courses as well as students who take courses but none of them CS112. Ultimately, you should return the following result set:

```
SNO SNAME          AGE
--------- ---------- ----------
    5 STEVE          22
    6 JING           18
    7 BRIAN          21
    8 KAY            20
    9 GILLIAN        20
   10 CHAD           21
```

MySQL and PostgreSQL

Use a CASE expression with the aggregate function MAX to flag CS112 if it exists for a particular student:

```
1   select s.sno,s.sname,s.age
2     from student s left join take t
3       on (s.sno = t.sno)
4     group by s.sno,s.sname,s.age
5   having max(case when t.cno = 'CS112'
6                   then 1 else 0 end) = 0
```

DB2 and SQL Server

Use a CASE expression with the window function MAX OVER to flag CS112 if it exists for a particular student:

```
1    select distinct sno,sname,age
2      from (
3    select s.sno,s.sname,s.age,
4           max(case when t.cno = 'CS112'
5                    then 1 else 0 end)
6           over(partition by s.sno,s.sname,s.age) as takes_CS112
7      from student s left join take t
8        on (s.sno = t.sno)
9           ) x
10     where takes_CS112 = 0
```

Oracle

For users on Oracle9i Database and later, you can use the DB2 solution above. Alternatively, you can use the proprietary Oracle outer-join syntax, which is mandatory for users on Oracle8i Database and earlier:

```
/* group by solution */

1   select s.sno,s.sname,s.age
2     from student s, take t
3    where s.sno = t.sno (+)
4     group by s.sno,s.sname,s.age
5   having max(case when t.cno = 'CS112'
6                   then 1 else 0 end) = 0
```

```
/* window solution */

1    select distinct sno,sname,age
2      from (
3    select s.sno,s.sname,s.age,
4           max(case when t.cno = 'CS112'
5                    then 1 else 0 end)
6           over(partition by s.sno,s.sname,s.age) as takes_CS112
7      from student s, take t
8     where s.sno = t.sno (+)
9           ) x
10     where takes_CS112 = 0
```

Discussion

Despite the different syntax for each solution, the technique is the same. The idea is to create a "Boolean" column in the result set to denote whether or not a student takes CS112. If a student takes CS112, then return 1 in that column; otherwise, return 0. The following query moves the CASE expression into the SELECT list and shows the intermediate results thus far:

```
select s.sno,s.sname,s.age,
       case when t.cno = 'CS112'
            then 1
            else 0
       end as takes_CS112
  from student s left join take t
    on (s.sno=t.sno)
```

```
SNO SNAME             AGE TAKES_CS112
--- ---------- ---------- -----------
  1 AARON              20           1
  1 AARON              20           0
  1 AARON              20           0
  2 CHUCK              21           1
  3 DOUG               20           1
  3 DOUG               20           0
  4 MAGGIE             19           1
  4 MAGGIE             19           0
  5 STEVE              22           0
  6 JING               18           0
  6 JING               18           0
  8 KAY                20           0
 10 CHAD               21           0
  7 BRIAN              21           0
  9 GILLIAN            20           0
```

The outer join to table TAKE ensures that even students who take no courses are returned. The next step is to use MAX to take the greatest value returned by the CASE expression for each student. If a student takes CS112, the greatest value will be 1, because all other courses are 0. For the solution using GROUP BY, the final step is to use the HAVING clause to keep only students with 0 returned from the MAX/CASE expression. For the window solution, you need to wrap the query in an inline view and then reference TAKES_CS112, because window functions cannot be referenced directly in the WHERE clause. Because of how window functions work, it is also necessary to remove duplicates caused by multiple courses.

Original solution

The original solution to this problem is quite clever and is shown here:

```
select *
  from student
 where sno not in (select sno
                     from take
                    where cno = 'CS112')
```

This can be stated as: "Find the students in table TAKE who take CS112, and then return all students in table STUDENT who are not them." This technique follows the advice regarding negation found at the end of Rozenshtein's book:

> Remember that real negation requires two passes: To find out "who does not," first find out "who does" and then get rid of them.

Question 2

You want to find students who take CS112 or CS114 but not both. The following query looks promising as a solution but returns the wrong result set:

```
select *
  from student
 where sno in ( select sno
                  from take
                 where cno != 'CS112'
                   and cno != 'CS114' )
```

Of the students who take courses, only students DOUG and AARON take both CS112 and CS114. Those two should be excluded. Student STEVE takes CS113, but not CS112 or CS114, and should be excluded as well.

Because a student can take multiple courses, the approach here is to return a single row for each student with information regarding whether the student takes CS112 or CS114, or both. This approach allows you to easily evaluate whether or not the student takes both courses without having to make multiple passes through the data. The final result set should be:

```
SNO SNAME           AGE
--- ---------- ----------
  2 CHUCK            21
  4 MAGGIE           19
  6 JING             18
```

MySQL and PostgreSQL

Use a CASE expression with the aggregate function SUM to find students who take either CS112 or CS114 but not both:

```
1  select s.sno,s.sname,s.age
2    from student s, take t
3   where s.sno = t.sno
4   group by s.sno,s.sname,s.age
5  having sum(case when t.cno in ('CS112','CS114')
6                  then 1 else 0 end) = 1
```

DB2, Oracle, and SQL Server

Use a CASE expression with the window function SUM OVER to find students who take either CS112 or CS114 but not both:

```
1  select distinct sno,sname,age
2    from (
3  select s.sno,s.sname,s.age,
4         sum(case when t.cno in ('CS112','CS114') then 1 else 0 end)
5         over (partition by s.sno,s.sname,s.age) as takes_either_or
6    from student s, take t
7  where s.sno = t.sno
8         ) x
9  where takes_either_or = 1
```

Discussion

The first step in solving the problem is to use an inner join from table STUDENT to table TAKE, thus eliminating any students who do not take any courses. The next step is to use a CASE expression to denote whether a student takes each respective course. In the following query, the CASE expressions are moved into the SELECT list and return the intermediate results thus far:

```
select s.sno,s.sname,s.age,
       case when t.cno in ('CS112','CS114')
            then 1 else 0 end as takes_either_or
  from student s, take t
 where s.sno = t.sno


SNO SNAME      AGE TAKES_EITHER_OR
--- ---------- --- ---------------
  1 AARON       20               1
  1 AARON       20               0
  1 AARON       20               1
  2 CHUCK       21               1
  3 DOUG        20               1
  3 DOUG        20               1
  4 MAGGIE      19               1
  4 MAGGIE      19               0
  5 STEVE       22               0
  6 JING        18               0
  6 JING        18               1
```

A value of 1 for TAKES_EITHER_OR signifies the student takes CS112 or CS114. Because a student can take multiple courses, the next step is to return only one row per student by using a GROUP BY with the aggregate function SUM. The function SUM will sum all the 1's for each student:

```
select s.sno,s.sname,s.age,
     sum(case when t.cno in ('CS112','CS114')
              then 1 else 0 end) as takes_either_or
  from student s, take t
 where s.sno = t.sno
 group by s.sno,s.sname,s.age


SNO SNAME      AGE TAKES_EITHER_OR
--- ---------- --- ---------------
  1 AARON       20               2
  2 CHUCK       21               1
```

3	DOUG	20	2
4	MAGGIE	19	1
5	STEVE	22	0
6	JING	18	1

Students who do not take CS112 or CS114 will have 0 for TAKES_EITHER_OR. Students who take both CS112 and CS114 will have 2 for TAKES_EITHER_OR. Thus the only students you want to return are those with a value of 1 for TAKES_EITHER_OR. The final solution uses the HAVING clause to keep only those students where the SUM of TAKES_EITHER_OR is one.

For the window solution, the same technique is used. You also need to wrap the query in an inline view, and then reference the column TAKES_EITHER_OR, because window functions cannot be referenced directly in the WHERE clause (they are evaluated last in SQL processing, prior only to the ORDER BY clause). Because of how window functions work, it is necessary to remove duplicates caused by multiple courses.

Original solution

The following query is the original solution (modified slightly). The query is quite clever and uses the same approach as the original solution in Question 1. The solution uses a self join to find students who take both CS112 and CS114, and then uses a subquery to filter them out of the set of students who take either CS112 or CS114:

```
select *
  from student s, take t
 where s.sno = t.sno
   and t.cno in ( 'CS112', 'CS114' )
   and s.sno not in ( select a.sno
                        from take a, take b
                       where a.sno = b.sno
                         and a.cno = 'CS112'
                         and b.cno = 'CS114' )
```

Question 3

You want to find students who take CS112 and no other courses, but the following query returns incorrect results:

```
select s.*
  from student s, take t
 where s.sno = t.sno
   and t.cno = 'CS112'
```

CHUCK is the only student who takes CS112 and no other courses, and is the only student that should be returned from the query.

This question can be restated as "Find students who take only CS112." The query above finds students who take CS112, but also returns students who take other

---

courses as well. The query should answer the question "Who takes only one course and that one course is CS112?"

MySQL and PostgreSQL

Use the aggregate function COUNT to ensure that students returned by the query take only one course:

```
 1  select s.*
 2    from student s,
 3         take t1,
 4         (
 5  select sno
 6    from take
 7  group by sno
 8  having count(*) = 1
 9         ) t2
10   where s.sno  = t1.sno
11     and t1.sno = t2.sno
12     and t1.cno = 'CS112'
```

DB2, Oracle, and SQL Server

Use the window function COUNT OVER to ensure a student takes only one course:

```
 1  select sno,sname,age
 2    from (
 3  select s.sno,s.sname,s.age,t.cno,
 4         count(t.cno) over (
 5           partition by s.sno,s.sname,s.age
 6         ) as cnt
 7    from student s, take t
 8   where s.sno = t.sno
 9         ) x
10   where cnt = 1
11     and cno = 'CS112'
```

Discussion

The key to the solutions is to write a query to answer both of the following questions: "Which student takes only one course?" and "Which student takes CS112?" The first approach uses inline view T2 to find students who take only one course. The next step is to join inline view T2 to table TAKE and keep only students who take CS112 (so what you are left with are students who take only one course and that one course is CS112). The query below shows the results thus far:

```
select t1.*
  from take t1,
       (
select sno
  from take
group by sno
```

```
having count(*) = 1
       ) t2
  where t1.sno = t2.sno
    and t1.cno = 'CS112'

SNO CNO
--- -----
  2 CS112
```

The final step is to join to table STUDENT and find the students who match those returned by the join between inline view T2 and table TAKE. The window solution takes a similar approach but does so in a different (more efficient) way. Inline view X returns the students, the courses they take, and the number of courses they take (the inner join between table TAKE and table STUDENT guarantees that students who take no courses are excluded). The results are shown below:

```
select s.sno,s.sname,s.age,t.cno,
       count(t.cno) over (
         partition by s.sno,s.sname,s.age
       ) as cnt
  from student s, take t
 where s.sno = t.sno
```

SNO	SNAME	AGE	CNO	CNT
1	AARON	20	CS112	3
1	AARON	20	CS113	3
1	AARON	20	CS114	3
2	CHUCK	21	CS112	1
3	DOUG	20	CS112	2
3	DOUG	20	CS114	2
4	MAGGIE	19	CS112	2
4	MAGGIE	19	CS113	2
5	STEVE	22	CS113	1
6	JING	18	CS113	2
6	JING	18	CS114	2

With the course and count available, the last step is to simply keep only rows such that CNT is 1 and CNO is CS112.

Original solution

The original solution uses a subquery and double negation:

```
select s.*
  from student s, take t
 where s.sno = t.sno
   and s.sno not in ( select sno
                        from take
                       where cno != 'CS112' )
```

This is an extremely clever solution, because nowhere in the query is the number of courses checked, nor is there a filter to ensure that students returned by the query actually take CS112! How does this work, then? The subquery returns all students who take a course other than CS112 and the results are shown below:

```
select sno
  from take
 where cno != 'CS112'

SNO
----
   1
   1
   3
   4
   5
   6
   6
```

The outer query returns all students who take a course (any course) and are not amongst the students returned by the subquery. Ignoring the NOT IN portion of the outer query for a moment, the results would be the following (showing all students who take a course):

```
select s.*
  from student s, take t
 where s.sno = t.sno

SNO SNAME          AGE
--- ---------- ----------
  1 AARON             20
  1 AARON             20
  1 AARON             20
  2 CHUCK             21
  3 DOUG              20
  3 DOUG              20
  4 MAGGIE            19
  4 MAGGIE            19
  5 STEVE             22
  6 JING              18
  6 JING              18
```

If you compare the two results sets, you see that the addition of NOT IN to the outer query effectively performs a set difference between SNO from the outer query and SNO from the subquery, returning only the student whose SNO is 2. In summary, the subquery finds all students who take a course that is not CS112. The outer query returns all students who are not amongst those that take a course other than CS112 (at this point the only available students are those who actually take CS112 or take nothing at all). The join between table STUDENT and table TAKE filters out the students who do not take any classes at all, leaving you only with the student who takes CS112 and only CS112. Set-based problem solving at its best!

Answering Questions Involving "at Most"

Questions involving "at most" represent another type of query problem that you'll encounter from time to time. It's easy enough to find rows for which a condition is true, but what if you want to place a limit on the number of such rows? That's what the next next two questions are all about.

Question 4

You want to find the students who take at most two courses. Students who do not take any courses should be excluded. Of the students who take courses, only AARON takes more than two and should be excluded from the result set. Ultimately, you want to return the following result set:

```
SNO SNAME          AGE
--- ---------- ----------
  2 CHUCK          21
  3 DOUG           20
  4 MAGGIE         19
  5 STEVE          22
  6 JING           18
```

MySQL and PostgreSQL

Use the aggregate function COUNT to determine which students take no more than two courses:

```
1 select s.sno,s.sname,s.age
2   from student s, take t
3  where s.sno = t.sno
4  group by s.sno,s.sname,s.age
5 having count(*) <= 2
```

DB2, Oracle, and SQL Server

Use the window function COUNT OVER, again to determine which students take no more than two courses:

```
 1 select distinct sno,sname,age
 2   from (
 3 select s.sno,s.sname,s.age,
 4        count(*) over (
 5          partition by s.sno,s.sname,s.age
 6        ) as cnt
 7   from student s, take t
 8  where s.sno = t.sno
 9        ) x
10  where cnt <= 2
```

Discussion

Both solutions work by simply counting the number of times a particular SNO occurs in table TAKE. The inner join to table TAKE ensures that students who take no courses are excluded from the final result set.

Original solution

Rozenshtein used the aggregate solution shown here for MySQL and PostgreSQL in his book along with an alternative solution using multiple self joins, shown here:

```
select distinct s.*
  from student s, take t
 where s.sno = t.sno
   and s.sno not in ( select t1.sno
                        from take t1, take t2, take t3
                       where t1.sno = t2.sno
                         and t2.sno = t3.sno
                         and t1.cno < t2.cno
                         and t2.cno < t3.cno )
```

The multiple self-join solution is interesting because it solves the problem without using aggregation. To understand how the solution works, focus on the WHERE clause of the subquery. The inner joins on SNO ensure that you are dealing with the same student across all columns of each row that can potentially be returned by the subquery. The less-than comparisons are what determine whether or not a student is taking more than two courses. The WHERE clause in the subquery can be stated as: "For a particular student, return rows where the first CNO is less than the second CNO and the second CNO is less than the THIRD CNO." If a student has fewer than three courses, that expression can never evaluate to true as there is no third CNO. The job of the subquery is to find students who take three or more courses. The outer query then returns students who take at least one course and are not amongst those returned by the subquery.

Question 5

You want to find students who are older than at most two other students. Another way to think about the problem is to find only the students who are older than zero, one, or two other students. The final result set should be:

```
SNO SNAME       AGE
---- ---------- ---
   6 JING        18
   4 MAGGIE      19
   1 AARON       20
   9 GILLIAN     20
   8 KAY         20
   3 DOUG        20
```

MySQL and PostgreSQL

Use the aggregate function COUNT and a correlated subquery to find the students who are older than zero, one, or two other students:

```
1  select s1.*
2    from student s1
3   where 2 >= ( select count(*)
4                  from student s2
5                 where s2.age < s1.age )
```

DB2, Oracle, and SQL Server

Use the window function DENSE_RANK to find the students who are older than zero, one, or two other students:

```
1  select sno,sname,age
2    from (
3  select sno,sname,age,
4         dense_rank( )over(order by age) as dr
5    from student
6         ) x
7   where dr <= 3
```

Discussion

The aggregate solution uses a scalar subquery to find all students who are older than no more than two other students. To see how this works, rewrite the solution to use a scalar subquery. In the following example, the column CNT represents the number of students that are younger than the current student:

```
select s1.*,
       (select count(*) from student s2
         where s2.age < s1.age) as cnt
  from student s1
  order by 4
```

SNO	SNAME	AGE	CNT
6	JING	18	0
4	MAGGIE	19	1
1	AARON	20	2
3	DOUG	20	2
8	KAY	20	2
9	GILLIAN	20	2
2	CHUCK	21	6
7	BRIAN	21	6
10	CHAD	21	6
5	STEVE	22	9

Rewriting the solution this way makes it easy to see that the students in the final result set are those for whom CNT is less than or equal to 2.

The solution using the window function DENSE_RANK is similar to the scalar sub-query example in that every row is ranked based on how many students are younger than the current student (ties are allowed and there are no gaps). The following query shows the output from the DENSE_RANK function:

```
select sno,sname,age,
       dense_rank()over(order by age) as dr
  from student
```

```
SNO SNAME           AGE         DR
--- ----------  ----------  ----------
  6 JING            18           1
  4 MAGGIE          19           2
  1 AARON           20           3
  3 DOUG            20           3
  8 KAY             20           3
  9 GILLIAN         20           3
  2 CHUCK           21           4
  7 BRIAN           21           4
 10 CHAD            21           4
  5 STEVE           22           5
```

The final step is to wrap the query in an inline view and keep only those rows where DR is less than or equal to 3.

Original solution

Rozenshtein takes an interesting approach to solving this problem by rephrasing it. Instead of "find the students who are older than at most two students," his approach is to "find the students who are not older than three or more (at least three) students." This approach is brilliant for those of you who want to learn how to problem solve in sets, because it forces you to find the solution in two passes:

1. Find the set of students who are older than three or more students.

2. Simply return all students who are not amongst the students returned by step 1.

The solution is shown below:

```
select *
  from student
 where sno not in (
select s1.sno
  from student s1,
       student s2,
       student s3,
       student s4
 where s1.age > s2.age
   and s2.age > s3.age
   and s3.age > s4.age
)
```

```
SNO SNAME      AGE
--- ---------- ---
  6 JING        18
  4 MAGGIE      19
  1 AARON       20
  9 GILLIAN     20
  8 KAY         20
  3 DOUG        20
```

If you examine the solution from bottom up, you see that step 1, "find all students who are older than three or more students," is performed first and is shown below (using DISTINCT to reduce the result set size for readability):

```
select distinct s1.*
  from student s1,
       student s2,
       student s3,
       student s4
 where s1.age > s2.age
   and s2.age > s3.age
   and s3.age > s4.age
```

```
SNO SNAME      AGE
--- ---------- ---
  2 CHUCK       21
  5 STEVE       22
  7 BRIAN       21
 10 CHAD        21
```

If you are getting confused by all the self joins, simply focus on the WHERE clause. S1.AGE is greater than S2.AGE so you know at that point any student who is older than at least one other student is considered. Next, S2.AGE is greater than S3.AGE. At this point any student who is older than two other students is considered. If you are stumbling at this point, try to keep in mind that greater-than comparisons are transitive. If S1.AGE is greater than S2.AGE, and S2.AGE is greater than S3.AGE, then it is also true that S1AGE is greater than S3.AGE. You may find it helpful to strip down the query to one self join and build the query once you understand what is returned by each step. For example, find all students who are older than at least one other student (all students except the youngest, JING, should be returned):

```
select distinct s1.*
  from student s1,
       student s2
 where s1.age > s2.age
```

```
SNO SNAME      AGE
--- ---------- ---
  5 STEVE       22
  7 BRIAN       21
 10 CHAD        21
  2 CHUCK       21
```

```
 1 AARON        20
 3 DOUG         20
 9 GILLIAN      20
 8 KAY          20
 4 MAGGIE       19
```

Next, find all students who are older than two or more students (now, both JING and MAGGIE should be excluded from the result set):

```
select distinct s1.*
  from student s1,
       student s2,
       student s3
 where s1.age > s2.age
   and s2.age > s3.age

SNO SNAME       AGE
--- ---------- ---
  1 AARON        20
  2 CHUCK        21
  3 DOUG         20
  5 STEVE        22
  7 BRIAN        21
  8 KAY          20
  9 GILLIAN      20
 10 CHAD         21
```

Finally, find all students who are older than three or more students (only CHUCK, STEVE, BRIAN, and CHAD are in this result set):

```
select distinct s1.*
  from student s1,
       student s2,
       student s3,
       student s4
 where s1.age > s2.age
   and s2.age > s3.age
   and s3.age > s4.age

SNO SNAME       AGE
--- ---------- ---
  2 CHUCK        21
  5 STEVE        22
  7 BRIAN        21
 10 CHAD         21
```

Now that you know which students are older than three or more other students, simply return only those students who are not amongst the four students above by using NOT IN with a subquery.

Answering Questions Involving "at Least"

The flip side of "at most" is "at least." You can often solve "at least" questions by applying variations of the techniques described for "at most" questions. When solving "at least" problems it is often helpful to rephrase them as "having no fewer than." In general, if you can identify a threshold in your requirement, you've already solved half the problem. Once you know the threshold, you can decide to solve the problem using one pass (aggregate or window functions typically using COUNT) or two passes (negation with subquery).

Question 6

You want to find students who take at least two courses.

You may find it helpful to restate the problem as "Find students who take two or more courses" or as "Find students who take no fewer than two courses." You can use the same technique used for Question 4: use the aggregate function COUNT or window function COUNT OVER. The final result set should be:

```
SNO SNAME        AGE
--- ---------- ----------
  1 AARON         20
  3 DOUG          20
  4 MAGGIE        19
  6 JING          18
```

MySQL and PostgreSQL

Use the aggregate function COUNT to find students who take at least two courses:

```
1 select s.sno,s.sname,s.age
2   from student s, take t
3  where s.sno = t.sno
4  group by s.sno,s.sname,s.age
5 having count(*) >= 2
```

DB2, Oracle, and SQL Server

Use the window function COUNT OVER to find students who take at least two courses:

```
 1  select distinct sno,sname,age
 2    from (
 3  select s.sno,s.sname,s.age,
 4         count(*) over (
 5           partition by s.sno,s.sname,s.age
 6         ) as cnt
 7    from student s, take t
 8   where s.sno = t.sno
 9         ) x
10   where cnt >= 2
```

Discussion

See Question 4 for a full discussion of the solutions presented in this section; the techniques are the same. For the aggregate solution, join table STUDENT to table TAKE and use COUNT in the HAVING clause to keep only those students with two or more courses. For the window solution, join table STUDENT to table TAKE and perform a count over the partition that is defined by specifying all the columns from table STUDENT. From there, simply keep only those rows where CNT is two or greater.

Original solution

The solution below uses a self join on table TAKE to find students who take two or more classes. The equi-join on SNO in the subquery ensures that each student is evaluated against his/her own courses only. The greater-than comparison on CNO can only be true if a student takes more than one course, otherwise CNO would equal CNO (as there is only one course to be compared with itself). The last step is to return all students who are amongst those returned by the subquery, and is shown below:

```
select *
  from student
 where sno in (
select t1.sno
 from take t1,
      take t2
 where t1.sno = t2.sno
   and t1.cno > t2.cno
)
```

```
SNO SNAME          AGE
--- ---------- ----------
  1 AARON          20
  3 DOUG           20
  4 MAGGIE         19
  6 JING           18
```

Question 7

You want to find students who take both CS112 and CS114. The students may take other courses, but they must take CS112 and CS114 as well.

This problem is similar to Question 2, except that in that case a student may take more than two courses whereas in this case they take *at least* 2 courses (AARON and DOUG are the only students who take both CS112 and CS114). You can easily modify the solution from Question 2 to work here. The final result set should be:

```
SNO SNAME        AGE
--- ---------- ----
  1 AARON        20
  3 DOUG         20
```

MySQL and PostgreSQL

Use the aggregate functions MIN and MAX to find students who take both CS112 and CS114:

```
1  select s.sno, s.sname, s.age
2    from student s, take t
3   where s.sno = t.sno
4     and t.cno in ('CS114','CS112')
5   group by s.sno, s.sname, s.age
6  having min(t.cno) != max(t.cno)
```

DB2, Oracle, and SQL Server

Use the window functions MIN OVER and MAX OVER to find students who take both CS112 and CS114:

```
1   select distinct sno, sname, age
2     from (
3   select s.sno, s.sname, s.age,
4          min(cno) over (partition by s.sno) as min_cno,
5          max(cno) over (partition by s.sno) as max_cno
6     from student s, take t
7    where s.sno = t.sno
8      and t.cno in ('CS114','CS112')
9          ) x
10   where min_cno != max_cno
```

Discussion

Both solutions use the same technique to find the answer. The IN list ensures only students who take CS112 or CS114, or both, are returned. If a student does not take both courses, then MIN(CNO) will equal MAX(CNO) and that student is excluded. To help visualize how this works, the intermediate results of the window solution are shown below (T.CNO is added for clarity):

```
select s.sno, s.sname, s.age, t.cno,
       min(cno) over (partition by s.sno) as min_cno,
       max(cno) over (partition by s.sno) as max_cno
  from student s, take t
 where s.sno = t.sno
   and t.cno in ('CS114','CS112')

SNO SNAME        AGE CNO    MIN_C MAX_C
--- ---------- ---- ----- ----- -----
  1 AARON        20 CS114 CS112 CS114
  1 AARON        20 CS112 CS112 CS114
  2 CHUCK        21 CS112 CS112 CS112
```

```
3 DOUG        20 CS114 CS112 CS114
3 DOUG        20 CS112 CS112 CS114
4 MAGGIE      19 CS112 CS112 CS112
6 JING        18 CS114 CS114 CS114
```

Examining the results, it's easy to see only AARON and DOUG have rows where MIN(CNO) != MAX(CNO).

Original solution

The original solution by Rozenshtein uses a self join on table TAKE. Following is the original solution, which performs extremely well with the proper indexes in place:

```
select s.*
  from student s,
       take t1,
       take t2
 where s.sno  = t1.sno
   and t1.sno = t2.sno
   and t1.cno = 'CS112'
   and t2.cno = 'CS114'

SNO SNAME       AGE
--- ---------- ----
  1 AARON        20
  3 DOUG         20
```

All the solutions work by ensuring that, regardless of the other courses a student may take, they must take both CS112 and CS114. If you are having trouble understanding the self join, you may find it easier to understand the following example:

```
select s.*
  from take t1, student s
 where s.sno   = t1.sno
   and t1.cno  = 'CS114'
   and 'CS112' = any (select t2.cno
                        from take t2
                       where t1.sno  = t2.sno
                         and t2.cno != 'CS114')

SNO SNAME       AGE
--- ---------- ----
  1 AARON        20
  3 DOUG         20
```

Question 8

Find students who are older than at least two other students.

You may find it helpful to restate the problem as "Find students who are older than two or more other students." You can use the same technique used in Question 5. The final result set is shown below (only JING and MAGGIE are not older than two or more students):

```
SNO SNAME          AGE
--- ----------  ----------
  1 AARON           20
  2 CHUCK           21
  3 DOUG            20
  5 STEVE           22
  7 BRIAN           21
  8 KAY             20
  9 GILLIAN         20
 10 CHAD            21
```

MySQL and PostgreSQL

Use the aggregate function COUNT and a correlated subquery to find students older than at least two other students:

```
1  select s1.*
2    from student s1
3   where 2 <= ( select count(*)
4                  from student s2
5                 where s2.age < s1.age )
```

DB2, Oracle, and SQL Server

Use the window function DENSE_RANK to find students older than at least two other students:

```
1  select sno,sname,age
2    from (
3  select sno,sname,age,
4         dense_rank()over(order by age) as dr
5    from student
6         ) x
7   where dr >= 3
```

Discussion

For a full discussion see Question 5. The technique is exactly the same for both solutions, with the only difference being the final evaluation on the count or rank.

Original solution

The problem is a variation of Question 6, the difference being you are now only dealing with the STUDENT table. This solution in Question 6 can be easily adapted to "find students older than at least two other students" and is shown below:

```
select distinct s1.*
  from student s1,
       student s2,
       student s3
 where s1.age > s2.age
   and s2.age > s3.age
```

```
SNO SNAME          AGE
--- ---------- ----------
  1 AARON           20
  2 CHUCK           21
  3 DOUG            20
  5 STEVE           22
  7 BRIAN           21
  8 KAY             20
  9 GILLIAN         20
 10 CHAD            21
```

Answering Questions Involving "Exactly"

You would think that answering the question of whether or not something is true would be easy. In many cases it is easy. But sometimes it can be tricky to answer questions of whether something is "exactly" true, especially when answering involves joining master/detail data. The problem stems from the exclusive nature of "exactly." It may be more helpful to think of it as "only." Consider the difference between people who wear shoes and those who wear only shoes. It is not enough to satisfy the condition; you must satisfy the condition while ensuring that no other conditions are satisfied.

Question 9

Find professors who teach exactly one course.

You can restate the problem as "Find professors who teach only one course." Which course they teach is unimportant; what matters is that only one course is taught. The final result set should be:

```
LNAME      DEPT       SALARY AGE
---------- ---------- ---------- ----
POMEL      SCIENCE       500  65
```

MySQL and PostgreSQL

Use the aggregate function COUNT to find the professors who teach exactly one course:

```
1  select p.lname,p.dept,p.salary,p.age
2    from professor p, teach t
3   where p.lname = t.lname
4   group by p.lname,p.dept,p.salary,p.age
5  having count(*) = 1
```

DB2, Oracle, and SQL Server

Use the window function COUNT OVER to find the professors who teach exactly one course:

```
1  select lname, dept, salary, age
2    from (
3  select p.lname,p.dept,p.salary,p.age,
4         count(*) over (partition by p.lname) as cnt
5    from professor p, teach t
6   where p.lname = t.lname
7         ) x
8   where cnt = 1
```

Discussion

By inner joining table PROFESSOR to table TEACH you ensure that all professors who teach no courses are excluded. The aggregate solution uses the COUNT function in the HAVING clause to return only professors who teach exactly one course. The window solution uses the COUNT OVER function, but notice that the columns from table PROFESSOR that are used in the PARTITION clause of the COUNT OVER function are different from the columns that are used in the GROUP BY of the aggregate solution. In this example it is safe for the GROUP BY and PARTITION BY clauses to be different, because the last names are unique in table TEACHER, i.e., excluding P.DEPT, P.SALARY, and .PAGE from the partition does not affect the COUNT operation. In solutions prior to this one, I purposely use the same columns in the PARTITION clause of a window function solution as I use in the GROUP BY clause of an aggregate solution to show that the PARTITION is a moving, more flexible kind of GROUP BY.

Original solution

This solution uses the same technique used in Question 3: perform two passes to find the answer. The first step is to find those professors who teach two or more classes. The second step is to find those professors who teach a course and are not amongst those returned by step 1. Please refer to Question 3 for a full discussion. The solution is shown below:

```
select p.*
  from professor p,
       teach t
 where p.lname = t.lname
   and p.lname not in (
select t1.lname
  from teach t1,
       teach t2
 where t1.lname = t2.lname
   and t1.cno   > t2.cno
)
```

LNAME	DEPT	SALARY	AGE
POMEL	SCIENCE	500	65

Question 10

You want to find students who take only CS112 and CS114 (exactly those two courses and no other courses), but the following query returns an empty result set:

```
select s.*
  from student s, take t
 where s.sno = t.sno
   and t.cno = 'CS112'
   and t.cno = 'CS114'
```

No row can have a column that is simultaneously two values (assuming simple scalar data types such as those used for table STUDENT), so the query will never work. Rozenshtein's book does a nice job of discussing how intuitive thinking when writing queries causes errors such as this one. DOUG is the only student who takes only CS112 and CS114 and should be the only student returned for this query.

MySQL and PostgreSQL

Use a CASE expression and the aggregate function COUNT to find students who take only CS112 and CS114:

```
1 select s.sno, s.sname, s.age
2   from student s, take t
3  where s.sno = t.sno
4  group by s.sno, s.sname, s.age
5 having count(*) = 2
6    and max(case when cno = 'CS112' then 1 else 0 end) +
7        max(case when cno = 'CS114' then 1 else 0 end) = 2
```

DB2, Oracle, and SQL Server

Use the window function COUNT OVER with a CASE expression to find students who take only CS112 and CS114:

```
1  select sno,sname,age
2    from (
3  select s.sno,
4         s.sname,
5         s.age,
6         count(*) over (partition by s.sno) as cnt,
7         sum(case when t.cno in ( 'CS112', 'CS114' )
8                  then 1 else 0
9             end)
10         over (partition by s.sno) as both,
11         row_number()
12         over (partition by s.sno order by s.sno) as rn
13    from student s, take t
14   where s.sno = t.sno
15         ) x
16   where cnt  = 2
17     and both = 2
18     and rn   = 1
```

Discussion

The aggregate solution uses the same technique found in Question 1 and Question 2. The inner join from table STUDENT to table TAKE ensures that any students who take no courses are excluded. The COUNT expression in the HAVING clause keeps only students who take exactly two courses. The results of the CASE expressions counting the number of courses are summed. Only those students who take both CS112 and CS114 have a sum of 2.

The window solution uses a technique similar to the window solutions found in Question 1 and Question 2. This version is slightly different as the value of the CASE expression is returned to the window function SUM OVER. Another variation in this solution is the use of the window function ROW_NUMBER to avoid using DISTINCT. The results of the window solution without the final filters are shown below:

```
select s.sno,
       s.sname,
       s.age,
       count(*) over (partition by s.sno) as cnt,
       sum(case when t.cno in ( 'CS112', 'CS114' )
               then 1 else 0
           end)
       over (partition by s.sno) as both,
       row_number( )
           over (partition by s.sno order by s.sno) as rn
   from student s, take t
   where s.sno = t.sno
```

SNO	SNAME	AGE	CNT	BOTH	RN
1	AARON	20	3	2	1
1	AARON	20	3	2	2
1	AARON	20	3	2	3
2	CHUCK	21	1	1	1
3	DOUG	20	2	2	1
3	DOUG	20	2	2	2
4	MAGGIE	19	2	1	1
4	MAGGIE	19	2	1	2
5	STEVE	22	1	0	1
6	JING	18	2	1	1
6	JING	18	2	1	2

Examining these results, you can see that the final result set is the one where BOTH and CNT are 2. RN can be either 1 or 2, it doesn't matter; that column exists only to help filter out duplicates without using DISTINCT.

Original solution

This solution uses a subquery with multiple self joins to first find students who take at least three classes. The next step is to use a self join on table TAKE to find those students who take both CS112 and CS114. The final step is to keep only those students who take both CS112 and CS114 and do not take three or more classes. The solution is shown below:

```
    select s1.*
      from student s1,
           take t1,
           take t2
     where s1.sno  = t1.sno
       and s1.sno  = t2.sno
       and t1.cno = 'CS112'
       and t2.cno = 'CS114'
       and s1.sno not in (
    select s2.sno
      from student s2,
           take t3,
           take t4,
           take t5
     where s2.sno = t3.sno
       and s2.sno = t4.sno
       and s2.sno = t5.sno
       and t3.cno > t4.cno
       and t4.cno > t5.cno
    )

    SNO SNAME       AGE
    --- ---------- ---
      3 DOUG        20
```

Question 11

You want to find students who are older than exactly two other students. Another way of stating the problem is that you want to find the third youngest student(s). The final result set should be:

```
    SNO SNAME       AGE
    --- ---------- ----------
      1 AARON       20
      3 DOUG        20
      8 KAY         20
      9 GILLIAN     20
```

MySQL and PostgreSQL

Use the aggregate function COUNT and a correlated subquery to find the third youngest student:

```
1  select s1.*
2    from student s1
3   where 2 = ( select count(*)
4                 from student s2
5                where s2.age < s1.age )
```

DB2, Oracle, and SQL Server

Use the window function DENSE_RANK to find the third youngest student:

```
1  select sno,sname,age
2    from (
3  select sno,sname,age,
4         dense_rank()over(order by age) as dr
5    from student
6         ) x
7   where dr = 3
```

Discussion

The aggregate solution uses a scalar subquery to find all students who are older than two (and only two) other students. To see how this works, rewrite the solution to use a scalar subquery. In the following example, the column CNT represents the number of students that are younger than the current student:

```
select s1.*,
       (select count(*) from student s2
         where s2.age < s1.age) as cnt
  from student s1
  order by 4
```

SNO	SNAME	AGE	CNT
6	JING	18	0
4	MAGGIE	19	1
1	AARON	20	2
3	DOUG	20	2
8	KAY	20	2
9	GILLIAN	20	2
2	CHUCK	21	6
7	BRIAN	21	6
10	CHAD	21	6
5	STEVE	22	9

Rewriting the solution this way makes it easy to see who the third youngest students are (those whose CNT is 2).

The solution using the window function DENSE_RANK is similar to the scalar subquery example in that every row is ranked based on how many students are younger than the current student (ties are allowed and there are no gaps). The following query shows the output from the DENSE_RANK function:

```
select sno,sname,age,
       dense_rank()over(order by age) as dr
  from student
```

```
SNO SNAME            AGE         DR
--- ----------  ----------  ----------
  6 JING               18           1
  4 MAGGIE             19           2
  1 AARON              20           3
  3 DOUG               20           3
  8 KAY                20           3
  9 GILLIAN            20           3
  2 CHUCK              21           4
  7 BRIAN              21           4
 10 CHAD               21           4
  5 STEVE              22           5
```

The final step is to wrap the query in an inline view and keep only those rows where DR is 3.

Original solution

The original solution uses a two-pass approach: step 1, find the students who are older than three or more students; step 2, find the students who are older than two students who are not amongst the students returned by step 1. Alternatively, Rozenshtein would rephrase this as, "Find students who are older than at least two students and are not older than at least three students." The solution is shown below:

```
select s5.*
  from student s5,
       student s6,
       student s7
 where s5.age > s6.age
   and s6.age > s7.age
   and s5.sno not in (
select s1.sno
  from student s1,
       student s2,
       student s3,
       student s4
 where s1.age > s2.age
   and s2.age > s3.age
   and s3.age > s4.age
)

SNO SNAME      AGE
--- ---------- ---
  1 AARON       20
  3 DOUG        20
  9 GILLIAN     20
  8 KAY         20
```

The solution above uses the technique shown in Question 5. Refer to Question 5 for a complete discussion of how extremes are found using self joins.

Answering Questions Involving "Any" or "All"

Queries involving "any" or "all" typically require you to find rows that satisfy one or more conditions completely. For example, if you are asked to find people who eat all vegetables, you are essentially looking for people for whom there is no vegetable that they do not eat. This type of problem statement is typically categorized as *relational division*. With questions regarding "any," it is crucial you pay close attention to how the question is phrased. Consider the difference between these two requirements: "a student who takes any class" and "a plane faster than any train." The former implies, "find a student who takes at least one class," while the latter implies "find a plane that is faster than all trains."

Question 12

You want to find students who take all courses.

The number of courses for a student in table TAKE must be equal to the total number of courses in table COURSES. There are three courses in table COURSES. Only AARON takes all three courses and should be the only student returned. The final result set should be:

```
SNO SNAME   AGE
--- ------- ----
  1 AARON    20
```

MySQL and PostgreSQL

Use the aggregate function COUNT to find students who take every course:

```
1 select s.sno,s.sname,s.age
2   from student s, take t
3  where s.sno = t.sno
4  group by s.sno,s.sname,s.age
5 having count(t.cno) = (select count(*) from courses)
```

DB2 and SQL Server

Use the window function COUNT OVER and an outer join instead of a subquery:

```
 1  select sno,sname,age
 2    from (
 3  select s.sno,s.sname,s.age,
 4         count(t.cno)
 5         over (partition by s.sno) as cnt,
 6         count(distinct c.title) over() as total,
 7         row_number() over
 8         (partition by s.sno order by c.cno) as rn
 9    from courses c
10         left join take t    on (c.cno = t.cno)
11         left join student s on (t.sno = s.sno)
```

```
12          ) x
13   where cnt = total
14     and rn  = 1
```

Oracle

Users on Oracle9*i* and later can use the DB2 solution. Alternatively, you can use the proprietary Oracle outer-join syntax, which is mandatory for users on 8*i* and earlier:

```
1    select sno,sname,age
2      from (
3    select s.sno,s.sname,s.age,
4           count(t.cno)
5           over (partition by s.sno) as cnt,
6           count(distinct c.title) over() as total,
7           row_number() over
8           (partition by s.sno order by c.cno) as rn
9      from courses c, take t, student s
10    where c.cno = t.cno (+)
11      and t.sno = s.sno (+)
12          )
13    where cnt = total
14      and rn  = 1
```

Discussion

The aggregate solution uses a subquery to return the total number of courses available. The outer query keeps only students who take the same number of courses as the value returned by the subquery. The window solution takes a different approach: it uses an outer join to table COURSES instead of a subquery. The window solution also uses window functions to return the number of courses a student takes (aliased CNT) along with the total number of courses there are in table COURSES (aliased TOTAL). The query below shows the intermediate results from those window functions:

```
select s.sno,s.sname,s.age,
       count(distinct t.cno)
       over (partition by s.sno) as cnt,
       count(distinct c.title) over() as total,
       row_number()
       over(partition by s.sno order by c.cno) as rn
  from courses c
       left join take t    on (c.cno = t.cno)
       left join student s on (t.sno = s.sno)
 order by 1
```

SNO	SNAME	AGE	CNT	TOTAL	RN
1	AARON	20	3	3	1
1	AARON	20	3	3	2
1	AARON	20	3	3	3
2	CHUCK	21	1	3	1
3	DOUG	20	2	3	1
3	DOUG	20	2	3	2

```
4 MAGGIE   19   2        3   1
4 MAGGIE   19   2        3   2
5 STEVE    22   1        3   1
6 JING     18   2        3   1
6 JING     18   2        3   2
```

The student who takes all courses is the one where CNT equals TOTAL. ROW_
NUMBER is used instead of DISTINCT to filter out the duplicates from the final
result set. Strictly speaking, the outer joins to tables TAKE and STUDENT are not
necessary, as there are no courses that aren't taken by at least one student. If there is
a course that no students take, CNT would not equal TOTAL, and a row with NULL
values for SNO, SNAME, and AGE would be returned. The example below creates a
new course that no students take. The following query demonstrates what the intermediate result set would look like if there exists a course no students take (for clarity, C.TITLE is included below):

```
insert into courses values ('CS115','BIOLOGY',4)

select s.sno,s.sname,s.age,c.title,
       count(distinct t.cno)
       over (partition by s.sno) as cnt,
       count(distinct c.title) over() as total,
       row_number()
       over(partition by s.sno order by c.cno) as rn
  from courses c
       left join take t     on (c.cno = t.cno)
       left join student s on (t.sno = s.sno)
  order by 1
```

```
SNO SNAME   AGE TITLE       CNT TOTAL  RN
--- ------  --- ----------  --- -----  ---
  1 AARON    20 PHYSICS       3    4    1
  1 AARON    20 CALCULUS      3    4    2
  1 AARON    20 HISTORY       3    4    3
  2 CHUCK    21 PHYSICS       1    4    1
  3 DOUG     20 PHYSICS       2    4    1
  3 DOUG     20 HISTORY       2    4    2
  4 MAGGIE   19 PHYSICS       2    4    1
  4 MAGGIE   19 CALCULUS      2    4    2
  5 STEVE    22 CALCULUS      1    4    1
  6 JING     18 CALCULUS      2    4    1
  6 JING     18 HISTORY       2    4    2
               BIOLOGY        0    4    1
```

Examining these results, it's easy to see no rows will be returned when the final filters are applied. Additionally, keep in mind that window functions take effect after
the WHERE clause is evaluated so it is necessary to use DISTINCT when counting
the total courses available in table COURSES (otherwise you get the total from the
result set, which would be the total number of courses taken by all students, i.e.,
select count(cno) from take).

The sample data used for this example does not have any duplicates in table TAKE, so the solution provided works fine. If there had been duplicates in TAKE, for example, a student that takes the same courses three times, the solution would fail. The workaround for dealing with duplicates in this solution is trivial; simply add DISTINCT when performing the count on T.CNO and the solution will work correctly.

Original solution

The original solution avoids aggregates by using a Cartesian product in a devilishly clever way. The query below is based on the original:

```
select *
  from student
 where sno not in
     ( select s.sno
         from student s, courses c
        where (s.sno,c.cno) not in (select sno,cno from take) )
```

Rozenshtein restates the problem to be "Which students are not among those for whom there is a course that they do not take?" If you look at the problem that way, you are now working with negation. Recall how Rozenshtein suggests handling negation:

> Remember that real negation requires two passes: To find out "who does not," first find out "who does" and then get rid of them.

The innermost subquery returns all valid SNO/CNO combinations. The middle subquery, which uses a Cartesian product between tables STUDENT and COURSES, returns all students and all courses (i.e., every student taking every course) and filters out the valid SNO/CNO combinations (leaving only "made up" SNO/CNO combinations). The outermost query returns only the rows from table STUDENT where the SNO is not amongst those returned by the middle subquery. The following queries may make the solution a bit more clear. To keep it readable, I'll use only AARON and CHUCK (only AARON takes all courses):

```
select *
  from student
 where sno in ( 1,2 )

SNO SNAME        AGE
--- ---------- ----
  1 AARON         20
  2 CHUCK         21


select *
  from take
 where sno in ( 1,2 )
```

```
SNO CNO
--- -----
  1 CS112
  1 CS113
  1 CS114
  2 CS112
```

```
select s.sno, c.cno
  from student s, courses c
 where s.sno in ( 1,2 )
 order by 1
```

```
SNO CNO
--- -----
  1 CS112
  1 CS113
  1 CS114
  2 CS112
  2 CS113
  2 CS114
```

These queries show the rows from table STUDENT for AARON and CHUCK, the courses that AARON and CHUCK take, and a Cartesian product that returns AARON and CHUCK taking all courses, respectively. The result set from the Cartesian product for AARON matches the result set returned for AARON from table TAKE, but CHUCK has two "made up" rows as a result of the Cartesian product that do not match his rows in table TAKE. The following query is the middle subquery and uses NOT IN to filter out the valid SNO/CNO combinations:

```
select s.sno, c.cno
  from student s, courses c
 where s.sno in ( 1,2 )
   and (s.sno,c.cno) not in (select sno,cno from take)
```

```
SNO CNO
--- -----
  2 CS113
  2 CS114
```

Notice that AARON is not returned by the middle subquery (because AARON takes all courses). The result set of the middle subquery contains rows that exist due to the Cartesian product, not because CHUCK actually takes those courses. The outermost query then returns rows from table STUDENT where the SNO is not amongst the SNO returned by the middle subquery:

```
select *
  from student
 where sno in ( 1,2 )
   and sno not in
       (select s.sno from student s, courses c
         where s.sno in ( 1,2 )
           and (s.sno,c.cno) not in (select sno,cno from take))
```

```
SNO SNAME        AGE
--- ---------- ----
  1 AARON        20
```

Question 13

Find students who are older than any other students.

You can restate the problem as "Find the oldest students." The final result set should be:

```
SNO SNAME        AGE
--- ---------- ----
  5 STEVE        22
```

MySQL and PostgreSQL

Use the aggregate function MAX in a subquery to find the oldest students:

```
1 select *
2   from student
3  where age = (select max(age) from student)
```

DB2, Oracle, and SQL Server

Use the window function MAX OVER in an inline view to find the oldest students:

```
1  select sno,sname,age
2    from (
3  select s.*,
4         max(s.age)over() as oldest
5    from student s
6         ) x
7   where age = oldest
```

Discussion

Both solutions use the function MAX to find the oldest student. The subquery solution first finds the greatest age in table STUDENT and returns it to the outer query, which finds student of that age. The window version does the same as the subquery solution but returns the greatest age for each row. The intermediate results of the window query are as follows:

```
select s.*,
       max(s.age) over() as oldest
  from student s

SNO SNAME        AGE    OLDEST
--- ---------- ---- ----------
  1 AARON        20        22
  2 CHUCK        21        22
  3 DOUG         20        22
  4 MAGGIE       19        22
```

```
 5 STEVE       22        22
 6 JING        18        22
 7 BRIAN       21        22
 8 KAY         20        22
 9 GILLIAN     20        22
10 CHAD        21        22
```

To find the oldest students, simply keep the rows where AGE = OLDEST.

Original solution

The original solution uses a self join on table STUDENT in a subquery to find all students who are younger than some other student. The outer query returns all students from table STUDENT who are not amongst those returned by the subquery. The operation can be rephrased as "find all students who are not amongst those students who are younger than at least one other student":

```
select *
  from student
 where age not in (select a.age
                     from student a, student b
                    where a.age < b.age)
```

The subquery returns use a Cartesian product to find all ages in A that are younger than all ages in B. The only age that would not be younger than any other age is the greatest age. The greatest age is not returned by the subquery. The outer query uses NOT IN to return all rows from table STUDENT where AGE is not amongst the AGE returned by the subquery (if A.AGE is returned, that means there is an AGE somewhere in table STUDENT that is greater than it). If you have trouble understanding how it works, examine the following query. Conceptually they both work in a similar way, but the following is probably more common:

```
select *
  from student
 where age >= all (select age from student)
```

Index

Symbols

% (modulus) function (SQL Server), 177, 277, 281
% (wildcard) operator, 13
* character in SELECT statements, 1
+ (concatenation) operator (SQL Server), 6, 297
_ (underscore) operator, 13
|| (concatenation) function (DB2/Oracle/PostgreSQL), 6, 296

A

abstraction, axiom of, 534
ADD_MONTHS function (Oracle), 191, 192, 230, 270, 287
ADDDATE function (MySQL), 230, 271, 280, 289
aggregate functions
  defining rows to perform operation on, 542–544
  grouping and, 538, 540
  multiple tables and, 50–54, 55–58
  NULL values and, 182, 536, 545
  WHERE clause, referencing in, 5
  window functions versus, 541
aliases
  for CASE expression, 7
  inline views, xxvi, 509
  referencing aliased columns, 4
  timing of application, 5
alphanumeric data (see strings)
analytic functions (Oracle) (see window functions)
ANSI standard, xix

anti-joins, 39
"any" or "all" queries, 583–590
AS keyword, 4
"at least" queries, 571–577
"at most" queries, 566–571
averages, computing, 157
AVG function, 157
axiom of abstraction, 533, 534
axiom of specification, 534
axiom schema of separation, 534
axiom schema of subsets, 534

B

bags, 536
Barber Puzzle, 533
business logic, incorporating, 310

C

calendars, creating, 251–269
Cantor, Georg, xiv
Cartesian products, 49
CAST function (SQL Server), 281
catalogs (see metadata)
CEIL function (DB2/MySQL/Oracle/PostgreSQL), 390, 391
CEILING function (SQL Server), 390, 427
COALESCE function, 11, 62, 158, 182, 309
columns
  adding headers to double pivoted result sets, 496–507
  concatenating, 5
  transforming to rows (see pivoting)

We'd like to hear your suggestions for improving our indexes. Send email to *index@oreilly.com*.

S

scalar subqueries
  converting to composite
    (Oracle), 507–509
  finding differences between rows
    using, 307
  joins and, 42
  referencing in WHERE clause, 5
  uses, 166, 167, 169
schemas (see metadata)
scripts, generating, 93
searching, 328–367
  duplicates, suppressing, 350–352
  forecasts, generating simple, 359–367
  highest/lowest values, finding, 340
  Knight values, finding, 352–359
  outer joins, OR logic in, 334–336
  reciprocal rows, determining, 337–338
  results, paginating through, 328–331
  results, ranking, 348
  row values, shifting, 345–348
  rows from table, skipping, 331–334
  rows, investigating future, 342–345
  for text not matching pattern
    (Oracle), 520–523
  top *n* records, selecting, 338–340
SECOND function (DB2), 233
SELECT statements
  * character in, 1
  conditional logic in, 7
  DISTINCT keyword and, 16, 351, 532
  GROUP BY and, 160, 538–540
  partial, xxiv
  (see also retrieving records)
self joins
  alternatives to, 298–300, 302, 304
  uses, 297, 337
separation, axiom schema of, 534
serialized data, parsing into rows, 509–513
set differences, 33
set operations
  generally, 28, 29, 33
  (see also specific operations e.g. MINUS,
    UNION ALL, etc.)
SIGN function (MySQL/PostgreSQL), 250
solutions (see recipes)
sorting records, 14–27
  on data dependent key, 26
  mixed alphanumeric data, 17–20
  on multiple fields, 15
  nulls and, 20–26

  on single field, 14
  strings, 116, 117–123
  by substrings, 16
specification, axiom of, 534
SQL Server
  cross-tab reports (see cross-tab reports)
  version discussed, xxiii
  (see also specific recipes)
START WITH clause (Oracle), 457, 465
Stoll, Robert, 533
STR_TO_DATE function (MySQL), 280
strings
  generally, 97
  queries, 97–156
    alphabetizing, 135–141
    alphanumeric status,
      determining, 107–112
    alphanumeric, sorting mixed, 17
    characters, removing unwanted, 102
    delimited lists, creating, 123–129
    extracting elements, 482–485
    initials, extracting from
      name, 112–116
    IN-lists, converting data to, 129–135
    IP Address parsing, 154–156
    numeric content, identifying, 141–147
    occurrences, counting character, 101
    ordering by number, 117–123
    ordering by part, 116
    parsing into rows, 509–513
    quotes, embedding, 100
    searching for mixed
      alphanumeric, 486–488
    separating numeric and character
      data, 103–107
    substrings, extracting, 147–153
    traversing, 97–99
subqueries
  converting scalar to composite
    (Oracle), 507–509
  forcing order of execution, 523
subsets, axiom schema of, 534
SUBSTR function
    (DB2/MySQL/Oracle/PostgreSQL),
    16, 117, 132
SUBSTRING function (SQL Server), 17, 277,
    281
subtotals
  calculating for all combinations, 412–421
  calculating simple, 408–411
  pivoting result set with, 439–443

About the Author

Anthony Molinaro is a database developer at Wireless Generation, Inc., and he has many years of experience in helping developers improve their SQL queries. SQL is a particular passion of Anthony's, and he's become known as the go-to guy among his clients when it comes to solving difficult SQL query problems. He's well-read, understands relational theory well, and has nine years of hands-on experience solving tough SQL problems. Anthony is particularly well-acquainted with new and powerful SQL features such as the windowing function syntax that was added to the most recent SQL standard.

Colophon

Our look is the result of reader comments, our own experimentation, and feedback from distribution channels. Distinctive covers complement our distinctive approach to technical topics, breathing personality and life into potentially dry subjects.

The animal on the cover of *SQL Cookbook* is an Agamid lizard. These lizards belong to the *Agamidae* family, which contains more than 300 species. Agamids can be found in Africa, Asia, Australia, and Southern Europe, and are characterized by strong legs and—in some varieties—the ability to change color. Unlike other species of lizards, agamids cannot regenerate their tails if they lose them. They can be found in a variety of environments, from arid deserts to tropical rainforests.

Several species of agamids are popular as pets. Among these are the Bearded Dragon (genus *Pogona*). Calm yet curious, these creatures grow to be only about 20 inches. However, they are still considered "giant" lizards, and therefore require ample space. Males are generally territorial and, although they are social animals, overcrowding can lead to stress, especially when the animals have no place to hide.

The head of the Bearded Dragon is triangular and features spikes protruding from its chin. These spikes resemble whiskers (thus the name). Bearded Dragons open their mouths and display their spiky beards to scare predators and other perceived threats. They also can flatten their bodies to appear larger. As pets, they may stop displaying their beards once they become comfortable with their owners and habitats.

The Flying Lizard (*draco volans*) is another species of Agamid lizard. Measuring slightly less than 12 inches, this lizard has a long, thin body with flaps of skin along its ribs. The male will claim two to three trees for its territory, with one to three females living in each tree. In order to transport itself from one place to another, it glides from trees or other high places by extending its skin flaps like wings. When threatened, the flying lizard may also extend its skin flaps to appear larger.

Another interesting variety of the *agamidae* family is the Red Headed Rock Agama (*Agama agama*), found in sub-Saharan Africa. These creatures often live in groups of 10 to 20 with an older male acting as the group's "leader." At night, their coloring is dark brown, but at dawn, their bodies change to light blue with a bright orange head and tail. Their skin coloring also changes with their mood. For example, when males fight, their heads will become brown, and white spots appear along their bodies.

Darren Kelly was the production editor for *SQL Cookbook*. Kenneth Kimball was the copyeditor, and Karmyn Guthrie was the proofreader. nSight, Inc. provided production services. Jamie Peppard and Genevieve d'Entremont provided quality control. Jansen Fernald provided production support. Beth Palmer wrote the index.

Karen Montgomery designed the cover of this book, based on a series design by Edie Freedman. The cover image is a 19th-century engraving from the Dover Pictorial Archive. Karen Montgomery produced the cover layout with Adobe InDesign CS, using Adobe's ITC Garamond font.

David Futato designed the interior layout. This book was converted by Keith Fahlgren to FrameMaker 5.5.6 with a format conversion tool created by Erik Ray, Jason McIntosh, Neil Walls, and Mike Sierra that uses Perl and XML technologies. The text font is Linotype Birka; the heading font is Adobe Myriad Condensed; and the code font is LucasFont's TheSans Mono Condensed. The illustrations that appear in the book were produced by Robert Romano, Jessamyn Read, and Lesley Borash using Macromedia FreeHand MX and Adobe Photoshop CS. The tip and warning icons were drawn by Christopher Bing. This colophon was written by Jansen Fernald.

Get even more for your money.

Join the O'Reilly Community, and register the O'Reilly books you own. It's free, and you'll get:

- $4.99 ebook upgrade offer
- 40% upgrade offer on O'Reilly print books
- Membership discounts on books and events
- Free lifetime updates to ebooks and videos
- Multiple ebook formats, DRM FREE
- Participation in the O'Reilly community
- Newsletters
- Account management
- 100% Satisfaction Guarantee

Signing up is easy:

1. Go to: oreilly.com/go/register
2. Create an O'Reilly login.
3. Provide your address.
4. Register your books.

Note: English-language books only

To order books online:
oreilly.com/store

For questions about products or an order:
orders@oreilly.com

To sign up to get topic-specific email announcements and/or news about upcoming books, conferences, special offers, and new technologies:
elists@oreilly.com

For technical questions about book content:
booktech@oreilly.com

To submit new book proposals to our editors:
proposals@oreilly.com

O'Reilly books are available in multiple DRM-free ebook formats. For more information:
oreilly.com/ebooks

O'REILLY®

Spreading the knowledge of innovators   oreilly.com

Have it your way.

O'Reilly eBooks

- Lifetime access to the book when you buy through oreilly.com
- Provided in up to four DRM-free file formats, for use on the devices of your choice: PDF, .epub, Kindle-compatible .mobi, and Android .apk
- Fully searchable, with copy-and-paste and print functionality
- Alerts when files are updated with corrections and additions

oreilly.com/ebooks/

Safari Books Online

- Access the contents and quickly search over 7000 books on technology, business, and certification guides
- Learn from expert video tutorials, and explore thousands of hours of video on technology and design topics
- Download whole books or chapters in PDF format, at no extra cost, to print or read on the go
- Get early access to books as they're being written
- Interact directly with authors of upcoming books
- Save up to 35% on O'Reilly print books

See the complete Safari Library at safari.oreilly.com

O'REILLY®

CPSIA information can be obtained at www.ICGtesting.com
Printed in the USA
BVOW031209080113

310072BV00006B/54/P